M000198947

Every-Name Index
for the Two Volumes of

HISTORY OF FREDERICK COUNTY MARYLAND

by T. J. C. Williams
and
Folger McKinsey

Compiled by Patricia A. Fogle

CLEARFIELD

Copyright © 2002 by Patricia A. Fogle
All Rights Reserved.

Printed for
Clearfield Company, Inc. by
Genealogical Publishing Co., Inc.
Baltimore, Maryland
2002

International Standard Book Number: 0-8063-5190-X

Made in the United States of America

Table of Contents

Introduction V

Index for History of Frederick County, Vol I 1

Index for History of Frederick County, Vol II 74

INTRODUCTION

In 1936, J. Merhling Holdcraft compiled a surname index of the two volumes of T. J. C. Williams and Folger McKinsey's *History of Frederick County.* It has survived and sufficed for 64 years, but I have a problem with surname indexes in that you have to go to every page with a specific page with a specific name listed to see if the one there is the one you are looking for. Therefore, I have compiled an *Every-Name Index*, hoping that others who feel as I do will appreciate this work and be able to use it much more efficiently. Mr. Williams and Mr. McKinsey did a wonderful work compiling this history, but it is not easy to use without an index.

Volume I of the *History of Frederick County,* containing pages 1 through 692, is a history of the growth of the county. It contains much information, however, about persons who lived in the county. There is much repetition, but the information is valuable to those who are interested in tracing their families. There is a modified index, which lists places, but not very many of the names included in the volume.

Volume II, pages 693 to the end, contains biographies of many of the leading citizens of the county, including much family information about their ancestors and descendants. It is an invaluable tool for family researchers and therefore should be indexed to make it more accessible to those wishing to use it. Again, there is an index of those whose names head the biographies, but it does not include the names of others therein.

I have tried to list every name as it is found in these books, but there are, doubtless, some that I have missed. I hope the researcher will understand those omissions. If you do not find a name with the spelling you believe to be accurate, please check other possible spellings. (Example: Brengle may be found under spellings such as Bringle, Brangle, Pringle, etc.) Remember, they spelled the names the way they heard them in earlier days. I have not listed names where there is no first name. You will find names such as Miss, Mr., General, Lieut.,

Dr., Rev., etc. with no first names listed, and I did not put them in the index because it is generally not possible to know who those persons are. However, I did list names where there was an initial. Also, I did not assume that initials alone were the same as names, even though I might believe them to be the same person. I leave that to the discretion of the researcher. As an example, under Harkey in the index you will find listed S. W., Simeon W., and Simon W. I would guess that these three could be the same person; however, I do not assume that to be true, so they are all listed. When I found a name of a female who was listed as Mrs., I used that to let the researcher know that it was not a maiden name. It is interesting to note that the compiler of this work frequently named the husband of females but did not as frequently name the wives of males. I assume that was due to the lack of standing in the community by female members of families as long as there were males living. Also, many women were simply listed as Mrs., using the husband's name instead of her own.

I know that many names are misspelled, but I did not correct them. My job was simply to index the names as I found them, and the researcher will have to use his or her discretion to decide whether the spelling is correct or incorrect. It is sometimes difficult to pick out who the children in a paragraph belong to, as the names were mixed together as children and children of children. I have done my best to sort them out, but there may be errors in my judgment, so let the reader beware.

Patricia A. Fogle

EVERY-NAME INDEX
HISTORY OF FREDERICK COUNTY - VOLUME I

Abbott, Edward, 458
Georg A., 541
Henry H., 437, 438,
506, 507
John H., 214
Abel, Russell, 604
Abrecht, Luther, 555
William, 555
Ackerman, George, 623
Acosta E., 185
Adams, A., 327
Andrew, 624
Ann, 632
Brooks, 113
Charles Francis, 111,
113
Dorsey, 560
George, 638, 646
J. F., 394
Jeremiah, 639
John, 35, 101, 103,
104, 109, 111, 112,
114, 123, 127, 177,
253
John Quincy, 102, 111-
114, 152, 154, 174,
185, 232, 253
Joseph, 626, 638
Louisa C., 112
Martin, 630
P., 327, 328
S. H., 394
Stophel, 641
Thomas, 630
Valentine, 409, 550,
552, 604, 605, 638
Addelspurger, Thomas,
626
Addison, Robert, 628
Adelsberger, D. G., 611
David J., 325
Michael, 611
Adgate, Elias, 661
Adkins, Charles, 643
William, 630
Adlum, John, 85, 95,
431, 638
Joseph, 167
Adolphus, Gustavus, 142
Agey, Jonathan, 630
Agie, Peter, 632
Agnew, David, 382, 601
Henry, 169

Robert, 82
Ahalt, Ezra, 281
Jacob, 503
Mathias S., 528
Mrs. Samuel, 497
Samuel, 497
Allbough, Simeon, 641
Ake, Jacob, 643
Alain, Joshua, 453
Albaugh, A., 266
Absalom, 169
Christian, 284, 624
Daniel, 628, 645
David, 163, 624
Edward, 606
Ephriam, 601
John, 624
John H., 469
Joshua, 468, 605
Lewis A., 468
Maurice, 391, 547
Maurice J., 535
N. H., 531
Peter, 624
Philip, 624
Solomon, 538
Sophia, 468
Susannah, 468
Thomas S., 485
Valentine, 469
William, 84, 85, 624
William A. , 550
William H., 169, 552
William V., 543
William, Jr., 624
Zachariah, 283, 624
Albert, Chas. S., 485
Albright, Henry, 636
Susanna R., 483
Alder, Frank E., 530
Aldridge, David C., 437,
438
Alexander, Ashton, 595
Eugene, 560
Henry, 641
Jacob, 166, 167, 636
John, 643
Thomas, 630
Valentine, 636
Algier, Rachel, 646
Alleman, M. J., 501
Allen, Benjamin, 4
Bennett, 430

E., 266
Edward P., 523
Ethan, 314, 435
Horatio, 160
John, 661
Mervin, 492
T. H., 266
W. F., 553
Allison, James, 634
John, 628
Allix, Michael, 136
Allnutt, J. Howard, 551
Allsock, John, 641
Alpendam, Jan Jansen, 69
Alvarez, Mrs. John M., 317
Alvey, Mrs. Richard H., 299
Mrs. T. Frederick, 317
Richard H., 319, 320
Amberson, Thos., 100
Ambrose, Catharine, 632
Christopher, 636
Henry, 634
Jacob, 84, 85, 90
Moses, 82
Peter, 167
Ambroser, Henry, 636
Ambrosier, Henry, Sr., 636
Amelung, Frederick M., 268
John Frederick,
268, 325, 536, 647
Ames, E. R., 458
Ammon, Charles Lee, 598
Ancell, Priscilla, 644
Ancrum, Jacob, 636
Richard, 636
And, Asa, 169
Anders, Aaron R., 599, 607
Herbert, 642
John, 628
Lawrence, 646
Moses, 489
Anderson, Archibald, 536
Daniel, 661
E. S., 546
Edward, 632
Franklin, 149, 597
G. W., 295
George W., 294, 481
James, 56
Jerry, 352
Jesse, 281
John, 661
Mrs. Lydia, 493

O. P., 352
William, 483, 628
Wm. P., 601
Andis, Matthias, 624
Paul, 624
Andrews, John, 597
Nicholas, 96
Solomon, Jr., 295
William, 630
Angel, Charles, 630
Jacob, 642
John, 626
Peter, 646
Philip, 626
Angelberger, George D, 483
Howard, 484
Jacob M., 483
John P., 484
Mary Susan, 483
Ward, 484
Angle, George, 640
Jacob, 632
Peter, 640
Angleberger, Philip, 469
Ankrom, Aaron, 636
Annan, A. A., 536
Andrew, 536, 585, 601, 605, 611
Andrew A., 607
E. L., 536, 548
Isaac S., 536, 610, 611
J. M. , 391
J. Stewart, 553, 606
James C., 536
R., 604
R. J., 536
R. L., 565, 566
Robert, 601, 605
Robert L., 582
Robert Landales, 585
Robert Lewis, 585
Samuel, 565, 585
Stewart S., 536
Anspach, J. G., 505
Apel, H. Wm., 647
Apfel, Peter, 479
Apple, Henry H., 419
J. H., 419, 438, 441, 509
Joseph H., 436, 437, 507, 510
Peter, 470
Susannah, 25
Theodore, 416
Thos. G., 414
Applebee, Hezekiah, 167, 169

Appleby, B., 503, 504
Appler, Jacob, 626
Archer, Stevenson, 319
Archley, Thomas, 85
Ardinger,
Christian, 146
Armis, Jacob, 628
Armstrong, Archibald, 211
James, 630
John, 634
Priscilla, 643
Wm., 110
Arnd, John, 632
Arnold, Alicia, 314
Andrew, 635
Anthony, 623
Archabald, 626
B., 330
Benedict, 329, 430
David, 641
Geo. V., 497
Henry, 636
James M., 547
John, 623, 636, 643
Martin, 497
Mrs. Joshua, 497
Samuel, 642
Thomas, 497, 535
William, 623
Zachariah, 642
Arnsperger, Mrs. Hanna, 456
Arter, Daniel, 626
Michael, 626
Arthur, Frederick, 642
Henry, 643
Artman, John, 636
Michael, 634
William, 634
Arvin, William, 661
Ashcom, Charles, 313
Ashmond, Henry, 636
Asper, John U., 484
John W., 482, 485
Athey, Jacob, 645
Wilson, 643
Atkins, Charles, 169
James, 169
Atkinson, Charles, 661
Joseph M., 450
Atlow, Priscilla, 643
Atman, William, 646
Atwater, Charles L., 492
Aubert, Jacob, 396
Lewis H., 541
Aughenbaugh, Geo. W., 486

Aughinbaugh, Edward, 348
Geo. W., 470
Ault, E. T., 549
Aunbert, Christian, 639
Aurand, Dietrich, 452
Ausherman, Charles
F.,460, 463, 529,530
Clement C., 599, 607
David, 497
Averhart, Jacob, 636
Averly, Adam, 635
Avery, George, 646
Axtel, Peter, 479
Ayle, Daniel, 632
Baare, F., 266
Bab, John, 638
Babs, William, 623
Babylon, Philip, 626, 642
Bachman, Henry, 6
Bachtol, Jacob, 454
Backenbaugh, Crate, 454
Eva, 454
Mary, 454
Backus, J. C., 449
Bacon, Stephen, 169
Thomas, 225, 429, 521
Bader, Anton, 647
Baer, Charles J., 585
David, 167
George, 133, 180, 182, 183, 225, 432, 527, 599, 601, 602
George C., 362
George, Jr., 600
Harry, 542
Henry, 536, 586
Jacob, 168, 169, 288, 542, 564, 566
Jacob S., 565, 585
Jacob Shellman, 586
Michael, 167
Michael Shellman, 586
William, 169, 550
Bager, John George, 466
Bageunt, William, 643
Baggel, Benjamin, 644
Bagle, Henry, 641
Bail, William, 646
Bailey, C., 266
John, 661
Joseph, 624
Mountjoy, 625
Wm., 327, 328
Bainbridge, Peter, 75, 78, 85
Baird, Frederick, 324
Peter, 468

Thomas, 90
William, 31, 84, 85, 600
Bakely, Henry, 642
Baker, Adam, 641
Albert, 555
Charles D., 586
Christian, 640
Conrod, 636
Daniel, 321, 456, 487, 518, 519, 528
Daniel, Jr., 487
David A., 524
Edward, 456, 524
Essie, 456
Francis, 628
Francis M., 492
Frederick, 327, 624, 632
Henry, 524, 601, 604, 605, 623, 632, 645
Holmes D., 519, 528
Isaac, 39, 86
J. D., 528
J. H., 487, 488
John, 383, 603, 625, 630
John H., 519
Jonathan, 460
Joseph, 625
Joseph D., 161, 292, 399, 402, 507, 519, 527, 528
Laura, 456
Martin, 641
Mary, 101, 111, 639
Mrs. Ann, 336, 340
Mrs. William,281
Nathaniel, 661
Peter, 640
Roger, 101, 111
S., 596
Samuel, 625
W. , 86
W. G., 487
William, 84, 85
William G., 519, 527, 528
William G., Jr., 519
William H. , 658
Balch, Hezekiah, 467
L. P. W., 177, 255, 450, 597
Stephen Bloomer, 448
Balderston, John, 167
Baldwin, Daniel, 630
Elijah, 630

Thomas, 628
Bale, Peter, 623
Balheim, H., 647
Ball, Daniel, 643
Henry, 638
John, 644
Ballinger, Cassa, 628
William, 602
Balsel, Jacob, 639
Baltsell, Jacob, 642
Baltzel, Christian, 639
George Jacob, 640
Baltzell, Charles, 8
Edward B. , 278, 550
George, 226, 536, 537, 603
I., 454
Jacob, 638
James W., 455
John, 169, 488, 565, 586, 589
Josephine, 315
W. H., 580
Wesley, 440
William, 210
Wm. H., 564, 566, 581, 583, 586, 592
Baltzer, John, 639
Bambridge, Absolam, 641
Peter, 636
Baney, George, 638
Bankard, Abram, 642
Christopher, 645
Henry, 642
Jacob, 630
Bankert, Abraham, 603
Bannister, James, 643
Bante, Henry, 167
John, 167
Bantz, Edward, 565
Gideon, 210, 275, 278, 525, 526, 550, 601, 603
Gideon, Jr, 271
H., 132
Henry, 536, 537
Mrs. Gideon, 374
Peter S., 541, 543
William, 537, 542, 586
William S., 271
Barber, Samuel, 447
Bard, Archibald, 46
Richard, 45, 46, 51
Bare, George, 85
Barger, Frederick, 636
Bargor, Philip, 638
Baringer, Widow, 59, 60

Barker, Fielder, 643
J., 271
John, 624
Thomas, 661
W. G., 459
Barnard, Luke, 327
Barnes, Abraham, 298
David, 643
Elisha, 642
George, 661
J. O., 531
James, 628
John, 628
John Thompson, 298
Joseph, 339, 340
Nachel, 641
Philip, 623
Samuel, 167, 180, 181, 187, 251, 537, 542, 601
Barnet, Jacob, 638
Luke, 625, 634
Barnett, Robert, 625
Barney, A. I., 603
Ai, 538
John, 182, 537
Joshua, 133
Mrs. Mary, 226
Barnhart, Anthony, 626
Benjamin, 624
David, 633, 642
George, 634
Michael, 630
Barnhold, Ann, 639
Barnot, James, 630
Barnover, George, 626
Barns, H., 266
Barr, Archabald, 630
J., 391
Barrack, Christian, 624
Elmer E., 485
Frederick, 624
George, 624
Henry, 624
Jacob, 624
Jacob (of Wm.), 624
John, 624
John, of Jno., 625
Peter, 625, 645
William, 625, 645
Barrackman, John, 661
Barrett, Albert, 524
Thomas, 661
Barrick, Christian, 327
Daniel I., 489
David, 475
George P., 489

4

Han., 327
Jacob, 327
John, 327, 328
John W., 365
Peter, 327, 328
Robert, 606
Wm., 327
Barrier, George, 661
Barry, William R., 520
Barshinger, D. A., 455
Bartel, Christian, 167
Bartgis, Hiram, 557, 602
James, 209, 556
M., 141
M. E., 537, 603
Mathias, 180, 246-249
Mathias E., 249, 538
Matthias, 181
Matthias E., 167, 602
William, 400
Bartholomew,
John, 636
Bartholow, John, 365,
603, 605
Bartle, Jacob, 640
Bartman, Christophel, 639
Bartol, James L., 296
James Lawrence, 319
Bartz, Martin, 90
Barwick, Thomas, 21
Bast, Simeon L., 607
Bateman, J. M. H., 575
Bates, L. N., 487
Battsell, Michael, 640
Baugher, Charles H., 391,
559
Eugene C., 391
H. L., 505
Isaac, 227
Baughman, C. C., 503
Charles H., 252
Corinne, 252
J. William, 552
John F., 598
John W., 251, 252, 290,
373, 597
L. V., 251
L. Victor, 159, 252,
290, 610
Louis Victor, 252, 373,
400, 562
Mary Lease, 252
Mrs. L. Victor, 561,562

Mrs. M. J. , 252
Baulus, J. Jacob, 453
Baum, John, 626
Peter, 626
Bauman, Sophia, 458
Baumgardner, George T., 524,
532
Jno., 620
Baumgartner, J. Hampton, 218
Baxter, Benjamin, 623
William E., 473
Bayer, Jacob, 537, 542
Jacob, Jr., 536
Lewis, 541
Bayler, M., 127
Bayley, Elizabeth Ann, 511
Francis R., 548
J. Roosevelt, 515
Montjoy, 137
Mountjoy, 138
Richard, 511
William, 86
William, Jr., 84, 85
Bayly, Mountjoy, 600
Bayplot, John, 642
Beachley, Daniel, 497
Geo. C., 497
H. D., 473, 548
John H., 497
Mrs. Ann R. , 497
Mrs. Catharine, 497
Mrs. Jno. D., 497
Beagle, Nicholas, 647
Tobias, 647
Beale, David J., 304
Beak, Jacob, 642
Beal, Samuel, 25
W., 455
William M., 534
Beale, Charles, 295
David J., 451
George, 635
Beall, Alexander, 661
Basil, 136, 603, 632
Brook, 84
Brooke, 85, 86
Charles, 85
Collimore, 632
Edward, 661
Elisha, 628
Harriet, 102
Henry D., 352
Ira H., 582

Ira W., 586
James, 644
John, 85, 86, 327, 625, 628
John, Jr., 623
Joseph, 75, 628
Joshua, 661
Josiah, 78, 600
Levin, 661
Nathan, 628
Nenian, 644
Ninean, 169
Rezin, 661
Richard, 86
Samuel, 75, 78, 86, 225, 521,
600, 602
Samuel, Jr., 84, 85
Tabitha, 628
Theadore, 643
Thomas, 85
Upton, 434
W. H., 547
Walter, 85
William A., 264
William D. , 166
William H., 541, 552
William J., 84
William M., 85, 431, 526, 602,
640
William Murdock, 196, 606
Wm. M., Sr., 433
Beam, Peter, 630
Philip, 626
Beamer, Adam, 624
Henry, 632, 645
Henry, Jr., 624
Matthias, 628
Philip, 630
Tice, 645
Bean, Mrs. Charlotte O., 491
Walter, 642
Beane, William, 169
Beanes, William, 306
Beans, Francis, 645
Bear, Catharine, 639
Christian, 462
George, 617, 632, 640
George, Jr., 138, 639
Gorg, 647
Henry, 141, 537, 538, 639
Hugh, 640
Jacob, 534, 537
Jacob, Jr., 638
Jacob, Sr., 638

John, 255, 628, 632
M. L., 501
Michael, 624
William, 639
Beard, Archibald, 46
Frederick, 645
Jacob, 169
James, 661
John, 467
M. L., 504
Margaret, 624
Paul, 627
Peter, 625
Samuel, 636
Bearshank, William, 169
Beatty, Alexander P., 334
C. W., 391
Charles, 80, 84-86, 95, 97,
  225
J. E., 581, 583
James, 624
John, 600
John M., 536
Joseph, 391
Joseph E., 566
Joseph Edward, 586
Thomas, 26, 27, 75, 78, 82,
  85, 86, 225, 227, 521,
  600, 605
Thomas, Sr., 128
William, 86, 95, 108, 125,
  127, 430, 600, 602, 625,
  638
Beaty, Jacob, 635
Thomas, 639
Beaumont, William, 644
Beaver, Jacob, 327
John, 635, 638
William, 636
Beavington, Henry, 643
Becel, Carl, 647
Beck, Johann Martin, 6
Beckenbaugh, George, 603
George W., 249
Leonard, 636
Becker, Charles, 411
H., 647
Beckett, Benjamin, 169
William, 641
Beckham, F., 347
Fontains, 353
Beckley, E. L., 535, 581, 584
Edward Luther, 586

G. Herbert, 586
Gabriel, 362, 371
Quitman S. J., 560
Beckwith, Benjamin, 636
Corydon, 597
Lamach, 646
Maurice G., 508, 509
Beckworth, Mary, 638
Becraft, George, 623
Peter, 86
Bedford, Gunning S., 522
John R. D., 543
Bedinger, Daniel, 338
Henry, 336, 338, 340, 341
Bedtman, M., 538
Beek, Adam, 489
Ludwig, 466
Wm., 489
Beeler, Daniel, 626
Behind, Jacob, 641
Beilfield,Jonathan J., 542
Beklote, John, 628
Belden, James, 227
Belknap, Wm. G., 266
Bell, Babby, 640
Cephas, 646
Edwin, 191
John, 363
Lewis, 272
Nathaniel, 640
Wm. M., Jr., 526
Belt, Alfred McGill, 586
E. O., 582
Edward Oliver, 586
Hickison, 632
Jeremiah, 490, 636
John L., 221
Lloyd, 167
McGill, 553
Beltser, Christopher, 626
Bend, Wm. B., 134
Bender, John, 556
Benfield, Samuel, 662
Benner, Alonzo, 606
Bennet, Benjamin, 623
John, 630, 662
Bennett, Al., 392
David, 169
David T., 392
John H., 547
O. P., 553
R. A., 546, 547
Robert A., 557

Samuel B., 548
Thompson, 250
Benson, Benjamin, 626
H. G., 520
R. E., 487
Bent, George, 85
Samuel, 646
Bentalon, Paul, 138
Bentley, Abner, 624
Eli, 630
Elijah, 624
Levi, 625
Solomon, 625
Benton, Thomas H., 252, 258,
  260, 558
Bentz, Ezra, 538
Frank L., 555, 560
Jacob, 24, 409
John, Jr., 169
Mrs. Gideon, 413
Benyan, Parslow, 662
Bergeseer, Jacob, 636
Bergstresser, Peter, 427, 501
Berkstresser, Peter, 485
Bernard, Edward, 601
Berry, Jeremiah, 430
W. R., 455
Besant, William S., 559
Best, John T., 552
Bevan, T. W., 266
Bevans, Charles E., 362
Bevington, Henry, 634
Bevins, Alex., 167
Biackston, Benj. H., 557
Bickley, Henry, 250
Biddle, Andrew, 628
George, 630
Bielfeld, Jonathan J., 543
Bierly, Frederick, 638
George, 624
Biershenk, Henry, 169
Bigelow, Horatio, 134
Biggerly, Henry, Sr., 636
Biggs, B., 132
Benjamin, 132-133, 600, 604,
  633
C. H., 547
Jacob, 630
James S., 535
John, 25, 632
Joshua, 600, 601, 611
Sheridan, 607
William, Sr., 630

6

Bigly, Henry, Jr., 636
Bigsler, Samuel, 630
Billmyer, G. W., 530
Bine, Adam, 632
Binford, Charles, 662
Binger, Michael, 628
Bird, Benjamin, 662
Birely, Charles E., 437
  Frederick, 457
  George, 532, 621
  J. W., 527
  J. William, 507, 525, 553
  Jacob M., 607
  John W., 556
  L., 230
  Lester S., 532
  Lewis, 604
  Lewis E., 527, 621
  M. A., 531, 581
  Morris A., 532, 548, 584, 586
  Samuel M., 531, 532
  Valentine, 169, 271, 275
  William, 227
  William C., 304, 312, 386, 541, 543
Birkbeck, Morris, 175
Birley, J. M., 547
Birnie, C., Jr., 597
Biser, Charles C., 535, 606
  Daniel, 476, 605
  Daniel G., 365
  Daniel S., 256, 288, 601, 602, 605
  J. Polk, 541
  Jacob, 476
  M. A. E., 440
  Tilghman, 586
Bishop, Charles A., 560, 561
  Henry, 467, 662
  J. Henry, 466
  John, 628
  John, Jr., 642
  John, Sr., 626
  Thomas, 662
  Vachel, 628
Bittle, D. F., 502
  D. H., 505, 543
  David F., 501
  George W., 529
  Thomas F., 529
  Thomas P., 530
  William M., 530

Bitzell, Henry, 90
Bixler, C. H., 506
Bizar, Daniel, 636
Black, Abraham, 642
  Adam, 626
  Andrew, 630
  Frederick, 630
  George W. Z. , 251
  John, 520, 638, 662
  Valentine, 25
  W. J., 603
Blackburn, Alexander, 634
  Richard Scott, 257
Blackfoot, Wm. M., 597
Blackford, John, 149
  Thomas, 167
Blackson, Harry, 542
Blacksone, Sir William, 80
Blackston, Harry, 541
Blair, David, 41
  John, 41
  Montgomery, 252
  Samuel, 647
  W. G., 611
  William, 75, 78, 82, 84, 86, 90, 95, 125, 602, 605
Blake, Mrs. Mary A. Robinson, 518
  Philip, 662
Blaxford, Oswald, 169
Blech, Carl Gottlieb, 6
Blenkinsop, Mother Euphemia, 518
Blentlinger, William H., 606
Blessing, Abram, 502
  George, 550, 641, 657
  Jacob, 636
  Solomon, 503
Blickensderfer, Jesse, 6
Blickenstaff, Cyrus W., 460
  Yost, 636
Blisse, Carl, 285
Blohorn, William, 643
Blois, John, 662
Blood, Wm., 450
Bloom, Adam, 642
Blueback, Benjamin, 626
Blukenstaff, Ulerick, 641
Blumer, F., 266
Boalus, Valentine, 636
Boane, James, 660
Boarden, Sephous, 623
Boarman, Mary, 314

William, 314
Boblitz, Ephraim L., 607
Bobst, Daniel, 169
Bockman, Andrew, 641
Boddington, William, 623
Bodenoe, David, 647
Bodige, Benjamin, 662
Boehm, Henry, 452
  Martin, 452
Boerly, Thomas, 353
Bogan, Frederick, 638
Boggis, Samuel, 628
Boghier, Peter, 641
Bohler, Franz, 6
Bohn, Otto, 647
Boiler, Joseph, 623, 624
Boller, John R., 658
  William, 658
Bolsell, Charles, 624
Bonaparte, Jerome Napoleon, 522
Bond, Dr. John, 165
  Frank, 400
  G. S., 266
  James A. C., 318
  Nicholas, 623
  Thomas, 313, 314
Boner, Geo, 635
Bonnet, Christian, 638
Bonsall, Jesse Stapleton, 521
Bontz, Adam, 640
  Henry, 640
Bonum, Malachia, 640
Boogher, B. C., 457
Booghier, Jacob, 643
Boohoup, John, 641
Booker, Frederick, 640
  John, 640
  John, Jun., 626
  John, Sr., 626
Bookey, Matthias, 632, 638
Boomwell, John E., 581
Boon, Abraham, 634
  Charles, 645
  J., 391
Boone, Benedict, 604
  H. Jerningham, 582, 586
  Jacob, 630
  Jerningham, 552, 565, 566
  Nicholas, 625
  Robert, 167, 169, 552
Boons, Robert, 603
Boos, John, 635
Booth, B., 332

Bartholomew, 10, 85, 225, 328-331, 430
Henry, 328
Mary, 328
Wm., 330
Boran, Lawrence, 645
Bordley, John Beale, 102
Stephen, 597
Bordly, Stephen, 298
Bore, Michael, 646
Borell, George, 628
Borgan, John N. C., 586
Borham, Mercy, 640
Borice, Laurence, 628
Bosenberg, Henry, 647
Bosler, David, 486
Bosley, Gideon, 626
Bossert, Samuel, 500
Bossler, David, 470
Bost, Felty, 626
Michael, 645
Bostian, Anthony, 624
Henry, 624
Michael, 625
Bostion, Philip, 628
Boswell, Edward, 662
Boteler, A. R., 340
Alexander R., 336, 338
Arthur, 604
Augustus, 292
Barton, 272
Edward, 603
Elias, 536
Henry, 210, 556, 557, 601, 605
Hezekiah, 272, 365, 491
Lucy, 396
Thomas, 175
William C., 535, 581
William H., 221
Wm., 566, 582
Wm. Clarence, 586
Wm. E., 587
Botts, Lawson, 353
Bouche,——, 647
Bouden, John, 630
Bougher, Jacob, 167
Bouquet, Henry, 41
Bourne, Wm. G., 587
Bouse, Christian, 632
Bouser, Stoph, 634
Boutsong, Adam, Jun., 641
Bovey, Adam, 454

D. E., 455
D. R., 454
Bowden, John, Jr., 645
Bowen, Christopher, 642
Bower, Abraham, 628, 645
George, 431, 492
John, 626, 630
Peter, 636
Bowers, George W., 353
Grayson E., 540, 543
H. G., 502, 503
Harry W., 440, 555, 558, 606
J. H., 489
Jacob H., 489
John, 645
John H., 530
R., 560
Stephen, 627
Wayne H., 486
William D., Jr, 227
Bowersmith, George, 636
Bowersock, Geo. A., 630
Bowie, Alexander, Jr., 85
Allen, 86
Allen, Jr., 84
Richard I., 397
Richard J., 375, 599, 600
Richard Johns, 218, 293, 319
Robert, 126
Thomas J., 82
Bowles, Betty L., 520
Noah, 598
Thomas, 84, 85, 225, 430, 602
Bowlus, David O., 560
E. L., 582, 587
Edward, 617
George, 332, 560, 601, 603
Jacob, 453
John, 454
John S., 497
Lewis H. , 606
Michael, 500
Mrs. Franklin L., 497
Noah, 601, 607
Stephen R., 601, 605
Bowly, Charles, 640
Jacob, 640
Bowman, J. C., 472
John C., 441
Bowser, Noah, 636

Bowsinger, Henry, 636
Boyd, A., 227
A. Hunter, 319
Abraham, 633
Andrew, 226, 457, 458, 525, 526, 639
Archibald, 84, 85, 86
David, 167, 457, 458, 525, 538, 552
John J., 226, 227
Marmaduke W., 149
Mary, 458
Mrs. Allen R., 82
Boyer, Adam, 487
Daniel, 460, 462
David, 624
Geo. W., 353
Henry, 647
Henry, Sr., 647
Jacob, 85
Jacob, Jr., 603
John, 169, 645, 647
Mary, 626
Michael, 8, 646
Mrs. John C., 497
Philip, 623
Robertus, 628
Teterick, 625
Wm. E., 469
Boyle, Daniel, , 630
Esmeralda, 107
Philip, 461, 462
Braddock, Edward, 53
William L., 492
Brade, George, 640
Bradey, James, 630
Bradley, B. J., 612
Bernard J., 523
Dominick, 82, 90
Thomas, 640
Wm. A., 158
Brady, H. L., 323, 617
Bragonier, A. C., 392
Braize, John, 641
Brake, Peter, 642
Brand, Christopher, 646
Brandenburg, John, 462
Samuel, 636
William, Jr., 636
Wm., 636
Brandenburgh, George, 640
Brandensburg, Jacob, 628
Brandensburgh, Frederick, 644

8

Brandt, C. H., 476
Christian, 647
James, 25
Brane, Benjamin, 453
C. I. B., 455
Braner, Henry, 634
Brangle, George, 640
Brantley, William T. , 320
Brantner, Z. T., 549
Brasford, Thomas, 630
Brashear, Belt, 592
Thomas C., 538, 603
Brashears, Belt, 326, 587
Henry, 400
Nathan, 625
Theodore, 454
Thomas C., 538
William, 350, 628
Brasilton, Isaac, 626
Braun, Frederick A., 524
Brauner, Frederick, 647
Brawner, Catherine Maria, 179
Elizabeth, 633
J. B., 611
John B., 582, 587
Joseph, 611
Thomas, 632
William, 82, 625
Brayfield, John, 630
Bread, George, 641
Bready, David, 169
G. P., 474
Guy P., 475, 548
Breckenridge, James, 190
Robert C., 449
Brednick, Henry, 632
Breidenbough, Kitty, 180
Breiner, Stephen, 645
Brendel, Henry G., 525
Brengle, Alfred F., 227, 228
Elmer, 463
Francis, 559, 598, 599, 601, 603
George L., 534, 556
John, 163, 167
L. J., 243, 520, 603
Lawrence, 128, 132, 167, 168, 252, 602, 603
Lawrence J., 159, 365, 524, 552, 554, 601
Peter, 602
Brent, George, 84, 641
Robert J., 252, 343

Sam'l., 167
Thos. C., 149
Brewer, John N., 371
John S., 372
Brian, James, 643
Martin, 643
Briar, Godfrey, 644
Brice, John, 646
Bricker, Henry, 628
Jacob, 626
John, 626
Bricket, John, 636
Bridges, Robert, 161
Brien, J., 434
John, 335
John McPherson, 265
Briger, Peter, 641
Briggs, John, 603
Bright, Sarah, 644
Brightwell, John, 624, 662
Richard, 638
T. W., 266
William, 623
Brim, Henry, 136, 139
Brine, Peter, 483
Briner, Abraham, 634
John, 644
Bringle, Laurence, 632
Brininger, Casper, 626
Brinkley, James, 662
Brinsfield, Zora N., 553
Briscoe, Gerard, 86
Ralph, 644
Robert, 643
Brish, David W., 271
Bristo, Samuel, 632
Britewell, John, 623
Britton, William, 632
Broadband, Joseph, 643
Broadrup, Eliza Ann, 483
Broadway, John, 662
Brodeback, Henry, 636
Bromett, Michael, 538
Bromwell, John E., 587
Brook, Henry, 82
Brooke, Hunter, 598
Isaac, 603
J. T., 597
Monica, 198
Ralph, 630
Rd., 86
Richard, 84-86, 597, 601

Roger, 198, 630
Thomas, 83-85
Brookover, Thomas, 644
Brooks, Chauncey, 242
Brother, Henry, 286
Val, 138
Valentine, 600, 602
Brothers, Henry, 640
Jacob, 626
John, 626, 640, 646
Val., 141
Brower, Emanuel, 623
Isaac, 603
Brown, Albert S. , 599
Ann, 642
Benj. F., 573
Cecilia, 313, 314
Charles H., 532
Daniel, 647
Dominic, 523
Francis, 169
Geo. S., 161
George, 232, 626, 662
Godfrey, 639
Gustavus, 313, 314
Hannah, 624
Henry, 626
I., 550
J. C., 353
J. Paul, 560
Jacob, 647
Jason, 356
Jeremiah, 461
John, 218, 287, 327, 346, 348, 349, 351-354, 356, 358, 359, 361-363, 397
Joseph, 502, 634
Joseph B., 605
Joshua, 626
L. E., 582
Louis Emmitt, 587
Mary Rutherford, 257
Michael, 639
Mrs. B. F., 396
Oliver, 352, 355, 362
Osawatomie, 362
Ossawattamie, 350
Ottawatamie, 360
Peter, 647
Peter H., 251
Richard, 662
Robert, 82, 90, 634
Robin, 640

S. Elmer, 451
Samuel R., 607
Simeon, 639
Stoffel, 636
Thomas, 328, 505
W. Hayes, 451
Walter, 352
Wilbur H., 541
William, 459, 604
William E., 501
William, Jr., 634
Wm., Sr., 505
Zachary T., 598
Browning, Benjamin, 645
  I. Thomas, 603
  Jeremiah, 603, 624
  Ralph, 582, 584, 587
Bruce, Andrew, 85, 86
  Norman, 10, 84, 314, 626
  Normand, 430, 600, 602,
    603, 605
  Upton, 128, 600, 601
Bruner, Catherine, 638
  Elias, 84
  John, 431, 632, 640
  Modelena, 640
  Peter, 634, 640
  Stephen, 632
Brunnar, John H., 227
Brunner, Edward A., 462, 463
  Elias, 85, 632
  Henry, 24
  Jacob, 24, 409
  James, 556, 603
  John, 24, 167, 406, 409
  John H., 559
  Joseph, 24
  Joshua, 413, 416
  Lewis, 292
  Rebecca, 469
  Valentine, 410
  Valentine S., 227
Brunt, Stoffel, 638
Brunton, Alexander, 662
Brush, John, 630
Brushier, Stephen, 646
Brust, Etta, 459
  Guy, 555
  Harry, 555
Brute, Simon Gabriel, 522
Bryan, David, 450
  Edward, 634
  James, 625

John L., 491, 492
Josiah, 630
William, 635
William Shepard, 318
Bryarly, Kate L., 520
Buchanan, James, 291
  James A., 396
  James M., 272, 290
  John, 235, 265, 298, 312,
    319, 320, 597, 630
  Lloyd, 597
  Mary, 342
  Thomas, 149, 265, 298, 312
  William, 635
Bucher, J. C., 464, 476, 485
Buchers, Richard, 639
Buck, Dudley, 304
Bucken, Robert, 625
Buckey, Basil V., 451
  D. P., 547
  D. Princeton, 599, 607
  Daniel E., 607
  Edward, 263, 278, 457,
    458, 550, 552, 601
  Geo. R., 469
  Geo. W., 469
  George, 169, 181, 321, 601
  George J., 541
  H. A., 469
  Jacob M., 221, 227
  John, 167
  Maynard, 469
  Michael, 321
Buckias, John, 640
Buckingham, G., 266
  Richard, 662
Buckler, H. Warren, 404
Buckley, George, 400
Buckstone, Brook, 658
Buesing, George, 556
Buffington, Jacob, 626
Buger, Bartho, 636
  Daniel, 636
Buhrman, Harvey, 566, 587
  Hiram, 601
  Upton, 601
Buley, B. F., 487
Bulfinch, B. S., 250
Bulkley, Olcutt, 492
Bullit, Eastburn, 597
Bumbgardner, John, 626
Bumgardener, Michael, 626
Bumgardner, Chrisley, 662

Bumgartner, Jacob, 181
Bunkley, Josaphine, 294
  Joseph, 294
Burbank, Isaac, 324
Burch, Albert S., 549
Burck, Lewis A., 587
  W. A., 303
Burgee, Thomas, 628
Burger, William, 644
Burgess, Edward, 84, 85
  Henry, 169
  Washington, 603, 605
Burgman, Christopher, 632
Burgoon, Jacob, 626
Burhart, Daniel, 167
Burhman, Harvey, 392
Burk, A. H., 505
  James, 635
Burke, James G., 523
  John, 630
  Thomas, 179
  Thomas V., 524
  William B., 249
Burket, Christian, 628
  George, 638
  George, Jr., 628
  Joseph, 628
  Nathaniel, 625
Burkett, Christopher, 85
  George, 497
  John, 639
  Stophall, 84
Burkhart, Anne Mary, 313
  Daniel, 169
  E. G. W., 266
  George, 25, 600
  J. W., 266
Burkitt, Newton, 587
Burkman, Henry, 604
Burlando, Francis, 517, 518
Burn, Henry, 640
Burns, George, 642
  Robert, 662
Burr, Aaron, 163, 164, 174
  F., 391
Burrall, J. M., 463
  Jesse M., 461
  Walter, 462
Burras, E., 560
Burrier, Leonard, 625
  Philip, 645
  William, 469
Burrnough, H. M. L., 266

Burshank, William, 647
Burtner, L. O., 453, 455
Burton, Elizabeth, 636
  Jacob, 636
Burucker, Oscar M. , 541
Busey, Charles, 628
  Henry, 630
Bush, John, 646
  Louis, 95
  Solomon, 662
Bushman, Henry, 630
  Jacob, 646
Bushong, T. F., 454
Bussard, Gideon, 469
  John M., 460
  Peter, 169
  Peter E., 528, 554
  Peter H., 534, 608
Busson, Benjamin, 645
Butcher, Charles, 555
Butler, Henry, 86
  John, 623, 662
  Joseph, 496
  Ormon F., 167
  Peter, 25, 602
  Richard, 86, 169, 431, 536,
    602, 603, 640
  Thomas, 142, 632
  Thomas R., 516, 523
  Tobias, 167, 431, 536, 537,
    602
  William, 645
Butt, George, 623
  John, 640
Button, David, 630
Butts, Charles, 500
  J. Frank, 599, 607
  S. F., 454
Buzzard, Andrew, 628
  Catha., 636
  Daniel, 327, 624
  Jacob, 636
  John W., 605
  Peter, 634
  Samuel, 636
Byer, George, 169
Byerly, Jacob, 632
Byers, Joseph, 601, 611
Byrd, R., 454
Byrn, S. L., 553
Byrne, John, 391
  Michael, 158
  William, 523

Byser, Frederick, 636
  Jacob, 636
  Jacob, Jr., 636
Cadwallader, John, 145
Cage, J. E., 549
Cain, Jacob, 639
  John, 636, 645
  William, 629
Caird, William, 492
Caldwell, James, 646
Calendar, Wm., 493
Calf, Jacob, 634
  John, 632, 634
  John, Sr., 635
Calfleash, John, 643
Calflesh, John, 632
Calhoun, John, 283
  John C., 326
Callaman, John, 636
  Moses, 641
Callaway, Frank H., 609
Callister, Sarah, 638
Calvert, Benedict, 10, 26, 27
  Benedict Leonard, 333
  Caecilius, 7
  Cecelius, 428
  Charles, 22
  Jesse, 462
  Leonard, 1, 335, 402
  Richard Lee, 26, 27
Camberlin, Martin J., 389
Camby, Samuel, 556
Cameron, Allan, 92
Camp, Peter, 629
Campbell, Aeneas, 84-86
  Ann, 625
  Carman G., 530
  Edward, 183
  James, 646
  John, 623, 625, 640
  Martha, 625
  Mrs. Mary Potts, 82
  William, 431, 662
Campton, John, 644
Canaday, Soloman, 643
Canadey, Ann, 643
Candle, Jacob, 639
Candler, David, 4, 420, 478
  Jacob, 646
Cann, Thomas M., 451, 507
Cannen, Jacob, 634
Cannon, Adam, 646
  Geo., 636

  Jacob, 169
Canon, Mary, 635
Cantour, Christian, 646
Caperoon, Richard, 662
Capiret, Paul, 78
Card, Benson, 662
  Sabriet, 662
Carey, Cyrus, 169
  John, 25
  John D., 600
  Mary, 632
  Robert C., 587
  William, 187
Carley, R. B., 266
Carlisle, John L., 598
Carlton, Thomas, 169, 187, 537
  William, 555, 556
Carmack, Ephriam, 598
  Evan, 458, 625
  Harry K., 541
  John, 430, 625
  S., 362
  Samuel, 168, 169, 458
  William, 625
Carmichael, Neal, 662
Carn, Balsum, 662
  Jacob, 636
  Michael, 638
Carnahan, B. R., 419, 468, 469
Carnegie, Andrew, 441
Carnegle, Catharine, 644
Carnes, John, 636
Carns, Jacob, 643
Carpenter, Emanuel, 169
Carper, James S., 221, 601
Carperton, John, 644
Carr, James, 631
  John, 643, 662
  Thomas, 538
Carrack, Samuel, 634
Carrell, John, 518
  Louisa, 518
Carrick, Joseph, 662
  Samuel, 85
Carrigen, Hugh, 662
Carringer, David, 641
Carroll, Albert Henry, 185
  Charles, 1, 3, 6, 10, 46, 80, 82,
    110, 116, 128, 129, 138,
    145, 171, 185, 201, 216,
    232, 240, 298, 321, 443,
    445, 496, 498, 519
  Daniel, 10, 46, 108, 123, 127,

443
Harriet, 115
Helen Sophia, 185
James, 1
John Lee, 116, 185, 321
Louisa, 185
Mary, 46, 185
Mary Lee, 185
Oswald, 185
Robert Goodloe Harper, 185
Thomas Lee, 185
Thomas William, 205
Carson, Charles L., 525
Carter, Bernard, 318
John, 636, 644, 646
Joseph, 169
Solomon, 646
Carty, Charles C., 541
Clarence C., 541
J. W. L., 527, 547
Jos. L., 440
Joseph W. L., 419, 541, 542
Carver, J. W. , 215
Jacob, 646
John, 643
Michael, 641
Carvil, William, 629
Cary, Cyrus, 169
George, 599
John, 84, 85
John D., 249, 269, 599
John Dew, 640
Jorn, 443
Case, Robert, 646
W. W., 389
Cashier, John, 646
Cashour, Charles W. F., 419
Casner, William, 642
Cassberry, Jane, 643
Cassel, Geo., 636
Henry, 642
Jacob, 627
Thomas, 636
Cassell, Abraham, 625
Charles E., 334
Wm., 167
Cassil, Martin, 85
Cassiman, William, 644
Caster, Thos., 635
Castle, C. Estelle, 583
Charles E., 610
Daniel, 603
David A., 541

E. C. B., 455
G., 376
George T., 391
John, 281
John A., 504
John C., 607
M. P., 426
Martin A., 542
Castleburg, Benja., 638
Cating, Joshua, 644
Caton, Richard, 321
Cattero, Jacob, 632
Caughman, Jacob, 646
Cavinaught, William, 662
Caywood, Thomas, 169
Cazenove, Anthony C., 151
Cecil, C. C., 487
William, Jr., 629
William, Sr., 629
Celler, Annie, 469
Cephas, Frederick, 646
Chadd, Samuel, 627
William, 642
Chaffee, A. E., 539
Chalhek, Andrew, 646
Chamberlain, D. L., 543
John, 225
Samuel, 26, 27
Chambers, B. D., 601
Chancellor, C. W., 571, 573,
575
Chandler, John, 492
Chaplain, Joseph, 26, 27
Chaplaine, Joseph, 600
Chapline, Col. Joseph, 33
Harry E., 607
Joseph, 75, 83-86, 225, 521
Thomas A., 534, 546, 555
Chapman, Joseph G., 272
N., 213
Nathan, 623
Charlten, John, Usher, 632
Charlton, Anne Phoebe Penn
Dagworthy, 314
Arthur, 314
Eleanor, 638
John N., 602
John U., 431
Thomas, 602
Charnal, Nicholas, 662
Chase, Jeremiah Townley, 199,
319
Richard, 597

Salmon P., 521
Samuel, 93, 103, 104, 108,
110, 145, 147, 343
Chatel, Thomas, 645
Cheeseman, Frederick, 644
Cheney, Charles, 628
Chew, Harriet, 185, 321
Samuel C., 306
Chilcote, James, 642
Richard, 271
Chilton, Robert, 662
Samuel, 353
William F., 541
Chism, John, 644
Thomas, 644
Chisolm, J. J., 592
Chiswell, J. N., 362
Lawrence A., 532
William T., 607
Chopper, Philip, 640
Christ, Michael, 632
Chriswell, Valerius, 598
Chunk, Joseph, 646
Citterman, John, 645
Clabaugh, Frank, 559
Clabough, Charles, 630
Frederick, 630
John of Fredk., 630
John of Jno., 634
Clagett, Alexander, 86
David, 342
Hezekiah, 342
Samuel, 342, 584
Sophia, 342, 490
Thomas, 101
William, 180, 299
Claggett, John, 306
Mrs. Anne, 493
Samuel, 587
Thomas John, 332
Thos. J., 601
William, 82, 597, 599
Z. S., 598
Clan, William, 623
Clance, Charles, 625
John, 630
Clantz, Charles, 488
Henry, 488
Clapham, Samuel, 111
Clapsaddle, Paul, 625
Clark, Charles H., 455, 456
Daniel, 129, 600
Daniel, Jr., 225

George Rogers, 88
Hugh, 169
James, 136, 639, 640, 647
John, 641, 643
Joshua, 643
Mother Xavier, 517
William Beverly, 263
Clarke, Clement, 623
Francis, 536
Hannah, 314
James C., 159, 227, 394, 403, 460, 558
Joseph, 635
Richard, 630
Robert, 662
William, 623
William Beverly, 290
Clary, Benjamin, 623
David, 623, 638
John, 629
William, 638, 641
Clay, Adam, 628
Henry, 31, 173, 185, 190, 193, 213, 264, 558
John, 628
Clegatt, Charles, 662
Charles, Jr., 662
Cleggett, Samuel, 582
Cleland, Samuel, 634
Clem, George, 632
George H., 344
Henry, 646
Michael, 646
Clements, William, 129, 138, 639
Clemm, Augustus, 485
Harvey, 484
John H., 484
Clempson, John, 604
Clemson, John, 627
Thomas, 326
Clew, Henry, 623
Clewell, L. P., 6
Clifft, James, 662
Climmer, Laurance, 646
Cline, Absalom, 221
Adam, 625
C. E., 528, 547
Casper, 458
Casper E., 553
Nicholas, 646
Peter, 636
Clingan, G. F., 396

John F., 227
Lewis S., 227, 539, 542, 552
Mrs. Frank, 396
Winchester, 210, 605
Clinton, Charles, 84-86
DeWitt, 134
Clipper, Felty, 641
Clise, Frederick, 632
Cloberry, William, 20
Cloninger, Philip, 636
Clothes, Geo., 630
Cloud, Mordecai, 643
Clunt, Adam, 630
Andrew, 630
Jacob, 630
Coad, Peter A., 523
Coagh, Henry, 623
Coale, James M., 157, 158, 252, 255, 276, 293, 316, 325, 326, 362, 601
Richard, 325, 326, 625
Richard, Sr., 212
William, 325, 587
Coblentz, Albert M., 535
C. R., 553
Calvin R., 612
Charles H., 465, 534, 535, 608
Emory L., 400, 465, 532, 533, 534, 535, 553, 599, 609, 612, 613
Horace B., 587
Jacob, 464, 587
John Philip, 464
Martin C., 553
Oscar B., 558, 599, 610, 613
Peter, 464
Coblin, James, 644
Cochran, John, 325
Cochrane, Sir Thomas, 301
Cock, Casper, 638
Henry, 84, 85
Samuel, 625
Cockey, John, 182, 587
John Paul, 587
Joseph Cromwell, 587
Joshua, 133, 134, 168, 181, 600
Sebastian G., 365, 602
Susunnah, 216
Cocklenkerg, Adam, 647

Cocklin, Thomas, 324
Cockran, Daniel, 635
Robert, 638
Cockrell, E. L., 617
Coe, John, Jr., 627
John, Sr., 627
William, 662
Coffman, John, 639
Cogan, John F., 524
Cola, William, 645
Colbert, W. T., 548
Colclaysier, Daniel, 627
Colden, Jacob, 642
Cole, Charles, 250, 364
Dennis, 630
H. A., 380
Henry A., 391
Humphrey, 169
James M., 159, 597
John, 662
William G., 364
Coleman, Chester, 450, 550
Colier, Edward, 645
Collamer, J., 354
Joseph, 357
Collard, Joseph, 643
Colleberger, Jacob, 628
John, 625
Collendine, Jacob, 630
Coller, Jacob, 639
Collier, Michael, 636
Colliflower, Bernard, 607
Lewis, 221
W. D., 549
W. F., 467
William F., 475, 485, 493
Wm., 489
Collins, Chas., 466
G. S., 503, 504
George S., 467
Hodijah, 632
Humphrey, 634
John A., 457
Mathias, 642
Matthew, 636
Patrick, 644
Robert, 644
William, 630, 662
Colman, Henry, 636
Colmure, George, 662
Colour, Jacob, 632
Colterbaugh, Frederick, 645
Columbus, Christopher, 558

Colvill, John, 333
Colville, Joseph, 662
Colvin, John B. , 249
Comb, Henry, 641
Combaugh, Michael, 645
Comber, Christian, 645
Combs, Henry, 641
J. W., 266
T. C., 266
Comercius, John Amos, 494
Comfort, H. I., 470, 471, 476
Common, George, 640
Comp, Peter, 627
Compter, Peter, 625
Compton, William, 623
Condall, William, 624
Condell, William (of Davy),
638
Zachariah, 625
Conine, Henry J., 389
Conley, C. H., 528, 582
Charles H., 404, 551, 587
Mrs. Helen Abell
Baughman, 562
Conly, John, 630
Connar, William, 640
Connelly, Hugh, 646
Thomas, 61
Conner, Atvill, 493
Atville, 468, 475, 542
William, 169
Connolly, John, 91, 92
Connoly, John, 662
Philip, 662
Connor, Atvill, 490
Edward, 630
James, 635
Thomas, 629
Conover, James W., 389
Conradt, G. M., 556
Conrod, Elizabeth, 640
Henry, 640
Jacob, 632
John, 641
Conroy, John D., 524
Contee, Benj, 127
Jane, 124, 166
Conway, Michael, 524
Cooe, David, 163
Cook, Benjamin, 169
George, 102, 111, 628
J. S., 432
John E., 352, 354, 356

R. A., 391
Cooke, Nathaniel, 662
William D., 397, 520
Cookerly, Jacob, 628
John, 128, 625
Cookery, James, 597
Coombs, Sister M. Anastasia,
510
Coomes, R. W., 391
Coon, Christian, 632
Henry, 640
Philip, 634
Coons, George, 646
Henry, 647
Jacob, 636
Nicholas, 646
Thomas, 641
Coonts, Baltser, 638
Henry, Sr., 630, 639
Coontz, George, 625, 632
Mary, 627
Paul, 630
William, 630
Cooper, Archibald, 634
Elton, 549
George, 623
J. S., 370
James, 372, 599, 634
James, Jr., 391, 634
John, 327, 625
Peter, 240
R., 400
Samuel, 513
Coopes, Chas. D., 434
Copeland, John, 352
Matthias, 634
Philip, 632
Copenhaver, John, 169
Coplin, Philip, 633
Coplinger, Jacob, 636
Coplintz, Adam, 636
Harman, 636
Peter, 636
Coppee, Edwin, 352
Coppersmith, Frederick, 597
George, 632
L. F., 244, 288
Lewis F., 226, 249, 525
Copple, Nicholas, 625
Philip, 645
Corbett, Emanuel, 543
Corbin, C. C., 303
Corcoran, W. W., 160, 551

William W., 280
Cormack, S. P., 371, 372
Cornelius, James, 642
Cornell, Benjamin, 630
Jacob, 632
Richard, 630
Cornickle, Daniel, 642
Cornicle, Danl, 638
Corrick, John, 82
Cossell, Daniel, 638
Cost, George, 636
Henry, 538
Jacob, 636
John, 604
Costley, Edward H., 281
Solomon, 281
Couden, Sarah, 623
Cough, George, 643
Coulehan, Mrs. Caroline, 112
Coursey, William R., 454
Courtney, William, 662
Coutz, Devalt, 645
Covel, John, 628
Cover, Abraham, 642
David, 473
E. G., 553
Earhart, 630
Eve, 627
Harry C., 535
Jacob, 630
John, 630
William, 471
Yost, 630
Cowart, E. L., 390
Cowen, John K., 243
Cowman, Anna, 338
Cox, Elisha, 641
Ezekiel, 86
Gover E., 587
Henry, 86
William, 629
Coy, Christopher, 644
Crab, Richard, 84
Crabb, Henry Wright, 600
Ralph, 647
Richard, 85, 86
Richard S., 134
Thomas, 638
Crabbs, Christian, 90
Frederick, 604
George, 630
Henry, 634
John, 90, 634

Crabell, Savilla, 458
Crabs, John, 82
Craft, Frederick, 636
Crafts, Thomas, 634
Craglo, George, 630
Craglow, William, 640
Craig, Ed., 448
  George, 662
  Kenneth M., 467
Craik, James, 299, 330
  William, 127, 128, 299, 330
Crain, Robert, 638
Craling, Teteril, 635
Crama, Jacob, 633
Cramer, Andrew N., 524
  Balth., 647
  Casper, 630, 644
  David, 475, 531, 551
  E., 605
  E. Lewis, 365
  Edward A., 437
  Ezra, 601
  Frederick W., 541
  Geo. Leslie, 541
  George, 625
  George H., 531
  George W., 543
  George William, 552, 553
  H. M., 547
  Harry M., 551, 552
  Harvey, 475
  J., 327
  J. Wm., 475
  Jacob, 628
  John, 4, 625
  John D., 454
  Leslie, 525
  M. C., 473
  Mary, 644
  Newton, 475
  Noah E., 524
  Oscar, 475
  Peter, 327, 625
  W., 327
  W. Stuart, 473
  William, 625
Cramphin, Thomas, 86
  Thomas, Jr., 83-85
Crampton, John, 663
  Oscar P, 607
  Thomas, 601, 605
Cranch, William, 597
Crane, A. Fuller, 397, 520

C. E., 547
Crapster, Abraham, 625
  John, 632
  Rudolph, 630
Craver, Clements, 169
Crawford, Charles, 663
  David, 623
  David, Jr., 623
  Elias, 642
  James, 623, 642
  John, 623, 628, 635
  Lewis, 605
  Lewis D., 607
  Moses, 633, 642
  W. H., 283
  Wm. H., 251
Crawl, Peter, 632
Crawle, Henry, 84, 85
Cray, William, 663
Craybill, John, 623
  Peter, 623
Creager, Adam, 488, 625, 646
  Conrod, 625
  Daniel, 163, 646
  Esau D., 370
  George, 278, 549, 603, 625
  George, Jr., 602
  George, Sr., 129
  J. Wesley, 532
  James, 334
  John, 323, 646
  Lawrence, 90, 334
  Lewis, 527
  Noble H., 560
  Phoebe Cath., 483
  Richard, 555
  Solomon, 163
  Valentine, 86
Creaver, Varney, 646
Crecher, George, 624
Creeger, M. L., 473
  J. Wesley, 535
  M. Luther, 535
  William, 588
Creel, J. P. H., 266
Cregar, Henry, 625
  John, 632
  Laurence, 632
  Valentine, 632
Cremian, Charles, 628
Cresap, Daniel, 21-23, 31
  Daniel, Sr., 136
  Elizabeth, 23

Joseph, Jr., 87
Michael, 22, 23, 31, 38,
  40, 87, 88
Sarah, 23
Thomas,14, 21-23, 26, 27, 31,
  39, 72, 75, 83-85, 88, 136,
  144, 225, 494, 521, 600
Cresman, Frederick, Jr., 627
  Frederick, Sr., 627
Cress, Simon, 642
  Valentine, 630
Cresswell, John A. J., 262
Creswell, Joseph, 663
Crice, John, 645
Crickbaum, Conrod, 632
Cridler, John, 635
Crim, John J., 530
Crimmins, William M., 312, 556
Crise, Henry, 634, 639
  John, 639
Crisher, Nicholas, 642
Crist, Geo. W., 482, 484, 485
  Jacob, 632, 634
  John, 634
  Philip, 632
Croan, Robert, 634
Crobough, Lodwick, 646
Crockett, Davy, 173
Croehan, J. M., 647
Croghan, George, 44
Cromer, Frederick, 646
  Jacob, 645
  John, 628
Cromrind, John, 647
Cromwell, Edith, 216
  Edward A., 588
  Eleanor, 115
  Joseph M., 526, 588, 601, 602,
    604
  Melville, 606
  Nicholas, 487
  Oliver, 216
  Robert T., 390
  William H., 440, 606
Cron, Alexander, 625
  Michael, 635
Crone, Conrad, 500
  Conrod, 636
  Jacob, 500
  Margaret, 323
  Robert, 638
Cronise, Albert Dewalt, 281
  Charles L., 526

Henry, 640
James, 461
John, 453, 640
Joseph, 534, 605
Mrs. John Calvin, 558
Crook, John A., 639
Crooks, Robert, 325
Cross, Henry, 632
Crossly, Philip, 663
Crothers, Austin L., 404
Crouse, Henry, 169
  Jacob, 473
  John, Jr., 632
  John, Sr., 630
  Philip, 627
  Rudolph, 555
  Russel O., 560
  Valentine, 630
Crow, Michael, 625
Crowell, C. H., 454
  C. J., 454
  Margaret, 625
Crowl, Devalt, 623
  Henry, 624
  Isaac, 632
  Margaret, 623
  Michael, 627
  Nicholas, 632
  Peter, 630
Crowle, Hobbs, 86
Croy, John, 638
Cruise, Paul, 627
Crum, Abraham, 169
  C. W. R., 582, 584
  Charles W. F., 541
  Charles W. R., 588
  Emory C., 542, 606
  George W., 542, 566, 606
  George W., Jr., 607
  George Washington, 588
  Henry H., 542
  Isaac L., 561
  John, 327, 625
  John Henry, 588
  John W., 485
  John, Jr., 625
  Josiah, 469
  William, 327, 431, 625, 632
Crumbaker, Jacob, 169
Crumbaugh, Conrod, 625
  John D., 370, 489
Crumbecker, Abraham, 623
  Catherine, 623

John, 624
Crumlish, John J., 524
Crumm, H. M., 547
Crush, Conrod, 639
Cruso, Robertson, 644
Crust, Henry, 646
Crutcher, Vincent, 169
Crutchley, Elias, 604
Cryer, William, 646
Cuddy, Henry, 632
Culb, Isaac, 632
Cullen, Victor F., 404
  Victor Francis, 588
Culler, C. C., 502
  Capt. Henry, 502, 503
  Clayton, 503
  Col. Henry, 503
  Daniel, 503
  Henry, 333, 601, 604, 658
  John Jacob, 588
  Lloyd T., 506
  Wm. L., 601
Culp, Philip, 642
Cumber, Christian, 625
Cumbridge, George, 643
Cumming, William, 298
Cummings, Robert, 129, 225,
  602, 624
  William, 623
Cummins, James, 623
Cumpston, Margaret, 623
  Mary, 625
Cunningham, Amos, 603
  B. A., 365, 534, 550, 603,
  605
  Benjamin A., 601
  James, 183
  William, 597
  William L., 523
Curns, James, 458
Curran, Michael, 642
  Wm., Jr., 90
Currans, William, 634
Current, James, 663
  Mathew, 663
Curtis, Henry, 625
  John R., 604
  S., 481, 483
Curts, George, 625
Cushing, Caleb, 266
  Thomas, 84
Custard, Adam, 602
  George, 636

Manuel, 643
Custis, G. W. Park, 149, 247
  George W. P., 248
  John, 164
Custus, Henry, 645
Cutsall, Geo. W., 483
Cutsell, Peter, 628
Cutshall, J. H., 547
  John H., 553
  W. B., 536, 547
  William B., 541, 553, 606
Cutting, Nicholas, 110
Cyphered, John, 628
Dabor, S., 266
Daddisman, Jacob, 642
Dade, Townsend, 492
Dadisman, Ezra, 556
  John, 400
Dagan, George, 645
Daganhart, Christian, 642
Dage, Jacob, 638
Dagworthy, John, 661, 663
Dahoof, Christian, 627
  Henry, 638
  Nicholas, 625
Dail, John, 645
Daily, John, 641
Daingerfield, Henry, 316
  Newbry, 352
Daker, Henry, 630
Dall, John R., 149
Dalton, Henry, 63
Daman, Frederick, 647
Damuth, Charles A., 392, 532
  Geo. J., 549
Daniel, John M., 325
Danner, Jacob, 623
  Samuel, 623
  Walter, 555
Dansey, Mrs. Martha, 313
Dant, G., 266
  Knowels, 72
Darby, Riggs, 541
Dare, Mary Ann, 218
Darnall, Henry, 597, 602, 644
  John, 75, 79, 85, 86, 225, 285,
  602, 644
  Philip, 644
  Thomas, 629
Darnell, Henry, 95
  John, 521
Darner, William E., 542
Darr, George M., 646

16

Darty, George, 63
Dashiell, Joseph, 145
Dashnall, George, 644
Daucherty, Elizabeth, 458
Daugherty, William, 250
Davidson, John W., 451
  Patrick, 449, 450, 467
  Samuel, 250
Davis, Amos, 623
  Barnet, 643
  Catharine, 458
  David, 663
  Elizabeth, 632
  Even, 663
  Francis, 638
  Frank E., 395, 416
  Garret, 623
  George L. L., 559
  Gilbert, 638
  H. Winter, 360
  Honical, 663
  I. L., 550
  Ignatius, 181, 601-603, 643
  James, 169
  James L., 450, 601
  James L., Jr., 451
  Jefferson, 354, 356
  John, 479, 627, 641, 644
  Joseph W., 375
  Joshua, 169, 170
  Luke, 643
  Meredith, 244
  Nathaniel, 644
  Philip, 623
  Phineas, 233, 240, 630
  Richard, 83-86, 629
  Richard, Jr., 84, 85, 87
  Thomas, 634
  W. C., 560
  Walter, 644
  William, 635, 639
  Wm. B., 556
Dawden, William, 645
Dawson, Jo., 328
  Nicholas, 644
  William, 644
Day, John, 663
  Latimer W., 531
  Leonard, 663
Days, Henry, 169
De la Vincindier, Demorest, 25
de Neale, Countess Pauline,
  117

de Schweinitz, Robert, 6
de Warville, Brissot, 337
Deakins, Frances, 86
  Francis, 85
  William, 85, 86
  William, Jr., 85
Deakus, John, 623
Deal, Benjamin, 463, 643
  Samuel, 645
Deale, George, 623
  John, 623, 625
  Leonard, 628
Dealsius, William, Jr., 84
Dean, Geo. W., 451
  George A., 534, 553, 606
  Hezekiah, 647
  John, 628, 645
  Joshua, 167
  Samuel, 663
  Thomas, 167
  W. W., 549
  William, 451
Deane, Robert, 632
Deaver, Henry T., 221
  Michael, 641
Deavers, W. P., 549
Decount, Mother Augustine,
  517
Deephy, John, 455
Deering, F., 284
Defauld, Rachel, 646
DeGrange, Garrett S., 541
  John, 169, 396
Delacour, Joshua Fredk., 638
Delander, John, 632
Delany, William J., 524
Delaplaine, Joshua, 168, 549
  Robert E., 542, 543, 555,
  621
  Theodore C., 524
  William T., 621
Delaplane, G. W. , 435
  John, 492, 625
  Joseph, 625
  Joshua, 601
  Theodore C., 601
Delashmet, Basil, 644
  Lindsay, 644
Delashmut, Elias, 636
DeLashmuth, E. L. H., 494
Delashmutt, A. J., 525
  Arthur, 382, 603
  E. L., 603

Elias L., 603
Mrs. A. J., 396
Otho, 169
Delasmutt, E. E., 401
DeLauter, H. Kieffer, 599
  James H., 606
Dell, Nicholas, 627
  Wm. H., 487
Delosier, Daniel, 634
Deloyder, David, 636
  Jacob, 636
  John, 636
Deluol, Louis R., 515, 517
Dempwolf, J. A., 528
Demuth, Jacob, 455
Denison, A. W., 560, 561
Dennis, George R., 221, 365, 391,
  395, 400, 435, 532
  George R., Jr., 541, 599
  Jacob, 632, 642
  John, 663
  L. Upshur, 598
  Mrs. George R., 180, 583
Denny, Stophel, 641
Dent, George, 603
Dern, Frederick, 627
  William, 603, 625
Derr, Bostian, 632
  Charles W., 598
  Daniel, 210
  Eugene L., 552, 606
  George, 632
  Hamilton K., 588
  Jacob, 632
  John Martin, 632
  Luther, 606
  Luther Z., 535
  Mrs. Mary C., 437
  Sebastian, 24
  W. H., 489
Dertzback, John, 167
Dertzbaugh, Geo. W., 547
  George, 552
  Lewis R., 560
Detro, John, 636
Deuker, John, 643
Devar, Abraham, 636
Devendall, John, 627
Deverbaugh, Christian, 627
Devilbiss, Adam, 623
  Casper, 623
  Chas., 163
  Christopher, 639

D. M., 580, 584
David, 605
David M., 581, 588, 607
Edwin, 535, 541
George, 327, 632, 645
George L., 659
John, 327, 588, 625, 632
Devilbliss, Edwin, 531
Devill, Geo, 327
Devitt, David B., 167, 450
Devoy, John, 638
Devoyer, Edmund, 632
DeYoe, Luther, 466, 467
Dick, Christian, 169
Joseph, 552
Peter, 625
Dickenson, John, 109
Dickenstree,
William, 623
Dickinson, Edward N., 272
Dickson, George, 25
J., 602
James, 25, 75, 78, 602
Diehl, Adam, Sr., 485
George, 396, 424, 425, 427,
502, 504
John, 531
John H., 506
Sam'l A., 484, 485
Dieterich, Daniel D., 389
Digges, Ignatius, 122
Mary, 115, 122
Diggs, James, 281
John, 26
Digman, Anne, 641
Dill, Andrew H., 598
Esther, 647
Ezra, 169
Joshua, 169, 603
Nicholas, 647
Diller, Chas. H., 582
E. D., 462
Jacob, 469
Dillon, Marmaduke M., 435
William, 644
Dimsey, John, 623
Dinges, Charles B., 549
Dinterman, George D., 528,
554
Harry, 485
Lincoln G., 606
Dittmar, David N., 486, 542
Harry F., 486, 541

Diver, Samuel, 556
Dixi, T. Freeman, 547
Dixon, Charles M., 437
Charles Mehrl, 438
Charles T., 392
Elmer E., 438
Howard Eugene, 400
James, 70, 167, 169, 200,
212, 285, 314, 597
Mrs. Fannie M., 437
Thomas, 394, 469, 487, 623
Dobb, Edward Brice, 65
Jacob, 636
Dodd, Morris, 663
Dodge, Francis, 244
Dodson, John, 623, 638
Michael, 627
Dogan, William, 663
Dolhammer, Uly, 625
Doll, C. J., 580
Charles, 556
Conrad, 136
G. J., 572
G. Jos., 573
George J., 524
James E., 534
M. E., 416, 534
Melvill E., 534
Michael, 167
Peter, 167
Samuel V., 551
Domer, George, 632
Donaldson, Charles F., 281
Donnebow, Hugh, 632
Donner, Jacob, 460
Donsife, H. L., 588
Doolittle, J. R., 354, 357
Door, William, 630
Doran, F. F., 523
Doratha, Patrick, 646
Dorchey, John, 646
Dorcus, Charles V., 536
Dorran, William, 85
Dorret, Garnet William, 663
John, 663
Dorsey, Basil, 84-86, 606, 629
Basil, Jr, 127
Daniel, 623
David, 638
Edward, 597, 600, 629
Edwin, 503, 504
Eli, 109, 623
Eli (of Edwd), 623

Elizabeth, 590, 623
Evan, 347, 643
Evan L., 353
Frederick, Sr., 342
H. W. , 550
Harry, 550
Harry W., 221, 588, 605
John, 325, 623
John (of James)., 638
John W., 538, 588
John, Jr., 326
Joshua, 175, 225, 431, 597,
600
Julianna, 109
Kate, 452
Lloyd, 168, 450, 538, 565,
588
Lloyd, Jr., 588
Mrs. Lucy, 562
Nicholas, 588
Rhoderick, 168, 169
Richard, 169, 226, 227, 565,
588
Sophia, 127
Thomas Beale, 319
W. Roderick, 542
William, 221, 562, 625
William (of Thos.), 623
William H., 131
William, Jr., 624
Wm. R., 548
Dosh, T. W. , 505
Doty, Elmer W., 541
Doub, Abraham, 456
Abram, 453
Enos, 454
Ezra, 256, 556
Florence W., 508, 509, 520
George, 601
Jacob, 456
Joshua, 453, 601
Lewis P., 454
Staley, 541
Valentine, 453, 456
William H., 525
William W., 535, 553
Dougherty, James, 41
W. E., 455
Douglas, Henry Kyd, 379
Robert, 493
Stephen A., 261, 291, 363
Thos. Fogerty, 635
W. Mitchell, 558

Douglass, Robert, 485
Doury, James, 167
Dow, Loreno, 453
Lorenzo, 537
Dowden, Michael Ashford, 75, 79
Downes, J. W., 548
Downey, Frank, 548
J. W., 548, 564, 581, 584, 590
J. W., Jr., 582, 588
Jesse Wright, 588
William, 172, 181, 536, 548, 601
Downing, Benjamin, 636
Dowson, Jos, 327
Doyle, Alexander, 311, 312
Henry, 264, 457, 527
John, 663
Lawrence, 169, 462
Draumer, Samuel, 63
Drill, Jacob, 636
Drine, Susannah, 641
Dromgoole, E., 482
Dronenburg, Charles, 498
Drumbar, Conrad, 627
Drumgole, Edward, 457, 458
Du Bois, John, 513-515
Du Bourg, William, 513
William V., 512, 517
Du Namel, Charles, 497
Duane, William J., 202
Dubel, Tyson D., 529
Duble, Isaac, 641
Dubois, John, 444, 522, 523
Dudderar, George W., 605
John, 183
Dudderer, William, 604
Dudrear, Mrs. Mary A., 485
Duer, Samuel, 556
Duffy, P. L., 523
Dugan, John, 635
Dugmore, Edward, 663
Duke, Basil, 663
Dulaney, Daniel, 1, 6, 10, 102, 327
Daniel, Jr., 597, 600
Patrick, 6, 406, 408
Walter, 25
Dulany, Benjamin, 84
Daniel, 22, 26, 27, 298, 494, 495
Patrick, 269

Dulen, Francis, 643
Dull, Conrod, 640
Joseph, 639
Peter, 641
Dumburger, Mary, 646
Dun, Barnet, 643
Dunbar, J. W. R., 353, 590
Duncan, John, 663
William, 644
Dungan, William H., 538
Duning, James, 629
Dunkin, Theodore, 644
Dunlap, Henry, 605
Dunlop, Elizabeth, 109
Henry, 257, 365, 550
Margaret H., 257
Dunn, Robert, 632
Dunning, Patrick, 635
Dunott, Daniel Zacharias, 588
Justus, 566, 588
Thomas, 566
Thomas J., 588
Dunphy, Edward J., 524
John C., 524
Dunstill, Charles, 663
Dunuman, William, 639
Durant, Clark J., 372
Durbin, Benjamin, 627
Cornelius, 642
John, 623
Mary, 628
Thomas, 627
Thos. Bond, 627
William, 627
Durf, Jacob, 639
Samuel, 640
Durst, Daniel, 169
Henry, 634
John, 169
Philip, 634
Dusinger, Jacob, 641
Dust, Isaac, 353
Dutro, Jacob, 468
Josiah, 468
Dutrow, H. V., 582
Howard V., 560, 588
R. P., 605
R. P. T., 493, 601
R. S. J., 419, 553
Richard P. T., 400
Richard S. D., 541
Richard S. J., 542
Samuel, 493

Samuel P., 541
Dutterar, George W., 603
Duttero, Baltser, 636
Conrod, 623, 631
Frederick, 642
George, 645
Jacob, 625
Dutteron, Jacob, 641
Dutterow, John, 645
Dutters, John, 627
Duval, Benjamin, 629
Grafton, 588
Lloyd, 565
Lloyd T., 589
Samuel, 25
Duvall, Chas, 462
Daniel, 185, 601, 604, 605
Gabriel, 200, 205
Geo. W., 531
Grafton, 604
J. E., 561
Lewis, 630
Luther, 417
Mareen, 630
Margaret, 459
Mary, 629
O. N., 541
Samuel, 431, 600, 603, 639
Samuel G., 528, 540, 543-545
Singleton, 542
Singleton W., 537
Thos. G., 437
W., 548
Walter, 560
Wilbur H., 527, 541-543
William, 86, 462
William H., 541
William, Jr., 629
William, Sr., 629
Wm. T., 547
Dwin, John A., 325
Dyer, Edward, 640
Martha, 639
Wm. H., 459
Eader, Abraham, 625
Charles, 348
Charles E., 384
E. M., 547
Elmer, 555
George, 625
Harry, 560
Jacob, 645
Mrs. A. L., 396, 584

P. M., 547, 561
Thomas S., 541
Eades, Samuel, 663
Eagenton, Sabriet, 663
Eagleston, Abram, 663
Earhart, Geo., 327
Earl, James, 641
Earley, Francis, 663
Early, Jubal A., 384, 562
Eastburn, Benjamin, 85
Easterday, Joseph, 504, 603,
  605
  Lewis, 503
  Louis, 504
Eaton, John H., 159
Eatry, Jacob, 663
Ebbert, Henry, 536
  John W., 251
Ebberts, Jacob, 169
  John, 169
  John M., 365
  Joseph, 169
  Joseph M., 364, 382, 602
Eberhardt, Nicholaus H., 6
Eberhart, John, 454
  Laurence, 453
Ebert, Adam, 638
  Eli, 167
  P., 482
Eberts, E. P., 556
Eby, Daniel, 455
  Lemuel, 456
Eccerhart, Martin, 647
Eccleston, Samuel, 516
Ech, Samuel T., 391
Eck, Conrod, 646
Eckard, Michael, 630
Eckart, Christian, 640
  Geo., 628
Ecker, Daniel, 462
Eckhart, Anthony, 625
Eckis, John, 630
Eckler, Jacob, 627
Eckstein, C. H., 437
  Christian, 559
  Christian H., 598
  Mrs. M. Kate, 437
Eddes, William, 73, 278
Edelen, Christian, 97
  Christopher, 600, 629
Edelin, Christian, 84
  Christopher, 85, 95, 285,
    602, 605, 606

Eden, Robert, 634
  William, 108
Edmeston, W., 467
Edmonds, Harry C., 560
  Joseph, 281
Edmondson, Roger, 629
Edwards, B. E. W., 266
  Bettie, 257
  Emory, 218, 491
  Henry, 491
  William, 663
Edzler, Daniel, 645
Egan, Michael De Burgo, 523
Ege, M. M., 342
Egerton, C. C., 353
  P., 331
Egg, Jacob, 627
Eichelberger, A. L., 266
  C. D., 589
  Edward S., 451, 598, 606
  Edward S. , 398
  G., 244
  G. M., 538, 549
  George M., 187, 227, 392,
    602
  Grayson, 226, 227, 365,
    398, 525, 597, 600
  James, 589
  James W., 589, 611
  James W., Jr., 589
  Joseph, 550
  Leonard, 642
  M., 605
  Martin, 604
  Mrs. Edward S, 82
Eickard, Joseph, 630
Eicker, Barnabas, 641
Eisenangle, Geoge, 343
Eisenhauer, John, 526, 556
  Joseph, 555
Eitly, Wm., 640
Elbert, Catharine, 640
Elberts, George, 639
Elder, Arnold, 634
  Basil Spalding, 324
  Charles, 170, 634
  Clementina, 634
  Elisha, 634
  Francis, 630
  Guy, 81, 632
  James A., 527, 611
  Joachim, 325
  John F., 605

Joseph, 643
Phebe, 634
Thomas, 324, 630
William, 10, 81, 90, 324, 497,
  634
  William Henry, 11, 324
  William, Jr., 632, 634
Eldridge, Charles D., 531, 541
Eldrige, Charles, 456
  George, 456
  Mary, 456
Elgar, John, 233
Elgin, Fisk, 581
Elkins, John W., 372
Elknand, Mary, 640
Ellengenger, Christian, 647
Eller, Elizabeth, 641
Ellicott, Evan T., 276
  Jonathan, 171
Elliott, C. M., 548
  Jesse D., 183
  Jno. A., 548
  Robert, 537
  Thomas, 642
Ellis, Charles M., 404
  E. M., 547
  Edwin H., 541
  James H., 389
  Zacharias, 85
Ellzey, William, 151
Ely, Charles W., 397, 398, 451,
  520, 567, 576
  Chas., 560
  Daniel, 169
  Grace, 82
  Grace D., 520
  Isaac, 400
  Wm., 167
Elzter, Daniel, 469
Embury, Philip, 457
Emery, John, 642
Emmart, W., 265
Emmert, G. F., 547
Emmet, Samuel, 85
Emmit, Samuel, 634
  William, 324, 634
Emory, Robert, 459
Emperor, ———, 352
Engelbrecht, P. M., 547
England, George, 110
  Jacob, 623
  John Jr., 623
  John, Sr., 623

Englar, Josiah, 606
Engle, Milton F., 437
  Milton T., 555
  Peter, 641
Englebrecht, George, 534, 552
  L. M., 547
  Philip M., 532
  William, 169
Englebright, Conrod, 639
Engler, Jacob, 623
English, George N., 535, 549
  Jonathan D., 603
Enniss, Wallis, 663
Enock, Henry, 59, 60
Ensey, Jacob, 623
Ent, George W., 168, 169, 292, 601
  John, 169
Epley, Jacob, 647
Epperd, Philip, 625
Epperly, Jacob, 625
  Jacob, Jr., 625
Erb, Christopher, 630
  John, 632
  Peter, 647
Erbach, Henry, 541
Erbaugh, Jacob, 635
  Laurence, 630
  Margaret, 627
  Wendle, 627
  William, 628
Erbin, James, 647
Erdman, F., 210
  George, 210
Erehart, George, 647
Erhart, Carl, 647
Ernst, Jacob, 645
Erskine, Robert, 536
Esburn, Jane, 642
Eschbach, E. R., 396, 408, 414, 415, 436-438, 441, 467, 469, 473, 474, 507, 510, 568
Estep, James, 630
  Thomas, 627
  William, 627
  Zachariah, 642
Etchison, H. D., 547
  H. Dorsey, 545, 546, 598
  H. N., 400
  Mrs. Marshall, 82
Etienne,
  J. B., 517

Etsler, George, 633
  John, 623
Ettinger, Jacob, 647
Etzler, A. H., 535, 536
  George W., 606
  J. H., 469
  John H., 606
Evan, John, 60
Evans, Allen, 352
  Ezekiel, 623
  Hugh W., 102
  John, 630
  Joseph, 169
  W. E., 506
  W. H., 353
Even, John, 59
Evens, Even, 663
  Thomas, 663
  William, 663
Everett, Edward, 363
  Valentine, 636
Everhart, Elijah, 589
  Lawrence, 138, 183, 322, 644
  Michael, 639
  Peter, 644
Everheart, Lawrence, 323
Everly, George, 645
  John, 623
Evers, A. M., 453-456
  Henry Samuel, 454
  Samuel, 454
Everton, Mrs., 25
Eves, Amanda, 468
  Basil, 281
  Mrs. Jane, 281
  Peter, 468
Evett, George, 167
Evit, Woodward, 638
Eyler, Benjamin, 455
  Charles, 455
  Charles A., 606
  Charles C., 607
  David, 455
  J. Albert, 473
  John, 169
  Perry, 455
  R. O., 549
  Thomas F., 535
Eyster, W. F., 503-505
Fagler, Henry, 646
  Jacob, 167
Fahee, Thomas, 663

Fahrney, H. P., 462, 463, 566, 584
  Harry P., 581
  Henry P., 589
  J. Welty, 463
  Mrs. P. D., 583
  P. D., 462, 463, 621
  Peter D., 589
Fair, Michael, 629
Faires, John, 90
Fairfax, Wm., 29
Faithful, William T., 376
Falconer, John H., 598
  William F., 551
  William H., 524, 552
Falkner, Alexander, 643
  Gilbert, 629
Falling, Henry, 636
Fare, Charles, 630
Fares, John, 82
Farguhar, Allen, Jr., 623
Faris, John, 634
Farmer, Golden, 284
  William, 642
Faro, Henry, 632
Faromite, Henry, 646
Farquhar, Allen, 627
  Benjamin, 603, 604
  James, 623
  John H., 599
  Moses, 627
  Poultney, 163
  Samuel, 623
  William P., 181, 549, 601, 604, 623
  William Jr., 623
Farrell, Thomas, 663
Farring, G. F., 487
Farthing, Aaron, 641
  James, 644
Farver, Margarett, 638
Faubel, F. Marion, 598
  Jacob, 168, 169
  John, 169
Fauble, Casper, 169
  George, 170
  James, 497
  John, 640
Faulkener, John, 663
Faulkner, C. J., 33
  John B., 536
Fauntleroy, Sally C., 77
Faupel, George H., 520

Faux, W., 176
Favorite, H. J., 266
Faw, Abraham, 127, 268, 600, 605, 638
Feaga, William M., 603
Fearake, Adolphus, Jr., 598
Fearhake, Adolphus, 459, 540-545
    Adolphus, Jr., 539, 606
    Adolphus, Sr., 536-539
    George, 536
    Rosa, 459
Feaster, George, 643
Featherbin, Jacob, 627
Feeser, Adam, 647
Feiser, P. L., 489
Feizer, P. L., 475
Fell, John, 663
Felty, Jacob F., 170
Ferguson, John, 627
    Samuel, 630
    Samuel, Jr., 630
    William, 636
Ferrel, John, 431
Ferrell, Kennedy, 285
Fessler, John, 174, 227, 638
Fest, Michael, 644
Fester, Daniel, 642
    George, 642
Feurhacke, George, 647
Fevery, Jacob, 634
Fickle, Jonathan, 630
    Matthias, 630
Fie, Henry, 640
    Joseph, 639
Fielding, John, 663
    Michael, 639
Fields, Henry, 663
    Mathew, 663
Fiery, Jacob, 348
Fife, Jonathan, 644
Filbert, H. W., 303
Filicchi, Antonio, 512
Filker, Jacob, 640
Filler, Jacob, 625
    William E., 541
Finch, John, 169, 630
    Thomas, 640
Finckel, Samuel, 466
    Samuel D., 467
Findlay, Patrick, 663
Fine, John, 170
    Peter, Jr., 628

Peter, Sr., 625
    Philip, 645
    Philip, Jr., 628
Finefrock, Henry, 647
Fink, Adam, 639
    J. R., 455
    J. W., 454
    Nicholas, 24
    Philip, Jr., 641
    Philip, Sr., 636
Firestone, Charles F., 541
    Jacob, 167
    Luther, 483
    M. L., 561
    Mary M., 483
    Mathias, 644
    Nicholas, 641
    Oscar F., 541
Firmwalt, Lawrence, 627
Firor, Calvin L., 473
    D. A., 473
    D. S., 471, 472
    Guy W., 560
    J. T., 472
    Jacob, 601
    James H., 473, 549
    Joseph T., 473
    M. D., 473
    M. L., 471
    W. L., 471, 472
    William, 473
Fishbrun, Philip, 625
Fischer, Adam, 170, 600, 605
    George J., 209, 226-228
    John, 536, 537
Fish, Charles B., 158
Fishburn, Philip, 84, 85
Fisher, Adam, 84, 85, 95, 565, 589
    Charles W., 454
    Christian, 632
    David, 606, 627
    Geo. J., 450
    George, 627
    George I., 552
    Henry, 636, 646
    John, 181, 375, 589, 601, 604, 640
    John Smith, 565, 589
    Mary, 627
    Moses, 541, 557
    Peter, 340, 636
    Philip, 646

S. R., 414
    Samuel, 486
    Samuel R., 470
    W. S., 476
    William, 643
Fisk, Charles B., 272
Fisnot, Peter, 327
Fisor, Jacob, 647
    Nicholas, 647
Fitch, G. N., 354, 357
Fitchtuck, John, 643
Fitsgerald, James, 643
Fitzgerald, James, 61, 62
    John, 663
    M. J., 381
    Morriss, 663
    Thomas, 530
Fitzhugh, B. G., 602
    Benj. G., 607
    Catherine, 342
    Clagett, 351
    James P., 335
    Mary Pottinger, 342
    Meta McP, 342
    Peragrine, 342
    William, 190, 342
    William H., 184
    Wm., Jr., 149
Fitzpatrick, James, 159
    Thomas, 663
Fitzwater, Levin, 663
Fivecoat, Peter, 642
Flanagan, Malachia, 646
Flannagan, Hugh, 632
    Lackland, 632
Flannegan, Richard, 663
Flautt, Christian, 324
Fleck, Lucas, 634
    Philip, 634
Fleet, Henry, 20
Flegle, Alty, 623
    Charles, 627
    John, 627, 642
    Valentine, 627
Flegleson, George, Jr., 627
Fleischmann, J. H., 555
Fleischmenn, Wm., 555
Fleming, Joseph, 450
    Thomas A., 589
Flemming, Arthur, 632
    James, 606
    John, 632
    Joseph, 646

Robert, 634
T. , 86
Thomas, 632, 643
Flenner, Daniel, 642
John, 625
Fleschmen, J. H., 561
Fletcher, Jacob, 630
John, 86
Fling, Owen, 169
Flint, Joseph, 86
Thomas, 225
Flohr, Chas. G., 462
Jeremiah, 473
John R., 462
Leonard J., 462
S. P., 462
W., 462
Flook, C. F., 304
Cyrus F., 456, 531
Dawson, 456
Elizabeth Eby, 531
Geo. W., 497
John P., 531
Jonas E., 497
Mrs. Mary, 497
Flora, Abright, 635
John, 634
Flower, Nicholas, 646
Floyd, Anna B., 559
Anna Beall, 82
James, 663
Fluehart, Massy, 630
Fluhart, Stephen, 642
Fluke, Barbara, 636
Henry, 636
John, 636
Peter, 640
Flynn, Dennis J., 523, 524
Mother Mariana, 518
Fock, Hugh, 642
Fogelson, George, 634
Fogle, Adam, 629
Baltzer, 625
Christian, 644
Frederick, 647
Henry, 625, 645
Matthias, 625
Michael, 627
Oscar M., 560
Fogler, Henry, 169
Foley, Henry, 640
Folke, George, 35
Folkner, Peter, 169

Forble, Jacob, 639
Force, Peter, 53
Ford, Edward, 663
John, 640, 643
Jose, 663
Joseph, 170, 630
Robert, 597
Stephen, 628
William, 642
Foreman, Edward K., 391
Forman, Edwin K. , 589
Forrest, Jonathan, 247
Solomon, 169, 604
Susan, 247
Forsythe, J. C., 502
James P., 541
Fortune, Charles, 634
Foster, Adam, 663
Nettie, 390
Foucht, Jacob, 563
Fouke, Michael, 340
Fountleroy, Sally Conrad, 508
Fout, C. Will, 555
Cyrus A., 437
John H., 538
Miss A. R., 396
Mrs. Martha, 437
R. C., 582
Foutch, John, 641
Fouts, Baltis, 632
Henry, 632
William, 645
Foutz, David, 604
Michael, 627, 645
Fowble, Jacob, 167
Fowler, James, 642
John, 629
O. P., 266
Zadock, 629
Fox, Baltzer, 625
C. F. Adolphus, 539,
541-543
Casper, 625, 647
Charles H. S., 437
Chas., 392
Elizabeth, 639
Frederick, 636
Geo. P., Sr., 505
George, 625
George P., 550, 605
Henry, 633, 644, 647
Jacob, 276, 605
Jeremiah, 606

John, 645
Matthias, 625
Michael, 625
Mrs. Mary E., 437
Peter, 625
Philip, 505
Thomas C., 535
Foy, Sister M. Aloysia, 510
Fralick, Henry, 632
Frame, George, 635
France, Daniel, 24
Francis, Earley, 663
Joseph, 663
Frank, George, 632
Frankenfield, Theodore, 408
Franklin, Benjamin, 3, 29, 41,
337, 341
Charles, 638
Thomas, 642
William, 42
Frasher, Henry, 636
Frasier, Henry C. , 365
John, 641
Sarah, 641
Frazier, David, 395
Henry, 491
John H., 557
Jonathan, 636
Luther T. O., 541
Peter, 663
Sarah, 490
Thomas, 636
William, 636
Fream, Richard, 634
Frease, A. P., 470
Andrew P., 489
Freberger, Peter, 167
Freck, Jonathan, 632
Frecker, Philip, 632
Freed, J. D., 454-456
Freeman, Aaron, 663
Benjamin, 664
Esias, 664
Jacob, 627
Nathaniel, 664
Richard, 629, 664
Samuel, 664
Thomas, 664
Freese, A. P., 493
Freeze, A. P., 465
Andrew P., 473, 475
D. P., 486
Freisogle, John, 163

French, Israel, 629
Thomas, 602
Freshour, Charles N., 530
G., 266
Freshower, Adam, 632
Mariah, 632
Frickburger, John, 646
Fridinger, Nicholas, 536
Friend, Charles, 12
Jacob, 86
Fries, W. O., 454
Frietchie, Barabara, 378
John Casper, 378
Frieze, A. P., 476
Michael, 625
Fringer, Jacob, 627
Nicholas, 630
Frink, Henry, 646
Frisby, James, 164
Perry, 164
Fritchey, J., 266
Fritchie, Barbara, 377, 379,
396
Caspar, 96, 97
Frock, Daniel, 627
Fromback, John, 642
Frombech, Jacob, 639
Fromke, A. J., 547
Augustus J., 526
Harry J., 541, 543
Frost, Eli, 561
George, 646
J. M., 266
Lucy, 459
Robert, 170
Frusham, Adam, 603
Frushour, Chas. N., 460
Jacob, 170
Fry, Anough, 636
Daniel, 646
Jacob, 646
Martin, 634
Fryer, Richard, 644
William, 664
Fukney, Peter, 645
Fulam, John, 635
Fulham, John, 635
Fulier, Robert, 636
Fulker, Christopher, 638
Fuller, Samuel, 634
Fulton, Clarence C., 531
Newton A., 531
Robert, 327, 337, 589, 604,

625
Fultz, Margaret, 639
Fulwiler, Jacob, 636
Fumenfelter, Phoenix, 647
Fundebaugh, Cath., 625
Daniel, 625
David, 625
Lazarus, 625
Funderbough, Walter, 632
Funier, Henry, 636
Funk, E. P., 455
Jacob, 85, 86, 92, 600
Peter, 636
Rudolph, 635
Furney, Abraham, 630
Nicholas, Sr., 627
Philip, 630
Furtney, Catharine, 645
Daniel, 645
Peter, 645
Fuss, Concord, 628
John, 627, 642
Philip, 627
William, 630
Fye, Simeon, 640
Gabble, Joseph, 629
Gabby, William, 149, 181
Gabler, H. Wm., 647
Gadultig, George, 170
Gaffney, John, 498
Gahart, Adam, 645
Gaither, Chas. D., 560
Ephraim, 134
Henry, 138
Henry, Sr., 86
John D., 601, 605
Stewart, 227, 534, 538
Stuart, 433, 434
William M., 606
Wm., 134
Galatin, Albert, 175
Gale, Edward P., 520
George, 127
Gall, Henry, 483
Gallagher, F., 391
M. P., 598
Philip J., 523
Galligher, M. P., 280
Galloway, Benjamin, 342
Galt, Matthew, 630
Galwith, P., 266
Gambrill, C. Staley, 541
James H., 396, 552

James H., Jr., 541
Mrs. Jas. H., 396
Robert G., 541
Stephen, 159
Games, Francis, 664
Gans, Edgar H., 318
Gansevoort, Peter, 163
Gant, Margaret, 644
Gantney, Adam, 646
Gantt, Fielder, 275, 600, 632
John, 536, 600
Thomas, 600
Gantz, Mrs. Mary, 285
Garber, Glenn O. , 542
John, 461
Gardiner, John, 314
Luke, 313
Susanna, 314
Susannah, 313
Gardner, John, 629
Lewis, 640
Tobias, 623
Garfield, James A. , 262
Garnhart, Henry, 640
Garret, Barton, 636
John R., 504
Garrett, John, 664
John W., 242, 347
Richard, 664
Robert, 242
Garrott, Edward, 272
John D., 589
Maria, 490
Nellie Carter, 559
Garsinger, David, 636
Gartland, Catherine, 316
Garver, Martin, 625, 645
Michael, 636
Samuel, Jr., 625
Samuel, Sr., 625
Gassaway, Robert, 625
Samuel, 628
Gassman, Jno, 510
Gaston, John, 641
Gates, Christian, 505
Horatio, 89, 328, 336, 341
Jacob, 634
Robert, 169
Gather, William, 638
Gatrell, Charles, 639
Gattin, J., 266
Gatton, Edgar M., 589
Gatzandanner, John, 168

Gauk, Christian, 632
Gault, Adam, 364, 451
Gaunt, W. A. , 462
Gaver, Christian, 625
    Daniel, 501, 636
    Elias, 567, 606
    George D., 531
    George W., 528, 554
    Henry, 501
    J. W., 547
    John, 642
    Joseph, 502
    Joseph W., 540, 543, 557,
        599, 607
    Otho J., 606
    Peter, 636
    Wm. E., 582, 589
Gay, Henry, 628, 645
Gaylor, Mrs. John, 497
Geasey, M. F., 531
Geering, John, 638
Geeting, George A., 452
    George Adam, 454
Geisbert, Charles, 456
Geisinger, Jacob, 452
    Samuel D., 603
Geisser, Melchoir, 464
Geissler, R., 441
Gelashee, Mathew, 641
Gelstrap, William, 664
Genater, John, 664
Genkins, Joab, 644
Genspur, John, 646
George, Samuel W., 530
Gephart, Geo. R., 547
Gerhard, ——, 647
Gerhart, Isaac, 412
Gernand, J. A., 473
    J. C., 473
Gessenger, Charles, 646
Gesty, Jacob, 645
Getert, Valentine, 640
Gethius, Hobson, 67
Getsentanner, George, 640
Getsingtanner, Baltser, 632
    Christian of B., 632
    Jacob, 632
    Jacob, Sr., 632
    John, 632
Gettes, Alexander, 645
Getty, Francis, 628
Getzendaner, Abraham, 221
    Daniel, 227

Edward T., 227
Getzendanner, Christian, 250,
    604
    George, 603
    Harvey F., 581, 589
    J. W., 582
    Jacob, 603
    John W., 589
    M. E., 620
Geyer, Hans Fred, 479
    Henry S., 252, 599
    J. M., 566
    J. W., 565, 589
    Jacob, 167
    James M., 601
    John W., 250, 256, 601,
        603
    Jonas, 167
    Joseph M., 601
Ghiselin, Reverdy, 602
Ghoslin, Ambrose, 170
Gibbons, John, 454
Gibbony, John, 603
Giboney, Richard, 546
Gibony, John, 536
Gibson, Hannah, 629
    John A., 582
    Joseph, 492
    Joshua Gregg, 589
    M. B., 510
Giddy, Peter, 633
Gilbert, Barnet, 632
    Bernard, 488
    Charles, 555
    Charles S., 389
    E. Marshall, 535
    Ezra, 460
    Francis, 647
    George, 454, 459
    Jacob, 623
    Jeremiah, 636
    Rachel, 647
    Thomas, 85, 636
Gilds, N. E., 470, 471
Gill, A. J., 543
    A. S., 303
    George A, 206
Gilleland, Hester, 630
    Philip, 639
Gilliland, David S., 324
Gilloegly, Michael A., 524
Gilmor, Henry, 384, 385
    Robert, Jr., 171

Gilmore, William, 625
Gilpin, Charles M., 598
Gilson, Albert, 459
    C. Albert, 527, 541
Gipps, Abraham, 640
    Nicholas, 639
Giraud, Eugene, 516
Girton, Sylvester, 634
Girty, George, 638
Gisbert, Hamilton, 658
Gisberts, Gisbert, 644
Giseberd, Andrew, 641
Giseler, George, 647
    John, 647
Gisert, Melchor, 636
Gist, Christopher, 216, 218
    Christopher, II, 216
    David, 216, 627
    Edith, 216
    Elizabeth, 216, 643
    Independent, 217
    J., 327
    Jemima, 216
    John, 216, 627
    Jonathan, 642
    Joseph, 218
    Joshua, 128, 216-218, 600,
        604, 623
    Mordecai, 216-218, 536
    Nathaniel, 216, 218
    Rachael, 216
    Richard, 127, 216, 218
    Robert, 218
    Ruth, 216
    Sarah, 216
    States, 217
    Thomas, 216
Gitt, Joseph S., 611
Gittinger, Edward A., 547
    Emma, 562
    Emma R., 396, 583
    George M., 613
    Henry M., 440, 526
    John, 623
    Z. James, 527, 540, 552
    Z. T., 292
Gittings, Colmore, 641
    George, 463
    Jeremiah, 636
    John S., 290
    W. T., 363, 601
    William, 556
Given, Jno. M., 621

Gladhill, J. S., 502
Glasby, Mathias, 640
Glass, Samuel, 642
Glazier, Frederick, 664
Glen, F. M., 454
Glenn, Lewis W., 184
Glessner, George W., 465, 560, 561
 Harry, 560
 William, 561
 Wm., 391
 Wm. T., 348
Glibra, John, 664
Gliston, John, 645
Gloss, George, 623
Glossbrenner, J. J., 454
Glover, John, 630
Gluck, A. M., 486
Godson, James, 664
Goebricher, Sussman, 540
Goering, Jacob, 501
Goldenburg, Henry, 539, 542
Goldsborough, C. W., 566, 584
 Caroline, 589
 Charles Henry, 589
 Charles W., 583, 589
 Chas. W., 581
 E. L., 603
 E. Y., 387, 390, 559, 561
 Edward Y., 560, 565, 598
 Edward Yerbury, 589
 Howes, 589
 John, 589
 John S., 589
 Leander Worthington, 589
 Marshal, 304
 Mrs. E. Y., 583
 Nicholas, 167
 Robert, 108
 William, 183, 227, 431, 527, 589
Goldshine, Arnes, 645
Gombar, Jacob, 638
 John, 638
 John, Jr., 640
Gomber, Ezra, 169
 Jacob, 600
Good, Adam, 630
 Eleanor, 630
 George, 630
 Isaac, 632
 Jacob, 85, 86, 95, 628

Goode, Mrs. Ignatius, 583
Goodell, C. F., 580-582
 Charles F., 546, 590
 Chas. F., 582
 Jessie, 459
Goodley, Henry, 642
Goodman, J. M., 582
 James M., 542
 James Munroe, 590
 Joseph, 644
 P., 556
 Philip, 634
 William, Jr., 634
Goodmanson, Peter, 210, 556
Goodwin, Mathew, 664
 Richard, 641
Gordon, Daniel, 634
 George, 26, 27, 602
 Harry, 284
 John B. , 389
 Joseph, 630
 Josiah H., 159, 371
Gorman, Arthur P., 159
 John, 664
Gorrell, James, 664
Gorson, Charles, 628
Gorsuch, Harry C., 531
 Thomas, 524, 601, 602
Goshour, John, 632
Goslen, Amos, 623
Goslin, Ambrose, 536
Gosling, Henry, 630
Gosnel, Joseph, 623
Gosnell, Alonzo, 549
Goss, Gideon, 639
Goswell, Charles, 645
Gotwald, Washington V., 466, 467
Gourley, Thomas, 602
Gouso, Jacob, 167
 John, 167
Gouvenier, Samuel, 332
Gouverneur, Samuel L., 251
Gower, Mary Ann, 212
Grabell, Peter, 550
Grabill, Moses, 169
 Peter, 601
Grady, Henry W., 311
Graeber, J. G., 501
Graff, George, 536
 Marcus Y., 167
Graham, John, 102, 601, 602, 640

Robert P., 609
Grahame, John, 110, 168, 431-433, 527
 Mrs. John Colin, 107
 Robert, 664
 Thomas, 167
Grambo, H., 647
Gramer, Jacob, 627
Grandadam, Francis, 627
Graser, Charles, 560
Grason, William, 159, 257
Grate, C., 325
Graves, Adam, 96
 Dietrick, 488
 George, 97
 James, 664
 John George, 96
Gray, C. H. , 266
 David, 341
 Earl, 328
 J. F. F., 487
 J. L., 266
 John, 272
 Mrs. Laura E., 493
 R., 266
 William, 170
Graybill, Henry, 41
 J. M. , 502
 Jacob, 630
 John, 183, 625
 Peter, 639
Greely, Horace, 551
Green, C. W. , 266
 Enoch, 400
 Francis, 629
 Frederick, 599
 H. T. C., 382
 John W., 541
 Lewis, 167, 182, 599
 Nathaniel, 89
 Samuel, 632
 Shields, 352
 Thomas C., 353
Greenhalt, Jacob, 627
Greenmeyer, William, 324
Greenwood, George E., 396
 Yost, 623
Gregg, Samuel U., 541
Gregory, Chas. R., 530
Greider, Eugene P., 6
Grey, James, 664
 Sabriet, 664
Grier, Robert S., 467

Griffin, Benjamin, 664
  Chas. W., 560
Griffit, William, 630
Griffith, Caleb, 629
  Charles G., 84, 86
  Elisha, 629
  Greenbury, 84, 85
  Henry, 80, 84-86, 600
  Henry, Jr., 84
  Lebbeus, 605
  Lebbius, 221
  Orlando, 629
  Patty, 630
  Philip, 629
  Richard, 431
  Samuel, 84, 85
  William, 26
Griffiths, William, 27
Grimber, John, 85
Grimes, Hugh, 664
  John, 625
  Joshua, 623
  Martin, 625
  Mrs. W. T., 472
  Nicholas, 623
  W. L., 3
  William, 625
  William G., 606
Grimm, Alexander, 491
  J. L., 453, 455, 456
  J. N., 455
  J. W., 454-456
Grinder, Eli, 392
  Eli D., 391
  John W., 607
Gring, M. A., 486
Gripencurl, Diderick, 647
Griswold, H., 353
Gritshall, John, 632
Grobp, John G., 466, 467
Groff, Charles D., 541, 560
  John, Jr., 630
  John, Sr., 630
  Joseph, 384, 391
  W. S., 560
Grose, Henry, 646
Grosh, Conrad, 84, 85, 95, 431
  Michael, 85
  Peter, 40, 84, 85
Groshart, Adam, 646
Grosheng, Abraham, 632
Groshon, Geo. A., 560
Grosman, Simon, 643

Gross, Charles, 605
  H. B., 590
  John A., 487
  Sarah, 639
Grossickle, George P., 606
Grossman, John, 639
Grossnickle, C. Upton, 531
  Chas. C., 460
  Elias, 460
  George, 460
  John, 636
  Martin, 460
  Peter, 636
  Tilghman F., 460, 529, 530
Groth, Conrad, 84
Grove, Daniel, 601
  George W., 561, 606
  Henry, 634
  Jacob, 636
  James H., 551, 598
  John, 635
  John H., 545
  John Mason, 528, 554
  John W., 541
  M. J., 401, 494
  Manasses J., 607
  Martin, 459
  Rachel, 640
  Reuben, 167, 396
  William, 605
Grover, Thomas, 629
Gruber, Jacob, 195
Grumbine, J. Allen, 541
Grushong, John, 646
Guedry, Felix, 517
Guilfoyle, Francis, 524
Gump, John, 90, 634
Gun, Alexander, 645
Gundy, Robert, 664
Gunsaw, George, 640
Gutridge, James, 664
Guyer, Adam, 639
  John, 640
Guyton, Mrs. Sarah, 497
  William L., 497, 528
Gwinn, Edward, 134
  John, 600, 605, 630
  Joseph, 636
  Thomas, 605
Gwynn, Allen, 128
  John, 128, 627
Gyer, George, 644
Haack, Charles F., 389

Haas, Fred, 481
  George, 606
  John, 84, 85, 95
  Michael, 638
Haase, I., 647
Habb, Richard, 646
Hack, John, 664
Hackalhorn, George, 181
Hackleton, James H., 507
Hackman, James, 602
Hackney, Jacob, 636
Haff, Abraham, 449, 450
  Jacob, 632
Haffler, Jacob, 646
Haffner, S. T., 547, 566, 580,
  581, 583, 584
  Samuel T., 558, 590, 606
Hafley, Stephen, 642
Hagan, Alexander, 634
  Andrew, 641
  Christian, 634
  Dennis, 597
  Francis, 604
  Hans Wendle, 634
  Harry L., 560
  John, 372
  Mary, 462
  Patrick, 631
Hager, A., 266
  Elizabeth, 343
  Jonathan, 80, 83-85, 144,
    147-149, 600
  M., 266
Hagerman, John, 630
Hagerty, John, 644
  Thomas, 636
Hagrader, Mary, 627
Hahecoh, Frederick, 646
Hahn, Frank, 456
  Lud, 647
Haidt, Valentine, 6
Hail, James, 327
Hain, Jacob, 639
Hainds, Edward, 631
Haines, Jacob, 340
  Mordecai, 604
Hains, Nathan, 642
  William, 642
Haire, Sylvester V., 517
Haldebrand,
  Joseph, 634
Hale, George, 640
  Thomas, 641

Hales, W.D., 547
Half, Abraham, 625
    Margaret, 639
Halkett, Sir Peter, 53-59, 61,
        63, 65-67
Hall, A., 266
    Anna, 342
    Benjamin, 623
    Catherine, 342
    Elisha John , 564
    Gabriel, 642
    James, 628
    Joel, 605
    John, 639
    John E., 134
    John G., 645
    John Stephen, 431
    Joseph, 629
    Margaret, 342
    Mother Etienne, 517
    Nicholas, 326, 629
    S. M. Etienne, 294
    Thomas Buchanan, 312
    Wilfred, 433
    William, 629
    William Hammond, 342
    William Murdock, 629
Haller, Charles, 435
    Charles W., 364, 365, 434,
        525
    David H., 364
    Grayson, 557
    Hemma H., 541
    John N., 541
    Michael H., 602
    Philip, 167
    Thomas, 227, 250, 251
    Thomas H., 507, 528, 541,
        573, 608-610, 612, 620
    W. Harry, 542, 560
Halley, Edward M. , 541
Halm, Frederic J., 524
Hambleton, Samuel, 159
Hamer, George, 643
Hamilton, Francis, 340
    James, 664
    John, 642, 664
    John Gardner, 597
    John H., 453
    William, 664
    William T., 261, 287, 288,
        293, 296, 598
Hammaker, P. N., 532

Hammer, Francis, 631
    Harry, 284
    Jacob, 634
    John, 634
    Jonas, 631
    Michael, 632
    Tobias, 625
Hammett, D. C., 473
    Robert, 629
Hammick, Sam'l P., 483
Hammond, Ariana, 313
    Charles, 26, 27
    Dawson, 276
    G., 230
    George, 281
    Grafton, 601
    John, 319, 623
    Nathan, 600
    Nicholas, 221
    Ormand, 136, 647
    Rachel, 313
    Rebecca, 314
    Richard P., 342
    Richard T., 566, 590
    Robert L., 582, 590
    Thomas, 601
    Vachel, 623
    W. S., 488
    William, 127
Hamner, J. G., 450
Hampson, James, 192
Hampton, Wade, 551
Han, Lewis, 630
Hancock, E. Frances, 520
Hand, Henry, 627
    Mathias, 627
    William, 627
Handley, John, 390
Hane, Daniel, 167
    David, 167
    Fannie B., 426
    Jacob, 647
Haner, George, 167
    Henry, 167, 169
Hanes, John, 647
Haney, John, 641
    Patrick, 82, 90
Hanhar, Martin, 624
Hanifer, John, 170
Hankinson, Henry B., 441
Hanks, John, 84
Hanley, Stephen, 646
Hann, Charles H., 109

Hannar, Marks, 634
Hans, George, 623
    Jacob, 623
    Martin, 627
    Michael, 623
    Mordecai, 627
    Nathan, 623
Hanseal, Barnabas, 25
Hansen, Geo. A., 543
Hanshew, Henry, 167, 271
    John, 169
Hansihl, Bernard Michel, 480
Hanson, A. B., 168, 169, 527,
        538
    Alexander C., 84, 85, 134
    Alexander Coatee, 106
    Alexander Contee, 96, 124,
        127, 165, 250, 599
    Alexander Contee, Jr., 133
    E. A., 372
    George A., 365, 542, 543, 598
    Jane, 638
    Jane Contee, 563
    John, 82-86, 91, 93, 95,
        122-124, 134, 137, 563,
        599, 600
    John, Jr., 91, 603
    Peter, 124
    Peter Contee, 137
    Samuel, 124
    William, 372
Hap, Frederick C., 536
Harbaugh, Charles, 475
    Daniel, 455
    George, 634
    Henry, 455
    J., 550
    Jacob, 634
    Jacob, Jr., 635
    John, 604
    Lodowick, 634
    S. W., 456
    T. C., 613
    Yost, 453, 455
Harbin, Anthony, 664
Harbough, Christian, 634
    John, 634
Harden, Wm., 458
Hardesty, Frank H., 384
Hardigel, Catharine, 629
Hardiker, Richard, 664
Hardin, J. L., 230
Harding, Elias, 629

Everest C., 551
Everest J. , 304
Gary, 644
James M., 542
John J., 598
John L., 167, 210, 527, 536, 603
Norman B., 602
Oliver P., 601
Richard, 639
William, 643
Zephaniah, 629
Hardinger, Christian, 642
Hardman, Christian, 639
Daniel, 641
Henry, 646
John, 627
Joseph, 640
Michael, 625
Nicholas, 644
Hardmar, William, 635
Hardt, John C., 312, 426, 547
Wm. M., 526
Hardy, Arnold, 623
Solo., 635
T. E., 582
Thomas Edwards, 590
William, 646
Hargat, Abraham, 644
Hargate, William, 658
Hargess, Elizabeth, 642
Harget, Peter, 645
Hargett, A. B., 547
Abraham, 437
Charles N., 552
Charlotte E. V., 437
D. H., 527
Douglass H., 606
John E., 469
Mrs. Catherine, 437
P. L., 528
Peter L., 541, 551, 607
Richard S., 469
Samuel, 605
Shafer T., 541, 542
Hargwager, Henry, 638
Harine, Lodwick, 642
Hark, George, 501
Harker, Cornelius, 625
Julot, 628
Harkey, S. W., 422, 423
Simeon W., 427, 483
Simon W., 250

Harkman, Abraham, 623
Harlan, James, 169
John, 327
Harley, Josephus, 475
Joshua, 641
Harlin, Daniel, 628
Joel, 625
Harling, Joshua, 491
Harman, David, 170
Jacob, 627
John, 627
Harmiss, Jacob, 657
Harmon, George, 605
Harn, E. Elmer, 607
Harne, James O., 535, 606
Overton C., 247
Wilberdear, 247
Harner, Gertrude, 509
Harney, W. S., 266
Harp, D. V., 456
David B., 383
George S., 460, 463
John, 453, 646
Reno S., 453, 529, 530, 545, 599
Harper, Charles Carroll, 522
Harpoke, John F. C., 647
Harrington, A. H., 547
E., 499
Harris, Daniel, 169
Elizabeth, 643
George W. , 31
Henry R., 601
James H., 459, 541
James P., 607
John, 631
Nathan, 623
Regin, 169
Samuel, 536
T. F., 266
Thomas, 631
Thomas G., 158
Z. G., 605
Harrison, Alex. C., 536
Benjamin, 109
Burr, 664
Catharine, 638
Eugene L., 607
James, 623
James W., 463
John, 602
Richard, 633
Robt. H. , 145

Thomas, 636
W. F., 548
W. H., 481
William, 400, 644
William Henry, 91, 173, 558
Wm. C., 242
Wm. H., 483
Zepheniah, 167
Harriss, Joseph, 664
Michael, 664
Harrisson, Benjamin, 642, 647
Harritt, J. H. , 266
John, 603
Harry, William H., 607
Harsh, Conrod, 628
Harman, 627
Harshberger, Barnabas, 636
Harshman, Christian, 460, 636
Susana, 456
Wm., 635
Wm. E., 531
Hart, Christian, 638
Ellis, 645
John C., 364, 386
Philip, 632
Susanna, 125
Hartman, I. I., 647
Heinrich, 8
Hartsock, Daniel, 627
Elizabeth, 625
George, 625
Henry, 623
J. S. B., 559, 602
John, 645
John (of Nichs.), 625
Lot, 601
Hartwick, John C., 480
Hartzog, W. T, 328
Harwood, John, 664
Richard, 664
Samuel, 86, 664
Thomas, 664
Hasler, Urith, 645
Haslet, William, 627, 646
Haslett, Albert, 352
Hassefross, John, 169
Hasty, Peter, 664
Hatch, Frederick, 432
Hathaway, William A., 389
Hatherly, Benjamin, 640
Hatter, George, 645
Hatting, John, 644
Hatton, Elizabeth, 313

Hauer, D. J., 503, 504
  Daniel, 25, 163
  Daniel, Jr., 138
  J. D., 504
  N. D., 534
  Nicholas, 25, 378
  William, 271
Haugh, E. G., 547
  Eli G., 541
Haupt, Jonas, 506
  Math, 647
Hauptman, Philip, 552
Hauver, Albert L., 535
  Peter, 601
  Roy V., 582, 590
Haven, Catharine, 640
Havener, Geo., 627
  Michael, 627
Havens, Farewell, 664
Haverley, Michael, 636
Hawk, Albert, Sr., 475
  George, 625
  John, 90
  Paul, 625
  Peter, 636, 642
Hawkins, Edward, 664
  Jacob, 501
  James, 169
  Mrs. James L., 491
  Philip, 281
  Thomas, 84, 85, 128, 129,
    132, 133, 168, 181, 600,
    601, 636
Hawks, B. F., 561
Hawman, Frederick, 169, 396
Hawn, Andrew, 627
  David, 627
  George, 627
  Jacob, 627
  John, 628
  Jonathan, 627
  Lodowick, 631
Haws, John, 646
Hay, C. A., 501, 504
  Daniel, 636
Hayden, J. O., 612
  James Oliver, 498
  John A., 316
Hayes, John, 630
  Jonathan, 634
  R. B., 382, 585
  Rutherford B., 322, 551
  Thomas G., 318

Hays, Charles, 664
  Joseph, 536
  Thomas C., 610
Hazard, Michael, 664
Hazel, W. J., 266
Hazlett, Albert, 356
Head, Biggar, 632
  Richard, 644
  Richard L., 536
  William, 633
  William, Jr., 633
  Wm. B., 604
  Zeal (Cecilius) , 169
Heagey, Jesse F. R., 599
Heard, Jno. Alger, 560
  John W., 249
Heatch, Elizabeth, 643
Heavener, Andrew, 642
Hebbard, Ebenezer Bradford,
  590
Heberly, M. J., 455
Heck, Andrew, 641
  Daniel, 638
  George, 631
  H. R., 557
  Hiram R., 541, 546
  James W., 541
  John, 505, 642
  Margaret, 638
Heckathon, Jacob, 632
Hecker, Barbara, 627
Heckman, Stephen, 639
Hedge, Andrew, 646
  Charles, 632
  Joseph, 636
  Mary, 625, 632
  Peter, 327, 625
  Shadrack, 642
Hedges, Andrew, 628
  Frank H., 555, 581
  Frank Hill, 590
  H. S., 530, 582, 584
  Henry Slicer, 590
  Jacob, 632
  John W. , 598
  Joseph, 603
  L. E., 227
  Lycurgus E., 524
  S. A., 503
  Shadrach A., 482, 484
  Solomon D., 541, 545, 558
Hedrick, Geo., 149
Heener, Conrad, 627

Heffner, ——, 6
  Catharine, 632
  David, 396
  Frederick, 632
  Frederick, Jr., 632
  Jacob, 167, 170
  Lewis C., 483
  Michael, 167
Hefner, Cutlip, 646
  Michael, 632
  Michael, Jr., 633
Hehl, George, 501
Heifner, Frederick, 431
Heigeman, John, 647
Heiler, A. J., 494
Heilman, W. H., 486
Heim, Andrew, 425
  David, 183
Heims, William, 555
Heiner, Elias, 413, 470, 486
Heinlein, Edward H., 459
  George H., 526
  George W., 459
Heinzman, Henry, 664
Heisler, M. L., 504
Heisley, Frederick, 174
Heistand, Mrs. Philip, 501
Heister, Daniel, 128, 171
Helbert, George, 643
Helchew, Nicholas, 647
Held, C. E., 506
Heldebridle, Jacob, 627
  John, 627
Heldebright, George, 627
Helfenstein, Albert, 411
  Cyrus, 227
  E. T., 491, 492
  Edward T., 492
  Jonathan, 408, 411, 464, 475,
    488, 493
  S., 464, 493
  Samuel, 411
Helfenstine, Samuel, 177
Helker, Christian, 641
Hellen, Johnson, 113
  Walter, 101, 111, 111-113
Heller, A. J., 493
Helman, Harman, 632
  James A., 467
Helms, Nicholas, 642
Helvery, Edward, 628
Hemlein, G. W., 547
Hemp, Abraham, 221

Abraham, Jr., 553
Henry, 453, 455
Peter S., 530
Philip, 645
Robert D., 542
Hempey, Henry, 169
Hench, S. M., 468, 474, 489
Silas M., 473, 475
Hendel, William, 411
Henderson, Andrew, 525, 526
Daniel, 664
James B., 607
Rd. H., 151
William, 664
Hendley, John, 665
Hendrick, Meriah, 627
Hendrickson, Ames, 459
Charles B. T., 541
Daniel, 456
Hendrix, J. O., 582, 587
James O., 541
John Oliver, 590
Hendry, Charles, 221
Henertt, H. S., 381
Henis, Samuel, 629
Henish, Jacob, 647
Henning, Casper, 634
Henninghausen, L. P., 7
Henop, Frederick L., 408, 409,
464, 475
Henry, Conrod, 640
Patrick, 104, 341, 522
Henshaw, David, 160
Henshew, John J., 607
Hensley, Leighton B., 467
Hensperger, M. S., 605
Hensy, John, 623
Hepner, John, 627
Herbert, Catharine, 639
Herd, Jacob, 625
Hering, Joshua W. , 404
Herkerthrow, George, 644
Herman, Alfred J., 474, 542
Augustine, 499
Herner, Christian, 631
George, 631
Michael, 630
Richard, 629
Herrin, Daniel, 645
Herring, Adam, 636
Casper, 632
Elijah, 624
John, 624

Lloyd, 221
Lloyd H., 603
Herriot, John, 85
Hersbeyer, Adam, 639
Hersey, Christopher, 643
Hershberger, Henry, 502, 641
John, 526, 541
Hershey, John, 452, 454
Hershperger, T. T., 227
Herwig, William, 542
Herzer, John H., 6
John Henry, 494
Hesler, William, 641
Hess, Charles, 631
Hesse, Ferdinand, 506
Hesselius, Mary, 102
Hesson, Baltzer, 630
Wendle, 630
Hester, William, 634
Hetherly, Benjamin, 643
Hett, Clarence H., 541
George M., 542
Heugh, Andrew, 75, 78
Heuser, W. L., 505
Hewes, Edward, 547, 599
Hewman, Benjamin, 665
Heyser, W., 172
William, 89, 172
Hibbert, Joseph, 623
Hichen, Jacob, Jr., 642
Hichew, Jacob, 627
Philip, 627
Hickenmiller, John, 647
Hickey, John, 497
Hickman, Geo. H., 548
Samuel T., 607
Hicks, J. W., 454
W. W., 457
Hickson, Thomas, 638
Thomas V., 169
Higbee, E. E., 414, 470, 471,
486
Higgins, James L., 604
Pat, 363
Patrick, 361
Higgs, John, 665
Highbarger, Otho S., 497
Highfield, Jonathan, 632
Hightman, Thomas, 606, 607
Higman, John, 603
Hilbert, Margaret, 642
Hildebrand, Erasmus, 632
Mary, 632

Hiler, Abraham, 86
Hilkey, George, 169
Hill, A. P. , 363
Abraham, 631, 634
Anthony, 630
Benjamin, 644
Cornelius H., 451
D. H., 379
G. J., 487
Henry, 665
Henry R., 644
Isaac, 631
James, 631, 665
Jonathan, 665
Joseph, 631, 644
Lewis H., 382
Penelope, 644
Richard, Jr., 631
Richard, Sr., 631
Robert, 644
Silvester, 665
Thomas, 643, 644
Thomas G., 548
William, 631
William J., 523
Hillary, Eleanor, 109
John, 636
Thomas, 629
Wm. H., 566
Hilleary, Anne Perry, 563, 590
J. W., 590
Jeremiah, 630
John, 490, 563, 590
John W., 530
Margaret, 630
Thomas, 590
William, 490, 492, 563, 565,
590, 604
William H., 606
Hillen, David, 665
Jacob, 665
John, 665
Thomas, 665
Hillery, Osborn, 629
Ralph, 629
T., 177
Hilliary, Howard, 461
Jno. W., 221
Hiltebrand, Henry, 641
Hilton, John, 643, 644
Miles, 167
Susanna, 630
Himbury, J. William, 541

Hime, Andrew, 645
Himes, Henry, 625
    Lawrence, 638
    W. A., 611
Himmell, John D., 556
Hinea, Henry A., 606
Hines, John, 625
    Martin, 627
    Peter, 276
    Philip, 625
Hinghew, Frederick, 639
Hinkey, John, 632
Hinkle, Baltis, 632
    George, 169
    John, 536, 623
Hinklehouser, Deterick, 636
Hinks, William H., 396, 601,
    606, 610
Hinsch, Lebrecht L., 486
Hinton, John, 629
    John, Jr., 641
Hireston, Michael, 327
Hirley, Frederick, 640
Hirsley, John, 167
Hisler, Nicholas, 638
Hitchcock, Franklin, 391
Hite, Jost, 4
Hitechew, P. M., 469
Hiter, William, 645
Hiteshew, D. C., 380
    P. L., 561
    P. Mehrle, 551
    Philip L., 607
    Wm. H., 547
Hitshew, D. C., 382
    P. L., 382
Hitt, Sam'l M., 149
Hoffmeier, John W., 475
Hobbs, Charles, 634
    Greenbury, 629
    John, 629
    M., 365
    Nicholas, 86, 623
    Regin, 169
    Samuel, 590
    Ulysses, 346, 348, 363, 601
    Warner, 590
    William, 84, 85, 225, 590,
    629
    William C., 276
Hobrick, John, 642
Hobson, Thomas, 665
Hockensmith, Conrod, 634

George, 634
    Jacob, 634
    Michael, 634
Hockersmith, George, 90
    Henry, 82
    Jacob, 90
    Michael, 90
Hockman, John, 623
    Mary, 623
Hocks, Frederick, 639
Hodge, Shadrack, 636
Hodges, John, 665
Hodgins, Robert, 665
Hodgkiss, Edward, 627
Hoen, Jacob, 479
Hoff, Abraham, 85, 86
    Garret, 625
    John F., 492
    Leonard, 642
Hoffman, Adam, 324, 634
    Andrew, 167
    Charles H., 292, 598
    Charles W., 558, 559
    Daniel, 134
    Francis, 603, 645
    Frederick, 646
    George, 406, 431, 639, 640
    George M., 479
    George, Sr., 169
    H. W., 360
    Henry, 627
    Henry W., 296, 297, 358,
    599
    J., 168, 560
    Jacob, 214, 281, 638, 640
    John, 128, 132, 136, 526,
    604, 640
    John N., 466, 467
    Michael, 169
    Nicholas, 646
    Peter, 24, 84-86
    Philip Rogers, 315
    S. J., 510
Hoffmeier, John W., 470, 489
    T. F., 469, 474, 493
    T. Franklin, 465, 468
Hofman, Adam, 644
Hofslette, Jas., 546
Hoft, Jacob, 479
Hog, Thomas, 84-86
Hogan, G. H., 530
Hogarth, W. H., 531
    William H., 606

Hogg, Samuel, 450
    Samuel R., 450
Hogmire, Conrad, 83-86
Hohne, Loohnd, 647
Hoile, George, 625
Hoke, B. H., 582
    Bradley H., 590
    Charles R., 548
    George B., 462, 463
    Martin, 469
    Samuel, 469
Holbruner, Paul, 489
    Thomas M., 603
Holbrunner, Thomas H., 547
Holce, Nicholas, 646
Holdumand, Frederick, 41
Hole, Jacob, 640
Holer, Jacob, 169
Holland, Jonathan, 636
    Otho, 636
    Ruth, 629
    Wm., 640
Hollebaugh, Joel V., 547
Holler, Henry, 167
    Peter, 643
Holliday, Clement, 239
    John, 640
Hollingsworth, J., 257
    Jacob, 642
    Samuel, 268
    Thomas, 268
Holliway, Edward, 645
Hollow, Christopher, 639
    Godfrey, 639
    Michael, 639
    Michael, Jr., 639
Holloway, Chas. T., 556
Hollyday, Mary, 115
Holmes, Peter, 633
Holsopple, Frederick, 641
    Mary, 637
Holt, Philip, 665
Holter, Daniel, 167
    George, 169
    M. Frank, 535
    William, 169
Holts, Benedict, 632
    Jacob, 632
Holtsman, Frederick, 632
    Jacob, 632
    Jacob, Jun, 632
Holtz, Clarence C., 474
    Nicholas, 282, 601, 603

Holtzman, Jacob, 500
Holtzople, John, 475
Homrick, Mary A.Isabel, 483
Hone, Michael, 632
    Samuel, 625
Honeburger John, 643
Honewalt, Lodowick, 631
Honig, George, 479
Honups, Michael, 635
Hood, James Mifflin, 508
    Margaret E., 508
    Mrs. Margaret E. S., 583
    Zachariah, 76, 78, 79
Hoof, John, 327
Hoofer, Jacob, 646
    Leonard, 645
Hoofnogle, Peter, 640
Hook, Daniel, 636
    James, 636
    James S., 536
Hooker, Alfred J., 389
Hooper, Charles, 605
    James, 625
    Thomas, 348
Hoover, A. D., 462
    Christian, 82
    Daniel, 604
    Francis J., 601
    Geo. A., 462
    Gideon, 453
    Jacob, 170, 635, 640
    John, 453, 456, 634
    Mary, 625
    Nicholas, 275
Hope, Esther, 623
    Henry, 665
    William, 643
Hopewell, Joseph, 41
Hopkins, H. H., 548, 590
    H. H., Jr., 590
    Howard H., 581
    Howard H., Jr., 581
Hoptman, Henry, 635
Hopwood, James, 394
Horine, A. G., 582, 590
    Arlington G., 530
    Daniel, 645
    M. C., 505
    Mrs. Bettie, 456
    Tobias, 641
Horman, William H., 606
Horn, David, 647
Hornacre, Isaac, 634

Horner, A. E., 536
    James, 665
    Joshua, 391
    O. A., 325, 391
    Oliver A., 536
Horsey, Outerbridge, 115, 116,
    122, 265, 365, 552, 605
    Thomas S. Lee, 122
Horwitz, Florence Gross, 315
Hoshouer, S. K., 505
Hoskins, George, 552, 602,
    603
Hosplehorn, George, 623
    Ludwrick, 623
Hoss, Margaret, 623
Hosselton, Edward, 625
Hosteter, Abraham, 85
Hostetter, Henry, 640
Hott, C. M., 454, 455
    J. E., 455
    J. W., 454
Houck, Ella V., 583
    Ezra, 210, 278, 525, 550,
    552, 556
    George, 524
    George E., 541
    Henry, 602, 603
    James, 524, 526, 553
    John, 167, 370
Houdin, Philippe, 285
Hough, E. G., 547
    John M., 469
    Samuel, 111
Houk, Jacobs, 640
    John, 632
    Peter, 633
Houke, Jacob, 647
Houp, Nicholas, 641
House, Franklin G., 606
    George, 636
    George C., 528
    Thomas, 639
    William, 636, 638
Houser, Michael, 639
Housman, Jacob, 632
Houston, James F., 537
    John, 536, 537
Houx, George J. , 169
Hover, Elizabeth, 625
    George, 634
    Jacob, 634
How, George, 639
Howard, Basil, 597

C. S., 621
Charles, 299, 302, 435, 630
Charles S., 543, 545
Charles T. F., 659
Cornelius, 644
Edward, 644
Elisha, 603
Elizabeth, 641
Ephraim, 84, 86, 623
Ephriam, 85, 430, 606
J., 168, 327
James, 644
John, 392
John C., 458
John Eager, 125, 138, 201,
    303
Joseph, 643
Joshua, 601, 605, 623
Julia McHenry, 304
Martha, 623
McHenry, 316, 396
Mrs. Ellen, 396
Mrs. Frances Dorsey, 562
Richard, 163
Sarah, 216
Thomas, 170
William, 315
Howe, Caleb, 636
    James, 169
    Samuel, 625
Howell, Stephen, 629
Hower, Daniel, 639
    Nicholas, 85, 638
Howman, Peter, 639
Howser, Margaret, 645
    Wm., 167
Hox, Mathias, 646
Hoy, Nicholas, 623
Hoyer, Jacob, 642
Hoyt, George H., 353
Hozier, Joshua, 665
Hubbert, Peter, 631
    Philip, Jr., 631
Hubert, Philip, 631
Huccle, John, 643
Huddersford, Geo., 328
Hudson, Jeremiah, 665
    Robert H., 590
Huebner, Samuel R., 6
Huey, James, 536
Huffer, Godfrey, 457
    Jacob, 453
Huffman, George H., 535

George W., 536
John, 170
Hufford, Chris., 327
  Christian, 625
  Philip, 625
Hugh, Andrew, 86
Hughes, Daniel, 227, 283
  Daniel, Jr., 172
  David, 534
  Elizabeth, 128
  Ezekial, 552
  Ezekiel, 249
  George, 256, 590
  Holker, 184
  Hugh, 170
  James, 61, 62, 324, 634
  Jesse, 642
  John, 631
  Joseph, 324, 634
  Joseph, Sr., 325
  Levy, 644
  Robert, 172
  S., 93
  Samuel, 83-85, 145, 600
  Thomas, 82
Hughs, Thomas, 665
Hull, Andrew, Jr., 631
  Andrew, Sr., 631
  Benjamin, 632
  George, 475
  Harry C., 560
  Jacob, 623
  John, 627
Humbert, George, 627
Hume, C. E., 590
  David, 45
Humm, John W., 551, 552
  William C., 542
Humphreys, John, 314
  Theodosia, 314
  Thomas, 84, 85
Hunichen, Mrs. Albert, 583
Hunk, Jacob, 84
Hunt, A. H., 226, 227
  Asbury, 292
  Asbury H., 457, 458
  Elizabeth, 459
  Job, 458
  John, 665
  William, 470, 481, 483
Hunter , George, 444
  James, 158
  John, 563

John C., 151
  Samuel, 46, 429
  Sister Mary Loretto, 511
  William, 640, 643, 665
Huntsbury, Howard M., 485
Hurley, B. F. M., 598
  Edmond, 665
  John, 169
  William, 641
Hurly, James, 630
Hurshberger
  William, 658
Hurst, Jacob, 665
Husband, Herman, 275
Huss, John, 494
  Michael, 169
Hutchin, John, 639
Hutchinson, William, 665
Hutrel, Peter, 636
Hutt, Samuel, 642
Huzzy, G., 266
Hyat, Eli, 629
Hyatt, Meshech, 629
Hyde, Jonathan, 627
  Philip, 665
Hyder, Isaac, 611
  Jas. O., 548
Hyner, Herbert, 627
Hyter, Phoeby, 627
Icough, Adolph, 636
Iford, Jeremiah, 641
Igo, John, 65
Ihleburger, Frederick, 643
Ijams, Jacob, 231
  John, 629
  Mary M., 520
  Plummer, 181, 601, 629
  Richard, 629
Ikenbread, Mary, 633
Iler, Conrod, 625
  Frederick, 634
  John, 625
Impson, H. Wm., 647
Inch, Peter, 631
Ingham, Joshua, 643
Ingle, Osborne, 77, 304, 390,
    435
  Peter, 638
  Peter, Jr., 639
Ingler, David, 638
Ingman, Edmund, 629
Ingram, A. P., 281
  James E., Jr., 609

John, 86
Ireland, Alexander, 636
  Jonathan, 636
Iron, John, 631
Ironmonger, John, 639
Irving, David, 170
Isburn, Robert, 636
Iseminger, Adam, 636
Isenberg, Jacob, 624
  John, 624
  Nicholas, 624
Isenberger, Henry, 638
  Nicholas, 628
Isenburg, Enoch, 623
  Gabriel, Jr., 623
Iser, George, 635
Israel, John, Jr., 623
  John, Sr., 623
Iter, Anton, 647
Ives, William, 665
Jackson, Andrew, 111, 173, 185,
    200, 224, 250, 251
  Henry, 632
  James, 641
  Samuel, 191
  Stonewall, 305, 363
  Thomas, 433
  W. A., 454
Jacob, J. E., 476
  John J., 22
Jacobs, Benjamin, 644
  Corbin, 169
  Daniel, 629
  George, 272
  Henry Barton, 404
  J. J., 89
  Joel, 641
  John, 169, 644
  John Conrad, 627
  John I., 89
  Philip, 169, 170, 625
  Richard, 643
  Samuel, 665
  Thomas, 665
  William, 644
Jacove, Jacob, 643
Jacques, Lancelot, 107
  Launcelot, 106
Jamelson, John, 167
James, Daniel, Sr., 625
  John, 632, 642
  Richard, 428
  Samuel, 630, 632

34

Thomas, 632
William, 638
Jameson, Benedict, 600, 636
Robert, 631
Jamison, B., 127
B. I., 531
Baker, 252
Benedict, 128
Brooke I., 590
Francis B., 523
Henry, 333
Ignatius J., 221
Mary Jane, 252
Janeth, Thomas, 646
Janney, Phineas, 151, 160
Janvier, William, 250
Jarboe, J. T., 590
J. W., 266
Mrs. J. S. W., 396
Thomas R., 606
Wilson T., 487
Jarrett, Abraham Lingan, 297
Jarvis, Zadock, 169
Jasinsky, Fred. W., 480
Jay, John, 109
Jefferson, John, 665
Thomas, 127, 175, 268,
449, 521
Jeffison, Henry, 644
Jenifer, Dan, 145
W. H., 145
Jenkins, B. S., 612
E. Austin, 292
Eliza Lucas, 518
Ellen M., 518
Francis De Sales, 292
George Carrell, 315
Michael, 518
Thomas C., 518
Wm., 167
Jenks, Joseph P., 597
W. D., 457
William D., 218, 525, 538
Jennings, Ann, 102
Edmund, 26, 27
Edward, 22
Joseph, 11, 429
Richard, 324, 634
Thomas, 102, 600
William, 665
Jerome, John Hanson Thomas,
291
Jessup, J. O., 276

James A., 276
Johannes, John G., 353
Johns, Henry V. D., 434
John, 433, 435, 598
Thomas, 85
Johnson, Adelaide, 112
Ann Jennings, 102
Arthur, 665
Baker, 84-86, 95, 101, 102,
106, 108, 110, 111, 335,
396, 402, 431, 590, 598,
600,
640
Balser, 84
Benjamin, 85, 95, 101, 111,
326, 431
Bradley T., 110, 111, 250,
371-373, 377, 382, 396,
538, 547, 590, 603
Charles, 109, 322
Charles W., 606
Chas. Worthington, 590
D. C., 605
D. T. , 221
De Witt C., 605
Dorcas, 102, 110, 111
Duncan, 665
Eleanor M., 82
Eleanor Murdoch, 82
Eliza, 102, 110
Elizabeth, 101, 110, 111
Erasmus, 169
Fanny, 180
Francis, 547
Geo., 582
George, 109, 111, 215, 538,
565, 590
George H., 221
Henrietta, 109
Henry, 315
J. T., 601
James, 10, 84, 85, 95, 96,
101, 102, 106, 108, 110,
111, 234, 335, 402, 431,
526, 549, 597, 601, 604,
606, 633
James T., 590
James Thomas, 110, 590
Jas., Jr., 431
Jno. L., 620
John, 111, 431, 590, 636,
644
John A., 221, 601

Joseph, 6, 109, 169, 170, 636
Joshua, 101, 102, 107,
111-113, 431, 644
Louisa, 111
Louisa Catherine, 113
Margaret, 110
Martin, 86
Mary, 101, 111
Mary Anne, 102
Mrs. Baker, 82
Otis, 111, 559
Peter, 646
Rafe, 247
Rebecca, 101, 102, 111
Reverdy, 132, 235, 241, 298,
370
Richard, 109-111, 274
Richard D., 161
Richard Dorsey, 110
Robert, 636, 647
Roger, 84-86, 95, 101, 102,
106, 108, 110, 111, 325,
335, 402, 629
Ross, 598
Samuel, 109, 590
Samuel A., 590
Sarah, 109
T. B., 581, 594
Thomas, 1, 10, 85, 86, 95,
101-106, 108- 112, 114,
127, 137, 138, 180, 181,
192, 248, 268, 282, 298,
333, 335, 396, 402, 411,
431, 559, 590, 597, 599,
600, 601, 605, 633, 636,
644
Thomas B., 533, 591
Thomas Jennings, 180
Thomas W., 591
Thomas, III, 431
Thomas, Jr., 95, 106, 107
Thos. B., 548
Tom, 110
Thos. J., 431
W. C., 580, 584
W. H., 548
William, 167, 192, 256, 333,
625, 630
William C., 158,578, 579,
58,1 601
William Cost, 185, 192, 218,
256, 258, 263, 307, 333,
538, 599 601, 605

William Crawford, 559, 583, 590
William F., 552
William H., 566, 583, 581, 591
William Thomas, 109
Johnston, Albert Sidney, 305, 311
Christopher, 313
E. S., 466, 467
George, 566
Johnstoun, Andrew, 665
Joliffe, Joseph N., 558
Jolly, Thomas M., 167
Jones, Abraham, 601, 604
Benjamin, 597
Charles, 75, 78, 86
David, 86, 635
Francis F., 365
Francis J., 221
Francis S., 276
H. M., 530
Howard M., 530
J, 328
J. Lawrence, 372
James G., 487
Jno. M., 546
John, 630, 631, 633, 665
John G., 532
John Peter, 606
Joseph, 665
Joshua, 630
Lewis, 630
Maris, 602
Morris, 167, 536
Nehemiah, 665
Richard, 334, 625
Spencer C., 520, 598
T., 132
Thomas, 84, 458, 601, 631, 642, 645, 665
Walter, 149, 194, 234
Walter, Jr., 163
William, 201, 277, 628, 657, 665
William A., 546
Zachariah, 630
Jordan, J. L., 547
John L., 606
Jordon, William, 665
Jose, George, 644
Jourdan, Charles H., 524
Judy, Martin, 638

Philip, 500
Jugerhorn, John, 84
Julian, John, 633
Jumper, Christian, 625
Jacob, 647
Mary, 647
Juright, Justice, 639
Justice, Aquila, 638
Elizabeth, 623
Ezekiel, 638
Griff, 623
Jessee, 624
Margaret, 624
William, 665
Kable, W. H., 584
Wm., 591
Wm. H., 582
Kachler, John, 501
Kagi, John, 352
Kahler, J. J., 546
Kailor, David, 221, 605
Kalbach, Mrs. Mary Wade, 518
Kalkloescher, Abraham, 167
Kaloria, J. B., 476
Kamp, Adam, 495
John, 496
Kane, George P., 371
William, 447
Kanodle, Luther, 400
Kantner, Jno. J., 459
Karaft, Valentine, 480
Karn, Adam, 537
Kauffman, G. L., 547
George L., 606
Henry, 167
John W., 251, 607
Kaufman, George L., 541
John W., 561
Keale, Peter, 636
Kearsley, John, 341
Keating, Sister Mary Joseph, 510, 511
Keech, John, 665
Keedy, Clayton O., 526, 598
Mrs. Clayton O., 82
Keefer, A. Eugene, 541
A. Kemp, 419
Abram Kemp, 541
Casper, 635
Charles H., 251, 400
Frederick, 627
Harry C., 251, 541, 542,

552, 607
Henry, 169, 631
Michael, 550, 605
Samuel, 221, 601, 605
Keele, Henry, 642
Keene, Edmund, 328
Robert, 328
William, 328
Keepers, Isaac, 629
Keeport, Capt. Geo. P., 8
Keever, Abraham, 635
Jacob, 635
Lodowick, 634
Kefauver, D. E., 527, 528
D. Edward, 465, 554, 608, 612
E. C., 473, 535
Elmer C., 548, 581, 591
Frank, 560
George W., 528
H. Milton, 419, 546, 606
Harry J., 442, 543, 545, 560, 607
J. Hollin, 528, 534
Jacob, 636
John, 538
Lewis F, 465, 612
M. Calvin, 437
Martin E., 551
Mrs. Annie A, 437
N. E., 543
Noah E., 555
Peter, 636
Philip, 500, 636
William Emory, 437, 438
Kefauvre, O. H., 281
Keifer, Philip, 647
Keil, Henry, 646
Keiler, George, 163
Keiser, C. W., 547
Keisler, George, 640
Keith, James, 597
Kelcholumer, Baltzer, 85
Kellar, Jno. H., 459
Kelleberger, George Adam, 625
Keller, Adam, 640
Catharine, 639
Charles, 167
Daniel, 624
E. L., 488
Ezra, 466, 467
George, 625
Henry, 606
J. B., 505

Jacob, 210, 327, 591, 625, 640
John, 167, 169, 636, 641
John H., 607
Juliana, 625
Mrs. Susan, 450
O. J. , 527
Otho J. , 494
Peter, 169
Philip, 636
Philip, Jr., 641
Philip, Sr., 636
Thos., 149
Willard, 558
Willard C., 598
Kelley, George, 90
Kelly, George, 82, 167, 631
Hugh, 633
Thos., 638
Kelse, Eccard, 646
Keltz, George, 169
Kemp, Abraham, 227, 282, 413
C. Thomas, 534, 537, 541
Catharine, 645
Christian, 527, 603, 604
Conrad, 24
Conrod, 636
D. Clayton, 541
D. Columbus, 400, 552, 610
Daniel, 163
Daniel S., 469
David, 601
Frederick, 84, 85, 633
Frederick, Sr., 634
Gilbert, 24
Harry, 181
Henry, 128, 129, 132, 163, 549, 600-603, 633
J. C., 454
James, 490
John, 170, 633, 647
Joshua, 454
Judith, 627
Lewis, 85, 86, 550, 552
Lodowick, 634
Lodwik, 645
Mary, 642
Peter, 452-454, 624, 633
Robert A., 532
Wm. Miller, 591
Kempton, Thomas, 665
Kendel, James, 629

Kenega, David, 525
Kenegey, John, 458
Kenly, John R., 372, 391
Kennedy, Ann, 635
Anthony, 296
Henry, 134, 632
J. Harry, 560
James H., 221
Mary, 642
Moses, 82, 90
R. F., 348
Thomas, 149
Kenop, Mary, 640
Kenouff, Chas., 459
Kenough, Henry, 636
Kensler, James, 624
Uley, 641
Kent, Joseph, 149, 151
Kenworthy, William, 627
Kephart, David, 627
Jacob, 636
John, 604, 640
Peter, 639
Simeon, 644
Kepler, Daniel C., 553
George, 642
Henry S., 434
Kepner, B. Evard, 541
Kercheval, Samuel, 18
Kern, Adam, 636
Kernhart, George, 636
Kerr, F. D., 391
J. J., 502
John, 639
Thomas, 640
Kershner, Martin, 172
Kesler, Andrew, 636
Jacob, 486, 631
John, 627
Kesseling, Ludwig, 603
Kesselring, Lodowick, 630
Kessler, A. P., 603
Absalom P., 602
Andrew, 371, 601
David, 169
Jacob, 163, 167
Kessner, Michael, 639
Ketcherside, James, 665
Ketsinderfer, John, 638
Ketterman, Stoffel, 634
Key, Anne Arnold, 315
Anne Phebe Charlton, 194
Arthur, 316

Edmund, 314
Edward, 313, 315
Elizabeth, 316
Elizabeth Rousby, 315
Elizabeth Scott , 315
Emily Louise, 315
Francis, 314, 316
Francis Eugenia, 315
Francis Scott, 193, 194, 227, 299, 303-306, 311, 313, 315, 431, 540, 559, 597
George Barton, 315
Henry Johnson, 315
Isaac, 316
John, 85, 86, 313, 314, 316
John R., 597, 599
John Ross, 97, 130, 137, 194, 227, 249, 269, 299, 313, 314, 600, 631
Josiah, 316
Louise Emily, 315
Mary, 313, 316
Mary Catherine, 315
Mary Lloyd, 315
Mary Tayloe, 304
Nicholas Sewall, 315
Philip, 127, 313, 314, 316
Philip Barton, 130, 133, 215, 299, 314, 315
Rebecca Ann, 315
Rev. Jonathan, 111
Richard, 313, 316
Richard Ward, 313, 314, 316
Susanna Gardiner, 314
Thomas, 314
Virginia Peyton, 316
William Thompson, 315
Keys, John, 627
Keyser, Jacob, 271
Kibler, Michael, 627
Kidd, John, 665
Milton Y., 371, 372
Kidwell, W. D., 549
Kiefer, Mathias, 303
Kieffer, Henri L. G., 419
J. Clarke, 558
J. S., 419, 468, 471
J. Spangler, 419, 465, 466
Jacob, 167
Michael, 25
Moses, 414
Kieft, Wilhelmus, 69
Kier, Jacob, 636

Kiger, John, 624
  Leonard, 624
Kile, John, 644
  William, 635
Kiler, Jacob, 603
Kilgore, John, 597
Kilgour, J. Mortimer, 221
  Robert, 134
  William, 371, 372
Kill, George, 634
Killer, Jacob, 636
Killgore, J. L., 488
Killian, Casper, 555
  J. M., 505
Killingsworth, John C., 542, 543
Kimbel, L. Frederick, 463
Kimberlain, J. M., 281
Kimes, Henry, 639
  Jacob, 642
Kimmel, A., 247, 538
  A. Z. , 221
  Anthony, 255, 288, 362, 363, 457, 539, 600
  Anthony, Sr., 212
Kimmerly, John, 275
Kindley, G. Wesley, 525, 532
King, Andrew, 636
  Charles, 625
  David, 541
  Francis, 665
  George, 635
  Herbert M., 404
  J. Bell, 541
  Jacob, 635
  James H., 469
  John, 629
  John Andrew, 483
  Mary, 636
  Robert, 665
  William, 665
Kingston, John, 389
Kinley, Shadrach, 629
Kins, John, 645
Kinsell, Mason, 272
Kintz, Frederick, 453
Kinzio, Henry, 625
Kipelrinjer, Martin, 639
Kiracofe, G. W., 454
  J. W., 454, 455
Kirby, H. H., 266
  John, 468
  Joseph, 627

Kirfover, Nicholas, 641
Kirk, Benjamin, 629
  Thomas, 630
Kirtsmiller, Leonard, 627
Kise, Abraham, 628
Kiser, Decus, 635
Kisinger, Francis, 639
Kisler, Henry, 642
Kitterman, Christian, 625
  George John, 625
  John, 628
Kitwilder, Jacob, 639
Kizer, J. D., 487
Klebs, Arnold C., 404
Klein, David, 462
  Fred, 462
  George, 462
  Jesse R., 461
  Peter, 169
Klein (Cline), Casper, 169
Kline, Allen, Jr., 555
  Daniel, 627
  David, 463
  Frederick, 639
  George, 643
  J. P., 505
  Mary, 639
  Stephen, 639
Klinehart, Francis, 640
Kling, J. Harry, 536
Klingender, Melchior George, 315
Klinger, O. G., 466, 467
Klink, Charles M., 501
  John, 169
Klise, Henry, 625
Kluet, John, 647
Kluge, Johann Peter, 6
Knauff, Adam, 90
  Charles E., 251
  Greenbury, 167
Knave, Bostian, 625
Knickerbocker, Diedrich, 69
Knife, Michael, 636
  Michael, Jr., 636
Knight, James, 591, 630
  Joshua, 630
  Samuel, 624
Kniver, John, 604
Knock, Charles F., 419, 541
  Mrs. Ada E., 437
  William H., 437
Knodle, Hiram, 502

Knop, Carl, 647
Knott, F. Columbus, 534
Knouff, Adam, 633, 636
  Jacob, 169, 640
  James, 325
  John, 634
  John, Jr., 634
Knox, James, 646
  John, 632
  Samuel, 138, 448, 449, 521
  Thomas, 603
Knu, George, 640
Koehler, Herman C., 552
Kohlenberg, Adam, 321
Kolb, C. Wm., 555
  Daniel, 537
  David, 292, 542
  David D., 541
  David H., 395, 555
  George, 250, 457, 458
  Isaac, 323
  John F., 170
  John W., 598
  Ramer, 169
  Thomas J., 462, 535
  W. , 546
  William, 210, 292
  William F., 167
  William O. , 541
  Wilson, 565
  Wilson W., 591
Koldenbaugh, Andrew, 628
Kontz, John, 167
Koogle, Daniel S., 535
  George, 607
  Jacob, 531
  Simon H., 541
Koon, Christian, 634
Koons, Abraham, 627
  C., 462
  Henry, 638
  Jacob, 642
  John, 601
  John A., 601
Koontz, Charles, 250
  Christian, 275
  Edward, 556
  George, 210
  Godfrey, 458, 532
  Henry, 210, 586, 638
  John, 170, 629
  William, 82
Kopp, Fred, 546

38

Korns, Henry, 169
Korr, Casper, 641
Kraft, Valentine, 420
Kramer, Abner R., 469
  George, 647
Krapf, D., 266
Kreh, Arthur, 560
  Charles F., 541
  Leonard, 555
Kreig, Wm., 494
Kreitzman, John, 479
Kremer, Abner, 489
  Abner R., 475, 486
Krider, Martin, 452
Krise, H. E. , 547
  Solomon, 605
Krogstrup, Otto, 6
Krug, John Andrew, 427, 480, 501
Krum, Christian, 452
  Henry, 452
Krumer, Adam, 641
Kubs, Walter E., 486
Kufer, Christian, 645
  Christian, Jr., 645
Kugle, Adam, 641
  Adam, Sr., 636
  John, 641
Kuhlman, Luther, 420
Kuhn, George, 90, 604
  Henry, 128, 132, 133, 526, 600, 602, 603
  L. H., 391
  L. M., 392
  Zebulon, 604
Kulp, Michael, 639
  Michael, Jr., 639
Kump, Peter, Jr., 642
Kunkel, J. M., 296
  Jacob M., 227, 314, 335, 597, 599, 600
  John, 210, 335, 552
  John B., 335, 342
  Philip B., 292
Kunkle, Jacob M., 261
  John B., 402
Kupers, Isaac, Jr., 643
Kurtz, B., 502
Kussmaul, Lewis F., 541
L'homme, F., 517
La Rowe, Henry C., 390
Labrouse, Benjamin, 665
  Jacob, 665

LaFayette, George
  Washington, 182, 183
Lairch, C., 266
Lake, O. E., 467, 473
  Orange E., 489
Lakin, Daniel, 490, 492
  Daniel T., 527, 528
  John, 169
  William, 169, 604, 605
  William Gerry, 437, 438
  William H., 507, 533, 567, 606, 607
Lamar, A. A., 582, 584, 618
  Austin A., 591
  John C., 533
  Lemack, 641
  Lewis, 591, 601
  R. I., 550
  Thomas, 642
  William, 625, 641
Lamb, Henry, 644
  John, 637
  Pearce, 627
Lambert, Christopher, 646
  Geo., 627
  John, Sr., 627
  Joseph, 641
  Peter, 645
Lambrecht, George, 169
  Michael, 169
Lampe, Allen R., 437
  Henry, 556
  J. Henry, 547
Lamy, L. J., 617
Landauer, A. M., 524, 573
  I. M., 560
Landerkin, Trago W., 541
  Trego, 578
Landers, Roger, 646
Landey, Richard, 643
Landis, Charles A., 545, 546
  Henry, 624
Landstreet, W. B., 492
Lane, John, 627
  John C., 550
  Peter, 628
Laney, John, 631
  Peter, 24
Lange, Carl, 408, 409, 475, 488
  Charles, 464
Lanius, W. H., 390
Lansdale, H. S., 548

Lanthrow, George, 630
Lantz, Cyrus, 456
  John, 641
Lap, William, 646
Lar, Henry, 630
Lard, William, 624
Larentz, Adam, 603
Larkins, George, 646
  John, 647
Late, Leonard, 633
  Michael, 625
  Orange E., 475
Lath, Henry, 628
Lathroun, J. B., 266
Latimer, R. B., 145
Latrobe, Benjamin H., 241
  John H. B., 235, 241, 398, 539, 541
Latz, Michael, 25
Lauber, Frederick, 500
Laugh, David, 627
Laurence, Jacob, 637
Lavely, Christian, 624
  Jacob, 638
Lawfer, Chanta, 644
Lawrence, Charles A., 221
  Elizabeth, 343
  Jacob, 604
  John, 84-86, 343, 606
  Jonathan, 343
  Martha, 149, 343, 624
  Mrs. Elizabeth, 214
  Otho, 179, 180, 597
  Upton, 172, 343, 597
Lawson, James U., 567, 606
  John, 531, 665
Layman, John, 170
Le Grand, John Carroll, 319, 320
Le Neve, Sir William, 111
Leace, William, 625
Leak, James, 629
Leaken, John, 637
Leakin, Abraham, Sr., 636
  Cerena, 490
  Emeline, 490
Leakins, Abraham, Jr., 641
  Daniel, 641
  William, 645
Lean, John, 645
Leap, William, 639
Lear, Daniel, 640
  Garrett, 643
Leary, Lewis L., 352, 355

Lease, Conrod, 627
　Edward, 547
　Harvey R., 606
　Jacob, 625
　John, 605
　M. F., 547
　Millard F., 540, 541
　Robert, 383, 602
Leason, Samuel, 665
Leathem, Charles N., Jr., 542
Leather, George, 641
　John, 644
　John, Jr., 644
Leatherman, Daniel, 460, 605,
　636
　Daniel I., 591
　George, 370, 460
　Godfrey, 636
　Henry, 640
　Jacob, 460
　John C., 460, 531
　Joseph, 641
　Marshall Edward, 591
　Wm. H., 531
Leatherwood, Samuel, 624
Lebherz, Harry J., 560
　William B., 560
Lee, Charles, 103, 329, 559
　Charles O'Donnell, 122
　Christiana (Sim), 114
　Columbus O'Donnell, 122
　Daniel, 665
　Dudley, 632
　Garrett, 170
　Henry, 134
　John, 181, 182, 184, 185,
　　293, 328, 600, 601, 666
　Joseph W. J., 122
　Mary D., 185
　Mary Digges, 116, 185, 321
　Mrs. Lawrence Rust, 82
　Philip, 10, 115, 127
　Richard Henry, 103, 104,
　　331, 332
　Robert E., 242, 311, 350,
　　352, 356, 362, 562
　Sarah, 127
　Thomas, 114, 331, 666
　Thomas Sim, 10, 82,
　　114-116, 126, 136-138,
　　181, 185, 248, 265, 321,
　　328, 559, 599, 605, 637
　Thos. S., 221

Leech, Benjamin, 631
　James, 631
　S. V., 396
Leek, William, 638
Leeman, W. H., 355
　William H., 352
Leese, M. F., 547
Lefever, Christian, 633
　Elias, 633
Legarde, Ernest, 523
Legare, Hugh S., 132
Leggs, Charles, 629
Lego, Charles, 666
Legrand, John Carroll, 260
Lehman, Adam, 453
Leib, J. H., 581, 582, 584
　Joseph H., 591
　Wm. J., 601
Leigh, Benjamin Watkins, 205
Leilich, Charles N., 541
　Jacob, 547
Leinbach, Christian, 496
Leister, Conrod, 647
　George, 642
Leman, W. M., 284
Lemar, Richard, 637
Lemaster, Abraham, 636
Leming, Elizabeth, 110
　John, 110
Lemmon, Adam, 624
　Jacob, 624, 627
　Richard, 634
Lemon, Adam, 625
　Jacob, 633
　John, 631
　Lodowick, 637
　Peter, 625
　Solomy, 627
Lengenfelter, George, 431
Lenginfelter, Barnet, 625
Lenmon, Abraham, 641
Lennis, Samuel K., 404
Lennon, Robert A., 517, 518
Lenox, Peter, 151
Lenport, George, 645
Leonard, Peter, 90
　Robert, 666
　William, 281
Lepper, George, 536
Leppo, Mary, 627
Lescalute, William, 642
Lester, Louis M., 525
Letroe, John, 666

Lett, Aquila, 629
　Daniel, 643
　Elijah, 629
　Jemima, 630
　Robert, 644
　Roselin, 643
　Zakariah, 643
Leuber, Francis, 252, 552
Levantin, S. H., 560
Levar, John, 666
Levatt, Henry, 225
Levy, C. V. S., 544
　Charles P., 524, 599
　Charles V. S., 524, 539, 543,
　　598, 608
　David, 639
　Jacob, 639
　Jonathan, 286
Lewis, Captain Joshua, 33
　Charles J., 524
　David, 644
　Frederick, 6
　Henry, 172
　Jacob, 639
　James R., 542
　Jas. R., 468
　John, 35
　R. Rush, 459, 533, 553
　Samuel A., 599
　Sarah, 631
　Wm., 138
Leyth, J. M. F., 391
Lezer, Zachariah, 641
Lice, Erasmus, 640
Lick, James, 303
Lickfetter, Joseph, 645
Lickfletter, George, 634
Licklider, Conrod, 633
　George, 633
　Peter, 633
Lidd, Henry, 646
Lidey, Geo., 488
Liggett, John J., 581, 591
Light, Elizabeth, 642
　Judy, 624
Lighter, Charles H., 465
　Henry, 637
　Russell E., 607
Ligon, Thomas W., 293
Lilly, Elias, 605
　Geo. W., 548
　Henry, 646
　Richard, 633

Samuel, 639
Thomas, 447, 511, 633
Limbreck, Daniel, 639
Limmon, John, 641
Limpley, John, 644
Peter, 644
Linch, Thomas, 666
Lincoln, Abraham, 250, 539
Linderman, John, 647
Lindsay, Hamilton, 606
Mrs Hamilton, 583
Oliver, 646
Line, John, 644
Linebaugh, Adam, 642
Christian, 633
Daniel, 90
Jacob, 634
John, 646
Samuel, 642
Lingan, James M., 134
Lingen, J., 327
Lingenfelter, Abraham, 24
Christian, 647
Daniel, 631
George, 406, 631
John, 639
Michael, 647
Peter, 647
Valentine, 631
Linger, John, 643
Linginfelter, Valentine, 637
Link, Adam, 625
Daniel, 391
Thomas, 628
Linn, William, 666
Linthicum, James Garrott, 591
John L., 601
Robert E., 601
Z., 86
Linton, Benjamin, 629
James, 666
Jeremiah, 629
John, 666
Samuel, 629
Samuel, Jr., 629
Zachariah, 629
Lioyd, Edward, 117
Lipps, William D., 557
Lips, Philip, 634
Lipsley, Peter, 167
Lischy, Jacob, 477
Lisler, William, 646
Lister, John, 627

Nicholas, 627
Litt, Henry, 647
Little, Barnet, 635
Charles J., 383
Horatio, 605
Joseph, 632
Littlejohn, Geo., 630
George W., 169
Leonard J. M., 169
Littleton, C. H., 488
Litzel, J. M., 486
Liver, Nicholas, 641
Livers, Anthony, 633
Elizabeth, 646
Ignatius, 646
Jacoba Clementina, 324
Mary, 634
Nathaniel, 633
Thomas, 634
William, 646
Livingston, W. O., 487
Llewellyn, ——, 314
Lloyd, Edward, 10, 26, 27, 303
Edward, IV, 313
Mary Tayloe, 313
Mary Taylor, 303
Rebecca, 313
Wm. A., 170
Loats, John, 226-228, 271,
365, 426, 525, 551, 552
Lochner, L. F., 469
Lochrey, Jeremiah, 46
Lock, John, 625
Locke, George, 167
Locker, Thomas, 666
Loffer, Lodwick, 645
Michael, 645
Lofflin, Joseph, 666
Logan, Andrew, 631
Daniel, 351
Logmire, John, 625
Logsdon, John, Jr., 627
Lombrick, Henry, 640
Long, A. P., 467
Albert, 469
B. F., 549
Baker, 666
Conrod, 647
Daniel, Sr., 631
Isaac, 452
J. A., 582
J. H., 266
J. W., 453

Jacob, 642, 643
James A., 591
James W., 536
John, 90, 637, 647
Joseph W., 485, 591
Josephus, 535
Patrick E., 612
Peter, 631
Samuel, 473, 548
Stoffel, 637
W. A., 582, 584
Wilson A., 581, 591
Longanecker, Daniel, 461
Longsworth, Robert, 643
Solomon, 625
Longwell, John K., 250
Lonk, Christopher, 644
Lontz, Leonard, 638
Lookenpeale, Jacob, 624
Peter, 624
Lopp, Henry, 641
Loree, L. F., 243
Lorentz, Adam, 604
Henry, 227, 228
Jacob, 323
Lorman, William, 172
Lott, Philip, 639
Loudenbaugh, Conrod, 634
Louder, Francis, 431
Loufer, Frederick, 641
Louff, ——, 325
Lough, J. P., 489
John Q. , 535
N. A., 436
U. A., 534
Loughridge, Wm., 272
Loval, I., 456
Love, Aaron, 666
Benjamin, 634
David, 634
Hugh, 634
James, 631
Philip, 666
Robert, 631
Low, Jacob, 639
Lowe, Adelaide Vincindier, 292
Andrew, 640
Bradley S. A., 290
E. Louis, 280, 363
Enoch, 559
Enoch L. , 597
Enoch Louis, 82, 261, 287,
288, 290, 292, 298, 365,

599, 601
Esther Winder, 292
G., 266
George, 169
Jacob, 170
John T., 603, 607
Mary Gorter, 292
Paul Emil, 292
Victorie Vincindier, 292
Vivian, 292
William, 603
Lowenstein, D., 572, 573
David, 558, 617, 620
Isaac, 541, 542
Lower, W. T., 454, 455
Lowery, David S., 549
Lowndes, Lloyd, Jr., 161
Lowry, David, 635
John, 628
Loy, Frederick, 634
Isaiah N., 541, 542
John George, 479
John R., 483
Loyd, Thomas, 625
Lucas, Barton, 666
Daniel Bedinger, 338
Luccessle, Michael, 646
Luckess, Luck, 639
Luckett, John, 86, 330
Lloyd, 598
M. B., 597
Mountjoy B., 536, 537
Nelson, 604
Otho H. W. , 169
William, 75, 78, 85, 95,
225, 430, 600, 637
William, Jr., 84-86, 606
Luckey, George J., 607
Ludith, Daniel, 625
Ludwick, E., 455
William, 84, 85
Ludy, John, 637
Lufft, George, 632
Lugenbeel, Peter, 400, 601
Lunday, D., 659
Luser, Daniel, 641
Luster, Michael, 645
Luther, George, 629
Jacob, 629
Lutz, George, 625
Mary E., 437
Nicholas, 645
Lye (Lay), John George, 24

Lynch, E. H., 254
Edward A., 250, 255, 601
Eugene H., 597
John, 637
John A., 170, 435, 530,
538-543, 559, 598, 600,
603, 607
Susanna, 638
William, 254, 255, 263,
550, 601, 604
Lynn, David, 75, 78, 82, 591
George, 591
Henry, 634
Michael, 631
Nicholas, 631
Lyon, James, 666
M'Bride, Hannah, 46
M'Cardell, A. C., 573
M'Curdy, Ira J., 583
M'kinsey, Folger, 614
M'Manimy, Daniel, 46, 47
MacCubbin, Richard C., 371
Macelfish, Charles, 630
Jane, 629
John, 629
Philip, 629
Macgill, Charles, 333
John, 249
Lloyd T., 557
R. H., 435
Wm., 565
Macguire, S., 499
Machen, Arthur W., 318
Mack, Alexander, 459
Mackabie, Allen, 642
Mackall, B., 328
Benjamin, 327
Mackechney, Jno, 392
Mackenzie, ——, 111
A. Ross, 591
Mackey, Robert, 639
Mackley, Charles M., 535
J. Irwin, 549
Macmannon, Hugh, 666
Mactier, Dolly, 109
Henry, 110
Madary, Andrew, 169
Madcap, Thomas, 624
Madding, Francis, 666
Mordecai, 666
William, 624
Maddox, C. Frederick, 206
Madery, John, 647

Nicholas, 639
Madison, James, 132, 430
Maffit, Newland, 458
Magawer, Patrick, 643
Magill, John, 250, 633
Magraw, William, 467
Magruder, A. C., 235
Alexander, 197, 198, 430
Benjamin, 198
E., 266
Howard, 198
John, 196, 197
Mary Lynn, 82
Nathan, 84, 85, 225, 521, 600
Patrick, 131
R. H., 551
Samuel, 85, 637
Samuel W., 84
Samuel Wade, 86
Susannah, 643
William, 637
Zadoch, 84-86
Maguire, Hugh, 136
Mahoney, Augustus B., 541
James H., 647
Sophia, 639
William, 364, 551, 552, 603
Mahony, Daniel, 629
Main, Adam, 637
Clinton E., 541
Daniel, 500
George, 462, 469, 633
J. Calvin, 461
J. Lewis, 541
J. W., 549
John, 169, 641
Maine, Frederick, 637
George, 637
Mainhart, Elizabeth, 483
Majors, Elias, 627
James, 631
Nathaniel, 627
Maken, John, 666
Makosky, E. C., 488
Maleve, Francis, 445
Maller, Mariano, 517
Malone, Lanchlan, 72
Maloy, J. E., 488
Manchey, John, 327
Mandine, Alexis, 517
Manery, Samuel, 666
Manklin, Benjamin, 643
Mann, Chas., 434

42

L. A., 501, 504, 534
Manning, Alex., 597
Manro, Jonathan J., 592
Mansfield, John, 641
Mantle, Michael, 632
Mantz, Alexander K., 555, 556
  Casper, 526, 538, 638
  Charles, 227, 557, 602
  Cyrus, 180, 532
  David, 167, 638
  E. Peter, 541
  Ezra, 166, 602
  Francis, 225, 313, 638
  Isaac, 640
  Jacob, 163
  Lillie M., 426
  Mrs. Anne, 583
  Peter, 169, 225, 450, 600,
    602, 605, 638
  Teresa, 313
Marburg, Charles L., 305
Marbury, Alexander M., 492
Margin, John, 638
Maris, G. W., 591
Mark, Ann, 341
  Christopher C., 541
  James, 603
  John, 341
  Joseph, 641
  Thomas, 629
Marke, Jacob, 631
Markel, Charles, 417
  George, 417, 473
  Mrs. Mary A E., 417
Markell, Charles F., 598, 607
  Edwin C., 534
  Francis, 435, 524
  George, 525, 552, 637
  J., 187
  Jacob, 169, 228
  John, 180, 227
  John U., 527
  Lewis, 534
  Louis, 417
  Mrs. Francis, 82
  Samuel, 227
  Thomas M., 524, 526, 597
  William, 251
Marker, Catharine, 634
  Christian, 644
  George, 637
  John, 627
Markey, D. John, 442, 560

David, 167
David J., 210, 525, 526,
  601, 605
F. A., 573
Frederick A., 542, 543, 552
Ida M., 612
  Mrs. Ida M., 437
  Mrs. Hanshew, 583
  Mrs. J. Hanshew, 559
Markland, John, 631
Markle, Nicholas, 647
Markley, Adam, 624
  Ephraim, 624
  Gabriel, 624
  John, 281
Marks, John, 626
Markwood, Jacob, 454
Marlow, Hanson, 169
  Horatio, 604
  Thomas, 490, 592, 641
  William, 637
Marmon, W., 391
Marquett, George, 396
Marriott, Barzelia, 250
Marsh, Alonzo P., 545
  Mary, 342
Marshal, William, 643
Marshall, J., 205
  Jacob, 25
  James, 322, 633, 666
  P. H., 170
  R. H., 433, 434
  Richard, 82, 599
  Richard H., 226, 227, 265,
    315, 532, 597
  Thomas, 666
  William, 632
Martin, Anthony M., 389
  Charles, 630
  David, 457, 458, 543, 634
  George, 476, 631
  J., 266
  J. T., 530
  Jacob, 453, 455, 604, 634,
    641
  James, 643
  James L., 492
  John, 643
  John A., 658
  John T., 530, 549
  L. W., 455
  Lenox, 88, 457
  Luther, 88, 179, 196, 298,

    333, 457
  Matthias, 634
  R. C., 493
  Robert N., 597
  Thomas, 82, 666
  Tobias, 461
  W. C., 288
  W. L., 454-456
  William A., 353
  William C., 605
Martineau, John, 245
Martz, Annie V., 483
  George, 638, 646
  John H., 606
  Mary Eliz., 483
  Wilson Nath., 483
Marvin, Wm., 458
Mason, Wm., 432
  Charles, 70
  Col. George, 22
  Edward, 666
  George, 298
  James M., 149, 354, 356
  John Thompson, 193, 290,
    293, 597
  John Thomson, 202
  Jonathan, 643
  Robert, 638
  Thomas, 298
  William, 372, 666
  William T. T., 133, 597
Mass, John Baptist, 666
Massey, J. L., 304, 546
  T. L., 547
Master, Rinehart, 646
Masterson, Hugh, 666
Mastetler, George, 644
Mates, Michael, 639
Mathery, William, 637
Mathews, John, 643
  Mrs. Belle, 583
  Peter, 646
  Philip, 634
  William, 666
Mathias, Jacob, 84, 85
  John P. T., 535, 607, 610
Matson, Ralf, 39
Matteny, George, 642
Mattern, Peter, 169
Matthes, Jacob, 494
Matthew, Chidley, 635
  Conrad, 90
  Conrod, 634

George, 90
Henry, 90, 634
James P., 261
Jesse, 490
John, 634
John Jr., 634
L. W., 454
Matthias, Jacob, 601, 604
John, 627
Joseph, 631
Mattingley, Gabriel J., 167
Maught, T. J., 504
Maugins, Samuel, 221
Mauk, Val., 327
Maulsby, Charles H., 598
Emily Nelson, 82
Mary Shriver, 82
W. P., 376, 561
William P., 82, 159, 170,
250, 365, 370, 373, 375,
391, 397, 525, 598-600,
605
William P., Jr., 375, 598
Maxell, Henry J., 606
S. J., 391
Maxwell, James, 250
John, 666
Thomas, 634
Wesley, 456
William, 627
May, Benjamin, 630, 647
Edward, 666
Frederick, 151
Henry, 252
Mayberrk, Israel, 169
Mayberry, Thomas, 335
Willoughby, 335
Mayer, Charles F., 7, 235
Christopher Bartholomew, 7
John, 643
Lewis, 407, 412
Maynadier, Henry, 315
Maynard, Albert, 442
H. G., 603
Henry, 624, 625
Horace, 262
John, 624
Nathan, 629
Richard, 629
S. S., 526, 566, 580, 582,
592
Thomas, 626
Thomas G., 601

Thomas, Sr., 629
Mayselles, M. L., 455
Maysellis, M. L., 454
Maywood, Margaret P., 520
McAfee, Daniel, 646
McAleer, Clara Louise, 317
Hugh, 206, 552
Joseph L., 382
McAlister, Alexander, 631
McAnair, Samuel, 642
McArdell, A. Leroy, 558
McAtee, George, 634
James, 630
McBee, Hugh, 643
McBride, Andrew C., 526, 606
C. A., 531
Daniel, 625
Foster S., 251
John, 268
L. E., 506, 530
Stella, 518
McCabe, S., 499
William K., 454
McCaffrey, John, 498, 523
McCahon, George, 557
McCalley, John J., 169
McCallister, John, 85, 86
McCally, John J., 169
McCannon, Eliza Asbury, 312
James, 312
Wm. H., 604
McCardell, A. C., 419, 436,
507, 510, 527, 552, 553
A. LeRoy, 541, 544, 545
Adrian C., 552
Albert N., 541
Edgar S., 542
H. C., 527
Mrs. A. C., 583
McCauley, C. F., 465
Charles, 476
McClain, William, 644
McClary, William, 85, 640
McCleary, Andrew, 25
Henry, 640
William, 84
McCleery, Caroline, 452
Henry, 432, 448-450
Martha E., 82
Perry B., 527
Robert, 169, 450
Wm.., 34
McClellan, William, 41

McCloskey, John, 523, 611
William George, 523
McClue, William, 643
McClure, John C., 353
McComas, Louis E., 89, 386
Walter P., 530
Wm. G., 592
McComb, William, 631
McCoombs, Patrick, 666
McCormack, A. Y., 451
Daniel, 634
John, 641
McCormick, George, 169
John H. M., 541
Philip F., 524
McCoy, James, 666
McCrackin, Isabelle Fitzhugh,
342
McCreer, I. F., 598
John T., 601, McCron
John, 425, 501
McCubbins, William, 666
McCulloh, Lewis, 643
McCullough, Archibald, 52
McCully, John J., 537
Joseph, 536
McCune, Samuel, 631
McCurdy, I. J., 580, 584
Ira J., 543, 545, 581, 582,
592
Irwin P., 451
McCusey, John, 645
McCusick, John, 634
McCutcheon, William O., 451,
541
McDanel, Alexander, 639
McDaniel, Ann, 629
C. B., 455
Francis, 646
James, 624
Joseph, 624
Mary, 643
Milton S., 462
Mrs. Elizabeth Pettingall, 562
Redman, 624
Walter, 560
Wm., 462
McDavitt, Harriet E., 483
McDead, Robert, 644
McDear, Patrick, 643
McDevitt, John, 169
McDonald, Francis, 629
Jacob, 633

James, 633
John, 65
Jonathan, 666
Margaret, 635
Samuel, 634
McDowell, James, 256
John, 597
Sallie Campbell Preston, 256, 258
McDudel, John, 643
McElfresh, Ariana, 314
David, 313
Henry, 292, 313, 314, 598, 643
John H., 227, 313, 601
John Hammond, 312, 313
McElroy, John, 189, 226
McEwen, Alfred, 622
McFarland, A. B., 154
Peter, 167
McFarren, Samuel, 86
McFear, Patrick, 635
McGafferty, Cornelius, 666
McGary, John, 634
McGee, John, 630
McGeehan, John, 604
McGerry, John, 523
McGill, Arabella, 490
Chas. B., 592
Eleanor, 256
Lloyd T., 599
Patrick, 133, 332, 602, 633
Robert H., 598
Rowland, 666
Samuel, 592
T. J., 365
Thomas, 565
Thomas J., 592
Wardlaw, 592
William, 592
McGinley, James, 46
McGinta, John, 666
McGlury, William, 83
McGorgan, John, 634
McGorvin, Dennis, 641
McGovern, John C. , 523
McGowen, James, 666
McGrah, James, 639
McGuire, Ross, 635
McGurgan, John, 324
McHaffie, James, 133
McHaffy, Jane, 627
McHenry, Henry, 634

J. H., 266
John, 327
S., 505
McIlroy, James, 635
McIntosh, D. G., 318
McKader, Sarah, 643
McKaig, Thomas J., 261, 288
McKain, William, 635
McKaleb, David, 645
Joseph, 631
McKalys, John, 604
McKan, Bartholomew, 640
McKaskill, Angus, 285
McKee, Samuel, 638
McKeehan, J. J., 604
James J., 601
Samuel H., 251
McKeen, William, 634
McKennon, Daniel, 430
McKensey, Eli, 627
Henry, 627
McKensie, David, 634
McKenzie, John, 626
Thomas, 101, 645
McKey, George, 666
McKierna, Charles B., 597
McKillip, Joseph, 95
McKinney, A. G., 531
D. F., 553, 582, 592
Matthew S., 541
McKinniss, John, 666
McKinny, John, 666
McKinsey, Folger, 304, 307, 312, 557
Lois, 304
McKinstrey, Evan, 604
M. C., 361
McKinstry, Evan, 601
McKissick, Margt., 635
McKnight, John, 467
McKogh, P., 647
McLain, George, 167
John, 630
Joseph, 638
Robert C., 541
Thomas L., 602
William, 629
McLaland, James, 666
McLamar, Archibald, 641
McLanahan, William H. B., 252
Wm. H. B., 251
McLane, R. A., 392

McLaughlin, James, 635
McLean, Daniel, 82, 90, 538
Donald, 304
E. L., 440-443, 469, 555
Eugene L., 436-438
Mrs. Donald, 304
Mrs. Donald, 77, 82, 310
Mrs. Donald R., 397
Thomas L., 524
McLocklin, Alexander, 643
James, 643
McMahen, James, 634
McMahens, James, 638
McMahon, John A., 599
John V. L., 32, 232
McMarti, Peter, 450
McMeen, Wm. H., 451
McMillan, O. D., 391
McMillen, Geo. O., 389
Jefferson O. , 389
McMin, George, 625
McMordy, Robert, 467
McMullan, Mary, 589
McMullen, Mary, 625
McMullin, Thomas, 169
McMurray, Louis, 400, 527
McNair, Samuel N., 325
McNeal, James, 666
McNeale, Archabald, 635
McNeill, W. Gibbs, 159
Wm. Gibbs, 157
McPherrin, Samuel, Jr., 631
Samuel, Sr., 631
William, 631
McPherson, Fitzhugh, 342
Horatio, 434
J., 532
James, 171
John, 136, 174, 180-184, 210, 212, 219, 225-227, 257, 265, 363, 450, 534, 549, 600-603, 640
John, Jr., 180, 182
Margaret Washington, 82
Maynard, 342
R. G., 167
Robert G., 601
W. S., 231
William S., 221, 534, 592, 605
William Smith, 342, 592
Wm., 167, 581
McRae, Duncan, 666
McRobie, Andrew, 184

45

McSheehan, J. J., 605
McSherry, Anna Gertrude, 316
  Barnabas, 632
  Caroline S., 317
  E. C., 573, 576
  Ed Coale, 316
  Edward, 316
  J. Roger, 552, 598, 607,
    609, 611, 612
  James, 77, 78, 292, 298,
    315-317, 319, 363, 395,
    396, 447, 527, 551, 552,
    554, 555, 567, 576, 597
  James Roger, 317
  James, Jr., 559
  Mary Alice, 316
  Mrs. James, 583
  Patrick, 316
  William, 592, 597
  William Clinton, 317
  William S., 316
McSwain, George, 666
McSweeney, Edward F., 523
McVicker, David, 167
McWilliams, John, 635
Meade, George, 383
Meadowe, Sir Thomas, 110
Mealey, Michael, 629
Mearns, Samuel, 666
Measel, Julia Ann, 483
Measell, Jacob, 169
Measle, Casper, 638
  Cynthia Ann, 483
  Frederick, 633
  Jacob, 638
Medairy, Summerfield Berry,
  544
Meddert, James, 640
Medoo, Henry, 645
Medtart, Lewis, 169, 219, 226,
  552
Medzler, Nicholas, 632
Meekle, J. M., 476
Meeks, William, 666
McElfresh, Henry, 592
  J. H., 592
Mefferd, John, 631
Mefford, Philip T., 643
Meier, Henry C. A., 542
Meinhard, Jacob, 647
Meister, P. A. , 412
Melcher, Philip, 640
Melius, Ella, 497

Melsheimer, Charles T., 250
Melton, Joseph, 626
Meminger, C. C., 361
Mensh, Adam, 637
Mensher, John, 626
Merady, Simon, 624
Mercer, C . F., 232
  Charles F., 151, 159
Merchant, Charles, 624
Meredith, William, 634
Merrick, Joseph I., 213, 275
  Richard T., 265
  William M., 244
  William V., 597
  Wm. D., 158
Merring, Wolfgong, 646
Merryman, William, 624
Mertz, George, 647
  Theobold, 25
Mesler, Ulrick, 624
Mesner, George, 634
Messeburg, Jacob, 637
Messenkop, C., 647
Messing, Christian, 647
Messner, Christian, 634
Metcalfe, Grace, 257
  Thomas, 658
Metre, Nicholas, 666
Mett, Francis, 645
Metz, Daniel O. , 461
Metzgar, William, 500
Metzger, John, 647
  W. M., 502
  William, 605
Metzker, Jacob, 639
Meyer, George Ernest, 541
Meyors, Robert, 645
Michael, Andrew, 644
  Barton F., 469
  Conrod, 641
  Daniel, 603
  George, 637
  Jacob R., 541
  Lodwich, 642
  O. E., 462
  Peter, 631
  William, 644, 645
Michaelhein, Francis, 628
Michel, Abraham, 484
Midhour, John, Sr., 631
Mikesell, Jacob, 628
  John, 642
Miles, D. S., 376

James, 454
Milla, John, 630
Millard, C. H. , 487
Miller, Abraham, 24, 627
  Abraham, Sr., 633
  Andrew, 638
  Anthony, 633
  Benjamin, 624
  Charles W., 601
  Chas. M., 450
  Clifford, 469
  Conrod, 637, 639
  Daniel, 462, 633
  Daniel B., 541
  David, 461
  Devalt, 647
  Edgar L., 545
  Elizabeth, 637
  Frederick, 634, 637
  Frederick, Jr., 637
  George, 170, 624, 631, 641
  George D., 249
  George W., 552, 603
  Godlip, 640
  H. N., 506
  Harrison, 607
  Harry, 555
  Henry, 455, 637, 646
  Henry, Sr., 646
  Ira, 558
  Ira L., 540, 543
  J. M., 504
  J. Marshall, 534
  J. O., 414, 416, 417
  Jacob, 8, 35, 85, 95, 136, 143,
    631, 633, 640, 646, 647
  Jacob F., 383
  Jacob J., 353
  Jacob T. C., 323, 605
  Jacob, Jr., 633
  Job M., 601, 607
  John, 167, 169, 450, 597, 626,
    627, 631, 633, 640, 643,
    646, 647, 667
  John F., 549
  John H., 544
  Joseph, 603, 624
  Joseph G., 276, 605, 606
  Lodowick, 634
  M. A. , 275
  Mahlon, 453
  Martin, 631
  Martin, Jr., 631

Mathias, 555
Michael, 637
Michael, Jr., 645
Nicholas, 637
Peter, 637, 647
Peter E., 462
Philip, 634, 647
Robert, 645
Robert H., 462
S. S., 419, 441, 468, 474, 493
Samuel, 461, 640
Sarah, 626
Simon S., 467, 468, 485, 541, 543
Stephen, 631
T. E. R., 580-582, 592, 601
Thomas E. R. , 610
W. T., 461
William, 604, 640, 667
William E., 372
William H., 603
William S., 552
Mills, D. Bernerd, 371
J. L., 488
John, 645
John R., 605, 607
Richard, 626
Thomas, 344
Mindt, Carl, 304
Mines, John L., 221, 552
W. W., 659
Minshe,
Joshua, 640
Minute, James, 634
Mire, John, 640
Mires, Jacob, 640, 641
Mirlvey, Michael, 645
Misker, Valentine, 636
Mitchel, Leonard, 641
Mitchell, Leonard, 169
Peter, 637
Stophel, 637
Theodore, 637
Thomas, 629
Thomas E., 592
Mitten, William, 169
Mitting, John, 627
Mixel, Peter, 647
Mixsell, Jacob, Sr., 167
Moaler, Jacob, 631
Solomon, 631
Moberly, Bradley, 592

Ed. M., 382
Eldred, 566, 590
Eldred W., 592
Eldrige, 565
L. Clinton, 400
William, 560
William L., 540, 542, 543
Mobley, Basil, 167
Edward, 348
James, 629
Lewis, 629
Mock, Thomas, 637
Valentine, 626
Mockett, Andrew, 637
Modden, William, 643
Moeller, John F., 421, 480
Moffett, Robert, 541
Moffit, Benjamin, 277
Molesworth, J. W., 531
Moling, Edward, 169
Noble, 169
Wm., 547
Monroe, Alexander, 667
James, 175, 522
Robert, 667
Thomas M., 598
Montgomerie, Thomas, 333
Montgomery, Edward, 633
John, 169, 486, 550, 603, 605
Thos., 642
Montgoney, John, 170
Monthland, Annie, 375
Montz, Jacob, 631
Mony, Richard, 627
Moodie, Hugh, 667
Mooney, William, 169
Moor, Wm., 647
Moore, Abraham, 627
Alexander, 633
Cato, 341
Charles, 169, 170
David, 84, 86
Edgar K., 459, 541, 543
James, 629, 635
John T., 525
Matthias, 642
Riley, 4
Robert, 541
Thomas H., 371, 372
Tobias, 624
William, 626
Moothers, Valentine, 637

Moran, Edmund, 41
John, 41
John J., 592
Martin, 225
Moray, George, 160
More, John, 644
Morehead, Samuel, 456
Morgan, Chas., 560
Conrod, 637
John, 220
Silas M., 598
Thomas W., 170, 177, 537, 538, 602
Thos. , 526
William, 169
Morhefer, Peter, 639
Morningstar, Philip, 633
Susanna, 633
Morris, Benjamin, 647
Capt. Roger, 54
John, 575, 577
John V., 389
Jonathan, 644
Robert, 118, 329, 331
William Thomas, 536
Morrison, Daniel, 82
J. G., 605
James, 604, 634
Jeremiah G., 383, 601, 604
John M., 607
Teresa, 490
William, 606
Morrow, Archabald, 643
Charles, 337, 341
Chas., 340
Mrs. Charles, 341
Teter, 640
Morse, S. F. B., 241
Morsel, Joshua, 434
Morsell, James, 164
William, 549, 604, 629
William P., 607
Mort, Conrad, 625
John, 626
Margaret M., 483
Matthias, 626
Peter, 647
Morton, Oliver P., 324
Moseback, Henry, 645
Moser, Conrod, 637
Jacob, 531
John, 497, 637
John H. , 462

Leonard, 633
Michael, 646
Peter, 627
Valentine, 637
Valentine, Jr., 637
Mosier, John, 169
Mossetter, Michael, 629
Motter, George Troxell, 592
Guy K., 543, 551, 552, 599
Henry D., 597
I. M., 440, 441, 468, 474, 493
Isaac M., 419, 438, 553
John C., 419, 525, 528, 541, 556, 598, 606, 607, 609-612
Joshua, 221, 254, 255, 325, 601, 605
Lewis, 324
Lewis M., 601, 611
Samuel, 325
Valentine, 500
William, 262
Mottor, Henry, 641
Valentine, 641
Mount, Elizabeth, 488
Thomas, 488
Mourer, Conrod, 643
Mower, Andrew, 643
Moxham, Frank B. , 542
Moyer, Christian, 645
Daniel, 647
John, 626
Joseph, 637
Joseph, Jr., 640
Michael, 638
Peter, 640
Samuel, 642
Moyers, Henry, 624
Joseph, Sr., 642
Peter, 624
Mozele, Charles, 667
Muckaberry, Abraham, 634
Mudd, George, 667
Sister Mary Rose, 511
Mueller, C. G., 141
Muhlenberg, H. E., 421
R. M., 479
Heinrich Melchor, 5
Mullen, Hiram H., 605
Mulhorn, J., 266
Mulinix, E. E., 566, 582
Robert, 638

Mullaly, Thomas, 447
Mullan, Nicholas, 646
Mullen, Nicholas, 634, 640
Muller, Hiram H., 383
Jacob, 647
Mullinix, E. E. , 590
Elisha E., 592
Frances, 82
Leonard C., 400
Mrs. Mary I., 459
Mrs. William T., 558
Thos. P., 548
William T., 558
Mumford, Jacob, 626
John, 624
Munday, Henry, 26, 27
Munford, E. M., 560
Munich, Daniel, 285
Munroe, William, 82
Munshour, Felix, 281
Nicholas, 631
Munshower, Elmer, 560
Murdoch, Eleanor, 128
George, 95, 327
John, 84
Mrs. Eleanor, 433
R. B., 531
Murdock, Bruce, 462
Bruce R., 463
George, 84, 86, 142, 221, 225, 227, 430, 431, 602, 640
H. V., 548
James, 598
John, 85, 603
Richard B., 167, 169
William, 634, 667
Murkle, William, 624
Murphew, William, 667
Murphy, J. J., 266
John, 193
Sister Mary Claudine, 510
W. R., 531
William, 604, 629
William C. , 541
Murquit, Michael, 639
Murray, Daniel, 134
Edward, 624, 642
Eli, 624
James, 624
Matthew, 537
Oscar G., 243
William Vans, 127

Zipporah, 216
Murrel, Robert, 629
Musgrave, Geo. W., 449
Musgrove, Benjamin, 248, 625, 667
Musser, C. J., 417
Mussetter, Christian, 629
Myer, Casper, 557
Myerhoeffer, Michael, 538
Myerly, David, 627
George, 627
Myers, Bostian, 633
Casper, 24
Chas. G., 451
Frederick, 625
Geo. W., 493
George, 271, 627, 628, 633
George Edward, 451, 606
Jacob, 627, 632
John, 39, 133, 624
Joseph, Jr., 642
Mary, 627
Melisia, 3
Nathan, 628
Peter, 638
Stephen, 633, 645
Thomas F., 541
Thomas H., 612
William, 325, 645
Nacviker, Archibald, 646
Nagle, Charles, 250
Nail, Daniel, 642
Jacob, 642
Philip, 631
Naile, David W., 550
Naill, D. W., 263
David W., 254, 255, 600, 601
H. C., 392, 520
H. Clay, 397
Henry Clay, 398, 601
Nale, Bosteon, 646
Nash, Thomas, 667
Nashbaum, John, 626
Nashorn, Conrod, 644
John, 644
Paul, 644
Nasman, Rev. G., 4
Nausbaum, Henry P., 461, 463
Samuel, 461
Nave, Balser, 645
John Henry, 24
Navel, Peter, 646
Naw, George, 645

Naylor, Alexander, 626
  Benjamin, 667
  George, 667
  James, 461, 463
  Joshua, 667
Nead, George, 90
  Rudolph, 82
Neaff, Abraham, 167
Neal, Alexander, 646
  Dennis, 643
  James, 537
Neale, James, 536
  John, 638
Neall, William, 667
Need, Christopher, 626
  George, 632
  John, 601, 603
  Magdalena, 631
  William, 334
Neff, Adam, 637
  Arthur S., 485
  Daniel, 637
  Henry, 637
  John, 637
Neghalf, Nicholas, 639
Neidig, William C., 541
Neighbors, E. D., 581, 582
  Eutaw D., 592
  Nathan O., 602
  Roger M., 607
Neike, George, 6
Neill, John, 449
Neilson, J. Crawford, 575
  William, 667
Neiser, George, 6
  Joseph, 6
Neith, Lorentz, 647
Nell, Philip, 631
Nelson, Arthur, 84, 85, 592, 644
  B. P., 266
  Burges, 638
  Elisha, 604
  Emily, 375
  F. J., 586
  Frederick J., 370, 598, 605
  Henry, 134, 626
  Howard, 78
  J. K., 454, 455
  John, 131, 132, 168, 174, 181, 215, 226, 298, 592, 597, 599, 600
  Madison, 82, 132, 250, 293,

    317, 375, 599, 600
  Nathan, 605
  Peter, 635
  Richard, 82
  Robert, 492
  Roger, 127, 128, 130, 131, 133, 141, 175, 179, 225, 248, 536, 537, 559, 597, 599, 600
  Roger, 635
  William, 645
Nestor, Jacob, 645
Nettle, R. H., 266
Neuwahl, Julius, 541
Nevin, Alfred, 413
Nevins, William, 315
Nevo, John, 667
Newby, Dangerfield, 355
Newcomer, Christian, 452, 454
  Samuel, 631
  Tobias, 438, 441
  William, 629
Newman, Francis J., 419
  Jacob, 635
  Jacob M. , 607
  John S., 530, 532, 535, 547, 598
Newport, David, 169
  James, 628
Niceinger, Magdalena, 642
Nichodemus, Valentine, 486, 631
Nicholas, George, 644
  Henry, 667
  John, 644
  Matthew, 41
  Mrs. Eliza M., 539
Nicholls, J. K., 487
Nichols, Adam, 167
  Edward, 597
  J. K., 488
  Jacob, 169
  James, 624, 644
  Philip, 641
  Samuel, 538
  Seth, 450
  Seth H., 525
Nicholson, Francis, 637
  Joseph Hopper, 313
Nicke, George, 494
Nickey, David, 628
Nickum, John, 486, 634
Nicodemus, A. W., 487, 605

Aubrey, 459
  Augustus W., 603, 607
  C. A., 531
  Edward B., 532
  Eli, 487
  Henry, Sr., 624
  John, 501, 624
  John D., 582, 593
  John L., 524, 601
  Mrs. William, 583
  Robert C., 541
  V. W., 531
  Wm. H., 526
Nidig, Benjamin, 453
Nieberg, Lars, 4, 5
Nienaber, Henry, 598
Nieuman, Frederick, 624
Night, George, 667
  Samuel, 667
  William, 629
Niles, Hezekiah, 249
  John, 169
  W. O., 230
  William Ogden, 249
Ninke, George, 4, 5
Nipple, Stephen, 631
Nisewanger, John, 637
Nisewarner, Christian, 637
Nixdorf, Henry M., 378
  Lewis M., 575
Nixdorff, G. A., 504
  Henry, 167, 169, 227
  Lewis M., 507
  Mrs. L. M., 396
  Sam'l, 527
Nixendurf, Samuel, 639
Noah, Conrad, 633
Noel, Blosius, 646
  John, 631
Noland, James, 634, 641
  Lawrence, 231
  Michael, 626
  Philip, 644
  Tho., 330
Nolley, Charles, 660
Norris, Barnet, 640
  Basil, 227, 434, 525, 593
  Benjamin, 626
  Edmund, 630
  J. Lawson, 251
  James L., 288
  John, 624
  John, Jr., 624

Mother Ann Simeon, 518
Nathaniel, 86, 647
Nicholas, 605
Samuel, 431, 639
William, 605
William H., 257
Norriss, John, 667
Northcraft, Richard, 85
Northrop, H. P., 523
Norton, Isaac, 638
Norwood, Frank C., 524, 533, 558, 559, 598, 606, 607
Samuel, 85
Notnagle, Adam, 400
Nowell, James, 667
Nowland, Thomas, 86
Noyer, Thomas, 667
Nublock, Geo., 630
Nugent, John, 63
Null, Chas. E., 549
Jacob, 631
Michael, 631
Valentine, 631
Wendle, 631
Nunemacker, Philip, 635
Nusbaum, Jacob, 525
Nuse, ———, 646
Michael, 640
Nusey, John, 634
Nussear, Jesse H., 611
Nusser, C. J., 441
Nusz, Ann R. E., 483
Jacob, 169
Millard N., 555
Oliver, 547
Peter E., 483
Nutter, Zacob, 631
Nyberg, Lars, 478
Lawrence, 494
Lorenz, 5
Lorenz Tharntansen, 6
O'Brien, Edward, 598
O'Bryan, Terence, 628
O'Conner, Joseph, 212
O'Conway, Cecilia, 513
O'Donnell, Charles Oliver, 185
Columbus, 256
O'Hara, Daniel, 642
Henry, 631
William L., 523, 610
O'Keefe, Mother Margaret, 518
O'Leary, A. D., 526
O'Neal, Archabald, 643

Bernard, 84, 85
H. G., 322
Patrick, 603
Singleton, 278, 550
Singleton H., 552
Thomas H., 525, 550, 601
O'Neil, Horatio G., 603
John F., 599
Lawrence, 602
Peggy, 201
Singleton H., 603
Thomas H., 603
O'Neill, John H., 597
Patrick, 604
Thomas H., 605
Obenderfer, F. W., 545
Occerman
Jacob, 626
Ocker, Christian, 633
Odd, Robert, 644
Offutt, Nathaniel, 84, 85, 86
Ogborn, John W. , 370
Ogburn, John W., 221
Ogden, Joseph, 637
Ogle, Alexander, 633
Benjamin, 86, 90, 95, 138, 431, 640
James, 90, 633
Joseph, 26, 27, 496, 634
Robert L., 535, 536
Samuel, 27
Sarah, 496
Thomas, 600, 638
Ogleby, John, 667
Ogly, Peter, 642
Ohr, Henry, 476
T., 476
Oland, Frederick, 660
Oldam, William, 643
Oler, Andrew, 634
Geo. Adam, 631
Laurence, 635
Peter, 631
Philip, 635
Oliver, Robert, 232
Thomas, 642
Olix, Adam, 639
Michael, 638
Ollick, Michael, 269
Onseller, Sarah, 624
Orand, Jacob, 626
Orbit, Philip, 634
William, 624

Ordeman, Daniel T., 540, 543
Orendorf, Christian, 84, 86
Peter, 631
Orendorff, Christian, 85
Organ, Thomas, 641
Orinand, Andrew, 629
Michael, 629
Orland, Frederick, 659
Orm, Archibald, 84
Ormant, Mary, 642
Orme, Archibald, 85
Robt., 54
Orr, John, 624
Nicholas, 642
Orrick, Nicholas, 335, 338, 339, 342
Ortner, John, 167
Osborne, Thomas, 353
Osler, Chas. H., 532
Ormond, 642
Reuben, 453, 455
Van B., 531
Osterday, Christian, 637
Christian, Jr., 637
Ott, Abigail, 635
Barnet, 644
Geo. M., 562
George, 634
George, Jr., 635
Jacob, 635
Mamie, 312
Mary Castle, 562
Michael, 635, 640
Peter, 169, 635
W. H., 266
Otter, A., 266
Otterbein, P. N., 475
Philip William, 408, 488
William, 452, 464, 494
Ould, Wm. L., 451
Oustler, Ormond, 628
Ovelman, George, 82, 624
Henry, 626
Jacob, 626, 642
Michael, 626
Overholse, George, 645
Overholts, Abraham, 634
Isaac, 624
Overholtz, Isaac, 642
Overs, Cephus, 281
Overton, John B., 539, 542, 543
Owen, J. W., 455
Thomas, 26

Owens, Thomas, 27, 600
Owings, Beale, 642
  Edward, 281
  F. D., 547
  John, 667
  Mrs. Nicholas, 396
  N. H., 538
  Nicholas, 395
  Nimrod, 183
  Richard, 482
Oyerly, D. H., 549
Oyler, Jonas, 634
Paca, William, 10, 104, 109,
  110, 145, 147
Pack, Simon, 667
Paddy, William, 642
Padgett, Daniel Z., 606
  George W., 606
Pagaent, William, 645
Pagan, John, 626
Page, C., 279
  Calvin, 210, 211, 552, 557
  Dudley, 547
  J. R., 520
  Thomas, 667
Pagget, Josiah, Jr., 644
  William, 644
Paggett, Josiah, 644
Paine, John, 169
Painter, John, 627
Paker, George, 641
Palmer, A. L., 543
  Chas., 560
  John, 143
  John Williamson, 101
  Joseph H., 398
  Joseph M., 221, 314, 525,
    597, 601
  Thomas F., 484
Pampel, J. E., 560
  P. Frank, 598
Pampell, John, 396
Pannebecker, J. H., 465
Panter, Henry, 631
Parah, Charles, 643
Paret, Wm., 491
Parish, Gilbert, 624, 638
  Richard, 624
Park, James, 82
Parker, Richard, 353
Parks, James, 90, 635
  John, 83, 638
  Lloyd B., 353

Parmley, Mrs. J., 82
Parnell, Bedwell, 644
Parret, Peter, 646
Parron, Samuel, 638
Parsins, John, 645
Parsons, Robert, 642
  W. Irving, 527, 528, 552,
    606
Pastorius, David, 406
Pate, Edward, 643
Pathoover, Edward, 643
Patterson, Albert L., 606
  Alida, 390
  Isaac M., 467
  John, 633
  John C., 390
  Joseph, 629
  Nathaniel, 635
  R. S., 485
  Thomas, 634
  William, 593
Paulin, Robert, 667
Paw, Abraham, 85
Paxton, Nathaniel, 640
  Thomas, 631
  William, 467, 631
Payn, Howard, 316
Payne, John Howard, 311
Peale, David, 631
Pearce, Fannie, 511
  Sister Mary Teresa, 511
Pearis, Richard, 661, 667
Pearre, F., 265
  Frank C., 599
  George A., 254, 597, 598
  George A., Jr., 599
  James, 221, 605
  James W., 598
  Merton S., 582, 593
  Mrs. Albert, 559
  Mrs. Nannie Dixon, 562
  Thomas O., 343
  William H., 607
Pearson, Isaac E., 598
  Isaac E., Jr., 598
  Thomas, 667
Peck, Charles M., 316
Peckenbaugh, Peter, 641
  Susanna, 637
Peddicord, J. C. , 473
  William, 667
Peiree, Peter, 667
Pelkington, Henry, 63

Pelshill, Uly, 646
Pemberton, Richard, 667
Pence, George, 639
  Margaret, 639
Pencoast, William, 629
Penders, Jacob, 639
Pendleton, Philip, 341
  Wm. N., 434
Penn, C., 266
  Richard, 71
  Thomas, 71
  William, 13, 80, 460
Pennel, John S., 383
Pennybaker, Samuel, 642
Penser, Godfrey, 646
Pentz, Jacob, 633
Pepper, Henry, 637
  John, 644
  John, Jr., 644
Pepple, Abraham, 638
  Jacob, 627
  John, 627
  Peter, 628
  William, 632
Perdon, Charles, 169
Perkins, John, 667
  Thomas, 667
  William, 667
  William H., 593
Perkinson, Edward, 627
Perril, Basil, 643
  Samuel, 643
Perrill, Thomas, 641
Perry, Benj. C., 593
  Charles, 86
  Henry, 453
  Jacob, 453, 455
  Jacob, Jr., 454
  James, 630
  James P., 606, 607
  Jonathan, 454
  Joseph, 83-86
  Roger, 597
  Sarah, 643
Perryman, Isabelle, 342
Peter, Enoch, 640
  Frederick, 646
  Johann Friederich, 6
  Warner, 624
Peterkin, Joshua, 434, 435
Peters, Charles, 167
  John, 639
  Michael, 169

Petit, Lewis, 667
Petre, Michael, 461
Petser, Samuel, 629
Pettenger, Benjamin, 97
Pettinger, Benjamin, 626
   Danl., Jr., 626
   John, 626
   William, 626
Pettis, John L., 250
Pettit, Belle, 452
   James, 631
Pfoutz, Isaac, 461
Pfrimmer, George, 452
Pharoah, Leonard, 634
Pheasant, Samuel, 627
Phebus, Peter, 169
Phelps, Eli, 641
   J., 266
   Philo F., 450
   Robert W. , 383
Pherson, Leonard, 646
Philbel, William, 638
Philberger, Frederick, 643
Philips, J., 560
   James, 641
   Noah, 550
   Reece, 631
   Samuel, 457, 493
   William, 470, 486
   Wm. D., 598
Phillen, Henry, 641
Phillip, Lycurgus N., 601
Phillips, Elizabeth, 458
   Jake, 362
   James, 536
   John, 454, 626
   Nancy, 458
   Noah, 221, 605
   R. H., 333
   Richard H., 492
   Samuel, 476, 485, 637
Philpot, Barton, 637
   Charles, 637
   G. Blanchard, 607
   Samuel, 536
   Zachariah, 637
Phipps, John, 667
Phleeger, John E., 607
Pickell, John, 158
Pickerell, Samuel, 667
Pickering, Timothy, 103
Pickett, W. W., 546
Picking, John B., 605

Pierce, Franklin, 266, 299
Pierpont, Amos, 646
Piester, Stephen, 170
Pifer, Philip, 638
Pigman, B. S., 181
   Beane S., 601
   Ignatious, 457
   R. S. , 597
Pilgram, Robert J., 442
Pillow, Gideon J., 266
Pinckney, Charles Cotesworth, 142
Pindell, Richard, 327
Pindle, Philip, 667
Piney, Henry, 169
Pingley, Christian, 633
Pingrave, Francis, 667
Pinkney, William, 127, 132, 196, 298, 311
Pintard, John, 268
Piper, D. A., 543
   Jackson, 575
   Jacob, 627
Pise, Charles Constantine, 522
Pitt, William, 28, 74
Pittinger, Jacob, 468
Pitts, Charles H., 597
   William, 556
Plain, David, 624
Plaster, Joseph, 638
Plata, Jean Baptiste, 33, 34
Plater, Anne, 315
   George, 26, 27, 104, 122, 315
   Rebecca, 313
Plecker, Yost, 96
Ploutz, Michael, 461
Plummer, Abraham, 629
   Eleanor, 643
   F. Berry, 454
   Isaac, 629
   James (of Saml), 629
   James (of Thos.), 629
   Jesse, 629
   Jonathan, 643
   Joseph, 629
   Joseph (of Saml), 629
   L., 86
   Moses, 629
   Robert, 629
   Samuel, 326, 629
   Sarah, 629
   Thomas, 629

   William, 326
   Yate, 629
Plunket, Robert, 667
Plus, William, 645
Pobst, John, 167
Poe, Adam, 343-345
   Andrew, 343-345
   Edgar Allan, 592
   George, 637
   Jacob, 251
   John P., 161, 598
   John Prentiss, 317, 318
   Neilson, 251
   Thomas, 52
Poffinberger, Samuel, 554
Pole, John, 647
   Thos. Samuel, 631
Poling, Elias, 642
Polk, Charles, 21
   Esther Winder, 292
   James, 292
   James K., 173, 264
Poll, George, 59
Polle, George, 60
Polston, Andrew, 624
   Cornelius, 624
   James, 624
Pontius, John W., 438, 465
Poole, Bushrod, 593
   Conrod, 626
   Cyrus W., 598
   Frederick, 167
   Henry, Jr., 638
   Henry, Sr., 624
   T. A., 582, 593
   Thomas E. D., 601
   William, 169
Poonsock, Jacob, 638
Poor, Abraham, 631
Poorman, Abraham, 505
   John, 631
Pope, Thomas E., 365, 573
Porter, John, 667
   John A., 167
   Nathan, 635
   Nathaniel, 603
   Philip, 504
   Samuel, 641
Ports, Sylvanus M., 475
Posey, Fabian, 560, 599
   George, 624
Pot, Benedict, 633
Pott, Fordyce, 563

Potter, Alonzo, 435
    Jacob A. , 281
    Thomas, 46
    William, 638
Pottinger, Mrs. Mary, 312
Potts, Arthur, 533, 552
    George M., 221, 227
    Philip, 167
    R., 230
    Richard, 10, 82, 127-129,
        225-227, 278, 299, 331,
        365, 431-434, 532, 540,
        541, 550, 593, 597,
        599-602, 605, 640
    Richard, Jr., 128
    Sarah, 638
    William, 128, 431, 433, 434
Poulter, Hugh, 667
Poultney, Anthony, 326
Pourtney, Anthony, 629
Powder, Jacob, 628
Powel, William, 646
Powell, Arthur Chilton, 404
    John, 667
    Joseph, 496
    Rev. R. , 6
    Samuel, 667
    Thomas, 641, 667
    William, 627
Powlas, George, 637
    Nicholas, 637
Powrigh, Lawrence, 626
Prangle, Christian, 638, 640
    Laurence, 640
Prather, Enoch, 637
    Henry, 668
    James, 84, 85
    John, 637
    John Smith, 600
    Thomas, 26, 27, 84, 85,
        430, 602, 668
Pratt, Enoch, 520
    Thomas G., 264
Prees, Henry, 668
Preine, C., 647
Preston, Samuel B., 275
    Sophia, 280, 281
    William T., 552
Price, Benjamin, 138, 182,
        597, 632
    Chas. S., 560
    Geo, 526
    George, 597

George E., 598
J. W., 598
Philip, 633
Thomas, 75, 78, 84-87, 136,
    225, 430, 432, 564, 603,
    630, 633
William, 158, 257
William B., 542
Prince, Thomas C., 250
Priner, Abraham, 640
Pringle, Christian, 639
    Margaret, 626
    Mark U., 134
Pringman, Michael, 638
Prinkman, John, 325
Pritts, Joseph, 46
Probst, J. F., 505
Proder, Conrod, 639
Proof, Jacob, 644
Protzman, Daniel, 90
    John, 90
    Lawrence, 90
Proutman, Jacob, 635
Prude, Conrad, 624
Prush, David, 644
Prutsman, Daniel, 633
    Elizabeth, 633
    John, 633
    Lodwick, 646
Pryor, James W., 593, 597
Pudiver, Thomas, 668
Pulbough, Joseph, 642
Pumphrey, Mary, 458
Pup, John, 633
    Peter, 633
Purcell, John D., 523
Purdie, William, Jr., 630
    William, Sr., 629
Purnell, William H., 451, 507,
    598
Putesbaugh, Peter, 626
Putman, John, 637
    Philip, 637
Putnam, George W., 350
Putonberger, Michael, 631
Pyfer, Philip, 167
    Philip H., 227
Quantrill, Thomas, 166
Queen, Richard, 668
Quicksel, Mary, 639
Quinn, Allen G., 292
    John T., 376
Quinner, Jacob, 632

Quinter, James, 462
Quitman, John A., 266, 538
Quynn, Allen, 141, 396
    Allen G., 527, 538, 539,
        541-543
    Allen, Jr., 600
    C., 230
    Casper, 537, 538, 555, 600,
        601
    Harry H., 541
    John, 644
Radcliff, A. Atlee, 541, 555
    Edith, 459
    Grace, 459
Radcliffe, A. A., 459
    A. Atlee, 543
Rader, Jacob, 628
Rady, Henry, 634
Radziwill, Ferdinand, 117
    Louise, 117
Raemer, Michael, 25
Ragan, Daniel, 630
    John, 629, 668
    R., 172
Rager, R. A., 547, 603
    Rufus A., 546, 606, 610
Rahauser, Frederick, 486
    Jonathan, 470, 486
    Theodore, 470
Railing, Geo. H., 547
Rakus, Henry, 643
Rally, Isaac, 668
Ramer, Michael, 638
Ramsay, Joseph, 635
Ramsbaugh, John S., 603
Ramsberg, George, 644
Ramsburg, Adam, 633
    Alexander, 610
    Alexander H., 606
    Christian, 604, 633
    D. E., 582
    E., 392
    Elias B., 540, 543-545
    Florence, 591
    Frederick, 169
    Henry B., 436
    Israel, 604, 605
    Jacob, 633
    John, 552, 633
    John E., 391
    John J., 593
    John S., 527
    John W., 606

John, Jr., 637, 640
Lewis, 170, 457, 500, 534
M. O. , 531
Sebastian, 256
Stephen, 24, 406, 431
Ramsburgh, Henry B., 542
Ramsey, John, 668
Ramsour, Adam, 629
Ramsower, Henry, 629
Randall, Mordacai, 169
Samuel, 645
V. W., 183
Randolph, Edmund, 105, 132
John, 165
Peyton, 91
Randthaler, Ambrose, 6
Edward, 6
Ransburg, Aaron, 628
Rasler, Henry, 626
Michael, 626
Rasor, Jacob, 433
Rass, Daniel, 646
Rate, Alexander, 639
James, 629
Rathell, Aaron, 668
Rattler, Wm. , 167
Raudabush, G. J., 454
Rawlings, Aaron, 637
John, 26, 27
Moses, 85
Raymer, Michael, 85, 431
Raymond, Calvin C., 598
James, 597
Rayner, Isador, 318
Razor, Jacob, 183
Read, Henry, 626
James, 165
Mary Cornelia, 185
Real, Michael, 631
Ream, George, 633
Sarah, 488
Rechard, Peter, 637
Reck, A., 502-505
Abraham, 501
Reckard, John, 634
Recop, Susanah, 646
Redburn, Henry, 637
Samuel, 668
Reddie, Wm., 553
Redick, Leonard, 638
Reece, Adam, 633
Adam, Jr., 633
Andrew, 627

John, 627, 631
Reed, Jacob, 631, 641
John, 633
Patrick, 325
Reek, A., 476
Reel, Frederick, 638
Reese, Aquila A., 457, 458
Joshua D., 483
Mrs. Catherine, 413
Reeside, John E., 173
Reeves, Prudence, 628
Regden, John E., 647
Reich, Benjamin F., 527, 598
Reid, Hugh, 628
James, 170
Upton Scott, 597
Reidenhorn, Barnet, 646
Reifsnider, John, 524, 605
Reighley, Charles, 493
Reigle, Benjamin, 520
Reilley, Richard M., 524
Reimensnyder, J. J., 481, 505
Reinecke, J. W., 549
Reineke, A. A. , 6
Samuel, 6
Reinewald, Chas., 466, 467
Reinhart, Andrew, 463
David, 624
David Jerome, 593
Really David, 463
William, 453
Reinkey, John, 505
Reisner, Michael, 72
Michel, 479
Reiter, Lewis, 416
Reitzell, Philip, 169
Rekenbaugh, George, 646
Remsberg, Albert S., 535
Amos, 465
C. Thomas, 465
Henry C., 553
J. Harman, 534
John W., 534
Singleton E. , 535
Walter L., 535
Remsburg, Benjamin, 454
Christian, 453, 454
Foster C., 534, 535
George C., 437
George W., 601
Henry, 453
Henry C., 553
J. Harmon, 465

J. J., 582
Jacob, 658
John, 85, 86, 464, 465
John S., 528
Singleton E., 606
W. L., 502
Remsburgh, Jacob, 550
Rench, A., 93
Daniel, 134
John, 86, 93
Peter, 25
S. M., 441
Reniker, Paul, 627
Renit, Robert, 635
Renn, Charles, 553
Eli Charles, 533, 541
John, 503
Renner, Charlotte, 645
F. C., 462
Isaac, 645
John, 327, 626
Michael, Jr., 645
William, 626, 644
Rentch, Daniel, 125
Renz, Mathaens, 6
Repp, John S., 383
Rerter, Felty, 641
Resser, Geo. B., 486
Reymour, Joseph, 668
William, 668
Reynolds, Edward, 164
George, 668
Hugh, 449, 633
J. F., 561
James, 641, 642, 668
John, 149, 343, 450
Luther M., 598
Thomas, 626
Rheam, Baltzer, 626
John, 626
Rhoads, Jacob, 456
Shafer L., 543
Rhoderick, Carlton, 323
Charles C., 419
Charles H. C., 541
Chas. K., 617
George C., 617
George C., Sr., 534
J. S. L., 326
Mahlen, 617
Mahlon D., 541
Rhodes, Chas. M., 459
Daniel, 321

F. T., 77
Francis T., 540, 541, 543
Geo., 327
Jacob, 626
Schaeffer L., 541
Thomas, 668
Rice, A. T., 415
Andrew, 631
Ann, 637
Benjamin, 490, 637
Casper, 631
Chas. A., 530
Dan, 284
George, 163, 211, 602, 631
George H., 485
Grafton J., 525
Isaiah, 485
J. E. B., 455
Jared, 491, 492
Joseph, 641
Lewis A., 312, 419, 534
M. L., 531
Marion C., 546
Michael, 642
Milton G., 541
Perry A., 598
Sarah, 491
Thomas, 647
Rich, Ernest A., 403
Richard, John, 635
Wm., 169
Richards, Aaron, 624
Caleb, 626
Catharine, 626
David, 84, 85
George, 134, 503, 504
George W., 419, 465
Jacob, 637
John, 628
Joshua, 638
Stephen, 275
William, 628
William L., 607
Richardson, David, 601
Davis, 185, 254, 255, 293, 603
George R., 160
Hester Dorsey, 313
John, 279, 627, 629, 638
Richard, 643
Thomas, 134, 165
William, 108, 221, 362, 550, 602

X. J., 505
Richer, Henry, 639
Richmond, Benjamin
Armstrong, 319
Benjamin H., 598
E. T. C., 319
Ephriam, 319
Violet, 319
Richter, Christian, 6
John, 167
Rick, Christopher, 627
Ricker, Conrod, 637
Ricksecker, Benj., 6
Riddle, Benjamin, 626
David H., 467
Riddlemoser, Michael, 327, 637
William, 593
Ridenour, Homer D., 541
J. R., 454
Rider, Frederick, 453, 455
G. I., 455
Ridge, Benjamin, 633
Cornelius, 635
Ephraim, 633
William, 633
Ridgely, Henry, 597
Jacob, 637
Richard, 637
Westel, 85, 86
Ridgeway, James, 644
Ridgley, Ann, 593
Anne, 564
Ridout, T. , 145
Rieghley, Charles, 408
Riehl, Jacob, 167
Rife, Christian, 645
Christopher, 642
Henry, 646
Riffle, Jacob, 624
Joseph, 646
Ludwick, 642
Riffly, Jacob, 635
Riffner, Henry, 635
Rigby, Townly, 597
Riggs, Amos, 85
Christopher M., 601
Edward, 469
George H., 581, 584, 593
John, 639
Right, John, 627
Rights, Anthony, 640
Rightstine, William, 353

Rigney, Frederick, 251
John, 166, 602
John T., 556
Wm. H., 556
Riley, E. S., 261, 325
Elihu, 372
James, 668
John, 642
Patrick, 640
Rimby, Peter, 632
Rimel, George B., 454
Rine, Casper, 629
Michael, 629
Rinedollar, Geo., 631
Henry, 631
Matthias, 631
Rinehart, Andrew, 461
David, 461, 601, 605
Felty, 631
George, 363, 631, 639
William, 454
William H., 206
Riner, William, 170
Ringer, Jacob, 626
John, 626
Mathias, 86, 633
Mathias, Jr., 633
Ringgold, Samuel, 127, 133, 165, 166, 168, 171, 307
Tench, 132
Ringland, John, 325, 635
Rinner, John, 169
Rip, Henry, 624
Rippen, Thomas, 629
Rippin, Thomas, 647
Riser, Charles C., 553
Jonathan, 606
Risner, Tobias, 638
Rister, Michael, 638
Samuel, 638
Ritchie, Abner, 128, 602, 640
Albert, 450, 458, 559, 565, 593
J., 132
John, 82, 166, 221, 310, 317, 346, 348, 362, 396, 450, 458, 598-600, 603, 640
Mary, 640
Mrs. John, 375, 559
Robert, 249
William, 598, 602
William, 640
Willie, 559

Willie M., 78
Willie Maulsby, 82
Riting, Andrew, 624
Ritinger, Ann, 628
    John, 627
Ritingmyer, Michael, 627
Ritter, Alfred, 598
    C. L., 505
    Elias, 635
    J. Alfred, 601
    John Alfred, 542
Rizer, Peter, 501
Roach, Robert, 458
Road, Christian, 640
Roadpouch, Frederick, Ser,
    642
Roads, Barbara, 639
Roar, Jacob, 640
    Philip, 640
    Rudolph, 640
Rob, Frederick, 633
Roberts, C. B., 575
    Henry, 627
    Isaac, 668
    John, 643, 668
    N. S., 154
    Richard, 629
    William, 601, 627, 635, 638
Robertson, Alexander, 167
Robinson, Charles, 82, 90,
    635, 668
    John K., Jr., 622
    John K., Sr., 621
    John M., 319
    William, 536
Roche, John, 90
Rochester, Nathaniel, 130,
    132, 171
Rock, John, 634
Rockwell, E. H., 276
    Elihu H., 249, 603
    Elihu Hall, 558
Roddy, John H., 535
Rodenpeler, Philip, 637
Rodensick, Henry, 647
Rodepouch, Frederick, 624
Roderick, Mahlon, 602
Rodock, Geo. S., 573
Roelke, Geo. A., 437
    George W., 437
    Richard J. D., 437
Roelkey, D. H., 530
Roelky, A., 266

Roemer, John M. , 479
Rogers, John, 324
    Owen, 631
    Patrick, 633
    William, 543
Rohr, George, 169
    Philip, 283
Rohrback, Jacob, 472, 510,
    534, 541, 542, 598, 607
    M. N., 527
Roller, John E., 507
Rolls, D., 538
Rolz, George, 479
Roman, James Dixon, 597
Romsburg, John, 84
Roop, Jesse, 461
    Joseph, 627
Root, Charles, 532
    Daniel, 624
    Daniel, Jr., 645
    Daniel, Sr., 626
    E. L., 334, 549
    Jacob, 221, 538, 601, 604
    John, 531, 532
Rop, Mary, 630
Ropp, Samuel, 169
Rosebaugh, Isaac, 635
Roseberger, Frederick, 630
Roseen, Swen, 6
Rosenberg, J. A., 501
Rosenour, Benjamin, 541
    Gerson, 543
Rosenplot, John, 631
Rosenstock, Aaron, 541
    Jacob, 541, 555
    Mrs. Aaron, 583
Rosier, Henry, 635
Ross, Anne Arnold, 314
    Charles W., 25, 292, 363,
        398, 532, 534, 542, 598
    Charles W., Sr., 540
    David, 597
    George, 668
    J. B., 450
    Jno. W. , 227
    John, 314
    Mrs. Ann Grahame, 559
    Mrs. Worthington, 180
    Richard P., 599, 609
    Richard R., 533
    William, 174, 180, 181,
        183, 212, 226, 432, 433,
        532, 597, 601

William J., 226, 227, 228,
    264, 319, 342, 365, 398,
    434, 435, 457, 520, 534,
    552
    Worthington, 538, 597
Rossiter, J. T., 419
Roszel, S. S., 458
Roszell, S. S., 457
Roth, Amos A., 593
    Henry, 24
Roud, Henry, 637
Roudabush, G. J., 455
Rouderbush, Daniel, 637
Rousby, Elizabeth, 315
Rouser, J. P., 601
Routson, Jesse H., 519
    Joseph, 271
    T. C., 488, 564, 582, 584
    T. Clyde, 582, 593
Routsong, Adam, Jr., 637
    Conrod, 647
Routzahn, Cyrus, 453, 531
    D. H., 603
    Enos, 502
    Ezra, 529, 530
    George, 499
    Herman L., 528, 534, 554, 608
    Isaiah, 529, 530
    John L., 528, 534, 554
    Jonathan, 524, 601
    Joseph, 524, 603, 605
    Nan E., 583
    William S., 528
Routzon, Jesse H., 541
Rouzer, Daniel, 334
    Harvey H., 598
    Henry, 470, 473
    John R., 392, 532, 602, 607
    Martin, 391
    Peter, 470
Row, Arthur, 82, 90, 635
    George, 635
    James, 639
    John, 170
    Michael, 635, 639
Rowe, Charles W., 601
    George W., 611
    Wm., 167
Rowland, Abraham, 627
Rowles, Francis, 668
    John, 668
    Thomas, 668
Roy, William, 626, 629

Royall, Mrs. Anne, 185
Ruble, Peter, 637
Rudicill, Jacob, 632
   Tobias, 631
Rudolph, Carl, 4, 5, 479
   Michael, 8
   Peter, 631
Rudolpus, Carl, 479
Rudy, Hanson J., 605
   Jacob, 322
   Peter, 637
   T. Carlton, 534
   William L., 535
Rue, Jacob, 642
Ruebush, John, 454
Rufcorn, Christian, 631
Ruff, Sabriet, 668
Ruffneck, William, 668
Ruger, T. H., 371
Ruland, Roy R., 560
Ruliff, Gilbert, 629
Rumsey, Benjamin, 319
   Charles, 338
   Clarissa, 342
   Edward, 338
   Edward, Jr., 338, 342
   James, 137, 335, 337, 338
   James, Jr., 342
   Susannah, 342
Rund, H., 647
Rundt, ———, 6
Runecker, H., 647
Runey, John, 638
Runkel, John, 593
   John William, 408, 464
   William, 410, 493
Runkle, J. W., 470
   John William, 475, 488
   William, 486, 640
Runkles, Jacob, 627
Runner, Abraham, 626
Rupley, F. A., 465
Rupp, Jesse, 463, 603
Russel, Jacob, 627
Russell, Abraham, 173
   Elizabeth, 102
   John, 668
   Thomas, 668
   William C., 184
Rutherford, Benjamin, 180,
   184, 432, 526
Ruthrauff, John F., 466, 467
Ryan, Edmund J., 524

James, 635
Joseph P., 598
   Matthew, 497
   Thomas, 630
Ryder, James, 447
Rye, Henry, 167, 626
Rylett, Edward, 645
Ryley, Doyle, 632
   Thomas, 635
Sables, A., 266
Sadler, Michael, 629
   William, 668
Sagaser, Jacob, 500
Sage, Samuel, 635
Saggersy, Jacob, 637
Sahm, John Jacob, 541
Sailer, Christian, 626
   Daniel, 626
Sailor, Frederick, 646
   Henry, 647
Sallers, Ellett, 169
Salmon, Catharine, 458
   Edward, 646
   George, 457, 538
   William E., 371, 601
Salter, Frank, 555
Sample, Cunningham N., 449
Sanbach, Francis, 628
Sandbaugh, Philip, 645
Sanders, Henry, 504
   Samuel, 645
Sanderson, Francis, 275
   W. R., 226, 593
   William R., 227, 450, 526
Sands, George W., 598
Sane, Philip, 631
   Philip, Jr., 629
Sap, Leonard, 628
Sapp, Robert, 668
Sappington, A., 365
   A. A., 361
   Augustus, 593
   C. T., 582
   Clifford T, 593
   F. B., 133, 556, 580
   F. D., 572
   Francis, 593
   Francis B., 540, 543-545,
   597, 601, 602, 626
   Francis Brown, 564, 593,
   600
   Frank B., 532
   G. R., 593

George K., 461, 462
   Greenbury, 566
   James C., 593
   Mrs. Louisa, 462, 583
   Richard F., 607
   Sydney B., 593
   T. P., 581
   Thomas, 169, 249, 593,
   600-602
   Thomas P., 593
   W. C., 601
   Wm. C., 597
Sargent, George, 645
Sargis, Frederick, 271
Sary, Caleb, 65
Sasser, Benjamin, 668
Saunders, George, 668
   John, 668
   Samuel, 211
   W., 363
   W. W., 555
   Walter, 304, 348, 362, 384,
   391, 547, 561
Sawer, Adam, 643
Sawers, Balser, 645
Sawyer, Matthias, 631
Saxe, Marshal, 142
Saxton, J. A., 547
   John A., 541
Saylor, C. E., 547
   Charles E., 606
   Daniel P., 460-462
   Daniel R., 462
   Daniel, Sr., 461
   Geo, 489
   Jacob, 461
   Thomas R. , 485
Scaggs, Isaac, 668
   James, 668
   Richard, 668
Scepter, Joseph, 632
Schaaf, Christian F., 6
Schaaff, Caspar, 85
Schade, John Julius, 647
Schaeffer, Chas. D., 441
   D. F., 177, 502, 503, 505
   David F., 227, 250, 427, 483
   David Frederick, 421
   James J., 468, 475
   William C., 419, 466, 510
Schafer, David F., 167
Schaff, Casper, 84
Schaffer, Charles D., 472, 473

Schaffner, Jacob, 167
Schamel, H. F., 593
Scharf, J. Thomas, 495
Schaum, I. H., 420
John H., 480
Scheel, Philip, 555
Scheffner, A. M., 486
Scheirer, A. C., 560
Schell, Charles, Jr., 169
Charlotte, 458
Elizabeth, 458
Ezra, 169
Harry, 555
Henry, 536
Jesse, 169
Joseph, 603
Schellas, F., 266
Schemich, Casper, 647
Schildknecht, Henry A., 528, 534
Schildnecht, C. N., 594
Schildtnecht, C. N., 581
Schildtz, Harry, 462
Schinder, Chas, 462
Schindle, David, 605
Schindler, David, 550
Schisler, Adam, 536
Jacob, 25
Schissler, John, 167
Schivaller, John, 167
Schlatter, Michael, 4, 407, 474, 479, 486
Schlegel, J. P., 6
Schley, A., 266
Alfred, 326, 391
B. H., 348, 391
B. Henry, 543
Benjamin, 372
Benjamin H., 541
Buchanan, 312
Charles, 597
David, 250, 251, 538, 601
Edward, 227, 597
F., 565
F. A., 597
F. Augustus, Jr. , 288
Fairfax, 227, 292, 400, 520, 552, 582, 594
Frederick, 296, 392, 527, 605
Frederick A., 6, 174, 181, 212, 221, 227, 293, 311, 312, 450

Frederick Augustus, 311
George, 158, 265, 312, 598, 601
George Jacob, 638
Henry, 169, 527, 602
J., 265
Jacob, 25, 134
James, 312
James M., 256, 601
John, 6, 132, 133, 168, 181, 225, 226, 527, 601, 602
John Jacob, 25, 311, 638
Louis H., 400
Steiner, 533, 541, 553
Thomas, 6, 25, 84, 225, 269, 406, 408, 409, 621, 638
W. S., 284, 305
William, 6, 182, 193, 212, 213, 306, 308, 309, 597, 599, 600
William L., 265, 598
William Louis, 6, 391
Winfield Scott, 81, 559
Wingfield Scott, 6
Schlosser, George, 221
Peter, 550
Peter G., 382, 605
Schmid, Empiricus, 420
Schmidt, Caspar, 495
Empiricus, 479
Jacob, 560
Schmitt, Jacob, 275
Schmucker, J. G., 501
S. S., 425
Schnauffer, Wm. , 530
Schnebely, Henry, 600
Schnebley, David, 149
H., 594
Schnebly, H., 565
Schneck, B. S., 470
Schnee, Jacob, 501
Schneider, Gerard Joseph, 593
Schnertzell, Sybila, 139
Scholl, Christian, 25
Henry, 167
Lewis V., 534
Schools, Thomas, 623
Schoto, John, 167
Schreiler, Henry, 647
Schriver, David, 84-86, 605
Jacob, 167
Schroder, Henry, 180

Schroeder, Harry O., 560
Wm., 134
Schuantiegel, Geo., 167
Schulman, Max, 549
Schultz, E. P., 6
Daniel, 25
David, 170
E. T., 2, 24
Ed. T. , 268
Edward T., 3, 25
Frederick, 90
John Christian, 477
Schweishaupt, Johannes, 6
Schwerdfeger, Samuel, 8, 480
Schwing, Henry, 416
Scofield, Jesse, 185
Scoggins, Ann, 643
Scotlowe, Augustin, 110
Dorothy, 110
Scott, Andrew, 84, 85
Dred, 205
George, 84, 85, 602, 606
Gustavus, 145
Thomas, 167
Upton, 563
Winfield, 266
Zachariah, 668
Screwel, George, 645
Scruble, Henry, 630
Seabrook, William L. W., 249, 250
Seabrooke, W. L. W., 296
Seacrist, M. Frank, 453
Seagler, Jacob, 643
Sealer, Henry, 640
Seaman, Christian, 271
Seattle, John Hamilton, 488
Sebold, Vincent, 531, 532, 598, 611, 612
Secafuse, John, 643
Sechrist, C. W., 505
Sechs, Henry, 479
John, 479
Sedge, Henry, 644
Sedgewick, Dorcas, 101, 111
Elizabeth, 111
Joshua, 111
Sedgwick, John, 196
Seeger, Chas., 547
Philip, 541, 547, 555
Segafuse, Peter, 643
Seibert, Joseph, 71
Seipe, Henry, 632

Seis, Geo., 633
  Paul, 633
Seiss, Joseph A., 424
Seitz, Henry, 647
Sekildler, I., 647
Selby, Samuel, 633
  William, 641
Seldner, John G., 479
Sell, Adam, 628
  Henry, Jr., 628
Sellers, Jacob, 85
Sellman, John J. M., 524
Selman, Adam, 624
  Gassaway, 643
  Thomas, 630
Semble, Jacob, Jr., 632
Semmer, Adam, 646
  Elizabeth, 640
Semmes, B. J., 598
Semple, Henry, 523
  James A., 540
Seney, Joseph, 127
Sengstake, Philip, 647
Sensebaugh, Peter, 637
Senseman, Gotleib, 6
Sensen, George, 626
Sentman, Solomon, 466, 467
Septer, Frederick, 647
  John, 647
Sergeant, Sarah, 641
  Snowden, 637
Serjeant, James, 637
Serr, James, 628
Setdown, Elizabeth, 643
Seton, Annina, 516
  E. A., 517, 518
  Rebecca, 516
  William Magee, 512
Settlemyer, W. H., 503, 505
Sewall, Maria Laura, 315
  Mary Brent, 315
  Nicholas, 315
  Robert, 315
Seward, William A., 287
  William H., 205, 296
Sewell, Thomas, 458
Sexton, Geo., 327
Seymour, Charles, 434
  William, 421
Shaaf, Arthur, 193, 194, 202, 597
Shaaff, Casper, 639
  George, 637

John Thomas, 594
Shad, William, 628
Shadd, Daniel, 627
  Philip, 635
Shade, W. G. , 166
Shaeffer, David F., 481
  Peter, 547
Shafer, Adam, 644
  Albert, 541
  Carlton, 598, 607
  Charles W., 535
  Conrod, 633
  Eve, 646
  George, 169
  Hamilton W., 530, 535
  Henry, 639
  Jacob, 645
  John R., 554
  John, Jr., 641
  Josephus W., 535
  Peter W., 466, 603, 608
  Philip, 637, 640
  Stephen, 630
  Theodore C., 465
Shaffer, G. R., 473
  John, 633
  Sanford L., 548
Shalt, Elizabeth, 636
Sham, Peter, 646
Shanam, Catharine, 643
Shaner, Peter, 631
Shanhols, Frederick, 639
Shank, Charles M., 535, 553
  Chas. M., 553
  Geo., 327
  George, 502, 626
  George W., 535, 605, 607
  John, 475, 488, 637
  Joseph L., 536
  M., 327
  M. , 489
  Michael, 489, 605, 626
Shankel, Philip, 169
Shankle, John, 453
Shankneer,
  John, 638
Shanks, Ignatius, 630
  Lewis, 257
  Thomas, 257
Shannan, Jos. P., 272
Sharetts, Mrs. Upton A., 583
Sharp, Geore (George?) W., 252

Samuel, 536
Sharpe, George W., 251
  Governor Horatio, 25
  Horatio, 107
  John, 668
Sharrer, Lodowick, 631
  Tobias, 631
Sharrett, John, 627
Sharretts, Upton A., 541, 594, 608
Shaukle, H., 266
Shaveler, George, 637
Shaver, George, 633
  Jacob, 633
  Peter, 633, 635
  Philip, 635
Shavock, Adam, 640
Shaw, John, 90, 220
  Moses, 536
  Robert, 668
  Samuel, 95
  Thomas, 278, 432, 532, 549, 550
  Victor, 631
  William, 604
  Zachariah, 220
Shawbaker, J. M., 531
Sheales, William, 86
Shealy, Christian, 631
Shean, Jacob, 637
Shearman, Jacob, 627
Sheckles, John, 637
Sheehan, Wm. Mason, 553
Sheets, Frederick, 635
  Henry, 643
  Jacob, 635
  Jacob Jr., 631
  John, 631
  Martin, 643
  Peter, 647
Sheffer, John, Jr., 637
  Peter, 641
Sheffey, Daniel, 84, 252, 599
  Madeline, 84
Sheffy, Adam, 640
Shelby, Evan, 124, 668
  Isaac, 124
Shell, Charles, 638
  Henry, 96, 97
Shellman, George, 382
  George K., 365, 598
  Jacob, 167
  James M., 182, 250

John, 136
Shelman, Anna Maria, 311
David, 629
Jacob, 639
John, 638
Shelmerdine, Stephen, 457, 633
Shelton, Michael, 65
Shemmy, John, 637
Shenkel, Sarah, 483
Sheon, David, 637
Nicholas, 633
Shepherd, Abram, 341
John, 604, 645
Mrs. Abram, 341
Mrs. Eleanor, 340
Solomon, 624
William, 604
Sheppard, Hayward, 353, 362
Sheradine, Thomas, 127
Upton, 127
Sherder, H., 647
Sheredine, Daniel, 127
Ellenore, 127
Paul, 641
Upton, 85, 86, 95, 96, 106, 430, 599, 600, 602, 605, 626
Sheridan, J. M., 488
Shethouse, Peter, 638
Sheuman, Aaron, 641
Shew, Jacob, 638
Shewbridge, C. D., 549
Shewen, Cornelius, 642
Shewmaker, George, 409
Shield, James, 266
Shields, E. W., 6
James, 635
James, Jr., 82
James , Sr., 90
Jefferson, 594
John, 90
Jonathan, 565
Patrick, 640
William, 82, 90, 95, 635
William, Jr., 635
Shielman, J. L., 230
Shiff, Godfrey, 633
Shilkinack, William, 637
Shilling, Charles, 560
Conrod, 647
John, 631, 647
Shine, Philip, 640

Shiner, Adam, 639
Philip, 631
Valentine, 639
Shingle, Laurence, 633
Shinogle, George, 641
Shipley, Geo. F., 573
Geo. Wm., Jr., 556
George E., 524
H. F., 547
Uriah, 624
Vachel, 624
William H., 560
Shipman, John, 538
Shippen, Edward, 329
Shirley, William M., 53
Shirvy, Modelena, 628
Shiseler, Jacob, 640
Shitoacre, John, 633
Shittenhelm, Frederick, 647
Shiveley, John, 644
Shivers, Richard, 645
Shoaff, James, 146
Shoemaker, Christian, 637
George W., 542, 546
Jacob, 647
John, 626
Peter, 628
Shoester, Joseph, 638
Shofe, John, 633
Sholl, George, 482
Shonce, Christopher, 632
Shontz, Jonas B., 466
Shooff, Caspar, 225
Shook, Daniel, 453
Peter, 453
Shope, Elizabeth, 458
George, 457, 458
George B., 167, 347
Shorb, Charles, 221
J. A., 594
Short, Hugh, 668
Shots, Michael, 645
Shotz, Henry, 169
Shoup, Christian, 633
George, 633
Henry, 646
John, 646
Matthias, 633
Shover, George, 643
Peter, 90, 470, 603
W., 328
Show, Conrod, 644
Conrod, Jr., 641

Showacre, George, 169
Jacob, 169
Shrader, Conrod, 637
Henry, 637
John, 631
Shreader, John George, 645
Shreeve, Jesse, 487
Shrieves, William, 630
Shriner, Abraham, 210
Edward D., 527
John, 628
Peter, 628, 643, 644
Shringer, Matthew, 634
Shriver, Abraham, 82, 181, 227, 527, 597, 599
Abram, 265
Abram F., 215
Andrew, 216, 218, 603, 604
Conrad, 627
David, 95, 128, 129, 282, 600, 606, 627
David, Jr., 132, 600
Dewalt, 128
E., 265
Edward, 221, 227, 263, 279, 288, 362, 365, 450, 551, 552, 555, 601, 602, 605
Ella, 396, 583
Frederick Wm., 633
Henry, 634
Isaac, 601
Jacob, 601
John S., 597
John Shultz, 163
Mary, 312
Shroyer, Jacob, 631
John (Tanner), 635
John, Sr., 635
Leonard, 626
Matthias, 631
Shryer, Christian, 637
Jacob, 637
Shryock, Christian, 633
Daniel, 633, 643
Thomas J., 540, 548, 549
Valentine, 604, 633
Shuey, George A., 454
Shuff, M. F., 549
Shuffler, Geo. T. M., 546
Peter, 641
Shuford, M. L., 476
Mortimer L., 475, 489
Shulenberger, A., 468

60

Anthony, 467, 469
W. C. B., 486
Shull, Catherine, 638
Frederick, 638
John, 631
Stephen, 631
Shultz, Catherine, 639
David, 640
F. , 266
Shuman, Jacob, 633
Shunk, Peter, 631
Philip, 637
Sicard, Mrs. William F. , 82
Sidwell, F. H., 582
Frank H., 594
Reuben, 221
Sifford, J. Edward, 394
John, 227, 228, 244, 457,
538, 601, 603
John E., 363
Sigafoose, Lawrence E., 548
Sigerfors, George, 628
Sigfrid, Geo., 630
Sigfrids, Godfrey, 629
Silance, J. Vernon , 524
Sile, Conrod, 638
Silenes, ———, 266
Sill, Henry, 627
Silver, Margaret, 629
Silvis, J., 266
Sim, Anthony, 626
J. T., 581
Joseph, 626
Joseph Thomas, 594
Patrick, 564, 626
Thomas, 319, 565, 566, 594
William, 626
Simmerly, Mathias, 643
Simmerman, George, 633, 644,
646
John, 639, 645
Michael, 645
Simmers, Thomas, 646
Simmon, Baltis, 633
Jacob, 635, 640
Simmons, A. H., 221
A. R., 605
Belinda, 629
Charles, 487, 547
Isaac, 628
Jacob, 626
James, 185, 256, 490, 492,
604, 637

John A., 603
John H., 256, 601, 604
Samuel, 221
Thomas Warfield, 594
W. A., 547, 555
William A., 545
Simons, John, 527
Simonton, Wm., 467
Simpson, Amos, 630
Anthony, 668
Basil, 626
Benjamin, 645
James, 668
John, 668
Richard, Jr., 626
Richard, Sr., 624
Solomon, 86
Thomas, 594, 668
Walter, 431
Sims, ,James, 668
Thomas, 641
Sin, Elizabeth, 633
J. T., 293
Jacob, 633
Sinclair, John, 137
Singer, Samuel, 635
Sink, George, 631
Jacob, 632
Sinn, Henry, 24
J. T. , 346
Thomas, 348
Siss, Godfrey, 646
Six, Geo., 631
Henry, Sr., 631
John, 631
Philip, 631
Skaggs, Ann, 490
Elinor, 491
Leonard, 490
Mahala, 491
Skinner, Henry, 541, 668
John S., 301
Samuel, 605
Skyles, N. H., 465, 467, 493
Nehemiah H., 486
W. H., 493
Slagle, C. S., 507
Slater, E. S., 505
Isaac, 668
John, 668
S. E., 506
Slaughter, Smith, 342
Sleeper, H. G., 598

Sleets, John, 626
Slemons, John, 467
Slice, Thomas, 628
Slicer, Henry, 457
Slick, John, 627
William, 628
Slider, Peter, 631
Simon, 631
Slife, John, 628
Slifer, Emanuel, 497
Ezra, 504
John, 637
Mrs. John M., 497
Mrs. Peter, 497
Peter, 497
Slingle, Jesse, 604
Slingluff, Jesse, 549
Sloan, Jas., Jr., 161
John, 167
Slonacre, Christian, 635
Sloregenhoupt, Philip, 642
Slumer, George, 645
Slush, Andrew, 635
John, 645
Sluss, Michael, 550, 605
Slye, F., 186
Robert, 313
Small, Jacob, 166
Smallwood, William, 147, 165
Smaltz, Catherine, 412
John H., 408, 411, 475, 488,
493
Smeak, Simon, 631, 633
Smedley, Samuel, 624
Smelser, Adam, 637
Smeltzer, Andrew, 641
J. P., 504
Smith, A., 327
A. J., 531, 582
A. M., 502
Adam, Jr., 626
Adam, Sr., 626
Albert, 448
Aloysius, 647
Alvey J., 594
Amos, 635
Andrew, 24, 637, 647
Ann, 458
Benjamin, 383
C. Edward, 475
Caspar, 85
Charles, 565, 566, 589, 594
Charles C., 497, 539, 543, 544

Chas. M., 476
Christian, 128, 183, 530, 626, 635
Christian, of Wm., 628
Christopher, 635
Clement, 151, 564
Conrod, 642
Daniel, 635, 668
David, 502
David M. , 251
E. D., 390
E. J., 547
Edward J., 599
Emma J., 583
F. B., 568, 582, 584
F. F., 581
F. Lester, 560
F. S. Key, 305
Francis, 643
Francis F., 566
Francis Fenwick, 594
Francis M., 391
Franklin B., 566, 567, 571, 572, 577-580
Franklin Buchanan, 564, 581, 583, 594, 597, 610
George, 227, 326, 538, 603, 629, 635, 647
George Edward, 390, 419, 541, 543
George F., 536
George William, 292, 386, 399, 527, 528, 608, 609, 612, 613
George, Jr., 635
Gerritt, 352
Harriet, 458
Henry, 169, 215, 473, 604, 628, 637, 644
Henry (of Henry), 637
Henry C., 473
Henry of Nies., 643
I., 348, 349
Isaac, 170, 354, 630
J., 350
J. F. D., 73, 92
Jacob, 502, 624, 631, 635, 637, 638, 645, 647
Jacob, Jr., 641
Jacob, Sr., 631
James, 24, 84-86, 93, 328, 430, 600, 604, 630, 639, 668

James H., 487
James K., 594
James M., 535, 536
James T., 250, 384
James W., 607
Jeremiah, 33, 629
John, 13, 82, 90, 169, 361, 461, 469, 479, 605, 628, 631, 633, 635, 637, 640, 645, 646
John (Cooper), 632
John (of Jno.), 641
John (of Philip), 626
John (Tanner), 626
John Christopber, 479
John Dinsmore, 167
John E., 598
John Francis, 556, 583, 599
John H., 601
John H. M., 181
John Hamilton, 630
John Walter, 404
John, of Jacob, 637
Joseph, 24, 75, 78, 84, 85, 450, 604, 644
Joseph L., 550
Joseph L., Jr., 183
Joseph Sim, 564, 632
Joshua, 215, 633, 643
Leonard, 85, 86, 239, 637, 643
Lewis C., 159
Lila, 583
Mary, 462, 628, 637
Mary E., 462
Math., 647
Matthias, 633, 635
McCarthy, 669
Michael, 324, 468, 635, 642, 668
Middleton, 628
Mother Reginia, 518
Mrs. Clemmie, 456
Mrs. Eliza, 497
Mrs. Francis Fenwick, 559
Mrs. Franklin B., 583
Mrs. Maria Lee Palmer, 562
Nicholas, 633
P. M., Jr., 486
Patrick S., 602
Patrick Sim, 600, 641
Peter, 328, 626, 635, 639
Philip, 328, 626, 639

R., 86
Richard, 85
Robert, 170, 467, 597
S. P., 158
Sampson, 641
Samuel, 133
Samuel H., 151
Samuel P., 564
Susannah, 468
T. A., 266
Thomas, 635, 669
Thomas A., 383, 487, 601
Tice, 628
W., 266
W. O., 455
Walter, 85, 151
William, 70, 170, 327 626, 628, 633, 658, 669
Wm. Prescott, 233
Wm. M., 582
Wm. Meredith, 594
Smouse, Henry, 624
Snarr, Philip, 628
Snavely, Henry, 83-85
Snebley, Henry, 83
Snell, S. H., 455
Snerr, Henry, 641
Snertzell, Geo. W., 638
Snider, Balsor, 328
Catharine, 647
Christopher, 643
Daniel, 658
George, 639, 646
Jacob, 34, 629, 639
Jacob, Jr., 627, 629
Jacob, Sr., 627
John, 626, 635, 642, 658
John, Jr., 626
Lodwick, 646
Peter, 638
Philip, 645
Snively, Jacob, 159
Snodyell, Jacob, 640
Snonk, Peter, 626
Snook, Charles S., 533, 536
John, 453
Snosinger, Joseph, 645
Snouffer, B. I., 552
B. J., 221
G. A. T., 548, 551, 552
G. Fenton, 400
George A. T., 606
J. J. , 266

William, 400
Snouk, Adam, 633, 642
John, 626
Snuer, Henry, 641
Snuffer, John, 627
Snuke, Adam, 327
Snyder, Baltzer, 626
G. C., 453
George Albert, 465
Henry, 167, 365
John Milton, 482, 484
Oliver P., 601
Samuel, 547
Soam, Peter, 624
Sohwen, John, 170
Sole, Peter, 645
Solmon, Geo., 167
Sombower, Adam, 641
Somersett, Thos., 639
Somerville, James, 167, 597
Sommer, Christian, 641
Sommers, Jacob, 637
Thomas, 643
Valentine, 637
Songor, Stephen, 644
Sook, Henry, 635
Souder, Adam, 633
J. M, 419
Souders, J. M., 467
Southerland, James, 669
John, 669
Southworth, Mrs. E. D. N., 377
Sowder, Adam, 646
Sower, Charles, 250
Geo., 628
Sowers, Frederick, 626
Jacob, 626
Sophia, 626
William, 628
Soyer, John, 647
Spake, Conrod, 640
Spalding, Elizabeth, 324
Spangler, George, 627, 638
John F., 389
Sparkes, Joseph, 631
Spates, Alfred, 159
Spaulding, Henry, 631
Speaker, John, 639
Spealman, Laurance, 646
Specht, Mrs. Elizabeth, 426
Speelman, Jacob, 637
Spencer, Francis, 669
Jervis, 275, 597

Samuel, 242
Spensinger, Michael, 626
Spessard, D. S., 454
Spigler, Israel, 643
Spikernal, Robert, 669
Sponceller, Michael, 632
Sponseller, Andrew, 626
Frederick, 169
George, 487
Jacob, 169, 645
Jacob, Jr., 647
Spoon, Conrod, 624
John, 633
Spotswood, Alexander, 142
Sprengle, David, 214
Sprigg, Edward, 600
James C., 89
Joseph, 84, 85
Michael Cresap, 88, 159, 181
Osborne, 88
Otho, 134
Samuel, 151
Thomas, 629
Spriggs, Otho, 604
Spring, Douglas, 669
Springer, Christian, 633
David, 167
Edward, 646
Jacob, 647
John, 640
Susanna, 626
Thomas, 594, 604
William, 431, 432
Springle, Peter, 647
Sproul, Jacob, 25
Spund, Joseph, 643
Spurrier, Eliza, 316
Levin, 624
Thomas, 624
Squires, Michael, 624
St. Clair, Sir John, 43, 55, 56, 58, 62
Stagner, Peter, 631
Stahl, Henry, 167
Stake, Anthony, 147
Edward, 162
Staley, Abraham, 169
C., 605
Cornelius, 453, 454, 550, 552, 601
Edward Garrott, 544
Elizabeth, 637

George, 476
George Lewis, 333
Henry, 633, 637
Jacob, 633, 637
John, 453
John R., 560
John, Jr., 633
Joseph, 633
Melchor, 633
Peter, 169, 633
Thomas Cornelius, 256
Victor A., 438, 440
Stalkman, Catharine, 639
Stallings, Benjamin, 163, 536
Richard, 169
Stallions, Benjamin, 645
Samuel, 626
Stambaught, A. A., 556
Stanley, Thomas, 647
Stansbury, Nicholas C., 606
William, 628
Stanton, C. A., 454
Staples, William, 632
Starner, Christian, 647
Starr, M. T, 605
Startzman, C., 502
Stattings, Phineas, 630
Statton, A. B., 453
George W., 454
I. K., 454
John F., 454
Statzler, George, 645
Staub, John W., 382
Staufer, Daniel, 639
Stauffer, David V., 552
J. H., 531
S. Theodore, 606
Simon W., 370
Staup, John W., 605
William E., 542
Stayman, George F., 250
Stearn, C. T., 454, 455
Steck, C. F., 482
Charles Frederick, 420
Daniel, 501
Steckle, Simon, 635
Steel, Abraham, 645
Hugh, 7
J., 266
John, 669
Steele, Guy, 404
James, 626
Stein, A. E. , 549

Steiner,
John A., 227
Josephus M. , 281
Bernard, 397
Bernard C., 559
Christian, 550, 552
D. T., 547
Daniel H., 541
Daniel S., 556
David, 534
Dr. Lewis H., 2
H. R., 451
Henry, 166, 167, 281, 527,
  602
Henry F., 545
J. A., 601
Jacob, 136, 214, 603, 640
Jacob, Jr., 638
Jesse, 468, 469, 475, 489
John A., 227, 312, 391,
  396, 547, 561, 602
John Conrad, 408, 475
John Conrod, 464
John Thomas, 167
L. H., 565
Lewis H., 227, 392, 396,
  397, 566, 600
Lewis Henry, 594
Stephen, 166, 210, 527, 604
Wm., 167
Steller, Ulrick, 628
Stem, John, 628
Matthias, 642
Stembel, Henry, 181
Stemble, Roger, 323
Stemple, Frederick, 248, 323,
  637
Stephens, Jacob, 536
Peter, 626
Stephenson, John, 626
Maryman, 642
Sterett, A. M., 597
Samuel, 127
Sterling, Jonathan, 631
Stern, Philip, 541-543
Sterret, Polly, 217
Stesch, E. H. J., 303
Stevans, J. C., 487
Stevens, Aaron C., 352
Adam, 559
Charles, 294, 626
Flavius J., 469
Rezin, 538

Richard, 276
Solomon, 669
Thaddeus, 316
William, 629
Stevenson, Charles, 603, 627
Daniel, 624
Edward, 624
Henry, 627
James, 635
John, 275, 635
Merryman, 603
Richard, 623, 644
Wesley, 169
William, 628
Stevins, Nancy, 488
Samuel, 488
Stewart, Adam, 333
Alexander, 82, 595, 635
Andrew, 151
Benjamin, 644
Charles, 555
James A., 575
Moses A., 476
Mrs. Harriet, 487
Posey, 643
Stidley, Frederick, 628
Stier, Hamilton, 548
Stile, Philip, 642
Stillwell, Nathaniel, 669
Stillworth, John, 669
Stimble, Jacob Sr., 631
Peter, 626
Stimmel, John B., 469
Stimmer, George, 640
Stinbrun, Charlotte, 628
Stine, Daniel, 468
F. L., 456
Stinespring, C. W., 304, 453-
  455
Stitely, Jacob, 626
John, 626
Stitley, Frederick, 626
Jacob, Jr., 626
Stober, Michael, 644
Stockdale, George W., 531
Stockman, George, 637
Russell, 546
Stocksdale, George W., 532,
  548
Stockton, George, 33
Isabella, 33
Wm., 33
Stoddard, Thomas, 669

Stoever, John C., 478, 480
John Casper, 420, 477
Stofer, Elias, 633
Stoke, Robert, 598
Stokes, Charles L., 541
George, 169, 453, 455
James, 634
Joshua, 455
Peter, 669
Robert, 607
Robert Y., 221, 227, 532, 550
Thomas, 669
William, 363
Stolmeyer, John, 479
Stomble, Joseph, 637
Stone, D. E., 553, 581, 582, 584,
  595
D. E., Jr., 582, 595
Daniel E., 548, 583
E. H., 536
E. R. H., 179
J. A., 266
Jacob, 641
John, 110, 637
John S., 433
L., 145
Michael Jenifer, 127
O. B., 581, 595
Sarah Jane, 483
Thomas, 145
Wm. M., 491
Stonebraker, William F., 530
Stonecypher, Daniel, 631
Jacob, 642
Martin, 628
Stoner, A. B., 471, 472
Ann, 624
Benedict, 633
Casper, 633
Christian, 169, 638, 645
David, 461, 624, 626
E. W., 461, 462
Ezra, 169
F. L., 547
Frank L., 536, 598, 607
George, 646
Henry, 646
Jacob, 24, 169, 626, 635
John, 85, 95, 624, 626, 633
John R., 531, 610
John, Jr., 626
Michael, 409
Solomon, 461

Wm. J., 532
Stoop, Margaret, 643
Stoore, George, 639
Storck, Charles Augustus
    Gottlieb, 421
Storep, Peter, 626
Storm, Harrie E. W., 546
    J. P. L., 560
    Leonard, 560, 639
    P. L., 557
    Peter, 169
    Peter L., 532
    Peter S. , 210
    Wendle, 641
    William B., 532, 557
    William M., 560
Storme, John, 631
    Joseph, 631
    Magdalena, 633
Stormes, Isaac, 638
Storp, George Adam, 644
Story, Asa, 595
    Wm. W., 305
Stottelmire, David, Jr., 641
Stottlemire, John, 286
Stottlemyer, David, Jr., 637
    Devalt, 637
    George, 640
    George R., 607
Stottlmyer, Jacob, 640
Stouder, John, 626
    Joseph, 643
Stouffer, B. F., 548
    Daniel F., 460
    John, 167
    W. Q., 548
Stouver, John, 647
Stover, Daniel, 169
    Philip, 644
Stowder, Joseph, 643
Strawbridge, Robert, 11, 457
Strayer, W. M., 488
Streaer, Jacob, 643
Streaver, Yockman, 633
Streavy, Paul, 634
Strevert, Edward, 643
Stribe, Peter, 626
Stricker, George, 8, 84-86, 95,
    286, 600
    Jacob, 628
    John, 8
    Michael, 635
Strickstrock, Jacob, 167

Strine, Adam, 626, 647
    Chas. M., 485
    John, 485
    Samuel M., 485
Stringer, George, 635
    John, 638
    Richard, 624
Stripe, Jacob, 624
Stripley, Peter, 624
Strisler, John, 646
Stroebel, William D., 501
Strouse, Nicholas, 624
Stuart, J. E. B., 351, 353, 382
Stubbs, J. C., 520
    Robert, 341
Stubs, Catharine, 644
Study, David, 271
    Lodwich, 647
    Martin, 647
Stuffle, Henry, 633
Stuffy, Andrew, 635
Stulk, James, 635
Stull, Adam, 408, 633
    Barbara, 408
    Christopher, 86
    Elizabeth, 408
    John, 83-86, 600, 633
    William H., 474, 549
Stuller, Ulrick, Sr., 628
Stults, Conrod, 627
    Henry W., 389
    John, 603
    Mary, 628
Stultz, C. A., 595
Stump, Adam, 632
    George, 631
    Leonard, 631
Stumpf, Michael, 25
Stuner, Frederick, 639
Stup, John, 483
    Mary Ann , 483
    Spencer, 484
    Wm. D., 483
Sturm, Jacob, 637
Stutt, Adam, 626
    Catharine, 626
Styer, Jacob, 630
Sueman, Eleanor, 637
    Peter, 96
Suitor, Charles, 669
Sulivane, Cornelius, 627
Sullivan, James J., 517
Suman, Isaac, 547

Israel W., 547
Summer, John, 669
Summerman, Michael, 643
Summers, David W., 535
    J., 482, 484
    Jacob, 500, 502, 641
    Joshua, 531
Summersfield, John, 669
Summervell, Alexander, 669
Summerwell, James, 643
Sumner, Charles, 262
Sumners, George W., 658
Sunbreen, John, 631
Sunday, Cornelius, 484
Surrat, Joseph, 669
Sutcliff, Robert, 143
Sutter, W. O., 549
Sutton, Robert B., 492
Swadener, Elizabeth, 624
Swadner, Andrew, 624
    Henry, 645
    John, Jr., 645
Swaggert, Daniel, 637
Swamley, Margaret, 626
Swan, John, 83-86
Swank, George, 530
Swarmley, Daniel, 487
Swartz, Daniel, 169
    Valentine, 638
Sweadener, H. Clinton, 542
Sweadner, Daniel, 169
    John, 602
Swearengen, Charles, 84
Swearingan, Jo., 526
Swearingen, Benoni, 341
    Charles, 83, 85, 86
    Joseph, 171, 175, 181, 341,
        537, 601, 603, 604
    Sam'l, 327
    Thomas, 637
Swearinger, Jacob, 25
    Margaret, 637
Swearingon, Joseph, 637
Sweeney, William, 635
Sweeny, John, 634
Sweinhardt, George, 479
Sweney, Edward, 635
    J., 266
Swikeffer, J. A., 266
Swimburger, Michael, 637
Swimley, George, 86
Swindley, Danl., 629
Swinney, E., 353

Switzer, Lud, 628
Matthias, 628
Rudolph, 647
Swomley, Daniel, 642
Swope, Barnet, 635
Henry, 632
Sydrich, Daniel, 6
Syester, A. K., 598
Andrew K., 296
Sykes, W. C., 476
William C., 542
Syphers, John, 90
Tabbs, Moses, 166
Tabler, Jacob, 643
Michael, 643
W. B., 363
William, 169, 645
William B., 602
Tagan, Jacob, 624
Talbot, Ann, 628
Benjamin, Sr., 629
James, 624
John, 629
Joseph, 629
Mahlon, 602
Talbott, Geo. E., 548
Joseph, 182
Wilson, 169
Talhelm, Henry, 454
Taliaferro, W. B., 353
Tall, E., 560
Tallhill, Henry, 646
Tandy, Richard, 669
Taney, Alice, 206
Anne, 206
Augustine, 595
Augustus, 325
E. S., 611
Frederick, 628
Henry, 635
J., 168
Joseph, 604, 631
Joseph, Sr., 601
Michael, 197
Octavius S., 82
R. B., 132, 298, 302
Robert B. , 201
Roger B., 197, 199, 206,
311
Roger Brooke, 129, 133,
163, 164, 181, 193, 241,
265, 299, 521, 527, 559,
597, 600

Thomas, 198
Tannehill, Carleton, 606
Tanner, David, 635
Jacob, 635
Tannin, Aquila, 647
Tansey, Lidia, 644
Tanzy, Arthur, 536
Tapp, George W, 353
Tarlton, Jeremiah, 644
Tarr, Philip, 641
Tarvin, Richard, 669
Tasker, Benjamin, 7, 10, 24,
26, 27, 333
Benjamin, Jr., 26, 27
Tate, James, 669
Mathew, 628
Tatler, Melcher, 645
Tayler, James, 669
Tayloe, Elizabeth, 313
John, 313
Taylor, J. Hiram, 606
Charles Philpot, 630
Clifford, 546
Conrod, 645
Enoch, 325
George Cavendish, 185
Henry, 629
Isaac, 629
John, 169
John K., 611
Joseph H., 567
Robert J., 597
Stewart, 352, 355
Thomas, 639
W. J., 266
William B., 169, 226
Zachary, 287
Zackary, 173
Tchan, John F., 598
Teater, George, 669
Samuel, 669
Templing, Samuel, 637
Tenbal, Jonathan, 637
Tenbell, Isaac, 637
Terrell, John, 669
Teshner, Jacob, 169
Testel, John, 639
Teter, Jacob, 643
Tetlow, Abraham, 640
Tetrick, Martin, 645
Thayer, William S., 404
Thirkpine, John, 628
Thomas, Amos, 642

B. C., 582
Benjamin, 644
Bernard O., 560, 595
Bernard W., 599
Bruce, 566, 595
C. F., 487
C. Herbert, 525
C. K., 322
C. Keefer, 551, 552, 605
C. M., 527, 528, 531, 567
Calvin A., 469
Caroline, 558
Catherine, 257
Cephas M., 606
Charles, 490
Charles F., 519
Charles G., 541
Christian, 552, 633, 635
Clinton C., 469
Cyrus, 438, 559
Daniel, 643
David, 550, 601
David O., 525, 541
Edward, 644
Elizabeth, 108
Evan, 84, 233
F. Granville, 607
Francis, 82, 159, 174, 182,
203, 247, 250, 256, 257,
261, 370, 373, 391, 431,
538, 542, 599, 601, 605,
633
Frank, 181, 192, 213, 221,
256, 283, 290, 291, 293,
298, 328, 364, 366
Gabriel, 644
Gabriel (of Felty), 644
Gabriel, Jr., 644
George, 365, 469, 605, 644
George P., 222
Grace M., 257
Hanson, 595
Hugh, 257
I. A., 145
I. Davis, 595
Isaac, 635, 642
J., 332
J. D., 493
J. Fenton, 524
J. Frank, 553
J. G., 582
J.Travers, 438, 440, 441, 507,
558

Jacob, 595, 635, 637
James, 563
John, 128, 133, 168, 218, 247, 256, 257, 280, 283, 490-492, 549, 600-602, 604, 628, 643, 644
John B., 221, 292, 312, 363, 400, 493, 601, 605
John Hanson, 129, 133, 163, 164, 168, 194, 227, 250, 431, 432, 595, 597, 601
John McGill, 257
Joseph Gaffney, 595
Josiah B., 493
Leonard, 637
Levy, 644
Lewis M., 552
Lloyd, 257
Mary Crabb, 257
Mrs. Cyrus, 583
Nellie, 311
Otho, 263, 601, 605
P. E., 230
P. F., 288
P. Henry, 85
Philip, 26, 27, 84, 86, 225, 227, 431, 432, 595, 600, 602, 638
Philip E., 151, 231, 232
Phillip, 563, 564, 590
Phillip E., 239, 240
Rebeccah, 644
Richard, 84, 108, 221, 260, 669
Robert F., 440-442
S. C., 493
S. F., 566, 580, 582
S. Frank, 559
Samuel, 169, 639
Samuel D., 606
Sarah Ann Eleanor, 257
Sarah Coale, 108
Stephen A., 493
Thomas, 321
Travers, 540
Valentine, 644
W. H., 488
W. R, 519
William, 257, 639, 643
William (of Wm.), 643
Thompson, B. , 266
Caroline, 185

Collin, 669
Dauphin, 355
Dolph, 352
Eleanor, 185
Evan, 486
Fielder, 488
Howard, 342
James, 669
John, 134, 275, 488, 669
John P., 249, 264, 450, 527
Leck, 646
Margaret, 110
Meta, 342
Samuel, 467
Thomas, 110
W. H., 355
William, 165, 352, 635, 645, 669
William E., 315
Wm.B., 158, 170
Thomson, Hugh, 631
Jno. of Wm., 635
Ralph, 635
William, 633
Thornicroft, John, 316
Thornton, Anna, 315
Sister Mary Rosalia, 510
Thrasher, Benjamin, 637
Threasher ,John, 669
Threlkeld, Joseph, 84, 85
Thresher, Elias, 641
Thomas, 502, 637
Throgmorton, Robert, 338
Thumb, Tom, 284
Tibbitts, Geo. F., 506
Tice, Nicholas, 85, 95, 136, 603, 638
Tidd, Charles P., 352
Tierney, John J., 523
Tilden, John, 595
Tilghman, Frisby, 134, 149, 151, 166
James, 127, 597
Matthew, 104, 109
Tench, 158
Tillard, Edward, 603, 638
Tillinghast, Mary E., 520
Timon, John, 517
Tippett, Charles B., 459
Tipple, John, 646
William, 275
Titcus, Jacob, 637
Titlow, Adam, 169

Christian, 639
Daniel, 169
Tobine, Michael, 630
Tobridge, John, 641
Todd, Alexander, 643
William, 550
Toffler, George, 645
Tofler, Peter, 633
Tolks, Catharine, 639
Tomlin, Hugh, 642
Tomlinson, Jessee, 629
John, 12
Richard, 669
Toms, Abraham, 641
Ezra, 605
George D., 529
Jacob, 453, 456, 641
John, 637
John H., 529
Lester, 560
Raymond, 560
Samuel, 637
William, 637
Toole, Catherine, 642
James, 641
Tootle, J. , 327
Topery, Joshua, 629
Tormey, Patrick, 552
Torrence, Halbert, 46
Touchard, Margaret, 342
Touchstone, Caleb, 500
Toughman, John, 635
Toup, George, 645
Townsend, George Alfred, 404
Towson, Nathan, 266
Tracey, Peirce, 669
Tradane, John, 4
Trail, Charles B., 553, 598
Charles E., 206, 210, 227, 312, 314, 373, 396, 400, 507, 526, 550, 552, 559, 600, 601
Chas., 292
Edward, 434, 524, 552
Trapnell, Jos., Sr., 434
Joseph, 435, 492, 598
R. W., 548, 584
Richard W., 581, 595
Traxall, Jacob, Jr., 645
Trayer, Jacob, 604
Tremble, Moses, 669
Trenton, Richard, 641
Trett, Paul, 637

Triemer, Lem'precth, 647
Trimble, Michael, 646
Trine, Susanna, 637
Trisler, George, 179, 180
  Michael, 640
Trisnen, Philip, 642
Tritapoe, Geo. H., 506
Trollope, Mrs. Frances, 188
Trostle, Jacob D., 461, 463
Trout, Jacob, 633
Troutman, Michael, 500, 637
  Peter, 169, 633
Troxall, David, 633
  Frederick, 633
  Jacob, 631
  Jacob, of Peter, 635
  John, 635
  John, Jr., 635
  Peter, 635
Troxel, Abraham, 452
  Frederick, 473
  M. D., 473
Troxell, A. A., 391
  Charles P., 438, 606
  Chas, 327
  Frederick, 82, 604
  George, 604
  J. G., 595
  John, 129
Trucks, George, 631
  John, 631
Truman, Richard, 669
Truscott, George, 541
Tschudy, Martin, 170
Tucker, James, 669
  John, 669
  Littleton, 669
  Morris W., 303
  Stephen, 644, 669
  William, 637
  Wm. J., 457
Tudor, John, 169
Tupir, Revd., 647
Tuppel, Christian, 647
Turbott, Nicholas, 537, 538
Turbutt, Nicholas, 601, 603
Turnbaugh, William, 635
Turnbull, Nicholas, 169
Turner, Catherine Contee, 257
  Charles, 629
  George W., 353, 355
  J. H., 504
  Jacob, 637

Jacob, Jr., 637
John, 629
Philip, 629
Solomon, 643
Thomas, 249, 601, 643
William, 629
William H., 524
William James, 629
Turney, Charles, 669
Tusnier, Andrew, 637
Tuttero, George, 633
  George, Jr., 633
Twiggs, D. E., 266
Twitcher, Jimmy, 284
Tycer, John, 669
Tyler, E. B., 387
  George L., 392
  John, 536
  Ira, 540, 560, 561
  John, 130, 132, 175, 178,
    182, 256, 431, 432, 532,
    537, 563, 595, 600, 640
  John B., 598
  R. Bradley, 595
  Samuel, 193, 197, 315, 450,
    565, 566, 586, 595, 597
  Samuel O., 550
  W. B., 226
  W. Bradley, 219
  W. Otis, 598
  William, 190, 201, 210,
    227, 397, 434, 526, 565,
    586, 592, 601
  William B., 184, 227, 228,
    254, 433, 434, 527, 532
  William Bradley, 174, 213,
    227, 264, 293, 565,
    592, 595, 600, 602
  William, Sr., 595
  Wm., Jr., 365
Tyng, Dudley A., 434
Tyson, Alex. H., 315
  Charles B., 227, 560
  G. Warren, 547
  G. W., 451, 547, 578
  G. Waring, 545
  Isaac, Jr., 276
  Jacob, 401
  Jacob B., 451, 541, 542
  Jonathan, 227, 450
  Mrs. Jacob B., 583
  Nathan S., 541
  Robert S., 566, 595

Ugly, Peter, 645
Uhler, Frederick, 281
Uhlry, Henry, 637
  Michael, 637
Uler, Andrew, 628
Ulith, Henry, 641
Ulrich, J. H., 303
Umber, William, 628
Umberger, J. S., 531
Umstead, Enoch, 638
  Jacob, 461
  Nicholas, 624
Underwood, I. M., 454
  William B., 249
Ungelby, Zachariah, 643
Unger, E. W., 473
Ungerfer, Frederick, 645
Unkefer, A., 276
  Abdiel, 538, 601
Unruh, John, 483
Unsuld, John N., 481
Unsult, Frederic, 478, 479
  Frederick, 6
Upcraft, Robert, 624
Upjohn, Richard, 434
Urner, Hammond, 397, 459, 507,
    546, 598, 607
  Helen, 459
  Milton G., 77, 318, 396, 398,
    459, 507, 553, 568, 598,
    599, 603, 607
  Milton G., Jr., 599
  Mrs. Hammond, 583
Utenwahle, C. H., 547
Utley, Richard, 6
Utto, Peter, 645
  William, 627
Utz, Charles M., 463
  Joseph, 463
  S. H., 461, 462
  Silas K., 463
Utze, Nathaniel, 68
Vaile, Charles, 189
Valens, Mary, 328
Valentine, Henry, 635
  Jacob, 82, 90, 635
  John, 635
  Josiah, 606
Valette, Alexander, 646
Vallo, F., 266

Van Buren, Martin, 224
Van Lear, J., 158
  Matthew S., 149

Van Meeter, Jacob, 4
Van Metre, W. H., 530
Van Swearengen, Weltner, 84
Van Swearingen, Joseph, 323
  Welner, 85
Vandiver, Murray, 404
Vandyke, Thomas, 563
Vanfenson, Arnold, 630
Vanfossen, W. H. , 266
Vanhorn, Benjamin, 638
Varner, Adam, 647
Vatgin, Stephen, 644
Vaughan, William, 669
Veach, James, 75
Veatch, James, 79
Venable, Nancy, 591
Venimel, A. K., 598
Verdries, Frederic O., 479
  John, 479
  Valentine, 479
Vernon, George W. F., 391,
  396, 561
  H. H., 391
Verterbaker, Jacob, 631
Vice, Francis, 24
Vickery, George, 641
Villiger, Burchard, 446
  George, 447
Vincendiere, Adelaide, 290
Vinson, John T., 607
Vogel, John, 479
von Zinzendorf
  Nicholas Lewis, 494
Voorhees, Daniel W., 352, 353
Vorhees, Daniel W., 551
Vredenburgh, Wm. H., 390
Wachtel, Geo, 502
  George W., 529, 530
  William S., 529
Wachter, A., 503
  Albert, 484
  Andrew J., 483
  C. L., 582
  Caleb, 483
  Cath. A., 483
  Catherine E., 483
  Charles L., 532, 596
  Chas. S. , 485
  Dan'l. M., 483
  Elizabeth, 483
  Elmer C., 485
  Ezra, 483
  G. H. Clay, 485

George, 271, 555
George H. C., 485
Granville L., 484
Henry, 483, 484
Isaac, 483
Jane R., 483
Jane Rebecca, 483
Leander W., 596
Lewis F., 483
Lewis H., 484, 485
M., 504
Mary A. , 483
Mary Ann, 483
Michael, 481, 483, 501
Millard, 596
Philip, 484
Wesley A., 484
Wack, J., 266
Wade, John, 638
Wadesworth, Henry, 504
Waesche, J. Theodore, 535
  James T., 535
  L. Randolph, 548
Wagaman, Samuel M., 596
Waggoner, Adam, 626, 633
  John, 624
  Joseph, 629, 646
  Michael, Jr., 628
  Michael, Sr., 628
Wagner, Daniel, 408, 410,
  411, 464, 493
  Jacob, 133
  Samuel, 475
  Tobias, 480
  William, 535
  Wm. H., 566, 581, 582,
  584, 596
Wain, George H., 384
Wait, Joseph, 632
Wakefield, R. C., 341
Waling, John, 639
Walken, C., 266
Walker, J. C., 531
  J. Dorsey, 400
  James E., 528
  Jesse, 463
  John, 639
  Nathan, 669
  Samuel D., 365, 370
  Sir Edward, 110
  William, 632
Wall, Edward, 491, 492
Wallace, George, 555

James, 497
Robert, 643
Samuel, 645
Walling, Julian, 458
Wallis, Albert E., 540
  Elizabeth, 645
  Renchart, 645
  S. T., 206
  S. Teackle, 206
Walls, William B., 275
Walp, S., 605
Walse, Samuel, 626
Walsh, P. W. , 446
  William, 263
Walter, Jacob, 634, 639
  Joshua, 611
  Michael, 642
Walters, Jacob, 175
Waltman, Emanuel, 504
  Joseph, 504
Walton, James, 444
Waltz, Thomas M. , 548
Wampler, Abraham, 604
  David, 624
  Jacob, 642
  John, 133
  Lod, 628
  Peter, 624
Wandell, Jacob, 639
Wane, Isaac, 639
Ward, Francis, 643
  John, 629
  Samuel, 669
Ware, Francis, 661, 669
Warehime, O. C., 553, 558
  Oliver C., 543, 551, 552
Warenfeltz, Joshua, 455
Warfield, Absolom, 628
  Alexander, 181, 596, 603, 604,
  626
  Anne, 644
  Basil, 626
  Charles, 84,85, 86, 604, 606
  Edwin, 77, 81
  Elizabeth, 624
  Henry, 218, 626
  Henry R, 171
  Henry R., 128, 537, 599
  Henry Ridgely, 128, 431, 600
  Jesse Lee, 596
  John, 629
  L. D., 605
  Peregrine, 134

S. D., 550
Warman, Andrew, 624
 Henry, 624
 Moses, 604
Warner, Clara, 437
 Ephriam, 437
 Joseph P., 353
 L. F., 488
 Mrs. Eph., 437
 Peter, 628
Warren, James, 643
 Thomas, 84, 85, 87
Warrenfeltz, Henry M., 530
 Uriah, 471-473
Warter, Job, 629
Warthen, A. , 266
 John, 169
Washington, Bushrod C., 149
 Catherine, 592
 Chas., 332
 George, 21, 22, 28, 101, 105, 109, 216, 247, 248, 333, 338, 410, 540
 George C. , 159
 Hannah, 329
 Lewis, 350
 Lewis W., 347, 353, 355
 Mary Ball, 298
 Samuel, 332
 William, 131, 138
Waskey, E. T., 493
Water, Horatio, 555
Waters, Andrew, 626
 Azel, 85, 86, 95, 626
 Charles C., 535, 543-545, 599, 607, 610
 Dyer, 643
 George, 639
 J., 132
 J. K., 473
 Jacob, 163
 James, 669
 James K., 535, 596, 606
 Joab, 600, 603
 Peter, 639
 Samuel, 629
 Susan, 589
 William, 596, 433, 564, 565
 Z., 86
Watgain, Christian, 645
Watkins, Christopher, 644
 Samuel, 642
 William, 605

Watson, F. G., 487
 Samuel, 634
 Thomas. Jr., 353
 Walter, 670
Watt, Robert, 170
 Thomas, 647
Watterson, Alfred D. V., 524
 Henry, 304
 John A., 523
Watts, Henry, 670
 Martin, 640
 Samuel, 670
Wattson, Henry, 670
Waugh, William, 630, 638
Way, Arnest, 628
Wayland, J. W., 9
Wayman, John, 630
 Thomas, 638
Wayne, Anthony, 139
Ways, Basil, 169
Weadle, Jacob, 637
Weagley, C. W. C., 596
Weakly, James, 637
 Ruth, 491
Wearry, Peter, 25
Weatherfield, Jacob, 637
Weaver, Christian, 638
 Daniel, 637
 George, 637
 George Jr., 635
 John, 628
 Peter, 327
 Philip, 626
Webb, Benjamin, 635
 James, 670
 Joseph B., 537
 William, 629
Webber, Robert, 629
 William, 458
Webbs, Benjamin, 643
Weber, George Richard, 250
 William, 250
Webster, Charles, 598
 Daniel, 235, 241, 366
 David, 167
 George F., 227, 556
 George H., 555
 Joseph E., 601
 Robert, 55
 Samuel, 167, 537, 538, 542
Wedrick, Marten, 646
Week, Michael, 647
Weelfly, David, 633

Wehel, Martin, Jr., 479
 Nicholas, 479
Weinberg, Hartog, 541
Weinbrenner, David, 25
Weise, Godfrey, 596
Weiss, L., 647
 Michael, 477
Weld, Isaac, Jr., 139
Welfley, John, 466, 467
Well, Joseph, 84
Weller, Jacob, 334, 453, 455, 478, 494, 604, 633
 Jacob, Jr., 633
 Jacob, Sr., 455
 John, 90
 John, Jr., 633
 Joseph, 334
 Philip, 82, 90
 Wm. T., 549
Wells, Ducket, 637
 James, 628
 Joseph, 85, 602, 603, 605, 624
 Thomas, Jr., 640
Welsh, Henry, 624
 Thos., 628
 Warner D., 382
Weltner, Ludwig, 8, 86, 95, 479
Welty, G. E. , 560
 John, 631
 Sourin, 546
Wend, Henry, 647
Wenner, Charles F., 601
Wenrick, John, 169
Wentz, Frederick, 628
Werble, Philip, 628
Werner, Elizabeth, 628
 Jacob, 633
 John, 628
Werns, Jacob, 626
Wertenbaker, Lewis, 453, 455
 William O.,549, 607
Wertheimer, Charles, 532, 533, 552, 610
Wertz, Michael, 643
Wesenger, Peter, 639
Wesley, John, 456
Wessley, Henry, 642
West, Benjamin, 332, 490
 Corbin, 603
 Erasmus, 490, 492, 641
 G. M., 491
 G. W., 595
 George M., 490

George W., 565, 566
George Washington, 596
Horace, 492
Jacob, 639
John, Jr., 333
Joseph, 629, 641
Levin, 169, 581, 584, 596
Mary, 490
Samuel, 86
Stephen, 75, 79, 145
Susannah, 490
Thomas, 641
William, 670
Westbay, Hugh, 631
Westenberger, Jacob, 637
Westenhaver, Christian, 633
Westerhaver, Christopher, 634
Westerman, William, 492
Westfall, John, 603
Samuel, 82
Westford, Thomas, 634
Westman, Jacob, 637
Wetsell, Jacob, 626
Wetzel, Jacob, 343, 344
James L., 281
Lewis, 343, 344
Martin, 479
Wever, Caspar W., 149
Casper W., 181,192, 271,
272
Weybright, John, 462
John S., 462
Samuel, 462
Weymer, Jacob, 486
Wharton, Jack, 299
Jesse, 299
John O., 299
Wm., 299
Whats, Susanna M., 483
Wheeler, Ann, 324
Charles, 670
J. A., 560
John, 110
Richard, 638
Robert, 630, 644
Samuel, 629
Wherritt, Bennett, 169
Whetcroft, Edward, 633
Whetherford, Thomas, 670
Whip, George T., 605
Jacob, 637
John, 644
Lewis O., 541

Martin, 644
Tobias, 644
Whipp, George, 169
George T., 554
Paul C., 560
Preston, 560
Whiskey, Augustus, 644
Margaret, 637, 645
Whitacre, Alex., 537
Whitaker, Alex., 86
Whitcraft, Wm., 327, 328
White, A. B., 338
Abraham, 631
Andrew, 631
Ann, 642
Benjamin, 625
Christopher, 631
D. G., 612
D. Grove, 554
David G., 528
Edward, 670
Elisha, 629, 646
Henry, 632
J. J., 561
James, 637
John, 450, 641, 670
Joseph, 633
Mother Rose, 517
Mrs. Elizabeth Keenan, 518
Nicholas, 431, 432
Rebecca, 458
Roscoe C., 599
Sarah, 635
Thomas O., 541
William, 4, 46, 450, 591,
596,601, 631
Whitecraft, Samuel, 626
Whitehead, Joseph, 638
Whitehill, J., 364
James, 226-228, 363, 457,
459
Maximus, 582, 596
Whitelock, George, 318
Whiteneck, John, 626
Whitenhaver, Christopher, 635
Whiting, Jos., 543
Whitman, John, 670
Whitmer, A. C., 419
Whitmore, Abraham, 635
Benjamin, 635
Benjamin, Jr., 635
Bruce C., 462
David, 635

G. A., 474
George, 628
George A., 3, 471, 472, 494
George H., 607
Henry, 635
Jacob, 635
Jerry, 475
Jno., 635
Michael, 639
S. L., 493
Whittier, John Greenleaf, 377
Whittington, William, 670
Whyte, William Pinkney, 293,
297, 318
Wickart, Christian, 628
Wickbawm, Nathaniel, 285
Wickes, Wm., 459
Wickham, Edith, 459
G. Roger, 541
Henry, 626
L. A., 520
Nathaniel, 26
Nathaniel, Jr., 26, 27
Robert, 25, 626
Widle, Peter, 637
Widrick, Christian, 169
Wier, P. , 327
R. F., 373, 381
Wiesenthal, Chas. Frederick, 564
Wiest, John, 170
Wigart, Andrew, 628
Wigel, John, 639
Wiggin, Walter W., 197
Wilar, John O., 463
Wilcoxen, A. J., 547
George, 558
Wilcoxon, H., 434
John, 552
William, 598
Wildbahn, Charles F, 466, 480
Charles Frederick, 421
Wile, Peter, 642
Wiles, A. G. P., 659
George, 637
James, 641
Thomas, 637
Wiley, Ephriam, 169
William, 264
Wilhide, Frederick, 479
Jacob, 454
Wilkes, Thomas, 629
Wilkinson, Alexander, 670
James, 134, 142, 163, 164,

168, 266
John, 225
Joseph, 164
Will, George, 631
  H., 647
  Henry, 624
  Nicholas, 631
Willar, Cornelius, 456
  David F., 456
  James L., 456
Willard, A. D., 440
  A. P., 353
  Arthur D., 599, 606
  Ashbel P., 348
  C. B., 555
  Clinton B., 542
  Dewalt, 475
  E. H., 596
  Elias, 475
  Ezra, 475
  Geo, W., 475
  George, 332
  George T., 538
  James, 566, 596
  John, 476, 503
  John Thomas, 596
  John, Jr., 476
  Paul Clarke, 558
  Peter, 596
  Thomas H., 602
Willer, Daniel, 646
  Jacob, 646
  Jacob, Jr., 646
  John, 646
  Mathias, 646
Willers, John, Sr., 646
Willets, John, 624
Willhide, Joseph, 605
Williams, O. H., 86
  Clement, 643, 646
  Daniel, 642
  David, 169
  Dunbar, 670
  Edward, 626
  Edward Greene, 166
  Eli, 83-86, 128, 169, 171
  Elisha, 600
  Elizabeth, 645
  Flora F., 111
  G. A., 266
  George, 492
  Henry, 90, 125, 134, 206,
    312, 520, 527, 532, 536,

552, 603, 604, 635
J. Windsor, 531
  Jacob, 635
  James, 597, 645
  Janie, 396
  John, 37, 125, 444, 629,
    639, 670
  John H., 125, 227, 251,
    292, 527
  Joseph, 89, 670
  Judge Ferdinand, 111
  M. Janet, 82, 583
  Mary, 125
  Mrs. Henry, 82, 396
  Mrs. John H., 396
  O. H., 166, 327
  Otho H., 149, 536
  Otho Holland, 81, 87, 89,
    313
  Prudence Holland, 89
  R. H., 396
  Richard, 37
  Robert H., 449, 451
  Thomas, 670
  William, 361, 644
  William E., 278, 549
Williamson, Hugh, 336, 339
  J. Allen, 541
  Joseph A., 558
  Mary A., 82
  Mrs. J. A., 583
  Peter, 34
  Thomas M., 524, 541
Williar, Augusta, 461, 462
Williard, Andrew, 635
  Davolt, 637
  Devalt, 603
  G. W., 485
  Geo. W., 493
  John, 635
  Peter, 635
  Philip, 502, 635
Willis, Henry, 278, 549
  John, 670
  William, 601
Willman, John S., 384
Wills, W. H., 598
Willson, John, 670
  Jona, 430
  Peter, 670
  Richard A., 550
  Thomas, Jr., 670
  Thomas, Sr., 670

Wilms, Frederick, 41
Wilson, Augustus W., 552
  Caleb, 631
  Charles L., 601
  Charles Light, 598
  Cumberland, 333
  David, 487
  Henry B., 607
  Isaac, 629
  J. D., 488
  John, 167, 170, 339, 497, 629
  Jonathan, 84, 85, 225, 600
  Joseph, 635
  Laura, 497
  Lawrence, 39
  Mary Elizabeth Ann Rebecca,
    534
  Michael, 635
  Mrs. Mahala, 497
  Otho, 169, 170
  Peter Lite, 487
  Robert, 497
  Thomas, 628, 635, 640
  William, 628
  William M., 596
Wilter, H. B., 547
Wiltshire, John C., 353
Wilyard, Elias, 637
  Philip, 637
Wimast, Henry, 647
Wimmer, Abraham, 631
Wimsatt, William Kurtz, 317
Win, John, 645
Winans, Ross, 233
Winbegler, Francis, 637
Winchester, B. F., 392
  George, 134
  H. F., 391
  H. T., 391
  Hiram, 450, 507
  Stephen, 628
  William, 84-86
Wind, George, 626
Windpigler, George, 170
Windsor, Arnold, 325
  L. T., 486
  Modelena, 634
  Zachariah T., 552, 603
Wine, S. K., 454, 455
Wineberg, Henry, 545
  Leo, 599
Winebrener, Mrs. D. Charles, 82
Winebrenner, Anthony, 626

D. C., 227, 348, 507, 526
D. Charles, 546, 552
David C., 610
David, III, 77
Philip, 77
Winecoff, Jesse, 503
Winegardner, Conrod, 628
Winemiller, Henry, 638
Winepegler, George, 644
Henry, 644
Wingert, Guenther, 467
Wingfield, Thomas, 670
Winkle, Rip Van, 267
Winkleman, Louis, 560
Winse, Michael, 642
Winter, Frederick, 629
John, 249, 639
Thomas, 605
Winters, Adam, 628
George, 624, 628
Harvey, 455
Jacob, 624
John, 481, 505, 642
Winton, H. B., 454
Wints, Jacob, 639
Wire, W. C., 504, 506
Wirt, William, 132, 298
Wise, C. E., 465
Godfrey, 593
Henry A. , 347
Jacob, 640
John, 642
Mary, 638
Wiseman, Conrod, 641
Wisher, Christian, 639
Wisner, John E., 555
Wissinger, Geo., 167
Peter, 167
Wissler, H. W., 473
Henry, 470, 471
Kate A., 591
Withero, John, 635
Witherow, John, 605
Withrow, John, 46
Witman, Frederick, 409
Witmer, John, 172
Witseller, John, 645
Witting, Sarah, 628
Wively, John, 647
Wogan, Henry, 670
Wolf, Adam, 644
Andrew, 647
D. J., 468

Daniel, 635
David J., 475
Geo. M., 534
George, 646
George D., 437
Henry, 629
J. Augustus, 478
Jacob, 488
John, 643
Michael, 647
Peter, 633
Simon, 633
Wolfe, Christopher, 631
Franklin, 462
Jacob, 626
John, 169, 463
Lewis W., 547
Martin, 624
Mary, 626
Samuel, 605
Thomas M., 391
Wm. N., 601
Wolfensberger, Isaiah, 334
Wolfkill, John, 645
Wolfy, David, 641
Wolgomott, John, 41
Wollsmecer, H., 647
Wondenbarker, Adam, 638
Wood, Abraham, 626
Alban M., 560
Alfred, 197
Basil, 624
Charles, 221, 628
Charles H., 598
Henry, 638
Isaac N., 593
J., 327, 328
James, 624
John, 599, 624, 628
John E. R., 598
Jonathan, 624
Joseph, 11, 84, 95, 225,
326, 430, 605, 624, 626
Joseph, Jr., 86, 606
M. G., 548
M. P., 531, 548
Melvin P., 607
Richard, 633
Robert, 84, 85, 99, 100
Sabriet, 670
William, 629, 670
Woodbridge, George, 251
J. E., 450

Woodman, Thomas, 644
Woodrick, George, 633
Woodroffe, John, 110
Woodrow, John, 603, 632
Thomas, 542
Woods, Robert, 275
Samuel, 537
Woodville, Mrs. William, 308
Woodward, Baldwin, 552
Benedict, 640
Branton, 169
Charles B., 249
M. A., 559
Woolart, Ludwick, 631
Woolery, Jacob, 628
Woolhide, Frederick, 633
Frederick, Jr., 633
John, 633
Woolridge, Roger, 670
Wooltz, Hezekiah, 169
Otho, 169
Wooman, Christian, 645
Wooten, John, 596
Wm., 566
Wm. Turner, 596
Wooton, Thomas Sprigg, 84, 85
Wootten, Singleton, 604
Thomas Sprigg, 80
Wm. T. , 365
Wootton, Thomas Sprigg, 86, 600
Worley, John, 214
Worman, Jacob, 624
Moses, 278, 450
Mrs. William, 583
Worman, 596
Wormley, James, 164
Worshall, Augustus, 642
Wortakel, George, 634
Wortal, John, 637
Worthington, C. N., 596
Catherine, 111
Charles E., 221
Glenn H., 557, 598, 606, 607
John H., 601
John H. , 292
Kitty, 106
Mrs. Julia Alvey, 562
Nicholas, 106, 111
T. C., 168
Thomas C., 169, 536-538,
597, 601
Thomas Contee, 166, 179,
181, 182, 184, 185

Upton, 221
William, 166
Wortz, Michael, 644
Wren, Catharine, 644
Wright, Anthony, 628
B. F., 598
C. W., 548
D. M., Jr., 549
D. S., 598
David, 642
George, 670
Henry, 633, 642
Isaac, 603
James, 170, 596
Joel, 624
Joseph, 628, 635, 643
Joseph, Jr., 638
Samuel, 642
William, 642
Wrightson, F. G., 553
Writing, Andrew, 624
Wyer, John, 632
William, 626
Wygart, George, 628
Wymert, Valentine, 628
Wynkoop, Benjamin, 341
Joseph, 341
Wyville, Stephen, 631
Yager, Charles, 169
Yancey, William L., 363
Yandes, George, 641
Yandis, Daniel, 626
John, 626
Yanits, Christian, 170
Yanser, Christopher, 646
Yates, B. , 266
C., 266
Ignatius, 638
Thomas, 640
Will, 332
Yeakle, William, 556
Yellott, John I., 390, 492
Yengling, Christopher, 642
Frederick, 632
Jacob, 632, 642
John, 628
Margaret, 632
Yerrick, John, 641
Yesterday, Margaret, 644
Martin, 643
Michael, 633
Yingland, Abraham, 647
John, 647

Yingling, Adam, 630
Yist, Philip, 643
Yon, John, 624
Yond, Jacob, 624
Yonker, Jacob, 647
Yonson, J. H., 473
Lewis, 453
Yonsy, John, 638
Peter, 638
Yont, John, 633
Yontz, Catharine, 638
Yorgen, Henry, 624
York, John, 169
Yost, George, 638
John, 646
Lodowick, 638
Young, Andrew, 167, 628, 640
Benjamin, 26, 27
Caspar, 90
Casper, 633
Charles T. K., 606
Conrad, 500
Conrod, 637
Crawford, 281
Daniel, 476, 633
David, 167
Elmer A., 529, 530
George, 633
H. D., 547
Henry, 210, 641
Howard, 560
J. D. S., 581
J. L., 476
Jacob, 84, 85, 136, 221,
454, 600, 605, 639
Jacob (of Conrod), 641
James, 596
John, 170, 325, 633, 635,
638
John D., 596
John G., 466
John Jacob, 640
John W., 546
Julia M., 520
Ludwig, 25
McClintock, 401, 542, 543,
622
Mrs. W. Nash, 396
Nannie, 459
Nicholas, 645
Oliver F. , 458
Peter, 633
Philip, 624, 626

Thomas, 167
W. Nash, 539, 543, 544, 552
William Nash, 400, 542
William R., 534, 535, 607
Wm., 31
Younger, Gilbert, 670
Youngman, Wm. H. , 170
Yourtee, George W., 582, 584,
596
Yousi, George, 641
Yudy, Philip, 640
Zacharias, Christian, 611
D., 469
Daniel, 227, 250, 408, 412,
493, 628
H. C., 527
Horace, 440
Horace C., 540, 541
`Janie, 416
John Forney, 596
Mathias, 635
Mrs. Annie, 426
Zahn, Johann Michael, 6
Zealer, Adam, 170
Yost, 644
Zeigler, Charles, 419
Susannah, 483
William H, 541 , 542
Zeiso, Geo., 167
Zellers, Calvin, 560
Zentz, Abraham S., 606
David G., 606
Newton M., 419, 524, 533
Zerger, J. E., 482, 484
Zieler, John D., 547
Zimmerman, A. H., 519, 541
Albert D., 485
B. H., 520
C. F., 493
Charles W., 606
Clayton M., 542
Daniel P., 606
David, 555
E. I., 469
Edward, 485
Ezra R., 610
Geo. M., 471
Geo. H., 620

EVERY-NAME INDEX
HISTORY OF FREDERICK COUNTY
VOLUME II

—— (No last name given)
Amelia, 773
Anna Elizabeth, 1425
Anna Mary, 1587
Betsey, 1534
Catherine, 1370
Delilah, 1274
Esther, 1032
Eve, 1342
Hannah, 1580
Harriet D., 1074
Ida, 1602
Janet, 765
John, 1074
Maggie, 768
Margaret, 1358
Mary, 1586, 1601
Mary Catharine, 1262
Mary Magdalene, 974
Naomi, 1355
Sarah, 1605
Susanna, 1425
Abbott, Edward G., 870
Eleanor D., 870
Eleanor V., 870
Flora, 1130
George A., 870
Henry H., 870
John H., 869, 870, 979
John H., Jr., 870
Julia E., 870
Abell, Arunah S., 699
E. Austin, 699
Helen, 699, 849, 1384
Abrahams, Charles E., Jr., 734
Abrecht, Elizabeth, 1174,
1190, 1265
Elizabeth Ellen, 746
Lutheran, 981
Adam,Abraham, 792, 1251
Henry, 1434
John Quincy, 824
Margaret, 1261, 1344
Mrs. C. R., 954
Thomas, 1344
William, 1047, 1071, 1520,
1606
Addison, Andrew, 1285
Anthony, 1233
Elizabeth, 1285

Frank, 1285
Frederick, 874
George Cook, 1285
George M., 1285
Isaac, 1285
Isabella, 1285
John, 1285
John D., 1285
Mary, 1398
Mary M., 1233
Matilda C., 874
Robert, 1285
Samuel, 1285
Sarah, 1285
Susanna, 1285
William, 1285
Ader, John, 1531
Adison, W., 948
Adkins, Charles, 746, 1174,
1265
Joseph, 842
Agnew,
Helen, 864, 1505
Maggie, 1275
Ahalt, A. S., 988
Albert M., 1102, 1265
Alonzo J., 1030, 1265
Alva Atlee, 1340
Amanda, 1164
Amanda A., 988, 1265, 1339
Anna Mary, 1573
Annie, 977, 1019, 1020,
1086, 1604
Arthur, 1030, 1265
Barbara, 1086
Benjamin A., 1182
Benjamin S., 988, 1045,
1265, 1339, 1475
Benjamin Singleton, 1474
Betsy, 988, 1086, 1265, 1339
Beulah, 1475, 1485
Beulah P., 1046
Blanche M., 1573
Bruce F., 989
California, 1573
Califronia, 1484
Carlton, 1086
Carlton P., 1164, 1569, 1573
Carrie Ellen, 1475
Catharine, 988, 1005, 1265,

1339, 1475
Catholine, 1573
Charles, 1005
Charles W., 1046, 1485
Charles William, 1045,
1475
Charlotte, 830, 931, 932,
1190, 1479
Charlotte M., 988, 1265,
1339
Chauncey A., 1265
Clara, 988
Clara S., 1339
Clarence Elvin, 1340
Clarence L., 988, 1339,
1379
Clifford, 988, 1339
Daniel, 1086
Dawson, 1265
Della, 1475
Mabel, 1164
Earl, 1475, 1485
Earl M., 1046
Edgar, 1030, 1265
Elizabeth, 1475
Ellen, 988, 1086, 1265,
1339, 1479
Emma, 1183
Emma C., 988, 1265,
1339
Ernest E., 1265
Ethel, 1265
Floied , 1573
Floyd, 1485
Floyd B., 1046
Foster, 1538
Foster M., 1339
Frances, 1164, 1265
George, 1573
Harold, 1030, 1265
Harriet, 1475
Harriett, 1484
Hazel, 1475, 1485
Hazel E., 1046
Henry, 857, 1086
Herman L., 1265
Homer, 1475
Huffer A., 1005
J. Guy, 1265

Jacob, 988, 1086, 1265, 1339, 1573
Jacob L., 988, 1265, 1339, 1481, 1575
Jennie, 1164, 1576
John, 988, 1037, 1265, 1339, 1378, 1484, 1573, 1621
John D., 1164, 1453, 1484, 1573
John Hilleary, 1573
John M., 1030, 1475
John R., 1265
John W. O., 1086, 1087
Joshua, 988, 1174, 1183, 1265, 1299, 1339, 1573
Joshua D., 746, 894, 988, 1265, 1339
Julia, 1164, 1475, 1485
Julia M., 1046
L. Calvin, 1379
Leroy S., 989
Lester R., 988, 1339
Lewis, 1126
Lilly, 1164
Lloyd Henry, 1339
Lola, 1164
Lucinda, 961, 988, 1086, 1339, 1483
Luretta, 1086
Luther, 1475
Luther Calvin, 1475
Luther M., 988, 1265, 1339
Lydia, 1086
M. Foster, 988
Olive E., 1340
Malinda, 1086
Margaret, 1126
Marshall, 1475
Martha E., 1062, 1189
Martha F., 988, 1265, 1339
Martha S., 989
Mary, 1086, 1316, 1475, 1485
Mary Elizabeth, 1164
Mary L., 989, 1046
Mathias, 1149, 1474
Matthias, 988, 1265, 1339, 1378, 1483, 1573, 1621
Matthias S., 988, 1078, 1265, 1339, 1538
May B., 1265
Merle, 1265
Mildred, 1475, 1486
Mildred N., 1046
Millard, 1030, 1265

Nannetta, 1265
Naomi, 1475
Nellie, 1005
Nora, 1164
Olive, 1164
Orpha, 1475, 1486
Roy M., 1265
Olivia, 1086
Ora, 988
Ora S., 1339
Orpha R., 1046
Paul, 1475, 1485
Paul E., 989
Paul R., 1046
Phoebe Ellen, 1149
Ralph, 1005
Rena, 1339
Samuel, 1573
Susan, 1086
Russell Matthias, 1339
Samuel, 988, 1086, 1164, 1265, 1339
Samuel Peter Willard, 1164
Sarah, 1086
Ura Viola Lucretia, 1126
Violetta, 1086
Virginia M., 1569
Wilber M., 988
Wilbur, 1339
Ahearn, Amanda, 1573
John, 1296
John C., 1457
Ahlbach, Johan Gearhardt, 1261
Johan Peter, 1261
Johan Wilhelm, 1261
Zachariah, 1261
Aiken, E.A., 1213
Aikin, George B., 1263
Akers, Milton T., 1341
Albaugh, Abraham, 1261
Alva, 1262
Andrew, 1070
Andrew H., 1284, 1519, 1527
Anna, 1262
Anna Susan, 1262
Annie L., 1213
Bertha M., 1284
Charles, 1052, 1248
Clarence, 1284
David, 1245
E., 1570
Edna, 1262
Edna Marie, 1520
Elizabeth, 881, 882, 1237, 1270, 1284, 1518, 1619

Ella, 1262
Ellen, 1058, 1537
Emma, 1284
Erwin, 1262
Esther, 1245
Eugene H., 1262
Eugenie, 1052
Florence, 1262
George, 1519, 1587
George W. M., 1283, 1284
Grace Asper, 1520
Guy, 1574
Guy M., 1284
Harriet, 1069, 1070, 1083
Harry E., 1284, 1519
Harvey, 1284
Hobart, 1262
Horace, 1262
Howard M., 1262
Ida, 1284
Ida M., 1284
Irving, 1134
Irving S., 1262
Jane, 1214
Johan Wilhelm, 1261
Johan Wilhelm, 2nd, 1261
John, 1284, 1286
John H., 1261
John Valentine, 1052
Joshua, 1052, 1207, 1261
Laura H., 1262
Laura M., 1532
Lillie, 1338
Luther Andrew, 1520
Lydia, 1020
Margaret Caroline, 1229
Margaret E., 902, 1317
Martha, 1546
Martha E., 703
Mary, 1527
Mary Catherine, 1520
Mary E., 1248
Mollie, 1284
Nina, 1262
Owen, 1262
Paul Eugene, 1262
Rachel Virginia, 1248
Raymond, 1284
Roger, 1134, 1262
Ruth, 1262
Sophia, 1354
Susan, 1134, 1262
Susie Irene, 1434
Thomas, 1052
Thomas F., 1262
Thomas H., 886

Valentine, 1213, 1262
Valentine A. , 1261
Walter A., 1284
William, 1052, 1134, 1262
William A., 1229
William L., 1262
Albright, Augustus, 1612
Albrunner, Maggie, 1306
Alcock, John, 1072
Aldridge, Clayton, 1601
Evan, 1162
Evan J. , 1305
Mark, 942
Willis, 1515
Alexander, Alverta, 1229
Andrew, 1054
Edna M., 1229
Ella, 1229
Emma, 1229
George, 1229
George C., 1228, 1229
Hugh, 885
Jane, 884, 885
Lawson, 1580, 1612
Mathias, 1229
Matilda, 1229
Melanchthon, 1229
Peter, 1229
Susie R., 1054
Tilghman, 1229
Allen, Ira, 1594
Thomas G., 1137
Allgire, Alfred, 1615
Grace, 1615
Allison, Jonathan, 830
Allnutt, E. L., 1102
George S., 1102
J. Howard, 1101, 1102
James P., 1102
Mary C., 1102
Mary E., 1102
Richard J., 1102
Robert D., 1101, 1102
William D., 1102
William P., 1101
Alsip, Josephus, 1496
Alvarez, John M., 695
Alvey, Julia, 729
Richard H., 713, 729
T. Frederick, 695
Ambrose, Bertha, 869
Catherine, 1011
Charles, 869
Clarence R., 869
Elizabeth, 1468
Emma, 869

Ezra, 869
George B., 869
George H., 869
John, 869, 1221
John C., 869
Katherin, 869
Laura, 869
Lottie, 869
Lottie V., 869
Marshall F., 869
Mary, 869
Mireno, 869
Rebecca, 869
Rene, 869
Amelung, John Frederick, 827
Ammon, William, 846
Anders, Aaron, 923, 1007, 1210
Aaron R., 924
Adam H., 850
Alice, 1498
Caleb Asbury, 1141
Calvin B., 924, 1229
Calvin Brown, 923, 924
Charles, 1434, 1537
Charles C., 924
Charles Clay, 923
Charles Henry, 1141
Charles May, 1327
Cora, 1200
Eliza Ellen, 1327
Elizabeth, 724, 725, 1141
Henry, 725, 1140, 1141
Henry Livingston, 1141
Jacob, 1218
John, 1587
Lizzie, 923
Margaret, 1048
Margaret Ruth, 1141
Mary Ann, 1141
Melvin J., 1328
Michael, 1200
Moses, 1327, 1384
Samuel, 729, 1458
Sarah Ann, 1141
Sarepta Jane, 1253
Thomas, 1141
Tillie, 1139-1141
Anderson, ——, 1028
Alexander Knight, 1029
Ann, 1028
Betty L., 1576
Blanch, 1576
Claudia, 1576
Elizabeth, 1025
Evan T., 1217
Henry Lee Hunter, 1029

Isabel Pettit, 1029
James R., 1576
Jane, 1576
Jennie, 1028
Jessie T., 1576
John H., 1028
Mary, 1095, 1355
Mary Ellen, 1095, 1542, 1543
Mary Priscilla, 1576
Robert, 1095, 1543
Samuel, 1576
Samuel B., 1028, 1029
Samuel H., 1028
Thomas T., 1029
Thomas W., 1028
Thomas William, 1028
William, 1028, 1029
William Turner, 1029
Zoe Lee, 1029
Andre, Hofrath Anthony, 802
Jean, 802
Andrew, Harry, 769
Andrews, Nicholas, 1211
Angel, Charles, 1620
Edgar, 1620
Edward, 1620
Ellsworth, 1620
Florence, 1620
Frank, 1620
John, 1620
Rosie, 1336
Susanna, 1564
William, 1620
Angelier, Frank, 1152
Angle, Charles, 1057
Angleberger, Ada May, 1609
Ann S., 902
Arthur O., 1609
Charles Joseph, 1468
Clara, 943
Edith M., 1609
Edward I., 1609
Fanny Estelle, 1336, 1468
George W., 1609
Grayson Clinton, 1468
Harriet A., 1609
Ida M., 1468
Joseph, 902, 1592
Julia J., 1609
Lola B., 1609
Mary S., 1609
Philip J., 1336, 1609
Phillip Jacob, 1468
Rhoda E., 1609
William D., 1609

Worthington R., 1609
Angleburger, Susan, 1333
  William, 1333
Ankleberger, Edward I., 1602
Annan, Andrew, 780, 864,
    1416, 1502, 1505
  Andrew A., 864
  Anna, 1503
  Anna E., 1505
  Anna Elizabeth, 864
  David, 864
  Edgar L., 864, 1503, 1505
  Edgar L., Jr., 1504
  Eliza, 1503
  Emily, 1503
  Helen, 1503
  Henry, 1024
  I. S., 864
  Isaac M., 1503
  Isaac S., 864, 1502, 1503
  J. Stewart, 864
  James C., 1502
  James Cochran, 864
  Jane, 864
  John E., 1503
  Lewis L., 1504
  Margaret, 864
  Pauline Ethel, 1504
  Richard Cochran, 1504
  Robert, 1417, 1502, 1503
  Robert L., 864, 1503
  Robert Lansdale, 1503
  Samuel, 1503
  Samuel McNair, 1504
  Sarah C., 1503
  William, 1252, 1503
Apple, A. T. G., 1000
  Charles A., 1000
  Charlotte Elizabeth, 1001
  Elizabeth, 1000
  Elizabeth Harner, 1002
  Emily Gertrude, 1002
  Emma Amelia, 1289
  Jacob G., 1000
  Joseph H., 1000
  Joseph Henry, Jr., 1000
  Miriam Rankin, 1001
  Susan M., 810, 1166, 1490
  Theodore, 1000
  Thomas G., 1000
Appleby, Alice B., 1339
  Bessie, 1305
  Bessie Alberta, 1339
  Crystal Estelle, 1339
  Dora, 1338
  Emma Lenora, 1338

  Fanny, 1338
  Florence, 1058, 1338
  Harriet, 1338
  Henry Carter, 1339
  Henry R., 1338
  Isabel, 1338
  James, 1338, 1339
  M. Lenora, 1339
  Margaret Loraine, 1339
  Martha, 1338
  Mary Jane, 1338
  Nicholas, 1338
  Rufus, 1338
  Sarah, 1338
  Somerset, 1338
  Viva, 1338
  Walter, 1338
  Wesley, 1338
  William, 1338
Appleman, A. G., 871
  Alpheus R., 871
  Catherine, 871
  Catherine C., 871
  Elizabeth, 871
  Jacob, 871
  John, 871
  John P., 871
  Lieghton F., 872
  Mary F., 871
  Philip, 871
  Rebeeca N., 871
  S. Philip, 871
  Sarah, 871
  Susan, 871
  William S., 871
Armacost, Mary E. A., 794
Armocost, Lester W., 755
Armour, P. D., 766
Arms, Ursula, 1136
Armstead, George R., 1614
Armstrong, Anna, 805
  Elizabeth, 805
  James, 805
  Jane, 805
  John, 805
  Robert, 805
  Samuel, 805
  William, 805
Arnold, Alvin, 1605
  Amanda, 1020
  Amanda Catherine, 1605
  Andrew, 932, 1479
  Andrew D., 1083, 1190
  Andrew Daniel, 1083
  Andrew David, 1189
  Annie, 1605

  Annie Louise, 1062
  Austin F., 1151, 1218
  B. G., 865
  Bessie, 1482
  Beulah, 1030
  C. M., 980
  Carrie V., 1101
  Carrie Viola, 1479
  Catherine, 1101
  Catherine Gertrude, 1078
  Charles Graham, 1078
  Charles Joseph, 1078,
    1189
  Claud, 1621
  Cora, 1062
  Daniel, 1020, 1605
  David, 1061, 1062, 1078,
    1083, 1122, 1150,
    1188, 1189, 1487,
    1540, 1605
  David Jacob, 1083
  Dorothy Grace, 1218
  Dorothy La Rue, 1151
  Edgar Franklin, 1151
  Edward, 1605
  Edith Anna, 1189
  Eliza, 1061, 1189
  Elizabeth, 1151, 1332,
    1549
  Ella, 1605
  Elmer, 1605
  Emma, 1605
  Eva Frances, 1062
  Ezra, 1062, 1189
  Fanny, 1189
  Frank, 1101
  George, 1061, 1188
  George V., 873, 1061,
    1062, 1101, 1189
  Gertrude, 1189
  Grace Naomi, 1101
  Harry, 1101, 1472
  Helen Adele, 1101
  Huldah, 1062, 1189
  Ida, 1605
  Inez, 1151
  J. Claude, 1151, 1217,
    1218
  Jennie May, 1062
  John, 1061, 1062, 1150,
    1188, 1189
  John H., 1189
  John J., 1101
  John Thomas, 1083
  Joshua, 1062, 1150, 1151,
    1189, 1217, 1482

Laura Bernadetta, 1189
Lena, 1189
Lester, 1605
Lydia, 870, 872, 1061, 1189
Mahlon, 977, 1062, 1101, 1189, 1479
Mahlon D., 1020
Malon, 1086
Margaret, 1100, 1103, 1125, 1540
Martha Ellen, 1101
Martin V., 1062
Mary, 866
Mary C., 1189, 1487
Mary E., 1605
Mary Elizabeth, 1083
Mary S., 1101
Maurice Lenord, 1083
Mrs. David, 1453
Nellie, 1101
Olivia, 1605
Otis, 1101
Peter, 1061, 1189, 1485, 1605
Robert Lee, 1062
Robert M., 1101
Sara, 1351
Sarah, 1062, 1189, 1351
Sarah Margaret, 1189
Thomas, 1061, 1062, 1189
Thomas D., 1062
Urner, 1605
William Wiener, 1189
Arrington, Jennie, 1271
Arter, Catharine, 796, 1414
Arthur, Camilla, 1143
    Celestia A., 1585
    Charles J., 719
    Minerva F., 1394
Asdale, Amandus, 917
Ashbaugh, Aquilla, 1039, 1377
    Charles B., 1040
    David L., 1039
    Ella G., 1040
    Elroy, 1040
    Fanny, 1040
    George, 1040
    Harrie, 1040
    Herbert M., 1040
    John, 1039
    Mabel, 1040
    Margaret, 1039
    Mary J., 1039
    Mina L., 1040

Repp, 1377
Ruth, 1040
Sarah Catharine, 1377
Violet, 1040
William E., 1040
William H., 1039, 1040
Atkinson, C. E., 1213
    Emma, 1577
    George, 1577
    George W., 1577
    Lydia M., 1577
    Robert, 1025
Atlee, Edwin, 911
    Mary A., 911
Aubert, Alfred H., 1599
    Annie, 1201
    Kate, 1599
Auld, Alice Chase, 818
    Amy, 1242
    Robert, 1242
    Robert E., 818
Ault, R. T., 926
Aultman, Alfred H., 1599
    George, 1283
    Mary M., 1469, 1474
Aumen, William A., 1519
Ausherman, Annie A., 873
    Charles, 1371
    Charles F., 870, 871
    Charles G., 1348
    Clement C., 872, 873
    David, 872, 1062, 1174, 1190, 1621
    Edward, 1474, 1621
    Eliza, 872
    Elizabeth, 871, 872
    Emma, 1062
    Emma M., 873
    Hanson, 1062, 1189
    John, 872, 1061, 1189
    John, Jr., 870
    John, Sr., 870
    Lydia, 872
    Martin, 872
    Mary, 872
    Mollie E., 873
    Sallie, 872
    Samuel, 872
    Samuel Q., 873
    Thomas, 872
    Tilghman, 872
    William, 872
Austin, Sarah, 965
Avirett, Philip William, 1395
Avis, W. L., 1381
    William L., 911, 1147

Axline, Elizabeth, 1460
Ayers, Rebecca, 1109
Babel, Caroline M., 1358
Babington, Amanda, 1472
    Joseph, 1472
Bacchell, Annie M., 868
Bachman, Frederick, 1395
    Rachel, 1395
Bachtel, Daniel E., 810
Bachtell, Charles, 1127
Bachter, Charles, 1457
Bachtol, Mary, 1361
Bacon, A. B., 906
    David, 906
    Henry M., 906
    Maria, 906
    Thomas Scott, 906, 1412
    William, 906
Baer, Adam, 962
    Annie C., 963
    Catharine, 962, 1043
    Eliza Ann, 1070, 1071, 1520
    Elizabeth, 897
    George, 945, 962
    Jacob, 831, 1281
    John, 1071, 1520
    John P., 962
    Mary E., 963
    Mary J., 831
    Michael, 962
    N. P. B., 723
    Philip, 897, 962
    William H., 963
Baile, Jeremiah, 1231
    Lydia, 1494
    Mary, 1231
    Nicodemus, 970, 1065
Bailey, Florence F., 925
Baill, Lena, 1209
Baille, Sarah, 966
Bair, George, 1203
    John E., 1246
    Lena Virginia, 1573
Baird, David, 842
    John, 1141
Baker, ——, 1450, 1452
    Aaron, 1075, 1438, 1493
    Alma G., 1390
    Almira, 1321
    Alice, 1493
    Amanda, 1462
    Andrew, 1231
    Andrew H., 802
    Annie, 1493
    Annie E., 1075

Augustus, 1493
Bertha, 1306
C. W., 932
Charlotte, 715
Christian, 965
Daniel, 711, 712, 1012,
	1029, 1081, 1277, 1320,
	1321, 1440, 1493, 1600
David, 1270
David A., 1493
Dorsey, 1216
Edward, 1493
Elizabeth, 1231, 1340
Ellen, 1321
Eva, 767
Ezra, 1493
Frederick, 1493
George, 932
Grace, 773
Greenberry, 879
Hiram, 1351
Holmes D., 715
Holmes Davenport, 1600
J D., 1231
J. L., 878
J. W., 1275
John, 759, 1231, 1493
John H., 1321
John R., 1321
John W., 1277
Joseph D., 713, 1321, 1600
Joseph Dill, 711
Joseph G., 1277, 1278
Lillian, 1278
Louisa, 1471
Maggie, 1493
Margaret, 1438
Marshall, 1306
Matilda, 1493
Mollie, 879
Mrs. Catharine, 915
Mrs. Frances, 1221
Sarah, 1075
Sarah C., 711, 1321, 1441
Sophia, 1493
Susan H., 1232
Thomas, 878, 1462
Vinton, 1094
Virginia, 932
W. Edward, 1278
William, 1231, 1279, 1306,
	1493, 1531
William D., 1075, 1493
William G., 711, 1320,
	1321, 1600
William G., Jr., 1321

Balch, Stephen B., 842
Balduer, Michael, 1210
Ball, Mary, 1072
	Mary S., 1072
	Walter, 1072
Baltzell, Alice B., 1072
	Edward, 982
	Eliza, 1072
	Ellen, 1072
	Fannie B., 1072
	I. Z., 708
	Jacob, 1211
	John, 1072
	Philip, 1211
	W. H., 1072
Bankard, Elizabeth, 1297, 1538,
	1565, 1566
	Jesse, 1141
Bankert, Carrie, 1356
	David, 1356
	Dennis, 895, 1273
	Josiah, 1273
Banks, Daniel F., 1330
	William Q., 1594
Bansen, Mrs. Eva L., 1544
Bantz, Gideon, 882, 1588
Barbara, Adam L., 1054
Barber, Margaret, 805
Bardette, Beckey, 1605
Barger, Henry, 1157
	Mary Elizabeth, 1435
Barker, Jeremiah, 942
	Margaret, 942
	Mary E., 942
Barkman, David E., 868
	Sarah, 1262
Barnes, ——, 1601
	Agnes, 965
	Alfred, 1462
	Amelia, 966
	Amidee, 967
	Andrew, 966, 967
	Ann, 983
	Asbury, 1462
	Augusta, 966
	Augusta Ann, 1155
	Carrie, 922
	Catherine, 966
	Cephas, 922
	Clara V., 965
	Clementine, 1462
	Darius H., 1496
	Ella L., 1275
	Elsie, 783, 784
	Emery, 1462
	F. Washington, 966

Florence Priscilla, 1462
Frances, 1462
Frank, 1279
Howard, 724
James Oliver, 1462
James P., 966
Jesse L., 1462
John, 814
John Randolph, 1462
John T., 1155
John Thomas, 966, 967
Josephine, 1462
Leroy Cress, 967
Levi, 1155
Levi Z., 1223
Levi Zadock, 966
Lewis, 967
Lizzie, 966
Lucretia, 966
Maggie, 967
Maggie H., 1223
Marion, 1495
Mary, 965
May Etta, 1462
Mollie, 967
Noah, 784
Nora, 967
Prudence, 966
Rachel, 966
Rachel E., 966
Sarah A., 966
Slingsberry, 966
Susan, 1462
Thomas, 965
Thomas P., 966
Tomsey Amelia, 1462
William, 1462
William Thomas, 1462
Zadoc, 966
Zedoo, 1223
Barnett, Ann, 1553
	Ann Elender, 1494
	Ann Elinor, 1298
Barnhiser Hannah, 862
Barnhold, Ann, 1329
Barrack, Alice, 1092
	Ann, 1163
	Anna, 1616
	Anna Catharine, 1616
	Barbara, 1266, 1301,
		1506
	Bradford, 1616
	Catharine, 1163
	Charles, 1163, 1597
	Claude H., 1230
	Cornelius, 1616

D. K., 1269
Daniel, 1267, 1507
David Michael, 1091
Edward, 1616
Elizabeth, 1133
Elizabeth (Betsey), 1163
Emma, 1616
Frederick, 1091
George, 1163
Grace, 1616
Harry, 1092
Hattie, 1092
Henry, 1163
Herbert, 1616
Jacob, 1091, 1163
John, 1163, 1218
John C., 1616
Kathleen, 1092
Katie, 1092
Levi, 1163
Lewis E., 885
Lillie, 1092, 1616
Mary, 1112, 1163, 1268, 1269
Mary A., 1270
Noah Edward, 1616
Peter, 1091, 1163
Rachel, 1597
Rebecca, 1163
Robert, 935, 1616
Samuel, 1111, 1133, 1268, 1269
Sarah, 1616
Simon, 1130
Wendel Michael, 1092
William D., 1092
William Robert, 1616
Barrick, Alice G., 1195, 1235, 1236
Carrie M., 1109
Catharine, 1236, 1604
Catherine, 1197
Catharine E., 1604
Charles, 1604
Charles J., 1195, 1196
Charles Late, 1196
Charles N., 1196
Chistian, 1604
Fannie C., 1195
Edward, 1614
Emma, 1614
George, 1197, 1353, 1409
George D., 1176
George Dix, 1196
George L., 1195
George W., 1195, 1236

Grover E., 1196
Harry W., 1196
Ida, 1236
Ida C., 1195
J. Wright, 1195
Jefferson D., 1195
John, 788, 1600
Lavinia Ellen, 1604
Margaret, 842, 843
Mary, 1236
Mary E., 1195
Michael, 1195
Morris V., 1196
Nannie S., 1196
Nathan, 755
Peter, 1604
Phoebe, 1353
Randolph, 1109
Randolph G., 1604
Robert, 1236
Robert E. L., 1195
Solomon, 1604
Susan J., 1195
William M., 1195
Barriger, Dorretta, 1454
Barrock, ———, 948
Ezra, 1493
Barron, Alexander, 1072
Bartgis, Albert W., 858
Byron. C., 858
Charles W., 858
Clara, 1273
Edith L., 858
Franklin, 858
James M., 858
John E., 858
Lloyd C., 858
M. E., 1160
Mary J., 858
Mathias, 858
Mathias, Jr., 858
Titus V., 858, 1061
Barthelow, Elisha, 1534
Jemima, 1534
Bartholow, Wiliam, 1358
Barton, Albert, 1585
Benjamin, 1506
Bessie, 1506
Charles, 1506
Gertrude C., 1506
Grace C., 1506
Henry, 1505
Ida, 878
Isaac, 1505
James M., 1506
John N., 1506

Leota, 1506
Margaret Ann, 1506
Ogle B., 1506
Russell, 1506, 1535
Samuel, 1505
Sarah, 742,1505
Sarah C., 1506
Thomas, 742, 1505
William, 1506, 1535
William A., 1505, 1506
Zora S., 1506
Bartry, Shain E., 1398
Bassford, Ellen, 763
Rosa, 763
Bast, Henrietta, 1487, 1488
John, 1488
Mrs. Mary, 1406
Susan, 1063
Bastian, David, 1500
Gladys, 1500
John, 1082
Margaret, 1500
Bates, Daniel W., 1298, 1495
Batonya, M., 1384
Battersby, George B., 1622
Baug, Anna, 1245
Baugher, ———, 1218
Anne, 1528
Amanda, 974
Clinton Augustus, 1528
Cora Irene, 1528
David, 775, 1406, 1523
David Hamilton, 1528
Elizabeth, 1527
George Washington, 1528
Isaac, 974
Jacob William, 1527
John, 1527
John D., 1527
John Martin Luther, 1528
Joseph, 1528
Lillie Florence Virginia, 1528
Lydia, 703, 704, 832
Mary, 1527
Michael Samuel, 1527, 1528
Oscar, 1137
Samuel, 1527
Savilla, 1527
William, 1528
Baughman, Charles H., 697
E. Austin, 1384
Frank C., 697
Helen Abell, 849
J. William, 697

John W., 696
L. Victor, 849, 1050, 1059, 1085, 1150, 1384
Lewis Victor, 1311
Louis Victor, 696, 697, 699
Mrs. L. Victor, 963
Victor, 841
William, 696
Baughter, Henry, 1599
Baumgardner, Abbie Irene, 1292
Ada, 1277
Barbara A., 1276
Carlton A., 1493
Catherine, 1276
Catharine E., 1493
Charles, 1276
Daniel, 1292
Edith Grace, 733
Edward T., 1277
Ella, 853
Emily Catherine, 1564
Emma, 1277
Fannie E., 1493
Fanny, 1452
Florence, 1277
George M., 733
George T., 853
Harry D., 853, 1492
Harry D., Jr., 1493
Henry, 1276
Ida A., 1277
Jacob, 1291
John, 733, 853, 1276, 1291, 1368, 1488
John F., 1492
John F. O, 1276
John Lester, 733
Kate, 830
Katie, 1277
Lizzie, 1276
Luther A., 854
Margaret, 853
Margaret L., 1493
Marian, 733
Marshall, 1291, 1513
Mary E. , 1291
Nora, 1277
Peter, 1291
Rachel, 1297, 1546
Ralph A., 1493
Raymond , 733
Sarah Catherine, 1292
Susie, 854
Thomas, 853, 1276

William, 853
Baumgartner, J., 856
Beachley, Albert, 1276, 1316
Albert C., 1379
Allen, 1477
Alvey L., 857
Amos, 1276
Anna, 857
Anna L., 1102
Anna Pauline, 1103
Annie, 1102
Annie M., 1077
Athene, 1276
Barbara, 857
Betty Blanch, 1316
Carlton Daniel, 1479
Carlton Paul, 1479
Catharine, 857
Charles Teddy, 1316
Clara V., 1102
Conrad, 857, 1476
D. Howard, 1482
Daniel, 857, 1102, 1147
Daniel V., 1102, 1103
Dorothy E., 858
Edgar M., 857
Edith M., 1273
Edith N., 1477
Edna, 1276
Edna E., 857
Elmer E., 1477
Emma, 1316
Emma V., 1379
Ethel, 1276
Eugenia, 1477
Ezra, 857, 955, 1102, 1103, 1477
Ezra W., 1102, 1103
George Daniel Dewey, 1316
George S., 1476, 1477
Grayson R., 857
H. J., 1477
Harvey D., 857
Henry, 857, 1086, 1102, 1316, 1339
Henson, 857
Howard, 1316
Howard D., 1315, 1316
Imogene Emma Prudence, 1316
J. H., 1248
J. Hanson, 1102
Jacob, 857, 1316
John, 857, 1276
John D., 1273, 1476, 1477
John W., 857, 1102

Jonas, 857, 1102
Jonas E., 1340
Joshua, 1476, 1477
Laura, 1316
Lester E., 1477
Lizzie, 1477
Lola, 1316
Lola E., 1339, 1379
Luther E. S., 1102
Macie, 1316
Martin H., 1379, 1425, 1612
Mary, 1476
Mary Esther, 857
Masie C., 1379
Matilda, 1062, 1189
Mazie, 1475
Merle, 1276
Merle V., 1103
Mildred, 1316
Millard R., 1379
Mollie, 857
Norma S., 1102, 1265
Oliver, 1174, 1190, 1316
Oliver O., 1019
Olivia, 1316
Oscar C., 857
Park, 1276
Peter, 857
Ralph, 1276
Rebecca, 857, 1102
Regina, 1103
Samuel, 1477
Sarah, 1476
Sarah Ellen, 1276
Tabitha, 1102
Vernon S., 857
Violetta, 1316
Beal, David J., 842
Beall, Basil, 1325
Elizabeth, 1326
J. W., 789
John Lee, 1216
Lucy R., 916
Matilda, 789
Mollie, 1231
Sarah, 1326
William, 1227, 1326
William Murdock, 777
Beam, Mrs. Lucy, 805
Bean, Arthur N., 1009
Thomas W., 851
Beanfelder, George H., 1150
Bear, ——, 866
Catharine, 927
Charles, 950

Charles D., 1403
Charles J., 745, 1354
David, 927
Elizabeth, 1598, 1599
George, 787, 1191
Henry, 1314
Jacob, 1599
James E., 868
Margaret, 740
Mary, 967
Mary E., 1193, 1611
William, 1314
Beard, Benjamin F., 859
Catharine, 1249
Catharine M., 860
Elinor L., 860, 977
Elizabeth, 859
Emma, 1260
George W., 1251
Haidee V., 860
Harlan, 1027, 1207
Howard W., 1252
Ida M., 1252
Isaac T., 859
J. Edward, 1252
Jacob, 859
James Calvin, 1252
James L., 1489
John, 1251, 1260
John B., 859
John D., 1251
John T., 859
John W., 860
Katie, 1210
Leola Grace, 859
Luther, 1260
M. L., 859, 977, 1046, 1394
Magdalena, 1100, 1103,
1125
Magdalene, 1293
Martha, 859
Mary Alice, 1252
Mary Maude, 860
Paul B., 860
Samuel M., 859
Susan M., 1572
Tillie, 859
William H., 859
Beasley, William J., 1153
Beatly, William, 1205
Beattie, Jane, 1199
Beatty, Catherine, 1328
Charles, 794
Eli, 1267
J. E., 911
Jane, 795

John, 795, 1329
Mary, 1329
Mary Middaugh, 1329
Robert, 795
Susanna, 782
Susannah Asfordby, 795
Thomas, 794, 1329
William, 794, 890
Beaty, Jeannette, 1279, 1280
Beavans, Charles A., 1073
Beaver, John K., 814
Martha J., 814
Beavers, Julia A., 1419
Julia Ann, 1420
Bechtal, Mary M., 1006
Bechtel, Catharine, 911, 1374,
1375, 1429, 1430
Catharine, 1296
Lewis, 1296, 1375, 1430
Sarah, 1296, 1375, 1430
Bechtol, Catharine, 1356, 1362
Daniel, 1050, 1059
Lewis, 1356
Lucinda F., 776, 952
Sarah, 1356, 1362
Beck, Daniel, 1445
Ida, 983
Mary, 821
Mary E., 1594
Nancy, 717
Nimrod, 1071, 1520
Osborn, 983
Beckley, Bertha, 1437
Becraft, Elizabeth, 1555
Emma, 1326
Beeler, Sarah, 812
Beeson, Drusilla, 737
Drusilla Hellen, 753
Henry, 753
Jesse, 753
Behen, Mrs. Aphaw, 1388
Beird, George, 1435
Beitler, Henry C., 1435
J. Allen, 1435
Jessie, 1435
Jessie J., 1435
John H. C., 1435
John S., 1435
Samuel, 1435
Samuel J., 1435
Sarah E., 1435
Sophia, 1435
William F., 1435
Belange, Rebecca, 1594, 1595
Bell Annie M., 1586
Benjamin, 1531

Cassandra, 796
Charles H., 1059
David, 1136
Earl, 1059
Florence V., 1227
John, 769, 796, 879,
1415,1620
Joseph M., 1347
Julia Ann, 1531
Mary E., 741
Sally, 762
Sarah Jane, 933, 1277
Viola, 1059
Wesley M., 1227
William, 741, 1277
Belleson, Annie, 1500
Catharine, 1500
Corrilla, 1500
George W., 1500
George Washington, 1500
Harriet, 1500, 1501
Henrietta, 1500
Lavinia, 1501
Lucretia, 1500
Mary, 1500
Mary Ellen, 1500
Milton, 1500
Rachel, 1500
Richard, 1500
Rosa, 1501
Thomas M., 1500
William, 1500
Belt, Alfred, 919, 920
Alfred Campbell, 920
Alfred M., 722
Alfred McGill, 919
America Macgill, 919
Ann Elizabeth, 920
Annie Oliver, 919
Carlton, 920
E. Oliver, 919
Edward McGill, 920
Edward Oliver, 919
Ellen Campbell, 919
Higginson, 920
Humphrey, 920
James, 920
John, 920
John D., 1367
John Lloyd, 919, 920
Julia, 919
Mary Charlotte, 919
Mary Ellen, 920
McGill, 919
Ruth Ann, 920
Sarah Virginia, 919

Sinclair, 920
William, 920
Benchel, William, 1063
Benchoff, Aaron, 1180
 John, 837, 1455
Bene, Anna Marie, 816
Benjamin, Parke, 721
Benner, Alonzo, 918
 C. M., 918
 Catharine, 1397
 Christian, 918
 George, 918
 John, 918
 M. W., 1320
Bennet, Martha, 1338
Bennett, Benjamin, 1338
 Edward, 1561
 Eli, 1181
 Eliza Eugenia, 783
 Emma, 1018
 Emma T., 1017
 George, 1561
 Helen, 1561
 Jennie, 782, 1561
 John T., 1561
 Lewis, 1018
 Margaret Reid, 1562
 Minerva, 1561
 Oliver P., 1561
 Thomas E., 1561
 Tilghman, 1561
 Washington A., 754
 William A., 1561
 William Besant, 1562
Benson, Benjamin R., Sr., 794
 Beulah Miller, 794
Bent, Magdalene E., 732
Bentz, Ann, 1314
 Catharine, 1375, 1376
 Elizabeth, 1067
 Gideon, 1313
 Jacob, 1376
 Laurence, 1548
 Lawrence, 1592, 1010,
  1021
Berger, John, 1095, 1543
Berrian, Hobert, 1045
Berry, Frank, 1221
 John, 752
Besant, G. Mantz, 1570
 James H., 1562
 Nellie G., 1562
 William T., 1570
Best, Catharine, 1427
 Charles E. T., 900
 Cora, 1554, 1596

Daniel, 900
David, 900
Edith, 1439
Elizabeth Ann, 900
Frank Lawrence, 900
Harry H. J., 900
John T., 899, 900
John T., Jr., 899, 900
Oliver D., 900
Simon, 1020
Simon David, 900
William H., 900, 1439
Betts, Josiah, 868
Biceline, Mary, 884
Biddinger, Albert, 1517
 Charles, 1215
 David, 1274
 Hester Marie, 1518
 Laura Othetta, 1518
 LeRoy McKinley, 1518
 Marie, 1215
 Othetta, 1215
 Thelma, 1215
 Thelma Elizabeth, 1518
Biddle, David, 1122
 Walter, 1383
Bidle, John, 1218
Biehl, James C., 1620
 John Bryant, 1620
 Katharine Lucille, 1620
Bielfeld, Herman, 855
 J. J., 855
Biggs, Caroline M., 1454
 Edmund, 1143
 Edward, 1587
 Eleanora, 788
 Emma, 1124
 James S., 750
 Martha, 794
 Mary, 1106
 Mary A., 850
 Milton A., 850
 Sarah, 706, 707, 1457
 Sarah D., 918
 William, 794
Billmyer, Annie, 922
 David, 901
 Edward E., 901
 Elise Selby, 901
 Ellen B., 901
 Francis Hamtramck, 901
 Frank L., 901
 George W., 900
 George Waters, 901
 George Waters, Jr., 901
 James Shepherd, 901

Jefferson Davis, 901
John R., 901
William H., 901
Birely, A. D., 1513, 1615
 Adam D., 1614
 Adam David, 1252
 Alice, 1614
 Alice P., 1615
 Amanda, 846
 Barbara, 703
 Bessie C., 976
 Bessie C., 764
 Caroline, 1461
 Catharine, 846
 Charles Irving, 1253
 Charles S., 1393
 Charles William, 703
 Charlotte, 702, 703
 Clarence E., 1253
 Daisy, 846
 David, 846
 Edward, 1036
 Elizabeth, 846, 976, 1048,
  1615
 Ella, 846, 1052
 Ella S., 1208
 Elmer B., 1253
 Fannie, 1035, 1036
 Fanny B., 1393
 Finkle Howard, 1253
 Frederick, 1252
 Frederick Adam, 1253
 George, 1036, 1393
 George K., 745, 1036,
  1037, 1252, 1354,
  1393
 George Washington, 1252
 Henry, 1252
 Henry Clay, 702
 Herbie Lee, 1253
 Jacob, 846, 1252
 Jacob M., 846
 James C., 1253
 Jane Zacharias, 703
 Jennie, 1052
 Jesse C., 1253
 John, 850
 John R., 1252
 John W., 1461
 John William, 702
 Katharine Elizabeth, 977
 Laura E., 850
 Laura V., 703
 Lester, 1048
 Lester C., 764
 Lester S., 860, 976

Lewis, 846, 1207
Lewis A., 1253
Lewis E., 1393
Lillie, 846
Lillie J., 976, 1048
Lloyd G., 976
Lottie, 846
Louis, 1052
M. A., 1252
Margaret, 702, 846
Margaret Elizabeth, 1252
Mary, 846, 1052
Mary Elizabeth, 702
Mary Rebecca, 1048
Mary Rosanna, 703
Merton Adam, 1253
Morris A., 976
Morris Alleman, 1048
Morris Franklin, 1048
Norris, 846
Oliver D., 1052
P. H. C., 702
Philip, 702
Phoebe Alice, 1253
Rebecca, 702, 976
Samuel, 764, 976, 1048,
    1252, 1253, 1615
Samuel M., 969, 976, 1048
Thomas F., 846, 1252
Victor M., 976
William, 702, 846, 1052,
    1208
William C., 703
William F., 1253
William K., 1393
Willie, 846
Birney, Roger, 1137
Biser, A., 1567
    A. E., 1361
    Albert C., 1059
    Annie, 951, 1576
    C. C., 1549
    Catharine, 951, 1050, 1059
    Catherine, 951, 1059, 1407
    Charles Bruce, 1051
    Charles C., 1050, 1059
    Claggett, 1030
    Cleggett, 1486
    Constance, 1562
    Cora B., 1562
    Cyrus, 1482
    Cyrus Carty, 951
    Cyrus T., 1006, 1050, 1059
    Daniel, 749, 790, 951, 952,
        967, 993, 1050, 1059,
        1186

Daniel G., 1144
Daniel S., 1566
Dorothy, 1562
Edith R., 1059
Elizabeth, 894, 951, 1050,
    1059, 1183, 1186, 1611
Ella, 1486
Emma F., 1050, 1059
Emma R., 951
Erie Calvin, 952
Ezra, 951
Florence E., 951
Floy Miller, 1051
Frances, 1562
Frank M., 952
Frederick, 951, 1050, 1055,
    1059, 1467, 1576
George, 1481, 1576
George C., 1187
George Cost, 1186
George Washington, 951
Glenn O., 1051
Goldie May, 1051
H. K., 1155
Harry, 1576
Henry, 951, 1050, 1059,
    1415
Henry C., 1256
Henry H., 1256
Ina, 1576
Ira E., 1562 Irma R., 952
Irvin S., 952
Irving, 951
Irving M., 952
Jacob, 951, 1050, 1055,
    1059, 1186
John, 951, 1050, 1059
John E., 1050, 1059
Jonas, 951
Jonathan, 1050, 1059, 1562,
    1616
Joshua, 951
Lauretta, 1093
Lawson H., 1050, 1059
Lillian Barrett, 952
Lydia A., 748
Mahalia, 1050, 1059
Malinda, 951
Maria, 791, 908
Mark Henry, 1051
Mary, 951, 1055
Mary C., 1415
Mary Catharine, 1050, 1059
Mary E., 1005
Mary M., 952
Melvin A. E., 952, 1006,

    1050, 1059, 1562
Meredith, 1562
Pearl, 812
Pearl H., 951
Peter, 951, 1050, 1059
Polly, 951
Reginald, 1562
Ruth A., 951
Sarah, 790, 967
Sarah T., 1050, 1059
Sophia, 1059, 1256
Thaddeus, 1366
Thaddeus M., 951, 1055
Thomas, 993
Thomas G., 1144
Tilghman, 1185
Victor R. S., 951
Virginia A. R., 1050, 1059
Bishop, Eva, 1277
    John, 1277
Bitler, Luther, 883
    Simon D., 1338
Bittle, Anna C., 1391
    Annie C., 877, 959, 1175
    Catherine, 896
    Charles J., 877, 1175,
        1390
    Charles Jacob, 1391
    D. P., 756
    Daniel F., 1175
    David Edgar, 876
    David F., 877, 1391
    Edward, 747, 955
    Emory M., 740, 1579
    Emry L., 877, 1176
    George, 876, 896, 1175
    George Matthias, 1390
    George Michael, 875
    George W., 875, 877
    Glenn E., 1176
    Henry, 875, 903, 904,
        1371, 1390
    J. Elmer, 875, 877
    J. Thomas, 875, 877
    John H., 876, 1175
    John O., 877, 1175, 1391
    Jonathan, 756, 876, 877,
        1175, 1390, 1391
    Lawson F., 877, 961, 1176
    Lawson F. A., 1391
    Malinda, 875, 876, 1175,
        1390
    Marah E., 876, 1175
    Margaret Lenore, 961
    Maria, 875, 1390
    Maria E., 1371, 1372

Marie, 871
Mary Ann, 759
Melinda, 756
Rachel, 875
Roy M., 876
Ruth Catherine, 961
Thomas F., 875-877, 913,
1175, 1390
Thomas W., 757
William, 959
William E., 877, 958,
1174-1176, 1391, 1524
William M., 757, 875-877,
1175, 1176, 1390, 1391
Bittler, Jesse, 1620
Bixler, Elmer, 814
Black, C. H. , 1506
Daisy, 856
Edith, 856
H. L., 971
Harry M., 856
Henry, 761, 999, 1060,
1447
Henry L., 1021
Howard J., 856
J. B., 856
Joseph, 787, 855, 1600
Joseph H., 855, 856
Julia, 855
Lizzie, 855
Lulu, 856
Mary, 855
Rebecca, 723
Rose, 856
W. Henry R., 856
William, 733, 787, 855,
1458, 1506, 1599
William A., 855, 856
Blacklar, Clinton C., 1045
Blackson, John, 1498
Blackston, Jennie, 1495
Blackstone, Harry, 819, 1560
Bladen, J. H., 823
Thomas, 832
Blain, W. S., 884
Blaine, James G., 1147
Blair, Montgomery, 696
Wm. B., 832
Blake, Ellen, 1589
Mary, 845
Blamey, Mary, 815
Blecker, Johann Conrad, 1404
Blentlinger, Charles C., 798
Blessing, Abraham, 1442
Ann Catharine, 861
Annie M., 1090

Benjamin L., 861
Catharine, 861
Ellen, 861, 1513
George, 861, 1478, 1513
George Philip, 861
George W., 1454
Lauretta, 861
Lewis, 861
Lydia, 861
Lydia Ann, 861
Margaret, 1442
Margaret Sophia, 861
Mary A., 1442
Mary Elizabeth, 861
Michael, 1442
Neri, 1090
Parker, 861
Penora, 861
Philip, 1442
Rebecca, 861
Sarah, 861
Sarah Jane, 861
Salome, 1479
Solomon, 1442
Susan, 861, 1519
Susan E., 861
Tilghman, 861
Tilghman L., 861
Blickenstaff, Bessie M., 862
Charles, 1471
Charles W., 862
Cyrus W., 862
Dorsey E., 862
Elias, 858
Elizabeth, 1013
Foster H., 862
George L., 862
Jacob, 862
Jacob R., 862
John, 862
John E., 862
Lidya, 858
Mandy B., 862
Margaret, 862
Mattie S., 862
Nellie L., 862
Susan, 862
Yost, 862
Blickerstaff, Margaret, 1221
Block, Earl L., 860
George G., 860
Goldie A., 860
Guyer, 860
Martha E., 860
Morris G., 860
William J., 860

Willis G., 860
Blocker, John, 1558
Blockley, Clinton C., 1303
Blockson, Henry, 1298
Jennie, 1298
Bloom, Granville, 1287
Bloomashine, Mary, 1614
Bloon, Rachel, 1514
Blume, Laura, 1058
Michael, 1059
Blunt, William, 1449
Boarman, Ann, 1215
Boden, Eliza, 1059
Boggs, R. J. B., 842
Sarah Ann, 1400
Bogner, Jacob, 759
John, 876, 1175
Mary Ann, 759
Rachel, 756, 876, 877,
1175
Bohn, Alice Joanna, 1181
Annie, 1053
Carrie, 1298, 1495
Clara Belle, 1182
Daniel, 1053
Daniel Oliver, 1182
David Richard, 1182
Derward, 1053
E. Frank, 1501
Earl Franklin, 1182
Elizabeth, 1181
Elizabeth Mary, 1182
Elmer, 1182
Elvin Richard, 1182
Emanuel, 1181, 1230
Ernest, 1053
Frances, 1182
Franklin Richard, 1182
Hamilton, 1053
Harvey, 1050, 1053
Helen Virginia, 1182
Henry, 1181
Ida, 1053
James, 1053
Jesse Marshall, 1182
John, 1053, 1513
John A., 1054
John C., 1053
John David, 1182
John H., 1053, 1054
Joseph, 1053
Lavinia, 1053
Lydia Ann, 1181
Maggie, 1214
Margaret, 1500
Michael, 1053, 1070

Nicholas, 1181
Olivia, 1557
Olivia R., 1054
Ora, 1053
Richard Simpson, 1181
Ruby F., 1054
Samuel, 1182
Saylor, 1053
Shirley Wilson, 1054
Solomon, 1053
Thomas, 1053
Wesley, 1181
Wilbur A., 1054
William, 1053
William M., 1181
Boileau, Charles E., 1146,
1220
Sophia K., 1220
Boland, J. D., 887
William F., 1073
Winifred, 887
Bolinger, Eve, 731
Boller, America V., 755
America Victoria, 1516
Anson E. W., 1516
Charles, 1516
Harry R., 1445
Henry, 755
Henry A., 1516
Hilda, 1516
Isaac, 1209
Isaiah W., 1516
Israel, 781, 1336, 1516
Jacob, 1516
Jeannette C., 1516
John, 729, 1458
John H., 1516
John R., 1516
Lee, 1445
Maria, 1516
Matilda, 755
Ross M., 1516
Sarah, 1516
Sherman T. G., 1516
Sophia, 1516
Spencer, 1516
Susan, 1516
William, 1516
Bollinger, Margaret, 733
Bolus, Joseph, 892
Mary, 1407
Stephen R., 1407
Bombaugh, C. C., 1264
Bond, Jane, 1109
Julia, 1435
Laura, 1377

Mary, 718
Thomas, 1279
Bonebrake, Mary, 718
Bonn. D. W., 1285
Book, David, 1402
Booker, Amos, 1515
Boon, Harvey, 1168
Boone, Alice J., 1231
Arthur Christian, 1240
Charles Franklin, 1230
Cora Isabella, 1240
Daniel, 1239
Dennis, 1239
Elizabeth May, 1230
H. Hanson, 1239
Harry William, 1230, 1231
Helen, 1231
Henry, 1230, 1231
James, 1230, 1377
Margaret, 940
Marshall D., 1239
Roy V., 1231
Ruth Naomi, 1231
William M., 1240
Bops, John, 1017
Bopst, Arthur C., 1170
Edna L., 1170
Fannie, 1170
Fannie M., 1044
G. S. C., 740
G. S. Clinton, 1170
Harrold S., 1170
Marietta, 1129
Sarah, 1044
William, 1044, 1170
William M., 1170
Boquet, Henry, 1068
Bosley, Margaret, 839
Samuel, 1355
Boss, Elizabeth, 865
Bostian, Sarah, 1517
Boston, Thomas, 1214
Bostwick, Frederick Howe, 1395
Boswell, Mary, 1443
Wm., 1274
Boteler, Benjamin, 1081
Benjamin A., 1080
Edwina T., 1081
Elizabeth, 977, 1081
Harry, 1080, 1081
Ida, 1081
Lingam, 978
Mary S., 1081
Robert S., 1081
Sarah, 1081
William L., 1080, 1081

Bottler, M., 1262
Boughner, Rachel, 1371
Bouldin, Wm., 1330
Bouquet, Henry, 1596
Boutler, Annie E., 1078,
1079
Oram, 1079
Bowden, Boyd, 1455
Bowen, Joseph, 1403
Bower, Adam, 1458
Catherine E., 1236
George, 949
William, 1012
Bowers, Albert, 942
Alice, 1513
Alice H., 943
Alice V., 1531
Allen T., 1508
Andrew Ralph, 1512
Anna Lee, 943
Bertha, 1533
Bertha E., 942
Charles Edward, 1531
Charles G., 1511
Charles H., 942
Charles W., 1531
Charlotte R., 785
Clara, 1531
Clara DeS. , 1390
Clyde Lewis, 1531
Cora E., 1110
Cora Elizabeth, 785
D. J., 1110
Daniel, 942, 1110
Daniel A., 1532
Daniel W., 1110, 1531,
1532
David, 1512
Earl, 1531
Edith, 1531
Edna B., 1512
Edwin, 1531
Elizabeth, 1110, 1111
Emory O., 1512
Fanny, 1513
Geo. R., 1512
George, 1251
George W., 942
Grace, 1531
Grayson E., 1110, 1111
H. G., 859
Harry Hubert, 1111
Harry M., 942
Harry W., 936, 1110,
1111
Henry, 942

Ida Loretta, 1531
J. E., 1532
Jacob, 1110
Jacob H., 1495
James H., 943
Jennie, 1495, 1508
John H., 1110
John W., 942
John W. Jr., 943
Jonathan, 800, 1511
Joseph B., 1531
Joseph Edward, 1110
Julia Ann, 1511
Katharine Sophia, 859
Leonard Millard, 1531
Lottie I., 1511
Lucy, 1271
Mahlon A., 1511
Margaret, 1110
Margaret Amelia, 1532
Margaret D., 943
Mary, 1110, 1205, 1448
Mary A., 1512
Mary E., 942
Mary Ellen, 1531
Mary L., 1531
Matilda, 800
Michael, 1390
Minnie May, 1512
Myrtle E., 1512
Nellie E., 1512
Nelson A., 943
Orba E., 942
Paul, 1531
Ralph R., 1110
Sarah Ellen, 1531
Stella V., 1511
Susan, 956, 987
Viola R., 1110, 1111
Washington, 1515
William A., 1531
William D., 785, 1110,
    1111
William H., 1108
Bowersox, Alice, 1518, 1619
    Henry, 1525
Bowhan, Lydia, 1597
Bowie, Clark, 966
Bowles, Edward, 1361
    Eliza, 1486
    Magdalena, 1190
    Morris, 1486
    Susan, 972
    William H., 1078
Bowlus, Adam, 994
    Annie, 1549

Catharine, 1094, 1255, 1423
Catharine C., 1379
Cora, 1276
Edward, 1191
Eliza, 1030
Eliza V., 1256
Elizabeth, 756, 757, 954,
    984, 1255, 1312
Ella, 1621
Ellen S., 1256
Esta E., 1549
Franklin L., 1256, 1275,
    1276
G. Grayson, 1549
George, 1423
John, 1276
Josiah, 1311
Julia, 913, 993
Julia A., 994
Julia K., 994, 1030, 1256
Katherine, 1276
L. H., 1275
Lewis H., 1030, 1255, 1256
Lewis L., 1540
Lucy Catharine, 1549
Luther Pearce, 1549
Madeline, 1177
Maria, 873, 1174, 1189,
    1190, 1255
Mary, 1276, 1549
Mary F., 1030, 1256
Mary Macie, 1549
Maurice A., 1332 , 1549
Maurice Hugh, 1549
Melissa Ellen, 1030
Nancy, 1332
Nicholas, 1030, 1255, 1275
Olive E., 1549
Salina, 1478
Samuel, 1238, 1276
Samuel L., 1030, 1255,
    1256, 1540
Simon, 1549
Stephen, 1030
Stephen R., 994, 1030, 1255,
    1256, 1275, 1479, 1540,
    1621
Susan, 1351
William, 1549
William D., 1549
Bowman, Allie, 946
    Bradley, 1210
    Bradley C., 946
    David M., 946
    Fanny, 946
    George, 1248

John, 1347
John A. E., 868
Laura, 946
Mrs. Jane, 736
Nancy, 1346
Nancy J., 1347, 1348
S. M., 925
Samuel, 946
Sarah, 946
Sarah E., 1129
William C., 946
William H., 946
Boyd, Allen Richards, 1330
    Andrew, 1346
    David, 794
    Nancy, 794
Boyer, Adam, 1479
    Albert, 957
    Albert Aretus, 1479
    Alice E., 797
    Amelia, 1486
    Amelia Margaret, 1486
    Annie, 1479
    Caroline Gertrude, 1479
    Carroll Eugene, 1479
    Catharine, 797
    Charles, 1131
    Charles Wesley, 1479
    Columbus, 1479, 1486,
        1131
    Conrad Arnold, 1479
    Cora Della, 1131
    Cordelia, 1605
    Daniel, 1221
    E——, 1605
    Eldredge C., 1485, 1486
    Eldredge Clark, 1486
    Eliza, 1058
    Elizabeth, 795, 1479
    Emma, 1478
    Emma C., 1467
    Emory, 1101
    Emory E., 1131, 1485
    Emory Eugene, 1479
    Ezra, 1605
    Florence, 1479
    Gabriel, 860
    George, 1336
    Georgetta M., 1584
    Georgetta Malissa, 1479
    Gertrude, 1486
    Greenberry, 796, 1605
    Hanson, 1131, 1173, 1479
    Harry, 1491
    Henry, 1605
    Herman, 1486

Herman Atlee, 1486
Hilda, 869
Hulda, 1221
James, 796, 965, 1382, 1572
Jesse, 1605
John, 795, 796, 879, 1467, 1475, 1479
John C., 894, 1046, 1485, 1486
John Everest, 1453
Julia, 1486
Julia E., 994
Lawson, 1478
L. H., 869
Leslie Slifer, 1486
Lester, 1336
Lora Ellen, 1479
Louisa, 1062, 1189, 1479
Marion, 1336
Martin Luther, 1131
Mary C., 1605
Mary E., 1173
Mary Eleanor, 1131
Merle, 1336
Michael, 1131, 1479, 1485, 1486
Millard Oliver, 1479
Milton, 796
Oliver, 1479
Oliver M., 1584
Paul Wesley, 1479
Pearl, 1475, 1485
Pearl M., 1046
Peter, 796, 797, 1595, 1605
Russell Levin, 1479
Sarah, 796
Thomas, 1578
Wesley, 795, 796
William, 796, 1336
William Edgar, 1479
Boyle, Albert Jones, 1452
Ann, 1451
Brooks, 1548
Catharine, 1451
Charles Bruce, 1451
Daniel, 1451
Daniel Scott, 1451
Dorsey Downey, 1452
Elizabeth Johnson, 1452
George Gather, 1452
Helen, 1451
Henrietta, 1451
Henry, 1451, 1452
Henry S., 1452
Henry Swope, 1452

James, 1451
James Downey, 1452
John, 1451
John Brooke, 1451, 1452
Joseph B., 1451
Joseph Bruce, 1452
Lillie Key, 1452
Margaret G., 1452
Mary, 1451
Mary Claire, 1452
Mary Simm, 1451, 1452
Matilda Swope, 1452
Norman Bruce, 1451
Robert E. Lee, 1452
Bradshaw, John, 1511
LaRu, 1511
Millard, 1511
Brady, H. L., 1191
Brafman, Nettie W., 1392
Brand, Wm. F., 1025
Brandenburg, Abram, 1055
Addie O., 1497
Alice, 849
Alice C., 1469
Alvey, 899
Alvey R., 866-868, 1470
Ann Priscilla, 879
Anna Myrtle, 879
Annie E., 1055
Austin M., 1471
Bertha R., 868
C. Upton, 867, 1470
Calmeda, 1471
Calvin R., 1055
Carrie L., 1055
Catharine, 951
Catherine, 1055
Charles H., 923
Charlotte, 879
Chester R., 867, 868, 1180, 1470
Cleveland LeRoy, 879
Cornelia, 923, 1101
Cyrus P., 867, 1470, 1471
Daniel, 923, 1038, 1055, 1474, 1536, 1552
David, 1055
Earl H., 1471
Edward F., 1055
Effie Clearfield, 879
Eli, 1055
Elizabeth, 879, 1055, 1467
Ellen F., 1536
Elmer, 738
Elmer C., 778, 867, 868, 1470

Elmer G., 1055
Emanuel, 879, 1497
Emily, 879
Emmert G., 1471
Emory M., 923
Erma F., 923
Esta, 1471
Eunice Estella, 879
Eva C., 869
Ezra, 879, 1531
Fannie, 923
Frank C., 1471
Garrison M., 878, 879
Garrison McLain, 879
George E. L. H., 879
George W., 1055
Glenn H., 923
Grace, 867
Grace R., 923
Harriett, 1055
Harry E., 1471
Henry, 866, 867, 951, 1050, 1055, 1059, 1470
Henry L., 1470, 1471
Hephzibah, 879
Ira, 1471
Ira C., 923
Isaac, 923
Jacob, 878, 1055
James, 1055
Jefferson, 1470
Jennie, 1471
Jesse, 878, 879
Joel, 923
John, 867, 878, 1470
John Michael, 923
John N., 1474
John W., 868
Jones, 779
Joseph, 1074
Katie M., 1471
Keefer, 827, 1471
Kerby, 879
Kelley S., 1471
Lemuel, 795, 878, 879
Lemuel Reece, 879
Lewis H., 740, 1055, 1579
Lizzie L., 923, 1552
Lloyd R., 1471
Lucinda, 879, 1474
Lucinda C., 1473
Lydia, 923
M. Lena, 1365
Mahala, 878
Malinda, 1055

Malinda C., 867, 1470
Mamie A., 1471
Marion G., 1054, 1055
Martin R., 867, 1470
Mary, 863, 923, 1272
Mary A., 1055
Mary E., 757, 867, 1470
Mary L., 1474
Mary Manzella, 879
Mary Polly, 878
Mathias, 878, 1055
Matilda, 879
Matilda May, 879
Maurice C., 923, 1359, 1552
Mildred E., 869
Nellie M., 1471
Nettie L., 1471
Norma Oleanda, 879
Oscar C., 1055
Oscar M., 879
Otha C., 1471
Peter, 1485
Priscella, 878
Rebecca, 1379
Rosco H., 869
Roy R., 1471
Russell T., 867
Ruth M., 869
Sadie E., 1471
Sallie V., 1471
Samuel, 757, 866-868, 1379, 1470, 1471
Samuel R., 867
Samuel Rue, 869
Samuel T., 867, 1470, 1471
Sarah, 879
Sarah E., 1471
Sarah Louisa, 878
Stella, 1471
Theodora M., 1055
William, 878, 1325
William E., 879
William H., 868
William W., 1055
Wilmer H., 1471
Brane, Charles Milton, 1218
Comodore I. B., 851
Daniel Ezra, 1218
Esta Grace, 1218
Ezra, 1218
George W., 1218
Henry, 851
John, 1254
Julia, 1218
Lydia Violetta, 1218

Margaret, 851
Mary C., 1218
Mary V., 1218
Rebecca, 1254
Brantley, William T., 696
Brantner, Z. T., 925, 926
Brashear, Belt, 1208
Laura, 1208
Thomas Cook, 1208
Brasheor, Hannah, 1555
Henrietta, 1555
Julia, 1555
Brawner, J. B., 802
Bready, Anna E., 1079
Calvin, 854
Charles E., 1079
Curtis, 854
Curtis B., 1079
Daniel C., 1078, 1079
David, 854
David F., 1079
E. T., 854
E. Tobias, 854, 1079
Edward, 1027
Eugene, 854
George, 854
George A., 854, 1078, 1079
George C., 1079
Guy P., 854
John, 854
John W., 1079
Kitty L., 854
Luther, 854
Luther M., 1079
Mary, 854
Molly, 1079
Naomi, 854
Orman, 1079
Ormond, 854
Richard, 854
Bream, Alice E., 1054
Harriet, 1054
William, 1054
Breckenridge, John C., 696
Breneman, Alice, 1607
Annie M., 1607
Daniel, 1607
Ella, 1607
Harry, 1607
John D., 1607
Lizzie, 1607
Lottie, 1607
Martha E., 1607
Mary, 1607
Monroe, 1607
Myra, 1607

Rhoda, 1607
Sallie, 1607
Brengle, Caroline E., 1560
Catharine, 1607
Charles, 1560
Daniel, 780
Ella C., 959
Emma, 1561
Eve Margaret, 1354
Fanny, 780
Francis, 936, 938, 941
George, 1096, 1561
George W., 959
John, 780, 1560
John W., 780
Lawrence, 780
Lewis, 1560
Margaret, 914
Margaret Eve, 745
Michael, 1156
Nicholas, 940, 1560, 1607
Rachel, 917
Robert, 780
Virginia, 780
William D., 941
William H., 821, 1560
Brenneman, Emma, 1262
Mattie, 1204
Brennerman, Mattie, 1219
Brent, Fanny, 1577
Brewbaker, Charles W., 1054
Brewer, Angeline, 1564
Hattie, 1209
Ida, 929
May G., 929
William G., 929
Brewster, Elizabeth, 1041
L. P., 906
Simon, 866
Bridges, Mrs. Cllifford, 919
Mrs. Robert, 919
Robert, 713
Brien, Ada, 825
Annie I., 825
John, 766
Isabelle, 1457
Lawrence W., 825
Luke T., 1296, 1457
Luke Tiernan, 824, 825
Mary, 825
Robert C., 825
Robert Coleman, 824, 825
William H., 825
Briggs, Caroline, 730
Brightbill, Annie E., 906
Elizabeth, 1335

Samuel L., 906
Brightwell, ——, 1223
  Josephine, 1014, 1222,
    1223
  Lyda, 1243
  Patsy, 1223
  William, 1305
Briscoe, Mrs. James, 809
Brish, A. C., 1603
  Annie, 1603
  Annie V., 1603
  Henry H., 1603
  J. Murray, 1603
  John, 1603
  Mary S., 1603
  Murray, 1603
  Nimrod, 1603
  William H., 1603
Brock, William, 730
Brockley, Lottie, 789
Brodrup, Charles, 1227
  George, 1132
Brooke, ——, 1451
  Baker, 1215
  Dorothy, 1215
  Edward, 1232
  Jane, 1215
  Leonard, 1215
  Robert, 1215
Brookery, Theodore, 1354
Brooks, Daniel, 1355
Broshear, Osborne, 1245
Brosies, Charles, 1035
Brough, Clinton, 1054
Brow, Daisy, 1548
Brown, Alice, 1391
  Alice M., 875, 969
  Alverta, 1179
  Amanda, 874
  Amanda M., 1443
  Andrew, 966
  Andrew J., 763
  Anna, 907, 1411, 1412
  Anna W., 997
  Arbelon, 1391
  Benjamin F., 1202
  Bessie M., 874
  C. Jane, 997
  Caroline, 1472
  Charles, 1534
  Charles A., 1391
  Charles C., 969
  Charles H., 873, 874
  Charles W., 875
  Cornelia A., 708
  David, 1221

E. E., 969
Edward, 1333
Effie L., 1391
Effie O., 874
Elisha, 963
Elizabeth, 874, 1535
Elizabeth Frick, 907
Elizabeth Grace, 964
Emanuel, 1511
Flora, 969
Florence, 1073
Frances, 1449
Francis L., 874, 875
Frank, 1096
George, 822, 1443
George A., 874
George F., 969, 1161
George J., 861, 1359, 1381,
  1541
Gulielma, 813
H. S., 874
Harry N., 755
Helen Miller, 964
Henry, 874, 1535
Henry C., 813
Hester A., 874
Hester E., 875
Ignatius, 1391
J. Newton, 1391
James, 873, 997
Jefferson, 1556
Jeremiah, 873
John, 1274, 1299, 1329,
  1346, 1398, 1485
John D., 969
John H., 874
Josephine, 1535
John M., 899
Joseph, 890, 960, 1019
Joseph B., 873, 874
Joseph L., 969, 1162
Joseph M., 969
Joshua, 798, 1338
Julia G., 875
Laura J., 813
Levi, 1179
Lucy, 1133
Mamie Grace, 963
Martha A., 874
Martha E., 749, 875
Mary, 809, 810, 1084, 1126
Mary C., 1162
Mary J., 969
Mary Magdalene, 1244
Mary N., 874
Mary R., 874

Mathew, 907
Matilda, 1180
Matthew, 1412
Mrs. Mary, 1459
Nannie M., 822
Newton V., 969
Orrae, 762
Payton, 1071, 1521
Pearl, 1434
Peter, 1376
Roger William, 1511
S. Elmer, 997, 1222
Sallie E., 1391
Samuel E., 970, 997
Samuel H., 997
Samuel W., 969, 1161
Servilla, 873
Sophia, 1369, 1370, 1376,
  1377, 1391
Susan, 1180
Titus, 878
Upton, 873
Wilford B., 874
William, 810, 813, 873,
  1084, 1126, 1133,
  1234
William A., 874, 1434
William B., 749
William E., 963
William J., 963
William Osbey, 1307
William Osbie, 970
William Roger, 1511
William T., 848, 969
Browning, ——, 878
  Agnes, 878
  Agnes Matilda, 878
  Algie, 878
  Annie, 865
  Arba, 866
  Archibald, 877
  Arnold, 866
  Avery, 865, 866
  Beriah Hopkins, 865, 866
  Charles Thomas, 1563
  Drusilla, 768
  Earl Harrison, 878
  Eldridge M., 878
  Elizabeth, 878
  Eunice, 865
  Eunice W., 866
  Fannie W., 1076
  Frank, 866
  George, 865
  George W., 865
  Hannah, 865

Harriet Ann, 878
Harriett Charlotte, 878
Harrison McGill, 878
Hephzi Edith, 878
Hiram, 866
Holly, 878
James Monroe, 878
Jedediah, 865
Jesse, 865
John, 865
Jonathan, 1076
Joseph B., 866
Lawrence, 878
Layman, 878
Lucinda, 866
Luther H. H., 878
Luther Henry Harrison, 877
Luther L., 878
Luther Martin, 877
Marie Elmer, 878
Mary, 865
Mary A. , 866
Mary E., 1145
Mattie, 866
Maud, 866
Melville Newton, 878
Morris, 878
Nathaniel, 865
Nellie, 866
Ralph, 865, 866
Raymond Atlas, 878
Richard, 1461
Rosella May, 878
Samuel, 865, 878
Sarah, 865
William, 865, 879
Brubaker, Frederick, 901
Paul, 901
Roy, 901
Virginia, 1234
Bruce, Robert, 1451
Bruchey, Charles, 1261
Frederick, 1261
George W., 1261
Laura, 1261
Mahalia, 1261
Margaret Ellen, 1261
Mary C., 1261
Susan Rebecca, 1261
Sidney A., 1608
Bruck, Roger E., 1306
Brunch, Maria, 871
Bruner, Rebecca, 1213
Brunner, Ann Barbara, 1456
Anna Catharine, 1425
Anna Katherine, 1423

Anna Mary, 752
Caroline, 917
Charlotte, 1250
Edward J., 917
Elias, 916
Elizabeth, 747, 1254, 1255
Ellen C., 917
Ellen Catherine, 736
F. M., 917
Frances, 1332, 1333
George, 1497
Henry, 747, 916
Isaac, 909
Jacob, 736, 916
John, 736, 916, 917
Joseph, 747, 916, 1254,
   1255, 1423, 1425
Lewis A., 917
Maria Elizabeth, 1378, 1415
Mary, 770, 917
Peter, 747, 1254
Rebecca, 1233, 1261, 1438
Valentine S., 916, 917
Virginia, 917
Brust, Bernhart A. H., 1437
Bryan, William J., 1384
   William Jennings, 698
Bryant, Elizabeth, 1305
Bubel, Christian, 1039
Buchanan, James, 1544
   Thomas, 766
Buck, Irvin A., 927
Buckenham, Harry, 730, 1458
Buckey, Ada, 1597
   Ann C., 1130
   Annie, 1143
   Annie Eliza, 1563
   Basil Vernon, 1130
   C. Gordon., 1597
   Carrie May, 1130
   Catharine Elizabeth, 1130
   Charles R., 1130
   Charlotte, 1130
   Clara, 1597
   Clara E., 1529
   D. Princeton, 854
   Daniel H., 1597
   Daniel E., 854, 1068, 1597
   Earl, 1597
   Edna, 1597
   Edward Dorsey, 1130
   Eli, 1130
   Elmer D., 854
   Ezra, 854, 1068, 1130, 1596,
      1597
   Ezra A. C., 1596, 1597

Ezra L., 854
Frank Leslie, 1130
George P., 854, 946, 1068,
   1069, 1132, 1279 ,
   1182 , 1597
George Peter, 1130
George Peter, 1596
George R., 1130
George William, 1118,
   1129, 1130
Guy Elmer, 1130
Gwendolyn, 1597
Hattie McElfresh, 1597
Herman Augustus, 1129,
   1130
Herman A., 1068
Jacob M., 1186
Jennie, 1597
Jennie A., 1279
John C., 1597
John William, 1130
Julia, 1315
Lula K., 854
Maggie, 1597
Margaret, 1596
Maria, 1130
Mary, 780, 1456
Mary L., 1118
Mary Louisa, 1130
Mildred, 1130
Minnie L., 854
Norma, 1130
Paul, 1597
Peter, 1456
Porten Norris, 1597
Richard R. , 1279 , 1529,
   1596
Richard Root, 1596, 1597
Ruth, 1130
Susan, 1130, 1133, 1266,
   1267, 1301, 1506
Susan E., 1130
Valentine, 1378
Vera Grace, 1130
Walter Maynard, 1130
William, 1133, 1266,
   1301, 1506, 1577
William Augustus, 1130
William G., 854
Buckingham, Agnes A., 798
   Alfred, 1556
   Amanda, 798
   B. W., 1243
   Eliza Florence, 798
   Lloyd, 1556
   Ruth Ann, 895

Buffington, Albert, 1239
Buffneyton, Jacob, 1221
Buh——, Silas, 749
Buhman, Elizabeth, 1084
   George, 1084
   Rebecca, 1084
Buhrman, Addie C., 984
   Albert L., 984
   Alfred, 983
   Alfred R., 984
   Alverta M., 863
   Ann, 984
   Cornelia, 863
   David, 863, 886, 984, 1058,
    1180
   Dinah, 873, 874
   E. M. Z., 984
   Elias, 984
   Elias M., 984
   Elsie I., 984
   Emory L., 984
   Hamilton, 1180
   Harry, 983
   Harry S., 984
   Harvey M., 984
   Henry, 863
   Henry, Jr., 983
   Henry, Sr., 983
   Ida, 863
   Isiah H., 863, 864
   Jacob, 863, 874, 886, 899
   John, 983
   Josiah, 863
   Kate A., 984
   Katie, 984
   Lewis A., 863
   Lizzie E., 1372
   Manzella, 984
   Martha E., 863
   Mary J., 984
   Minnie M., 984
   Rebecca, 1083
   Ruth A., 867, 899
   Sida E., 983
   Sida H., 984
   Silas, 952, 983
   Sophia, 863
   Tipton, 983
   Upton, 1372, 757
   Vernon M., 984
   William, 707, 1180
   William H., 863
Bullinger, Emma J., 860
Buntz, William S., 917
Burall, Adam, 862, 863
   Alberta, 1468

Anna, 1468
Bessie, 863
Cameron, 1468
Clara, 1468
Clementine, 1468
Edna Irene, 1468
Emma, 1468
Harvey A., 1468
Henry Oscar, 1468
Irving, 863
Jesse Marcellus, 862, 863
Josephine, 1468
Laura, 1468
Lizzie, 1468
Margaret, 1468
Marshall, 863
May Luetta, 1468
Ruth, 863
Sally, 863
Samuel, 863l, 1468
Samuel P., 1468
Walter, 863
William, 862
Burch, Ida May, 1390
   John, 1029
   Raymond M., 1067
Burdett, Charles M., 1488
Burdette, James, 1325
   Lillie, 1306
   Rebecca, 723
   Webster V., 1540
Bure, Frances, 1219
   Harry, 1219
   Pauline, 1219
   Ray, 1219
   William, 1219
Burgee, Amon, 1228, 1461,
   1462, 1475
   Catherine Eliza, 1476
   Clara E., 1461
   Clyde Elmore, 1476
   E. McSherry, 1475
   Eldridge, 1461
   Eli, 1461
   Eli McSherry, 1461, 1462
   Elinor, 1228, 1286
   F. Lawson, 1228
   Frederick, 1228, 1461, 1475
   Gabriel, 1462
   Gabriel L., 1475
   Gabriel Lewis, 1228
   Grace Elizabeth, 1476
   Guy, 1461
   Hilda E., 1461
   Leanthe Ellen, 1228
   Leathe Ellen, 1475

Leslie Ray, 1476
Letha Ellen, 1461
Lizzie, 1461
Madge, 1462
Martha, 1227
Maud Esther, 1462
Mayme E., 1461
McKendry Riley, 1461
McSherry, 1228
Mehrl, 1069
Miel, 1227, 1228, 1460,
   1461, 1475
Miel Day, 1462
Miel E., 1475
Miel Eldridge, 1228
Nellie Pauline, 1462
Orville Norris, 1461
Osie D., 1228, 1475
Osir Delilah, 1461
Ralph McSherry, 1462
Rebecca, 1228, 1461,
   1475
Singleton, 1285, 1286,
   1460
Sydney Lanier, 1461
Thomas, 1460
Vallie, 1310
William K., 1461
William Keefer, 1460,
   1475
William Kieffer, 1228
Worthington, 1461
Burgenwald, Kossuth, 1391
Burger, Annie Margaret,
   1105
   Annie Rosetta, 1105
   Catharine C., 1318
   Charles Edward, 1105
   George P., 1318
   Henry C., 1105
   William A., 870
   William Alexander, 1105
   William H., 1105
Burgess, Bryce, 1556
   Eva R., 1008
   Joshua, 1248
   Ruth, 716, 1008
   Sarah Virginia, 1248
   Washington, 1008
Burian, Hobert, 1303
Burier, Annie M., 1014
   Philip, 1014
Burk, James, 1411
Burke, Christiana, 1150
   Elizabeth, 1150
   Theodore, 1150

Burkett, Phoebe, 1236
  Sarah Jane, 883, 1589
Burkhart, Albert W., 943
  Albert Wilson, 1397
  Charles, 943
  Charles H., 1397, 1606
  George, 1397
  Margaret, 1397
  Peter, 1397
Burkholder, Annie, 799
  Lulla Vinton, 799
  William H., 799
Burkitt, Henry, 1566
Burnett, Margaret, 1068, 1360
  Robert, 1360
Burns, Edward, 1256
  Eleanor, 1003
  Eleanora, 1256, 1311, 1312
  Jacob, 827, 1606
  Lornie, 1058
Burnside, Ann, 915
  John Nelson, 915, 916
  Joseph, 916
  Olivia, 762
Burrall, Cora Edith, 731
  Henry Oscar, 1467
  Jesse M., 731
  Mary Lucinda, 731
  Susan, 1245
  Walter E., 731
Burrell, Caroline, 1152
Burrier, Ada Cordelia, 1261
  Allen J., 1533
  Amanda E., 1533
  Amy Lease, 1533
  Anna Belle, 1260
  Barbara, 1252
  Barbara Ellen, 1260
  C. Frank, 703, 1537
  Calvin, 1537
  Carrie Lucinda, 1261
  Charles Daniel, 1537
  Charles William, 1260
  Clara L., 1260
  Clarence Calvin, 1260
  Daniel, 1537
  Daniel Luther, 1260
  Darwin Denton, 1261
  David Jesse, 1260
  Edith Grace, 1537
  Ella Lavinia, 1260
  Emerson, 1533
  Fanny May, 1261
  Fanny Rebecca, 1537
  George, 1260
  George Edward, 1260

George M., 1260
  Gideon L., 1533
  Harry, 1260
  Helen Virginia, 1537
  Howard Milton, 1260
  Ida Bell, 1533
  Jacob, 1533
  Jacob S., 1566
  James Levi, 1260
  Jennie Elizabeth, 1261
  John, 1252, 1533
  John Edward, 1261
  John Howard, 1537
  John Philip, 1260
  John William, 1260, 1261
  Jonas, 1534
  Jonas L., 1260
  Josiah, 1260
  Kate, 1531
  Katie, 1533
  Lavinia, 1260
  Mahalia, 1260
  Mary, 1537
  Mary Edna, 1533
  Mary Rebecca, 1261
  Mayme Lenore, 1260
  Murray, 1260
  Nannie Hoke, 1537
  Naomi Catharine, 1537
  Nellie May, 1537
  Nettie Rose, 1537
  Nevin S., 1403
  Pearl May, 1533
  Robert Wesley, 1260
  Sally, 1533
  Samuel Robert, 1537
  Sarah, 1260
  Wesley, 1512
  William Hanson, 1261
Burton, Grace, 1293
  W. Rodney, 1503
Burucker, Lewis, 1359
Buse, Mary J., 1459
Bush, Catharine, 909
  Clara, 922
  Elizabeth, 1134
Bushey, Bertha, 1048
  Elizabeth S., 1367, 1368
  Franklin, 1048
Bushnell, Charlotte, 703
Bussard, Alma Elizabeth, 1383
  Amy Viola, 1383
  Annie Kate, 1541
  Annie V. C., 1382
  Benjamin P., 1359
  Carrie Susan, 1542

Catherine, 861, 1541
  Charles L., 1382, 1383,
    1542
  Charlotte, 961
  Danie(l), 861
  Daniel, 1359, 1381, 1541
  Daniel L., 1382, 1469,
    1542
  Daniel W., 1474
  David, 1474
  David F., 860, 861,1541
  Earl Albert, 1384
  Elizabeth, 1270, 1474
  Elmer Franklin, 1383
  Emma V. F., 1382
  Enos, 861, 1359, 1381,
    1541
  Ezra Lee, 861, 1381
  Fannie Rebecca, 1383
  George, 800, 1359, 1381
  George H., 1359, 1360
  George Hiram, 1359
  George Washington, 861,
    1541
  Gideon, 768, 1359
  Gideon B., 861, 1381,
    1541
  Gorman Santee, 1541
  Hannah, 967
  Harry E. L., 1383
  Howard Wesley, 1360
  Ida Estella, 1541
  Ida May, 1382, 1542
  Ira B., 1359
  Isaac, 1474
  J. W., 759
  James O., 726, 1126, 1300
  James Oliver, 861, 1541
  John, 899, 1359
  John A., 861, 1541
  John E., 1349
  John Franklin, 861
  John H., 1359
  John W., 965, 1300, 1370,
    1381, 1382, 1542,
    1572
  John Wesley, 860, 861,
    960, 1381, 1541, 1542
  Joseph H., 1382, 1542
  Lawson, 1474
  Lee, 1359
  Lewis, 861, 1359, 1381,
    1541
  Loretta C., 861
  Lydia, 861, 1359, 1381,
    1541

Margaret Catharine, 1359
Martha A., 923, 1359
Martin, 800, 1359
Martin T., 798
Mary, 1359, 1407, 1541
Mary Catharine, 861, 1381, 1541
Mary Charlotte, 1542
Mary Elizabeth, 1382
Mary M., 1474
Maurice Luther, 1384
Melvin F., 1383
Nellie, 1101
Newton A. S., 1382, 1383, 1542
Newton S., 849
Olive, 1541
Peter, 861, 1359, 1381, 1541
Peter E., 1006, 1361, 1382, 1383, 1542
Peter H., 961, 1428
Peter Hanson, 861, 1359, 1381-1383, 1541, 1542
Rosa M. C., 1382
Ruth Amanda, 1382 , 1542
Samuel, 861, 923, 1014, 1359, 1360, 1381, 1541
Samuel D., 740, 1382, 1542, 1579
Samuel M., 861, 1359, 1381
Samuel Peter, 1359
Samuel R., 1541
Sarah A., 1359
Savilla, 1527
Sophia, 738, 861, 899, 1127, 1359, 1381, 1541
Stanley R., 1360
Stella C., 861
Susan, 861, 899, 1300, 1307, 1309, 1343, 1359, 1381, 1541
Susan A. M., 961
Susan Ann, 768, 1382, 1542
Susan E., 861, 1381, 1541
Titus T., 768
Ulstey, 861, 1381, 1541
Wesley, 1359
William A., 1383
William H., 758, 1382
Butler, Arthur R., 1413
Benjamin, 772
Dennis, 1305
Elsie, 1613

James Henry, 1461
Lula May, 1461
Mary, 1298, 1495
Butts, Annie M., 1485
Bessie May, 1485
Beulah LaRue, 1485
Carlton M. C., 1485
Charles Earl, 1485
Charles H., 1484, 1485
Isaiah, 1484
J. Franklin, 1485
James, 1484
James O., 1485
Joseph, 1484
Minnie K. L., 1485
Raisen, 1484
Butz, Mrs. Samuel A., 1544
Buxton, Ada, 1034, 1310
Amy, 1034
Basil, 1034
Brook, 1034
Brook, the 2nd, 1034
Carrie B., 1034
Edgar, 1034
Eugene, 1034
Frank, 1034
James, 1034
John, 1034
Lizzie, 1034
Mary, 1034, 1555
Samuel, 975, 1034
Susan, 1034
Susan P., 893
Thomas, 1034
Upton, 1034
William, 1034
Byerly, Charles, 927, 928
Davis, 915
George K., 819
Henry, 927
J. David, 1315
J. Davis, 1105
Jacob, 927, 1047
John Davis, 927, 928
John F., 928
Mary C., 915
Mary Catharine, 928
Rebecca, 1387
Susan, 1298, 1495
Byers, Blanche G., 860
Caroline, 860
Carrie J., 860
Catherine, 860
Charles Robert, 860
David, 860
David A., 1612, 1613

David Ezra, 1613
Edward, 1613
Eliza Jane, 1613
Elizabeth, 860, 1612
Ellen, 860, 1613
Frances Anna, 860
George, 860
George Franklin, 1613
George G., 860
Gilbert G., 860
Grace L., 860
Harry Bryan, 860
Henry, 1612
Jacob, 860
Jacob K., 860
Jesse Ernest, 1613
John, 860, 1612, 1613
John Henry, 860
Joseph, 860
Joshua, 860
Luther , 860
Margaret Ann, 1613
Margaret E., 860
Mary, 1612, 1613
Mary Janette, 860
Maud E., 860
Michael, 860, 1612
Peter, 1612
Polly, 860
Samuel, 1613
Sarah, 860
Susan, 859, 1612
Thomas, 1613
William Henry, 1613
Byrd, Alfred H., 1544
Jane, 1551
William, 1551
Byrne, William, 803
Cadwallader, Anna Maria, 1343, 1386
Cain, Joseph J., 1326
Caine, Calvin, 855
Callahan, Rose, 1231
Callas, Mary, 796
Calvert, Ann, 1215
Cecelius, 1216
Charles, 832, 1210
Frederick, 1210
George, 1215
Leonard, 697, 1215
Campbell, ——, 1323
Abner, 1571
Aeneas, 920
Amelia, 1531
Anne, 920
Bonaparte, 866

Elizabeth, 1508, 1571
Margaret E., 883, 884
R. H., 851
Sarah, 865
Sarah Elizabeth, 866
Susan, 1282
William, 884
Camwell, Lizzie, 1203
Carl, David, 875
Ellen C., 875
Mary Ellen, 1048
Carlin, Frank, 1575
Carlisle, C. A., 925, 1590
Carrie, 1576
Charles, 1576
John S. , 1211
Laura, 1576
Mary E., 1211
Robert, 1576
Carmack, Alice, 1514
Ephraim, 1514
Hanson, 1514
James, 1237
John, 1035, 1141, 1514
Joshua, 1514
Margaret, 1514
Mary Catharine, 1514
Sarah, 1514
Sophia, 1514
William, 1270, 1237, 1284,
1514, 1518, 1619
Carmock, William, 1558
Carnahan, Elizabeth, 1152
Carney, John, 1525
Carpenter, Andrew Jackson,
898
Annie E., 898
Clarence Stanley, 898
Flora Elizabeth, 898
Franklin Buchanan, 898
Grover Nelson, 898
Hattie Jane, 898
John C., 898
John Markell, 898
Mabel Floyd, 898
Marcia, 770
Margaret Ann, 898
Mark C., 898
Martha, 898
Martin Flook, 1229
Mary, 898
Mary Edna, 898
Mat, 852
Maud Lillian, 898
Peter J., 898
Roger Ruley, 898

Carr, Amos, 1064
Isabella, 892
John, 812
Mary, 934
Thomas, 892
Carrel, Christian, 804
Carroll, Charles, 914
Carry, Joseph, 891
Cartee, Charles F., 1617
Frisby G., 1348
Jennie C., 1348
Carter, Albert, 1231
Alcelia, 1231
Anna, 1059
Barbara A., 1339
Bessie, 1231
Charity, 1231
Charles, 1231
Charles H., 1339
Cora, 1231
Edith, 1231
Elizabeth Jane, 1231
Emily Florence, 1339
Emma, 1073
Fanny, 1231
Frank, 1339
Frisby, 1373
Grace, 1338, 1339
Grafton, 1231
Henry, 1059, 1231, 1339,
1545
John Milton, 1231
Kate Clay, 1339
Laura, 1058
Laura Jane, 1339
Lucinda, 1231, 1545, 1546
Margaret E., 1339
Mary C., 1339
Milton, 1231, 1235, 1516
Milton G., 1546
Milton, Jr., 1231
Myrtie, 1231
Olivia, 938, 1231
Robert Hugh, 1231
Susie, 1339
Carty, Alton B., 845, 881
Arthur C., 881
Charles C., 710, 881
Charles P., 845, 881
Clarence C., 845, 880, 881
Cora M., 881
Daisy E., 845, 881
Eleanor G., 881
Frank R., 881
Harry E., 881
Joseph W. L., 845, 880, 881

Joseph W. L. , 844
Margaret A., 881
Mary Virginia, 845
May, 881
Nannie Roberta, 845
Ruth, 881
William A., 881
William P., 844
William Proctor, 880
Cartzendafner, Virginia, 716
William, 716
Carwood, McClane, 1067
Cash, E. O., 1597
John C., 1232
Lewis, 846
Truman, 1597
Zula, 1597
Cashour, Charles W. F., 793,
1253
Emily, 1204, 1310
George A., 1130
Margaret, 1546
William, 1546
Cassell, Catharine, 1437
David, 1535
Nancy, 1534, 1535
Olivia, 1054
Cassin, John, 745, 1354
Casso, Libie, 1324
Castle, Annie Viola, 1340
Bessie, 1481, 1576
C. Estella, 851
C. Phillips, 851
Catharine, 728
Catherine, 727
Charles, 1095
Charles A., 850, 851
Cora B., 851
Cordelia, 851
Daisy, 1078
Daniel, 850, 851, 1340
Daniel O., 1340
David, 1509
Edgar C., 1340
Elizabeth, 1340
Emma F., 851
Frank A., 851
George T., 851
Henry, 1340
Ida V., 851
John, 1005, 1045, 1299,
1605
John Albert, 1340
John Calvin, 1340
John W., 1540
Joseph, 1340

Leonard, 728
Lewis O., 851
Luella, 1340
Mahlon, 1340
Malinda, 1340
Martin, 932, 1332
Mary E., 851
Matilda, 1120
Nancy, 1509
Otho, 1340
Randolph, 1340
Thomas, 850, 851
Vandelia, 1299
Wilhelmina, 1340
Wilhelmina B., 1340
William, 1340
William E., 851
Caton, Jeannette, 914
Richard, 914
Catrow, Joseph, 1400
Lewis Paul D., 1400
Caulliflower, William, 1620
Causten, Josephine, 744
Ceas, Nathaniel, 1513
Seraphine Elizabeth, 1513
Cease, Charles Allen, 966
Cloyd, 966
Samuel, 966
Cecil, Agnes, 933
Amanda, 915
Catharine, 915
Levin, 915, 933
Mary, 915
Morga, 1335
Morgan, 769
Samuel, 915
Chamberlain, Edith, 1616
Chambers, Alco, 1574
B. D., 919
B. Duvall, 919
B. T., 1099
Eleanor McGill, 919
Mrs. Lottie Belt, 919
Chaney, Dorcas, 1434
Nathan, 1326
Chapline, Ann Elizabeth, 914
George Markell, 915
Harry Eugene, 913, 914
Isaac, 913
Isaac Thomas, 913, 914
James Augustus, 914
John, 913
Joseph, 914, 1403, 1404
Laura Schley, 1583
Margaret, 914
Moses, 914

Rosa, 914
Rose Schley, 1583
Thomas, 745, 1354, 1583
Thomas A., 914, 928
Thomas Augustus, Jr., 915
William, 913, 914
William, 2nd, 913
Charlton, Earl, 1565
Olivia, 1423
Susan, 1483
Chase, Jane, 1242
Janet, 818
Salmon P., 818, 1242
Chatman, Laura, 1203
Chelecker, Christina, 1290
Cheneworth, Martha, 1557
Chew, J. H., 1345
Jeanette Benson, 1345
John, 1581
John, Sr., 1582
John H., 798, 1345
John Hamilton, 1344
Mary, 1581, 1582
Mary R., 1130
Rosa Dulany, 1345
S. C., 1213
Thomas J., 1345
Chilcote, Delilah, 1354, 1355
Elijah, 1355
Childs, A. K., 1232
Chiles, C. C., 1291
Mary Carr, 1291
Chislin, Reverdy, 704
Chisolm, J. J., 1213
Chissell, George, 1137
Chiswell, Jemima Eleanor,
781-783
John A., 782
John Augustus, 783
Sarah Newton, 783
Thomas, 1115
Christ, Eliza Ann, 1606, 1607
Grafton B., 947
William, 947
Clagett, Cynthia Norwood, 865
Jesse, 865
Jesse C., 864, 865
Margaret B., 1038
Nathan, 878
Thomas, 864, 865, 1038
Claggett, Ann, 1073
Ann Mary, 1282
Ann Perry, 1281
Edward, 1344
Eliza M. R., 783, 1073
Elizabeth, 1256

Genevieve Louise, 1282
Honorie Martin, 1281
John Fraser, 1345
John Heugh Martin, 1345
Laura Eliza, 1344
Louis Benoit Keene, 1345
Louisa, 1259
Martha Matilda Ann, 1345
Mary Martin, 745, 1281
Mary Maud, 1282
Mary Priscilla, 1344
Minnie West, 1345
Richard, 1344
Robert, 1073
Samuel, 1344, 1345
Samuel, Jr., 1345
Sarah, 1344
Sarah M., 948, 949
Sophia Eliza, 1345
Sophia Genevieve, 1344
Thomas, 1259, 1344
Thomas J., 745
Thomas John, 949, 1281,
1282, 1344
Thomas John Chew, 1345
Thomas West, 1345
Thomas West, Jr., 1345
Violetta, 1344
Claiborne, William, 920
Clance, Mary, 1070, 1520
Clantz, Mary, 1071
Clapp, Albert, 909
Henry Clay, 909
Robert E., 1258
William S., 909
Clark, James C., 748, 825
Mary, 823, 824
Sherman, 1347
Clarke, James C., 747, 1254
Richard, 836
Clary, Alice, 1239
Cordelia, 1437
Dora, 1239
Fanny, 1239
Frederick, 1324
Henderson, 1555
Henrietta, 1556
Ida, 1239
Jesse E., 733
Jesse Edgar, 1239
Jesse T., 1239
John, 1122
John M., 1410
Lina, 1239
Lizzie, 1239, 1324
Mary Ann, 1076

Mrs. F. S., 1557
Nathan, 1557
Ollive Irene, 1326
R. W. , 1326
William H. H., 1076
Clay, Annie, 1463
Calvin, 1463
Catherine, 1310
Charles, 1547
Cinderella, 1463
Coral, 878
Cornelius, 1463
Edna, 1546
Ellen, 1463
Eveline, 1463
Grafton, 1462, 1463
Henry, 824, 1116, 1462,
1463
Jackson, 878
Jesse, 1217
Joanna, 1463
John, 1546
John N., 1326
Joseph W., 1310
Lina, 1547
Linda, 878
Louisa, 1463
Mabel, 878
Margaret, 1547
Martha J., 1326
Mary, 1547
Milton, 1463
Nellie, 1463
Nimrod, 1463
Sadie, 1547
Stella May, 1547
Sterling, 878
Susan, 1463
Thelma, 878
Wilanna, 1463
Wilbur, 1546
William, 1547
Zebulon, 1462, 1463
Claybaugh, Catharine, 1245,
1246
Cleaver, Sarah, 1594
Cleggett, Jane, 972
Thomas, 972
Clem, Altah S., 1023, 1598
Augusta, 724, 1616
Bradley, 1022
Bradley E., 1022, 1023,
1598
Catherine, 1023, 1598
Chester G., 1023, 1598
David, 1023, 1598

Earl J. H., 1023
Florence, 1023, 1598
George, 1284
George J., 1023, 1598
Harvey S., 1023, 1598
Jacob, 1022, 1597
John H., 1022, 1023, 1597,
1598
Lillian, 1023
Margaret, 1023, 1598
Mary C., 1023, 1598
Miranda, 1284, 1519
Samuel E., 1023, 1598
Thomas M., 1023, 1598
Walter G. H., 1023, 1598
Clemens, Samuel L., 1331
Clements, Caroline, 836
Clemm, Catherine, 1300
Miranda P., 1527
William, 1300
Clemson, C. C., 734
Emily, 1076
Frank C., 734
Frederick Wilson, 734
James, 945
John Walter, 854
Margaret, 847
Nicholas H., 1270
Paul Hamilton, 734
Cleveland, Grover, 728, 1096,
1225
Clinck, G. F., 1477
Cline, Adam A., 1467
Alexander, 1087
Alice V., 1469
Amanda C., 1308, 1529,
1530
Anna Grace, 1088
Barbara, 1530
Benjamin, 827
Bessie S., 1088
C. E., 959, 1346
Carrie J., 1469
Caspar, 1016
Casper, 1087, 1088
Casper E., 1088
Casper E., Jr., 1088
Charles L., 1468, 1469
Charles R., 1469
Clarence E., 1469
Elias, 1530
Elinor Frost, 1088
Elizabeth, 826, 1530, 1605,
1606
George, 1530
George T., 1016, 1017, 1087,

1088
Harriet, 1087
Harry T., 1469
Hezekiah, 1530
Jacob E., 1469
John, 1087, 1530
John F., 1469
John L., 1469
John W., 810, 1530
Laura E., 1469
Lawson, 1530
Lawson C., 1308
Lewis, 1177, 1530
Lewis A., 1469
Maggie, 1534
Margaret, 1088
Mary, 1346, 1469, 1530
Mary L., 1016
Mary Louisa, 1087
Nicholas O., 1087, 1088
P. H., 1173
Philip, 826, 1468, 1530
Philip H., 1469
Rebecca, 1530
Rebecca D., 1467
Ruby M., 1088
Ruth M., 1088
Samuel, 1530
Sarah, 1530
Sophia, 1530
Thomas, 1468, 1469,
1530
Victor R., 868
Virginia N., 1088
William, 1087
William H., 1469
Clingham, Lewis, 1548
Clopper, Sophia C., 1405
Clory, Frederick S., 1344
James B., 1018, 1365
Nathan, 1344
Cloud, Catharine, 1614
Clough, Serena, 916
Cloyd, Mary, 1092
Clugston, Robert, 837, 1455
Clutz, Bertie, 831
Harry E., 823
Coale, James M., 693, 1450
James Mc., 1452
Richard, 1449
Sally, 1449, 1450, 1452
Coatam, Thomas, 1404
Coblentz, Albert Martin,
1536
Alice, 1289
Alice G., 985

Ann Maria, 1289
Ann Mary, 1100
Anna R., 1536
Ava A., 776
Benjamin Carlton, 1288
Bertha F., 776, 952
Bertha Frances, 1080
Bertha Francis, 1289
Byron George, 1290
C. Frank, 985
Calvin R., 776, 923, 1552, 1584
Carrie L., 1290
Catharine, 1288, 1378, 1379, 1411, 1425
Charles C., 732, 984, 985
Charles H., 776
Charles Henry, 1288-1290, 1536, 1552, 1584
Charles Herman, 1289
Charles William, 1289
Cleantha R., 776
Colantha, 1584
Cornelia, 1288
Cornelia A., 1283
Daniel Perry, 1289
David, 1100
Dorothy Elizabeth, 1290
E. Kathleen, 985
E. L., 1028
Edward Franklin, 1289
Edward L., 776, 952, 1080, 1584
Edward P., 953
Elinor, 1289
Elizabeth, 1006, 1037, 1059, 1283, 1288, 1289, 1378, 1379
Elizabeth J., 1100, 1103, 1104, 1125
Ellen Ann, 1288
Elmer L., 1289
Elmira, 1289
Emory L., 776, 911, 952, 1375
Ethel R., 985
Eugene, 908
Eva, 911, 1375, 1584
Eva Ruth, 1289
Eve, 1288, 1379
Fannie C., 1051
Frances, 1288
George, 1310
George G., 776, 791, 908, 1356, 1361, 1430, 1584
George H., 908

George Richard, 1289
Germanus, 908
H. B., 1038
Harmon, 776, 952
Helen R., 985
Henry, 761, 1288, 1289, 1379, 1446, 1536
Henry Milton, 908
Henry Philip, 1289
Herman, 1236, 1288, 1290, 1536, 1552, 1584
Horace B., 1289
Imogene, 1300
Imogene Frances, 1289
Jacob, 1037
Jennie M., 776, 952
Joanna, 1289
John, 1037, 1104, 1125, 1283, 1288, 1378, 1379, 1411
John Calvin, 1289
John Harmon, 1290
John P., 1006, 1289
John Philip, 776, 952, 1288, 1289, 1584
John Vernon, 1552
Joseph Daniel, 1289
Katherine Reid, 953
Lena, 1091, 1288, 1361, 1538
Lenore, 1486
Leslie N., 1552
Lewis P., 1317
Lewis Philip, 1288, 1289
Lewis Philip, Jr., 1289
Lizzie Adeline, 1537
Lloyd E., 1288
Lloyd Grayson, 1584
Lora E., 1290
Louisa A. C., 1379
Lucinda F., 1080
Magdalena, 1379
Mahalia, 1584
Mahalia Ann Rebecca, 1437
Mahalia F., 776 , 1293
Mahlon Calvin, 908
Margaret, 951, 1050, 1059
Martha, 1289
Martin C., 923, 1536
Martin Calvin, 1288
Mary Edith, 1290
Mary Elizabeth, 908
Mary Ellen, 776, 1584
Mary Manzella, 1584
Mary Ruth, 777
Maurice, 1289

Maurice Daniel, 1536
Millard C., 1552
Miriam Amy, 777
Morris Henry, 1289
Naomi F., 777
Oliver P., 984, 1474
Oliver P. Jr., 985
Oliver Z., 776, 1290, 1552, 1584
Ora Elizabeth, 1289
Oscar B., 776, 952, 953, 1549
Oscar P., 985
Perry, 827
Peter, 984, 1255, 1288, 1378
Philip, 776, 791, 908, 952, 1085, 1288, 1290, 1293, 1356, 1361, 1375, 1379, 1430, 1552, 1584
Philip Oliver, 1584
Richard, 1289
Rosco Zacharias, 1584
Rose C., 1317
Rose Mary, 1289
Ruth, 1289
Sarah, 1288, 1289, 1379, 1428
Sophia, 908
Thomas Theodore, 908
Victor C., 1536
Walter B., 1584
Walter C., 1536
William Emory, 908
William H., 1536
William Keefer, 1584
Cochran, Bertha Ellen, 929
Cornelius, 929
Julia A., 913
Louis, 994
Malinda Catherine, 1283
Margaret, 1422, 1503
William, 1503
Colbert, William T., 1161
Cole, Charles, 1395
Sarah, 1013
Coleman, Jennie, 1071, 1521
Coles, Eliza R., 1263
Colgate, Jennie, 1207
Collier, Vernon, 1565
Colliflower, Albert, 837, 1455
Barney, 1238
Clarence Wilson, 1239
Edith, 1239
Elizabeth, 1588

Elmer E., 1238
Hazel M., 707
Henry, 1123
Herbert, 1460
Jago, 1238
John, 1238
John T., 707, 1238
Joseph Howard, 1239
Laura M., 707
Laura May, 1239
Lloyd, 1239
Lloyd Ross, 1239
Lottie D., 707
Lula, 707
Lula Catharine, 1239
Mary Isabel, 1239
Mary Jane, 1238
Michael J., 1238
Ross, 1239
Ruth, 1239
Samuel, 1238
Susan Elizabeth, 1238
Viola, 1239
William F., 1064
Collins, Ella, 1597
Mary, 1239
Samuel, 1597
Comfer, Mollie, 1602
Compher, Christiana, 1113
Christiana S., 1108, 1114
Elmer, 931
Hannah A., 970
John, 891, 1108, 1114
Samuel, 970
Conard, John, Jr., 789
Susan, 813
Condon, Catherine, 941, 942
D. John, 941
James W., 1556
John, 942
Nimrod, 1547
Ruth, 1547
Susan, 1547
Zachariah, 1555
Conger, Edward, 1359
Conklin, William, 881
Conkling, Roscoe, 852
Conley, Charles Henry, 848
C. H., 699
Charles Henry, 849
Charles William, 848
Clara B., 848
Edgar Thomas, 848
Helen Abell, 849
Helen Mary, 848
Thomas Y., 848

Connard, Joseph, 1460
Conner, Atvill, 1097, 1098,
1205
Atvill, Jr., 1097
Catherine, 1097
Cora V., 1097
Dorotha, 1097
Evelin, 1097
Fannie R., 1097
George Atvill, 1098
James, 1097, 1445
John, 1097
Morgan, 1097
Polly, 1097
Rebecca, 1097
Samuel, 1097
Thomas B., 1097
William, 1097
Conrad, August M., 717
Conway, Margaret C., 954
Richard, 1275
William, 955
Cook, Andrew A., 1503
Annie, 1488
Christiana V., 1488
Edna M., 1488
Edward, 1057
Frank, 1488
George, 1122
George A., 1503
George E., 1487, 1488
George E., Jr., 1488
George H., 1503
George W., 1068
Henrietta, 1488
Isaac S. A., 1503
John, 1207
John W., 1364, 1488
Jonathan F., 1488
Lester E., 1488
Louisa, 1488
Mary, 1488
Matilda, 1488
Raymond F. B., 1488
Robert G., 1503
Susan C. E., 1488
William F. N., 1488
Cookerly, Jennie, 1297, 1366
Lewis C., 1297
Virginia, 1361, 1362
Cookson, John C., 1563
Cooledge, George R., 761
Cooper, Charles, 969
Savilla, 1434
Sophia, 1434
Cope, Jacob Erdman, 907

Copeland, Alice, 931
George W., 931
Copelin, Frances V., 1349
Copland, Fannie, 850
Cork, Charles, 830
Cornell, Ann, 1367
Edward B., 1061
Corry, James, 1108, 1114
Coshgan, A. B., 1211
Cost, Elizabeth, 977
Frederick, 1409, 1414
Jacob H., 917, 1614
Mary E., 1316
Mary Irene, 917
Thomas J., 1316
Courlander, M., 1428
Covell, John, 1555
Cover, Cassandra, 1438
Enos, 1438
J. H., 1394
John, 1614
Minne B., 1053
Nellie, 1285
William F., 1053
Cox, Elizabeth, 1194
William, 1194
Cozens, Albert Owen Casper,
1088
Anna Winifred, 1088
Bessie B., 1088
W. J., 1088
William J., 1088
Crabbs, Elizabeth, 816
John, 816
Mary, 1394
Crall, Henry, 794
Cramer, A. N., 1108
Absalom, 1485
Ada Mary, 1268
Agnes, 1112, 1268, 1269
Airy May, 1134
Alice, 1376, 1530
Alice Josephine, 1270
Alva B., 746
Amanda, 1484, 1485
Amos, 812
Amy, 1134
Andrew, 1200, 1315,
1507, 1511
Andrew N., 746
Ann Rebecca, 1205
Anna Barbara, 812
Annabel, 1268
Annie, 883, 1270
Annie Louise, 1302
Baxter, 1268

Belva A., 764
Belva E., 976
Bessie, 1270, 1302
Bettie, 881
Bradley T. Johnson, 1270
Catharine Reynolds, 929
Charles, 1133
Charles Christian, 1112, 1268, 1269
Charles G., 929, 1232
Charles Henry, 1270
Charles Leslie, 1267, 1507
Clarence, 1266, 1301, 1507
Cora, 1532
D. K., 1268
David, 929, 1111, 1163, 1268, 1269, 1315
David J., 1135
David Kemp, 1111, 1112, 1268
E. L., 792
Edith, 1134
Edna, 1134
Edward, 1133, 1266, 1301, 1506, 1507
Edward D., 1145
Elfie I, 883
Elfie I., 1302
Eli, 935
Elizabeth, 935, 1235
Elizabeth May, 1270, 1302
Elsie, 1134, 1262
Emma, 1133
Emma Barbara, 1266, 1301, 1507
Emory Kemp, 1267
Etta, 1112, 1268
Eva, 1616
Ezra, 1111, 1112, 1212, 1268, 1269, 1294, 1342
Ezra D., 1133, 1266, 1267, 1498, 1506, 1507
Ezra Lewis, 1111, 1112, 1267-1269
Floyd A., 1434
Frank Ridgely, 1267
Franklin, 1219
Frederick Worman, 928, 929
George, 883, 929, 1232, 1493
George H., 1135, 1270
George Henry, 1133
George L., 710, 928, 929, 1232, 1357, 1424
George W., 881

Glenn, 1134
Guy Ramsburg, 1267
H. M., 1320
Haller, 1597
Harriet R., 929, 1232
Harry Emery, 1507
Harry Ralph, 1267
Harvey, 1302
Helen, 1268
Henrietta, 1268
Henry, 1111, 1266, 1267, 1269, 1301, 1376, 1506, 1507
Herbert, 1236
Hilda, 1266, 1301, 1507
Hugh, 1597
J. Henry, 1112, 1205, 1268, 1269
Jacob, 1336, 1532
James Houck, 1232
Jeremiah H., 1112, 1268
Jeremiah Henry, 1269, 1270
Johannes, 1232
Johannus, 929
John, 1111, 1267-1269, 1578
John D., 929, 1232, 1268
John David, 1434
John E., 1268
John George, 1111, 1267, 1269
John Philip, 1112, 1268, 1269
John William, 1133
Joseph, 1577
Josephus Elijah, 1112, 1268, 1269
Katharine Reynolds, 1232
Laura Nettie, 1266, 1301, 1507
Lewis, 1000, 1111, 1251, 1267, 1269
Lewis Glenn, 1268
Louisa, 1133, 1214
Margaret, 812
Margaret A., 812
Margaret Ellen, 1118, 1119
Margaret Jeanette, 1259
Mary, 1134
Mary A., 1145
Mary Agnes, 1212
Mary Alice, 1266, 1301, 1507
Mary Annabel, 1434
Mary Elizabeth, 1270
Mary L., 1080
Mary M., 1437

Mary Reynolds, 929
Mary Rosanna, 702
Maud, 1302
Maud M., 1427
Minnie, 1266, 1301, 1507
Morris, 1266, 1301, 1507
Mrs. Jacob, 1527
Newton, 1266, 1301, 1507
Noah, 1133, 1302
Noah E., 929, 1091, 1231, 1232, 1530
Oscar, 1134
Philip, 1130
Phoebe, 709, 1266, 1301, 1341, 1342, 1507, 1604
Richard R. T, 1112
Richard T., 1268
Robert, 1109
Robert Lee, 1270
Rush, 1266, 1301, 1507
S. Clinton, 929, 1232
Sadie Elizabeth, 1267, 1507
Samuel, 1130, 1133, 1266, 1267, 1301, 1506
Steiner, 1266, 1301, 1507
Theodore, 1516
Theodore F., 1287
Thomas, 1270
Thomas L., 1302
W. A., 1267
William A., 929, 1111, 1232, 1269
William A. , 1267, 1533, 1597
William H., 1219
William J., 976
William Jacob, 1112, 1268, 1269
William L., 929
William Thomas, 1112, 1268, 1269
Willie Clayton, 1434
Zoe Amelia, 1267
Zoie Ameilia, 1507
Zoir, 1498
Crampton, Annie, 1478
B. P., 1032
Bessie, 1478, 1479
Charles, 1478
Claude, 1478
Elizabeth, 1478
Elmer, 1478
Emma, 1478

Floyd J., 1238
Harry, 1238
Howard, 1478
James F., 1238, 1478
Jennie, 1238
Jennie E., 1540
Jennie Elizabeth, 1478
John, 1478
John C., 1238
John D. G., 1345
John Heugh, 1345
Joseph, 1478
Joshua, 1238, 1478, 1540
Josiah, 1478
Kate, 1478
Katie, 1238
Kieffer, 1478
Luther, 1478
Melvin, 1478
Nancy, 1478
Oliver, 1478
Oscar, 1345
Sarah, 1174, 1478
Susan, 1478
William, 1478
Crapster, Gustavus, 1263
Craver, Caroline, 1525
  Charles E., 1399
  Clara V., 1049
  Elizabeth, 1399
  George, 1508
  Margaret, 1525
  Minnie, 1508
  Simon P., 1049
Crawford, Alice, 718
  Basil, 1073
  Blanche S., 850
  Bruce L., 850
  David, 718
  Emma, 831
  Ethel L., 850
  George H., 850
  George M., 850
  Harriet Thomas, 1072, 1073
  Helen K., 850
  John H., 832
  John S., 1326
  Lewis D., 850
  Maud M., 850
  Olive, 884
  Sarah E., 1227
  Thomas, 892
  Thomas H., 850
  Thomas L., 831
  William, 1471
Creager, Anna, 1436

Carroll, 1436
Daniel, 1448
Edwin C., 1436
Effie, 1545
Ellen, 1436
J. Frederick, 1436
J. Howard, 1436
James, 1436
John, 1436
John M., 1436
John Wesley, 1436
Leo M., 1436
Lottie, 1545
Lottie E., 1436
Luther, 1436
Lydia, 1537
Margaret, 1436
Roy, 1436
Sarah, 1164
Savilla, 1436
Saville, 1447
Susan, 1490, 1130
Susan E., 1520
Wesley, 1545
William, 1448, 1196
Crebs, Joseph H., 1062
Creswell, John A. J., 755
Crist, Adam, 883
  Alice, 884
  Catharine, 1530
  Catherine, 883, 884
  Daniel, 883, 884
  Daniel Alfred, 884
  Daniel, Jr., 884
  David, 883, 884
  David Monroe, 885
  Elizabeth, 884
  George Bruce, 885
  George W., 883, 884
  Harriet, 884
  Irene, 1468
  Jacob, 883
  Jacob Adam, 883
  John, 883
  John George, 883
  Laura, 884
  Laura Alice, 885
  Margaret, 884
  Mary, 884
  Mary Ann, 883
  Michael, 884
  Nancy, 884
  Philip, 883, 884
  Rebecca, 884
  Robert O., 885
  Rosanna, 1035

William, 883
Criswell, Sarah, 932
Crockett, John, 940
Cromwell, Agnes D., 1301
  Arthur A., 1300
  Etta, 1140
  F. Vera, 1301
  Lucy, 1300
  Melvill, 1301
  Melvill C., 1300
  Neva K., 1301
  Nicholas, 1300
  Nicholas C., 1300
  Oliver, 719, 920
  Philamon, 1300
  Richard, 1301
  Thomas, 1205, 1259
  Virginia, 1530
  William, 724, 1530
  William E., 1300
Crone, Catherine, 1177
  Elizabeth, 964, 1157,
    1177, 1572
  Garfield, 889
  Magdalena, 994
Cronis, Mary C., 1169
Cronise, Adell A., 1438
  Albert, 1272
  Americus, 1438
  Americus C., 1054
  Andrew F., 1054
  Ann M., 980, 1002
  Ann Maria, 1039
  Anna, 1039
  Anna Mary, 1054
  Calvin, 1493
  Catharine, 1205, 1259
  Catherine, 1139
  Charles, 1438
  Charles E., 1054
  Charles L., 1233
  Clayton H., 1054
  Clyde, 1234
  Edwin H., 1054
  Elsie M., 1054
  Emma J., 1054
  Eva, 980, 1003
  Frederick, 980, 1003,
    1039, 1054, 1139
  George, 1039
  George Wesley, 1234
  George Wilbert, 1234
  Gertrude E., 1438
  Grace E., 1054
  Hannah A., 1054
  Hannah Sophia, 1039

Hanson Monroe, 1234
Harriet E., 1234
Harriet M., 1054
Henry, 1003
J. C., 1054
J. Calvin, 1233, 1438
Jacob,
    882,1039,1054,1305,
    1396, 1536, 1589
Jacob L, 1054
Jane, 1054
Jennie M., 1054
Johannes, 1139
John, 1139
John, 2nd, 1139
John F., 1537
John L., 1054
John P., 1039
Joseph, 1233, 1438
Lenna, 1234
Lillie R., 1233
Louisa, 1305, 1536
Lydia, 1039
Marshall C., 1054
Mary, 1305, 1536
Mary E., 1190, 1191
Mary M., 1054
Milton A., 1054
Minnie Belle, 1234
Mrs. Clayton, 815
Nannie K., 1234
Netta E., 1233
Octavia, 1305, 1536
Rebecca, 1039, 1139
Rebecca L., 1054
Samuel, 1139, 1305, 1536
Simon, 1304
Sophia, 929
Susan, 1003
Susan H., 1303, 1304
Susan Henrietta, 1305, 1536
Susie, 1234
Webster N., 1054
Wilbert E., 1233, 1234
William, 799, 1054
Willie H., 1234
Crooks, Lottie, 916
    Mary C., 799
    Maymie C., 916
Cross, Arabella, 1073
Crothers, Austin L., 714, 1241
Croun, Curtis, 1079
Crouse, Eliza, 933, 1491, 1492
    Frank E., 1560
    Gertie, 1533
    James, 1490

John T., 778
Lela, 1182
Lillie, 911, 1375
Mary, 1614
Michael, 1492
Crow, Sarah, 1568
Crown, George W., 838
    Mary, 947
Crum, Ada, 1320
    Albert W., 1526
    Alcinda, 1226, 1319
    Alcindia, 1526
    Alice, 1574
    Anna Belle, 1320
    Annie, 1106, 1145
    Annie M., 912
    Casper, 1574
    Catharine, 1574
    Charles, 789, 1574
    Charles E., 1198, 1294, 1526
    Charles V., 1145
    Charles W. R., 912
    Claud R., 1320
    Edward, 1058
    Elizabeth, 1145
    Ella, 1145
    Elmer, 1023, 1598
    Emery, 1507
    Emory, 1266, 1301
    Emory C., 1145, 1146
    Ezra, 1226, 1319
    Ezra R., 1526
    Florence C., 1253
    Florence V., 1226, 1319
    Florence Virginia, 1526
    Frank, 1574
    Frederick, 1319
    George C., 1574

George W., 911, 912, 957,
    1511, 1592
Hanson E., 1319, 1320
Harry, 1110, 1574
Henrietta, 1320
Henry, 911, 1266, 1301,
    1507
Henry H., 1145
J. David, 1145
Jacob, 1226, 1531
Jacob L., 1319, 1320, 1526
Jacob Lincoln, 1320
James H., 1168
John E., 1603
John Emory, 1320
John H., 912
John Michael, 1320

John W., 1145
Josiah, 1058, 1226, 1319,
    1526
Kathrine Ellen, 1526
Lee, 1532
Lenora Alice, 1526
Leslie Regnald, 1526
Lillian I., 1320
Lillie, 1531
Mary C., 1226
Mary Catherine, 957
Mary Kate, 912
Mayme, 1507
Myrtle, 1252
Mollie, 1574
Nina Elizabeth, 1320
Noble, 1266, 1301, 1507
Noble D., 1145
Paul, 1266, 1301, 1507
Paul E., 1145
Paul L., 1320
Paul Leroy, 1512
Ray, 1320
Roy L., 1320, 1512
Solomon, 1226, 1319,
    1526
Solomon C., 1525, 1526
Stephen B., 1087
Virgie L., 1320
Walter, 1266, 1301, 1507
Walter C., 1526
William, 1134
Zoie, 1145
Crumbaugh, Elizabeth, 1318
    Gideon, 1318
    John D., 1218, 1292
    Phoebe, 1218
Crumbaugh-Shank, Phoebe,
    1292
Crumpacker, Rachel, 1155
Crune, E. C., 1166
Crutchley, Fannie Estella,
    925
    John William, 925
    Milton, 1023, 1598
Culler, Albert F., 1207
    Alma, 1502
    Alta Virginia, 1383
    America A. C., 1086
    Ann Rebecca, 1027, 1207
    Anna, 1091
    Anna Rebecca, 1028
    Anna V., 1091
    Annie, 1502
    Annie V., 1266
    Annie Virginia, 1104

Blanch, 849
Captain Henry, 1173, 1206, 1288
Catharine, 1378
Catherine, 1416
Charles H., 849
Charlotte, 1091
Charlotte E., 1123
Colonel Henry, 1206
Daniel, 1085, 1086, 1143, 1173, 1206, 1430
Daniel Milton, 1086
David, 1086, 1206
Dorsey, 1502
Dorsey S., 1266
Dorsey Spangler, 1091
Elizabeth, 1085, 1288, 1289, 1584
Elizabeth Agnes, 1028
Ella, 1091, 1266, 1502
Ella E., 1207
Ellen, 1165
Ellen R., 1086, 1143
George, 1091
George B., 1027, 1207
George C., 1444, 1501, 1502
George Carlton, 1265, 1266
George W., 849
Harmon, 1361
Henry, 1027, 1085, 1086, 1095, 1206, 1406, 1543
J. J., 1046, 1206, 1572
Jacob, 797, 1085, 1091, 1266
Jacob A., 1501, 1502
James H., 1207
James Henry, 1027
John, 1085, 1091
John H., 1006, 1266
John Harman, 1501
John Harmon, 1091,1265, 1502
John Henry, 1086, 1173
John J., 1027, 1086, 1206, 1207
John M., 849
John W., 1091, 1266, 1411, 1502
Lavinia, 1406
Lewis M., 1006
Lillian Margaret, 1028
Lloyd, 849
Lloyd C., 1027, 1207
Martin Luther, 1086
Mary C., 1086

Mary E., 1091, 1502
Mary Matilda, 1027, 1207
Mary R., 1207
Michael, 1085, 1086, 1173, 1206, 1266
Millard, 1423
Millard F., 1086, 1173
Millard Filmore, 1085, 1086
Milton, 1308
Morris L., 849
Oscar, 1570
Oscar Daniel, 1173, 1174
Peter, 1104, 1125
Philip, 1027, 1085, 1086, 1206
Ralph E., 1207
Samuel, 1086, 1411
Silas, 1266
Silas H., 1502
Silas Harmon, 1091
Susan, 1085
Thelma Regina., 1028
Thomas P., 1207
Virginia, 1086, 1362, 1430
William, 723, 849, 1206, 1383
William L., 849, 1027, 1086, 1207, 1420
Culp, David, 1082
Cummings, George, 1160
Cundiff, Hattie H., 1431
Cunningham, Emma, 1600
Emma N., 715
Jacob V., 1186
Curfman, Charlotte M., 1381, 1383, 1542
Elizabeth, 1082
William, 1382, 1542
Curren, Elizabeth, 805
Currens, Mabel, 1436
Sophia, 733
Curry, Theodore, 966
William, 895, 1278
William R., 966, 1223
Curtin, A. G., 852
Curtis, George, 737
John R., 883, 1589
Josephine, 883, 1589
Custard, Adam, 947
Mary C., 947
Susan, 1533, 1534
Cutsail, Hattie, 1577
James H., 1577
Cutshal, William B., 1520
Cutshall, Anna B., 1285
Annie, 1176, 1237

Catharine, 1176
Catharine E., 1177
Gail L., 1177
George M., 1176
John H., 1176
Louisa, 1176
Mary J., 1177
Neva M., 1177
Philip, 1176
Sarah Louise, 1177
William, 1176, 1285
William B., 905, 951, 1028, 1070, 1176, 1285
D'Orbin, Margaret, 948
Dagenhart, John, 1617
Daggy, Zacheus, 893
Dahlgren, Madeline Vinton, 1192
Dailey, Theresa, 1449
Dall, James A., 1487
Dallam, William A., 1331
Daly, Carrie, 1028
Robert, 1028
Damuth, Amanda, 1394
Charles A., 1393, 1394
David, 1393, 1394
Emma, 1394
Herbert Ross, 1394
Jane Elizabeth, 1394
Jason, 1394
Jerry, 1024
John, 1394
John Carl, 1394
Josiah, 1394
Lester Blaine, 1394
Sarah, 1394
Stanley R., 1394
Warren Keifer, 1394
Wiiliarn, 1394
Dance, Alexander, 1355
Joseph, 1355
Phoebe, 1355
Daniels, Denis M., 1437
Mitchell E., 982
Danner, Edward, 1355
Fanny, 1007, 1499
Hannah M., 928
Henry J., 1443
Irene, 752
J. B., 1538
Joel B., 752
Joseph, 1104, 1125
Julia, 990
Darby, William, 768
Dare, Abigail, 1594

Almarine, 1594
B., 1594
Benoni, 1594
Caroline, 1594
Catherine, 1012
Catherine R., 1595
Charles, 1595
Constant, 1594
David, 1594
David Dayton, 1594
Elizabeth, 1594, 1595
Elizabeth M., 1595
Elizabeth Rose, 1594
Emeline Eliza, 1594
Emma E., 1594
Enoch Fithian, 1594
Ephraim, 1594, 1595
Francis Munford, 1594
Freelove, 1594
Harriet, 1594
Isaac, 1594
Jane Elizabeth, 1594
John, 1594, 1595, 1012
Jonathan, 1594
Jonathan Dayton, 1594
Lemuel, 1594, 1595
Levi, 1594
Lizzie, 1605
Lydia Ann, 1594
Mary, 1594
Mary E., 1594
Mary Hay, 1594
Mary Jane, 1595
Mary M., 1594
Philip, 1594
Rachel, 1594
Rebecca, 1595
Robert, 1594
Robert Harris, 1594
Sarah, 1594
Susan, 1595
Susan (Hershberger), 1605
Susan M., 1595
William, 1594, 1012
William H., 1594
Darkis, Leafy, 1385
Darling, Mary G., 944
S. R., 944
Darner, Alonzo Koogle, 1325
Calvin, 1324
Calvin E., 1332
Charles, 1324
Charles B., 1332
Elizabeth, 1324
Florence, 1324
Frederick William, 1325

George, 1324
George F., 1332
Gertrude, 1332
Henry, 1324, 1332
Henry J., 1324
Howard, 1324
Howard F., 1332
J. S. W., 1332
James C., 1324, 1332
John J., 1324
Lydia, 1324
Mary, 1332
Mary Katherine, 1325
Rodney J., 1325
Samuel, 1324
Sarah, 1324
Thomas, 1324
Warren, 1324
William, 1324
William E., 1332
Daub, Enos, 1077
George, 958
Daugherty, Catharine C., 1422
Dauson, Charles W., 1099,
    1107, 1114
John, 948
Martha Ann, 948
P—— Ann, 948, 949
Davidson, Joseph, 773
Davis, A. Maria, 1171
Aaron, 1091, 1170
Anna M., 1385
Annie, 1461
Annie C., 1437
Aubrey Gaffney, 840
Bernard Martina, 840
Bessie, 1228
Catharine, 765
Catharine C., 766
Catherine, 1328
Catherine Lackland, 1328
Charles G., 839
Charles Spalding, 840
Charlotte, 839
Clara C., 1437
Cyrus, 869
David Franklin, 1436, 1437
Donald Neil, 1296, 1457
E. Carlton, 1461
Edgar T., 1437
Edith, 1069
Edward Aaron, 1171
Edward T., 1171
Eli, 839, 1295, 1456
Ephraim, 1069, 1461
Etta, 1613

Felissa, 1296, 1457
Flora A., 1171
Frances Isabelle, 840
Franklin H., 1437
Gassou, 840
George, 839, 1069
George H., 1090, 1170,
    1171, 1437
George W., 839
H. L., 769
H. Stanley, 1296, 1457
Harry L., 1457
Harry Leslie, 1296
Henry Clay, 839
Hepsie E., 1069
Ida, 1228, 1461
Ignatius, 1328
Isaac, 839, 933
Isaac, 1457
Isaac T., 839
Jacob, 795
James, 1449
James B., 1045, 1303
James L., 1412
James Milton, 1461
Joab W., 1069, 1461
Joab, Jr., 1069
John, 839
John Edward, 1296, 1457
John F., 839
John Franklin, 1295,
    1296, 1456
John N., 766
John Neil, 1296, 1457
John W., 1171
Jonathan C., 1170, 1171
Joseph, 1171
Joseph C, 1437
Julia Ann, 839
L. Kate, 1437
Louis D., 840
Louis Detrick, Jr., 840
Margaret, 898
Marjorie Earle, 1296
Mary, 839, 845, 865
Mary C., 1437
Myrtle, 1390
Nellie May, 840
Rachel M., 840
Rebecca G., 1437
Richard, 839
Robert Lee, 839, 840
Robert Leslie, 840
Robert Spalding, 840
Rufus, 839
Ruth R., 1437

Sadie E., 1228, 1461
Samuel, 742, 1058
Samuel B., 839, 1461
Samuel Byron, 1461
Thomas, 845
Vernon, 1069
Victoria, 1058
W. K., 1228
Walter H., 1437
William, 731, 839, 1171
William K., 1069
William M., 839
William O., 1171
Zachariah, 1437
Davison, Patrick, 842
Daw, Nannie, 1547
Dawson, Mary, 1321
  Philemon, 802
  Thomas, 1286
Day, Abbie R., 1301
  Celeste, 1604
  Elizabeth, 795, 796, 1460
  Hattie E., 1462
  James, 796, 1301, 1462
  Jefferson, 1462
  Lola A., 839
  Luther, 1462, Nettie J.,
    1228
  Nettie Jane, 1461, 1462
  Richard Riley, 1604
  Rufus K., 879, 1295, 1456
  Sarah Ann, 879
  T. G., 1461
  Titus, 724
Dayhoff, Milton, 1547
de Gylpyn, Richard, 823
De Laplaine, Ephraim, 1265
  Margaret, 1265
De Lauder, Annie Lee, 1363
  Benjamin T., 1363
  Daisy L., 1363
  Eli, 1220
  George S., 1363
  Gertrude J., 1363
  Harry Luther, 1363
  Margaret E., 1363
  Norma Mary, 1363
  Paul George, 1363
  Robert, 1339
  William H., 1363
De Ller, Casper, 1118
de Marmien, Agnes, 948
de Marmusin, Alex, 948
De Pritot, Jane, 948
Dean, Alice, 843
  Alice R., 1198

Annie, 843
Bella G., 1198
C. H., 776
Carlton H. , 1584
Catherine Reynolds, 1198
Estella, 1174, 1190
George A., 843, 1197
George W., 842, 843, 1307
Hezekiah, 1006, 1220
James H., 1197, 1198

John, 842, 843
John A. , 1198
Margaret Barrick, 1198
Marian, 1198
Nellie, 843
Robert, 1197
Roberta W., 843
Stewart, 843
William, 1197
William G., 1198
William H. R., 1197
Deaner, A. V., 1073
Deardorff, Mrs. Horace, 1452
Deater, William, 1150
Debring, H. F., 907
Deckerbough, John, 1531
Deems, J. M., 738
Deeter, John C., 1474
Deets, John, 1287
Defawn, Anne, 1258
  Annie, 1497
Degrange, David, 1169
  Elizabeth, 1171
  Elizabeth E., 1170, 1171
  Henry, 1411
  John, 1169, 1171, 1602
  Thomas, 1333
  William, 1527
Dehoff, Carrie, 1246
  John, 1309
  Nelly, 1221
Deihl, Alice, 788, 1600
  Harry, 1199
  Julia Ann, 1324
Deitrich, Jacob, 816
Deitrick, D. W., 838
Delaplaine, Caroline, 1441
  Edward Schley, 1036, 1037
  George Birely, 1036, 1037
  John H., 1124
  Joseph, 1035
  Maymie, 1243
  Robert Edmonston, 1035,
    1036, 1037
  Rosanna, 1036

Theodore Crist, 1035,
  1036
Theodosia, 1036
Wesley, 1436
William T, 1035
William T., 1036
William Theodore, 1036,
  1037, 1563
Delaplane, Caroline, 770
  Charles, 789
  James, 1252
  Joseph, 1614
  Ross, 789
  William T., 745, 1393
DeLashmut, Edward T. H,
  1365
  Edward T. H., 1018
Delashmutt, Arthur, 930
  Elias, 930, 1109
  Rebecca, 944
  William, 1109
Delauder, E. Stanley, 1453
  Elias, 1006
  Lydia, 1031
  Margaret, 1297
  Mary M., 1031
  Samuel, 1031, 1149
  Sarah, 1149
Delaughter, Amanda D. ,
  1611
  Susan Ann, 1381, 1382,
    1541, 1542
DeLauter, George H., 868
  George N., 868
  Henry, 1326, 1369
  James H., 868
  John, 1044
  Otho V., 868
  Robert, 1453
  Susan Ann, 861
Dell, Rufus, 1500
Delovier, Phoebe, 835
Delphia, Catherine, 1458
Delphey, Ada, 1221
  Catharine, 1221
  Clara, 1221
  George, 1221
  Grant, 1221
  Hannah, 1221
  John, 1221
  Joseph, 1221
  Katie, 1221
  Laura, 1221
  Margaret, 1221
  Minerva, 1221
  Missouri, 1221

Philander, 1221
Sally, 1221
Thaddeus, 1221
Washington, 1221
William, 1221
Demory, Alvira, 1031
Annie B., 1031
Daniel P., 1031
Decora D., 1031
George Theodore B., 1031
Henry E., 1031
Luther L., 1031
Walter M., 1031
William W., 1031
Demuth, Jason, 755
Jerry, 830
Denegre, Antinette Morgan, 1211
William O., 1211
William P., 780
Denison, A. N., 1242
Dennis, Anne Grahame, 834
Archibald R., 809
Charlotte Patterson, 834
Dannock, 808
George R., 834, 1211, 1291
George R., Jr., 809
George Robertson, 808
John, 808
John M., 809, 1291
John M., Jr., 1291
Littleton, 808
Littleton U., 808
Mary F., 1291
Mrs. A., 1045
Sarah Robertson, 808
Thomas, 809
Dent, Addison, 1122
William, 1058
Denton, Jennie, 1620
Minna, 1620
Deppy, Catherine, 730
Dern, George W., 935
Hammond, 1221
Roy, 1058
Susan, 1270
Derr, Abraham, 844
Ada, 844
Alice V., 1247
Amanda, 1006, 1086
Amanda L., 1173
Ann Elizabeth, 1612
Ann Mary, 1220
Ann Rebecca, 1006
Anna L., 1154
Bessie, 844

Betsy, 715
Beulah J., 844
C. Edward, 996, 1153, 1154
C. Paul, 844
Catharine, 1157, 1246, 1382
Charles, 1247
Charles H., 1005, 1006, 1361
Charles H., Jr., 1006
Charles M., 1154
Charlotte, 1006
Charlotte C., 961
Cornelius, 761, 767, 999, 1447
Cornelius E., 843, 844, 961, 1220
Daniel, 1006, 1059, 1173, 1220, 1288
Daniel C., 843, 1077, 1220
David, 996, 1003, 1153
David E., 1154
Dorthy, 1543
E. L., 1534
Elizabeth, 1006, 1024, 1078, 1246, 1456, 1612
Ella C., 996, 1003, 1154
Ella M., 1154
Elmer S., 997, 1043
Emma, 1220
Erma, 1006
Estella, 844
Esther, 964
Esther C., 964, 1572
Eugene L., 1246, 1247, 1591
Ezra Z., 1247, 1591
Frances E., 1591
George D., 1006
George N., 788, 1600
Harold E., 1006
Harry S., 1154
Jacob, 843, 1006, 1220
Jane M., 1157
Joanna, 838
Johanna M., 996, 1154
John, 996, 1006, 1153, 1157, 1220, 1246, 1353, 1456, 1475, 1591
John C., 706, 755, 883, 997
John Peter, 1247
John Sebastian, 1591
John T., 843, 1006, 1220
Kate Norman, 1591
L. Z., 953, 1146
Laura J., 996, 1154
Lena J., 1154
Lewis E., 1158
Lewis Edward, 1157

Lizzie A., 883
Lucinda, 1006
Lucinda F., 843, 1220
Lulu B., 844
Luther C., 1150
Luther E., 844
Luther Osmond, 1220
Luther Z., 843, 1220
Lydia, 1006, 1220
Maggie E., 1220
Mamie F., 844
Manzella C., 843
Margaret, 1247, 1270, 1271, 1352
Margaret A., 1353
Margaret E., 749, 843
Mary, 741, 1006, 1246, 1247, 1277, 1456
Mary A., 843
Mary Ann, 1222
Mary E., 997, 1006, 1220
Mary L., 1353
Mary Oneida, 1220
Marzella C., 1220
Maurice M., 844
Mildred Rebecca, 1220
Milliard, 1006
Oliver C., 1006
Philip, 934, 964, 1157, 1572
R. Scott, 996, 1063, 1148, 1153, 1154
Rebecca, 1157, 1220
Richard, 1543
Rosie, 1271
Roy D., 997
Roy V., 844
Samuel, 843, 1006, 1220
Samuel J., 1220
Sarah, 1006
Sarah A. E., 1157, 1158
Sarah A. R., 1059
Sarah E., 1045
Sarah Elizabeth, 1475
Sebastian, 1246, 1425, 1591
Solomon, 1271
Susan S., 1154
Thomas, 1157, 1247, 1591
William, 1247
William R., 1591
William S. T., 844
Willie May, 1591
Willis E., 1154, 1543
Dertzbaugh, Charles, 1017

Ella, 1017
Fannie, 1017
Frank, 1018
Hallie, 1017
Harry B., 1018
Jane, 1017
John, 1017
Lewis R., 1017, 1018, 1305
Mabel, 1018
Mary B., 1018
Pearl, 1018
William H., 1017, 1018
William Lee, 1018
Detrich, Lewis F., 806
Detrick, Frederick Lewis, 941
  Jacob S., 1251
  John U., 941
  Louis F., 941
  Margaret Jane, 941
  Sophia Markell, 1251
Detrow, Samuel, 943
Devilbiss, Abner C., 1508,
  1509
  Ada, 1509
  Adam, 1230, 1258
  Adam A., 1297, 1298,
    1494, 1553
  Adam C., 1298, 1494
  Adam Clark, 1297, 1298,
    1495
  Adam W., 1323, 1508
  Albert, 1298, 1495
  Alberta, 1298
  Alverdia, 1495
  Ann Maria Josephine, 1298,
    1495
  Annie H., 1304
  Arthur Risdon,, 1298, 1495
  Bayard, 1118
  Casper, 1298, 1494, 1495,
    1553
  Catharine, 1314, 1315
  Catharine M., 1322
  Cecelia A., 1278
  Clayton, 1263
  Columbus Cervera, 1553
  Cora, 1304, 1305, 1536
  Cyrus Fletcher, 1298, 1495
  D. M., 1230, 1231
  Daniel Ellsworth, 1553
  David, 1303-1305, 1315,
    1323, 1508, 1535, 1536
  David A., 1304
  David M., 1229
  David Marshall, 1323, 1324
  Deborah, 1298, 1495

Edna C., 1324
Edward, 1209
Edward Thomas, 1298, 1495
Edwin, 733, 1323, 1508,
  1509
Elizabeth, 1304, 1508, 1536
Ella Pearl, 1553
Ellis, 1305, 1536
Ellis K., 1304
Ford, 1298, 1495
Francis, 1298, 1495
Frank William, 1275
George A., 1519
Hannah, 1277, 1278
Hazel, 1298, 1495
Henry, 1304
Hilda, 1118
Howard H., 1279
Isaiah, 1278
James, 947
Jane Rebecca, 1270
John H., 1270, 1508
John Hanson, 1118
John W., 1278
Katharine, 1304, 1536
Lucretia, 1315
Maggie, 1553
Marga, 1377
Margaret T., 1324
Maurice Martin, 1275
May, 1270
Oliver P., 1303, 1304, 1525
Otis Belmont, 1298, 1495
Parker, 989, 1004, 1049,
  1305, 1536
Preston, 1130
Preston S., 1118
Rachel Annie, 1553
Reuben, 1298, 1495
Rodger M., 1324
Roger B., 1118
Rosanna, 1323
Samuel H., 1553
Samuel Sherman, 1275
Solomon, 1536
Solomon D., 1303, 1304
Solomon David, 1304, 1535,
  1536
Susanna, 1425
Thomas M., 1304
Wilbert, 1298
William, 1275, 1553, 1556
William S., 1553
William Sherman, 1275
Devilbliss, ——, 965
Devine, Sarah E., 1161

Devries, B. F., 1509
Dewall, William, 1532
Deweese, Edward, 1460
Diamond, Constantine, 835
Dice, John, 917
Diehl, Adam, 1568
  Alice, 1568
  Cora M., 1159
  Elizabeth, 947
  George, 1395, 1525
  Jacob, 1050
  Jacob H., 1159
  John, 1159, 1532
  John Henry, 1159
  John W., 1182
  Magdalena, 1210
  Martin, 1159
  Matilda, 1292
  Mattie V., 1159
  Moses, 1050, 1159
  Mrs. Nelson, 1456
  Sarah E., 1050, 1159
  William Clarence, 1159
Dielman, Adelaide, 801
  Francis, 802
  Henry, 801
  Jacob, 802
  Jean, 802
  John Casper, 801
  John Casper Henry, 801
Dietrich, D. W., 1056
  Lewis F., 848
Dietrick, John H., 938
  John U., 937
Diffenball, Catherine, 860
  Eva, 860
  John, 860
Diffenbaugh, Jas. A., 1476
Diffendal, J. M., 844
Diffendall, Samuel M., 837 ,
  1455
  William, 1195
Diffindall, Mary, 1250
Diggs, Edward, 1216
  William, 1216
Dillard, Malissa, 1183
  Melissa, 1482
Diller, Annie, 1119
  Augustus Bradford, 1119
  C. H., 1124
  Charles Donald, 1119
  Charles H., 1118, 1119
  Charles W., 1119
  Clara Virginia, 1119
  Coral B., 1124
  E. Dorsey, 1124

Edwin Dorsey, 1119
Eliza, 1119
Enos, 1118
Francis A., 1119
George Emory, 1119
Jacob, 1119
Jacob M., 1119
John, 1118, 1119, 1201
John Hanson, 1119
John Willie, 1119
Levi, 1119
Martin, 1119
Martin, Jr., 1119
Mary, 1119
Merle T., 1124
Roland R., 1119
Ursa M., 1119
Verna Saylor, 1119
Walter Cramer, 1119
William H., 1119
Willie C., 1119
Dinsey, Guy, 1275
Dinterman, Alfred, 1110
Annie L., 961
Caroline, 961
Catharine, 961
Charles E., 1512
Clyde Atwell, 1535
Eliza E., 961
Ella, 1110
Elsie, 1110, 1533
Ernest E., 1512
Etta May, 1535
Fannie, 1512
George, 961, 1091, 1382, 1512, 1535, 1542
George B., 1512
George D., 961
George H., 961
George H. P., 961, 1512, 1535
Hattie, 1320
Hattie A., 1512
Ida, 1512
Ida Elizabeth, 1110
Jacob, 1110, 1320
Jacob B., 961
Jacob E., 1512
John, 1340
John M., 1512
John Mathias, 1535
John P., 961, 1006
Katie, 1110, 1320
Lillie M., 1512
Lincoln G., 1273, 1320
Lincoln Grant, 1512

Malinda, 1512
Mary, 1506, 1512
Minnie C., 961
William H., 1512
Dixon, Agnes Virginia, 763
Alice, 1030
Alice S., 763
Ann, 1027
Ann Rebecca, 1206
Annie, 1074, 1086
Benjamin F., 1015
C. M., 841
C. Merle, 842
Charles F., 764, 787, 845
Clayton, 1442
Clayton T., 841
Devitt, 1095
Dewitt, 1543
Eberly T., 763
Edwin T., 763
Eliza, 842
Elmer E., 841, 842
George, 763
Georgianna, 1031
Harry H., 841
James, 1206
James E., 762
Jesse W., 762
John Hatton, 763
John T , 762
Joshua, 1074
L. Minnie, 762
Lee, 1397, 1610
Lyda, 842
M. E., 1204
Marie, 842
Mary M., 762
Minnie R., 845
Miriam, 763
Nannie E., 764
R. May, 841
Rebecca, 842
Rebecca O., 1222
Roberta H., 787
Samuel, 1442
Samuel F., 763
Sarah, 842
Susan, 1438, 1493
Thomas, 762, 807, 842, 1030, 1150
Thomas Freeman, 842
Thomas O., 841, 842, 1222
William T., 841
Doll, Alexander H., 998
Annetta, 844
B. Frank, 998, 999

C. Mantz, 844
Charles, 928
Charles D., 1403
Charles J., 1080
Daniel, 911
Elizabeth W., 1080
Ellen Virginia, 1080
Ezra, 844, 928, 1080
Frank A., 1080
G. J., 1026, 1080, 1424, 1527
George J., 1080
Hannah, 1151
Harriet, 844
Harry, 999
Henry W., 1080
J. Hood, 999
James E., 844
Joseph, 844
Joseph G., 928
Joshua, 989, 998, 1420
Kate, 989, 1525
Leander, 844
Lewis H., 844, 928
Louisa, 844
Louisa B., 928
Margaret E., 999
Marianna, 1080
Mary Susan, 911
Mary W , 1420
Melville E., 928, 1080
Melvin E., 844
Mrs. M. E., 815
Roger A., 1080
Samuel V., 844, 928
Domer, George H., 811
Sarah E., 811
Donaldson, Emma Virginia, 925
Fannie Ebert, 1563 F., 1213
J F , 1228
John Lyttelton, 925
Rebecca, 1160
Donnelly, John, 1024
Donsife, Catharine Mary, 1140
Henry C. , 934
Sarah A., 934
Dorcas, Catharine, 1199
Charles, 1218, 1292
Jacob, 1566
Dorcus, Edward T., 703
Dorff, Julia A., 869, 870
Dorner, David, 772
Elizabeth, 772

John, 1483
Lydia, 901, 1483
Dorsey, Achsah, 1072
    Amanda, 1445
    Ann, 1445
    Anna M., 1446
    Arthur, 940
    Basil, 938, 940, 941
    Basil D., 941
    Basil, Jr., 936, 939-941
    Caleb, 940
    Caroline, 1115
    Carrie V., 1445
    Charles, 1620
    Charles A., 1445
    Charles L., 1446
    Cleggett, 1293
    Corbin, 940
    Cordelia, 936, 938-940
    Cordelia H., 941
    Cordelia Harris, 1452
    Deborah, 1072
    Edward, 940, 1448
    Eli, 1448
    Elizabeth, 845, 1154, 1448,
        1449
    Emma, 1445
    Evan, 940
    Fanny A., 803
    Frances, 1445
    Frances Charlotte, 1563
    Grafton Duvall, 1345
    Harry, 940
    Harry W., 941, 1448
    Helen, 1095, 1543
    Hettie A., 1445
    Humphrey, 940
    Ignatius W., 1448, 1449
    Joanna, 900
    John, 940, 966, 1072, 1271,
        1344,1445, 1448, 1449
    Joseph, 940
    Joshua, 940, 941, 1448
    Julia, 1445
    Lucy, 941
    Lula, 1239
    Marie, 941
    Martha, 1072
    Mary A. E., 1497
    Mary E., 966
    Philemon, 940, 1072
    Pottinger, 1449
    Rachel, 1337
    Richard, 940, 1072
    Samuel, 940, 1449
    Sibyl C., 1446

    Sophia, 941
    Vachel, 940
    Susan, 1449
    Vernon W., 1448
    W. H. B., 1563
    Walter R., 1445, 1446
    William, 940
    William B., 900
Dotterer, Annie, 1262
    David Roop, 1263
    Edna Alice, 1263
    Elhannan, 1262
    Elsie Anna, 1262
    Franklin, 1262
    Frederick, 1262
    Henry, 1262
    Hezekiah, 1262
    James Raymond, 1263
    Jesse, 1262
    Jesse Vernon, 1262
    John, 1262
    John Ezra, 1263
    Joshua, 1262
    Josiah, 1262
    Martha, 1262
    Mary Ann, 1262
    Mary S., 1262
    Orren J., 1262
    Ruth Marie, 1262
    Sophia, 1262
    Washington, 1262
    William H., 886, 1262, 1263
Doty, Abner, 807, 1046
    Abner Delos, 1046, 1047
    Abner Wilard, 1047
    Claude P., 1047
    Elmer Crum, 1047
    Elmer W., 1047
    Erma Elizabeth , 1046
    Eugene Delos, 1047
    Eva O., 1047
    Guy D., 1047
    Howard D , 1047
    John, 1162
    Josephine Marie, 1047
    Lettie G , 1047
    Louise, 1543
    Louise R., 1047
    Margaret, 1047
    Mary, 1047
    Maud S., 807, 1047
    Mildred Emily, 1046
    Nettie G., 1047
    Robert W., 1047, 1543
    Volney Leonard, 1046
    Walter C., 1046, 1047

    William B., 1047
Doub, Abraham, 838
    Abram, 836
    Amanda M., 1426
    Amy A., 777
    Annie E., 838
    Catherine, 836
    Donald J., 838
    Elizabeth, 904, 1033
    Enos, 838
    George, 1524
    Harvey L., 838
    Isaiah, 1476
    J A , 913
    Jacob, 904
    James E., 838
    John, 1391
    John W., 838
    Jonas A., 838
    Joshua, 1154
    Lemuel, 1077
    Mary, 836, 1391
    Sophia, 746, 955, 958,
        1176, 1374, 1391,
        1523, 1524
    Virgil W., 838
    William Warren, 838
Doubt, Joshua, 996
Dougherty, Alice, 1508
    Baxter, 1508
    C. Thomas, 1508
    Carrie, 1508
    Charles, 1508, 1515
    Charles E., 1237, 1270,
        1284, 1508, 1518,
        1619
    Cleveland, 1508
    Emma, 1508
    J. Frank, 1508
    James, 1508
    Jennie, 1508, 1515
    John, 1508
    Laura, 1508
    Mollie, 1508
    Raymond, 1508
    William, 1508
Doughty, Sarah, 1594
Dove, Zodoc, 820
Dover, A. Albaugh, 1349
Downey, Abram Jones, 1452
    Ann, 939
    Basil, 936, 938
    Basil D., 941
    Basil Dorsey, 1452
    Bessie, 1548
    C. A. Lawrence, 938

C. Augustus Lawrence, 941
Cordelia, 941
Cordelia Dorsey, 1452
Edmund, 936, 938, 939
Eliza, 782, 937, 938, 941
Eliza Johnson, 783
Elizabeth, 937, 941, 1074
Emma, 941
Frances, 1452
Francis J., 941
Frank, 937, 938, 940, 941
Harriet, 936, 938, 939, 941
Harriet D., 941
Ima, 1452
James Atlee, 1452
Jesse W., 936, 938, 941
Jesse W., Jr., 937, 941
Jesse Wright, 937
John, 782, 936, 938-941
John Johnson, 941
Lidie, 941
Lydia Jones, 1452
Margaret, 937
Margaret Jane, 938, 941,
   1224
Margaret Mantz, 938, 941,
   1224
Maria, 936, 938, 941
Rebecca, 936, 938
Robert, 936, 939
Ruth, 939
Samuel, 936, 939
William, 863, 936,
   938-941, 1074, 1224,
   1452
Downing, Julius, 1576
Doyle, Catharine E., 1249,
   1250
Christena, 894
Drehr, Annie M., 1105
Drenner, Charles, 1469
Dreyer, Henry, 976
Mary L., 976
Driver, Henry, 785
Dromgold, John, 814
Dronberg, Thomas, 1294
Droneberg, John, 1320
Nancy E., 1320
Nancy Elizabeth, 1319
Dronenberg, Mary A., 762
Dronenburg, Lillie G., 1074
Cora, 1074
George T., 1102
Jacob, 1074
Jane, 1074
John J., 1074

John T., 1074
Joseph M., 1074
Lucy A., 1074
Lucy D., 1074
Margaret E., 1074
Mary S., 1074
Drummond, Jane, 1081
John, 804
Du Val, Catharine, 1399
Dubbs, Joseph H., 1042, 1395
Mary, 1395
Dubel, Lawson A., 1360
Dubell, Upton, 1394
Duckwall, John, 773
Duckworth, Maria L., 1294,
   1295
Dudderar, ———, 1223
Austin, 1015
B. F., 966
Benjamin, 1015, 1223
Benjamin F., 1223
Benjamin Filmore, 1222,
   1223
Betsie, 1222
Charles, 1015
Clara A. , 1223
Clifton, 1015
Conrade, 1222
Cora J., 1223
Daisey A., 1014, 1015, 1223
Daisy A., 1155
Eliza, 895, 1222
Ellen, 1222, 1343
Emma L., 1223
Flora M., 1223
George W., 762
George Washington, 1223
Helen, 1015
John, 1545
Margaret, 895, 1222, 1223
Margaret E., 930, 931
Martha R , 1223
Peter, 1014, 1155, 1222,
   1223
Peter Clifton, 1223
Philip, 931
Russell, 1015
Sally, 1222
Sarah, 1155, 1222
Susan, 1239
Susanna, 955, 1222
Theodore, 1223
Warren E., 967, 1223
Washington, 1222
William, 895, 1015, 1155,
   1222

William Westwood, 1223
Duderar, Eliza, 763
Maynard, 1516
Dudrear, Amelia Catharine,
   1266, 1267
Ella V , 1333, 1334
Emory, 1267
John, 1333
Randolph, 1267
Dudrow, Maynard, 1235
Dufer, Risbeth, 1200
Dugan, Frank, 1248
Dulaney ,Daniel, 792, 1026,
   1210, 1211, 1253
Edward, 804
R. H., 1137
Dulany, Bladen, 1345
Dull, Charles, 950
Dumest, Elizabeth, 1072
Dummick, J. N., 814
Dunbar, John R. W., 1212
Duncan, John M., 1212
Dunlap, G. B., 1295
George, 957
Henry, 957
Horace, 1245
Dunn, Thomas, 1286
Dunsife, Genoah, 1277
Duple, Margaret, 1529
Durbin, David, 1527
Durnin, Mrs. Josephine, 872
Durr, Mrs. Josepha, 1187
Dusing, Jennie, 760
Stanley, 868
Dussing, Elizabeth, 737
Dutloyd, Edward, 858
Dutrow, Ada Rebecca, 1283
Amelia Catharine, 1507
Catharine, 1332
Catherine, 715
Charles D., 1006
Columbia, 982, 1283
Columbus, 726
David, 1304, 1346, 1536
Edward, 1006
Eliza, 1346
Elizabeth, 860
Emory, 1507
Fannie Elizabeth, 1283
George, 781, 1200
H. V., 1346
Jacob, 1283
John, 1282, 1283
Katie, 1283
Kitty, 1283
L. B., 1283

Laura, 1013
Laura R. C., 983
Leslie E, 1158
Lu, 1286, 1532
Mahilia, 1283
Margaret, 1283
Margaret E., 1412
Marie M., 1200
Markel, 1266, 1301, 1507
Martin C., 868
Mary, 1283, 1299
Mary A., 892
Mary Grace, 1006
Nannie, 1266, 1301, 1507
Olive R, 1006
Parthenia E., 983
R. Claude, 982, 983
R. O. Lee, 854, 983
Randolph, 1507
Rebecca, 982, 1283
Rebecca E., 1282
Richard, 1283
Richard P. T., 982, 983
Richard S. J., 1283
Samuel, 759, 982, 1013, 1282, 1283
Samuel P., 1283
Sarah, 1507
Surah, 1266, 1301
Susan, 781
W. S., 1048
Dutson, Joshua, 855
Duttera, Louisa C., 854
Duttrow, Mary, 1167, 1311
Dutz, Francis Asbury, 1282
Duval, Augusta, 1567
Gabriel, 1567
Joseph, 1567
Julia, 1039
Marcellus, 1443
Mary, 1567
Rector, 1567
Zelophehed, 1443
Duvall, Alex. Thomas Hawkins, 949
Algernon, 949
Alice, 724
Annie, 999
B. D., 925, 926
Benjamin, 846, 948, 999, 1577
Cordelia, 846
Elizabeth, 1072, 1555, 1556
Elizabeth Lawrence, 949
Emma E., 998, 999
Gabriella, 949

Graflon, 948
Grafton, 949, 982
Grafton Allen, 762
Henry Claggett, 948, 949, 1344
Houston, 949
James L. Hawkins, 949
John, 948, 1555
John C., 1557
Julia, 949
Lawrence, 948
Lewis, 1072
Mareen, 948
Mary Elizabeth, 949
Massiot, 948
Medora, 1557
Mrs. Columbia, 1282
Pearl M., 762
Preston, 1262
Robert, 948
Samuel, 948, 949
Sarah, 1245
Sarah Ann, 949
Sieur Hugh, 948
Susanna, 948
Thomas, 948
Thomas Hawkins, 949
Trovilla A., 762
Virginia Claggett, 949
William, 853, 948
Zara, 1557
Dyer, John A., 1040
Martha J., 1040
Eader, Amelia, 1104
Annie, 1104
Annie Elizabeth, 1105
Annie M., 1607
Augustus L., 1104
Bernard J., 1104
Bessie O., 1608
Catharine Rebecca, 1105
Charles E., 1607
Charles M., 1104
Daniel R., 1607
David, 1607
David N., 1607
Eliza C., 1607
George D., 1608
Jennie, 993
John, 1104, 1105
Jonathan, 1607
Lewis B., 1607
Louise, 1105
Margaret, 1105
Nora, 1344
Pauline R., 1105

Pearl A., 1608
Peter M., 1607
Rachel L., 1607
Rosa, 1104
T. S., 822
Thomas S., 1104
Thomas Stephen, 1105
Walter G., 1608
William, 1104
William H., 1607
Eagle, Lauretta, 1035
William, 1035
Eaker, Bertha C., 1058
Early, Jubal, 1242
Jubal A., 720
Eastee, H., 856
Easter, Betsy F., 994
Easterday, Alvey, 868
Charles I., 1478
Charles O., 1477, 1478
Christian, 1477
Clarence E., 1478
Conrad, 1477
Conrad P., 984
Daniel, 1477
Elizabeth, 1478
Ellen, 1478
Emma V., 998
Fannie S., 740
Francis, 1570
Gamaliel, 1570
George, 1568, 1611
Jacob, 898, 1477
James H., 1477
Joseph, 740
Josephus, 1418
Julia Ann, 1569, 1570
Lavania, 1477
Lawrence, 748, 1477
Lillie K., 1418
Mary, 1541
Mary C., 1570
Michael, 1477
Samuel, 1477
Sarah, 1477
Sarah A., 1467
Sarah A. C., 898
Sarah R., 820
Susan, 861, 1513
Tracy, 1477
Easters, Mrs. Sewell, 1245
Easton, Andrew, 1564
John, 1145
Eaton, Joseph, 1023, 1598
Eaves, Ida, 1260
Ebaun, Henry H. , 1223

Ebbert, Susan, 1388
  William, 707
Eberly, Elizabeth, 1006, 1007,
  1499
Ebert, ——, 1270
  August, 1276
  Benjamin, 1461
  Catharine R., 1105
  Harry, 1018
  John, 1461, 1462
  Rebecca, 839, 1462
  Rebecca M., 1461
Eby, Daniel, 1221
  Elizabeth (Shideler), 1033
  Jacob, 1033
  Lemuel, 1221
Eccard, Allen, 1084
  Effie, 1084
  Frederick, 743
Echison, Rebecca, 1325
Eckard, William, 707
Eckenrode, Henry, 1013
Ecker, Aaron, 1155
  A. W., 1508
  Albert W., 1514, 1515
  Bertha, 1601
  Bertha C., 1155
  Carrie, 1515
  Catharine, 1155
  Charles L., 1155
  Clarence, 1515
  Clyde William, 1155
  Cordelia, 1515
  Daniel, 1155
  David W., 1155
  Deborah, 1155
  Eliza Jane, 967
  Elizabeth, 1155
  Ella, 922, 1601
  Ella Virginia, 1155
  Frank Hull, 1515
  Harrison, 1155
  Henry, 1155
  Herbert B., 1155
  Ida, 1515
  Ida M., 1230
  Jacob, 1155, 1222
  Jane, 1243
  Jennie, 1515
  John, 1155
  Jonas, 1155
  Katy, 1155
  Levi, 1230, 1514, 1515
  Lillian, 1546
  Lillian A., 1155
  Margaret, 1614

  Mary, 1155
  Mary C., 1155
  Merhl, 1515
  Myra L., 1015, 1155, 1223
  Peter, 1155
  Samuel, 1053, 1155, 1515
  Sarah Susan, 1155
  Sidney, 1053
  Thomas, 1515
  William, 966, 967, 1015,
    1155, 1601
Eckes, Charles, 1320
  Jane, 1320
Eckinrode, Caroline, 1013
Eckstein, Annie, 1096
  C. H., 1097
  Christian, 1096
  Christian H., 1096
  Christian T., 1097
  Elizabeth, 1096
  Ella V., 1096
  Louis V., 1097
  Louisa, 1096
  Mary, 1096
  Mary C., 1593
  Maude S., 1097
  William F., 1096
Edelen, Mary Roberta, 1472
Edmons, Mary, 1332
Edmonston, Eden, 1036
Edmunds, Benjamin, 1324
  Mary, 1324
Edwards, B. F., 830
  Fannie, 1418
  Irene, 1448
  James, 1418
  Maria, 1418
  Maria M., 1417
  Rachel E., 1155
  Susan, 1583
Eichelberger, A. J., 1357
  Abram Ralph, 1357
  Adam L., 1357
  Alice L., 1357
  Anna, 846
  Charles, 974, 1024
  D. S., 1564
  Edward, 853, 974
  Edward C., 1225
  Edward Gray, 974
  Edward L., 1357
  Edward S., 974, 991
  Emma J., 1196
  Francis M., 1357
  George M., 974
  Grayson, 816, 974, 991

  Hershey F., 948
  J. D., 1187
  Jacob, 788
  James, 1614, 806
  James W., 1416
  Joanna, 1614
  John, 1496
  Joseph, 1614
  Jane Grayson, 974
  Jod Dix, 1196
  John, 974
  Joshua, 974
  Leonard, 974
  Louis Edward, 1357
  Lucinda, 1357
  Margaret Grayson, 974
  Marian, 1614
  Mary, 1195
  Mary D., 1564
  Mary Elizabeth, 1614
  Philip Frederick, 974, 975
  Thirza G., 1357
  William H., 1357, 1496
Eldridge, E. J., 1603
Eigenbrode, Cameron, 1263
  Charlotte, 1620
  Phoebe, 733
Eisenhauer, A. S., 1202
Eisenhaur, John, 928
  Regina, 928
Eisenman, M., 1118
Elautt, Ann, 746
Elder, Aloysius, 834, 835
  Anna, 835
  Anna Frances, 835
  Anna Rose, 835
  Anne or Nancy, 836
  Annie, 767, 768
  Arnold, 835
  Basil Spalding, 836
  Basil T., 836
  Benjamin, 835
  Catharine, 836
  Charles, 835
  Charles D., 836
  Christiana, 836
  Clara, 835
  Clara Elizabeth, 835
  Clementina, 836
  Edward, 835
  Eleanora, 836
  Elizabeth, 835, 1450,
    1453
  Frances W., 836
  Francis Xavier, 835
  George, 835

Guy, 835, 836
Hazel Virginia, 835
Ignatius, 835, 836
James, 835, 836
James A., 802, 834
James B., 835
James Basit, 834
James C., 836
Joachim, 834
John Dubois, 835
Joseph, 835
Joseph E., 836
Joseph Edward, 835
Judith, 835
Maria M., 836
Martha Alice, 835
Mary, 835
Mary Bernardine, 835
Mary Catherine, 835
Mary Elizabeth, 836
Pauline Eleanor, 835
Polly, 835
Priscilla, 835
Richard, 835
Theresa, 836
Thomas, 835, 836
Thomas Richard, 836
Thomas S., 836
William, 835, 836
William Henry, 836
William Pius, 836
Eldridge, Charles C., 904
George D., 904
James F., 982
John W., 1148
Mary, 904
Elgin, Augusta, 1245
James, 1094
Eli, Miranda Waters, 975
Elinor, 1069
Elkins, Evaline, 702
Ellen, Kathrine, 1094
Elliott, Agnes, 828
Elizabeth, 804
James, 828
John, 1583
R., 743
T., 1612
William J., 751
Ellis, John, 1216
John Francis, 1563
Phoebe, 935
Susan Rebecca, 1548
Ely, Charles, 833
Charles R., 944
Charles Wright, 944

Charlotte V., 793
Cornelia M., 944
Elias H., 944
Elias Sanford, 944
Grace Darling, 944
Isaac, 793
Mabel D., 944
Richard Grenville, 944
Emerick, Elizabeth, 1377
Emmert, Joseph, 1207
Susan, 1098
Engel, Caroline, 1527
Catharine, 1527
John, 1527
Joseph H., 1527
Mary M., 1527
Nicholas, 1526
Sarah, 1527
England, Charles, 831
Charles Edward, 831
Edwin Hood, 831
Frank, 831
George Marion, 831
Georgia D., 1014
Georgie, 724, 1231
Harriet E., 831
Harriet Elizabeth, 831
Henrietta, 831
Imogene, 831
James, 831
John, 1286
John W., 831
John Walter, 831
Joseph, 831
Lavinia, 831
Mary Ellen, 831
Mary Rebecca, 831
Mildred Jane, 831
Nathan, 831
Nathan J., 831
Nettie, 1286
Roland Lee, 831
Walter Alexander, 831
Englar, Ann Elizabeth, 1085
Edith Grace, 1085
Elhanan, 1596
Ezra, 1209
Engel, Caroline, 1527
Catharine, 1527
Jessie, 1597
John, 1527
Joseph H., 1527
Mary M., 1527
Nicholas, 1526
Sarah, 1527
George P. B., 1279

Hannah, 970
Helena, 1085
John D., 1085
John Hamilton, 1085
Josiah, 1085
Lydia, 1085
Margaret Rebecca, 1085
Nathan, 1085
Nathan Addison, 1084, 1085
Engle, Annie, 1044
Fannie, 1607
John, 1044
John D., 903
Joseph, 1284
Joseph H., 1526, 1527
Nicholas, 1545
Engleman, Eden, 1476
Eliza, 1476
Emily, 1007
Mary Elizabeth, 1476
Mayme, 1461
Engler, David, 970, 1065
Hannah, 1065, 1509, 1534
John, 732
John W., 1083
Philip, 971, 1065
Susie, 732
English, Jonathan D., 743, 868
Ennalls, ——, 1241
Ennis, Franklin, 1351
John, 1351
Joseph, 1350, 1351
Mary Catherine, 1351
Thomas, 1110
William, 1079, 1350, 1351
Enoch, Jennie M., 942
John P., 1546
Sarah, 1546
Ensminger, Archibald, 1116
Ensor, Abraham, 1355
Betty, 1355
Delia, 1355
E. Betty, 1355
E. Clarence, 1355
Edward, 967
Edward C., 1354, 1355
Elijah, 1355
Elizabeth, 1355
George, 1355
Gilbert, 1355
John, 1354, 1355
John B., 1355
John H., 1355

Joseph, 1355
Lillie Ann, 1355
Luke, 1354, 1355
Polly, 1355
Rachel, 1355
Sally, 1355
Samuel, 1553
William, 1355
Epler, Bessie, 1204
Eppard, Lavinia, 1286
Epperly, Emma, 1298, 1495
Erb, Alice, 1315
David, 1315
Eli, 1246
Elias, 1298
Mary Jane, 1246
Ericson, John, 701
Ersholtz, Ada, 1533
Anderson, 1533
Calvin, 1533
Grace, 1533
John, 1533
Lillian, 1533
Lula, 1533
Raymond, 1533
Eschbach, Anthony, 909
Catherine E., 911
David, 909
David J., 909
E. R., 1593
Edmund R., 910
Elizabeth B., 909
John, 909
Mary C., 909
Mary S., 911
Eshleman, David, 1120
Nancy, 1119, 1120
Essen, Hezekiah, 1245
Estep, Catharine, 1012
Richard, 1069
Etcheson, Henry, 1069
Etchison, Elisha, 795, 1026
Elizabeth Simpson, 1026
Ephriam, 1026
George Johnson, 1113
H. Dorsey, 1113
Henry, 1358
Henry N., 1113
Hepsabah, 795
Ida, 731
J. Garrison, 913
James Milton, 1113
Lenora, 1047
Marshall L., 1026
Mary, 913
William, 1074

William H. B., 763
Etzler, A. H., 1230, 1515, 1622
Ada V., 1230
Adam Taylor, 1058, 1339
Albert, 1613
Alice C., 1339
Alice M., 1229
Anderson Hicks, 1229
Anna R., 1535
Annie Pearl, 1059
Archie, 1613
Aubrey Taylor, 1059
Augustus, 1515
Charles, 1338
Charles Ellsworth, 1059
Charles H., 1058
Cora V., 1230
Daniel, 1058, 1229, 1297, 1535, 1546
Daniel Henry, 1059
Daniel W., 1058
Dorsey P., 1230
Elizabeth, 1130, 1273
Ella, 1058, 1613
Ezra, 1229
Florence, 1058
George Albert, 1058
George L., 1230
George W., 1229
Harriet, 1229
Harriet V., 1229
Ida B., 1229
Ignatius, 1613
James, 1058, 1339
Jeremiah W., 1022, 1229, 1230
Joel, 1273
John, 1058, 1546
John David, 1613
Laura, 1058, 1531
Lettie R., 1059
Lydia, 1229
Lucy Ann, 1613
Malachi, 1229
Margaret Gertrude, 1059
Mollie, 1058
Nimrod, 1546
Polly, 1229
Rachel, 1058
Roscoe E., 1230
Selma J., 1613
Silas W., 1230
William, 1229
William H., 1613
William Henry, 1613
William N., 1059

William Taylor, 1059
Eury, Annie, 1305, 1339
Benton, 1339
Cecil, 1305, 1339
David Washington, 1305
Harry, 1305
Jesse, 1305
John William, 1305
Lydia, 1305
Margaret, 1293, 1305
Mary Ellen, 1305
Samuel, 1305
Samuel A, 1305
Stanley Benton, 1305
Susan, 1305
Eustis, George, 1211
Marie Clarice, 1211
Evans, Catharine, 1016, 1089
Corilla, 1087, 1089
D. G., 1088
Job, 1089
John, 1089, 1442
Robert, 1087, 1089
Theodore, 1293
Everhart, Ann Eliza, 1107
Daniel, 890
Eliza, 1099, 1114
Elizabeth, 889, 890
Jacob, 889, 890
Laura, 1099, 1107, 1114
Laurence, 889, 890, 1107
Lawrence, 1099, 1114
Philip, 1099, 1107
Everett, Harriet English, 1422
John E. , 1422
Eves, Peter, 1020
Ewing, Samuel, 1351
Eyler, Aaron, 836
Adam H., 769
Alice, 1231
Amanda, 836
Amanda, 1514, 1598
Amelia Ann, 780
Amos, 1511
Anna B., 966
Anna Elizabeth, 1215, 1517
Anne, 1532
Annie E., 829, 1618
Annie L., 1265
Arbelon C., 837
Arbelon Clementine, 836
Benjamin, 836, 1367
Caroline, 837, 1455
Charles R., 1455
Edward, 1512

Catharine, 1082
Charles, 1458
Charles A, 837, 1455
Charles F., 1456
Charles H., 829, 1618
Clarence Wilbur, 1050
Cyrus, 1336
Daisy, 1140
David, 836
David F., 836
E., 755
Edna May, 1050
Edward Ross, 837, 1455
Eliza, 1082
Elizabeth, 1292
Ellen I., 837, 1455
Elmer, 1445
Emma Almira, 1327
Emma C., 837, 1455
Enrezetta Virginia, 836
Etta, 1367
Frederick, 837, 1455
George, 836
George Allen, 733
George B., 1050
Gordon I., 1456
Harriet, 836
Hazel M., 838
Hazel Rebecca, 733
Henry, 1214
J. C., 1458
J. Frederick, 837, 1455
J. O., 730
Jane E., 1455
Jennie, 1549, 1550
Jacob, 1082
John, 769, 1082, 1500,
    1514, 1533
John C., 730, 781
Jonas, 1110
Judith, 836
Lavenia, 836
Lizzie E., 837
Luella Catherine, 733
Lulu M., 1456
Lydia, 1620
Key Margaret, 1456
Margaret, 836, 1286, 1500
Maria, 1455
Marie, 837
Markwood, 836
Martha A., 730
Mary A., 1238
Mary J., 1455
Mary Ingle, 1327
Mary Veda Grace, 733

Michael, 1215
Milton, 1528
Mrs. John, 1132
Murray E., 733
Myra Ethel, 1050
Norman Elwin, 1050
Oliver, 733
Perry, 836
Peter, 1286, 1327, 1532
Rachel, 836
Raymond E., 1456
Raymond Oscar, 1050
Rebecca, 837, 1455
Ross R., 837
Ruth Catharine, 1050
Samuel, 729
Susan, 836, 979
Susan E., 1150
Tacie E., 1238
Thomas, 725
Thomas F., 837, 1455
Thomas R., 1455
Tracy, 836
William, 836, 837, 1168,
    1455, 1533
Eylor, Simon, 1458
Faber, George, 734
    Minnie F., 734
Fagan, Charles T., 1150
    Elizabeth, 1150
Fahrney, Elmer G., 1439
Fahs, Charlotte M., 863
Fair, Lauretta R., 1368
    M. Ross, 1368
    Mary, 862
Fairfax, Lord Thomas, 1460
Faith, Ellen, 961
Falconer, Elisha, 1216
Fales, Edward, 871
Faller, Henry, 1555
    Stella, 1555
Farior, John C., 1455
Fauntz, Barbara, 1200
Favorite, Amelia Ann, 1123,
    1124
    Cyrus O., 1009
    George, 837
    Henry, 811
    Samuel, 1620
    Sophia, 1609, 1610
    Sophia R., 1397
Fawley, Catharine, 1113
    Catherine, 1099, 1107
    George, 1099, 1107, 1113
    Henry, 1172
    Howard C., 1444

Margaret, 1172, 1298,
    1299
Mary C., 1040
Susan, 1108, 1114
Feaga, Catherine M., 800
    E. B., 1609
    E. C., 1308
    Elmer B., 908
    George, 800
    Josiah, 800
    Philip, 800
    Uriah V., 908
    William M., 800
Fearhake, Adolphus, 827
    George, 827
    Rose, 827
Feaster, Annie, 1047, 1086,
    1206
    Annie M., 1238
    Ann Maria, 1478
    Catharine, 768, 1086
    Edgar, 1047
    Ella V., 1174
    Hazel, 1047
    Jacob, 807, 1040, 1086,
    1174
    John, 1238, 1478
    Lillie E., 1040
    Marguerite, 1047
Feeser, Ella, 846
    John, 846
    Mary Ellen, 1254
Feidt, Matilda A., 859
Feinour, Mary K., 1097
Feiser, Alice, 1292
    David, 1292
    Ella, 1292
    Ella Estella, 1294
    Emma, 1218, 1292
    Henry, 1292
    Jacob, 1218, 1292
    Kate, 1292
    Laura, 1218, 1292
    Leah, 1292
    Louisa, 1292
    Maria, 1292
    Mary, 1292
    Parmalee, 1218, 1292
    Peter, 1292, 1294
    Rebecca, 995, 1271, 1284,
    1292, 1619
    Sarah, 1292
    Susan, 1218, 1292
Felix, Lydia, 1555
Felton, Anthony, 1119, 1120
    Blaine, 1120

Edisto, 1120
Edna, 1120
Ephraim, 1119
Estella, 1120
Frank, 1120
George, 1120
Grant, 1120
Holden, 1120
John, 1119
John L., 1120
Laura, 1120
Thaddeus M., 1119, 1120
William, 1120
Felty, Margaret, 1395
Fentenwenner, Charles, 1122
Fenwick, Cuthbert, 1215
Elizabeth, 1215
Ignatius, 1215
Ferguson, Ruth, 1552
Ferrell, Abraham, 1442
Benjamin Franklin, 1442
Eliza, 1442
James Clinton, 1442
James R., 1442
John, 1442
John William, 1442
Laura C., 763
Laura Catherine, 1442
Lela, 1442
Richard, 1442
Sarah Virginia, 1442
Susan, 1442
William Fenton, 1442
Ferry, Mary, 1405
Fessler, Caroline Rebecca, 784
John, 784
Rosanna C., 979
Fetcher, Dorothy, 1047
Elmer, 1047
Samuel P., 1047
Fetterling, Christiana, 1468
Fidler, Ezra, 1534
Fiery, Alburtus, 1299
Catharine, 859
Figgin, Ann Eliza, 894
Filler, Jonathan, 1460
Thomas, 1533
William E., 815
Fillinger, Mary, 922
Michael, 922
Susan, 922
Finenran, Mary A., 1160
Finger, Ann Catherine, 711,
1320, 1321
Fink, Annie Eliza, 1351
Elizabeth, 1351

Emanuel, 972, 1351
Esta L., 972
George, 1351
George Washington, 1307
Jacob, 972
John, 1062, 1189, 1351
John D., 1351
Joseph, 1351
Mary E., 1351
Millard, 1351
Richard, 972, 1351
Samuel, 988, 1265, 1339
Sarah, 1351
Susan, 1351
Susanna, 1191
Finley, Frances Ann, 1024, 1025
William, 1025
Firestone, Mary M., 724
Firor, Daniel, 727
John, 727
John C., 837
Peter O., 1585
Sophia, 1436
Sophia B., 1336
Susannah, 727
Z. U., 800
Firstone, Mary, 1000
Fisher, A. E., 829
Abraham, 829, 1324
Ada N., 930
Agnes, 828, 1618
Alice, 828, 1618
Allen G., 828, 829, 1617,
1618
Alvaretta Jane, 1324
Amanda, 828, 1618
Archie, 1038
Calvin V., 829
Calvin W., 1618
Catharine, 828, 1618
Charles, 829
Charles A, 1324
Clara I., 930
David, 828, 930, 1618, 1620
Effie M., 762, 829, 1618
Elinor, 950
Emma E., 930
Frederick C., 930
George, 930
George Newton, 930
George W., 828, 1618
Henry, 1326
I. M., 930
Irwin J., 930
Isaac, 828, 1324, 1617
Isaac Newton, 1324

James B., 1028
John, 829
John D., 1324
John M., 762, 828, 1600,
1617, 1618
Laura, 829, 1618
Lucy A., 828, 1618
Mahala, 1326, 1327
Maria, 930
Mary, 1300, 1326
Mary E., 897, 1618
Nathaniel, 828, 1618
Nellie M., 1618
Newton, 829, 1556
Ralph M., 829
Ruth, 829
Samuel, 1435
Sarah, 828, 1618
Sarah E., 829, 1218, 1600,
1618
Susan, 828, 1618
Thomas, 828, 1324, 1617,
1618
Thomas S., 1102
Vanburn, 828, 1618
Willis E., 829, 1324
Fiske, Moses, 760
Wilbur, 760
Fissler, Jacob, 886
Fitch, Emma, 1119
G K., 1187
Fithian, Rebecca, 1594
Fitzhugh, B. F., 880, 935
Benjamin, 1233
Fitzsimmons, Charles, 1076
Ignatius, 1349
James F., 1553, 1596
Flair, Amanda, 1481, 1576
Flanagan, A. Lycurgus, 1234
Adam, 1234
Adam H. E., 1385
Aida Belle, 1385
Belva Frances, 1234
Edith Minerva, 1234
Edna, 1385
Ernest W., 1385
George H., 1385
Harry J., 1385
Hazel Irene, 1234
Hilda Theresa, 1385
Hugh, 1384
James, 1384
John, 1234
John F., 1384, 1385
John M. O., 1385
Lycurgus L., 1385

Lycurgus Levi, 1234
Margaret, 1384
Mary Ann, 1384
Mary R., 1385
Minerva T., 1385
Noah, 1234, 1385
Noah E., 1384, 1530
Ralph Green, 1385
Reda May, 1385
Russell Noah, 1385
Sherman Edward, 1385
William H., 1385
Flanigan, Adam H. E., 1385
Hugh, 1385
John, 1385
William, 1385
Flant, Mary, 873
Flaught, Clara I., 1240
George, 1240
Flautt, Carrie, 959
Gilmore, 959
Gilmer R., 1437
H. R., 959
Hattie B., 959
L. C., 959
Virginia, 959
Virginia Catharine, 959
Walter L., 959
William C., 959
Fleet, Charles, Bennett, 783
Howard McKim, 783
John Alexander, 783
Lucy Broddus, 783
Nellie, 783
Thomas Maynard, 783
Fleiger, Rhoda, 1501
Fleming, Alvertia E., 1402
Charles F., 1548
Della, 878
Ida M., 1548
J. Alfred, 1402
Joseph, 965
Susan, 1547
Flemming, Alfred, 812
Alice, 1197
J. W., 734
Jennie, 1094
Jennis, 1093
Susan Ann, 1559
Walter Wolf, 734
William, 1557
William Randolph, 1047
Fletcher, John, 1140
Flickinger, Aaron, 1244
Christianna, 949
Clarence L., 1245

Daniel, 1244
Ellen, 1244
Emma May, 1245
George, 1053, 1244
George Albert, 1244
Grace C., 1245
Howard, 1092, 1244
John, 1244
Levi, 1244
Louisa, 1244
Louisa E., 1053
Mary, 1244
Noah, 1244, 1396
Peter, 1244
Raymond D., 1245
Rufus, 1244, 1245
Flinkinger ,Howard, 1110
Flohr, Carroll M., 1124
Josiah, 730
M. C., 1124
Mary K., 1124
Rosie, 957
Flook, Albert D., 830
Anna K., 994
Annie E., 1030
Barbara, 857
Betty D., 1033
Carlton H., 1032
Catharine, 1030, 1032, 1620
Cyrus, 829
Cyrus F., 830, 904, 1032,
1033
Cyrus Rudolph, 1030
Daniel, 1030, 1032, 1475,
1620, 1621
Daniel Charles, 1621
Dawson F., 829, 830, 1032,
1352
Dawson Y., 830
Elizabeth, 1030, 1032, 1407,
1620
Elizabeth D., 830
Elmer S., 830, 1033
Emma E., 830, 1033
Emma Evelyn, 1621
Esther, 1019
Eveline, 1030, 1032
Evelyn, 1620
Fanny E., 1621
Frances, 1475
Hanson, 791, 908, 1030,
1032, 1356, 1361, 1375,
1430, 1620
Hattie, 1265
Hattie M., 1030
Henry, 1032

Howard H., 1032
Jacob, 1030, 1032, 1481,
1575, 1620
John, 857, 932, 953, 986,
1032, 1129, 1479,
1621
John P., 829, 830, 904,
1033, 1157, 1190
John P. T., 1030
Jonas, 1486
Joshua, 1033
Joshua M., 830
Josiah, 953
Lewis, 1621
Lewis Martin, 1030
Luther, 1474
Margaret, 1621
Mary, 830, 1191
Mary C., 1033, 1351,
1352
Mary Louise, 1621
Millard F., 1621
Millard Benton, 1030
Millard F., 1256
Millard Filmore, 1030
Nena Adele, 1621
Norah, 1621
Oliver, 1299
Oscar B., 1030
Percy C., 1032
Perry, 829, 1030, 1620
Perry C., 1033
Philip, 1019
Philip E., 1174, 1190
Ridgely, 1621
S. Grace, 1151, 1218
Sarah Grace, 1621
Staley M., 1030
W. S., 1218
Wilber, 1621
William, 1621
William S., 1030, 1169
William Snively, 1620,
1621
Floyd, Catherine, 757, 877,
897, 1175
Elizabeth, 756
Jacob, 877, 1175
Jennie, 1086
John, 756, 757
Joseph W., 992
Margaret, 911, 1375
Mary, 958, 1028, 1522,
1524
Mary L., 992
Fogle, Aaron David, 1319

Abner Eugene, 1083
Adam, 1082
Alice M., 1215
Alice Margaret, 1517
Andrew, 1318
Annie, 1082, 1083
Balser, 1214
Barbara, 1082
Calvin Earle, 1083
Catharine, 945, 1082, 1318
Charles H., 1319
Charles P., 1319
Chester Lynn, 1083
Clarence Ellsworth, 1319
Daniel, 1318
David E., 1318
Della, 1518, 1619
Elias, 1214, 1517
Eliza, 1082
Emanuel, 1214, 1318, 1319
Ephraim, 1083
Etta May, 1215
Eva, 1215
Francis, 1214
Frederick, 1082
George P., 1261
George W., 1512
Grayson B., 1261
Harriet, 1214
Henry, 1082
Hezekiah, 1214
Hiram, 891
Isaac, 1082, 1083
James, 1214
Jesse Emanuel, 1319
John, 1082, 1083, 1238
John Henry, 1083
John T., 1176
John W, 1273
John W., 1244, 1274
Joseph, 1214
Joshua, 1251
Josiah, 1491
Laura, 1215
Lewis, 1083
Lucy Ann, 1214
Lula May, 1083
Margaret, 1082, 1215
Martha L., 1491
Martin M., 1214
Mary, 1082, 1318
Mary Ann, 1214
Mary Ellen, 1083
Mathias, 1082
Nancy, 1082, 1491

Nicholas, 1319
Oscar Arthur, 1083
Rema Larue, 1261
Ruby Estella, 1083
Samuel Edward, 1319
Sarah Alice, 1083
Susan, 1082, 1273, 1274, 1298, 1501
Susanna, 1318
Thomas William, 1082, 1083
William, 1082, 1083
William H., 1318
Font, Margaret, 1035
Ford, A. W., 780
Alice, 1067
Alice L., 1067
Alonzo, 1445
Charles, 1327
Emily C., 900
Ignatius, 1067
Ignatius P., 1067
James Edward, 900
Joseph C., 1067
Laura M., 1067
Margaret S., 1068
Mary E., 1067
Parran B., 1067
Paul W., 1067
R. G., 1360
Raymond G., 1067, 1068
Robert, 1072
Sister Mary Claud, 1067
Washington, 1067
William F., 1067
Foreman, Albert, 1262
Clara, 1514
Edward, 1212
George W., 728
Mary Martha, 728
Forney, Mary, 1245
Forsyth, A. P., 1188
Anna C., 1188
Fortney, Rebecca, 1165, 1419
Fout, Charles, 821, 1594
Daniel, 1008
George, 771
Grafton, 822, 894
Isadora V., 822
Lewis, 1335
Lucretia C., 822
Margaret, 1314
Marietta, 1594
Mary E., 821
Peter S., 1431, 1528
Rebecca, 894
Foutz, Isaac, 731

Fowler, Ann, 1454
David, 1404
Lucretia, 1500
Mrs. Susan, 1404
Thomas, 839
Fox, Adolphus, 1531
Alice, 1531
Ann M., 899
Anna I., 1111
Anna Julia, 1531
Annie A., 1531
Balser, 1082, 1083, 1512
Baltazar, 1491
Calvin O. C., 1358
Catharine, 1083
Catharine Susanna Isabelle, 1620
Charles B., 1111
Charles M., 1531
Daniel, 946
Dorothy R., 1491
E. A. C., 1019, 1358
E. August, 1358
Edward, 1221, 1306
Eliza M., 899
Elizabeth, 749, 1083
Ella, 899
Ellen A., 738, 868
Ellen S., 778
Emily, 1083
Emily Jane, 1083
Emily R., 1491
Ernest M., 1157
Estella E., 899
Estelle E., 867
Frank, 1219
G. S. J., 1491
Gazella G., 899
George, 861, 899, 1359, 1381, 1541
George H., 810, 899, 1084, 1126
George P., 738, 899, 1127
Grant, 1221
H. K. C., 1358
Harry, 1306
Henry, 946, 1531
Henry C., 1530, 1531
Hezekiah, 1083, 1271, 1491
Howard, 1152
Ida, 1358, 1534
Irving A., 899
Jacob, 946, 1083, 1298, 1495
Jeremiah, 1122, 1251,

1273
Jerry, 1007, 1181, 1499
Jesse, 1151, 1207, 1377, 1491, 1531
Jesse F., 1491
Jesse R., 946, 1615
Joanna Elizabeth, 881
John, 946, 1017, 1531
John P., 899
John Philip, 1620
Joseph J., 899
Leah N., 1491
Lena Elizabeth, 1083
Lewis, 951, 1358
Lewis M., 1277
Linda, 1221
Lizzie, 1358
Louisa, 946
Lydia Ann, 1083
Mabel, 1221
Marcella, 1491
Margaret A., 899
Margaret Ellen, 1083
Martha, 1491
Martin L., 1491
Mary, 946
Mary Ann, 1083
Mary L., 1531
Maryetta, 899
Minnie, 805
Rachel Sophia, 1083
Reuben, 1491
Robert, 1491
Samuel W. , 1437
Sarah Susan, 1083
Singleton, 1531
Sophia, 899
Sophronia, 1531
Susan M., 1126
Susan W., 1439
T. C., 867
Thomas, 867
Thomas C., 899
Victoria, 1531
Washington, 946
Wilhelmina, 1358
Fraley, Addie M., 1150
Augustus, 1149, 1150
Bertha, 1150
Charles H., 1150, 1521
Clara N., 1150
Cora, 1150
Francis, 1561
Henry, 1090, 1150
John, 1238, 1443
Lewis H., 1149, 1150

Mabel, 1071, 1521
Mary, 1238
Nettie, 1150
Robert A., 1150
Utokeia, 1150
Victoria, 1150
William H., 1150
France, Isaac, 883
Frank, Sallie T., 1302
Silas, 1302
Franklin, Ann, 1462
Anne Rebecca, 701
Benjamin, 1428, 1581
Charles, 1462
David, 1279
Fabian, 713
George E., 701
John, 1581
L. A., 799
Louisa, 784
Maria C., 701
Rosie, 1613
Frantz, Lydia, 1332
Fraser, F. L., 1389, 1390
Frazier, Elizabeth C., 885
David, 885, 935
Edward, 1160
Estella V., 1160
Etta, 1160
Florence V., 935
George Edward, 1160
George W., 1160
John H., 1160
John H., Jr., 1160
Louisa S., 1160
Marie Aileen, 1160
Mary, 1160
Walter, 1160
Freats, Samuel, 1442
Frederick, Rosetta Grace, 1332
Samuel, 1332
Free, Samuel S., 1588
Freeman, Rebecca, 842
Freeze, Joseph, 754, 1620
Josiah, 1394
Mary, 1168
Nora G., 1239
Freitchie, Barbara, 940
French, John, 1248
Freshour, Amanda, 1610
Eli, 1610
Elizabeth, 1132
Frey, Edward, 1146
Enoch, 797
Jacob, 1476
John, 743

Leanore, 1476
Susan, 1173, 1467
Fries, Sarah, 903
Fritchie, Ann, 1462
Barbara, 1211, 1462
Barbara (Hauer), 870
John, 1462
John C., 1047
Fritz, Andrew, 891
Elmer E., 1157
Frizen, Anna, 797
Frizzel, David, 874
Frizzell, Bertha Oswald, 1355
Dudisell, 1355
Gordon, 1355
Raymond Lewis, 1355, 1356
Susan, 1344
Walter, 1355
Frock, Elizabeth, 1237, 1270, 1284, 1518, 1519, 1619
Howard, 1501
Minnie, 1520
Frost, Eli, 1088
Minerva J., 1088
Frubridge, Mary Ann, 1263
Frushour, Charles N., 1349
Henry A., 862
Robert, 1163
Fry, Addie C., 891
Albert, 1460
Alice A., 1460
Annie, 890
Cecilia, 1460
Charles M., 891
Charles W., 890
Curtis J., 891
Daniel, 1460
David J., 891
Edward F., 890, 891
Effie M., 1460
Eli A., 1459, 1460
Ella V., 891
Florence K., 1460
George W., 890
Grace, 1460
Harvey, 1416
Howard, 1460
Isaac, 1570
John, 1459
John D., 1460
John E., 1460
Joseph, 1459, 1460
Joseph C., 1460
Joseph W., 1460

Lydia J., 890
Luther, 1460
Mabel, 1460
Margaret E., 890
Mary, 1162, 1460
Mary A., 890, 1460
Mary Jane, 969
Matilda, 1460
Maud, 1460
Nellie V., 891
Olie M., 891
Pearley B., 891
Peter, 890
Robert E., 1460
Rose, 1460
Samuel, 969, 1099, 1107, 1114
Samuel F., 890
Samuel L., 891
Scott L., 891
Susan, 1460
Viola, 1460
Fuller, Aaron, 848
Elizabeth, 1389
Helen Mary, 848
Fulmer, Fannie A., 1106
Jacob, 1250
John, 1106
M. C., 979
Marshall, 723
Fulton, Barbara, 1066
Barbara A., 971, 1065
Catherine, 1304, 1535, 1536
Charles Henry, 1260, 1287
Clay, 1315
Henry, 1342, 1493
John, 971, 1066
John S., 925
N. A., 1322
Newton, 1205, 1532
Fultz, Katy, 1324
Lewis, 863
Fumstine, Frederick, 1278
Fundeburg, Solomo, 995
Funk, Clara T., 1031
Daisy D., 1031
Edward D., 1031
Eliza C., 1031
Eva Viola Irene, 1031
Harry B., 1031
John B., 1031
Lewis R., 1031
Malinda A., 1404
Millard, 1177
Raymond D., 1031

V. B., 1031
William, 1031
Funston, John, 1155
Furgueson, Jane, 773
Furney, John, 780
Furrey, Elizabeth, 812
Furry, Edward, 1472
Edward D., 885
George Wilber, 885
Martha, 1404
Mary, 1472
Mina, 1472
Myrtle, 885, 1472
Paul, 885
Samuel, 1472
Samuel B., 936, 1472
William, 1472
Fuss, Albert, 830
Annie, 831
Asbury, 830
Berry, 804
Ezra, 830
Hettie, 830
John, 830
John I., 831
John T., 830
Kate, 830
Mead, 830
Missouri, 830
Virginia, 830
William H., 830, 831
Gaither, Henry C., 1243
Henry Chew, 1076
Julia E., 1076
Juliet E. Maynard, 1076
Samuel, 1181
Sarah, 1180, 1181, 1216
William H., 1494
Gaithers, Frank, 840
William, 840
Gale, E. P., 1251
Gall, Barbara, 810, 1166
Charles M., 727
Anna E., 1526, 1527
Barbara, 1490
Carl, 1436
Carl S., 1545
Charles M., 1545
Edward, 1545
Elizabeth, 1527
Eva, 1545
Glenn N., 1545
Henry, 1545, 1592
Henry Lloyd, 1545
John, 1545
Louise, 1436, 1545

Lula Katharine, 1545
William, 1527, 1545
Gallagher, Airy, 1153
Lucy, 1153
Norris, 1153
T. D., 1153
Galt, Mary, 1247
Mary J., 1033
Matthew W., 1033
Sterling, 1033
Galway, Jane, 1259
Gamble, David, 773
Gambrill, C. Staley, 963
Horace G., 745, 1354
James H., 1036, 1441, 1589
James H., 3rd, 1057
James H., Jr, 709, 1056
James H., Sr., 1056
Susan May, 1057
Gammon, Adelaide, 1264
Gankeri, William, 858
Gannon, George, 1306
Sarah E., 1306
Ganso, Laura, 843
Gantt, Mary, 1344
Garber, Abraham, 1136, 1259
Abram, 1219
Addison, 1377
Amanda, 1259
Amon, 1151
Ann Louisa, 1071, 1520, 1521
Annie M., 1136
Catharine Elizabeth, 1151
Charles, 1220
Christian, 1135
Della, 1220
Earl, 1220
Edward, 1219, 1498
Effie, 1151
Emma, 1220
Fanny, 1220
George W., 1230
George Washington, 1151
Glenn O.,1109,1127, 1128
Hannah, 1151, 1194
Henry, 1151
Ida, 1220
J. William L., 1151
John, 1219
John D., 1127
John G., 1151
Joseph, 1220
Julia, 1220

Lena, 1151
Lulu R., 1128
Martin, 1219
Mary, 1220
Mary E., 1151
Minerva, 1127
Mrs. Rachel (Repp), 1007,
    1499
Paul, 1220
Rachel, 1298, 1495
Samuel, 936
Solomon, 1219
Thomas J. McClelland,
    1151
W. Scott, 1127
William, 1071, 1521
William H., 1222
Gardiner, Elizabeth, 1462,
    1463
    Emily Ritchie McLean,
    1331
    Francis, 836
    John, 1463
    John deB. W., 1331
    Joseph, 836
Gardner, Keziah, 798
    L. S., 934
Garfield, James A., 852
Garling, Samuel, 1448
Garnand, Catherine, 737, 738
    Daniel, 738
    Daniel J., 1377
    Daniel S., 868
    David T., 781
    Preston, 1373
Garner, Annie Adelia, 925
    John A. P., 1171, 1396
    Mary, 1040, 1106
Garnes, Effie, 1155
Garret, Emma, 1093
Garrett, Jennie, 1320
    Laura, 1452
Garrettson, Catherine, 1025
    Garrett, 1025
Garrison, Benjamin F., 1594
    Edmund, 1595
Garrott, Aden Anderson, 1576
    Allen Franklin, 1576
    Barton, 1576
    Barton Van Buren, 1576,
    1577
    Cora Miller, 1577
    Edward, 1282
    Ellen Catherine, 1576
    Emily A., 1577
    Emma, 1576

Frank, 1576
George Barton, 1577
George Barton, Jr., 1577
Hannah, 1227
Hannah Frances, 1282, 1576
Harry, 1576
Jacob Brent, 1577
Jerard Rice, 1576
Jessie Talbot, 1576
Julia, 1576
Julia Ann, 1227
Laura, 1576
Laura J., 1450
Lee, 1576
Mabel, 1577
Martha E., 748
Mary Elizabeth, 1576
Matt, 1576
Nellie, 1576
Nicholas, 1227
Sarah, 1576
Susan Matilda, 1576
Virginia, 1576
Warren, 1483
Garry, M. M., 1595
Gartland, Catharine, 693
Garver, Benjamin, 1532
    Harry, 1558
Garvick, Elizabeth, 1319
Gassman, John, 1481, 1575
Gatch, Thomas, 735
Gather, Emma M., 1452
    Florence B., 1452
Gattrell, Martha Ellen, 1326
Gaugh, Ann M., 1445
    Hannah E., 1236
    Jesse, 800, 829, 1618
    Jonathan A., 1236, 1445
Gaver, Alfred W., 1289, 1300
    Alice H., 1371
    Ann Rebecca, 759
    Anna Viola, 1300
    Annie M. E., 1028
    Annie R., 826, 1606
    Austin Wilfred, 1146
    Catharine M., 1299
    Charles, 826, 1606
    Charles B., 1299, 1485
    Charles H., 1370
    Charles L., 1146
    Charles R., 1383
    Daisy, 1606
    Daniel, 826, 993, 1144,
    1473, 1605, 1621
    David T., 827, 897
    Della, 1383

Effie, 1606
Elias, 877, 994, 1175,
    1371, 1372
Elias H., 826, 1606
Elizabeth, 1383
Elizabeth V. A., 827
Elsie M., 1492
Ephraim, 1273
Ernest, 1252
Estie O., 1028
Fannie C., 827
Flora E., 994
Floyd F., 1312
Frances C., 1289
Franklin E., 1383
George, 826, 1605, 1606
George D., 826, 1605,
    1606
George E., 827
George W., 861, 1028,
    1146, 1299, 1311,
    1541
Grover Cleveland, 1383
H. L., 761, 999, 1541.,
    1447
Harmon, 1492
Harry S., 827
Henry, 826, 904, 1605
Henry P., 826, 1606
Hiram, 1514
James W., 827
Jeremiah, 1299, 1311,
    1383, 1606
Jerome, 820
Jerome E., 1383
John, 826, 1605, 1606
John P., 826
John T., 744, 826, 827,
    1606
John W., 827
Joseph, 959, 1146, 1177,
    1299, 1311
Joseph W., 1299
Josephus, 1146
Kitty V., 1606
Laura, 1146, 1606
Lee J., 1370
Leslie W., 1146
Levi, 826, 1606
Lewis P., 743
Lola E., 744, 827
Louisa, 826, 1606
Mary, 827, 1606
Mary Etta, 1473
Melancthon, 1146
Minnie E., 1383

Nellie L., 827
Orma Catherine, 1312
Oscar F., 1300
Otho J., 1299, 1311, 1312
Philip F., 826, 1383, 1606
Pierce Horatio, 1146
Rebecca, 1146, 1220
Roland Melancthon, 1146
Roy V., 827
Sadie E., 1312
Samuel D., 1028, 1146
Scott, 1260
Singleton E., 1146
Susan E., 1471
T. F., 1146
Tilghman, 986, 1005, 1538
Tilghman F., 889, 890, 952
Virgie, 1383
Virgie G., 1312
Wade Victor, 1312
William, 1471
William E., 992
William H., 1383
Gear, George, 1431, 1528
Geasey, Martha, 1539
Geasy, Catharine, 755
Geesey, Alton, 1271
Edward, 1167, 1271
Elizabeth, 1167
Hannah, 1267
John, 1166
John A., 989, 1049
Susannah Rebecca, 735
Thomas, 775, 1132
Gehr, Nancy, 1348
Geiger, Elizabeth Ann, 1000
Jacob, 1000
Mary, 1057
Geigis, Mathias, 915
Geiman, Charles, 1058
Edna, 1058
Eugenia, 1058
Harry, 1058
Lottie Lee, 1058
Madeline, 1058
May, 1058
Rose, 1058
William H., 1058
Geisbert, Elizabeth, 982
Elizabeth Ann, 1282, 1283
Michael, 1507
Geisburt, Catherine, 740, 741
Jonathan, 741
Geiselman, Clara Ann, 1214
Daniel, 1214
Geisleman, Charles, 1338

Clara A., 1164
Samuel, 1533
William, 1499
Geisler, William, 763
Gelwicks, Detta, 1040
George, 1351
George, James W., 978
Gephart, John, 716
Gelwicks, James, 1445
Germand, Grace I., 1500
Gernand, Addison, 1135
Amanda C., 1135
Andrew, 1302
Andrew Augustus, 1135
Annie, 1135, 1270, 1302
Caroline, 1477
Charles E., 1135
Daniel, 727
Daniel J., 1136
Daniel Josiah, 1135
Ernest Joseph, 1136
Fannie M., 1135
Frank D., 1136
Grace I., 1136
Helen, 1136
Ida L., 1135
Jacob, 811, 1135, 1490
John D., 1220
Joseph A., 798
Leslie D., 1136
Lillie, 1136
Margaret Alice, 1135, 1302
Mary A., 810, 811, 1490
Susan J., 1135
William C., 1135
Gernard, Andrew, 745, 1399
Gerry, Mary, 1012
Michael M., 1012
Gesey, Alice L., 1525
Catharine, 1524
Elias, 1524
John, 810, 1490, 1525
John Albert, 1524, 1525
Martha, 1524
Mattie Rebecca, 1525
Millard F., 1525
Myrtle Oland, 1525
Sarah, 1524
Theodore, 1524
Getting, George, 1404
Getty, Ann, 860
Getzendanner, Abraham, 1456
Adam, 1456
Addie, 1456
Alice May, 822
Anna Mary, 997, 1222

Christian, 822, 1456
Daniel, 709, 821, 1222,
1246, 1342, 1456
Daniel J., 1456
E. Grace, 1361
Edward T., 1354, 1456
Elizabeth, 874, 1443
Eugene, 1368
Eugene M., 1361
Harriet M., 1061
Harvey, 1456
Harvey F., 822, 1443
J. W., 822
Jacob, 874, 1456, 1559
John, 822, 1456
John D., 822
John Harvey, 822
John W., 1456
Jonathan, 822, 1222,
1246, 1456
Joseph, 1534
M. E., 832, 1488
Mary, 1074
Nannie May, 1354, 1456
Susan V., 1559
William Reese, 1456
Ghiselin, Reverdy, 832
Gibbons, Susan, 1363
Gibson, Ida E., 1614
J. Gregg, 848
Nannie Pottinger, 848
Giddings, Elizabeth, 1230,
1514, 1515
George W., 1515
William, 932, 1484
Giesbert, Miranda C., 1064
Gilbert, Ada, 1268
Adam, 860
Albert, 1223
Allen Sellman, 1162
Catherine, 1310
Charles, 1133
Charles Ezra, 1268
Charles W., 1134
Charlotte, 1214
Clarence, 1268
E. Marshal, 1214
Eli, 1213, 1214
Elizabeth, 956, 1305
Ellen, 860
Fannie O., 1213
George, 860
George Henry, 1162
George K., 1575
George Stanley, 1162
Harry E., 1214

Henry, 1133, 1162
Henry Calvert, 1162
John, 1162, 1555
John W., 1162
Lizzie, 1162
Margaret, 1162, 1268
Mary Elizabeth, 1162
Mary Jane, 1518, 1519,
　1619
Michael, 1518, 1619
Nora Maybelle, 1162
Russell Meade, 1162
Walter, 1162
Webster, 1205
William H., 1213
Gilds, Rebecca, 983
Gill, Jennie R., 963
Gilland, John, 804
Gillespie, Catherine, 731
Gills, John, 882, 998, 1410
Gilmore, Ellen, 1488
Gilpin, Ann M., 743
Bernard, 823
C. M., 748
Charles M., 823, 824
George F., 823, 824
Gideon, 823
Joseph, 823
Gilsin, Richard, 773
Gilson, Amanda, 794
Ann Rebecca, 794
Carrie M., 823
Charles A., 823
Charles Abraham, 794
Charles Albert, 823
Elizabeth M., 823
Ella B., 823
James William, 794
John Emory, 794, 823
Mary P., 793
Mary Priscilla, 794
Myrtle E., 823
Richard, 793, 804, 823
Richard Gibbons, 794
Robert, 794
Robert Newton, 794
Sarah, 794
Thomas, 794
Thomas J., 823
Thomas Smith, 794
Gise, Mabel, 955
Gissinger, Cora, 1358
Gittinger, Clara M., 978
Daniel F., 978
E. A., 1357
Frances, 1591

George, 978
George William, 978
Henry M., 978
John E., 843, 978
Laura C., 978
Lewis C., 978
Margaret J., 978
Mary E., 978
Minnie G., 1357
Samuel J., 978
Sarah, 978
Z. J., 1016
Gittings, Edwin, 1511
George W., 892
Henrietta F., 892
Gladhill, Catherine, 1358
Daniel L., 985
Elizabeth, 759
Jane, 1373
Glaze, Catharine, 812
David, 812, 1022
Elizabeth, 812, 1022, 1023,
　1603
John, 812
John H., 812
Joseph, 807, 812
Maggie, 812
Margaret, 812
Maria, 812
Mary, 812
Mary A., 1402
Samuel, 812
Sarah, 812
W. O., 1165
Wendell, 812
Worthington, 1166
Worthington O., 812
Glessner, Mary, 1146, 1147
Mary C., 1381
Glisen, R., 1057
Glissen, Rodney J., 1243
Gluck, A. M., 735
Aaron Manns, 825, 826
Henry, 825
Gockley, Mary, 1590, 1591
Goetz, Margaret, 1121
Golding, James A., 830
Joseph, 773
Goldsborough, C. W., 1422
Charles, 1241
Charles W., 1533
E. Y., 1243
Edward Ralston, 1242
Edward Yerbury, 1241
John, 1241
Mary Catherine, 1241

Nicholas, 1241
Robert, 1241
Robert Henry, 1241
William, 1241
Gonso, Amy E., 822
Henry, 822
Goodell, Asa, 760
Charles Fremont, 760
Charles Graham, 761
Harriet E., 760
Hosea B., 760
Jessie R., 761
John H., 760
Mary, 760
Raymond D., 760
Robert F., 761
William F., 760
Goodhart, Charles, 1099,
　1114
Charles W., 1107
Goodman, Edward, 1274
Florence, 1274
Helen Lucile, 1274
J. M., 814
James Hammond, 1274
James M., 1274
John H., 1274
Mattie, 1274
Sallie, 1274
Silas M., 1274
William, 1274
Gordan, John, 810
Margret, 810
Martha Ellen, 810
Gordon, Blanche, 1333
Callie, 831
Nevin, 1333
Wilbur, 1333
Gorman, Arthur P., 1311
Clema, 1335
Elizabeth I., 1335
Elmer C., 1335
Emma M., 1335
Jacob, 1335
Jacob H., 1335
Jacob R. , 1335
Steward J., 1335
Vera, 1253
Gorrell, Mary, 1142
Gorton, Emma V., 1198
Gosnel, Sarah Ellen, 1555
Goswell, John Thomas, 1245
Beale, 1245
Benjamin, 1245
Charles, 1245
Christiana, 1245

Hanson, 1245
James Dawson, 1245
Jesse Edward, 1245
Louisa, 1245
Lydia Hammond, 1245
Margaret, 1245
Susan Mary, 1245
William H., 1245
William Henry, 1245
Gouff, Mary C., 1496
Gough, Harry Dorsey, 940
Govman, Philip, 719
Grabell, Wm. H., 1497
Grabilk, W., 1135
Aaron M., 1259
Abraham, 1258
Abraham Webster, 1258
Albert, 1258
Annie, 1258, 1259
Edna, 1259
Frank, 1259
John, 1258
Magdalena, 1209
Mary, 1259
Nora, 1259
Reuben S., 1501
Samuel, 1258
Warren, 1258
Graff, Charles B., 1412
Elizabeth E., 1412
John P., 1411, 1412
John P., Jr., 1412
Mary W., 1412
Roger E., 1412
Sophia T., 907, 1412
Theressa A., 1412
William, 907, 1411, 1412
Graham, Ada V., 761
George A., 1490
Jordan Wenner, 1590
Lizzie, 1507
Robert H., 761
Sarah E., 811
Sarah I., 1490
Grahame, Ann Rebecca, 1224, 1225
Grasty, Charles H., 713
Graves, Adam, 1211
John George, 1211
Gray, Charles Warren, 974
John, 1344, 1414
Mary, 1485, 1486
Miriam, 974
Sarah Elizabeth, 974
Graybill, A. K., 1151
Fanny, 1214

Savilla, 1116
Greeley, Adolphus W., 700
Greely, Horace, 898
Green, Ann Rebecca, 1529
Annie, 1108
Benjamin L., 1108
Charles, 1529
Clay Z., 1530
Conrad, 727
Cora, 1530
Douglas, 1108
Everett C., 1489
George, 1108
George W., 1108
Harlan, 1529
Harry, 1530
Ida, 1108
J. Randolph, 1109
James L., 1108
John L., 1108, 1109, 1128
John T., 1108
John William, 1529, 1530
Joseph D., 883, 1108
Lewis T., 868
Lillie U., 1108
Louis, 787
Louisa, 1529
Mahlon B., 868
Maria C., 1108
Martha, 1529, 1530
Martha E., 1385
Mary, 1151
Maud Estella, 1530
Mervin, 1530
Monica, 836
Norman Clyde, 1530
Parker P., 1529
Perry, 1500
Rosie Amanda, 1530
William E., 1108
Zachariah, 1529, 1530
Zachariah T., 1385
Greenbury, Elizabeth, 1241
Mary, 1212
Greentree, Ezra, 839
Mary Elizabeth, 795
Greenwald, Annie M., 1090
Henry, 962
Susan, 1154
Greenwell, Priscilla, 1067
Greenwood, Alfred, 1546
Ann Maria, 1298, 1495
Carrie, 1546
Catherine, 1367
Horace, 1546
Philip, 1298, 1495

Gregg, Charles S., 1040
Harry C., 1040
James W., 1040
John, 1040
Myrtle, 1040
Samuel U., 1040
Sarah C., 1040
Gregory, Anna Virginia, 1574
B. Louis, 1574
Charles R., 1573, 1574
Edwin M., 1574
Estella, 1574
Eugenia, 1574
George M., 1574
Gertrude, 1574
H. E., 1539
Josephine, 1574
Julian S., 1574
Logan, 1574
Lula, 1574
Mahetable C., 1574
Malcom, 1574
Martha G., 1574
Mary, 1574
Richmond, 1573, 1574
Samuel J., 1574
Greybill, Jacob, 961
Greinder, John, 1614
Grier, Ann Margaret, 1505
Robert, 1505
Griesemer, Louisa Rothermel, 854
Griffin, Harry, 1221
Laura, 1057
Griffith, Airy, 1153
Annie, 1153
Annie M., 1008
Auralea, 1153
Charles, 1153
Eleanor, 782, 783
Elinor, 716
Elizabeth, 1153
Fannie H., 1041
Greenberry, 1153
Harry, 1153
Henry, 845
Howard, 783
John, 1153
John Burgess, 716
John L., 1153
John McElfresh, 1152, 1153
Lillian, 1153
Mordica J., 1008
Mrs. Philemon Howard, 716

Nacy, 1152, 1153
Nacy L., 1153
Philemon, 716
Philip, 1153
Philomon, 1008
Rachel, 1153
Rebecca, 1153
Roger, 1153
Ruth, 716, 781, 783, 845, 1069, 1073, 1461
Samuel, 1041
Sophia, 948
Victor, 1153
William, 1153
Grimes, Adeline C., 1009
Amelia, 1235, 1516
Anna May, 1071, 1521
Beatrice Virginia, 1071,1521
Belva Irene, 107, 1521
Catharine, 1604
Charles, 1071, 1520
Clinton, 1071, 1520
Edgar L., 956
Eliza Martin, 1520
Ephraim, 1274
Ephraim D., 1071, 1520
Evelyn Irene, 1071, 1521
F. H., 1089
Francis E., 1071, 1521
Frank, 1007
Franklin, 1530
Frederick, 1071, 1520
Gladys Irene, 1071, 1521
James, 1071, 1520
James Blaine, 1071, 1521
Johanna, 1071, 1520
John Hayden, 1071, 1521
Joseph H., 1071, 1521
Josephine, 1071, 1520
Kitty, 1555
Leoda, 1071, 1521
Mary, 1071, 1181, 1230, 1498, 1520, 1555
Mary Ann, 1071, 1520
Mary E., 1009
Mary Elizabeth, 1071, 1521
Maurice Ellsworth, 1071, 1521
Oscar Sherman, 1071, 1521
Rachel, 1555
Rena, 1071
Reno, 1521
Roland, 1071, 1521
Russell, 1071, 1521
Samuel, 1009

Sarah Jane, l071, 1521
Sarepta E., 1009
Scott, 1071, 1520
Susan, 1071, 1520
Taylor, 1071, 1520
Warner T., 1009
Washington, 1500
William B., 1070, 1071, 1520
William C., 1070, 1071 , 1520
William C., 2nd, 1070, 1520
William C., 3rd, 1071, 1520
William G., 735
William Grant, 1071, 1520, 1521
Grimm, Abraham, 1094
Mary, 1094
William, 922
Grinder, Alonzo M., 1002
Annie, 1527
Emma C., 1002
John S., 1002
Joseph S., 1002
Maggie, 1002
Mary W., 1002
Michael, 1002, 1116
Regina C., 1002
Samuel, 1002
Susan, 1116
Grines, Eliza Ann, 1613
Gring, David, 1574
Grisbert, Jennie, 930
Grise, Barbara, 1559
Groff, Doris, 1619
Joseph, 1237, 1270, 1284, 1518, 1619
Newton, 1517
Groh, Joseph, 1403
Grosh, Hattie A., 1380
Mrs. Amelia W., 1380
Gross, Anna Louyse, 978
Catharine, 977
Charles, 977
Charles A., 978
Clemma B., 1193
Daniel, 977
Edward Lynch, 978
Elizabeth, 977
Flora, 978
Flora Clarke, 978
George, 977
Gertrude, 1472
H. B., 978
Harry, 977
Henry, 977

John, 1181, 1460
Johnathan, 977
Urias, 1496
William Boteler, 978
William L., 977, 978
Grossnickle, Albert, 869
Amanda, 1371
Anna Elizabeth, 1182
Anna Mary, 1377
Annie C., 1373, 1522
Annie E., 1371
Benton, 1513
Bertie, 1371
Bertie G., 1374
Bettie M., 1372
Blain, 1471
C. Upton, 958, 1373, 1374, 1524, 1580
Caleb T., 1377
Caroline, 871, 1371
Caroline A., 1371
Carrie, 994, 1374
Catherine, 1370
Charles, 725, 877, 1175, 1371
Charles C., 1148, 1371
Charles E., 1372
Charles W., 1370
Christianna, 1369
Clara, 1374, 1513
Clay V., 892, 1372
Cora M., 1373
Daisy U., 1374
Daniel, 756, 1369, 1374, 1513
Daniel R., 1374
David, 1135, 1136, 1370, 1376, 1377, 1499
David Roy, 1377
Edith, 1371
Effie E., 1370
Elias, 1148, 1373, 1374
Elizabeth, 771, 819, 903, 1347, 1369
Elmer, 1500
Emmanuel, 1477
Etta M., 1373
Flora, 1371
Florence B., 1372
Foster E., 1372
George, 862, 1374
George F., 1373
George P., 1370, 1470
George Peter, 1376
Hanna, 1369
Hannah, 1376

Harry, 1471
Harry M. G., 1370
Harvey R., 1372
J., 1349
Jacob, 1369, 1374
John, 1148, 1373
John Adam, 1377
John D., 1370
John M., 1373
John P., 1371
John, Jr., 1370, 1373
John, Sr., 1369, 1370, 1374
Jonathan, 1371, 1374
Joshua Carmack, 1514
Joshua R., 1377
Julia, 1470, 1513
Julia C., 866-868, 1470, 1471
Kansie Grace, 1514
Lidye, 1617
Louie, 1513
Louisa C., 1348, 1373, 1470, 1471
Lydia, 1369-1371
Mahlon, 1371
Mahlon W., 1371
Margaret, 862, 1349, 1371
Margaret E., 1371
Maria Alverta, 1371
Martin, 1369, 1370, 1373, 1377
Mary, 1369, 1370
Mary C., 1370
Mary E., 1136
Mary Elizabeth, 1377
Mary Key, 1514
Mary R., 1372
May R., 1372
Meadie, 1513
Melissa L., 1373
Mrs. John, 1373
Nannie, 1374
Nannie M., 1580
Nellie, 1513
Nellie N., 1374
Nettie H., 1370
Oliver Franklin, 1377
Parker, 1513
Paul, 1374, 1500
Peter, 871, 875, 876, 903, 1175, 1349, 1369, 1371-1374, 1376, 1377, 1390
Peter, Jr., 1369, 1370
Peter, Sr., 1369
Phoebe Ellen, 1514

Raymond, 1374
Rebecca, 1369, 1374
Retta, 1292
Rettie, 1513
Rhoda, 1514
Richard H., 1370
Richard Hilliary, 1377
Robert G., 1374
Rosco B., 1372
Russell H., 1373
Salome A., 1370, 1373, 1522
Sarah, 1376, 1513
Sarah Ann, 1470
Sarah E., 756
Susan, 1369, 1370, 1374, 1513
Susan R., 1148
Susan S., 1370
Thomas, 1371
Tilghman F., 1370, 1373, 1522
Tilghman L, 1513
Upton, 747, 883, 955, 1589
Upton W., 1374
Ursula Blanche, 1377
Vada E., 1148, 1372
Vernie, 1371
Wade, 862
Welty K., 913, 1371
Wilbur Luther, 1514
William Clayton, 1377
William H., 1371, 1372
Grove, John H., Jr., 1135
Anna M., 1011
Annie, 895, 1134
B. L., 1187
Barbara, 1134
Benjamin F., 1134
Bernard L., 1187, 1188
Carrie E., 1187
Catherine, 1134
Charles, 1129
Charles B., 1570
Charles D., 1409
Charles L., 951
Charles R., 1135
Charles W., 1134
Chrissie V., 1134
Cora Pauline, 1135
Daniel, 977, 1021, 1031
Daniel R., 748
David, 1129, 1134
E. D., 1187
Edward D., 1187, 1188
Elias, 1134, 1523
Elizabeth, 1047

Elizabeth J., 1186
Ella M., 748
Emma, 1186
Emma M., 1134
Eugene, 1129
Eugene A., 1188
Eugene Ashby, 1187
F. F., 1599
Fannie M., 1129
Frances, 1186, 1568, 1611
Francis H., 1134
Fullerton, 894
George, 894, 1183
George E., 1135
George W., 1186, 1568, 1611
Grace, 1134
Grace H., 1523
Greenberry Dillard, 1482
Henry, 1134
J. Harry, 1188
J. R. , 1047
Jacob, 893, 894, 1186, 1563
Jacob F. T., 894
James A., 1011
James H., 1187, 1188
James H., Jr., 1188
James K. P., 894
Jennetta, 1129
Jeremiah, 894
Joan Eliza, 1563
Johanna, 894
John, 894, 895, 1129, 1130
John H., 1135
John M., 895
John Mason, 893-895
John S., 1076
Joseph, 950
Kathleen M., 1135
Laura, 1186, 1187
Leonard, 894, 1511
Loretta, 894
Louisa, 1366
Louisa E., 1010, 1365
Lydia, 1134
M. J., 745, 761, 999, 1035, 1186, 1187, 1188, 1447, 1568
M.. J.
Mabel M., 1135
Manasses J., 1187
Manasses Jacob, 1186, 1188
Manzella, 894

Margaret, 1134
Marshal L., 1134
Martin, 894, 1366
Martin Franklin, 1186, 1187
Mary, 1182, 1183, 1186, 1482
Mary Ann, 894
Mary Catharine, 1144
Mary Evelyn, 1135
Mary Magdalene, 894
R. C., Jr., 901
Reine E., 1135
Reuben, 1129, 1134
Rosa B., 1134
Samuel, 894, 993, 1093, 1144, 1621
Sarah Alice, 894, 895
Susan, 1134
Templeton, 895
Virginia, 894
Virginia E., 1094, 1095
William, 894, 895, 1129
William J., 1187, 1188
William Jarboe, 1186
Grover, M., 1164
Grubbs, Emory, 1462
James H., 1462
Lindley, 1462
Vivian, 1462
Gruder, Frank, 1336
Grumbine, Alice V., 1359
Calvin J., 1359
Charles F., 1359
Daniel G., 1359
Daniel M., 1358, 1359
Ella N., 1359
Enoch L., 1359
J. Allen, 1358, 1359
Jacob, 1358
Lillian Rae, 1465
Marshal S., 1359
Marshall, 1465
Mary M., 1359
Rose C., 1359
Sarah J., 1359
Grumling, Isaac, 899
Gue, James, 1325
Gurley, Charlotte L., 837, 1455
Mary, 954
Pleasant, 1549
Thomas, 837, 1455
William, 954
Gush, Ella, 1567
Guthing, George Adam, 1404

Guting, Heinrich, 1403
Ludwig, 1403
Gutting, Johann Heinrich, 1404
Guttrell, Lydia, 1153
Guyer, John, 1075
Guynton, E. E., 994
Julia Loretta, 994
Velma, 994
Guyton, Charles T., 1045
William, 1549
Gwyn, Ellen, 1388
Haak, Carrie, 830
Hack, A. A., 1417
Hacket, Caleb, 1002
Hackney, Philip, 1275
Haden, Thomas, 1365
Hafer, Samuel, 1134
Haff, Abraham, 734, 794
Abraham, 3rd, 794
Abraham, Jr., 794
Amy, 734
Lawrence, 794
Haff-Biggs, Martha, 793
Haffner, Austin F., 801
George W., 800
Jacob, 800
John, 1443, 1483
Lewis, 1609
Martha W., 800
Samuel P., 800
Samuel T., 800, 936
Sarah, 1286
Ward C., 801
William F., 800
William W., 800
Hagan, Annie H., 1559
Charles, 1558
Charles Mc., 1558, 1559
Henry J. D., 1559
Michael, 1559
Michael P., 1558
Norman B., 1558
Richard, 1558, 1559
Hageddorn, Jennie M., 1551
Hagen, Adam, 1469
Margaret, 1469
Hagenbouzer, Louisa, 779
Hager, Jonathan, 1025, 1262
Hahn, Abraham, 772
Adolph, 818
Adolphus, 1560
Alice B., 1526
Annie C., 819, 1560
Bessie V., 819
Caroline, 818, 819
Carrie Marie, 1511

Catherine, 1009
Charles M., 1560
Charles N., 819
Clara A., 1560
Clara C., 819
Edgar A., 1511
Elizabeth, 1246
Ellen C., 1560
Henry, 1514
Henry A., 818, 819, 934, 1560
Jacob, 787, 1511, 1599
James, 1215, 1448
John, 1516
John Michael, 1526
Lena V., 1560
Marcella, 1511, 1514
Margaret, 1511
Margaret A., 1560
Margaret E., 1130
Mary, 1252
Matilda, 1516
Michael, 1511
Monroe B., 1130
Newton M., 1130
Oliver F., 1511
Phillip, 805
Sadie C., 819
Sarah E., 1357
William, 891
William A., 819, 1560
William E., 1511
Haines, Albert, 1613
Albert L., 1203, 1204
Catherine, 798
Charles, 1203
Charles Norris, 1076
Charles S., 1076
Charles W., 1129
Daniel, 1194
David, 1203
Edith, 1203
Ephraim, 1194
Etta Pearl, 1555, 1556
Francis W., 1203, 1204
Israel, 1203
Jesse, 1610
Jessie, 1204
John, 1203
John M., 1203
Lizzie, 1556
Pearl, 1204
Thomas, 1463
William, 1555
Hains, Jesse L., 821
Halbruner, Mary Louise,

1312
Thomas, 1312
Hall, B. Franklin, 898
    Hattie V., 898
    Jane, 1329, 1608
    Joel, 1068, 1247
    John, 1329, 1608
    Sidney A., 1122
Hallabaugh, Susan, 1612
Haller, Alice, 1141
    Charles, 1096
    Clara, 784
    David, 1095
    Edward F., 784
    Elizabeth, 784, 1439
    Eugene, 784
    Grace V., 785
    Harriet, 880
    Hemma H., 784
    Henrietta, 844
    John M. , 784
    Lucy, 784
    Mary Elizabeth, 1454, 1577
    M. C., 823
    Nettie, 784
    Ruth E., 785
    Thomas, 784
    Thomas H., 784, 914, 1357, 1368, 1488
    Thomas Stewart, 785
    Tobias, 784
    Violetta, 1454
    W. Harry, 785
    Wm., 1096
Hallowell, Ben, 1582
    Benjamin, 744
Halter, Charles R., 1541
Hamaker, B. F., 1273
Hames, Lillie, 1538
Hamilton, John, 789
    Lloyd, 789
    Raymond, 959
Hammaker, B. F., 920
    Mary C., 920
    Peter, 920
    Peter N., 920, 921, 973
    Solomon, 920
Hammerick, Asger, 1428
Hammett, Blanch, 858
    David C., 858
    D. C., 1436
Hammitt, Susan Brunner, 812
    Thomas P., 812
Hammond, Ann, 946
    Ariana, 1153
    Augustus, 1453

Carroll, 1263
Charles, 1212
Denton, 937, 941, 946
Edgar, 1452
Edgar, Jr., 1452
Emma, 1214
Eugene, 1450, 1451, 1480
Fannie Lenore, 1214
Frances Willard, 1214
Frank, 1450, 1453
Harold Dorsey, 1214
Henry Bruce, 1452
Horace, 1214
John, 1212, 1264, 1273
Julia Anne, 1263
Laura A., 991, 992
Margaret B., 1008
Mary Marie, 1214
Mary W., 937
Mrs. Nick, 716
Nathan, 1212
Paul B., 1214
Philip, 1212
R. L., 1214
Reason, 1263
Reginald G., 1214
Richard, 1112, 1268, 1269
Richard T., 991, 1212
Robert Garrison, 1214
Robert Lee, 1212, 1213
Walter Charles, 1212
Wellington, 1596
Hamner, James G., 842
Hamtramck, Florence, 901
Hanawalt, H. C., 1484
Handly, Albert, 1284
    Martha E., 1284
    Mary, 1284
Handy, Wm. W., 1212
Hane, Fannie B., 1017
    George F., 1438
    Jacob D., 1017
Haner, William, 1314
Hanes, Ann Eliza, 1611
    Charles W., 987
Hankey, A. J., 761, 999, 1446
    Alva, 1167
    Amanda A., 811, 1490
    Anderson, 1167
    Anna, 1167
    Barbara, 810, 1166, 1490
    Carrie, 1167
    Cora, 1167
    Elizabeth, 810, 1166, 1490
    Frederick, 810, 1166, 1490
    Frederick W., 811, 1490

George, 810, 1166, 1167, 1490
George W. A., 1167
Ida A., 811, 1490
Isaac, 810, 1166, 1490
Isaac L., 1166, 1167
Isaac L., Jr., 1167
Jacob, 810, 1166, 1490
Jacob A., 811, 1490
James, 788, 1600
James M., 1167
John, 810, 1166, 1167, 1490
Mary, 1167
Mary A, 810, 1490
Mary A., 811, 1166
Mary C., 1167
Mary Catharine, 1167
Myrtle, 1167
Ora A., 1167
Peter, 810, 1166, 1167, 1490
Ralph, 1167
Roy W., 1490, 1491
Sarah E., 811, 1490
Susan, 810, 1166, 1490
William, 1167
Hanks, Florence, 1120
    Nancy, 1120
Hann, Henry, 1039
    Martha, 1039
Hanna, Clinton, 1556, 1601
    George, 1344
    Isabella, 1388
    Jean, 1601
    Milton G., 1557
    Sarah, 1379
Hansell, Margaret, 718, 719
    Morris, 719
Hanshew, George B., 1318
    Henry, 870
    Julia M., 870
Hanson, Abrilla, 806
    Alexander Contee, 1211
    Grafton D., 1232
Harbaugh, Ada B., 1180
    Agnes W., 1180
    Allen, 1179
    Allen Edgar, 1336
    Alva Steiner, 1336
    Amanda, 1180
    Amie M., 1180
    Andrew, 1179
    Ann, 1336
    Ann Catherine, 1178
    Ann Margaret, 1178

Ann Maria, 781
Anna Margaretta, 1178
Anna Maria, 1178
Arben, 1179
Barbara, 1178
Benjamin, 1178
Bertha, 838
Calvin, 769
Caroline, 1179
Carrie, 1200
Catharine, 973, 1264, 1336
Catherine, 781, 918, 1178-1180
Cecelia A., 730
Celia Ann, 781, 1336
Celiann, 1179
Charles, 1179, 1468
Charles H., 1335, 1336
Charles L., 1179
Charles Norman, 1336
Charlotte, 1179
Christian, 1179
Clarence, 1179, 1336
Clemence, 1179
Cora M., 1179
Cornelia, 1180
Cornelius, 1180
David, 1178-1180
David Keller, 1180
Delilah, 781, 1336
Diana, 1336
Diana Agnes, 1179
Elbert, 1179
Electus, 1179
Elias, 1178, 1446
Elizabeth, 769, 1178-1180
Emily, 1180
Emma J., 780, 781
Emma Jane, 1336
Ephriam, 836
Esther M., 1180
Frederick, 1178
George, 781, 899, 1178, 1180, 1446
George Ludwig, 1178
George M., 873
George Martin, 1179, 1336
Hamilton, 868, 886, 1179, 1180
Harry, 780, 781
Harry C., 1179
Harry R., 1179
Helen S., 1336
Henry, 1178, 1179, 1195, 1336, 1446
Herman, 1179

Hiram, 760, 1178, 1179, 1446
Ignatius, 1180
Isabel, 1336
Isabella, 1180
Jacob, 1178, 1179, 1446
James, 715, 1180
Jefferson Lewis Franklin, 1179
Jeremiah, 1179
Jerry, 1619
John, 1178-1180, 1336
John H., 1180
John Henry, 781, 1179
John Henry Franklin, 1179
John I., 874
John Ignatius, 1180
John M., 1179
John Nicholas, 1180
Jonathan, 1178, 1180
Joseph, 1097, 1178
Josiah, 1180
Juliann, 1178, 1179
L. C., 717
Leonard, 717, 1178, 1446
Leonard C., 1178, 1446
Levi C., 973
Lewis, 1180
Lewis C., 1178, 1179, 1446
Lewis E., 1179
Louis C., 1446
Ludwig, 1179
Lula E., 1179
Lydia Ann, 1179
Mansella, 1336
Manzella, 781
Margaret, 1178, 1179
Marthia Delia, 1179
Martin, 1180
Martin L., 1180
Martin Ray, 1336
Mary, 1178, 1179
Mary Ann, 1178
Mary B., 1180
Mary Catherine, 1179
Mary Elizabeth, 1178
Mary I., 781
Mary Isabella, 1179
Mary Jane, 1180
Matilda, 1178
Mettie G., 1180
Milton Wesley, 1180
Minnie, 733
Morgan M., 995
Nancy, 1178
Nannie, 1143

Oscar, 886
Rebecca, 1179
Rosina Elizabeth, 1180
Sabilla, 1179
Sabina, 1179, 1252
Sadie E., 1336
Samuel D., 1179, 1180, 1446
Samuel Milton, 1180
Sanford, 769
Savilla, 781, 1179, 1336
Simon W., 838
Simon Washington, 1178, 1446
Solomon, 1178
Stanley Lee, 1180
Susan, 868, 1178-1180
Susan C., 717
Susan D., 1180
Susan E., 1178, 1446
Susannah, 1178
T. C., 1193
Thomas, 1180
Thomas Chalmers, 995
Valentine, 1178, 1446
Vincent C., 1179
Virginia K., 1179
Wilbur H., 1179
William, 781, 1179, 1336, 1518, 1619
William A., 1179
William F., 1336
William Henry, 1180
Yost, 715, 1178
Youst, 1180
Hardey, May, 1188
Harding, Basil, 1355
Cora, 1355
John B., 722
L. R., 1469
Lewis, 1440
Mary, 1440
Mary A. R., 1440
Hardt, Margaret C., 845, 880, 881
Hardy, Catharine Rebecca, 1219
John, 1219
M. C., 1100
Thomas E., 1122
Hargett, Abram, 1256
Ann, 1494
Ann Maria, 1085, 1086
Barbara, 1086
Bessie M., 1258
Burns, 1258

Calvin, 1256
Catharine, 1561
Charles, 923
Charles N., 807
Claude, 1004, 1092
Cyrus, 1313
D. H., 1092, 1311
Della, 1561
Douglas H., 1004
Douglass, 1243
Douglass H., 923, 1256, 1312
Earlston Lilburn, 1258
Edna Maud, 1092
Effie S., 1004, 1092, 1366
Eleanor, 1092
Eleanor M., 1004
Hiram, 1020
John, 1003, 1004, 1086, 1256, 1366, 1416, 1431, 1528
John E., 1003, 1004, 1090, 1092, 1256, 1312, 1366
John L., 1561
John W., 1561
Julia A., 1432, 1528
Julia Ann, 1366, 1431, 1528
Levin, 987
Margaret A., 1561
Mary, 1416
Mary C., 1004, 1256, 1311, 1426
Mary Ellen, 1561
Minnie J., 987, 1561
Othalia, 1561
P. L., 965, 1004, 1311
Peter, 1256
Peter C., 1004
Peter L., 1256
Peter Lilburn, 1312
Richard S., 1004, 1092
S. F., 1561
Samuel, 1003, 1004, 1256, 1312
Samuel L., 1004, 1256, 1311, 1312
Sarah, 1143
Schaeffer T., 1256, 1312
Shafer T., 1004
Walter S., 1258
William, 987, 1561
William D., 1561
William S., 1004, 1092
Harley, Charles Mortimer, 1453

Cornelius F., 1567
Cornelius Franklin, 1453
Eliza, 1566
Elizabeth, 1185, 1566
Francis Dunbar, 1567
George Trueman, 1567
Harriet Catherine, 1453
Henry Tilghman, 1567
John H., 1567
John Willard, 1453
Josephus, 1177, 1453
Josephus E., 1566, 1567
Joshua, 1566
Julia Frances, 1453
Lucy Marcissa, 1453
Mahlon, 1566
Margaret , 1453
Margaret Frances, 1453
Mary, 1567
Mary Christine, 1567
Otho, 1453, 1566
Sophia, 1567
Thomas, 1566, 1567
Trueman, 1453
Virginia Theodosia, 1567
William, 1566
Harling, Charles, 974
Fannie, 974
Harmis, Annie, 1274
Charles W., 1274
Delilah, 1274
George W., 1273, 1274
Jacob, 1274
Laura E., 1273
Margaret, 1274, 1538
Mary J., 1274
Mary Jane, 1517
Oliver, 1274
Susan, 1274
Harmiss, Ann, 1071
Harmon, Edward, 1588
Elizabeth, 1171
Eugenia, 743
Holly, 1209
Isaac, 1151
Mary Ann, 746
William, 746
Harn, Abner, 1293, 1305, 1557
Albert, 1557
Alice, 1293
Annie L., 1293
Augustus, 1557
Carilla, 1558
Cordelia, 1558
Denton, 1557
Edward Elmer, 1558

Elisha, 1557
Elizabeth, 1557
Ellen, 1558
Evan, 1557
Isabella, 1557
Johanna M., 1557
John H., 1557
Kenley, 1293
Laura, 1293
Letha, 1557
Letha Zelma, 1558
Levi, 1557
Louisa, 1557
Luther, 1305, 1558
Luther E., 1557, 1558
Maria Cordelia, 1557
Mrs. John H., 1162
Rachel, 1557
Samuel, 1293
Singleton, 1557
Thomas W., 1067
Wesley J., 1557
William, 1053, 1557
William D., 1558
Harne, Albert E., 1014
Alonzo J., 1014
Charles O., 1014
Cordelia, 1611
Cora M., 1014
Creola V., 1014
Cyrus F., 1014
Gideon O., 1014
Henry, 1013
James G., 1014
James O., 1013, 1014
Maggie B., 1014
Oliver G., 1014
Roy M., 1014
William D. L., 1014
Harner, Alfred, 828, 1618
Gertrude, 1002
James W., 1620
Harnie, Newton, 1312
Harnish, Webster, 1119
Harp, Caroline, 904
Catharine, 904, 993
Catherine, 1148, 1373
Charles W., 757
Clara E., 905
Clara M., 852
Daniel, 903, 904
Daniel V., 904
Elizabeth, 829, 830, 904, 1032, 1033, 1352
Emma Victor, 905
George, 903, 904

Hannah, 903, 904
Jacob, 903, 904
Jennie M., 905
John, 829, 830, 903, 904, 1033
John Michael, 903
Joshua, 852, 904
Lizzie, 1133
Louise J., 1186
Lydan, 770
Lydia, 904
M. D., 893
Madaline V, 906
Maria, 903
Markwood D., 905
Mary, 903
Mary A., 904
Mary Ellen, 1077
Michael, 903
Reno S., 706, 903-905
Reno S., Jr., 906
Roy S., 1229
Sarah, 946
Sarah C., 876
Silas, 1374
Susan, 870
Susanna, 1147, 1148
Susannah, 903, 904
Harper, C. W., 1391
Charles, 764
James, 805
Harr, Joseph, 1181
Harreld, Patsey, 1417
Harrington, George, 1134
Harris, Addie, 866
Amanda, 1206
Chapin A., 1051
Cordelia, 940, 1073
Eliza Ann, 1533
Elizabeth, 940
Elizabeth B., 815
G. W., 735
George, 1206
Harriet, 939-941
Henry R., 1091, 1206, 1389
Israel, 866
James H., 815
James H., Jr., 815
Johnson, 940
Joshua, 940
Julia Amanda, 1389
Lizzie, 1501
Louisa, 922
Mary Elizabeth, 815
Nathan, 939-941
Thomas, 815, 940

William H., 1227, 1294
Harrison, Charles, 778
Charles W., 1134
Eugene Lincoln, 925
George Otho, 925
Jessie, 1605
L. F., 1118
Mary, 1245
Mary Josephine, 925
Napoleon B., 1389
P. L., 1607
Robert L., 1544
Sally, 1555
Thomas, 1172, 1299
Thomas P., 949
William Carleton, 925
William Franklin, 925
William Henry, 918, 1048
Harry, Ann R., 1310
Eleanora, 1311
Irwin, 1311
Stephen R., 1310
William H., 1004, 1256, 1310
Harshman, Adie C., 1148
Alvey P., 1347, 1348
Amy A., 820
Annie A., 1347
Aquilla, 1347
Aquilla A., 1348
Catherine, 771, 819, 1347
Charles, 1471, 1606
Christian, 1346
Cordelia M., 820
Cornelius, 819, 1347
Daniel, 749, 819, 1347, 1369, 1371, 1617
Daniel C., 1148
Daniel H., 1349
Elias, 819, 820, 1347
Emanuel, 1371
Emma V., 1349
Emmerson E., 820
Estella M., 1349, 1617
Ezra, 819, 1347
Flora V., 1349
Florence E., 1148
Frank, 1336
Franklin, 1110, 1512
Franklin B., 1622
Ida S., 820
Ira V., 1347, 1371
J. Frank, 1348
J. Lloyd, 1347
John, 771, 819, 1346, 1347, 1369

John E., 819, 820
John F., 1332, 1347
John T., 743, 819, 1346-1348
John W., 1348
Jonathan, 819, 1347
Lauson P., 819, 1347, 1348
Lawson P., 726, 1617
Louisa C., 820
Mary, 1061, 1371
Mary A., 1349
Mary E., 820
May L., 1348
Millard A., 1348
Missouri A., 820
Nancy, 1348
Nina E., 820
Polly, 1189
Sallie M., 1347
Sarah O., 820
Susan, 1524, 1617
Susan E., 820
Susan R., 1149, 1616
Upton W., 1346-1348
Waldo L., 820
Wilbur C., 1348
William, 1371
William E., 1348, 1349
William Ivan, 1349
Harshmon, Mary, 1605
Hart, Maria, 1516
Hartman, H. H., 814
Hannah, 727
Sarah E., 814
Stewart, 1244
Washington, 1151
Hartow, Elizabeth, 783
Hartsack, Lavina, 1556
Hartsock, Ann, 1217
C. L., 927
John, 946
Julia Ann, 1142
Sarah, 1263, 1571
Hartz, Clinton, 1335
Harvey, Harry C., 1099
James, 1099, 1107, 1113
Margaret, 887
Susanna, 1285
Harwetter, Ella, 1253
Harwood, Clinton B. G., 973
Clinton B. J., 972
Eleanor, 1510
Etta, 1565
George M., 973
Henrietta, 972

Jessie M., 973
M. Noble, 972
Margaret E., 973
Thomas, 972
Thomas Noble, 972, 973, 1102
Virginia Noble, 972
William Thomas, 972
Hasemeyer, Caroline, 840
Haslup, E. L., 1428
Hatcher, E. B., 1389, 1390
Hauck, Caroline, 1602
  James, 1270
  Peter, 1602
Hauer, Agnes Rebecca, 1048
  Barbara, 1047
  Catharine, 1047
  Catherine Zealer, 1047
  Daniel, 1047
  E. Irene, 1048
  Elizabeth, 1047
  George, 1047
  Harriet, 1047
  Henry, 1047
  Ira Clarence, 1048
  Lillian M., 1048
  Margaret, 1047
  Mary, 1047
  Matilda, 1047
  Nicholas, 1047
  Nicholas D., 1047
  William, 793, 1253
Haugh, Abalonia, 1219
  Addison, 1498, 1513
  Addison G., 935
  Adeline, 1207
  Albert C., 1245
  Amy, 1219
  Annie, 1052
  Arthur, 1052
  Arthur A., 1208
  Benjamin Frank, 1498
  Catharine, 1219, 1261
  Catherine, 935
  Charles, 981, 1052
  Charles Cornelius, 1208
  Charles E., 936
  Cora, 1052
  Cora M., 1208
  Cora Myrtle, 1125
  Cornelius, 935
  David, 935, 1052, 1053, 1141, 1219
  Donald C., 1053
  Edna, 1498
  Eli G., 935, 936

Eliza Ann, 1498
Elizabeth, 1207
Ellen, 1498
Emma, 1052
Flora, 1052
George B., 1053
Hamilton, 1333
Henry, 1497, 1513
Hezekiah, 1052
Hilda E., 936
Irving, 1052
Isaac, 1152
Isaac Wallace, 1497, 1498
Isabelle, 1219
J. A., 1207, 1262
Jacob, 935, 1052
John, 935, 1052, 1207, 1261
John H., 1498
John W., 935
John W. A., 1052, 1053
Joseph, 1071, 1520
Josiah, 1498
Judith, 935
Julia, 1052
Julia Ann, 1207
Julian, 1219
Laura, 1052
Louisa, 1052, 1207, 1498
Margaret, 1136, 1219, 1259
Mary, 1052, 1498
Mary Ann, 1207
Mary C., 1141
Neill, 846
Nellie B., 936
Paul, 1052
Powell, 935
Rebecca, 1498
S. C., 1262
Samuel, 1052
Samuel C., 846, 935, 1125, 1207
Solomon, 1052, 1207
Solomon E. E., 1052, 1053
Sophia, 1219
Susan, 1052, 1207, 1219
Susannah, 1261
Thelma, 981
Thomas, 1207
William, 935
William H., 1052, 1207, 1469
Haupt, Emma C., 892
  John H., 951
  Lawson, 892
  Lydia, 1538
  Orpha M., 1158

Susan A. R., 1062
Hause, Levi, 1129
  Naomi, 734
Hauver, Albert L., 1126, 1127
  Albert P., 1127
  Alvey W., 810
  Amy C., 810
  Annie M., 1127
  Charles C., 810
  Chester M., 1083, 1084
  Christian, 809, 810, 1084, 1126, 1370, 1373
  Clara S., 1127
  Clyde L., 1084
  Elizabeth, 810, 1084, 1126
  Ella, 1084
  Emma, 1127
  Ephraim D., 809, 810, 1084
  Ephriam D., 1126
  George P., 1127
  Grace T., 1127
  Hannah, 810, 1084, 1126
  Ida T., 887
  Ira H., 1127
  Jennie F., 810
  John, 886
  John C., 810, 1084, 1126
  Marietta M., 1127
  Mary, 1370
  Masie N., 1084
  May T., 810
  Melancthon, 810, 1083, 1084, 1126
  Peter, 809, 810, 899, 1083, 1126, 1127
  Rebecca, 1373
  R. V., 1426
  Roy V., 1379
  Ruth M., 1084
  Sarah A., 1127
  Stanley E., 1127
  T. L., 757
  William, 749, 810, 887, 952, 1084, 1126
Hawk, Albert Calvin, 1246
  Albert Lee, 1246
  Alvill Clifford, 1246
  Andrew, 1245
  Barbara, 1245
  Delana, 1245
  Elizabeth, 1246
  Henry, 1245
  James, 1245

John, 1245
John William, 1246
Joseph, 1245
Josiah, 1245, 1246
Lucinda Jane, 1246
Martha Adelaide, 1246
Mary, 1245
Oda Marie, 1246
Samuel, 1246
Sarah, 1245
William, 1245
Hawker, Minerva, 1086
Hawkins, Richard, 724
Thomas, 949, 1083
Hawthorne, Elizabeth, 1503
Samuel, 1503
Hax, Elizabeth, 1315
Hay, Nancy, 1530
Hayden, Thomas, 1420
Haydon, John A., 694
Hayes, Abram, 805
Benjamin, 806
Deborah Weimer, 805
Elizabeth Elliott, 805
Hayes, Jonathan, 804
Henrietta, 1011
Jahue, 804
James T., 805
John, 804-806
John Coffee, 804
Jonathan, 804, 806
Joseph, 804, 805
Mary, 805, 854
Samuel, 806
Samuel Elliott, 805
Thomas, 805
William, 805
Hays, Caroline, 840
Denton, 1370
Elizabeth Armstrong, 806
George R., 1027
Harry W., 805
Hattie A., 1027
James T., 806
John O., 899
John Ross, 805
John W., 805
Lizzie Ross, 805
Marietta M., 951
Mary, 886
Samuel C., 805
Sarah Margaret, 805
Sarah Weimer, 805
Thomas, 806
Thomas C., 805
William E., 805

Hazard, Anna, 865
Hazel, Catherine Thorn, 1343
Heagey, Annie, 1139
Calvin G., 1139
Elmira F., 1139
Elmyra M. J., 1139
George W. G., 1139
H. F. C., 1139
Hannah M. C., 1139
Isaac T., 1139
Isaac T. W., 1139
Jacob, 1139
Jesse F. R., 1139
Martha J., 1139
Mary A., 1139
William H., 1139
Heagy, Henry, 1139
Heard, Samuel, 805
Hearn, Lola, 1244
Sarah, 1242
William, 1244
Heath, Charles C., 1140
Steven P., 1385
Heatuale, Ethel May, 1495
Heberlig, Adam, 1199, 1280
Anne Laura, 1199
George B., 1199
Janet, 1199
John, 1199
Martha Elizabeth, 1199
Mary Amantha, 1199
Myra Beaty, 1199
William Mervin, 1199
Hechert, J. C., 1167
Heck, Margaret, 929
Heckathorn, Almeda, 922
Hedge, Mrs Emma, 1287
Hedges, Alice, 1315
Amelia, 1158
Amy C., 1563
Charles, 1061, 1322
Charles Henry, 1314, 1315
Charles Wade, 1315
Daniel, 1304, 1314, 1315
Daniel A., 1322
Daniel Ford, 1315
David, 1315
David L., 1322
Edith Virginia, 1563
Eleanor M., 1061
Enos, 1314
Eva Catharine, 1315
Glenn Harold, 1315
H. S., 925, 926
Harry, 1322
Harry H., 1061

Harry S., 1563
Harvey L., 1322
Helen Charlotte, 1061
John H., 1061
John S., 1563, 1564
John W., 1563
Joseph, 791, 858, 908
Joseph H., 1061
Leslie E., 1061
Lillian G., 1061
Margaret Erb, 1315
Margaret Hazel, 1322
Mary, 858
Mary Alice, 1315
Mary Elizabeth, 1564
Mary M., 1061
Minnie, 1315
Miriam Sophia, 1061
Ralph David, 1315
Samuel, 1563
Shedrick, 1061
Solomon, 1322
Solomon D., 881
Thomas, 1061
William Harper, 1563
Heely, Roy, 1498
Heeter, E. E., 725
Heffelbower, Annie, 1151
Daniel, 1151
Heffling, Robert, 1418
Heffner, Alice, 1333
Amanda, 1333
Charles Henry, 979
Clayton, 1333
Daniel, 979
Delia, 1333
Della L., 1482
Ellen, 1333
Elmer, 1333
Elsie, 1333
Frank, 1333
Frederick, 979, 1332
Ida L. C., 979
Irma, 1333
John, 1609
John D., 979
John H., 1332, 1333
John P., 1333
Lewis, 1482
Lewis C., 1332, 1333
Lillie May, 1333
Lulu, 1333
Luther, 1333
Mary, 1333
Matilda A., 979
Maud, 1333

Nettie, 1333
Ruth, 1333
Samuel, 1333
Samuel T., 1482
Staley Grover, 1333
Walter, 1333
William, 1333
Hefner, Catherine, 1099
Samuel T., 1213
Sophia, 1213
Heidelberger, Isabella, 1392
Heider, Sarah, 1145
Heightman, Blanche, 1435
Jennie C., 1005
Joseph, 1005
Heim, Charles, 1108, 1114
Heiner, Elias, 909
Heines, James, 1100, 1103, 1125
Helfenstein, Allen Trail, 963
Anna Trail, 963
C. G., 963
Charles, 1155
Charles M., 963
Cyrus, 963
E. T., 963
Ernest, 787, 963
Fanny, 963
J. C. Albertus, 963
Jonathan, 963
Mary G., 963
Nannie, 963
Helier, Clara M., 1307
Jacob, 1307
Heller, Caroline, 1413
Mary A., 1170
Hemp, A., Jr., 1477
Abraham, 806, 1443, 1487
Abraham, Jr., 806, 807, 1046, 1047, 1487
Abraham, Sr., 807
Alex, 1502
Bettie W., 807
Clara Lee, 807
Clarence, 1570
Clayton R., 957, 1621
Cora A., 1477
David, 807
Elizabeth Ann, 1487
Ellen, 807
Ellen Catherine, 1064
Frederick, 807, 1064
Helda M., 1047
Hilda Maud, 807
John, 807
Julia C., 807

Julia Catherine, 1487
Laura G., 807
Mary Hannah, 1487
Michael Arnold, 1487
Mollie V., 807
Nena, 1621
Peter, 1189
Peter S., 807, 1137
Peter Slifer, 1487
Rebecca, 807
Richard Lee, 807, 1047
Robert D., 807, 1047
Robert Douglass, 807
Samuel, 807
William, 1477
William A., 807
William F., 1123
Hempston, Alexander, 1338
Frances, 1045, 1303
Hempstone, Cephas, 920
Hench, Ada L., 814
Adella S., 814
Allison L., 814
Annie K., 814
Bandina, 814
Charles L., 814
George W., 813, 814
George William, 814
Inez L., 814
Jeremiah, 814
John, 813
Margaret, 814
Marguerite, 814
Martha J., 814
Mary Elizabeth, 814
Samuel, 813
Samuel N., 814
Sarah A., 814
Silas M., 813
Henderson, Janet, 1137
R. B., 845
Hendrickson, Mary I., 1026
Abraham, 1141
Amanda, 1141
Carroll Henshaw, 1142
Charles B. T., 843, 1141
Daniel, 1141, 1219
Daniel R., 1026
Ephraim, 1141
John, 1141
John D., 1141
John Hunt, 1142
Lydia, 1141
Mary, 1141, 1142
Mary C., 1026
Molly, 1151

Rebecca, 1141
Russell Ames, 1142
Hendrix, Arthur D., 803
Augustus W., 803
Bertha, 803
C. W., 803
Elmer D., 803
George T. Whipp, 804
Irvin N., 803
Jessie, 803
John O., 803
Joshua, 803
William L., 803
Hendry, Burrel, 1286
Charles, 831, 1228, 1286
Emily C., 1286
Isaac S., 1286
Isabelle, 1286
Jane, 1286
Martha C., 1286
Mary Ellen, 831, 1286
Nathaniel B., 1365
Rebecca, 1286
Sarah Amanda, 1227, 1228, 1286
Hennecke, Frederick, 1290
Lena, 1290
Rosina, 1290
Henry, Joseph, 801
Nina, 783
Rebecca, 1309, 1310
Samuel T., 1310
Henshaw, Margaret, 973
Herbert, Fannie S., 1363
John W., 1363
Herbst, John L., 868
Herd, Annie Ethel, 1149
Hergisimer, Emma, 1130
Herman, George, 1591
Isiah, 1590
Isiah L., 1591
Sallie E., 1590
Herr, Ellen, 1477
Emanuel, 1477
Herring, Edward, 912, 923, 955, 1168
George, 1595
Mary S., 1101
Robert R., 1101
Hersberger, Henry, 1378
Hershberger, Aaron, 1573
Bernard, 1595
Catherine, 1595, 1605
Clarissa, 943
David, 943
Dorothy, 792

Elizabeth, 1595
Helen, 944
Henry, 1595
Hiram, 943
Janet, 1573
John, 943
John, Jr., 944
John B., 1595
Joseph C., 943
Joseph C., Jr., 943
L. S., 943
Mary, 1595, 1605
Mayette, 944
Missouri, 943
Mollie, 943
Myrtle, 944
Naomi, 944
Rebecca, 943, 944
Susan, 1595
Thomas, 1595
Tilghman, 1412, 1573
William, 944
Hersperger, Harriet, 1453
Henry, 1453
Julia, 1144
Hertsock, Ernest, 955
Hess, Abraham N., 1367
Carrie, 1367
Charles, 1367
Charles M., 1367, 1368
Charles W., 1367, 1368
Clara A., 1367
David H., 1367
Effie E., 1367
Emma J., 1367
George W., 1367
J. Henry, 1367
Johann Jacob, 1404
John E. E., 1367
Lillie B., 1368
Maria, 718
Nannie E., 1368
Samuel, 1367
Samuel F., 1367
Sarah B., 835
Hessen, Jacob P., 1534
Hesser, Belle, 707
George, 1238, 1239
Lillie, 1239
Mary, 1239
Mary I., 1238
Susan, 1239
Hessin, Edna, 1260
Jacob, 1260
Hesson, Alice, 1009
Alpheus, 1009

Andrew, 1009
Catherine, 1009
Lydia, 1009
Sarah, 1078
Sarah E., 1009
William, 1009
Hessong, Elizabeth, 1443
Ezra, 896
James, 1471
John, 896
Rachel, 1492
Hessongs, John, 1606
Martha E., 1606
Hett, Charles E., 821
Charlotte E., 822
Clarence H., 821
Ethel M., 822
George M., 820, 821
Henry, 821, 1135
John, 821
John D., 821
Margaret J., 821
Melvin C., 822
Heummer, Sarah S., 1589
Hewes, Edward, 1354
Hickey, James D., 802
Hickman, Alberta, 1099, 1107,
1114
Alice, 1099, 1107, 1114
Charles D., 931, 1108, 1114
Eliza, 1099, 1107, 1113
Elizabeth, 1099, 1107, 1113
Ella, 1099, 1107, 1114
Ella M., 1108, 1114
George H. C., 1098, 1099,
1107, 1114
George H., Jr., 1100, 1162
Harry C., 1098-1100
John, 1098, 1099, 1107,
1113
John P., 931, 1099, 1107,
1113, 1114
John W., 1108, 1114
Laura J., 1099, 1107, 1114
Lillie M., 1100
Lottie C., 1100
Maggie V., 1108, 1114
Margaret, 1099, 1107, 1113
Margaret A., 1100
Margaret V., 1099, 1107,
1114
Martha, 1099
Mary A., 1108, 1114
Mary C., 1099, 1107, 1114
Millard F., 1099, 1107, 1114
Nina B., 1108, 1114

Rosie Lee, 1099
Roy S., 1108, 1114
Samuel L., 1099, 1107,
1114
Samuel T., 1108, 1113,
1114
Sarah, 1099, 1107, 1113
Sidney, 1099
Thomas, 1099, 1107
Thomas F., 1099
Thomas W., 1107, 1114
Thornas, 1113
Walter M., 1108, 1114
William, 1099, 1107,
1113, 1114
Hicks,Thomas H., 1399
HienaCalvin, 930
Higgiaames L., 941
William, 1471
Hightfilarence, 1332
George, 1095, 1543
Hannah, 1496
Helen, 1543
Hightmann, John, 1611
Mary E., 1611
Hildebrand, Laura, 1221
Hildebrand, Amanda, 971,
1020
Annie, 971
Annie B., 1021
Blanche Susan, 972
Charles R., 971, 1021
David, 1021
Elizabeth, 1018, 1364
Florence, 971, 1021
George L., 971, 1021
Grace Esta , 972
Isadore, 971
Isadore V., 1021
John, 971, 1018, 1020,
1021, 1364, 1391
John T., 1391
Joseph, 971
Joshua, 1020
Laura, 971
Laura A., 1020
Lewis, 1251
Lewis A., 971, 1021
Louisa, 1020
Lydia, 971, 1020
Lydia C., 1021
Naomi, 972
William, 971, 1020
Hilderbiddle, ——, 1263
Anna, 1262, 1263
Hilderbridle, Frank, 1528

Hill, Anna, 1616
Anna Margaret, 745, 746
Annie, 1342
Annie M., 896
Annie May, 1129
Caroline, 921, 973, 1616
Catharine, 1562, 1583
Christian, 1603
Christopher, 896
Clay, 1200
Frederick J., 848
John, 896, 1129, 1616
Joseph Kent, 848
Julia Ann, 1616
Kitty, 1616
Lillie, 1275
Margaret Ann, 1399
Mary, 1346
William H., 1418
William Kimmel, 848
Hilleary, Abraham, 1116
Ann Cornelia, 1115
Ann P., 1281, 1344
Ann Perry, 1115
Anne Perry, 1115
Betsy, 1442
Caroline, 1115
Charles W., 1115
Clarence, 1115
Clarence W., 1137
Clarence Worthington, 1137
Cornelia Williams, 1115
Eliza Rachel, 1116
Elizabeth, 1115
Ellen McGill, 1115
Ellen Rebecca, 1137
Emma Williams, 1115
Harry Wheeler, 1138
Isiah, 1116
Jeremiah, 1217
John, 1115, 1116, 1137
John Henry, 1115
John William, 1115
Joseph, 1137
Laura Gray, 1115
Leila, 1115
Louisa, 1115
Lucy Baker, 1115
Marshall, 1115
Mary T., 1115
Mortimore Theodore, 1116
Mrs. Charles, 1078
Odell, 1115
Rheumaha, 1115
Russell Paxton, 1115, 1116
Ruth Elizabeth Magruder,

1137
Sallie, 1137
Sallie Worthington, 1138
Sarah, 1154
Sarah Ann, 1137
Thomas, 1115, 1154
Thomas Jackson, 1115
Tilghman, 949, 1115, 1116,
1137
William, 1115, 1208, 1281
William Perry, 1137
Hillegase, Margaret, 1120
Hillery, Eleanor, 1551
Hilliary, Charley Waters, 1596
Ida F., 1596
John Hanson, 1554, 1596
Lizzie, 1059
Mary Elizabeth, 1596
Sarah Ann, 1596
Susan Rebecca, 1553, 1554,
1596
Thomas, 1596
Hilt, Neal, 1326
Hilton, Benjamin, 1338
Hime, Edward, 1426
Himes, Annie, 1062, 1189
John S., 979
Mrs. John S., 979
Nancy J., 1221
W. A., 969
Himlein, Laura V., 815
Hinea, Daisie M., 1123
Elizabeth, 1584-1586
Emma E., 1123
William, 1585
William C., 1123
Hineman, Wm., 718
Hinkle, Jennie, 1576
Hinks, C. D., 818
Caroline, 818
Charles Dent, 817
George M., 818
Janet Chase Dent, 818
Josephine, 818
Josie L., 1323
Louis Edgar, 818
Marian, 818
Samuel, 765, 817, 818, 1323
Samuel M., 818
Susan, 1323
William, 817
William H., 817, 818
Hipsley, Hannah, 1292
Hiteschew, John, 1484
Hiteshew, Anna, 1116
Anna M., 1117

Annie Mary, 889
Charles P., 808
Daniel, 1116
Daniel C., 1116
Ellen, 1116
Floy May, 808
George, 1116
Jacob, 1116
James M., 1116
Julia, 841, 842
Julia A., 807
Laura, 1116
Mary, 1116
Mary M., 1022, 1023,
1597, 1598
P. L., 889
P. M., 1166
Philip, 807, 1023, 1117,
1598
Philip L., 1116
Philip M., 807
Phillip, 898
Savilla, 1116
Sophia E., 807
Webster, 1117
William H., 1116
Hobbs, Alverta, 1560
Charles, 807
E. A., 942
Edward, 1546
John, 965, 966, 1238
Laura, 1449
Martha, 965
Mary, 965
Mrs. Margaret, 1560
Sarah, 1462
William, 940, 941, 1449
Hockensmith, Columbia, 773
Robert, 773
Hodges, Elizabeth, 1227
Hoff, Alice, 1262
George, 1514
I. F., 949
Hoffman, Barbara, 912
Catharine, 1049, 1497
Elizabeth, 858
Franklin, 1127
Henry, 984
Jane E., 984
John, 892
Margaret, 1049, 1497
Mary, 1262
William, 1070
William H., 886
Hogan, David, 1032
Ella, 1032

George H., 1031, 1032
Michael, 1031, 1032
Richard, 1032
Thomas, 1032
Hogarth, Alice A., 806
Annie B., 806
Donald Walter, 806
Emory N., 806
Percy S., 806
Wi lliam H. , 806
William A., 806
William N., 806
Wm. H., 1008
Hoge, H. F., 1230
Hoges, Mary, 1214
Hohf, Elizabeth, 731
Mary, 1318
Michael, 1318
Hohman, Louise, 1168
Hohn, Jacob, 1007
Missouri Victoria, 1007
Hoke, Alice, 1024
Amanda, 1024
Anna, 814
Anna Mary Grons, 1024
Annie, 1024
Bradley H., 814
Bradley Hartman, 815
Catharine, 814, 1537
Catherine, 1545
Clara, 1533
Clarence, 1024
David, 814, 1214
David H., 1164
Edward LaMar, 815
Effie, 1024
Elizabeth, 1024
Fanny, 1214
Fanny L., 1164
Flora, 1024
George, 814, 1024, 1214, 1496
Harvey, 1214
Henry, 1024
Henry G., 1545
Ira L., 814
Jacob, 1023, 1024
John, 814, 1024
Kramer J., 1024
Lee, 1214
Lena, 814
Lillie, 1024
Lloyd, 1545
Lottie, 1024
Martha Catharine, 814
Martin, 814

Mary C., 1024
Mary Elizabeth, 1024
Mary Estella, 814
Mary Estelle, 1274
Mattie, 1214, 1302
Mayne, 1092
Milton, 1214
Mrs. Clara A., 1163
Nancy, 814
Peter, 1023
Rebecca, 814
Robert LaMar, 815
Samuel, 814, 1274, 1537
Samuel Earl, 815
Samuel, Jr., 1353
Sarah, 1024
Sarah Elizabeth, 815
Holbrenner, John M., 1140
Holbruner, Henry, 1566
Sarah, 1566
Thomas, 1237, 1619
Holbrunner, Elizabeth, 1271
Thomas, 1270, 1284, 1518
Holder, Peter, 1584
Holland, John, 915
William, 1471
Holmes, Charles R., 1560
Ephraim, 1594
Robert, 1560
Holt, Benjamin, 1286
Harrison, 1594
Holter, Albert Edward, 1104, 1126
Alma Sarah, 1104, 1126
Ann Perry, 745
Annie Elizabeth, 1104
Annie Mary C., 1101
Catharine, 1100, 1103, 1125
Charles E., 1293
Charles R., 1125
Charles Richard, 1104, 1126
Charlotte Virginia, 1101
Daniel, 1100, 1103, 1125
Daniel Vernon, 1104
Edward Franklin, 1104
Elise Virginia, 1104
Elizabeth, 1100, 1103, 1125
Ella, 1293
Florence Virginia, 1104, 1126
George, 1103, 1125
George B., 1100, 1103, 1125
George M, 1293
Harry T., 1293
Hazel, 1294
Helen L., 1294

Ima E., 1294
Irma E., 1294
Jacob, 1100, 1103, 1125
John, 1100, 1103, 1125
John William, 1104, 1126
Lucy Viola, 1126
M. F., 1430
Magdalene, 1100, 1103, 1125
Mamie Elizabeth, 1101
Margaret, 1100, 1103, 1125
Mary, 1100, 1103, 1125, 1293, 1565
Mary W., 1294
Melvin F., 1103
Melvin Franklin, 1104, 1126
Morris, 1103, 1125
Morris R., 1100, 1101
Naomi Frances, 1101
Peter, 776, 1100, 1103, 1125, 1293
Ruth K., 1294
Ruth Rebecca, 1101
Samuel, 743, 1006
Samuel L., 1100, 1103, 1125, 1308
Samuel W., 1293, 1453
Sarah, 1100, 1103, 1125, 1307
Susan, 1100, 1103, 1125
Viola Gwyndolyn, 1104
William,1100,1103, 1104, 1125, 1289, 1293
William P., 798, 1293
Holtz,——, 1401
Agnes, 1403
Albert B., 1602
Ann R., 950, 1402, 1403
Clarence, 908
Ellen B., 1567, 1568
Granville, 1132
Jacob, 950, 1403
John, 1568
Mary, 1043, 1085, 1407
Michael, 1399
Nicholas, 1212
Oliver, 1305, 1536
Holtzapple, Rebecca, 1219
Homes, Ann Eliza, 1456
Honkey, Daniel P., 830
Hood, Alexander, 1029
Annie, 1555
Basil, 1555
Benjamin, 1555

Catherine, 1555
Effie J., 1153
Elizabeth, 1555, 1557
Ella Daisy, 831
Ellen, 998, 1420, 1556
Emma, 1324
Ephraim, 1555
Fanny Temple, 831
Ford Emory, 1555
Frances Emma, 1556
Gassaway, 1555
George, 1555, 1556
George A., 831
George Emory, 1555, 1556
Henry, 1555
James, 1400, 1555, 1575
James M., 1353
James Mifflin, 1400, 1401
Jason, 1293
John, 1555, 1556
John M., 1162
Joshua, 1555
Julia A., 1029
Margaret V., 1556
Marion, 831
Martha, 1556
Mary, 1555
Mary Catherine, 1556
Mrs. Margaret, 1266
Rachel, 1162l, 1555, 1556
Sarah, 831, 1555
Sarah Elizabeth, 1555
Sophia, 1556
Susan, 1556
Thomas, 1555
William, 1245
William Albert, 1556
Hooge, Annie, 1597
Hoogereff, Samuel, 949
Hooper, Elizabeth, 1383
  Elizabeth E. F., 1382
  James Oliver, 1382
  Mary Catharine, 944
  Minnie A., 1348
  Susan E., 1150
  William, 944, 1348
  William H., 1150
Hoopes, Jefferson, 1613
Hoover, Allen D., 929, 930
  Annie Catharine, 930
  Apelonia, 1554
  Asbury E., 868
  Catharine A., 930
  Catherine, 1178
  Clara Catharine, 930
  Daniel, 930, 1178

David, 1554
Edna Missouri, 930
Emma Elizabeth, 930
George A., 930
George David, 930
Jacob, 828, 1178, 1618
John, 930, 1554
Joseph, 1554
Josephine, 1554
Levi, 820, 1477
Lillie, 930
Margaret, 1178
Maria Elizabeth, 930
Mary, 767, 1554
Rachel, 1178
Rebecca, 1554
Samuel, 1467
Sarah, 1554
Sophia, 1178
Susan, 748
Theodore Allen, 930
Vallie A., 820
Wilbur Newton, 930
Hopkins, Benjamin V., 1166
  Carrie G., 1166
  Carrie M., 1146
  Charles, 1074
  Fanny, 937
  H. H., 1008
  H. H., Sr., 937, 938
  Howard H. , 941
  Howard Hanford, 1223, 1224
  James S., 941
  James Stephenson, 1224
  John R., 1223
  Lawrence, 937
  Margaret D., 941
  Margaret Downey, 1224
  Marion, 1166
  Mary McConkey, 941, 1224
  Robert M., 1224
  William D., 941
  William Downey, 1224
Hopwood, Daisy R., 1380
  F. T., 1358
  Lizzie E., 1358
  William, 1038
Horine, A. G., 925, 1164, 1611
  A. J., 1033
  A. Lee W., 1569
  Ada Marguerite, 1009
  Alvey J., 830, 904
  Amos, 1568, 1611
  Annie, 1091
  Arlington Grove, 1568
  Baxter, 1164, 1611

Baxter F., 1611
Caroline May, 1009
Carrie M., 720
Catherine, 1086
D. Grove, 1569
Daniel Carlton, 1009
Edna B., 779
Edwin M., 1568
Effie, 1568, 1611
Elizabeth, 739, 985, 1578
Emma, 1568, 1611
Ezra, 1568
Ezra S., 1611
Florence, 994, 1611
George Theopilus, 1009
Jacob, 1611
Joel, 1091, 1568, 1611
John, 1611
John A., 1186, 1568
John Alpheus, 1611
John H., 905
John T., 1568
John V., 1611
Joshua, 1611
Joshua D., 779
L. A. S., 1299
L. A. T., 1078
Lottie, 1568
Louise, 1569
Luther, 720, 1502, 1568,
  1611
Luther A., 1091, 1266
Luther A. T., 1009
Luther Keller, 1009
Malinda, 1481, 1575,
  1611
Martha E., 1611
Martin Luther, 1611
Mary, 1568
Mary Ann, 1611
Mary C., 1487
Mary Magdalene, 1009
Matilda, 1611
Maurice Sheffer, 1009
Melancthon, 1611
Millard H., 1091
Norma, 1091
Samuel, 1611
Sarah, 1568, 1611
Stephen E. F., 1611
Susan, 1131, 1611
Tobias, 1009, 1104, 1568,
  1611
Tobias, 2nd, 1611
Virginia, 1569
Horman, Alice, 1577

Augustus F. C., 1454
Augustus R., 1454
Bessie, 1577
Charles E., 1454
Dora V., 1454
Eliza A., 1396
Elizabeth, 1396
Ella, 1577
Ella May, 1454
Frances, 1577
George, 1396
George William, 1454, 1577
Henrietta, 1454
Katie Adella, 1454
Lena, 1454
Lenora, 737
Lewis, 1455, 1577
Lewis Edward, 1454, 1577
Lizetta, 1454
Mary E., 1454
Walter, 1577
William H., 737
William Henry, 1454, 1577
Horn, Eva, 1074
Hannah, 1075
John R., 868
Samuel, 1546
Valentine, 1075
Horner, Andrew Annan, 1505
David W., 1504
Elizabeth Motter, 1505
O. A., 864, 1502
Oliver A., 1503
Oliver Alexander, 1505
Sarah J., 997
Horning, Elizabeth, 1319
Moses, 1319
Samuel, 1318
Horsey, O., 1577
Outerbridge, 1046
Hortig, Gustave, 947
Hoskinson, Anna Rebecca, 1093
Hospelhorn, Hettie, 1445
Hospilhorn, Henry, 995
Martha M., 995
Hossler, Jesse, 1273
Hott, Charles Eldon, 837
Charles M., 837
Charles Martin, 836
David, 837
Dwight Kingston, 837
Ellen F., 837
Francis, 837
G. Dwight, 837

George P., 837
Isabella S., 837
Jacob F., 836, 837
Jacob W., 837
James M., 837
James William, 837
John E., 837
Mary Vada, 837
Virginia Evangeline, 837
Hottle, Anna M., 1097
Houck, Alice, 1530
Alice E., 1376
Bertha Eugenia, 812
Caroline, 1609
Catharine, 752, 753, 1376, 1530
Charles, 1530
Charles S., 1376, 1530
Daniel, 1592
Daniel J., 1201, 1590
E. Kate, 1376
Edwin Stone, 811, 812
Elenor Hillman, 812
Elizabeth, 1376
Ella, 1376
Ella , 1232
Emma, 1376
Eva Hammitt, 812
Ezra, 720, 1375, 1376, 1530
George, 966, 1375, 1376, 1530
Georgianna, 1376
Henry, 811, 812, 1547
Henry C., 811
Henry J., 811
Henry Stone, 811
Isaac, 1010, 1021, 1592
Isabella, 1530
Isabella Virginia, 1376
James, 1232, 1375, 1376, 1530, 1538
James W., 1376
John, 752, 753, 789
Margaret Earley, 812
Mary, 789
Mary Edna, 812
Mary Eugenia, 811
Matilda, 1376
Matilda Ogle, 812
Maud, 1297
Morrison F., 1297
Murray, 1297
Viola, 1297
William, 1530
Houff, Joseph, 1538
Hough, Alverda, 1299

Amy, 1034
Mac. , 1244
Houghton, Florence, 1339
House, Andrew, 916, 1182
Annie Mary, 916
Charles J., 1005, 1183
Charles T., 916
David, 1005, 1183
Dillard Grove, 1482
Eli C. H., 1183
Eli P., 1182, 1183, 1475
Eli Pierpont, 1169
Elitha, 916, 1182
Eliza, 1611
Elizabeth, 916, 953, 1182, 1183
Frank G., 1182
G. J. R., 1186
George, 915, 916, 1182
George C., 1183
George Elijah, 915
George Thomas, 916
Greenberry, 915, 1151, 1453, 1482
Greenberry J. R., 1182, 1183
Grove, 1183, 1482
John Valentine, 916, 1182
John William, 916
Joseph, 916, 1182
Joseph A., 916
Joshua Wilmer, 1482
Laura, 1183, 1453
Lee Arnold, 1482
Levi, 953, 986
Levin B., 916
Lillian Ermina, 1482
Mabel, 1183
Martha, 916, 1182, 1183
Martha Elizabeth, 915
Mary, 1183
Mary Catherine, 1183
Maryan, 1183
Perry Thomas, 915
Rachel, 898
Rebecca Annie, 915
Ruth, 1183
Sarah, 1621
Sarah A. R., 1543
Sarah Ann, 1183
Stephen, 894
Thomas Nathen, 1482
Ulysses Grant, 916
William, 916, 1182, 1183
William R., 915
William Richard, 915

Householder, Anna C., 978
  Dorothy, 963
  Henry, 963
  Salome, 963
  Silas, 978
Houser, Paul, 962
Housman, Rebecca, 1062
Houston, Katie, 1616
Houver, Calvert, 892
Houx, Ann Elizabeth, 1507
  John, 1507
Hovis, James, 1384
Howard, Annie, 1143
  Annie Eliza, 1563
  Annie V., 1414
  C. S., 745
  Charles, 894, 1562
  Charles Edward, 1562
  Charles Sothoron, 1562, 1563
  Charles Sothoron Jr., 1563
  Dorothy V., 1143
  Edward, 705, 1143, 1563
  Edward Buckey, 1563
  Ella B., 1143, 1165
  Ellen, 1295, 1457
  Ellen H., 1143
  Emily, 1563
  Flavius, 1602
  George R., 1143
  Hannah, 1212
  Harry, 989
  Harry O., 1144
  Harry M., 1143
  Irene E., 1143
  J. E., 824
  James, 1310
  John, 836, 1072
  John Eager, 940
  Lillian, 1563
  Mary, 965, 1563
  Mary E., 1143
  Mary L., 1143
  Nellie, 839
  Rachel, 1072
  Susan V., 1060
  Susan Virginia, 705
  Victoria, 1563
  Virginia, 1563
  W. T., 1213
  William, 1086
  William C., 1004, 1092, 1143, 1414, 1563
  William H., 1165
  William Summerfield, 1563
Howell, Stephen, 942, 1344,

1557
Howes, Abraham, 1241
Howlard, Mary, 1183
Hoy, Clementine, 1508
  Elizabeth, 1075, 1076
  Mary, 806
Hubbard, Elizabeth, 1240
Hubley, Frederick, 1254
Hudson, E. J., 1291
Huff, Catharine, 813
  Charles, 1063
  Charles J., 1135
  Cora E., 1135
  Edgar, 1463
  John, 813
  Mary, 1135
  Sarah, 1547
Huffer, Alberta, 1005
  Amanda S., 812
  Angie Venola, 812
  Anna Mary Cordelia, 1605
  Annie, 1147
  Arthur, 1005, 1147
  Arthur Howard, 977
  Carrie, 1147
  Carrie May., 977
  Catharine, 812
  Charles M., 1149
  Charles S., 1005
  Charles Singleton, 1005
  Clara Belle, 1149
  Clara La Rue, 1605
  Clarence Arlington, 1605
  Clarence Filmore, 1005
  Clay Webster, 1005
  David, 977, 1019, 1020, 1030, 1604, 1605
  Davison, 977
  Dawson, 1174, 1189
  Edward, 1335
  Eliza, 977, 1030
  Elizabeth, 812
  Elva Amanda, 1605
  Emma, 977, 1020
  Ethel, 1005
  Fannie, 1335
  George, 977
  George C., 1030, 1031, 1149, 1190
  George S., 1005
  Harrie G., 812
  Harry, 894, 1005, 1149
  Harry G., 951
  Howard M., 977, 1019, 1020, 1605
  J. L., 746

Jacob, 812, 894, 977, 988, 1031, 1086, 1265, 1339
  Jacob M., 812, 1149
  Jacob T., 977, 1147
  John, 977, 1030, 1031, 1086
  Joseph, 977, 1019, 1020, 1174, 1265, 1335
  Joseph D., 1031
  Joseph Dawson, 1004, 1005
  Joseph L., 977, 1004, 1030, 1149
  Josephus, 1147
  Josephus Theodore, 977
  Joshua Samuel, 1149
  Josiah B., 812
  Julia, 748, 977, 1031
  Lovetta Catherine, 1605
  Mamie Leona, 977
  Martin Luther, 1149
  Mary, 1147, 1149
  Mary Ellen, 812
  Mary Etta, 1005
  Naomi, 952
  Naomi Margaret, 812
  Oliver, 977
  Oliver Augustus, 1020, 1604, 1605
  Oliver Garland Beard, 1605
  Ralph, 1005
  Ralph Singleton, 1005
  Robert, 1149
  Roy Augustus, 1605
  Ruth, 1005
  Ruth Elizabeth, 1005
  Silas M., 812
  William E., 1031
  Wm. H., 1152
Huffman, David H. , 1124
  Elias, 1367
  George Henry, 1367
  George W., 1269, 1367
  George Washington, 1367
  Henry, 1367
  John, 1367
  John H., 1367
  John Philip, 1367
  Kitty, 1367
Huggins, Dora, 1547
Hughes, Barnabas, 1342
  Daniel, 1353
  Edward, 745, 1152
  Elizabeth, 1342, 1463

Susie, 981
W. O., 929, 1232
Hull, Andrew, 1604
    Anna Catharine, 1604
    Barbara Ellen, 1604
    Catharine, 1231
    Catherine, 1167
    Cyrus J., 1515
    Daniel L., 811, 1490
    Edna, 1167
    Frederick, 844
    H. C., 1507
    H. Clay, 1604
    Harry C., 1604
    Harry Clay, Jr., 1604
    Henrietta, 1176, 1285
    Ida, 1515
    J. C., 1570
    Jacob, 1604
    John, 1604
    Julius C., 1604
    Margaret, 1265
    William, 1167
Humerick, J. H., 1527
Humm, Annie C., 820
    Benjamin F., 820
    Claude F., 820
    Edward, 820
    Emma J., 820
    Grace M., 820
    Harry E., 820
    Helen, 820
    John W., 820
    Mamie E., 820
    Nannie, 820
    Robert D., 820
    Samuel M., 820
    Susan A., 820
    William C., 820
Hummer, Adam, 1286
    Agnes, 1286
    Alice E., 1286
    Annie Myrtle, 1287
    Charles O., 1514
    Denda Irene, 1287
    Georgianna Missouri, 1286
    Grayson Joseph Langley,
        1287
    Harriet Ann, 1286
    Henry, 1286
    Ivy Ruth, 1287
    Jacob Peter, 1286
    John, 1286
    Joseph, 1286, 1387
    Joseph Hamilton, 1286
    Julia Estella, 1287

Margaret, 1387
Mary, 1286
Raymond Miller, 1287
Sarah, 1286
Sarah S., 1387
Susan, 1286
Virgie Viola, 1287
William Henry, 1286
Humphreys, Jeannette, 1591
    Milton, 1591
Humrichouse, Catherine E.,
    1248
    Frederick Post, 1248
Humrick, Lewis, 799
Hunsicker, Clara A., 774
Hunt, David B., 1142
    Louise A., 1142
Hunter, George Ross , 1029
    Henry Lee, 1029
    Romanas, 1556
    Zoe Lee, 1029
Huplett, Edward, 812
Hurley, Elizabeth, 858
    Lucinda, 1295, 1456
Hurst, John E., 954
Hutzel, Lyla, 1012
Hutzell, Susan, 955
Hyatt, Annie, 1217
    Bradley, 1466
    Clyde, 1467
    Eli, 1466
    Elizabeth, 839
    Emma, 1466
    Henry, 1466
    Irene, 1466
    James, 1467
    Jennie, 1466
    Lottie, 1467
    Martha, 975
    Mary Ann, 1216
    Maud, 1467
    Nettie, 1466
    Olivia, 1467
    William B., 1466
    William E., 1466, 1467
Hyder, Alice Olivia, 1210
    Amos, 947
    Anna Mary, 1210
    Catharine, 1050, 1159
    Edna S., 948
    Elsie Grace, 1209, 1210
    Harry Pfoutz, 1210
    Henry, 1209, 1210
    Jacob, 947, 1159, 1210,
        1266, 1301, 1507
    Jacob W., 903

Jacob W. , 1210
Jacob Wachter, 947
John, 947, 1249
Margaret, 903
Mary Ann, 946
Samuel Preston, 1210
Sarah, 1266, 1301, 1507
Sarah Elizabeth, 1210
Theodore, 947
Hymes, George M., 1032
    Henry, 1032
    John, 1032
    John H., 1032
    Mary V., 1031
    Mary V. , 1032
    Samuel, 1032
Hyndman, Edward K., 813
    Howard William, 813
    Hugh, 813
    Roy I., 813
Ifert, Abraham, 1356, 1375,
    1430
    Charles E., 1011
    Ira, 1095
    John J., 776
    Joshua, 1584
Ijams, Jane, 1285
    John, 975
    Plummer, 975
    Richard, 975
    Ruth, 845, 975
Ingle, Charlotte Rhett, 1233
    Frances, 1232
    Henry, 1232
    James Addison, 1233
    James Addison, Jr, 1233
    John H., 1232
    John P., 1232
    Maria, 1232, 1233
    Mary, 1232
    Mary Addison, 1233
    Osborne, 1232
    Susan B., 1232
Ingleman, Mary E., 1228
Ingram, Mittie, 1453
Inskeep, A. M., 1186
Irwin, P. H., 1451
Isanogle, A. M., 1093
    Alva M., 800
    Amanda, 1335
    Ann E., 799
    Bessie V., 800
    Charles, 883, 1589
    Charles W., 799, 1335
    Clara, 800
    George M., 799

Ida E., 1335
Jacob O., 799
James R., 799
Jane E., 799
John T., 799
Joseph A., 799
Mamie G., 800
Mary C., 799
Michael, 799
Samuel D., 799
William H., 799
Isnogle, Clara, 1387
Israel, G. W., 1510
Jackson, ———, 1120
　Adolph, 1406
　Andrew, 744, 1398
　Clara Virginia, 1530
　Elizabeth, 799
　H. M., 774
　John A., 1417
　Marie J., 775
　Mary, 1511
　Mary C. L., 1489
　Stonewall, 766, 1313, 1478
　Thomas, 1530
Jacob, Jemima, 783
Jacobs, Adam, 1142
　Betsey, 1479
　Caroline, 1560
　Elizabeth, 1131, 1485
　George, 1336
　George W., 781
　Henry, 1139
　Jonathan, 879
　Leah A., 1406, 1523
　Salina, 1143
　Washington, 706
James, Daniel, 847, 1073
　Helen, 1448
　Margaret, 1073
　Pratby, 848
　Sidney Ann, 847
　Virginia, 1263
　William A., 931
Jamison, A. L., 1553, 1596
　Baker, 697
　Brook I., 1553, 1554, 1595, 1596
　Brook I., Jr., 1596
　Brook J., 1553, 1554
　Eliner, 1554
　Elizabeth, 1215, 1216
　Elmer, 1596
　Elmo, 1554, 1596
　Emily, 1554, 1596
　Henry, 1215

Jane, 717
John, 1553, 1596
John H., 1554, 1596
John Ignatius, 1553, 1596
John V., 1553, 1596
Julian Waters, 1554, 1596
Lena May, 1596
Leonard, 1215
Liggett Johnson, 804
Mary Jane, 696, 697
Mary Louise, 1067
Nina May, 1554
Sylvester B., 1067
Sophie C., 1553, 1596
Teresa, 1553, 1596
Janney, Jonathan, 1035
Jarbo, Henry, 1030
Jarboe, Henry, 1035
　J. S. W., 1599
　John, 1187
　John S., 1035
　Margaret, 1035
　Susan, 1035, 1186-1188
　Thomas, 1187
　Thomas R., 1034, 1035, 1620
　William, 1034, 1187
Jenkins, Matilda Dale, 1444
Jennings, Mrs. J. W., 954
　Samuel K., 1212
Jett, Lavinia, 805
Johns, J., 1212
Johnson, Anna, 879
　Annie, 1497
　Annie F., 897
　Baker, 766, 1225, 1385
　Bradley T., 1353
　Caroline Grahame, 1225
　Carrie E., 897
　Catharine W. R., 1225
　Catharine Worthington, 1385
　Charles, 1353
　Charles E., 897
　Charles W., 896, 897
　Clara V., 1489
　Clinton, 1199
　D. C., 1276
　D. V., 1442
　David H., 1141
　David L., 1489
　Edwin L., 897
　Eleanor Grahame, 1225
　Elizabeth, 782, 936, 940
　Elizabeth D., 941
　Ella H., 1489
　Fanny, 809

George, 853, 1225
Henry, 745, 1399
Jacob, 896
James, 1208
John, 757
John Grahame, 1224, 1225
John Llewellyn, 1488
John Price, 1488
John W., 896, 897
Julia Ann, 896
Laura, 1264
Laura J., 1208
Lennie, 1259
Louise, 1208
Mary, 1606
Mary Ann, 896
Mary E., 897
Nannie, 875
Nellie A., 897
Polly, 1244
R. D., 1105
Rebecca, 733, 734, 740, 1579
Rebecca Ann, 896
Rebecca E., 997, 1147, 1148
Reuben A., 1443
Richard, 713, 1225
Richard P., 1225
Roger, 1208
Ross, 1225
Samuel, 1208
Thomas, 762, 809, 834, 883, 915, 940, 941, 1026, 1208, 1225, 1232, 1236 , 1589
Thomas B., 1554
Thomas Brashear, 1208
Thomas W., 1225
W. P., 705
William B., 1433
William C., 1208
William Cost, 1443
William H., 1208
Worthington, 1225
Worthington Ross, 1224, 1225
Johnston, Christopher, 1213
　Robert, 770
Johnstone, David, 1333
　Elizabeth, 1333
　Martha, 880
　Robert, 880
Jolliffe, Dorothy Elizabeth, 799

Edith M., 799
J. J., 799
John W. , 799
Joseph, 799
Joseph L., 799
Mary Louise, 799
Neill, 1240
T. S., 1240
Walker N., 799
Walker Neill, 799
Walker Neill, Jr., 799
Jones, ———, 734
Abraham, 936, 938, 941, 1452
Albert, 941, 1053
Alice, 1073
Aubrey, 1222
Charles, 941
Clara Virginia, 1248
Daniel, 989, 1049
David, 1109
David T., 1321
Elizabeth, 1340
Elizabeth Virginia, 1240
Ella, 1321
Ellen, 1510
Eugene, 848
Evelyn Marvin, 1241
Florence G., 1584
Francis, 936, 938, 941
Gertrude, 1248
H. M., 799
Howard Douglas, 1241
Howard Marvin, 1240, 1241
J. Harry, 881
James, 1305, 1536
James G., 1247
James Howard, 1248
Jane Emily, 1553, 1596
John, 804, 1240, 1247
John Dorsey, 941
Louis R., 1240
Lydia, 936, 938, 941, 1452
Mabel Christine, 1241
Marion Adele, 1241
Marjorie, 1241
Mary Elizabeth, 1248
Mordecai, 1240
Morris, 1266, 1301, 1507
Mrs. Betsy, 972
Nancy, 1463
Ohio F., 1584
Paul B., 1248
Raphael, 1163
Rosa P., 896

Sarah Ruth, 1248
Virginia Audrey, 1241
Washington B., 1240
William, 1247, 1466
William A., 1561
William D., 941
Jordan, John L., 925
Jourdan, Antoine, 801
Charles Henry , 801
Edith, 801
Flora, 801, 1013
Frances, 801
Francoise, 801
Francoise Bremond, 801
Henry J., 801
Jerome, 801
Joy, Chester, 986
Herbert, 1488
Ida, 1060
Ida R., 1446, 1447
James, 1060
John, 707, 1447
John J., 1134
John T., 1077
Rose Ann, 1060
Kable, Charles H., 1333
Clarence, 1333
Elinor D., 1333
Gertrude, 1334
Helen A., 1333
Ida, 1333
John, 1333
John Hartman Massey, 1334
John J., 1334
John James, 1333
Madge V., 1334
Margaret, 1334
Mayme, 1333
William Hartman, 1333, 1334
Kabrick, John, 1460
Kadle, John W., 1534
Kahle, William H., 1437
Kahler, Adam, 797
Kailor, David, 739, 985, 1579
Kanauf, Catharine, 1584, 1585
Jacob, 1584
Kane, Margaret, 1112, 1268, 1269
Martin, 1322
Mary Ann Darby, 768
William J., 1321, 1322
Kanode, Catharine, 1319
Jacob, 1319
Kantner, George, 1454
Sarah M., 1454

Karley, Clotilda, 887, 888
Karn, Catharine, 1480
Effie, 1183
Etta, 1407
Elizabeth, 1621
Emma, 1486
George, 1351, 1621
Grace, 1362
Harry Lee, 1362
J. P., 925
Josephus, 1096, 1568, 1611
Lewis H., 1351
Maud, 1362
Mozell V., 1362
Mrs. Mary C., 1351
Rebecca, 1362
Roy C., 1362
Sarah, 1061, 1188, 1189
Vernie, 1096, 1543
William C., 1362
Karney, John, 989, 1049
Kauffman, Elsie, 836
Henry, 1548
Jesse D., 747
Kaufman, Annie Katherine, 1202
Bessie Marie, 1202
Charles O., 1200
Clinton, 1458
Conrad, 1200
George L., 1200, 1201
Grayson H., 1200
Hiram, 1200
Hiram G., 1200
Jesse, 1201
Jesse D., 1200
John, 1145
John C., 1200
Joseph, 1200
Mary C., 1200
Violet Roberts, 1202
William C., 1200
Keedy, Anne, 1403
Barbara, 1403, 1405
Barbara Ann, 1405
Betsy or Elizabeth, 1405
Clayton O., 925, 1201, 1403, 1405, 1428, 1570
Cornelius L., 1405
Daniel, 1403-1405
Daniel George, 1404
Daniel, Jr., 1405
David D., 1405
David H., 1404

Elizabeth, 1404
George Adam, 1404
Henry, 1403-1405
Henry H., 1405
Jacob, 1404, 1405
John, 1404
John A., 1404
John D., 1404, 1405
Jonathan, 1404
Joseph E., 1403, 1405
Lowowick, 1403
Mary, 1404
Reuben M., 1405
Samuel, 1404
Samuel H., 1405
Susan, 1404
Keefer, A. Kemp, 911
Ed. , 1160
Lewis, 1556
Ludwig, 1556
Nannie C., 881
Phillip Nusbaum, 1556
Samuel, 1556
Keefhauver, D. Edward , 1086
Keenan, C. H. F., 1390
Mattie R., 1390
Keeney, Alice, 1260
Cora, 1511
Eunice, 1007
Wesley, 1082
Kefauver, Albert, 911, 1375
Albert C., 1361
Alden C., 1297, 1362
Alma, 1538
Amanda, 1361
Amanda C., 1296, 1356,
1362, 1375, 1430
Amanda Lenore, 1487
Amy A., 1380, 1381
Ann, 908
Annie C., 1104, 1362, 1430
Annie M., 1538
Arthur Roland, 1297
Bessie C., 1356
Calvin, 911, 1375
Carrie Bell, 791
Catharine Bechtol, 1380
Charles Henry, 1538
Charles L., 1297, 1362
Charles Philip, 1537, 1538
Charles R., 791
Clarence C., 1362
Clarence D., 1430
Curtis, 909
Curtis R., 921
D. Edward, 1061, 1104,

1265, 1296, 1361, 1362,
1380, 1429, 1430, 1580
Daisy V., 1297, 1362
Daniel, 791, 908, 911, 1104,
1296, 1356, 1361, 1374,
1375, 1380, 1428-1430
Daniel C., 911, 1289, 1375
Daniel Carlton, 791
Daniel Edward, 1296, 1356,
1375, 1430
Daniel Edward William,
1362
De Lauder, 1363
Dessie M., 1361
Elizabeth, 791, 908, 1296,
1356, 1361, 1362, 1375,
1430
Ella Frances, 1357
Elmer C., 911, 1375
Emma A., 1362
Emma Amanda, 1297
Emory, 1487
Eugene, 791
Eva, 911
Eva Frances, 1375
Eva Ruth, 1289
Floyd S., 1361
Franklin T., 1362
George, 791, 908, 1296,
1356, 1361, 1362, 1375,
1429, 1580
George H., 791, 1361
George William, 1357
Germanus, 791
Grayson N., 136
H. B. , 1146
Harmon, 1538
Harmon C., 1361
Harry J., 909, 921, 1538
Henry, 791, 908, 921,
1061, 1296, 1356, 1361,
1362, 1375, 1430
Henry Augustus, 1487
Henry Milton, 791
Horatio, 1375
Horatio B., 1147, 1296,
1356, 1362, 1381, 1430
Howard D., 1297, 1362
Ida, 1147
Irene Virginia, 1362
J. Hallen, 1078
J. Hallin, 1580
J. Orvrille, 1297, 1362
Jacob, 791, 908, 1091, 1266,
1288, 1296, 1356, 1361,
1362, 1375, 1430, 1486,

1502, 1538
Jacob W., 1361
John, 791, 908, 1177,
1296, 1356, 1361,
1362, 1375, 1429
Jonathan, 791, 908, 1296,
1356, 1361, 1362,
1375, 1429
Joseph H., 1296, 1362,
1375, 1430
Joseph Hollin, 1356, 1357
Julia O., 911, 1375
Katie F., 1538
Laura Etta, 1375
Lauretta, 911
Lesley F., 703
Lester F., 1538
Lewis, 1366, 1367
Lewis F., 1296, 1356,
1361, 1362, 1375,
1430
Lewis H., 756
Lillian S., 911
Lizzie, 1361
Lloyd A., 1357
Lu DeLauder, 1297
Lucinda, 1361, 1501,
1502
Lucinda C., 1091, 1266,
1265
Luella V., 1146
Luther Melvin, 1487
M. N., 1486
M. Calvin, 791
Mahala, 1375
Mahalia, 1296, 1356,
1362, 1430
Mahlon C., 908, 921
Manville, 1297
Manville E., 1362
Martha E., 1296, 1356,
1362, 1375, 1428,
1430
Martin E., 1362, 1363,
1430
Mary, 791, 908, 1293,
1538
Mary Ann, 791, 1290,
1296, 1356, 1361,
1362, 1375, 1430,
1552, 1584
Mary Alice, 1297
Mary Elizabeth, 791
Mary Ellen, 791
Mary V., 777, 911, 1375
Mary Virginia., 777

Maurice D., 1357
Mehala M., 1009
Melvin Easterday, 1487
Mildred, 1538
Millard T., 1361
Minnie E., 1362, 1430
Morgan, 1479
Morgan N., 1361
Myrtle Estelle, 1487
Naomi Sheffer, 1357
Newton R., 911, 1375
Nicholas, 791, 908, 911,
  921, 1296, 1356, 1361,
  1362, 1374, 1375, 1429
Noah E., 911, 1375
Nora M., 1361
Norman O., 1361
O. H., 1486
Oliver, 1006, 1538
Oliver H., 1361
Olivia, 1361
Orpha Ruth, 1357
Orville H., 1361
Oscar C., 748, 909, 921
Phillip, 1429
Rebecca, 791, 908, 1296,
  1356, 1361, 1362, 1375,
  1430
Richard C., 911, 1296,
  1356, 1362, 1374, 1375,
  1430
Robert A., 1486, 1487
Robert J., 1361
Roy J., 1361
Russell, 1621
Sallie E., 1366
Samuel, 1363
Samuel M., 1296, 1356,
  1362, 1375, 1430
Sarah Ann, 1430
Sarah E., 1362
Sarah Ellen, 1297
Scott, 1361
Sophia, 791, 1061
Stella V., 1362, 1430
Theodore Clinton, 791
Thomas Franklin, 1297,
  1362
Viola E., 1362, 1431
W. S., 1183
W. Scott, 1611
Walter E., 1297, 1362
William, 1356, 1375, 1430,
  1580
William D., 1296
William Emory, 791

William J., 1297, 1362, 1363
  Wilmer Jacob, 1538
Kehn, Charles, 1359
Kehne, Chrissie, 1134
  Frederica, 1523
  Frederick, 1134
  Henrietta, 1134
Keilholtz, Mary Elizabeth,
  1024
  Benjamin, 1024
  Carrie O., 1119
  Grace E., 1586
  James, 706
  John D., 1586
Keilholtz, Henry, 1514
Keiser, Frank, 706
Keisicker, Katharine M., 881
Keiter, M. F., 837
Keith, William, 1388
Kelbaugh, Jesse B., 868
Kell, Joseph, 814
Keller, Amos Remsburg, 1580
  Anna A., 1612
  Anna May, 1482
  Annie D., 790, 967, 1429
  Annie L., 1160, 1360
  Barbara, 1055
  Bertha L., 1360
  Betty E., 1234
  C. E., 1360
  C. Weagley, 1161
  Calvin, 1612
  Carlton, 1266
  Catharine, 1580, 1612
  Charles, 807, 1006, 1361,
    1612
  Charles A., 1612
  Charles E., 1160, 1161
  Charles E., Jr., 1161
  Charles Ernest, 1580
  Charles H., 808
  Charles K., 1160
  Charles M., 791
  Clarence P., 1612
  D. Rupley, 790, 967, 968
  Daniel, 790, 967, 1580
  David, 967, 1580, 1612
  De Witt Clinton, 770
  E. L., 1360
  Earl R., 968
  Edgar B., 967
  Edgar M., 1612
  Edith E., 1612
  Edward L., 1602
  Elizabeth, 1475, 1580, 1612
  Elizabeth Grace, 1361

Elmer E. R., 1522
Elmer L., 968
Elmer W., 1612
Elouisa, 1161
Emanuel, 860
Ethel M., 968
Ezra, 756, 1475
Francis J., 1160, 1360
Frank M., 791
George, 1612
George W., 1580
George W. M., 1050, 1059
Grace, 1091, 1266
Grace A., 1502
Grant, 1006, 1361
H. Melvin, 790, 967
Hannah, 790
Hannah V. E., 790, 967
Harlin E., 1580
Harry C., 968
Henry, 790, 967, 1429,
  1580, 1612
Isaac, 951, 1580, 1612
J. Charles, 1379, 1426
Jacob, 1234
Jane R., 1161
Joel, 1580
John, 807, 1059, 1612
John C., 1580
John Charles, 1580
John F., 1360, 1419
John H., 1580
John M., 1160, 1360
Jonathan, 1050, 1160,
  1360, 1580
Josie S., 791
Julia, 807, 1064
Laura, 1612
Lillie M., 1360
Lydia, 1580, 1612
Lyda C., 790, 967
Malinda, 1580
Margaret, 808
Martha, 1612
Martin, 1488
Mary, 1580
Mary E., 1612
Mary Louise, 770
Mattie J. B., 1068, 1360
Michael, 1160, 1360
Milton, 1612
Molley F., 1444
Mozelle C., 1612
Naomi O., 791
O. J., 1068, 1161
Otho J., 1160, 1360

Sarah, 787, 1599
Simon, 1612
Sumner, 739, 740, 1579
Sumner K., 790, 967
Thomas C., 1483, 1502
Thomas H., 1160, 1360
William, 723, 1160, 1287,
   1360, 1580, 1612
William C., 1612
William H., 1611, 1612
William O., 1360
William O., Jr., 1361
Kelley, Alice, 922
Ernest, 1221
Jas. M., 1152
Jerry, 1468
John, 731
Lucinda, 730
Lucinda M. J., 731
Thomas, 803
Kelly, Emma, 1306
Ethel, 1306
Gladys, 1306
Glenn, 1306
Howard, 1306
Jesse, 1306
Johnnie, 1306
Marcella M., 792
Mary, 1322
Walter, 1306
Kemp, ——, 746
Alexander, 1515
Abraham, 792, 1335
Abram, 1020
Allen D., 793
Amy, 1251
Amy R., 792
Anna, 793, 1253
Anna Walcutt, 1251
Annie, 1426
Annie Brunner, 1425
B. M., 1424
Barbara A., 976, 1048
Barbara Ann, 1048
Brent, 1093
C. Thomas, 1109, 1128,
   1358, 1424, 1425

Carl Mercier, 1113
Caroline, 815
Catharine, 1315
Catherine, 1217
Charles Edwin, 793, 1253
Charles Wesley, 793, 1253
Clayton E., 746
D. C., 1056

D. Chester, 792, 1251
D. Columbus, 791, 792,
   1251, 1253
Daniel, 1205, 1259
Daniel E., 1426
David, 791, 792, 1112, 1251,
   1268, 1269
David M., 792
Dorothy, 1113
Elizabeth, 883
Ellen, 792, 1251
Eve, 1139
Ezra L., 902, 1317
Fanny, 1472
Fanny Kate, 793, 1253
Frederick, 792, 793, 1253
George W., 1426
Gilbert, 792, 1253
Harold A., 1254
Harriet Markell, 1251
Harrison M., 792
Harry, 863, 1267
Harry M., 1251
Henrietta, 792, 1111, 1112,
   1251, 1267-1269
Hester A., 1426
James F., 1426
John Conrad, 791-793, 1253
John E., 1426
Joseph, 792
Julian, 1255
Laura T., 1267
Lewis, 779, 1129
Lewis G., 1211, 1424
Madge E., 1426
Malinda, 1426
Martha A., 1254
Martin, 1416
Martin C., 1426
Mary, 867, 1470
Mary Margaret, 1424
Mildred V., 746
Mrs. C. Thomas , 909
Nellie I., 1426
Paul E., 1426
Peter, 793, 898, 976, 1253
Reno M., 1426
Rhodes, 1159
Rhodes R, 793
Rhodes R., 792, 1253
Robert A., 792, 793, 1253
Sarah Ann, 792, 1251
Stoll Detrick, 1251
Susan E., 1267
Susan Nelson, 1113
Thomas L., 1426

William, 784, 1426, 1497
William E., 1426
Kengla, Blanche, 1119
Kennedy, John, 766
Sandy, 1442
Kenny, Samuel, 1275
Kent, Joseph, 1398
Kephart, Catharine, 1485
Elizabeth E., 1027
John, 1420
Louisa, 977, 1146, 1147
Mattie, 1181
Peter, 1147
Kepler, Alonzo, 1191
Alto Zero, 1487
Annie May, 1077
Augusta, 1077
Catharine, 1077
Charles, 1077
Charles L., 1340
Clara Elizabeth, 1077
Daniel, 1077, 1157
Daniel C., 1077
Earl Ray, 1077
Fannie K., 1077
Fannie Oneida, 1077
Flora Augusta, 1077
Grayson Edgar, 1077
Harry E., 1077
Henry, 955, 1077
Henry M., 1487
J. Luther, 1408
Jacob Hanson, 1077
John, 889, 1077, 1086
John Luther, 1077
Loyd, 1005
Lucie L., 1408
Malinda, 1077
Martin, 1077
Mary, 1077
Mary M., 889
Merle, 1340
Myrie Kathleen, 1077
Naomi Grace, 1077
Rebecca, 1077
Susannah, 917
Vincent S., 873
William, 857, 1102
William J., 1077
Keplinger, Adam, 1378
Mamie, 1047
Kepple, Elizabeth, 1096
Kerns, George, 1534
Sophia, 733
Kesecker, Jacob, 1556
Kesselring, Elizabeth, 1308

Samuel, 1369
Kessler, Cromwell C., 1045, 1303
John H., 1300
Lloyd, 1563
Kesslering, Julia A., 757
Ketler, Catharine, 981
Frederick, 981
Mary E., 981
Ketrow, Rhoda, 1468
Key, Elizabeth, 1451
Francis, 750
Francis Scott, 1437, 1451, 1613
John Ross , 1613
Joseph, 1072
Keyser, Leonard, 1247
Richard, 1575
Samuel, 1156
Kidd, Brunner, 1063
Kieffer, Ann Cecelia, 1553
Calvin Luther, 1553
Clementina, 1553
Daniel, 1553
Elizabeth Clarke, 1395
J. Spangler, 1394
Jacob, 1082
James Clarke, 1394, 1395
James W., 1553
John, 1553
Lewis, 1553
Ludvig, 1553
Margaret, 1553
Mary C., 1553
Mary Catherine, 1275, 1553
Philip, 1553
Samuel, 1553
William, 1553
Kiholtz, Alfred, 788
Kiler, Elsie, 1613
Joseph, 1223
Killey, Annie, 1467
Killian, Mary A., 1575
Kimball, Henry, 1329, 1608
Susan, 892
Kimber, Helen K., 1434
Kimmel, Agnes Gibson, 848
Anthony, 846, 847
Anthony Z., 846-848
Eleanor James, 848
Elizabeth Marshall, 848
Ellen, 848
Mary, 848
Mary Morgan, 848
Michael, 847
Pratby James, 848

Thomas Morgan, 848
William W., 848
Kindlay, Jacob, 1216
Kindley, Bradley Willson, 796
Charlotte, 795, 878
Charlotte R., 796
Elvira, 1461
Elvira W., 795, 1069
Frederick, 795, 878
George F., 795, 1069
George Frederick, 796
George Wesley, 796
John Newton, 795
Mabel Elizabeth, 796
Miranda, 795
Nellie Norris, 796
Oscar Murray, 796
Sebastian, 795
Wilbur Augustus, 796
William, 795
William E., 971, 1066
William Ernest, 796
William Jacob, 795, 796
King, Edwin, 1024
Ella, 922
Estella, 724
George, 1024
Hannah Ann, 877
Harold, 1024
Harriet Ann, 878
Hicks, 1564
Jemima D. J. E., 763
John E., 1228
John W., 868
Louisa, 1609
Luther, 1534
Mattie, 723
Pauline, 1024
Phillip, 1024
Sarah, 1272
Walter J., 763
Kinna, Atlee, 1327
Charles E., 1326, 1327
David, 1326, 1327
Dewey Sampson, 1327
Ella, 1327
Elmer, 1327
Esta, 1327
Fannie P., 1327
Grace, 1327
Ida M., 1327
John, 1327
Mary, 1326
Sadie, 1326
William, 1326
William E., 1326

Kinney, Samson, 757
Kinper, Anne, 1057
Kinty, Jamima, 1325
Kinzer, Betsy, 923
Margaret, 1085
Theressa, 1412
Kipe, John, 769
Washington, 1457
Kirecofe, Alice Needy, 893
Augustus, 893
Bertha, 893
C. H., 893
Charles M., 893
Clifford O., 893
George W., 893
Henry, 893
J. H., 893
Jacob H., 893
John, 893
John W., 893
John Wesley, 893
Joseph H., 893
Lillie V., 893
Mary J., 893
Nellie Grace, 893
Nimrod, 893
William O., 893
Kirkham, Joseph, 751
Kirkpatrick, J. C., 1233
Kiser, Annie B., 1414
Charles W., 1414
Jennie, 1414
William, 1414
William K., 1414
Kissel, Jonathan, 1487
Mrs. Emma, 1487
Kissinger, Edgar, 1048
Kittinger, Jennie, 1622
Kitzmiller, Anna M., 1139
Emma C., 779
Frisby, 779
Kizer, Philip, 1333
Sophia, 1333
Klein, Alexis R., 798
Andrew J., 798, 1379
Charles E., 798
Charles S., 797, 1294
E. Frederick, 797
E.Frederick, 797
Fannie L., 798, 1294
George J., 797
Henrietta, 797
Jesse R., 798
Louisa, 885, 1449
Louisa C., 797
Rosa E., 798

Kline, Amanda E., 1385
  Andrew, 1426
  Christian, 1221
  Delilah, 1502
  Elizabeth, 1221
  Ella, 1515
  Jesse R., 886
  John, 1534
  Laura, 1053
  Louisa, 1309
  Malinda, 1471
  Nicholas O., 931
  Paul, 759
  Paul, Jr., 868
  Thomas, 1373
  William, 1574
Kling, Ann Maria, 1235, 1515
  Anna Elizabeth, 1235,
    1516
  David, 1235, 1515
  Eliza Ann, 1235, 1515
  Elizabeth, 946, 1377
  Emma, 1235, 1516
  George, 1235, 1515
  J. Harry, 1234, 1235, 1516
  Jennie, 1235
  John, 946
  John D., 1234, 1235, 1338,
    1515
  Roger, 1235
  Roscoe, 1516
  Samuel, 1235, 1515
  Susan Alice, 1235, 1516
  Thomas, 1235, 1516
  Virginia, 1231, 1516
Klipp, Annie, 1363
  Bertha I., 1363
  Charles, 1363
  Charles H., 1363
  Elizabeth, 1363
  Goldie R., 1364
  Henry, 1363
  John, 1363
  Lillie H., 1364
  Margaret L., 1364
  Mary E., 1363
  Minnie M., 1363
  Nellie M., 1364
  Paul, 1318, 1363
  William A., 1363
Knadler, Lydia S., 1482
Knapp, Caroline, 990
  Mary M., 1329
Knauff, Amy, 1238, 1239
Knight, Daniel, 1333
  Lillie, 1326

T. J., 1333
Knill, Charles, 1250
  William T., 1409
Knipple, Harry, 1588
Knode, John, 1219
  Lydia A., 1577
  Mary Catherine, 1526
  Oliver, 859
  Rebecca, 1249
Knodle, Benton, 820
  Hiram, 913
  Loretto, 990
Knott, Alexander B., 1244
  C. Elizabeth, 1571
  Caleb, 1570
  F. Columbus, 1570
  Frances, 1137
  Francis, 1137
  Francis A., 1570
  James, 965
  Jane, 1570
  Laura, 1570
  Nannie C., 1571
  P. Henry, 1570
Knouff, Mary B., 729, 1457,
    1458
Knox, Samuel, 842
Knuff, Catharine, 1506
Kolb, Charles, 1167
  Charlotte A., 822
  David, 1123
  David H., 1575
  David R., 1123, 1124
  Ellen Rebecca, 1124
  Florence E., 1124
  George W., 1124
  Henry Isaac, 1167
  Jesse, 1052, 1208
  Jesse Wilbur, 1124
  John, 1360
  John E., 1124
  John W., 1123
  Martin, 1124
  Mary, 1167
  Mary Jane, 1124
  Rosa A., 1119, 1124
  Samuel, 1123
  Susan A., 1124
  Thomas J., 1123-1125
  Wilbur A., 1208
  Wilbur Allison, 1125
  William G, 1167
Koogle, Adam, 1192, 1325
  Alice, 1576
  Ann Maria, 1538
  Bruce S., 1078

Calvin R., 1078
Charles, 1131
Chauncey, 1576
Christopher, 1121
D. Sampson, 1131
Daniel, 859, 1538, 1611
Daniel L., 1131
David H., 889, 890
Dessie D, 1078
Edgar, 1576
Effie, 1120, 1121
Effie J., 1478
Ellen, 1131
F. M., 1123
Fanny, 859, 1131
Flossie K., 1078
Frederick, 1333
George, 1131, 1311, 1361
George W., 1078
Henry, 843
Henry A., 1220
Ida, 1131
John, 1131, 1478, 1481,
    1576
John W., 1078
John W. D., 760
Joshua D., 1538
Laura A. S., 1538
Martin, 1131
Mary, 996, 1131, 1154
Mary E., 1191, 1193,
    1479, 1576
Mary Ellen, 1192
Susan, 1158, 1173, 1479
Susan M., 1131
William H., 1102, 1131
Koon, Sarah, 1150
Koons, Abraham, 1613
  Alfred Reno, 1616
  Alice, 917
  Alice Louisa, 1614
  Arthur, 1221, 1615
  Barbara, 1615
  Belva, 1614
  Belva A., 1615
  C. Blanche, 1517
  Catharine, 1614
  Clara, 1614
  Clara B., 1614, 1615
  Clyde O., 1517
  Cora Hill, 1616
  Daisy May, 1616
  Daniel L., 1614
  Delila, 1221
  Dorothy, 1616
  E. H., 1124

Edward, 1615
Edward J., 1616
Edward John, 1614
Emma, 1615
Emma Jane, 1616
Ethel, 1614
Ethel Jane, 1616
Florence Estelle, 1517
Frank Sheridan, 1616
Frederick, 1500
George, 1517, 1613, 1614
George T., 945
George U., 1517
George W., 1517, 1614
Georgiana, 1614
Georgianna, 1616
Georgianna Celista, 1614
H. E., 1622
Harry Eichelberger, 1615
Helen, 1614
Helen D., 1616
Henry, 1613, 1614
Hulda, 1221, 1615
Irene, 1614
Isaac, 1614
J. Ross, 1517
Jacob, 1614
James Alfred, 1221, 1615
James Arthur, 1616
James Hamilton, 1614
Jennie, 1614
John, 1613
John A., 976, 1614, 1615
John Alfred, 1613, 1614
John Reno, 1221
John Russell, 1615
Joseph, 1614
Joseph M., 1616
Joseph Maryland, 1615
Josephine, 1615
Julia, 1614
Julia Barrack, 1616
Lillie, 1614
Madge, 1124
Margaret, 1614
Mary, 1614, 1615
Mary Ann, 1614
Mary Eva, 1616
Mary Martha, 1517
Mervin, 1615
Milton, 1517
Mrs. Emma, 1616
Oscar Sherman, 1615
Paul, 1615
Peter, 1517, 1614
Peter D., 1253, 1615

Peter D., Jr., 1614, 1615
Peter Donaldson, 1614
Robert, 1615, 1616
Robert L., 976, 1048
Robert Livingstone, 1615
Russell, 1124, 1221
Ruth Estelle, 1517
Sarah Catharine, 1517
Savilla, 1614
Saxton, 1615
Susie, 1614
Thomas, 1614
William, 1615
William George, 1614
William M., 1221
William Mervin, 1615
Koontz, Albina C., 725
Catherine, 1091
Charles, 1339
Edward, 1096, 1593
Fannie, 1088
George W., 725
John, 993, 1540
John A., 1195
Lydia, 992, 993
Lydia Ann, 1540
Margaret, 1518, 1619
Mary, 793
Mary Benson, 794
Mary Magdalene, 1593
Richard Gilson, 793
Wm. A., 1613
William A., 793
Korrell, Anna Mary, 1318
Charles, 1318
Elizabeth, 1318
Frank, 1318
Gideon, 1318
Grover, 1318
Jesse, 1318
John, 1317
John A., 1317, 1318
John P., 1318
Mary, 1318
Noah, 1318
Reda May, 1318
Tresia C., 1318
Koser, Joseph, 1199
Kramer, Susanna, 1435
Krantz, Charles E., 797
Cleo D., 1420
Cora B., 1420
Edward C., 797, 1414, 1415
Ethel A., 1420
Frederick B., 1415
Frederick J., 796, 797, 1414

Goldie B., 1420
Harry C. E., 797
Hazel R., 1420
Henry C., 1415
Henry C. E., 1573
John D., 796, 1414, 1419
Katie C., 1415
Julia E., 1420
Laura V., 797, 1415
Margaret A., 797
Mary C. E., 797
Mary M., 797, 1415
Sarah C., 1420
W. Donald, 1420
W. Raymond, 1420
Walter B., 1419, 1420
William H., 796, 797,
    1415, 1419
Kready, Peter, 1139
Krebs, Peter, 1255
Kreglo, Ida, 1119
Kreh, Charles, 1315
Elizabeth, 1315
John F., 1315
Leslie B., 1315
Lewis T., 1315
Mary, 1315
Nora, 1315
Peter, 1315
William H., 1315
Kreidler, J. M., 1244
Kreitzer, Herman, 1286
Kresh, Christine, 1113
Dorothy, 1113
Herbert, 1113
Krise, Charles H, 926
Edward E., 811, 1490
Elias, 1262
Frederick, 882
H. E., 1160
Henry W., 1167
Jacob, 1195
Mary A., 1166, 1167
Susan, 1195
Kroh, Margaret, 1519
Krone, Henry, 1009
Krontz, Edward, 1050, 1059
Kuch, Polly, 749
Kuhn, Mary, 731
Kumm, Karl, 1591
Kump, Amy C., 842
Annie, 842
L. H., 842
Kunkel, Ada Serene, 1417
John J., 1386
Philip B., 917

Theresa, 1386
Kunkle, Ellen, 1110, 1320
    J. B., 728, 730, 1458, 1533
    Pauline, 1138
Kuntz, Susan, 1619
Kurfman, Elizabeth, 1029
Kurtz, Benjamin, 1212
    Clara, 1128
LaBarre, Angeline, 845
    George Royal, 845
Lafevre, J. A., 1051
Lagarde, Ernest, 802
Laidley, Thomas, 1581
Laken, Daniel, 792
    Ruth, 791, 792
Lakin, Abraham, 1011, 1012
    Abraham, 3rd, 1012
    Alberta, 1012
    Cephas E., 1012
    Charlotte B., 880, 1012
    Daniel T., 703
    Elizabeth, 1012
    Frances Isabella, 1012
    Francis, 880, 1064
    Francis Dare, 1012
    Francis T., 1011, 1012
    H. A., 1012
    Henrietta, 1012
    Henry B., 1012
    John, 1012
    John Henry, 929
    John S., 1012
    John Sebastion, 929
    Lucretia, 982, 983
    Lucretia C., 1012
    Mary Ellen, 1012
    Mary L., 1012
    Ruth, 1112, 1268, 1269
    Susan A., 1012
    Susan Julia, 1064
    William, 880, 929, 983,
        1011, 1012, 1064
    William Cochran, 929
    William G., 1012
    William H., 807, 1012,
        1483
    William Hilleary, 1064
    Wm. H., 880
Lakins, William, 1586
Lamar, Abraham, 1184
    Alice M., 814
    Angie V., 1185
    Anne, 1184
    Annie M., 1027
    Archibald Smith, 1184
    Asa F., 1185

Austin A., 1185
Austin Flint, 1185, 1186
Benjamin, 1184
Benoni, 1026, 1027
Benoni Smith, 1184
Bruce Snyder, 1185
Clarence H., 1027
Daisy, 1554, 1596
E. S., 815
Eliza, 1185
Elizabeth, 1184
Ellender, 1184
Emma, 1185
Emma E., 1185
George A., 1027
Henrietta, 1184
John, 1184
John C., 1026, 1027
Laura V., 1565
Lewis, 1184, 1185
Loretta, 1184
Louise C., 1185
Louise Catherine, 1186
Lucius Q. C, 1184
Mareen, 1184, 1185
Mareen Tyler, 1184
Marion T., 1027
Mary, 1184
Mary Ann, 1184
Maximillian, 1184
Mirabeau B., 1184
Peter, 1184
Priscilla, 1184
Rachael, 1184
Rachel, 1184
Rebecca, 1184
Rhoda E., 1185
Richar, 1184
Richard, 796, 815, 1184,
    1415
Robert, 815, 1005, 1184,
    1185
Robert G., 815
Robert J., 1540
Samuel C., 1027
Sarah, 1184
Susannah, 1184
Thomas, 1009, 1027, 1045,
    1184, 1185, 1573
William, 1184, 1185, 1566
William B., 1027
William Bishop, 1184, 1185
Lamb, Melton, 1528
Lambert, David, 1204, 1519
    Elizabeth Ann, 1203, 1204
    George G., 894

Mary, 1613
Susan, 1204
Lambricht, Harriet, 1548
Lamore, John, 1183
    Peter, 1183
    Thomas, 1183
Lampe, Allen R., 907, 950
    Blanche, 907
    Christine, 907
    Frank B., 907
    Harry R., 907
    Henry R., 907
    J. Gerhard, 907
    John Henry, 907
    Julius, 907
    Lewis T., 907
Landers, John, 751
    Phoebe, 751
    Landers
    Julia, 1503
    William C., 1503
Landes, Eve, 1591
Landis, Susan, 1279
Lang, James, 934
Langdon, P. R., 1391
Lantz, Albert, 873
    Maria, 1134
    Mary, 900
    Milton, 874
Larrick, Martha E., 848
Lashorn, Catharine, 1402
Latch, Jane, 719
Late, Emma, 1196
    George, 747, 1254
    Michael, 1420
Latham, Julia, 1591
Latimer, Elizabeth Swan, 914
    Hugh, 914
Lauman, Jacob, 851, 1254
Laurence, Lucy, 920
Lauterbough, Matilda, 1119,
    1120
Lawrence, Annie, 1434
    Augustus, 1231
    C. A., 938
    C. Augustus, 940, 941
    Frances, 938, 940, 941
    John, 940
    Levin, 940
    Margaret, 940
    Rachel, 940
Lawson, Clara E., 1228 ,
    1460, 1461
    Clara Elizabeth, 1475
    Delila, 1540
    James H., 1224

John W., 1228
Margaret, 1228, 1461
Uriah F., 1228
William, 1455, 1577
William P. N., 1475
Layman, Clara, 1397, 1610
Clarence, 1277
Colonel, 1609, 1610
Earl W., 1397
Ella, 1540
Florence R., 1397
George M., 1397
George W. , 1397, 1609, 1610
Jacob, 1397, 1609
Jacob A., 1397, 1610
Leonard, 1277
Marion, 1397
Mary R., 1397, 1610
Roger J., 1397
Savilla, 1397
Sophie C., 1397
Survilla, 1610
William H., 1397, 1610
Layton, Ann Louisa, 840
Leatha, 1461
Leathe, 1228
U. Cora, 840, 1461
Uriah, 840
Lazer, Mary A., 725
Le Fevre, Mary, 1119
Leakins, Daniel, 1070
Lease, Amos, 789
Andrew Jackson, 789, 879
Anna May, 1110
Annie M., 1235
Austin Riner, 1142
Blanche, 790
Catharine, 1110, 1130
Cathrine, 1578
Charles, 789, 1512
Charles H., 789
Clara, 789
Daniel, 1109, 1578
Davis, 1142
Edwen, 789
Effie, 790
Elizabeth, 789, 827, 863, 1122
Ella, 789
Ellen, 1110, 1577, 1578
Elma, 789
Emery, 1533
Etta, 789
Fanny, 789
George, 1142

George C., 790
George D., 1109, 1110
Gideon, 1110, 1533
Harry, 789
Harvey R., 789, 790, 1095
Howard Gwynn, 1142
Jacob, 827
Jemima, 1142
John, 789, 1468
John William, 1142
Joseph, 789
Josiah, 1110
Lloyd N., 789
Mamie, 789
Martha, 1110
Mary, 789, 790, 1110
Mary Agnes, 1142
Mary C., 1533
Mildred, 790
Nannie Camilla, 1142
Nellie May, 1110
O. D., 1235
Oliver D., 1110
Oliver Daniel, 1109
Pearl Sanner, 790
Rachel A., 1496
Rachel Ann, 1110, 1294
Reuben, 790
Reuben S., 790
Robert, 789, 790, 1165, 1166
Sarah, 1170
William, 790, 1142
William Henry, 1142
William McAlister, 1142
William N., 1110
Leather, Annie, 1469
David W., 1469
Edward E., 1469
Emily, 1136, 1539
Emily Catharine Elizabeth, 1469
George, 1136, 1469, 1539
Henrietta, 1469
Henrietta L., 1052
James, 1469
John, 1052, 1469
Margaret, 1469
Mary, 1469
Mary Catharine, 1136, 1539
Millard F., 1136
Leatherman, Adam, 1149, 1524, 1616, 1617
Albert Calvin, 994
Alfred J., 1148., 1617
Amanda A., 883, 1589
Anna Mary, 994

Annie, 1506
Charles T., 1148
Clara F., 1617
Clara R., 1148
Clare E., 1148
Clarence G, 883, 1302
Clifford, 1387
Clifford Roy, 1589
Daniel, 727, 758, 882, 883, 993, 1054, 1147, 1149, 1374, 1532, 1588, 1616
Daniel E., 1149
Daniel I., 883
David O, 1148
Della I., 994
Edgar G., 1617
Edna E. A. R., 1617
Elias, 1370
Elizabeth, 870, 993, 1148
Ella, 1374
Elmer D., 1617
Elmer W., 1617
Emory Daniel, 1149
Ethel Elizabeth, 994
Ethel Rebecca, 1149
Floyd, 994
Foster, 994, 1374
Franklin, 1148
Frederick, 867
Gardiannis O., 883, 1589
George, 740, 896, 960, 993, 997, 1147, 1148, 1579
George C., 1617
George Carlton, 1148, 1149
George U., 1148
Glenn, 994
Godfrey, 882, 1588, 1616, 1617
Hannah, 1148
Harry, 1387
Harry C., 1149
Harry F., 883, 1588, 1589
Harvey I., 1349, 1616, 1617
Isaiah, 1617
Jacob, 870, 882, 993, 1147, 1148, 1351, 1370, 1373, 1409, 1588, 1616
James, 1488
Jennie R., 1149
John, 993, 1148
John C., 1147-1149, 1374

John W., 993, 994
Josephine Curtis, 1588
Josiah, 781, 1617
Julia Ann, 1148
Laura E., 913
Laura Ellen, 994
Levi C, 882, 883, 1588, 1589
Lewis Carlton, 1149
Lillie, 781
Lizzie E., 1524, 1617
Luther E., 883, 1589
Mahala, 1616
Marshall, 1040, 1589
Marshall E., 883
Martha C., 1617
Martha E., 883, 1589
Mary, 993, 1148, 1373, 726, 1617
Mary C., 1617
Mary E., 740, 758, 883, 951, 1542, 1578, 1579, 1589, 1617
Mary Elizabeth, 1148
Mary Ellen, 1148, 1149
Matrona, 1387
Matrona M., 1589
Nannie R., 1148
Nellie M., 1617
O. F., 1396
Ollie L, 883
Orests F. E., 883, 1589
Paul, 1302
Paul C., 883
Paul R., 883
Peter, 913, 993, 994, 1147, 1148
Robert Lee, 883, 1589
Roy, 1372
Roy L., 1148
Sarah, 1617
Sarah C., 997, 1148
Susan, 1351
T., 1589
Upton, 1348
V. Ward, 1148
Vernon W., 1148
William H., 994, 1148
Leatherwood, Elizabeth, 1245
John, 1245
Mary, 1047
Ruth, 1245
Leazer, Samuel, 1147
Lebherz, Joseph, 981
Ledwidge, Ann Victoria, 1271
Daniel, 1271

Franklin Pierce, 1271
Isabel, 1271
John, 1271
John Allen, 1271
Martha Jane, 1271
Owen, 1271
Lee, Charles O'Donnell, 1444
Dodridge, 1099, 1107, 1113
Edgar E., 1607
Fitzhugh, 825, 1410, 1558
John, 1567, 1573
Joseph Jenkins, 1444
Maria, 879
Philip, 1342, 1444
Robert E., 1069, 1398
Richard, 1444
Sarah, 1342
Thomas, 879
Thomas S., 1351, 1417
Thomas Sim, 1444
W. H. H., 825
Leedy, Mary, 1291
Legatus, Hervey, 1388
Richard, 1388
Leggatt, Henry, 1388
Legget, James, Jr., 1388
James, Sr., 1388
Leggett, John, 1237, 1270, 1284, 1518, 1619
Legore, Bruce, 1481
Catharine Louise, 1481
Edna Ray, 1481
Emma Jane, 1481
George R., 1480
George Randolph, 1481
Harry William, 1481
James Alton, 1481
James W., 1480, 1498, 1533
John, 1480
John Lewis, 1481
Lelia, 1481
Mildred Irene, 1481
Walter Clay, 1481
Wilbur Corthell, 1481
LeGore, Walter, 1271
Wilbur C., 1271
Lehman, Rachel, 1058
W. H., 1565
Leib, J. H., 1093
James, 1119
Leister, William A., 1543
Leloup, Charles A., 802
Lemmon, John, 1604
Lenhart, Mary, 1469
William, 724
Leopold, Susan, 756

Lerew, Joseph, 742
Lether, John, 1469
Levy, Arthur E., 787
C. V. S., 708, 1113, 1608
Charles P., 786, 963
Charles V. S., 786, 787, 963, 1350
Elizabeth S., 787
Mary G., 787, 963
P. J., 1055
Perry J., 786
Roger S., 787, 1012
Walter V. S., 787
William S., 787
Lewis, Ada B. E., 1444
Alfred B., 975
Alfred Henry, 1545
Amelia, 1444
Ann Eliza, 1462
Ann M., 1561
Anna Elizabeth, 1444
Barnard, 1196
Basil, 1266, 1443, 1444
Basil C., 1444
Berdie, 1136
C. M., 1199
Charles L., 1444
Clara Virginia, 1444
Cora M., 1196
David, 1092, 1196
David J., 1384
Elizabeth, 1510
Elizabeth Laura, 1093
George, 849
George E., 1443, 1444
George Jacob Benton, 1444
Helen, 1444
Henry Walker, 1444
Ida H., 1444
Jacob, 1092, 1093
Jeremiah, 1217
John, 1081
Joseph Hooker, 1196
Lee, 1196
Lillie M., 1444
Margaret A., 1443
Margaret C., 1444
Martha Ellen, 1444
Mary F., 1444
Mary Margaret, 1444
Maud, 1444
Paul, 1444
R. Rush, 1056, 1092, 1093
Ransom, 1093

Rita, 1444
Robert Nelson, 1444
Roberta I., 1444
Rosa H., 1444
Rose, 1091, 1266
Ruth E., 1444
Samuel A., 1196
Samuel W., 1196
Sarah, 1443
Sidney, 1196
Survinna E., 1196
Walter Raleigh, 1444
William, 1196
William Basil, 1444
William H., 1607
William M., 1196
Lichtenberger, Levi, 718
Lidia, Julia, 730, 1458
Samuel, 730, 1458
Ligget, Clara Harris, 1389
Henry H., 1389
J. J., 1388
John E. H., 1387
John Enoch Hanna, 1388
John James, 1387, 1388
Liggett, Clara Elizabeth Harris, 1206
Henry H. , 1533
Henry Harris, 1206
John L., 1206
Lighter, Alice V., 889
Alma C. V., 1095
Barbara, 889, 890
Beulah O., 1095
Catharine, 889, 1094
Catherine, 890
Charles D., 1095
Charles E., 889
Charles H., 1094, 1095
Daniel, 890
Daniel J., 889
Daniel W., 889
Edith S., 1095
Edna K., 890
Edward, 1486
Edward M. L., 1094
Elizabeth, 889, 890
Emma K., 889
Frank R., 890
Gertrude F., 889
Grayson E., 1095
Hannah, 889, 890
Henry, 889, 890
Hiram, 1095
Irene B., 1095
J. Calvin, 889

Jacob, 889, 890
John, 889, 890
John H., 890, 1077
Joseph, 889, 890
Lawson, 1094, 1255
Lora M., 1297
Lorenz Carlton, 889
Lorenzo, 1541
Malinda, 889, 890
Martha J., 889, 890
Mary, 889, 890, 1094
Mary B., 889
Mary Catharine, 1541
Mary E., 889, 890, 1316, 1379, 1425, 1426
Mary Elizabeth, 1580
Mary Grace, 1541
Mary M., 1095
Mrs. Amanda E., 1430
Norma R., 890
Olive G., 1095
Peter, 889, 890
Richard Carlton, 1541
Russell E., 889, 890
S. L. H., 776
Samuel, 1584
Samuel L. H., 1094
Sarah Catharine, 1095
Simon P., 889, 890
William E., 889
Zorah V., 1095
Lightner, John, 1235, 1515
Mary Clark, 1563
Samuel, 893
Sarah, 947, 1159, 1210, 1266, 1301, 1507
Likens, Myra, 1548
Lillich, Anna R., 797
Frederick, 797
Lilly, Richard, 835
Samuel L., 1394
Limbert, Herman, 820
Limebaugh, Benjamine, 1369
Lincoln, Abraham, 826, 870, 1099, 1107, 1114, 1163, 1484, 1549, 1606
Lindsay, Adam, 1355
Almer, 1194
Benjamin, 895
Edward, 1546
John, 966
John Dallas, 1310
Julia, 895
Lula Elizabeth, 1194
Marian, 763
Mary Margaret, 1194

Sarah, 895
Susan, 1223
Lindsey, David, 1222
Hamilton, 966
Susan, 966, 1155
Line, John, 857, 1102
Linebaugh, Catherine, 1276
Mary, 952
Susan, 1476, 1477
Link, George, 1294
Mary, 1023, 1024
Linn, Catharine, 1498
Isaac, 1498
Linthecum, George, 1136
Hannah, 768
Mary, 1069
Linthicum, Annie, 1228
Burwell, 1228
C. H., 1461, 1475
Charles F., 1228
Charles H., 1227, 1228
Charles Hamilton, 1228
Elinor, 1228
Elizabeth, 1227
Ellen, 1227, 1461, 1475
Frederick, 1227
Garrott, 1228
Hannah F., 1228
James G., 1227
John, 1286
John H. S. McElfresh, 1227
John Hamilton Smith McElfresh, 1227
John W., 1227, 1228
Julia, 1228
Lydia, 1227
Martha E., 1228
Mary E., 1228
Nicholas, 1228
Otho, 1227
Paul Winstin, 1228
Philemon, 1227
Slingsberry, 1227
Stannie F., 1228
Thomas, 1227
Thomas S., 1228
William T., 1227
Linthum, Garrot, 1074
Linton, Frank, 1399
Reuben M., 752
Lipps, George, 740
Lippy, Emma, 1511
M. H., 1230
Michael, 1513
Mollie, 1506

Little, Augustus, 742
   Charles, 1333
   Charles J., 1540
   Jennie, 1057
   Mariah, 1349
Littles, Ann Catheran, 1168
Livers, Arnold, 835
   Jacoba Clementina, 835
Lizer, George, 749
Lloyd, Ada, 990
   Edward, 1026
Loats, John, 712
Lochner, Nicholas, 1276
Lock, Adeline, 1511
   Charles E., 1274
   Clarence, 1274
   George F., 1274
   Ira D., 1274
   William L., 1274
Locke, Fred, 1251
   George, 1082
   Harriet, 1491
   Howard, 1534
   Mary Ella, 1367
   Sarah, 1251
Lodge, Henry, 1124
Lohr, Abraham, 707, 788
   Calvin Simon, 789
   David, 788
   Effie G., 707
   Elizabeth, 788
   Emma Zena, 789
   James, 788
   John, 788
   Joseph, 788
   Joseph N., 788
   Mary, 788
   Mary E., 789
   Minnie C., 789
   Rosa Kate, 789
   Simon, 788, 1513, 1619
   Stewart, 788
   Virginia, 733
   William Edgar, 789
Long, Abraham, 750, 787, 788,
     845, 1599
   Abraham S., 788, 1600
   Absalom, 1274, 1538, 1566
   Anna, 1123
   Annie M., 1424, 1558
   Arabella V., 788, 1600
   Barbara, 787, 850, 851,
     1599
   Beulah M., 1600
   Blanche, 1600

   Catharine, 887
   Charles M., 1123
   Christopher, 994, 1123
   Clora, 1538
   Cost, 1531
   Cyrus Green, 1558
   Daisy E., 1123
   Daniel, 1558
   Daniel James, 1558
   David, 1244
   Edgar M., 1600
   Edward, 787, 1179, 1599
   Elizabeth, 883, 1123
   Emma I., 788
   Emma J., 788, 1167, 1600
   Ephraim, 1086
   Estella G., 1600
   Eva Rosina, 1309
   Frederick C., 1600
   George P., 1558
   Howard A., 788
   James, 887, 1297, 1538,
     1565
   James W., 1274, 1297 , 1538
   John, 787, 1340, 1469, 1599
   John A., 1600
   John C., 1123, 1379
   John H., 1260
   John L., 1558
   John S., 787, 788 , 1600
   John W., 1091, 1123, 1177,
     1424, 1538
   Joseph, 1123
   Joseph W., 1123
   Josephine, 1558
   Josephine C., 1558
   Josephus, 1297, 1565, 1566
   Kate, 1260
   Laura P., 788 , 1600
   Lavinia, 1260, 1566
   Lillie, 1260
   Lolla Lee, 1600
   Lottie R., 1123
   Malissa, 1110
   Margaret, 887, 1006, 1123,
     1566
   Mary, 787, 1162, 1599
   Mary (Polly), 1162
   Mary A., 1600
   Mary A. C., 1558
   Mary A. R., 994
   Mary E., 1123, 1297
   Mary Elizabeth, 1566
   Minnie, 788, 1600
   Minnie E., 750
   Mollie, 1123

   Nannie M., 1123
   Nettie E., 788
   Patrick E., 887
   Philip, 787, 1599
   Pauline, 1600
   Reuben, 1297, 1546, 1566
   Samuel, 788, 1600
   Samuel A., 1600
   Sarah, 787, 1123, 1336,
     1599
   Sarah A., 788, 1340 ,
     1600
   Sarah Ann, 1203
   Susan, 1123, 1244, 1442
   Theodore D., 788
   Theodore R., 1600
   Thomas W., 1558
   Uriah, 1566
   William, 1260, 1566,
     1617
   William D., 1558
   William H., 788, 829,
     1599, 1600, 1618
   Wilmer L., 788
Long-Snyder, Eva Rosina,
    1308
Longenecker, Solomon, 1230,
    1231
Longman, Lula, 1533
Longnecker, Solomon, 930
Lookingbill, Alberta
    Josephine, 1298
   Alverdia Josephine, 1495
   Barbara, 1222
   Belindas Jane, 1495
   Emily Louisa, 1298
   Emily Louise, 1495
   John Henry, 1557
   Malinda Jane, 1298
   Margaret Ann, 1298, 1495
   Peter, 1298, 1495
Lorah, Mary A., 1041
   Mary Amanda Griesemer,
    1042
Lord, George K., 1100
   Marian, 1151
   Marion, 1377, 1615
Lortz, Lewis, 1044
Loub, Milton, 1431
Lough, Ada E., 950
   Charles W., 950
   Edward, 1273
   Edwin G., 950
   George, 949
   Grace, 950
   J. Q., 1273

John, 949
John Q., 950
John R., 1176
Margaret, 950
Myrtle, 1177
Sarah C., 950
Uriah A., 949, 950
William A., 950
Louthan, John, 1113
Mary E., 1113
Louts, John, 1318
Loutzenhauser, Moses, 917
Lowe, Charles, 768
Enoch Louis, 1338
Louis E., 696
Mollie, 1510
Lowell, James Russell, 720
Lowenstein, Amelia, 1463
David Amelia, 1463
David, 888, 1368, 1463,
1488
Isaac, 1368
Lower, ——, 1522, 1524
Lowman, Florence, 1204
Frank, 1204
Harry, 1204
Stella, 1204
Lowndes, Lloyd, 1067, 1096,
1242
Loy, C. W., 811, 1490
Irvin W., 926
Luckett, William F., 725
Luckner, Beulah, 1261
Edward, 1261
Herman, 1261
Lewis, 1261
William, 1261
Ludy, Charles W. M., 781
Cyrus M., 781
Emma C., 781
Grace E., 781
Joseph A., 781
Manzella M., 781
Nicholas, 726, 781
Susan, 726, 1348
William, 781
Lugenbeel, Ann Elizabeth,
1085
Elizabeth, 1246, 1247, 1591
Emily, 1083
Mary, 1305
Mary M., 844, 881
Peter, 1247
William, 1305
Lupton, Sarah, 799
Luther, Martin, 1247

Lutz, Annie C., 1409
Elizabeth, 1363
George, 1409
John, 956, 988
Lewis, 953
Mary E., 1409
Lynch, John A., 827
Lynn, Addison, 1009
Peggy, 1513
Lyons, Joanna, 1076
John, 894
Mary, 894
Robert, 936, 938, 939
Lyzar, James, 952
MacGill, Basil, 1154
Charles, 919
Charles G., 1155
Eva, 1155
Henrietta D., 1154
James, 919, 1154, 1551
John, 1154
Lloyd T., 1154, 1155
Lloyd Thomas, 1154
M. G., 1154
Mary, 919
Nannie E., 1155
Richard Edwards, 1155
Robert, 1553
Robert Henry, 1154
William E., 1155
MacKenzie, Mrs. Joan Fraser,
1345
Mackey, Samuel, 1547
Maclefresh, Sarah, 716
MacMunn, Geo., 1608
Maddox, Thomas Notley, 1344
Madery, Mary M., 1074
Magalis, Bessie L., 1032
James, 1032
Richard, 1032
MaGraw, Francis, 1554
Magruder, America F., 1510
Charles L., 1510
Columbia M., 1510
Eleanor E., 1510
Felissa, 1296, 1457
James, 1259, 1510
Matilda Noble, 1259
R. H., 724
R. Harwood, 1510
Rufus H., 1510
Rufus K., 1296, 1457, 1510
Zachariah Claggett, 1510
Mail, David H., 820
Main, Allen, 1101
Annie, 1576

Annie E., 1481
Austin, 1576
Austin L., 1482
C. F., 1333
Catharine S., 1575
Catherine, 1409
Catherine S., 1481
Charles F., 1481, 1576
Cora E. R., 1101
Daniel, 1481, 1575
David, 1101
Edward, 1101
Elizabeth, 1261
Emeleine L., 1481
Emeline L., 1575
Emma, 1481
Emma E., 1576
Floyd, 1576
Floyd C., 1482
Frederick Tobias, 1481,
1575
George, 1283, 1289, 1334
George D., 1481, 1576
George W., 1481, 1575
Grayson, 1576
Grayson E., 1482
Guy, 1576
Guy P., 1482
Harry P., 1481, 1576
Henry P., 1481
Henry R., 1575
John D., 1481, 1575
Jonathan, 923, 1101, 1573
Josephine, 1481, 1575
Lewis, 1576
Lewis H., 1015
Lewis T., 1482
Lorenzo, 1481, 1576
M. G., 1101
Martin Luther, 1481, 1575
Russell, 1576
Russell W., 1482
Sallie, 1481, 1576
Sarah E., 1481, 1575
Susanna, 1055
Tobias, 1101
Tobias F., 1147
William, 1055
William Z., 993
Zacharias, 1541
Mainard, John, 782
Mainhard, Charles, 1611
Mainhart, C. C., 1568
Clara V., 820
Daniel, 820
Frank N., 1198

Lewis D., 1568
Mary A., 1198
Maize, Elizabeth Garvin, 1113
Malohan, John, 1500
Manahan, Mary, 1179
  Urith, 1557
Manard, Scott, 1053
Mangins, Jacob, 1369
Mann, Annie M., 1104
  Daniel, 1611
  Dora J., 1390
  John, 730, 1484
  L. A., 1325
  Sarah, 1484
  Sarah V., 1476, 1483, 1484
Manning, Charles, 802
Manns, Anna Margaret, 825
Manson, James, 805
Mantz, Casper, 1450, 1453
  Catharine, 770
  Charles, 1343
  Eliza C., 939
  Emanuel, 894
  Ezra, 940
  Gideon, 940
  Hiram, 1118
  Irene, 1449, 1450, 1452,
    1453
  John, 939
  Margaret, 937-940, 1047
  Mary, 1607
  Peter, 770, 937-940, 1047
Marhisser, Henry, 1556
Mariott, Alfred, 1497
Markell, Annie, 710
  Charles, 715, 770, 940
  Conrad, 1441
  Edwin C., 1441
  Francis, 770, 1201, 1441
  Francis H., 770, 1441
  Francis Willard, 770
  Frank, 940
  Frederick, 1431, 1528
  George, 710, 721, 770, 927,
    940
  Harriet, 1251
  Jacob, 962
  John, 710, 770, 940, 1441
  John U., 1068, 1441
  John Usher. Jr., 1441
  Lewis, 705, 940
  Louis, 770
  Marcia Carpenter, 770
  Mary, 770, 915, 927, 928
  Mrs. Mary G., 1068
  Samuel, 870

Sophia, 710, 770
Virginia, 715
William, 770, 1441
William A., 1441
Marken, Ann Buhrman, 817
  Annie, 778
  Effie Buhrman, 817
  Ellen, 1019
  John, 1019
  Josiah, 817, 984
  V. M., 855
Marker, Ezra, 1474
  Mary, 757, 760
  Matilda, 869
  Michael, 757
  Paul, 727
  Rebecca, 1612
Markey, D. John, 772, 1026
  Daniel J., 772
  David J., 709, 772
  Eleanor, 772
  John H., 772
  Rebecca B., 708, 709
  Susan M., 772
  Willard, 772
Markin, Rebecca, 1013
  Victor M., 745
Marlow, Tuisco, 1344
Marlowe, Gertrude, 1078
Marr, Mary, 1244
Marriott, John, 845
Marsh, George P., 1443
Marshall, Andrew, 805
  John, 1115
  Mary Elizabeth, 1115
  Rheumaha, 1115
Martin, ——, 733
  Abiah, 733, 741
  Adam B., 868
  Adelia Bruce, 733
  Anna Barbara, 861
  Annie B., 707
  Barbara, 733, 855
  Bessie, 1457
  Catharine, 1537
  Charles T., 707
  Cora, 733
  David, 1546
  David H., 733
  Edna, 1457
  Eliza, 1071
  Elizabeth, 733, 754
  Ella, 1200, 1585
  Ellen, 707
  Emma C., 955
  Emma Rebecca, 707

Fannie, 1435
Florence, 1457
G. T. M., 734
George, 733, 861
George T., 813
George Thomas Marshall,
  733
George W., 955
Gertrude C., 707
Grace R., 733
Hannah E., 1390
Harvey, 733
Henrietta, 1514
Henry, 734
Honore, 1344
Howard K., 733, 773
J. Edward, 1390, 1585
Jacob, 1457
James P., 733
Jeremiah, 930
John, 733, 754, 1457
John T., 925, 926, 954
Joseph, 733, 1277
Joseph Pentz, 733
Joshua A., 707
Laura, 1013
Mabel, 1457
Margaretta, 727
Mary, 733, 1394, 1416
Morris, 733
Murray, 733
Nettie B., 707
Nevin, 733
Rachel, 733, 1280
Rachel Hope, 754
Russell, 733
S. H., 1280
Sallie N., 1280
Sophia, 949, 1344
William, 1017, 1310,
  1620
William H., 707
William N., 780
Martz, Albert T., 1010, 1021,
  1592
  Allen B., 775
  Allen S., 1022
  Anna V., 1592
  Annie V., 1010, 1021
  Caroline, 1592
  Caroline C., 1010, 1021
  Catharine S., 1545
  Catherine, 1592
  Charles C., 1010, 1021,
    1592
  Charles W., 1592

Clarence H., 775
Daniel, 1082, 1592
David H., 1010, 1021, 1592
David S., 1010, 1021, 1592
Eleanor Catherine, 1593
Elias, 1077
Elizabeth, 1592
Elizabeth B., 902
Ethel V., 1011
Eugene A., 1022
Fannie E., 1022
Fanny, 1229
Fanny E., 1230
G. Maynard, 1011
George, 902, 1010, 1591, 1592
George D., 1081, 1082 , 1591, 1593
George J., 1592
George S., 1010, 1011, 1021 , 1592
Harvey D., 1150 , 1593
Helen Whitmore, 1593
Ida R., 1022
Jane E., 1081, 1082
Jennie, 1575
Jennie P., 1592
Joanna, 1082
John H., 1010, 1021, 1521, 1591-1593
John Wilson, 1593
Joseph D., 1022
Julia, 1592
Julia A., 1010, 1021
Katie E., 1253
Lewis J., 775, 1010, 1021, 1022, 1230, 1592
Lola Jane, 775
Maretta E., 1010, 1021
Mary Ann, 1592
Maryetta, 1592
Margaret R. , 908
Meharl Edgar, 1011
Mrs. Wilson N., 1592
Randolph N., 1592
Rebecca, 1592
Ruth Eckstein, 1593
Samuel B., 1022
W. N., 898
William H., 1252
William H., 1022, 1082
Wilson N., 1010, 1021, 1575, 1591, 1592
Mason, Elizabeth, 976
John, 1503
John S., 975

Julia A., 739
Rebecca, 1604
Massey, John E., 1334
Mathews, John, 869
L. G., 1212
Mathias, Abbie, 927
Alice, 926
Eliza J., 926
Elizabeth, 926
Ella J., 926
Etta S., 927
Griffith, 926
John P. T., 926, 927
Laura, 926
Park G., 927
Philip, 926, 927, 1270
Rose, 926
Rose Ann, 926
Susan, 927
Matthews, John, 751, 754
Julia, 750, 751, 754
Lena, 1221
Lycurgus G., 1133
Margaret, 763
Mauabam, Mary, 1434
Maught, Andrew, 1123
Andrew C. H., 994
C. C., 1541
Catherine, 1183
Charles C., 994, 1030, 1256
Conrad, 1478
Conrad Jacob, 1479
Daniel, 994
E. Maud, 994
Eliza, 993
Eliza A. E., 1541
Frank, 1478
Henry, 994
James, 1541
John, 993, 994, 1478, 1611
John A. E. H., 994
John W., 1478
Katy, 994
Lucinda, 1478
Mary Ann, 994
Mayme, 994
Roy, 994
Roy N., 1486
Samuel, 994
William, 932, 994, 1569
Maugruter, Margaret, 749
Maulsby, Bettie H. M., 1608
Betty Harrison, 1329
Emily N., 1609
Emily Nelson, 1608
Henry Hanson, 1609

Israel David, 1329, 1608
Mary S., 1609
William P., 1329, 1330
William, Jr., 1314
William Pinkney, 1211, 1329, 1608, 1609
William Pinkney, Jr., 1608, 1609
Maxell, Albert H., 773
Ann Eliza, 773
Francis A., 773
Frank Phillip, 773
Henry, 773
Henry F., 773
Jane Maria, 773
Julia, 773
Margaret, 773
Mary A., 773
Maud Amelia, 773
Roy F., 773
Samuel, 773
Samuel J., 773
Thaddeus Augustus, 773
William, 773
Maynard, Albert, 785
Augusta, 783
Augusta C., 783
Benjamin, 782, 783, 1073
Benjamin T., 782
Benjamin Thomas, 783
Brice, 785
Catharine, 783
Clara Hobbs, 753
Clinton, 785
Dawson Stevenson, 783
Eleanor, 782, 783
Ephraim, 783
Fanny, 782, 783
Florence E., 783
Florence Elizabeth, 783
Frank N., 783
Frank Nathan, 781, 782
George Edwin, 783
Grafton, 1073
Henry, 782
Howard, 1073
Howard Griffith, 783
Irwin Oliver, 1073
James, 782
James R., 753
Jemima, 783
John A., 783
John Augustus, 783
John Newton, 782, 783
Joseph Thomas, 783, 784
Lavinia, 785

Leah Ellen, 1073
Lewis S., 783
Lewis Shull, 783
Mittie, 1263
Nathan, 781-783
Rachel, 782, 783
Rachel A., 783
Rachel Thomas, 1073
Richard M., 783
Robert Claggett, 1073
Ruth, 782, 1073
Ruth Eleanor, 783
S. Laura, 753
S. S., 785
Sarah, 782, 783
Sarah Howard, 783
Susan, 783
Thomas, 781-783, 1073
Thomas B., 785
Thomas Greenberry, 785
Virginia, 785
Warren, 785
William J., 783
William Jay, 783
Mayne, Annette, 1044
Annie, 1044
Daniel, 1092
David, 1044
David F., 875, 1044, 1170
Delia, 1529
Edward C., 1044
Enos L., 1044
Jacob, 1529
John H., 1044
John J., 1044
Joseph H., 1044
Lillie, 1092
Ruie V., 1044
Sarah, 1044
McAfee, Elizabeth, 1391
John, 1196
McAleer, Clara Louise, 695
Hugh, 695
McAlister, Anna Martha, 1142,
1143
James, 1143
John, 1143
John Alexander, 1143
John W., 1142, 1143
Lavinia, 1143
Mary, 1143
Scott, 1053, 1143
Virginia, 1143
McAllister, May, 1058
McBee, Daught, 1390
McBride, A. C., 1173

Albert H., 987, 1129
Alice, 1129
Allan C., 954
C. A., 1008
Carrie E., 954
Catharine, 953, 986, 1129
Charles L., 987
Clara A., 987
Clara E., 1129
Clarence, 1093
Cyrus Samuel, 1129
Edgar H., 954
Elizabeth Catharine, 953
Ellsworth, 1299
Elsie Viola, 1129
Fannie V., 953
George, 953, 986, 1129
George W., 953
Henry, 953, 986, 1129
Henry C., 953, 986, 1129
Laura, 1129
Laura F., 987
Lewis, 986, 1005, 1050,
1059, 1129
Luther, 1299
Martha F., 953
Mary, 953, 986, 1129
Mary A., 953
Maynard, 987
Millard F., 986, 987
Millard P., 1129
Minnie F., 987
Philip, 953
Sallie, 986, 1129
Samuel E., 987, 1129
Sarah, 953
Sarah A., 987
Sarah E., 953
Sidney V., 953
William, 953, 986
McCallister, Amanda, 922
McCardell, A. C., 943, 1121,
1141, 1176
Adrian C., 1248, 1249
Adrian L., 1249
Albert N., 1249
Alburtus, 1248
Annie, 1248
Courtney, 1248
Edgar S., 1249
Ernest W., 1249
Lucretia P., 1248
Mary A., 1248, 1249
Odelo D., 1248
Pauline E., 1249
Rebecca, 1248

Richard P., 1248
Thomas, 1248
Thomas E., 1248
Upton, 1248
Wilfred D., 1248
Wilfred S., 1249
Willoughby, 1248
McClain, Catherine, 1179
Elizabeth, 1179
Isabella, 1179
John, 715, 1179
Margaret Savilla, 1179
Mary Jane, 1179
Peter, 1179
Susan, 1179
McClaine, Ann, 769
Catherine, 769
Da— N., 770
Elizabeth, 769
Ellen S., 769
Isabella, 769
Jane, 769
John, 769
John R., 770
Joseph, 769
Letha N., 770
Lewis B., 769
Margaret, 769
Mary, 717
Peter, 769
Simon, 769
Susan, 769
William, 717
William F., 770
William H., 769
McCleary, Elizabeth, 722
George B., 787
McCleery, C. R., 1360
McClure, A. K., 1395
McComas, George W., 796
Lewis E., 755
Louis E., 697, 960, 1311
McConaughy, David, 1139
McConkey, George W., 1263
Marian Livingston, 1263
Mary A., 1223
William, 1223
McCormac, Anna M., 1131,
1226, 1489, 1593
McCoy, Nannie, 1496
Robert, 1496
Washington, 1496
McCrea, Isabella, 1217
McCulloh, George, 823, 824
Maria L., 823, 824
Robert, 824

McCurdy, Charles, 927, 1550
Elizabeth Agnes, 927
George, 1550
Ira J., 1549, 1550
Irwin P., 842
James, 1549
James Crawford, 1549, 1550
John, 1550
McDaniel, Elizabeth, 1530
George A., 731
Mary Alice, 731
S. Alton, 731
McDeavit, Sarah, 1333
McDermott, Mary, 1024
McDeviett, Ada, 1022
John E., 1022
McDevitt, Cornelius, 965, 1572
Harriet, 952
Margaret, 1414
Sarah A., 1021
McDewitt, Cornelius, 1382
McDonald, Jacob, 1270
McDuell, Ann Elizabeth, 1159
Anna Elizabeth, 1138
Charles W., 1087
Henry, 1087
James, 1087
Jennie, 1087
Julia Staley, 1159
Mary Magdalena, 1087
Robert, 1159, 1576
McElfresh, Annie, 1153
Ariana, 722
Arianna, 1336
Henry, 1153
John, 783, 1153, 1337
John H., 722
Rachel, 1128
Ruth, 1152, 1153
McFadden, Michael, 1024
McFarlan, F. A., 1274
McFarland, James, 1359
McGaga, Alice Jane, 1435
Almstead, 1299, 1434, 1435
Bernard Heightman, 1435
David, 1434
Dorcas Chaney, 1435
Duenna, 1434
Ellwood, 1299
Fredie Lee, 1435
Irvin Connard, 1435
John, 1434
Joseph, 1434
Leanna, 1434

Louise, 1299
Luther Franklin, 1435
Mabel Viola, 1435
Malcolm Edgar, 1435
Mary, 1434
Mary Ellen , 1435
Mattie Elizabeth, 1435
Nellie Irene, 1435
Thomas, 1434
William, 1434, 1435
William Connard, 1435
William Edgar, 1435
McGill, Eleanora, 872
Elenora A., 841
Eleanor West, 1550, 1551
Ernest, 766
Georgia Pearre, 809
James, 872
John, 813
Mary Worthington, 809
Sarah Eleanor, 919, 920
Thomas, 809
Thomas J., 1551
Wardlaw, 809
McGinnis, Samuel M., 1071, 1520
McGowan, Patrick, 1313
McGraw, John T., 1384
McGruder, Margaret, 952
Matilda Noble, 1205
McHenry, Charles, 1363
McIllhany, Harriet, 1137
McIlvains, Thos A., 919
McIntire, Catherine, 723
Edward, 723
William, 1302
McKaig, Wallace, 1211
McKay, David, 995
Norman, 1127
McKechney, John, 1558
McKevitt, John T., 914
McKiel, Albert Ludlow, 1330
McKinley, Mrs. William, 1230
William, 801, 905
McKinney, Andrew C., 1552
Annie, 1075
Armstrong, 1075
David Ferguson, 1552
David Trego, 1553
Hester G., 1552
James Harris, 1552
John, 1552
M. M., 1552
Matthew, 1552
Nancy G., 1552
Priscilla, 1552

Walter, 1075
William Harris, 1553
William W., 1552
McKinstry, Annie M., 733
Evan, 1076
Joseph, 733
Margaret, 733
Mary Ann, 1075, 1076
McKinzer, Wilbur, 1245
McKissick, Rebecca Ann, 1513
McKown, Mary Ann, 1116
McLain, Daniel, 1041
Mary N., 874
McLaine, Fannie, 1229
John, 1229
McLaughlin, William, 1264
McLean, Bettie Maulsby, 1331
Daniel, 1042
Donald, 1330
Elizabeth, 1042
Emily Nelson, 1331
Emily Nelson Ritchie, 1331
Eugene L., 1042
Eugene Lorah, 1041
James, 1041
James B., 1041
John, 1041
Mary Margaret, 1042
Mrs. Donald, 1331
Oliver, 1502
Rebekah McCormick, 1331
Samuel, 1041
McLeod, Hester Ann Rogers, 1138
McMurray, L., 833
Lewis, 704, 1386
Louis, 715
McMurry, Lewis, 1150
McNair, Agnes, 1142, 1143
Alexander, 1143
Harry, 1143
Helen, 1143
Hiram, 1143
Pauline, 1504
Samuel, 1143
William, 1143
McPentz, Mary, 733
McPhearson, J., Jr., 787
McPherson, Alexander, 766
Alice, 809
Edward, 766
Elizabeth, 766

Fannie, 1291
Fanny, 809
Harriet, 766
Horatio, 766
James, 766
John, 765, 766, 809, 1211, 1386
Libbie K., 767
Mary, 766
Maynard, 766
Robert, 765, 766
Thomas Buchanan, 766
William S., 766, 1211
William Smith, 766
Williarn, 765
Williarn S., 765
Wm. S., 1264
McSherry, Ann Ridgeley, 695
Anna Gertrude, 694
Bertha Stuart, 695
Caroline Spurrier, 695
Charles E., 1452
Clara Louisa, 695
Edward, 693
Edward C., 694
Grace, 1553
J. Roger, 1293
James, 693-695, 713, 729, 833
James Roger, 695
Kitty, 1449
Mary Alice, 694
Patrick, 693
Richard, 1213
William Clinton, 695
William S., 694
McWilliams, Amy, 1505
Mealey, Charles E., 1610
Isa, 882, 1588
Isaac, 797, 1415
Laura V., 797, 1415
Measel, Emma I., 1335
George W., 1335
Rebecca, 1575
Measell, Clarence, 1135
Cynthia A. C., 1132
David L., 1490, 1520
Fannie A., 1490
George, 882, 908, 1592
Julia Ann, 882
Mary A.C., 908
Rosie, 1520
Measle, Virgie, 1387
Medairy, Ellen, 1280
Medtard, Barbara, 833
Medtart, Susan, 764

Meherling, George, 1157
Margaret, 1157
Mehring, Franklin, 1367
Lydia, 1587
Mehrling, Anna Mary, 778
August, 777
Ellizabeth, 777
George W., 778
Henry, 777
John Lewis, 777
Lewis W., 777
Lewis William, 778
Margaret Elizabeth, 778
Philipina, 778
Mehrring, Upton, 1518
Meier, August, 1290
Gustav, 1290
H. F. August, 1290
Henry C. A., 1290
Herman, 1290
Mary, 1290
William, 1290
Menchey, Rebecca P., 984
Menchy, Daniel, 985
Mary, 985
Rebecca, 985
Mengis, Amanda, 750, 787, 788, 1599, 1600
Jacob, 788, 1600
Mentzer, Amos, 1514
Ann R. C., 1157, 1158
Annie, 1514
Barbara, 1157
Catharine, 1157
Charles, 1514
Christian, 859
David, 718
Elizabeth, 1157
Ellen, 1514
George, 1514
George Michael, 1514
Hannah, 718
J. C., 1513
Jacob, 1157
John, 1157
Joshua E., 1514
Kitty, 1514
Laura, 1532
Mary, 1157
Mary Ellen, 1310
Peter, 1514
Polly, 1514
Rachel, 1514
Roy W., 1514
Samuel, 1157, 1605
Susan, 1157, 1514

Mercer, Albert M., 775, 1406, 1523
Alice, 775, 1406, 1523
Clara S. V., 775, 1406, 1523
Clara V., 1578
Earl W. H., 1406
Eliza, 1072
Elizabeth, 1248
Ercelle L., 1406
Fanny, 1268
Florence L., 775, 1406, 1523
Gracen, 1134
Grayson H., 775, 1406, 1522, 1523
Howard D., 775, 1406, 1523
Ida G., 1406
Ida M., 775, 1406, 1523
John, 1067
Leana G., 1523
Mae L., 1523
Mary Elizabeth, 1066, 1067
Melvin L., 1406
Victor S., 1523
William, 775, 1287, 1405, 1522, 1578
William C., 775, 1405, 1406, 1523
William E., 774, 1405, 1406, 1522, 1577
Mercier, Adam, 1534
Annie, 1260, 1534
Archibald, 1181
Azel, 1181
Bertie, 1534
Cordelia, 1181
Cornelius, 1180, 1181
Eli Washington, 1181
Fannie, 1534
Fanny, 1112, 1534
George, 1534
Iola, 1534
John, 1181, 1534
John William, 1533, 1534
Katherine Tivis, 1181
Keturah, 1181
Minnie, 1534
Mollie, 1260, 1534
Nancy, 1534
Rachel, 1181
Richard, 1180, 1181
Richard Cornelius, 1180, 1181

Robert, 1122, 1181
Robert Shipley, 1112
Ruth, 1534
Ruth Elizabeth, 1181
Tivis, 1181
Walter, 1534
Washington, 1112
William, 1534
William F., 1533, 1534
Meredith, Ellen, 1557
Hannah, 1093
Margaret, 1216
Meridith, Fenton, 1162
Merring, Upton, 1619
Messler, Anne, 1007
John, 1007
Messner, Ann Rebecca, 772
Charles E., 772
David, 772
Effie M., 772
George, 772
Jacob, 772
Jacob H., 772
Josiah G., 771, 772
Sophia, 772
Metcalf, Calvin Reese, 1194
Clinton, 1235, 1516
Gaven Edgar, 1194
Isaac Francis, 1194
Lena, 1159
Reese , 1194
Thomas, 1506
Metz, Catherine, 1017
D. O., 1231
Daniel O., 886
John, 1477
Metzgar, Sarah, 1357
Metzger, Daniel, 767
Elizabeth, 1351
George, 767
Henry J. P., 767
J. L., 1391
J. William, 767
Jacob, 767
John, 767
John L., 767
John Luther, 961
Lewis, 1563
Louisa C., 767, 960
Louisa Catharine, 961
Lydia (Tomes), 843
Mary E., 767, 844, 961
Mosheim M., 767
Mosheim Morris, 961
Philip, 767
Samuel, 767

William, 767, 844, 960, 961
William S. T., 767, 961
Michael, Abraham, 1602, 1609
Albertus, 947
Alice, 931
Andrew, 930, 947
Andrew, 2nd, 930
Anna A., 931, 1088
Annie A., 931
Annie E., 1602
Annie M. E., 1609
Bertha V., 931
Beatrice V., 1602
Bessie, 947
Burns M., 1602
Caroline, 758, 882, 883,
  1374, 1589
Catharine E., 964, 1340,
  1341, 1572
Catherine, 985, 1572, 1579
Catherine R., 739
Charles, 1234
Charles E., 1602
Charles F., 1602
Conrad, 883, 1377, 1589
Curtis, 947
Daniel, 930, 947, 960
Daniel J., 931
Daniel W., 1485
Deborah, 1275
Eliza, 930, 947, 1109
Elizabeth, 883, 947, 1377,
  1589
Ella, 931
Elmer E., 931
Emily, 947
Ernest D., 1602
Eugenia, 931
Ezra, 930, 931, 947, 1038,
  1088, 1171, 1364, 1396,
  1422, 1427
F. E., 1273
Florence, 1602
Florence E., 1603
Frank, 1022
Franklin E., 1320
Franklin Esterday, 1602
George, 1602
Grace E., 931
Granville, 1081
Granville J., 1602
Hallie V., 1602
Harry, 957
Harry N., 931
Henry, 739, 964, 985, 1114,
  1341, 1572, 1579, 1601

Henry S., 930, 947
Hester C., 1603
Horace Z., 1602
Isaac, 1370, 1467
Isabella M., 947
J. Edwin, 1213
J. Ezra, 758
Jennie M. C., 706
Jerome, 947
John, 923, 947, 1316,
  1602
John Lambert, 947
Joshua, 947
Katholyn, 1602
Laura, 947
Leah M., 1602
Leo H., 1602
Louisa, 1140
Lucretia, 911, 1375
Marion S, 1114
Marion S., 930, 931, 1108
Martin B., 931
Mary E., 947
Maurice W., 1602
Mayme Viola, 1603
Mollie V., 1485
Oliver, 1485
Pauline E., 1602
Pearl C., 947
Phoebe, 947
Samuel, 947, 1341
Samuel A., 930
Sarah, 930, 947
Sarah A., 1341
Simon P., 1602
Stella V., 1320, 1603
Susan, 1313
Upton S., 1602
Virgie Ella, 1603
Walter M., 931
William H., 947, 1601,
  1602
William O., 1601, 1602
Michaels, Daniel, 759
Isaac, 758
Marie, 789
Roy, 789
Russell, 789
Mickley, Abram, 1347
Sarah, 830
Middlekauff, Isaiah, 1075
Mifflin, Elizabeth, 1400
Thomas, 1400
Mikesell, Margaret, 1007
Miles, Catherine, 839
Elvira, 933

F. T., 1213
George E., 926
Nelson A., 1017
Sarah, 1152
Milford, Samuel, 763
Millard, Almira, 1030
  Charles H., 1107
  Charles R., 1030
  Lucy A., 1107
  Margaret, 1107
Millbourne, L. R., 1389
Miller, ——, 779, 882, 1588
  Abner, 1463
  Adam, 897, 898, 1469
  Alice V., 901
  Amelia, 1614
  Andrew, 1082
  Ann, 968
  Ann A., 770
  Ann M., 717, 1063
  Ann Margaret, 1122
  Anna Belle, 780
  Annie, 780, 1205, 1614
  Annie C., 1051
  Annie F., 1158
  Augustus, 1614
  B. F., 1360
  Bertie, 1155
  Beulah E., 964
  C. H., 973
  Caroline, 1483
  Carlton C., 1051
  Carrie, 1094
  Carrie A., 1158
  Carrie M., 1051
  Carrie May, 1051
  Catharine, 1158, 1514, 1614
  Catherine, 1158
  Charles, 1403, 1614
  Charles A., 1360
  Charles D., 973
  Charles E., 779
  Charles M., 765
  Charles Philip, 1483
  Charles S., 1157
  Charles W., 901, 1483
  Charles William, 1482, 1483
  Christian, 1089
  Christopher Columbus, 780
  Claude L., 779
  Clementine, 1620
  Columbia Victoria, 1614
  Cora M., 1618
  Daisy, 901

Daniel, 1158, 1288, 1573
Daniel A., 1484
Daniel B., 780
Daniel C., 1051
Daniel M., 1476, 1483, 1484
Daniel, Jr., 1484
David, 1543
David J., 1589
Edgar Allen, 781
Edith M., 974
Edna E., 1158
Edward, 1060
Effie, 1093, 1124, 1360
Eliza P., 765
Elizabeth, 780, 946, 1605, 1614
Ella C., 1158
Ellen, 1483
Elmer Vernon, 781
Emma, 1614
Emma Etta, 781
Erma Adella, 781
Etta, 1614
Evaline V., 780
F. Clayton, 1483
Frances A., 1122
Frank, 1324
Frank L., 1158
Frederick, 901, 1071, 1333, 1483, 1520
Frederick Clayton, 901
G. L., 739 , 1579
George, 779, 1158, 1264, 1336
George D., 1252
George E., 1158
George Heilman, 781
George L., 1158
George M., 779
George M. D., 779
George N., 973
George W., 781, 921, 973, 1264, 1511
George Washington, 780, 1616
George William, 780
Georgianna, 1615
Georgianna Celista, 1614
Georgianna Celistia, 1613
Gertrude, 1483
Girtude, 1158
H., 1290
Hannah, 1252
Harrison, 1287
Harry A., 1158
Harvey, 789

Harvey C., 1614
Harvey Ernest, 781
Hattie, 1501
Helen Gertrude, 780
Henry, 955, 1158, 1443, 1483
Hicks, 1418
Hiram, 780
Howard, 1614
Ida, 1484
Ida C., 921, 973
Isabella, 780
J. L., 1264
J. Hunter, 1583
J. Marshall, 921, 973, 1264
J. Michael, 859
Jacob, 1511
Jacob H., 1212
Jacob L., 973
James, 1506, 1614
James A., 1360, 1533
James W., 1360
Jane, 1158
Jane Ione C., 1089
Jane R., 1580
Jennie, 1075
Jessie, 1614
Joanna, 1614
Jobe, 1483, 1484
Jobe M., 1476, 1484
John, 717, 734, 780, 842, 897, 973, 1157, 1158, 1242, 1264, 1271, 1483, 1513
John A., 780, 1360
John C., 1158
John D., 1157, 1158
John F. D., 1614
John H., 779
John Henry, 1484
John I., 973, 1264
John M., 1476, 1484
John P., 1360
John S., 812
John W., 1287, 1360, 1614
Joseph, 1614
Julia, 796
Julia Ann, 1350, 1351
Julia Elizabeth, 1287
Kate B., 1484
Kinney, 715
L. F., 1513, 1514
L. Frank, 1614
Lewis D., 1158

Lewis E., 973, 1264, 1618
Lewis P., 1051
Lizzie, 1520
Lucinda, 1483
Lucy, 1537
Luella M., 1158
Luther Townsend, 1484
M. C., 1334
M. Martha, 1614
Margaret, 1484
Margaret Adella, 1360
Margaret Virginia, 1476
Martin, 1397
Martin Matthias, 901
Mary, 717, 780, 973, 1178, 1360, 1446
Mary A., 1397, 1533
Mary Grace, 1484
Mary M., 1061
Mary O., 1158
Matilda, 764
Matilda Catherine, 1242
Mattie, 1614
Maud Manzella, 781
Mildred, 1158
Miller, 858
Minerva, 973, 1614
Minnie Elsie, 1614
Miranda, 1360
Miss A., 1616
Morris, 1614
Naomi I., 1158
Niles, 1614
Olive M., 779
Ora Grace, 781
Oscar C., 1158
Otho J., 951
Rachael, 898
Rachel, 1298
Ralph, 1051
Roy, 1614
Roy M., 1484
S. S., 907
Sally, 1501
Samuel, 897, 898
Sarah, 1424, 1483
Sarah A. E., 898
Sarah Ann, 780
Sarah E., 1360
Sarah Louise, 1484
Sarah V., 1158
Silas V., 964
Sophia, 1405
Susan, 780, 781, 850, 1200
T. E. R., 1022, 1243, 1402, 1597

T. W., 1089
Thomas E. R., 973, 1264
Townsend, 1484
Viola G., 1158
Virginia, 918
Virginia H., 974
Washington, 780
William, 779, 780, 1094, 1614
William A., 780
William C., 1158
William E., 761, 1000, 1447
William H., 1264
William H. C., 779
William L., 973
William S., 779, 780
Zacharias, 1614
Millineaux, Sarah, 879
Mills, Albert N., 1051
Hannah, 965
John R., 1051
Mary, 920
Pauline B., 1051, 1217
William R., 1051
Miltenberger, Geo. W., 1213
Milton, Tabitha, 1239
Mines, John, 777
John Louis, 777
William Willson, 777
Minnick, Julia, 934
Minor, Dona, 1221
John B., 857
Margaret L., 1419
Spencer, 1419
Miss, Lewis, 1363
Sarah, 1363
Mitchell, Hamilton, 1299
P., 1228
Sophia, 1029
William, 1116
Mitten, Catharine, 828, 1617
Elizabeth, 1221
Moats, John F., 1469
Mobberly, E. W., 937
Helen, 1343
Moberly, Ann E., 1118
Annie, 1118
Charles E., 1117, 1118
Charles E., Jr., 1118
Daniel, 1017
David, 1118
E. W., 745
Edward, 1118
Elizabeth, 1306
Hiram, 1118
Levi, 1117, 1118

Lewis, 1118
Louisa, 745
Margaret, 1306
Mary, 1118, 1560
Mary L. F., 1118
May M., 1118
Mehrl, 1560
Merhl F., 1117, 1118
Mollie K., 1118
Mrs. Edmund, 815
Rachel, 1040
Susan, 1306
Thomas, 1306
William, 1118
Mobley, A. Clyde, 1548
E. S., 1548, 1549
Edward, 1548
Ella, 1548
Eli, 1548
Frank H., 1548
George L., 1548, 1549
J. C., 1548
Jesse B., 1548
Laura, 1548
Mary E., 1548
Moffett, Benjamin, 1323
Ellen, 1323
Ellen E., 1322
J. T., 1109
Mrs. Robert, 1208
Mohler, Annie M., 771
Dolly V., 771
Eva, 1565
Franklin A., 771
George, 1565
Gertrude M., 771
Harry, 1173
Harry E., 771, 1061
Homer S., 771
Jacob, 771
John L., 771
Ruthford H., 771
Thomas G., 1061
Moler, George, 972
Molesworth, Annie Lois, 942
Archley R., 942
Columbus, 1547
Edward, 1344
Eldridge, 768
Elizabeth, 1326
Florida Virginia, 769, 1296
Gassaway, 1547
George, 768, 1326
Gurney C., 941, 942
Helen M., 942

Henrietta, 1547
James, 768
James P., 1338
Jessie, 840
John, 769
John Joseph, 941, 942
John W., 941
John Wesley, 1547
John William, 768, 1296
Joseph, 768
Joshua, 1547
Laura Virginia, 1547
Louisa, 1547
Margaret, 768
Margaret Earl, 769
Martha, 1326
Mary Thomas, 769
Mathias, 941, 942
Matthew, 768
Minnie R., 769
Rachael R., 942
Roger Wright, 769
Samuel, 768, 769, 941,
    1547
Susan, 768
Susan C., 942
Thomas, 768, 769
William, 768, 1547
Zachariah, 1547
Molinix, Ann, 795
Monath, August, 1261
Moncrief, Alexander, 1503
Mong, Elizabeth, 1178
Monkur, John C. S., 1212
Monn, Ida, 1605
Montgomery, Oliver P., 1552
Moore, Dollie C., 973
    Hannah, 1076
    Jacob M., 800
    Josephine E., 1255
    Margaret, 1262
    Martha, 1024
    Valentine, 973
Moos, Elise, 841
    Elise W., 840
    Johan Adam, 840
Moran, James, 1024
More, C. F., 1224
    Von Herman, 1224
    Willis L., 1224
Morelock, Mary Ann, 860
Morgan, Alice D., 893
    Annie L., 892
    Annie S., 778
    Benton M., 892
    Clair N., 779

Clinton, 892
Dale, 893
David, 778, 892
Della E., 892
Edward L., 778
Ethel V., 893
Franklin, 892
George, 745, 1072, 1354
Grace, 893
Ida R., 779
Irving, 738, 867
Irving R., 778
J. Page, 779
James W., 778
Jefferson E., 778
John, 1156
Leslie I., 779
Levi, 827
Margaret, 892
Margaret E., 778
Mary, 848
Mary A., 779
Mary Jane, 892
Mary S., 892
Ralph E., 779
Randolph, 892
Rufus R., 778
Ruth E., 779
Saline, 892
Samuel, 1221
Silas, 892
Susan, 892
Thomas, 848
Vernon S., 779
Wesley, 892, 1311
Morningstar, Anne, 1181
    Elizabeth, 1208
    Fannie, 1135
    Jasper, 1140
Morris, Arthur, 889
    John G., 1212
    Sarah, 1582
    Thomas, 1582
    Thomas J., 1242
Morrison, Elizabeth A., 864
    Harriet E., 823
    Helen Bruce, 1505
    John, 1116
    Margaret M., 1253
    Richard, 892
    Susan, 778, 892
    William, 864, 1505
Morse, Samuel F. B., 760
Morsel, William P., 1143
Morsell, Caroline M., 1413
    Charles K., 1413

George, 839
Hester A., 1413
Margaret, 1413
Mary Howard, 1414
Mary T., 1413
Rachel, 839, 1295, 1456
Rebecca, 1414
Sarah, 1413
William, 839
William B., 1413
William P., 1413, 1414
Morselle, Tabitha, 1223
Mort, Bessie, 1060
    Bessie N., 1447
    Charles S., 1418
    Daisy, 1418
    Eliza Jane, 1418
    Frances Anna, 1513
    Fransanna B., 789
    Frederick, 789, 1447,
        1513
    George, 1132, 1512, 1513
    George A, 1418
    John, 1418
    Laura, 1418
    Matthias, 1052
    Philip F., 1418
    Samuel, 1418
    Sarah E., 1418
    Spencer E., 1419
    William, 717, 789, 1512,
        1532
    William Henry, 789, 1512,
        1513
Moseley, Wesley, 1075
Moser, ———, 771
    Alpha, 957
    Bettie, 1158
    Daniel, 771
    Eleanor, 957
    Elias, 770, 771
    Elizabeth, 771
    Ephraim, 743
    Ezra F., 771
    Fannie E., 957
    George, 771
    Ida M., 957
    Jacob, 819, 1347
    Jacob L., 770, 771
    Jennetta, 957
    Jennie, 1479
    John, 957
    John E., 771
    Joseph, 771
    Leonard, 770
    Lucinda, 957

Mary, 771
Mirah, 771
Olivia C., 957
Samuel C., 957
Vallie L., 957
Wallace, 804
Mosser, Frederick, 1363
Motter, Alan, 817
  Alice, 1417
  Amie, 817
  Anna, 816, 864
  Anna M., 1416
  Anna Maria Eber, 815, 816
  Barbara, 1416
  Bessie, 817
  Carrie May, 1417
  Elizabeth, 1416
  Ellen, 1417
  Emily, 817
  Ernma, 816
  George, 815-817
  George T., 816
  Grace, 1417
  Guy Kunkel, 1417
  Helen, 817
  I. M., 907
  Isaac, 1097, 1416
  Isaac M., 1416, 1417
  Jacob, 815, 816
  Jessie, 817
  John, 816
  John C., 816, 889, 890, 896,
    1201, 1408
  John Christian, 1417
  John Columbus, 815, 816
  Joshua, 1416
  Joshua S., 1417
  Lewis, 780, 1416
  Lewis Edwin, 1417
  Lewis Martin, 1416
  Lillian Elizabeth, 1417
  Lolo, 817
  Margaret Rudisel, 1417
  Mary, 1417
  Rachel, 1417
  Roger, 817
  Samuel, 1033, 1416
  Samuel Lewis, 1417
  Serene, 1417
  Valentine, 1416
  William, 1416, 1417
Mough, Mrs. Myra L., 1612
Mought, William, 1190
Mount, Edith, 724
  John R., 942
  William, 724

William T., Jr., 1272
Moxley, Harvey, 1590
  Jemima, 1271, 1272
  Leah, 1555
  Sarah E., 1162
Mudd, Eugene, 1473
Muir, John, 1428
Mulfinger, Mrs. J. P., 975
Mulkey, Mary, 1124
Mull, James, 980
  Laura M., 980
  Lillie A., 1495
Mullen, Charles, 1559
Mullendore, Arnold Lee, 1062
  Catharine, 1030
  Catherine, 1149
  Clifford, 1062
  David, 1473
  Ellis Clifford, 1062
  Etta, 1486
  Eva Pauline, 1062
  George B., 1062
  Grace, 1062
  John, 1031
  Mabel Marie, 1062
  Mary Annabel, 1062
  Olive Virginia, 1062
Mullenix, Kitty, 1034
  Leonard C., 1025
Mulliken, Anna, 763
Mullindore, Catherine, 1004
Mullinix, E. E., 759
  Elisha E., 1026
  Frances A., 1026
  Kate, 1245
  Kitty, 1034
  L. E., 773, 784, 1026
  Leonard C., 1026
  Lorenzo E., 1025, 1026,
    1141
  M. Edna, 773
  Sybelle M., 1026
  Thomas, 1026
Mullnix, Frances Elizabeth,
    1026
  Helen Alberta, 1026
  Mary Edna, 1026
  Ruth Simpson, 1026
Mumford, E. Carl, 860
  Martin, 1012
Mumma, Elizabeth, 1620, 1621
  Elizabeth Susan, 1030
  Henry C., 1405
  Isaac, 1335
Mundbach, Catherine, 869
Munford, Richard, 1594

William, 1594
Munn, Edna Alberta, 1616
Murdoch, Benjamin, 1280
  Eleanor, 1342, 1343
  Ella, 1280
  George, 1343
  Howard V., 1280
  John, D., 1280
  Richard B., 1272
  Richard Bruce, 1272,
    1280, 1281
  Richard Howard, 1280
  Sallie R., 1280
  William Buoy, 1280
Murdock, Alexander, 711
  John, 771, 1460
  R. Bruce, 1008
Murphy, Alice, 768
  Ann, 768
  Annie C., 768
  Belle, 768
  Betsy, 768
  Carrie, 768
  Charles E., 768
  Elmer, 1537
  Enoch Lewis, 768
  Frances, 1169
  Frances S., 768
  Hattie B., 768
  Horace L., 767, 768
  Ira Edwin, 768
  J. Oliver, 768
  James, 767
  Jefferson D., 768
  Mary E., 768
  Maud, 768
  Milton A., 768
  Ollie Augusta, 768
  P. C., 768
  Patrick, 767, 768
  Priscilla, 768
  R. R., 915
  R. W., 1358
  Roger, 768
  Sophia, 768
  William, 767, 768
  William G., 768
  William R., 767, 768
Murray, Ann K., 774
  Ann Kirkwood, 773
  Anna Mary, 1028
  Barbara F., 774
  Clara H., 774
  Edgar, 1275
  Emeline, 774
  Esther, 774

James, 773, 943, 1074
John Gardner, 773
John Gardner, Jr., 774
John T., 798
Joshua, 1028
Joshua J., 1003
Ruth, 774
Murry, Silas, 1416
Musgrove, Amy, 1564
Bessie, 1565
Eliza, 1564
Francis M., 1564
James L., 1564
Mary, 1564, 1565
Minnie, 1565
Nellie, 1565
Walper G., 1564
William, 1565
Zacharias, 1564
Musselman, Aaron, 718
William, 957
Mussetter, Ann, 975
Barbara, 975
Becky, 975
Betsy, 975
Christian, 845, 975
Christoper, 975
Christopher, 975
Elizabeth, 975
Harriet, 975
Henry Percival, 975, 976
Hobson Schley, 976
Jemima, 975
Jennie, 975
Joel, 975
John, 975
John H., 976
Lemuel, 975
Martha Elizabeth, 976
Mary Ruth, 976
Nancy, 975
Plummer, 975
Rebecca, 845
Ruth, 975
Myer, Ann C., 1048
Mary, 1282
Myerly, Frederick, 1518, 1619
Myers, A. V., 1166
Abraham, 946
Annie M., 813, 1165, 1166
Augusta Catharine, 1439
Bernard, 1333
Bernice E., 1165
C. E. Victor, 1166
C. Victor, 1143
Casper, 1425

Charles, 1358
Charles B., 1419
Charles E. Victor, 1165
Charles F., 1439
Charles G., 1439
Charlotte, 1461
Christian, 1164, 1294
Christiana, 1488
David, 946
Elizabeth, 1472
Emma B., 1439
Ephraim, 843
Ethel M., 1146, 1166
F. Ross, 1166
Francis M., 1419
G. Ed., 735
George, 1439, 1602
George C. F., 1165, 1166
George E., 999
George Ed., 735
George Edward, 1439, 1440
George R., 1419
George W., 813, 1165, 1166, 1364
Hannah, 1258
Harry, 1108, 1114
Hattie L., 1419
Henry, 1083, 1554
Jacob, 1472
James E. B., 1419
Jessie D., 884
Joel, 734
John, 1318
L. F. M., 1419
Lee, 1273
Lena M., 1419
Maggie, 1320
Maggie E., 1419
Margaret, 1018, 1364
Margaret P., 1165
Mary, 1305, 1536
Mary E., 1166
Mary Elizabeth, 946
Mary I., 1165, 1166
Mary R., 1419
Melvin E., 1439
Miss A., 1554
Mollie M., 1472
Peter, 1165, 1419
Robert I., 1439
Ruth M., 1419
Susan, 1101
Theodore, 1199
Thomas F., 1146, 1165, 1166
Tilghman P., 1416
Wesley, 886

Myesli, Solomon M., 860
Naill, David W., 1279
Jacob, 1279
Maggie, 1278
Maggie L., 1279
Naille, Dora, 1220, 1498
John, 1495
John Peter, 1223
Louisa, 1495
Nash, Elise, 1211
Lalitte, 1211
Minnie Lucile, 759
Minnie Lucille, 1210, 1211
Mrs. Isabelle, 1210, 1211
Naylor, Albina, 1063
Annie, 1063
Catherine M., 1063
George C., 773
John R., 1063
Mary A., 1063
Reuben R., 1063
Roscoe, 1063
William, 717, 1062
William H., 1062
Neale, Elizabeth, 1215
James, 1215, 1216
Neart, Lizzie, 1221
Neely, George Macbeth, 773
George Macbeth, Jr., 773
Neff, Ann, 970
Ann March, 1065
Cordelia, 1042
Mary Harnish, 1042
William, 1042
Neidhardt, Annie, 1560
Augustus, 1560
Joseph William, 1560
Lena, 1560
Louisa, 1560
Lucy, 1560
Margaret, 1560
Mary, 1560
Mary E., 1560
Minnie, 1560
Rudolph, 1560
William Joseph, 1560
Neidhart, Mary E., 1118
Neidig, Clara, 1098
Clara A., 1205
Isaac, 1205
William, 1342
Neighbors, Elizabeth, 1606
Elizabeth R., 1397
Eutaw D., 1607
Fleet R., 1201, 1607

John O., 1607
John T., 1606
John W., 1607
Lolla A., 1607
Martha, 1606
Martha R., 1607
Nathan O., 1606
Reta E., 1607
Roger M., 1606, 1607
Sarah, 1606, 1607
William, 1606
Neikirk, Albertus, 1006
  Alburtus W., 1361
  Annie, 1462
  Cecilia, 1361
  Charles E., 1006, 1361
  Clara, 1006
  Clara V., 1361
  Earl, 1362
  Emma, 1006, 1383
  Emma S., 1361
  Esta, 1006
  Esta M., 952
  Esta W., 1361
  Fannie J., 1361
  Fannie L., 1006
  George, 1006, 1361, 1382,
    1383
  George D., 1361
  George Lewis, 1006
  Laura, 1006
  Laura A., 1361
  Lillie, 1006, 1361
  Lillie M., 1361
  Margaret Ann, 1006
  Martha E., 1361
  Martha Ellen, 1006, 1361
  Mary, 965, 1361
  Mary C., 1006
Neil, Isabelle, 1296, 1457
Nelson, Basil, 783
  Benjamin, 1073, 1122
  Elisha, 1122
  Ella, 1205
  Emily, 1329, 1330
  Emily C., 1329, 1608
  Frederick J., 968
  Hanson, 1122
  Henrietta, 1122
  Henry, 941, 1122, 1123
  Jesse, 895
  John, 833
  Madison, 694
  Margaret, 1122, 1152
  Maria, 1122
  Marian, 1122

Marian R., 1123
Markell Henry, 1123
Mary Jane, 1122
Matilda, 1112, 1122
Miranda, 1122
Nathan, 1073, 1112, 1122,
  1531, 1533
Rebecca, 1510
Robert, 1122
Robert W., 1510
Roger, 1329, 1330, 1608
Sophia, 1122
Susan Rebecca, 1122
Verdie Jane, 1123
William B., 1096
William Pinkney, Jr., 1329
Ness, George T., 1198
Neviett, Robert R., 1413
Newahl, Julian, 1354
Newcomer, B. F., 1564
  Catherine, 920
  Henry E., 1186
  Isaac, 1405
  Lena E., 1185, 1186
  Samuel, 1239
Newell, Daniel, 1329
Newkirk, Anna Mary, 1025
  George, 1025
Newman, Charles, 946
  Emma Catherine, 856
  Francis, 744
  Francis J., 856, 857
  Helen Elizabeth, 856
  Jacob, 856
  Jacob M., 856, 857
  Jacob N., 1360
  John, 946
  John Nicholas, 856
  John S., 856, 857
  Mary Henrietta., 857
  Parsons, 857
  Susan Bird, 744
Newton, John B., 1551
  Sarah North, 1550
Nicholas, George, 1231
Nichols, Agnes, 1389
  Charles E., 1045, 1302, 1303
  Charles Ernest, 1045
  Edward, 1044, 1045, 1302,
    1303
  Edward, Jr., 1045, 1303
  Elsie M., 1303
  Estell, 1303
  Harriet A., 1303
  Harriet A.., 1045
  Harriet E., 1303

Harriet Ellen, 1045
Jacob, 1044, 1045, 1302,
  1303
John, 1044, 1302
Julia Estelle, 1045
Mary E., 1045, 1303
Otho, 1303
Otho Trundle, 1045
Sarah E., 1045, 1303
Sophia E., 1045, 1303
Thomas, 1045, 1303
Tillie, 965
William, 1045, 1303
William Anna, 1045
Willie A., 1303
Nicholson, Asa, 763
  Cassandra, 763
  Cordelia, 763
Nickum, John, 804
  Sarah, 805
Nicodemus, A. W., 1021
  Allen W., 956
  Albert, 1546
  Alice, 1546
  Anna, 1054, 1139
  Annie, 980, 1003, 1509,
    1535
  Asbury, 1545
  Augusta, 1546
  Augustus W., 1065, 1441,
    1509, 1534
  Augustus, Jr. , 1065
  Augustus W., Jr., 971,
    1065, 1066
  Augustus W., Sr., 970,
    1066
  Bradley, 1546
  Bradley T., 955, 1272
  Bud, 1545
  C. A., 1537
  Catherine Gertrude, 1546
  Chancy S., 956
  Charles, 1545
  Charles Albert, 1509,
    1534, 1535
  Clara, 1546
  Clinton C., 1545, 1546
  Clinton Roscoe, 1546
  Conrad, 1509, 1534
  Edgar R., 971, 1066, 1365
  Edith, 1509, 1510
  Edith M., 1535
  Edward B., 1535
  Eli, 971, 1065, 1509,
    1534
  Elias, 1314

Eliza, 955
Elizabeth, 1510
Ellen, 1510
Emeline, 1545
Emma, 1509, 1535
Emma L., 956
Eva S. E., 956, 1145
Fanny, 1546
Felty, 1545
Frank C., 1535
Grace H., 1066
H. C., 1515
Hannah Elizabeth, 1509, 1535
Harry O., 971, 1066
Henry, 970, 1546
Henry L., 1065
Isaac, 1222
Isaac C., 955
J. D., 1294 , 1515, 1537
J. V., 1515
Jesse, 955
John, 970, 1195, 1509, 1534
John Allen, 1546
John D., 1509
John H., 955
John L., 832, 970, 971, 1065, 1509, 1534
John Lewis, 1509, 1534, 1535
John Luther, 704
John V., 1510
Kent Castle, 1510
Lona L., 956
Mamie, 796
Mamie E., 971, 1066
Margaret, 1059, 1231, 1339, 1545
Martha E., 1546
Martin, 1231
Martin L., 1545, 1546
Martin Luther, 1545, 1546
Martin R., 812
Mary, 1510, 1545
Mary L., 956
Morgan, 1545
Mrs. Jess, 1243
Murry D., 1546
Nancy, 1278
Nanie, 1546
Nannie, 1293
Nathan, 971, 1065, 1509, 1534
Nava E., 956
Olive V., 1546

Olivia, 1058, 1546
Percy O., 956
Peter, 955, 1145
Ralph, 1546
Robert, 1510
Robert F., 1066
Sarah A. E., 1145
Sarah E., 955
V. W., 1008
Valentine, 1509, 1534
Vernon W., 955, 956
Wilbur P., 956
William, 1155, 1546
William H., 955
William T., 1546
Nikirk, Cecelia, 1380
George, 1380
Nixdorf, George, 1473
Nixdorff, George, 1314
George A., 765
Henry, 704, 764, 832, 833
Henry M., 765, 784
Henry V., 765
John George, 764, 832
Julia M., 765
Lewis M., 764, 765
Mary, 704, 832, 833
Mary E., 765
Samuel, 833
Susan, 765, 817, 818
Noble, A., 1503
Anna Catharine, 1088
Bessie Cline, 1088
Charles, 1088
Charles Casper, 1088
Nicholas Dwight, 1088
Nogle, Annie, 1248
Charles, 1588
Noland, B. T., 782, 783
Timothy, 783
Noll, Catherine, 759
Noonan, John, 1251
Joseph, 792
Norfolk, Arthur, 1454
Norris, ——, 1597
A. Henry, 1075, 1076
Amon T., 856
Amos, 991, 1075, 1076
Ann, 915
Basil, 1076
Carrie, 1076
Carrie Urner, 1077
Clara G., 1076
Cordelia, 1547
E. O. , 1207, 1513, 1615
Edna Clary, 1076

Edward O., 903
Elizabeth, 1076
Evan, 1076
Helen Monroe, 1077
Henry, 1338
Henry G., 1076
Israel, 1076
Jacob.Bohn, 1053
Joanna, 1076
Joanna W., 1076
Joel, 1547
John, 1153
Jonathan, 1075
Joshua, 953, 986, 1129
Margaret E., 1076
Mary, 856, 925, 1076
Mary Eugenia, 1076
Mary J., 1076
Mary T., 1076
Matilda, 856
Matilda C., 855
Milton McK., 1076
N. Dorsey, 1076
Nellie, 795
Nicholas, 1075, 1076
Nicholas Browning, 1076
Nicholas E., 1076
Nicholas Edgar, 1076
Paul, 1077
R. L., 1310
Rachel Ann, 1153
Rebecca L., 903
Richard H., 1217
Sally, 731, 1151, 1219, 1377
Samuel, 1076
Samuel McKinstry, 1077
Susan, 1076, 1130
Susanna, 990
Susannah, 991
Tabitha, 1076
Tabitha R., 732, 733
Wash., 1053
Norton, Mary, 1237
Norvell, Emily W., 919
Norwood, Anna, 1216
Arianna, 1216
Aubrey E., 1094
B. M., 879
Barbara A., 1217
Belt, 1216
Benjamin Franklin, 933
Centhia, 1038
Charles, 1223
Charles A., 1217
Chester H., 1217

Clarence, 1094
Cynthia, 864
Edward, 1094
Eleanor, 1216
Elizabeth, 1216
Ella, 1094
Eula Irene, 933
Frank C, 1217
Frank C., 1216, 1217
Isabella V., 1217
Isiah, 1217
James, 1216
Jeremiah, 933, 1216
John, 1216
John T., 1094, 1344
Joshua, 1216, 1540
Lorenzo B., 1093, 1094
Martha, 1217
Martha Jane, 1540
Mary, 1216
Mary E., 879
Mary Ellen, 1217
Matilda, 1216
Nettie, 1094
Olivia, 1217
R. Nelson, 1051, 1216,
  1217
R. T., 933
Rachel, 1217
Ralph, 1216
Ruby Estelle, 933
Rufus, 1217
Ruth, 1072
S. Belt, 1217
Samuel, 1072, 1216
Sarah C., 1217
Sarah E., 1217
Sarah M., 1216
Susan, 1216
Thomas, 1216
Virginia, 1094
William, 879
Notnagle, Adam A., 1561
  Ellen Sophia, 1561
  Franklin Leonard, 1561
  Frederick J., 1561
  Jacob, 1561, 987
  Jacob William, 1561
  Leonard, 1561
  Mary, 1561
  Sophia, 1561
Null, Harriet A., 1002
  Jacob, 1613
  James, 762
  Mary, 965
  Roy, 962

Susan, 1221
Nusbam, Isaiah, 1278
  Marshall Naill, 1278
Nusbaum, A. F., 1294
  Abram, 1297, 1546
  Abram Washington, 1297,
    1546
  Adam, 1297, 1546
  Adam F., 1566
  Adam Francis, 1297, 1546
  Alice M., 1279
  Amy E., 1309
  Angeline, 1297, 1546
  Ann, 1203, 1556
  Barbara, 1260
  C. Edgar, 1279
  Charles, 1260
  Chester, 1597
  Chester M, 1279
  Clara May, 1297
  Clinton, 885
  Delia, 1534
  Elizabeth, 1279
  Ella, 1309
  Ezra, 956
  Fanny, 1279, 1546
  Florence, 1546
  Florence B., 1279
  George, 1546
  Gladys, 1597
  Gladys S., 1279
  Harvey, 1279
  Henry, 1297, 1546
  Ida, 1297
  Isaac, 966
  Isaiah, 1279
  Jacob, 1279
  John, 1309, 1498
  Laura, 1279
  Lola, 1546
  Margaret, 1297, 1546
  Margaret E., 1130
  Marshall, 1597
  Marshall N., 1279
  Marshall Naill, 1279
  Mary, 1279, 1283
  Mary Angeline, 1058
  Mary S., 1279
  Mayme, 1546
  Minnie, 1546
  Nettie, 1059
  Oswa Irene, 1297
  Rachel, 1553, 1556
  Samuel, 1130, 1297 1546,
    1578
  Samuel A., 1508

Simon, 1468
Susan, 1279
Nusbaum
Nusz, Annie, 1204, 1205
  George, 1276
  Joseph, 1283
  William, 1205
O'Connor, William, 1221
O'Donnell, J. C., 1543
  Oliver, 1282
O'Neal, George, 1060
O'Neil, George, 761, 999,
  1447
O'Riley, Lillian, 753
Oahr, Mollie, 1311
Oaks, Catherine, 1384
Obenderfer, Augustus, 1559
  Caroline, 1559
  Catharine, 1559
  Christina, 1559
  F. W., 1308
  Frederick W., 1559
  John L., 1559
  John William, 1559
  Mary, 1559
  Nellie, 1559
  Sabean, 1559
Odein, William, 763
Odell, Sarah A., 842
  William C., 842
Oden, Tony M., 768
Offley, Mattie, 1497
Offutt, Clara Courtnay, 1259
  James, 1259
  Sarah, 940
Ogburn, Laura, 1112, 1268,
  1269
Ogden, William, 1367, 1447
Ogle, Ada M., 922
  Albert, 922
  Alfred, 922
  Allen G., 1585
  Annie H., 844
  Archie A., 841
  Benjamin, 1401, 1506,
    1584-1586
  Beulah, 1585
  Catherine E., 1586
  Charles Abraham, 922
  Christina Elizabeth, 1427
  Clara, 1585
  Clara L., 1506
  Edward, 922
  Ephraim, 922
  Evan, 922, 1143
  George, 922, 1427

George W., 1584-1586
Grant, 1092
Harry, 922
Harvey B., 1585, 1586
J. B., 926
James H. B., 1585
John G., 1586
John S., 1585
Julia A., 1585
Laura, 922
Lewis C., 1584-1586
Lydia Wolfe, 922
Margaret, 1401
Margaret M., 1586
Mary, 922
Mary C., 1585
Mary E., 1427
Mary O., 1585
Mary V., 922
Matilda, 812
Nora I., 922
Pauline I., 1586
Rachel, 1586
Rebecca, 922
Robert L., 1585
Samuel, 1401
Sidney, 922
T. A., 1468
Thomas, 922, 1210
Thomas A., 1585
William, 922, 1512
William B., 1585
William C., 922
Oglebee, J. D., 1590
Ohland, Alice, 1305, 1536
Ohler, Catharine, 789
    George, 1540
Oland, Alice D., 1049
    Alice E., 989, 1049, 1304
    Alice Elizabeth, 1525
    Annie L., 1049
    Augustus F. H., 1525
    Carlton E., 989, 1049
    Carlton Edward, 1525
    Charles E., 989
    Charles F., 989, 1049
    Charles Franklin, 1525
    Daisy A., 1049
    David, 1143
    David P., 989, 1049
    David Peter, 1525
    Ellen D., 989
    Fannie I., 989, 1143
    Frances, 989, 1049
    Frances Catharine, 1525
    Frederick, 747, 989, 1049,

1254, 1304
    Frederick Henry Augustus,
1525
    Henry F. A., 1525
    Ida Etta V., 1525
    Jacob L., 989, 1049
    Jacob Luther, 1525
    Lena, 989
    Lucretia, 989, 1049
    Lucretia Sophia, 1525
    Millie, 989
    Minnie, 1143
    Olie M., 1049
    Olive O., 989
    Sharetts, 989
    Susie V., 1049
    Thomas J., 1537
    Virginia, 989, 1049
Oler, Catharine, 1512, 1513
    Frederick, 1513
    George A., 741
    Nicholas Cronon, 741
Olinger, Anna, 884
Oliver, John, 824
Olmsted, William, 1583
Orbison, R. A., 1574
Ordeman, Charles Lee, 1439
    Charles O., 1459
    D. T., 1098
    Daniel T., 1439, 1459
    David, 1439
    Emma C., 1459
    Frederick A., 1459
    Georgiana, 1459
    H. D., 1098, 1459
    Helen Catherine, 1439
    Herman, 1439
    John H., 1459
    Mary C., 1098, 1459
Orison, Mary Louise, 1189
Orms, Ursula, 1539
Orndorf, Catherine, 1275
    Eliza, 1024, 1025
    Elizabeth, 1025
    James, 860, 1620
Orr, Anna B., 884
    Anna Baum, 885
    Henry, 885
    James Monroe, 885
    Mary Priscilla, 885
    Mollie, 1306
    Robert, 884, 885
Orrison, Arthur, 1099, 1107,
1113
    Charles, 1020
    Edward, 1078

Harry, 746
    Mary Louisa, 1078
Osborn, Eugene, 1438
    Sherard, 1581
Osborne, Abraham, 1581
    Balaam, 1581
    Daniel, 1581
    David, 1581
    Ephraim, 1581
    John, 1581, 1582
    Jonathan, 1581, 1582
    Josiah, 1581
    Nicholas, 1581, 1582
    Peter, 1581
    Randall, 1581, 1582
    Richard, 1581, 1582
    Samuel, 1581
    Sarah, 1581
    Stephen, 1581
Osburn, Adelina Beatrice,
1583
    Adeline, 1582
    Ann, 1582
    Atwood, 1582
    Clara Louise Williams,
1583
    Clarissa Elliott, 1583
    Elizabeth, 1582
    Frank C., 1582
    Frank Chew, 1583
    Franklin, 1582, 1583
    Harry G., 1582
    Henry Augustus, 1583
    Henry Griswold, 1583
    James W., 1582
    James Warner, 1583
    Jennie M., 1582
    Jennie Maria, 1583
    John, Jr., 1582
    Laura Schley Chapline,
1583
    Louise W., 1582
    Margaret, 1582
    Mary E., 1582
    Mary Elliott, 1583
    Richard, 1582
    Richard, Sr., 1582
    Robert, 1582
    Robert Dudley, 1583
    Rosalie Warner, 1583
    Samuel, 1582
    Sarah, 1582
    William, 1582
    William W., 1582
    William Warner, 914,
1583

Ott, Clarence, 1614, 1614
  David, 1329
  Eli, 1262
  Elizabeth, 1614
  George, 1614
  Henry, 1614
  Ira, 1614
  John, 1614
  John Jacob, 1614
  John T., 1231
  John Willlam, 1614
  Lena, 1614
  Margaret, 719
  Mary, 1081, 1082, 1517
  Mary Ann, 1614
  Nora, 1380
  Susannah, 1614
  William, 1614
Otte, Augusta, 1138
  Charlotte, 1138
  Lewis, 1138
  Louisa, 1138
  Minnie, 1138
  Robert Adolph, 1138
  Theodore, 1138
  William, 1138
Otto, Catharine, 1517
  Edna E., 1517
  I. Forrest, 1472
  Sallie, 1207
  Thomas G., 1517
  Wilbur H., 734
Ould, William L., 842
Ovelman, Reuben, 855
Overholtzer, Christina, 788
  Maria Louisa, 831
Overhultz, Elizabeth, 749
Owen, Nancy, 824
  Robert, 824, 1404
Owens, James, 1534
  Lottie, 1258, 1497, 1597
Owings, Beall, 940, 1073
  Edward, 1089
  Elisha, 1122
  Hannah, 1548
  Miranda, 1089
  Rachel , 1073
  Rebecca, 1548
  Samuel, 939, 940
  Washington, 1548
Oxley, Emma D., 1181
  Thomas, 1181
Pabst, Caroline, 732
Packard, Benjamin D., 1328
  Charlotte, 1328
  Louisa, 1328

Padgett, George W., 1079
  Maggie E., 1079
Page, Calvin, 870
  Dudley, 1395
  George, 1306
  Ignatius, 1074
  John, 1573
  John W., 885, 949, 1281
  Mary Mann, 1551
  Robert, 1551
Paine, Lizzie, 1534
  William, 1231
Palmer, Amanda, 764
  Anna, 764
  Carlton, 759
  Charles, 1326
  Edgar Birely, 764
  Elmyra, 1508
  Flora M., 862
  Florence, 764
  Franklin, 764, 1132, 1226,
    1283, 1489, 1593
  G. Lloyd, 764, 1242, 1243,
    1265
  George, 764, 1242
  Grayson E., 764
  Hezekiah, 862
  Jacob E., 764
  Jacob Ezra, 1234, 1242
  James Armstead, 1216
  John, 1234
  John C., 764, 1471
  Jonas, 1012
  Joseph M., 720, 1241, 1247
  Josephus, 1011
  Lawson, 749, 952
  Mamie E., 764
  Maria, 1229
  Maria Lee, 1215, 1216
  Maud, 1295
  Michael, 903
  Millard J., 764
  Nancy, 1012
  Peter, 1229
  Potter, 825
  Upton, 1474
  Upton W., 868
  Uriah M., 868
  Virgie A., 764
Pampel, Elizabeth, 982
  F., 982
Pangborn, J. J., 1100
Parcell, Russell, 990
Parish, Nicholas, 1355
Parker, W. H., 1389
Parrish, Emma K., 751

  Nicholas M., 751
Parsons, Amy R., 857
  Mason, 1214
  Simon, 1141
  W. Irving, 1141, 1214
Parvin, Holmes, 1594
Patterson, Harriet, 1195
  Nettie G., 860
  Sarah, 1344
Patton, William, 727
Paxson, J. S., 1100
Paxton, Oden, 1099
Payne, Frances, 1476
  Irvin J., 1168
  Joseph, 1168
Paynter, Edward, 1352
Payton, Henry, 1418
Pearl D., 724
  George W., 953
  John T., 953
Pearman, Lulu, 1264
Pearre, Albert Austin, 764
  Albert L., 763
  Alexander, 895
  Annie M., 763
  Aubra, 895
  Caroline, 895
  Cecelia, 895
  Charles, 895
  Charles B. , 945
  Claudia, 763
  David, 896
  David C., 924
  David Dudderar, 895
  Edward, 1531
  Eliza, 895
  Ernest, 895, 1239
  Geo. A., 945
  George A., 809, 960, 1201
  George A., Jr., 944, 945
  Hixon, 896
  James, 763, 895, 944, 945,
    1222
  James W., 763, 1563
  Josephine, 763
  Joshua, 895, 1450
  Lemuel, 895
  Leona, 895
  Margaret, 895
  Mertin S., 896
  Miranda, 895
  Oliver, 763, 895
  Otho, 895
  Peter, 895
  Rachel B., 1051
  Sally, 763

Sarah, 895
Sarah Elizabeth, 1421, 1450, 1452
Walter, 895
William, 944, 945
William H., 895
Peck, Charles M., 694
Peddicord, Annie M., 1067
Arthur A., 1066, 1067
Caleb, 1066
Catherine A., 1067
Charles W., 1067
Emma Louise, 1067
Harry A., 1067
Henry Adolphus, 1066, 1067
Louis Victor, 1067
Marie E., 1067
Peier, Ann M., 856
Henry, 856
Mary C., 856
Peitzel, Catherine, 729, 1458
Pembroke, Alice, 1067
George W., 1067
Pendleton, Martha, 783
Martha C., 783
Penn, Harry, 768
William, 719, 858, 1552
Pennel, Mary, 942
Pennell, Henry, 1091
Pennington, Edgar, 1558
Rebecca, 1500
Pentzer, Anna Catherine, 1178, 1446
Percy, Hugh, 791, 1253
Perkins, Elsie, 1297
Perkey, David, 1511
Louisa V., 1511
Perry, Ann, 1116, 1137
B. C., 1211
Benjamin Cissel, 758
Elizabeth E., 1227
George W., 1255
Iva M., 1255
J. J., 1539
J. P., 1539
Jacob, 1524, 1539
Jacob S., 1539
Katharine, 1539
Mattie E., 1539
Patrick, 1275
Peter, 1083
Richard Humphrey, 758
W. E., 1539
William K, 1539
Petcher, Malissa, 1336

Peter, George, 991
Peters, Caroline Frances, 763
Charles Otis, 763
Christina, 763
Elizabeth, 1390
Ella, 763
Esther M., 763
George W., 762
Helen, 762
Horace, 763
James Johnson, 763
John, 762, 763
John R., 763
John T., 763
Lavinia, 762
Lillian, 762
Martha Cordelia, 763
Mary E., 762
Mary Virginia, 763
Miranda, 763
Olie May, 763
Olive, 762
Samuel G., 763
Sarah Ellen, 763
Susan, 763
Thomas, 762, 763, 915
Travella E., 762
Walter, 762
William H., 763
William T., 762
Zora Viola, 763
Petrie, Catherine, 1477
Pettingall, Martha, 1424
Pettingill, Benjamin, 1340
Pettit, Elizabeth, 1029
Pfaffenberger, Adam, 759
Christianna, 759
Christopher, 759
Daniel I., 759
Elizabeth, 759
George, 759
George F., 759
George, Jr., 759
Jacob, 759
Pfoutz, Chrissie, 936
Donald, 924
Donald Warfield, 1250
Elmer Pittinger, 1250
Esther, 1210
George, 1210
Hannah, 1058
Hester, 1007
Hetty, 1210
Isaac, 1070, 1135, 1210, 1249, 1250, 1499
Isaac D., 1250

Jesse, 924, 1249, 1250
John, 1007, 1058, 1070, 1210
Lydia, 1249
Margaret, 1601
Mary, 1209, 1210, 1249
Mary Ann, 1209, 1210
Peter, 1210, 1494
Rachel, 1007, 1070, 1249, 1499
Sallie, 1210
Samuel, 1210
Sarah, 1124
Thurston, 924
Thurston Jesse, 1250
Phalen, Daniel, 1274
Ella, 1275
Ella M., 1275
John, 1275
Maggie L., 1275
Maria, 1275
Martin W., 1274, 1275
Mary, 1275
Thomas H., 1275
Phebus, B. E., 1255
Phelps, Philo F., 842
Philips, Emma I., 788
Lycurgus N., 788
Margret, 1013
Phillips, Alexander, 1083
Amelia, 741-743
Annie, 851
Benjamin, 1385
John, 741, 1076
Lycurgus N., 851
Minnie, 1130
Noah, 741
Thomas, 1338
Thomas R., 815
Phipps, Samuel, 1133
Phleeger, Guy O., 1308
Hermie C., 1308
J. E., 821
John, 1307
John E., 1307, 1308
John, Sr., 1308
Nannie M., 1308
Samuel Keefer, 1308
Sara E., 1308
Phlegar, Arabella, 1089
Frederick, 1086
Phoebus, Elsworth, 849
Phreaner, D. H., 1248
Pieffer, P. H., 745
Piele, Friederecke, 855
Pierce, Alfred Newton, 1241

Franklin, 1621
Lucinda, 1306
Mabel Clarke, 1241
Mary Elizabeth, 1241
Pierpont, Sarah, 1183
Pierson, Hannah, 1225
Pigman, Abraham, 1184
Hanson V., 1609
Jacob, 1184
Rebecca, 1184
Susannah, 1184
Pincen, Frank, 1158
Pine, Mary Elizabeth, 1605
Pitt, William, 1211
Pittinger, Andrew Levi, 1507
Charles M., 1507
Clarence, 1531
Elmer W., 924
George, 922
George W., 1507
Hezekiah, 1514
Hezekiah B., 1507
Ida, 1053
Jacob N., 1142
James W., 1507
John, 1620
Lydia Ann, 1214
Malla Dean, 1250
Mallie, 924
Minnie Mabel, 1142
Mrs. Maud C., 924
Newton, 924, 1250
Sabina, 1620
Sabine, 1619
Samuel, 717
Samuel B., 1507
William, 1083, 1546
Pitts, Annie, 1208
Pitzer, Eliza A., 1400
George D., 1172, 1400
Loretta V., 1400
Mayme E., 1172
Michael, 1396, 1400
Plain, Maria, 769
Plary, Elizabeth, 1343
Plecker, Yost, 1211
Plummer, Amelia, 972
Emma E., 972
F. Berry, 830, 1033
Rachel, 1547
Wilmer, 814
Poe, Edgar Allen, 1300
J. P., 818
John P., 1300
Neilson, 818
Poffenberger, Amanda Ellen,

759
Ann Maria, 1496
Annie Cordelia, 759
Annie F., 760
Arthur, 1173
Catharine, 861, 1300, 1541
Catherine, 759, 860
Clara E., 899
David, 1229
Elizabeth, 759, 1496
Elmer, 820
Emma Cora, 760
Enoch, 759
George, 899
George David, 961
George Franklin, 760
George O., 899
George W., 757, 1496
H. Isabella, 1496
Hannah Patricia, 1496
Henry, 867, 1470
Hezekiah, 759
Isaac, 759
Jacob, 759, 1496
Jacob Reno, 760
John, 759
John H., 1496
John Henry, 759
Josiah, 1496
Laura Geneta, 760
Lawson, 1496
Lillie Catherine, 760
Lloyd, 760
Mary, 759, 1496
Mary C., 760
Mary Susan, 759
Maud, 1496
Nellie E., 760
Rachel, 759
Rebecca Alice, 759
Reese St. Clair, 1495, 1496
Reno B., 961
Roger F., 760
Rowanna, 759
Samuel, 1496
Sarah, 1496
Sarah A., 899
Simon, 1496
Sophia, 1496
Susan, 1496
Thomas, 1496
Thomas L., 1496
Viola Catherine, 961
William, 759
William H., 1495, 1496
Poffenburger, ——, 1013

Polsen, Elizabeth, 966
Pomeroy, John, 805
Pontius, John W., 953, 1042
Margaret E., 953
Poole, Benj., 734
Bushrod, 1073
Charles Edgar, 1073, 1074
Claire B, 1073
Cordelia O., 1073
Daniel, 1073
Edward, 1073, 1558
Henry, 1073
Henry Thornton, 1073
Hester, 1151
Joseph James, 1073
Lucy, 782, 783, 1073
Lucy Elizabeth, 1073
Mahalie, 789
Margaret, 1073
Margaret F., 1073
Matilda, 1073, 1112, 1122
Narcissa, 1073
Sarah, 1531
Thomas E., 797
Thornton, 1073
Poor, Theresa, 1567
Porter, B. D., 1389, 1390
Emily J., 1047
Jane, 1046
Nathan, 1604
Philip, 1047
Robert, 1047
Samuel A., 1389
Sophia, 1604
Vernon C., 875
Porterfield, James S., 1076
Posey, Adrian, 1472
Cataldus H., 1472
Ella, 1473
F., 1035
Fabian, 1472
Francis A., 1473
J. Clarence, 1472
Regina, 1473
Washington A., 1472
Post, Merritt, 871
Pottinger, Anne, 1184
Henry, 1184
Potts, Annie R., 1343
Arthur, 1343, 1386, 1487
Cornelia Ringgold, 1343, 1386
Eleanor, 1343, 1386
Eleanor Murdoch, 1343
Elizabeth, 1342
George, 1343

George M., 1342, 1386
George Murdoch, 1343
Harriet Murdoch, 1343
John Lee, 1342
Louisa, 1343
Mary Jane Fitzhugh, 1343
Philip Thomas, 1342
Rebecca, 1342
Richard, 1342, 1343
Rienard, 1386
Samuel, 1342
Sarah Ann, 1342
William, 1342
William, 2nd, 1342
William, 3rd, 1342
Powel, Florence M., 1385
Powell, Albert, 1234
Clara E., 1511
Cramer, 1134
Curtis N., 1237
Elmer M., 1236
Elwood, 1134
Ernest R., 1236, 1237
Estella C., 1236
Florence M., 1234
Lawrence B., 1237
Lewis J., 1236
Lillie B., 1236
Luther C., 1134, 1236
Margaret, 1134
Naomi E., 1237
Samuel L., 1236
William, 1134, 1236
Power, Edward, 783
John, 860
Praeter, Thomas, 1210
Pratt, Thomas G., 1398
Preston, Ann R., 1413
Charles, 1413
Price, Abbie, 906
Charles, 1460, 1461
Edgar, 1115
Eli, 1228, 1461, 1475
Elizabeth, 839
J. E., 1409
Jacob, 1098
John E., 1088 , 1439, 1459
John Emmert, 1098
Sterling, 1208
Thomas W., 865
Prince, Mary, 1610
T. C., 1359
Pritchard, America, 1510
Benjamin, 1510
Protzman, Rosanna, 952
Proudfit, James, 1503

Proyer, Cornelia, 1180
Samuel, 1180
Prunett, Priscilla, 948
Pryor, Alfred, 886, 1127
Annie M., 886
Cornelia, 1179
Cornelia A., 886
David, 886
Eliza, 886, 899
George, 886
Hannah, 886, 984
Ira E., 868
Jane, 886
Joseph, 886
Mary C., 886
Oliver, 868
Peter, 886
Peter C., 868
Samuel, 886
Samuel C., 868
Samuel H., 886
Seraphyne, 886
William S., 887
Wilson L., 886, 887
Purcell, Frank, 1346
Nora E., 1346
Purdum, Albert Marriat, 1326
Arthur Monroe, 1326
Charles E., 1326
Edmund Winfield, 1326
Elizabeth, 1325
Emma C., 1326
Frances Cullum, 1326
Isabelle, 1326
Jacob, 1162
James, 1325
John, 1325
John F., 1326
John Mason, 1325
Joseph A., 1326
Joshua, 1325
Josiah W., 1325, 1326
Josiah Washington, 1326
Keziah, 1325
Luther, 1280
Maggie V., 1326
Margaret, 1325
Margaret C., 1326
Mary Amony, 1326
Nathan, 1325
Priscilla, 1325
Rachel, 878, 1325
Rufus, 879
Sally, 879
Sarah Beall, 1325
Vergie Maybelle, 1326

W. L., 1461
William, 1344
William Joshua, 1325,
1326
William W., 1326
Purnell, William H., 815,
1330
PurselΒalen, 1582
Hannah, 1582
Joab, 1582
Joel, 1582
John, 1582
Mary, 1582
Milly, 1582
Morris, 1582
Precilla, 1582
Richard, 1582
Sarah, 1582
Thomas, 1582
Pusey, Mary, 1447, 1513
Putman, Amanda, 1446
Annie E., 761, 844, 999 ,
1446, 1447
Arthur F., 762
Calvin, 1060
Calvin L., 761, 829, 1000,
1447, 1618
Charles, 1060
Charles C., 1446, 1447
Dessie, 1060
Dessie E., 1000 , 1447
Dessie G., 761
Earl C., 762
Elizabeth, 1060
Elmer, 1060
Elmer E., 761, 999 , 1447
Estella, 1061
Frederick, 724
Glenn L., 762
Greenberry H., 761, 999,
1000, 1060 , 1446,
1447
Hezekiah, 761, 999, 1318,
1364, 1446
J. Frederick, 761, 1000,
1447
Jacob F., 1060
James Oscar, 1060
John, 739, 985, 1060
John Allen, 1061
John J., 999, 1000, 1060,
1134, 1447
John J., Jr., 761, 999,
1446
John J., Sr., 761, 999,
1446

John Jerome, 1060
Julia, 761, 999, 1038, 1060,
    1422, 1446
Julia Catharine, 1171, 1427
Julia M., 761, 999, 1447
Laura, 1060
Laura C., 761, 999, 1447
Lewis, 1060
Lewis W., 761, 999, 1447
Lula, 1506
Luther, 1506
Malinda, 761
Margaret L., 762
Mary C., 1061
Minnie, 761, 999, 1060,
    1447
Minnie M. , 1364
Raymond, 1090
Raymond C., 1060
Robert E. L., 1000
Roy G., 1060
Samuel, 761l, 1446
Putnam, Israel, 1060
    Julia Catharine, 758
    Nathan, 1418
Pyfer, Ann C., 917
    Margaret M., 917
    Philip, 917
    Philip H., 917
    William, 917
Pyle, Pearl, 1200
Quantrell, Mary, 1462
Quinn, John, 1472
Quynn, Allen G., 1047
Radcliff, Ralph, 706
Radcliffe, Mollie, 1130
Rader, Amanda, 933
Raifsnider, William, 1171
Railing, Adam, 1156
    Catharine, 1156
    Christian, 1156
    Elmer C., 1157
    Elsie M., 1157
    George H., 1116, 1156,
        1157
    Henry, 1156
    Lewis D., 1156
    Margaret C., 1157
    Peter Z., 1156
    Wilford F., 1157
    William, 1097
Raith, Barbara Ann, 1212
Raitt, Rachel, 1263
Ramsay, Charlotte, 1161
Ramsberg, Addie, 1416
    Albert J., 1416

Ann Margaret, 1431, 1528
Anna, 1416
Anna A., 1416
Bessie, 1416
Calvin F., 1416
Catharine, 1416
Catherine, 1416
Clinton, 1416
Elizabeth, 1416
Elizabeth R., 1416, 1432
Ella, 1416
George, 1431, 1528
George P., 1415, 1416
Gideon J., 1416
Gidon, 1313
Jacob, 1415, 1416
Lottie, 1416
Lucinda, 1416
Philip A. W., 1416
Sebastian, 1416
Susanna, 1416
Washington Z., 1415, 1416
Ramsberger, Jane, 1091, 1266
Ramsburg, Adaline V., 1038
    Albert, 1022
    Alex., 1054
    Alexander, 758, 1038, 1171,
        1201, 1396
    Alice, 755
    Allen B., 1427
    Alta I., 902
    Alva S., 902, 1317
    Annie, 1396
    Annie E., 758, 1427
    Annie H., 1426
    Annie M., 1054
    Annie M. , 1054
    Bessie E., 1038
    Calvin A., 902, 1317
    Casper, 1396
    Catharine A. C., 1038
    Catharine Pitzer, 1172
    Catharine R., 1105
    Charles Garrett, 1172
    Charles J., 1171, 1396
    Charles S., 755
    Charles T., 1037, 1038
    Clagett E., 1038
    Claggett, 854
    Clara H., 758, 1427
    Clarence L., 755
    Cornelius, 947, 1527
    Daisy C., 1039
    Daniel, 1527
    Danno F., 1039
    David J., 755

Dennis, 882, 956, 987,
    998, 1396, 1410
Drusilla H. Anna, 753
Earl Howard, 758
Edward, 1396, 1561
Elias, 752, 753
Elias B., 753
Elias Zacharias, 752
Eliza, 758, 1038, 1171,
    1396
Elizabeth, 1015, 1037
Elizabeth M., 1038
Elizabeth R., 753, 1207
Ellis Orlando, 1427
Elmer, 1271
Elmer K., 902, 1317
Elmer K., Jr., 1317
Elsie F., 758
Emory, 1366
Erma E, 902
Estella May, 1267
Florence V., 902, 1317
Frederick, 902, 1317
Frederick P., 902
George, 1015, 1044
George L., 1302, 1427
Georgiana L., 1038
Gertrude, 1164
Gideon, 1578
Grace, 758, 1070
Grace S., 1317
Harlan, 1258, 1267
Harriet, 1396
Harriette M., 753
Harry Edgar, 1427
Hellen, 753
Henry, 758, 1037, 1038,
    1171, 1427
Henry B., 753
Henry B., Jr., 753
Henry T., 1038
Howard, 755, 883, 1589
Howard P., 758, 1427
Ida B., 1039
Ida R., 753
Ida Rebecca, 737
Ira C., 902
Irvin J., 1317
J. Richard, 753
J. Stephen, 753
Jacob, 1038, 1171, 1396,
    1427
Jane, 753
Jesse H., 753
John, 752, 755, 1037,
    1574

John J., 758, 1427
John S., 737, 753, 863
John Stephen, 752
John W., 1038
Jonas, 1516
Jonas A., 755
Josiah A., 902, 1317
Lewis, 1396
Lewis P., 758, 761, 999,
   1038, 1171, 1427, 1446
Lillie R., 1038
Lucretia, 1262
Luther, 1397
Luther F., 1039
Lydia A., 1038
Lydia Christine, 720
M. O., 1294, 1511
Mamie, 758
Mamie J., 902
Marian, 753
Marshall, 1585
Marshall Orlando, 758,
   1427
Martha H., 1039
Mary, 1037, 1171, 1396
Mary B., 755
Mary C., 753
Mary Catharine, 752
Mary I., 753
Mary Lottie, 758
Mattie B., 755
Melvin U., 1317
Merhl H., 902
Minnie, 758, 1427
Mirian R., 1317
Morris M., 1317
Mrs. Elizabeth, 1396
Mrs. Margaret, 723
Myrtle, 758
Nellie L., 1038
Nelson A., 758, 1038
Nelson D., 1171, 1396
Nevin O., 1317
Ninian H., 1038
Oscar C., 758
Sally, 1037
Samuel, 1164
Samuel C., 1038
Sarah, 755
Steiner, 1529
Thomas, 829, 1396
Thomas C., 758, 1038,
   1171
Tina F., 758
Urias D., 902, 1317
Vallie E., 829, 1038

Viola, 758
Vernon, 1472
William, 1346
William H., 1121
William P., 1038
William S., 901, 902, 1317
Washington Z., 1426
Zoe Estella, 1427
Ramsburgh, Anna, 752
Catharine, 752
Elizabeth, 752
Jacob, 752
John, 752
Mary, 752
Peter, 752
Stephen, 752
William, 752
Randall, Vachel, 940
Ranels, Lillian, 1351
Rankin, Mary E., 1001
Ranneberger, Robert, 1049,
   1303
Rannesberger, Mary M., 993
Robert, 993
Rapp, John S., 1076
Rass, John B., 842
Raughter, Henry, 787
Raute, Mary, 1258
Rautzahn, Phoebe, 988, 1265,
   1339
Ray, Annie L., 1062
W. S., 1140
William S., 849
Raymer, Jennie, 759
John, 904
Walter, 716
Raymor, Elmer, 757
Mary, 826, 1606
Ream, Rebecca, 946
Rebert, Emanuel, 758, 1422
Guy, 1054
Rechee, Johanna, 984
Recher, Ann Sophia, 768
Delilah, 778
Joanna, 951, 952
Johanna, 748, 749
John, 749, 778, 952
Josiah, 868
Peter, 952
Reck, Charles, 955
Recker, Sophia, 1460
Reddick, Calvin B., 883
Laura Jane, 883
Rena I., 883
Redgrave, Martha, 738
Redmon, Mattie, 1390

Reece, Catherine, 1010, 1021
M. G., 1086
Reed, Lottie, 965
Mary, 799
Reely, James, 1621
Reese, Catharine, 1130,
   1131, 1226, 1593
Catherine, 1489
Catherine E., 1592
Ellen, 966
Jacob, 1246
John, 1131, 1226, 1283,
   1489, 1592, 1593
Luanna A., 881
Rebecca, 724, 1225, 1226
Susan R., 1131
Susanna, 988, 1132, 1226,
   1283, 1489, 1593
T. P., 881
William, 1294
Reeser, Catherine, 1097
Elizabeth, 1097
Peter, 1097
Reich, Annie, 1109
Benjamin F., 1132, 1133
Benjamin F. William,1133
Charles S., 1109
Edna A., 1109
John, 1133
John H., 919
Lillian, 1109
Lucy B., 1133
Mary, 1109
Philip, 1004, 1109
Philip V., 1133
Phoebe, 1109
R. Eugene, 1109
R. H. Lee, 1109, 1225
Raymond C., 1109
Sarah, 1109
Virginia, 1109
William, 1133
William G., 1109
Reichard, C. W., 1347
Reid, Athelaine, 1046
Bertie, 1299
Daniel, 1261
Margaret, 1445, 1562
Reider, Rebecca, 1554
Reifsnider, David, 950
Margaret, 950
Mary E., 829
Reifsnyder, Molly, 1324
Reigle, Harvey S., 1139
Reinecke, Anna Harriette,
   1149

Clara Belle, 1149
Ernest, 1149
J. W. , 1149
John Jacob, 1149
Mary, 1149
Ruth, 1149
Reinewald, Charles, 751, 752
Emma, 751
Henry J., 751
Joseph Lewis, 751
Mary M., 751
Matilda, 751
Reinhart, Andrew, 769
Hattie, 1434
Margaret, 769
Margaret Maria, 1296
Reisler, Edward, 1350
Remberg, Arthur R., 1381
Roscoe C., 1381
Remensberger, George, 1377
Remmell, Anna, 921
Annie, 909
John, 909
Susan, 909, 921
Rempy, Mary, 1532
Remsberg, Aaron, 1379
Addie M., 1433
Albert S.,1379, 1425, 1426
Alda F. C., 1379, 1426
Amos, 1426
Amos E., 1425
Amos L., 1379
Amos W., 1379
Ann R. E., 1379
Ann Rebecca, 1425
Anna, 1425
Anna Margaret, 1378
Anna Maria, 1378
Annie, 1380
Annie M., 1379
Annie V., 1379, 1426
Arthur S., 1426
Barbara, 1378
Carlton R., 1426
Casper, 1425
Catharine, 1378-1380, 1425
Catherine, 1595
Charles, 1379, 1380
Charles H., 1380 , 1426
Charlotte, 1378, 1425
Christian, 1425
Daniel E., 1010, 1380
Elias, 1425
Elizabeth, 1378, 1425
Elmer C., 1379
Elmer W., 1380

Elsie E., 1426
Elsie Florence, 1382
Emma, 1380
Emory C., 1009, 1010, 1380
Emory E., 1010
Estelle M., 1379
Estie, 1380
Foster C., 1380
George, 1377, 1378, 1380, 1425
George C., 1380
George I., 1379, 1425
George Peter, 1378
George, I, 1381
George John, 1425
Harold A., 1426
Henry, 1378, 1425
Henry C., 1009, 1010, 1377, 1380, 1381, 1379, 1425
Howard P., 951
Israel, 1425
J. Homer, 1426
Jacob, 1425
Janie, 1379
Jennie R., 1379
Jessie, 1426
Jesse W., 1379
John, 1378, 1425
John C., 1379
John D., 1379
John George, 1425
John H., 1380, 1425, 1426
John Harman, 1379, 1425
John Jacob, 1425
John, II, 1378
John, III, 1380
Josephus, 1062
Joshua P., 1379, 1425
Laura M., 1426
Lewis H., 1379, 1425
Loren H., 1010
Lottie A., 951
Lucy, 1379
Lucy M., 1010, 1379, 1426
Mahlon R., 1379, 1380, 1425
Margaret, 1425, 1426
Margaret E., 1379
Mary, 1378
Mary C., 1379
Mary E., 1379, 1426
Maurice F., 1380
May C., 1426
Oscar Z., 1010
Samuel, 1380, 1425
Sarah, 1378, 1380
Sebastian, 1378

Simon H, 1379
Stephen, 1378, 1425
Stephen C., 1425
Stephen Carlton, 1379
Susan, 929, 1425
Susan S., 911
Susanna, 1011, 1012, 1378
Vara Montrose, 1379
Walter, 891
Walter L., 1379
Washington, 1433
Winnie, 1380
Remsburg, AdalineVirginia, 1423, 1424
Alice, 1177
Alexander, 1422
Amanda, 1174, 1190
Amanda L., 873
Amos, 894, 1174, 1190
Ann Caroline, 994, 1255, 1275, 1540
Ann Rebecca, 1423
Anna, 1423
Anna V., 1580
Annie, 1086, 1177
Annie E., 1422
Asa, 1129, 1423
Asa M., 1423
Barton, 1423
Beckey, 1177
Benjamin, 1482
Caroline, 1030, 1256
Caspar, 1423
Catharine, 1146, 1358
Charles, 1177
Charlotte, 1174, 1189
Charlotte Frances, 1190
Chistian, 1177, 1423
Clara H., 1422
Clarence Ivan, 1190
Clinton Oscar, 1177
Daniel, 1423
Edward, 1177
Effie, 1177
Elias, 1423
Eliza, 1422
Elizabeth, 1005, 1174, 1189, 1190, 1423, 1481, 1576
Elizabeth C., 1423
Emma, 873, 1174, 1190
Emory, 1123 Emory R., 1423
Emory Richard, 1422, 1423

Estelle, 1177
Frank, 1423
George Edward, 1423
George I., 1612
George W., 838
George William, 1423
Gilmer, 1354
Hanson, 1077, 1423
Harmon, 1094
Harriet E., 838
Harriet S., 1400
Harry, 1177
Henry, 873, 1104, 1422,
    1423
Henry C., 1174, 1356,
    1375, 1422, 1423 , 1430
Hiram, 932, 1004, 1149,
    1174, 1479
Hiram E., 1190, 1189
Howard P., 1422
Ida Emma Jane , 1482
Ida Kate, 1177
Irving, 1354
Isaac, 1423
Israel, 1275, 1423
Jacob, 1177, 1422, 1423
Jennie, 1174, 1177, 1190
John, 1288, 1289, 1423
John Harman, 1580
John J., 1422
John W., 1177, 1422, 1424
John Wesley, 1423
Joseph, 1174, 1177, 1190,
    1423
Josephus, 1177
Josiah, 1423
Katherine, 1423
L. Roy, 1424
Levi, 1177
Lewis, 1423
Lewis Elbert Gilson, 1422
Lewis P., 1422
Lillian, 1177, 1183
Lloyd A., 1423
Lottie, 1423
Luther Singleton, 1190
Luther V., 1424
Lydia A., 1536
Lydia A. R., 923, 1552
M. O., 1422
Mahlon, 1006, 1361
Margaret, 1354, 1423
Maria Catharine, 1174,
    1190
Mary, 1423
Mary A., 1424

Mary Lizzie, 1177
Mary Susan, 1174, 1189
Maud, 1177
Millard, 1177
Minnie, 1422
Morgan H., 1423, 1424
Nelson A., 1422
Paul Edward, 1190
Rebecca, 1316, 1339
Robert, 1610
Roger, 1177
Samuel, 873, 1005, 1174,
    1190, 1255, 1354, 1423,
    1189
Samuel Leroy, 1190
Sarah, 1104, 1125, 1289
Singleton E., 873, 1174,
    1189, 1190, 1265
Solomon, 1423
Stephen, 1423
Susan, 983, 1064, 1423
Thomas, 1354
Thomas C., 1422
Wesley, 1497
William, 977, 1423
William P., 1031
Renn, Alice, 1095
Alva Vernon, 1289
Annie E, 1169
Asa B., 1123
Beulah Charlotte, 1289
Callie, 723
Catherine, 1169
Charles, 1308
Charles C., 1169
Daniel W., 1458
E. C., 1308
Effie, 1516
Elizabeth, 1016
Elizabeth R., 1559
Elmira Virginia, 1289
Emma E., 1169
George, 1169
George C., 1169, 1191
George Calvin, 1169
George E., 1169
Grayson S., 1170
Ida E., 1169
John, 1289
John H., 1169, 1621
John Hanson, 1543
John Harmon, 1289
John L., 1169
Luther, 1488
Margaret G., 1170
Martha Alice, 1169, 1543

Mary E., 1169
Mary L., 1170
May I., 1379
Meridith E., 1170
Ralph H., 1170
Roy J., 1169
Ruth A., 1169
Ruth Lucinda, 1289
Sarah A., 1169
Stella V., 1170
Thelma A., 1170
Wilbur H., 1170
William H., 1169
William Z., 1170
Renner, Abraham, 749
Annie, 749
Beryl K., 750
Daniel, 730
Elias, 799
Eliza, 749
Francis, 749, 1082
Francis C., 750
George I., 749
George Isaac, 750
Grace, 1240
Isaac, 749
James, 965
Jane R., 820
John, 749
Joseph, 749
Kate, 749
Laura N., 750
Milton O., 750
Noah, 749
Sarah, 1210
Sophia, 749
Susan, 749, 1119, 1124
Valentine, 1559
William, 1234
Wilford A., 750
William, 749
William I., 749 , 1600
William T., 788
Repp, Aaron, 924
Abbie, 1258
Annie Mary, 924
Bessie, 1498
Charles, 1135
Charles C., 1220, 1498
Charles David, 1498
Charles Ezra, 1267
Christian, 924
Elizabeth, 1182
Ellen, 1007, 1499
Elva, 1498
Ephraim B., 1219

Guy O., 1267, 1507
Guy Oliver, 1498
Harold F., 1159
J. Hamilton, 1182, 1230
John, 1499
John H., 1219, 1220, 1309
John Oliver, 924, 1181,
   1258
John S., 1057, 1068, 1135,
   1497
Lela, 1220
Leila, 1498
Lenora, 1159
Margaret P., 1501
Mary, 924, 1498
Maud C., 1250
Rachel, 1499
Rachel Jane, 1377
S. O., 1258
Samuel, 886, 1070
Samuel George, 1501
Wesley, 924, 1070, 1501
William O., 1159
Resley, Horace, 991
Resser, Geo. B., 1417
Ressler, Daniel, 1513
Retgering, Matilda J., 807
Reynolds, Alice, 1197
   Ann, 1197
   Catharine, 929, 1232
   Eleanor, 1197
   Elizabeth, 1197
   Frances, 1117, 1118
   Hugh, 1197
   James, 1197
   Jane, 1197
   John, 1197
   John F., 1117
   Lillie, 1197
   Louisa, 1566
   Malinda, 1197
   Margaret, 1197
   Maria, 1197
   Samuel, 1197
   Sarah, 1197
   William, 1197
Rhein, Mary, 1057
Rheolkey, David H., 1169
Rhinehart, Andrew, 1462
Rhoades, Jacob, 708
   Mary A., 708
   Mary Ann, 707
Rhoads, Catherine, 1180
   David, 1180
   Emily, 1180
   Frederick, 1180

John, 1180
Lewis, 1180
Samuel D., 1180
Rhoderick, Benjamin, 1191
   Bernard J., 1192
   Charles C., 1538
   Charles K., 1191-1193
   Elizabeth, 1118, 1129, 1130
   Frank, 740
   Frank N., 1192
   G. Carlton, Sr. , 1191
   George C., 1191-1193
   George C., 3rd, 1193
   George C., Jr., 1191
   George Carlton, 1193
   George Carlton, Sr., 1191,
      1192
   Helen Margaret, 1193
   Henry F., 1191
   J. Morris, 1431, 1528
   James, 1605
   John L., 1130
   Joseph T., 1167, 1294
   Joshua, 1324
   Lee Ella, 1294
   M. Dorsey, 1191
   Mahlon, 1191
   Margaret E., 1192
   Morris H., 1191
   Paul R., 1538
   Ralph Mahlon, 1193
   Rebecca, 1191
   William, 775, 1406
   William C., 1533
Rhodes, Anna Mary, 1318
   Annie M., 1014
   Columbia A., 793, 1253
   Elmira, 1046
   J. Lewis, 860
   James, 943
Rice, Aaron F., 957
   Anna, 915
   Anna R., 956, 988
   Arthur B., 957
   Catharine, 800
   Charles, 843, 1023, 1418,
      1479, 1598
   Chase W., 1220
   Clay E., 1011
   Cyrus L., 1011
   Daniel J., 956, 987
   David, 814, 1156
   Edward, 1487
   Edward A., 988
   Eli D., 956, 988
   Ella May, 957

Elmer F., 1011
Emma, 1487
Emma F., 1011
Ernory E., 957
Evva M., 1011
Frances R., 813
Frederick C., 956, 988
George, 1479
Goldie G., 957
Henry, 987, 1011
Henry, 2nd, 1011
Ida M., 1011
Ilga M., 1011
Jacob D., 956, 987, 988,
   1132, 1226, 1283,
   1489, 1593
Jeremiah D., 1011
John W., 956, 987, 988
Joseph A., 956, 988
Joseph O., 957
Joshua A. L., 956, 957,
   988
Katharine, 988
Levin, 1333
Manzella, V., 1011
Margaret Ann, 1334
Margaretta, 1584
Martha M., 1479
Mary C., 1144
Mary Catharine, 1144
Mary Jane, 956, 987
Matilda, 956, 988
Milton R., 1325
Mrs. Maggie Lee
   (Massey), 1334
Nettie, 1219
P. Luther, 988
Perry, 915, 1324
Perry G., 1443
Reno C., 1011
Roy J., 957
S., 1594
Samuel, 956, 987, 988
Samuel B., 988
Susan E., 1011
William H., 956, 988
Richards, Albert Glenn, 962
   Ann, 836
   Daniel, 782
   Edward L., 962
   Ellis, 962
   Frank, 962
   Helen, 962
   Isaac, 961
   Rachel, 782, 783
   Raymond, 962

Richard, 1141
Ruth, 962
Walter, 962
William L., 962
Wlliam L., 961
Richardson, Mrs. J. Lynn, 809
Robert Ridgely, 1072
Richmond, Lavenia, 1574
Rickard, B. F., 814
Ricksicker, Elizabeth, 1058
Riddlemoser, Charlotte M.,
1250
Emma E., 1250
Ephraim, 1250
Estella M., 1250
Francis, 1250
Francis Marion, 1250
Grover L., 1251
Howard E., 1250
Jacob, 1250, 1531
Joseph L., 1251, 1341
Lewis W., 1250
Louise, 1297
Lula E., 1251
Margaret S., 1531, 1532
Marion F., 1250, 1334
Millard T., 1251
Ruth C., 1251
William E., 1250
Ridenour, Barbara, 1157
Benj. S., 1390
Daniel, 1157
Elmer, 1196
Frederick, 874, 1157
Henry, 1157
J. R., 843, 1220
Jacob, 1077, 1157, 1448
John, 1157
Mary, 1157
Nettie, 1448
Rebecca, 1157
Sarah, 1157
Solomon, 828, 1618
Susan, 1157
Washington, 707, 869
Ridge, George, 730, 1458
Ridgeley, Ann, 1420
Deborah Dorsey, 1344
Ridgely, Ann, 1449
Catharine D., 1073
Charles, 1072, 1344, 1449
Charles C., 783, 1072
Charles Carnan, 1072, 1073
Elizabeth, 1072
Elizabeth Dorsey, 1072
Frank, 1072

George K., 1072
George W., 1072
George Washington, 1072
Henrietta, 1072
Henry, 948, 1072
Henry K., 1072
Irwin Oliver, 1073
Jernima Ruth, 1073
John, 1072
John R., 1072
Julia, 1072
Lucretia, 1072
Martha, 880, 1072
Oliver Dorsey, 1072
Robert, 1072
Ruth, 1072, 1183
Samuel, 1072
Susan, 1072
Thomas, 880
Thomas P., 1072
William, 1072
William A., 1072
Ridgley, Hiram, 890
Ruth, 1169
Rife, Fanny, 1214
Hannah, 1013
Henry, 1013
Rigdon, James, 1575
Riggs, Amon, 845
Betty, 898
Christopher M., 845
Christopher Mussetter, 845
Edward, 1218, 1292
Edward B., 1092
Elma May, 1219
Evelyn Rebecca, 846
Florence, 1292
George Henry, 845, 846
Henry, 845, 975
John, 845
Laura Maud, 1092
Lizzie, 1468
Mary, 1155
Plummer, 1292
Ralph, 845
Winfield, 1219
Winfield Ralph, 1219
Riley, Agnes, 1301
Annie, 1275
Bettie, 1275
Charles, 1275
James, 1275
Louise Hoffman, 1275
Rine, Elizabeth, 878
John, 762
Lucy A., 762

Mary, 762
Rinehart, Andrew, 1163
Becky, 1194, 1219
Charles Peter, 1163
Daniel, 902
David, 1163, 1556
David Jacob, 1163
Florence Jennie , 903
Frederick, 1163
George, 1163
George P., 1091
George Philip, 1163
Grace L., 903
Harriet Amanda, 1163
Hattie, 1200, 1234, 1537
Israel, 902
Joseph P., 903
Lucy N., 903
Mary, 903
Mrs. Rebecca, 922, 1091
Olivia, 903
Philip, 1163
Susan, 1163
Thomas M., 903
William, 1091, 1163
William G., 860
William H., 1091
William Henry, 1163
Riner, Mary, 1142
Ring, May, 1392
Ringgold, Cornelia, 1342,
1343, 1386
Samuel, 1343, 1386
Rinker, Frederick, 1099,
1107, 1114
Ripon, Silas, 1007
Rishel, Elizabeth B., 909
Ritchie, Abner, 1329
Albert, 1328-1330
Annalanah, 1329
Anne Meredith, 1330
Betty Maulsby, 1330
Edith, 1330
Eleanor, 709
Emily Nelson, 1330
George H., 1099
Georgia Johnson, 1330
Henrietta Hanson, 1330
Jane Hall Maulsby, 1330
John, 694,
709,1328-1330, 1428,
1608
Katharine Lackland, 1330
Lynn Ursula, 1330
Margaret Davis, 1330
Mary, 1329

Mary E., 1098, 1099
Mary Harrison, 1330
Mary Louisa, 1328
Mary Zachariah, 1329
Matthew, 1329
Roger Nelson, 1330
Susanna, 1329
Thomas, 1329
William, 1328, 1329
William Neilson, 1329
Willie Maulsby, 1330
Ritter, Alfred, 1405
Irene, 1405
John B., 814
Roadeniser, Catheran, 1435
Jonathan, 1435
Robbins, Frank A., Jr., 1417
Roberts, Clinton, 1349
Edith M., 753
Henry, 965, 1382, 1572
John, 1451
Michael, 1489
Rebecca Naylor, 753
Sanford, 1014
Victoria E., 1489
William E., 753
Robertson, B. P., 1390
Susan, 1504
Robinson, Austin F., 1240
Fanny, 796
Henry, 1399
James W., 1271
Jane, 1398, 1399
John K., 843
Roby, Barbara E., 1390
James P., Jr., 1390
Rockwell, Elihu H., 941
Rhodie, 1341
Roddy, Abraham, 1013
Anne, 1013
Annie I., 968
Catherine, 1013
Daniel, 1013
Daniel Francis, 1013
Frank, 1013
Frank A., 801
Hugh, 1013
John, 1013
Joseph, 1013
Margaret, 1013
Martha, 1013
Mary, 1013
Peter, 781, 1336
Simon, 1013
William, 1013
Roderick, Ada, 1578

Andrew McClellen, 1578
Annie, 1578
Bessie Gertrude, 1578
Charles, 1578
D. W., 1590
Edith W., 1578
Elizabeth, 1577
Elmer Ellsworth, 1578
Fanny, 1578
Florence O., 1127
George, 1577
George S., 1128
Gertrude, 1578
Harry McComas, 1578
Jane, 1170, 1578
Jennie, 959
John, 1577, 1578, 1610
Joseph, 1127, 1577
Mary C., 1578
Mollie, 1578
Nellie Mercer, 1578
Polly, 986
Raymond, 1578
Ruth Gray, 1578
Sarah, 1477
Susan, 1577
Susie, 1578
William, 1577, 1578
William McClellan, 1577, 1578
Rodes, Kate, 1351
Rodock, George S., 1383
Roelke, Annie, 1095
Augustus, 1095
Charles Robert, 1096
Chrissie, 1095
David, 1095
Eliza, 1095
Emma, 1095
Harmon, 1095
John, 1095
John Peter, 1096
John R., 1095, 1096
Laura, 1095
Lawrence, 1095
Lloyd, 1095
Minnie, 1095
Olive May, 1096
Peter, 1095
Sophia, 1095
William, 1095
Roelkey, Alice, 1543
Anna Kate, 958
Annie, 1543
Augustus, 1542
Blanch, 1543

Chrissie, 1543
David, 1543, 1576
David H., 1543
David Henry, 1542, 1543
E. L., 882
Eliza, 1543
Emma, 958, 1543
Harmon, 1542
John, 1542, 1543
John R., 1543
John Thomas, 958
Julia, 958
Julia S., 882
Laura, 1543
Lawrence, 958, 1543
Lew Milton, 882
Lillian, 1543
Loyd, 1543
Margaret M., 882
Maud, 1543
Minnie, 1543
Nina, 1543
Peter, 1542, 1543
Ruth, 1543
Sophia, 1543
Sue, 958
William, 1542
Roemig, Barbara, 909
Rogan, Catherine Susan, 1528
Daniel, 1431, 1528
Henry, 1528
Rebecca, 1431, 1528
Thomas, 1528
Roger, Thomas, 1442
Rogers, Bessie, 1040
Mrs. Henry W., 809
Rachel, 1040
William F., 1040
William Herbert, 1040
Rohrback, Allen, 736
Charles, 736, 1035, 1473, 1473
Lauretta Jarboe, 1473
M. N., 1570
Ellen B., 1035
Francis E., 1035
Jacob, 736, 753
Lauretta J., 1035
Lauretta Jarboe, 1473
M. N., 1570
Margaret J., 1035
Martin N., 736
Martin N. , 917
Thomas J., 1035
Rohrer, Mariah, 1479
Sarah, 1124

Rolkey, Alice, 1047
    D. H., 875
Rollington, Mary, 848
    William, 848
Roltenheffer, Annie M., 986
    Christina, 986
    Lawrence, 986
Roman, J. Dixon, 1211
Rooch, Mary, 1274, 1275
Roop, Abraham, 1571
    Annie A., 1040, 1041
    Catharine, 1263
    Clara, 1571
    Daniel, 1263, 1571
    David, 924, 1262, 1520
    David R., 1571
    Elizabeth, 1263, 1571
    George, 1263
    Henry, 1263
    Jacob, 1263, 1571
    James, 1263
    Jesse, 1041, 1263, 1571
    Joel, 1263, 1571
    John, 742, 1209, 1263
    Joseph, 1262, 1263, 1571
    Kitty, 1571
    Lewis, 1263
    Mary, 1263
    Mary C., 1262, 1263
    Mary E., 1209
    Nancy, 742
    Samuel, 1263, 1494, 1571
    Sarah, 1263
    Susan, 1571
    Susan R., 1494
    Urith, 1041
Roosevelt, Theodore, 906, 1445
Root, Amanda, 1394
    Ann, 1068, 1596, 1597
    Charles, 1614
    Daniel, 831, 1263
    Edward, 1614
    Elihu, 1596
    Fannie, 1394
    Harry, 1614
    Helen, 1394
    Henrietta, 1394
    Jacob, 1394, 1613
    James, 1394
    John, 1394, 1457, 1614
    Mary Elizabeth, 1394
    Richard, 1068, 1394
    Sarah, 1124, 1394
    Susan Alice, 1394
    Tillie, 1263
Roots, George, 1179

Ropp, Emma F., 985
    Louisa C., 1028
    Ludwig, 732, 985
    Magdalena, 985
    Magdalene E., 732
Ropley, Florence, 1547
Rose, Elizabeth, 1594
    Frederick C., 1335
    Samuel, 1471
Rosenberg, Mollie Macgill, 919
Rosenour, Abraham, 1392
    Amelia, 1392
    B., 1149
    Belle, 1392
    Benjamin, 1392, 1393
    Bernard, Sr., 1392
    Celia, 1392
    Gerald, 1392
    Gerson, 1392
    Jennie, 1392
Rosenstock, Aaron, 1391
    Adilade Susan, 1392
    Benjamin F., 1392
    Jacob, 1391
    Joseph, 1391
    Lewis, 1392
    Solomon, 1392
    Sophia, 1391
Roser, Adam, 1110, 1513
    Guy C., 1437
    Robert D., 874
Ross, C. W., 1572
    Caroline, 1386
    Charles W., 776, 809, 1133,
        1216, 1544
    Charles Worthington, 1385,
        1386
    Charles Worthington, 3rd.,
        1386
    Charles Worthington, Jr.,
        1386
    Charles Worthington, Sr.,
        1343
    Cornelia Ringgold, 1386,
        1387
    Eliza, 1385
    Elizabeth M., 907
    George Johnson, 1386
    George M., 1386
    Jane, 805
    John, 1385
    Mrs. Charles W., 1255
    Richard P., 1386
    Richard P., Jr., 1387
    William, 1385
    William Davis, 1385

William J., 1386
    William J., 1133
    William Johnson, 1385
    Wm. J., 847
Rossman, F. C., 703
Rothenheifer, Lawrence, 1602
Rouche, Kate, 1577
Rout, I. L., 1339
    Isaac L., 1200
Routson, Caroline, 995
    Charles W., 1041
    Frank I., 1041
    George H., 1106
    George H., 1040
    George. H., 1041
    Gover M., 1041
    Harvey T., 1041
    Henry, 1040, 1106
    J. Kenly, 1041
    Jesse H., 1040, 1041
    John, 1040, 1106
    Melvin W., 1041
    T. Clyde, 1106
    T. Clyde, Jr., 1107
    Thomas H., 1040, 1106
Routzahn, Adam, 756, 1193,
        1428
    Addie S., 756
    Alvy, 1266, 1301, 1507
    Amanda, 1316, 1482
    Amanda E., 756
    Ann Magdalena, 1288,
        1289, 1536
    Anne E., 1217
    Annie, 757
    Annie B., 756
    Annie E., 757, 954
    Benjamin, 1288
    C. B., 926
    Caroline, 756, 757, 896,
        897
    Catharine, 1390, 1391
    Catherine, 757, 877, 959,
        1175
    Charles, 1266, 1301,
        1361, 1507
    Charlotte, 757, 1317
    Charlotte C., 757
    Charlotte E., 1110, 1289
    Clara E., 1379, 1426
    Clara F., 1146
    Daniel, 951, 1050
    Delana, 829, 1480
    Edna M., 756
    Edward, 812
    Eli, 1059, 1316, 1482,

1612
Elias, 756, 875, 876, 1175, 1390
Elias E., 756
Elias S., 756
Elizabeth, 757, 760, 790, 967, 1288, 1372
Elizabeth A. B., 756
Elizabeth E., 757
Elizabeth R., 756
Elmer, 1177
Elmira, 756
Elsie M., 1482
Emma Blanche, 1482
Estella Pearl, 1482
Eva, 1391
Ezra, 876, 1288, 1289
Fannie Virginia, 1288
Frances Lucinda, 1482
Franklin, 756
Frederick, 756
George, 851
George H., 967
H. H., 1481, 1575
Harry, 1507
Harmon, 1356, 1375
Harmon L., 1289
Harry, 1266, 1301
Herman, 1095
Herman L., 1428, 1430, 1482
Hezekiah, 757, 954, 1312, 1372
Isaiah, 757
Jacob, 757, 897
Jacob L., 757, 867, 1470
Jennetta E., 968
Jennette E., 967
Jennie, 1391
Johannes Ludwig, 1428
John, 1059, 1288, 1366, 1428
John H., 1482
John Henry, 1426
John Lewis, 1428
John Renolds, 1482
Jonathan, 1077, 1146
Joseph, 821, 926, 1110, 1288
Josephine A., 1622
Joshua, 1030
Laura C., 1055
Lavina, 1618
Lawson, 757
Lewis, 1288, 1391, 1474

Lucinda, 1485
Ludwick, 756, 757
Ludwick, Jr., 757
Ludwick, Sr., 756
Ludwig, 760
Luther, 756, 1611
Ludwig 2nd, 1428
Lydia, 1473
Lydia M., 1482
M. Calvin, 1482
Magdalena, 1611
Magdalene, 1009
Margaret, 757
Maria, 1019
Martha E., 1372
Martha G., 757
Martha M., 757
Mary, 1009, 1077, 1078, 1356
Mary A., 1429
Mary C., 757
Mary E., 876, 1428
Mary Olive, 1482
May, 1266, 1301, 1507
Mellia F., 757
Melvin A. E., 951
Minnie B., 756
Mollie M., 757
Moor, 739
Naomi E., 756
Noah, 1055, 1579
Peter Benjamin, 1428
Phoebe, 1149, 1266, 1301, 1474, 1507
Roscoe, 812
Roy Glenn, 1482
Ruth J., 758
Samuel L., 757
Sarah J., 1482
Simon D., 1482
Solomon, 737
Sophia, 1059
Sophia C., 1312
Susan, 850, 851
Theodore S., 1482
Wilber M., 1482
William, 1077
William F., 757
Wolfgang, 1428
Routzen, John, 1382
Routzhan, Isaiah, 923
Sarah, 1086
Rouzer, Arthur Lee, 751
Barbara Ann, 754
Catharine Jane, 754
Charles W., 751

Daniel, 743, 750, 751, 754
Daniel Riley, 754
Eliza Adeline, 754
Ernest Russell, 751
Frank Key, 751
Gertrude, 743
Horace C., 755
Howard C., 751
James Madison, 754
John, 750, 751, 754, 1545
John M., 751
John R., 754
Margaret C., 755
Martin Luther, 751
Martin R., 1394
Mary Catharine, 755
Mary Elizabeth, 754
Morris L., 751
Mrs. Emma K., 750, 754
Oliver F., 1139
Peter, 754
Sarah, 751, 754
Simon Henry, 754
Sophia, 727
Sophia Margaret, 754
Uriah A., 754
William H., 751
Rowe, A., 1508
Catherine, 769
Charles, 773
Daniel, 828, 1347, 1348, 1618
E. May, 1348
George W., 1502
Mary E. , 828, 1618
Nathaniel, 805
O. V., 743
Sarah, 734
Rowland, Bertha, 1276
Joseph, 1276
Rowlings, Sarah, 1044, 1045, 1303
Royer, Fanny, 1324
John T., 932
Ruch, Myrtle, 1138
Rudisel, Alice, 1416, 1417
Ludwig, 1417
Rudy, Amanda, 1103
Amos, 1147
Amos W., 1131
Anna K., 1316
Annie M., 1316
Bertha May, 1131
Blanche C., 1316
C. W., 1147
Charles, 1361

Charles M., 1103
Clarence, 977, 1538
D. W., 871
Edgar C., 1316
Erma, 1147
Ernest, 1147
Frances, 1316
Frank H., 1316
George E., 1316
Hanson T., 1316
Jacob, 1059
John, 731, 895, 1538
John H., 1045
John T., 1005
Joshua, 1129
Laurence, 1190
Lettie, 1147
Louisa, 1147
Mary L., 1103
Paul, 1147
Rebecca, 1316
Susan, 1316
T. C., 838, 889, 890, 1316
W. L., 1289
Walter R., 1316
William L. , 1316
Rundle, George H., 1041
Runkle, Albert, 1164
Runkles, Alice, 1310
    Annie, 1310
    Basil, 1290, 1309, 1310,
        1343
    Basil Thomas, 1310
    Brice, 1343
    Clara, 1310
    Clara E., 1290
    Daniel, 1343
    Dorsey, 1344
    Edith, 1344
    Edith E., 1326
    Edward H., 1344
    Elizabeth, 1343
    George, 1310
    Harry C., 1204
    Herbert, 1310
    Herbert Augustus, 1204
    John, 1343
    John B., 1343
    Joseph, 1309, 1343
    Joseph Henry, 1204, 1309,
        1310
    Katy, 1310
    Marion V., 1344
    Mary, 1290, 1310
    Minnie L., 1344
    Mollie, 1310

Nancy, 1343
Nettie, 1310
Orry F., 1344
Oscar H., 1310
Raymond, 1344
Ruth Ann, 1310
Samuel, 1162, 1310, 1343
Samuel T., 1343
Sarah E., 1343
Susan, 1344
Theodosia, 1344
Upton, 1343
Walter, 1034
Walter G., 1310
Wilford, 1310
William, 1343
William H., 1326, 1343,
    1344
Willis Burnside, 1310
Rupley, Theodore, 1346
Rupp, David, 1007, 1071, 1091,
    1140, 1218, 1301
    William, 1573
Ruse, John, 1460
    Mary J., 1460
Russell, Henry R., 1122
    James, 1122
    Robert M., 1552
    Susan, 1089
Rust, James, 1099, 1107, 1113
Rutherford, Benjamin, 1088
Sadler, N. Agnes, 871
Sager, Annie Catharine, 946
    Charles, 945
    Elizabeth, 945
    Elmer Myers, 946
    Harvey, 945
    John, 945
    Mathias, 945
    Tacie Idella, 945
Salter, Annie, 1575
    Catherine, 1575
    Charles, 1575
    Elizabeth, 1575
    Emma K., 1575
    Frank C., 1575
    George E., 1575
    George W., 1575
    Mamie R., 1575
    William E., 1575
Saltzgiver, George E., 725
Sam, Abraham, 1367
Sams, M. Betty, 1274
Sanders, E. L., 1080
Sanderson, Eleanor, 1225
    Francis, 1225

John P., 1225
Julia P., 1225
Lucy Jane, 1225
Margaret, 1225
Mary Pierson, 1225
Thomas, 1225
William R., 1225
Sanks, Abner, 975
Sanner, Alma P., 790, 1095
    Alta, 955
    Amanda, 955, 1487
    Charles, 958, 1524
    Charles C., 746
    Charles V., 747
    Charles V. C., 955
    Daniel, 790, 955
    Daniel Grayson, 1095
    Daniel W., 1095
    E. Chauncey, 955
    Ella, 955
    Emma, 955
    Florence, 955
    Georgia, 955
    Grayson T., 955
    Jennie G., 1095
    John, 955
    John Edward, 1095
    Keefer E., 955
    Malanchton, 955
    Mary, 955
    Milton, 955
    Nettie, 955
    Newton, 955
    Roger, 955
    Sarah E., 1102, 1103
    Susan, 955
    Tabitha, 955
    Vernon L., 955
    Vincent, 955, 1095
Sanogle, William J., 771
Sappington, Adelaide, 1450
    Amy V., 885
    Ann Ridgely, 693, 1449
    Augustus, 1421, 1449,
        1450, 1452
    Charles, 1450, 1452
    Charles B., 1421
    Claire E., 1451, 1453
    Clara E., 1421
    Clare, 1450
    Clifford, 1422
    Clifford T., 1420, 1421
    Cordelia Downey, 1451
    E. Clare, 1422
    Eden, 1576
    Edna Rosella, 1450

Emma, 1450
Ernest F., 885
Eva Elder, 1450, 1453
Frances, 1450, 1452
Francis, 1420, 1449
Francis Brown, 693, 885,
    1420, 1449
Francis Leo, 1450
George C., 1449
George K., 885, 886, 1136,
    1231
Greenberry, 1243, 1338,
    1449, 1450, 1452
Greenberry R., 1420, 1421
Greenberry Ridgely, 1421,
    1449, 1450, 1452
Harriet, 1449
Helen, 1450, 1576
Helen M., 885
Irene, 1450
Irene Loretta, 1450, 1453
James, 1240, 1450
James C., 1421, 1422
James C., Jr., 1422
James Coale, 1450, 1451,
    1453
James Coale, Jr., 1451,
    1453
James M., 1421, 1450,
    1452
John, 885
Josephine Kavanaugh, 1450
Katie, 1450
Katy, 1450
Kitty Ann, 1449
Lillian R., 885
Lizzie, 1450, 1452
Louisa M., 885
Lydia Ridgely, 1449
Madge, 1576
Mary, 1576
Mary Angela, 1450, 1453
Mary Margaret, 1450
Matilda, 1449
Nannie E., 885
(Nellie) Jinder, 1576
Paul Richard, 1450
R. Frank, 1450
Richard, 1450, 1452, 1576
Richard C., 1421
Richard D., 1449
Richelieu, 1449
Roger, 1449
Ross F., 885
Sally, 1449
Sally Elizabeth, 1450, 1453

Sidney, 1058, 1421,
    1449-1452
Sidney Reaney, 1450
Sidney S., 1450
Sidney St. John, 1451, 1452
Sidney St. John, Jr., 1451
Thomas, 797, 885, 1420,
    1421, 1449, 1450, 1452
Thomas Augustus, 1451
Thomas P., 1420-1422, 1451,
    1453
Thomas Pearre, 1421
Sarah Grace, 1276
Wentworth, 1449
William, 1421, 1449, 1452
William A., 1450
William C., 1450, 1515
William Coale, 1449
William Cole, 1450
William Gilmore, 1450
Sauble, Addison, 1057
Anne, 1057
Belle, 1057
Catherine, 1057
Daniel, 1057
George, 1057
Grace, 1057
Hannah Mary, 1058
Harrison, 1057
Henry, 1057
Jacob, 1057
John, 1057
John Henry, 1057
Lydia, 1057
Maggie, 1057
Margaret, 1057
Mollie, 1057
Peter G., 1057
Peter G. , 1058
Wesley Emanuel, 1057
William, 1057
Sauer, C. F., 1334
Saum, Elizabeth, 1139
Sawyers, Mary Drake, 1321
Saxten, Alvie V., 1622
B. W., 1519
Benjamin William, 1622
Dessie, 1230
Dessie J. W., 1622
John A., 1230, 1622
Lulu R., 1622
Mary E., 1622
William, 1622
Saxton, John A., 1615
Lulu, 1615
Sayler, Abram, 1070

Ann, 1070
Betsy, 1070
Clara Rebecca, 1070
Daniel, 1070
Daniel Oliver, 1069, 1070
Emma Jane, 1070
Frank Roy, 1070
Granville Calvin, 1070
Harriet Rosie May, 1070
Hester Ann, 1070
John, 1070
Leana Capitola, 1070
Mary, 1070, 1071
Sarah, 1070
Solomon, 1069, 1070
Saylor, Abraham, 1182
Abram, 1219
Amy Virginia, 1182
Anna Virginia, 1119
Annie, 1053
Annie Elsworth, 933
Annie V., 1124
Becky, 1194
Benjamin Franklin, 1140
Betsy, 1194
C. C., 1140
C. E., 733, 1472
C. Preston, 1194
Catharine, 1210
Catherine Elizabeth, 1140
Catherine Margaret, 1194
Charles Clay, 1140
Charles E., 936
Clarence O., 1194
Claude William, 1497
D. Oliver, 1499
Daniel, 1124, 1271
Daniel I., 1194
Daniel Johnston, 1140
Daniel P., 1058, 1068,
    1124
Daniel R., 922, 933, 1124,
    1182
David Hanson, 1124
E. C., 1352
E. W., 1049
Edward, 923
Emery W., 1497
Evelyn Louise, 1140
Ezra , 1141
Ezra J., 1139
Ezra James, 1140
Ezra Willard, 1140
Frank J., 1194
George, 1140
Gertie Irene, 1050

Gladys Marie, 1497
Hannah O., 1497
Harry E., 703
Helen Marie, 1050
Henry, 1140, 1151, 1194
Henry L., 1140
Isaac W., 1124, 1194
Jacob, 1119, 1124, 1135,
    1193, 1194
John, 1049, 1159, 1194,
    1271, 1497
John Hamilton, 1049
Katie, 1194
Lizzie May, 1194
Marie E., 1194
Martha Ellen, 1124
Mary, 1194, 1521
Mary Ellen, 1140
Mary Margaret, 1124, 1125
Millard Edward, 1497
Myra, E., 1194
Paul Emery, 1497
Reuben, 1194, 1501
Reuben, Jr., 1194, 1195
Reuben, Sr., 1194
Roland Oscar, 1050
Rosella May, 1050
Ruby Virginia, 1194
Samuel Jacob, 1194
Sarah, 922, 1007
Sarah Ann, 1140
Sarah Susan, 1124
Solomon, 1049, 1497
Solomon Jonas, 1124
Thomas R., 1139, 1140
Walter, 1194
Willard Cromwell, 1140
William B., 1194
William Henry Harrison,
    1124
Schade, Joahanna Christina,
    1278
Schaaff, Arthur, 1553
Schaeffer, Ada E., 1106
    Adam, 1016
    Anna, 1254
    Barbara, 1003, 1004
    Catharine, 1456
    Charles Edward, 1254
    Charles M., 1254
    Daniel, 1254
    David, 1254
    David F., 1017
    David L., 1415
    Elizabeth, 1254, 1415
    Emma A., 1254

Hattie Anne Estella , 1132
Howard R., 1106
Jacob, 1254, 1359
Jasper E., 1106
John, 1254
John H., 1105
Jonathan, 1254
Laura V., 1016
Mamie E., 1415
Marshall A. , 1132
Mary A., 1358, 1359
Mary M., 1106
Nathan C., 1042
Newton R., 1105, 1106
Peter, 1254
Rebecca, 1254
Roger S., 1106
Simon, 1254
Sophia, 1254
Susan, 1254, 1304, 1359
Wesley F., 1106
William C., 1042, 1106
Schaff, Ray, 1411
Schaffer, ———, 747
    Anna, 747
    Annie, 747, 989, 1049
    B., 909
    Charles Edward, 747
    Charles P., 747
    Daniel, 747
    David, 747
    Elizabeth, 747
    Frederick C., 747
    Jacob, 747
    James Clark, 748
    John, 747
    Jonathan A., 747, 748
    Margaret, 1034
    Martha O. M., 748
    Nicholas G., 747, 748
    Peter, 747, 1049
    Rebecca, 747
    Roy C. W., 748
    Simon, 747
    Sophia, 747
    Susan, 747
Scheinflew, Charity, 1231
Schell, Alice, 1548
    Charles, 1548
    Charles David, 1548
    Ezra, 1548
    George, 1548
    Harriet Rebecca, 1548
    John E., 1548
    John Edward, Jr., 1548
    Lewis, 1548

Mary M., 1548
Nicholas, 1548
Samuel Duvall, 1548
Schellman, Ann Maria, 1314
    Catherine, 1314
    Elizabeth, 1314
    George K., 1314
    Jacob, 1314
    John, 1314
    Lewis, 1314
Schildknecht, Abraham, 1020
    Alice R., 779
    C. E., 829
    Charles E., 1019
    Charles L., 1019
    Emma, 1020
    Emma Catharine, 1019
    Harlen, 1019
    Harlen R., 1019
    Helen Frances, 1019
    Hellen, 791
    Henry, 791
    Henry Abraham, 1019
    Jacob, 1019
    Jacob Luther, 1019
    John, 1019
    Josiah, 1019
    Lena, 1019
    Lena C., 1391
    Lenah C., 1391
    Louisa, 1019
    Louise M., 1019
    Sarah Ann, 955
Schildnecht, Joshua M., 781
Schindler, Ann C., 1028
    Mary C., 1028
Schingler, Peter A., 756
Schley, John Thomas, 710
    Alice, 745, 1354
    Anne Perry, 745
    Annie, 745, 1354
    Annie E., 1393
    B. H., 745, 1354
    E. Louise, 1354
    Edward, 745, 914, 1354
    Ellen E., 745, 1354
    Eve Margaret, 1354
    Fairfax, 734
    Fannie, 745, 1354
    Franklin, 745, 1354
    Fred A., 1314
    Frederick, 784
    Gilmer, 745, 1354
    H. Florence, 1354
    John, 745, 1241, 1314,
        1354

John T., 1158
John Thomas, 700, 745,
    914, 1354, 1560
Laura, 745, 913, 914, 1354
Margaret, 745, 1241
Mary, 1354
Mrs. Ann, 1454
Nathaniel Wilson, 1354
Rose, 745, 1354
Steiner, 923
Stiner, 728
Thomas, 1037, 1281, 1314,
    1354, 1454
William, 711, 787
Winfield S., 745, 1354
Winfield Scott, 700, 701,
    943, 1022, 1365, 1393,
    1589, 1597
Schlosser, Ann E., 838
    Annie, 913
    Elizabeth, 913
    George, 1121
    Mary, 1573
    Mary Ann, 1164
    Peter, 913, 1573
Schlousser, Annie, 877
Schmaul, Catherine, 1459
Schmid, John, 703, 704, 832
Schnauffer, Carl H., 840
    Carl Heinrich, 840
    Elise W., 841
    Emma, 841
    Johan Heinrich, 840
    Levin West, 841
    Lillie, 841
    Patrick McGill, 841
    William, 840, 841, 872
Schnebel, Caroline, 1291
    Charlotte, 1291
    William, 1291
Schofield, William, 1566
Scholl, Charlotte, 978
    Christian, 1353, 1401
    Daniel, 1400, 1401
    Lewis V., 783
    Margaret Elizabeth, 1400,
        1401
    Rebecca, 1353
Schooley, Roxana, 978
Schover, Peter, 751, 754
    Sophia, 751, 754
Schreiner, Hans Adam, 1352
    Johan Martin, 1352
    Johan Michael, 1352
    Michael, 1352
    Michael, Jr., 1352

Pieter, 1352
Schrieber, Magdalena, 816
Schriver, Augustus, 1492
    Keener, 1492
Schroder, Zourie, 1549
Schroyer, Amanda, 1084
    Caroline, 743
    Daniel, 743
    Edmund K., 743
    Edwin C., 744
    Elizabeth, 743
    Elma M., 744
    Gordon O., 744
    John, 743
    John F., 744, 868
    Katie, 743
    Lawson, 743
    Lewis, 743
    Luther M., 743, 868
    Mary G., 744
    Minnie V., 743
    Sarah, 743
    Thomas L., 744
    Trenton C., 743, 744
    William H., 744
Schuler, Bessie, 855
    Elizabeth, 855
    Taylor, 855
Schultz, Georgia Ardella, 1390
    Mary C., 821
Schwalen, Catharine, 1560
Schwarber, Linnie Irene, 1070
Scott, Daniel, 1451
    Elizabeth, 1045
    Elizabeth M., 1452
    Elizabeth Maynadier, 1451
    Ella, 1620
    Julia, 1595
    Lavinia, 1143
    Margaret, 1451
    Norman Bruce, 1451
    Upton, 1451
    Winfield, 1576
Scribner, Charles, 701
Seabrook, Minnie, 1615
Seabrooke, James A., 1220
    William, 1620
Seachrist, Lettie, 1512
    Mary, 1472
    Michael, 1512
Sebold, Bennett, 1555
    Catherine, 1554
    Francis E., 1554
    Francis Raymond, 1555
    Gertrude, 1555
    Henry Allen, 1555

James, 1555
James V., 1554
John D., 1554
Joseph Gray, 1555
Louise, 968
Margaret, 1555
Margie, 1554
Marion, 1555
Maysie, 968
Nicholas, 1554
Peter, 968, 1554
Ray, 1555
Samuel, 968
Vincemtia, 968
Vincent, 968
Sebrid, Vincent, 1013
Sechrist, Catherine, 1041
    Charles, 1427
    Frank, 1468
Sefton, Bready, 1447
    Charles G., 1447
    Clellin, 1447
    Donald, 1447
    Edward Brook, 1447
    Elizabeth, 1447
    Harry, 1447
    Ivey, 1447
    Joseph W., 1447
    Maria, 1447
    Paper, 1447
Seibert, John, 826
Seidenstricker, Abraham,
    1248
Seidling, George, 1150
Seiss, Daniel L., 1139
    George, 788, 1600
Selby, William, 1221
Sellman, Amanda, 1162
    Ellen G., 1292, 1293
    Ida, 1310
    J. J. M, 920
    Joshua, 1293
    Miranda, 1293
    Rufus, 1162
Selsum, John, 987
Sencil, Alice I., 1121
    Isabella, 1121
    John, 1121
Sennott, James, 1221
Sensenbaugh, Malinda, 1521,
    1522
Septer, John, 1024
Seward, Anna Catherine,
    1472
    Charles E., 1472
    Charles H., 1471

Cleggett R., 1472
Emma Jane, 1471
Isabel, 1471
Isabelle, 1472
James C., 1471
Joseph, 1471, 1472
Laura, 1472
Margaret, 1471
Mary, 1471, 1472
Solomon, 1471
William, 1538
William H., 1472
William Joseph, 1471, 1472
Seyes, Ida M., 1306
Seyler, Martin, 1045
Shafer, ———, 1174
    Addie E., 746
    Albenia, 993, 1144, 1621
    Alexis, 993
    Alta F., 746
    Amos, 1622
    Ann Elizabeth, 746
    Ann Maria, 1147
    Ann Rebecca, 1144, 1621
    Anna Louisa, 1147
    Annie, 977
    Annie Mary, 746
    Caroline, 993, 1144, 1621
    Carrie Sophia, 746
    Catharine, 746
    Charles E., 746
    Chas. H., 1131
    Clara Virginia, 1147
    Daniel, 746, 1147
    Delphina, 993
    Delphina L., 1541
    E. T., 993
    Edna Grace, 746
    Edward C., 1144
    Edgar Y., 1622
    Elias Talbot, 1144
    Elizabeth, 1544
    Elmmert L., 746
    Emma E., 977
    Emma Eleanor, 1147
    Emma V., 1408
    Ethel May, 1147
    Fannie V., 746
    Fanny Jane, 1147
    Flora, 850, 1622
    Frances, 746, 1174, 1265
    Frances Ellen, 1189, 1190
    Franklin, 993, 1541
    Franklin A., 1335
    George, 746, 1146, 1174,
        1190, 1265, 1332, 1481,

1576, 1621
George C., 746, 955
Glenn C., 746
Grace Mildred, 1147
Hamilton, 1189
Hamilton J., 992, 993, 1144,
    1540
Hamilton W., 993, 1541
Hamilton Willard, 1540
Harry, 1541
Hanson, 746, 1146
Harry B., 993
Harry P., 1622
Hellen R., 993
Henrietta, 993, 1144, 1621
Henry, 992, 993, 1144, 1621
Howard Rupley, 1147
Ida, 1174
Ida E., 746
Ida Elizabetb, 1265
Ira, 1622
Jennie, 1265
John, 1544
John P., 1543, 1544
John Randolph, 1408
John T., 992, 993
John T., Jr., 993, 1541
John W., 1144
John Willard, 1621
Joseph, 746, 891, 1146,
    1174, 1265
Josephus, 977, 1621
Josephus W., 1146
Josephus W., 1147
Laura, 1174
Laura Emily, 1265
Lauretta, 746
Lester E., 746
Luther, 1147, 1622
Lydia, 1363
Lydia E., 1149
Martin, 993
Martin T., 1144, 1621
Mary, 993, 1147, 1174,
    1265, 1541
Mary Ann, 746, 1481, 1576
Mary Eleanor, 1544
Mary Hamilton, 1540
Mary Louisa, 1147
Mary R., 993
May, 1622
Mollie May, 746
Naomi Catherine, 1147
Nora Margaret, 1540
Oda Anzonetta, 746
Oscar, 1622

Peter, 746, 993, 1174,
    1190
Peter H., 1144, 1621
Peter W., 973, 1543, 1544
Ralph Alexis, 1540
Rebecca, 746, 993, 1147
S. Lesley, 1437
Salie B., 746
Samuel, 746, 977, 1146,
    1147
Sarah, 891, 993
Sarah E., 1540
Talbot, 1621
Thomas Carlton, 1147
Thomas K., 993, 1541
Vada, 746
Virginia, 993
Shaff, ———, 1569
    Abraham, 1444, 1570
    Annie Maria, 1570
    Catherine, 1569
    Daniel, 1416, 1569
    Elizabeth, 1569
    Fannie E., 1040
    Frances, 1046, 1570
    George, 1569, 1570
    Grover Cleveland, 1570
    Ida C., 1444
    Jacob, 1569
    Jacob C., 1569, 1570
    John, 1569, 1570
    John G., 1570
    Julia Ann, 1569
    Luther, 1570
    Madora I., 1046
    Margaret, 1569
    Mary, 1570
    Morris Eugene, 1570
    R. L., 1595
    Samuel, 1569
    Sarah, 1569
    Solomon, 1570
    Susan, 1569
Shaffer, Augustus, 1399
    Caroline, 1473
    Edward, 1612
    Elizabeth, 908
    Emma, 1020
    Fanny, 1590, 1591
    George, 932, 958, 1096,
        1324, 1479, 1524
    Grayson, 1438
    Gustavus W., 745
    Hanson, 1621
    Jacob M., 1116
    John R., 1486, 1487

Joseph, 1471
Lavinia, 1234
Margaret, 1288, 1289
Mary, 1481, 1621
Mary Ann, 956, 987, 988, 1525
Newton, 1027
Peter, 1525
Rebecca, 894
Samuel, 956, 987, 1020
Sophia, 1333
Thomas, 1487
William E., 1123
Shanabrough, Joseph, 1564
Shank, Amanda D., 1078
Anna, 1218
Annie E., 1219
Carlton P., 1429
Charles M., 790, 967, 1429
Clara M., 1219
Elmer, 994
Emma C., 1219
Franklin P., 1055
Frederick, 1218, 1292
George, 1429
George A., 1429
George D., 1285, 1495, 1566
Hannah, 1218
Helen, 731
Jacob, 1429
Jennie, 989, 1519
John, 959, 1291
John H., 1429
John Robert, 1219
John W., 1292
John William, 1218
Joseph L., 1622
Lewis, 989
Lillian, 1495
Marion, 1495
Martin L., 1429
Mary B., 1622
Michael, 1495
Otho, 1218
Otho A., 1271, 1292
Otho Augustus, 1218
Peter, 1078
Phoebe, 1292
Raymond R., 1495
Richard Leonius, 1218
Susannah, 1167
William, 1218, 1519
Shankel, Sarah, 1528
Shankle, Luther, 1609
Shann, Sarah A., 1105

Shannon, Arthur, 1295
Charles, 1294
Emma, 1295
Frank, 1295
Ida, 1295
L. C., 1294
Lucille, 1295
Margaret Palmer, 1295
Minnie, 1295
Sarah Louise, 1295
Thornton, 1295
William, 1294
William E., 1294, 1295
Sharer, Charles, 1616
Cora, 1616
Ersia, 1616
John, 1616
William, 1616
Sharretts, Albert, 1553
Della, 1553
Esther, 1553
Samuel, 1553
William, 1024
Sharp, Sarah, 1595
Sharrer, Ernest, 1436
Minnie, 1436
Shaubaker, Jacob M., 1008
Shauer, Mary Jane, 1291
Shaum, Julia Ann, 1287
Shaw, Catharine E., 856, 857
Cora E., 1177
Elijah E., 724
Elizabeth, 1290
Francis, 856
Frank T., 856
George, 1081
Jacob, 1095
John, 956, 987, 1036
Mary, 1235, 1515
Mrs. W. Potter, 1544
Nancy, 1195
William, 1466
Shawbaker, Annie M., 806
Caroline, 1276
Catharine, 1277
Emma Elizabeth, 956
Jacob, 1277, 1543
Jacob M., 956
Shawbecker, Bessie, 1320
Shawberry, Nora, 1262
Shawn, D. L., 1307
Martin L., 1420
Sheaf, George, 932
Shearer, Allen S., 930
Lydia, 784
Susan E., 930

Shebbitts, Henrietta E., 994
Sheeler, Conrad, 873
Katharine E., 873
Mary, 873
Sheeley, John, 1135
William, 1135
Sheely, Aaron, 1139
Elizabeth, 734
Sheerer, L. P., 1080
Sheetenhalm, Delilah, 863
Reuben, 863
Sheetenhelm, Catharine, 1109
Delilah, 789
George, 1109
Mary, 789
Sidney Ann, 898
Sheets, Abraham, 968
Ann, 1066
Anna Mary L., 1234
Sheffer, Betty, 1077
Catharine, 1146
Catherine, 1077
Charles, 1480
Charlotte, 1483
Daniel, 905, 1009, 1077, 1078, 1356
Edgar L., 1078
Edna M., 850
Esta M., 1078
Esther, 756
Frank, 1078
Frank D., 1078
George P., 1077, 1078
George W., 1078
James, 829
Jonas, 904, 905, 972, 1077, 1480
Julia, 901, 1483
Kittie, 1077
Laura E., 1356
Laura F., 1078
Lugenia Frances, 904
Martha, 988
Martha J., 1078, 1339
Martin L., 1480
Mary, 838, 1078
Mary C., 1078
Maurice, 850
Maurice E., 1078
Morris, 1229, 1622
Myrtle, 1078
Philip, 901, 961, 988, 1077, 1265, 1339, 1483
Phoebe E., 961
Rebecca, 720

Rebecca R., 1078
Sallie, 1077
Sallie K., 1078
Sarah C., 1078
Susan Rebecca, 1009
Theodore, 1480
Willa M., 1078
Sheffield, Andrew, 1357
Crescent, 1357
Edward, 1357
Frank E., 1357
John, 1357
Joseph, 1357
Maria, 1583
Naomi, 1358
Ruth, 1358
Welty, 1358
Wilbur, 1358
Sheffler, Margaret, 1276
Shell, Henry, 1211
Shellman, Alice V., 1313
Charlotte, 1313
Daniel J., 1090, 1313
Della, 1313
George K., 1313
Hester L., 1313
Ida, 1313
Jacob, Jr., 1313
Jacob, Sr., 1313
John, 1313
Lewis E., 1313
Maria, 1313
Shelman, James M., 787
Shepard Ephraim E., 1594
Shepherd, Elise Hamtramck, 901
Eliza Catherine, 901
James H., 901
Nicholas, 845
Shepley, John, 1370
Ruth, 1181
Melvin F., 1485
William S., 1011
Sheppard, E. C., 735
Harry, 1434
Mary, 1087
Sheridan, Philip, 1582
Sheredine, Upton, 941
Sherman, Elizabeth, 1317, 1318
John, 852
Shibbetts, Barbara A., 722, 723
Henry, 722
Shideler, Elizabeth, 1033
Shields, Charles E., 1229

Ebenezer, 1024
Thomas, 1202
Shietenhelm, Reuben, 1122
Sidney A., 1122
Shifler, George, 812
Shilling, John, 1081
Shinaflew, Charity, 1545
Shiner, Sarah, 757
Shinmel, John, 1285
Shipes, Henrietta, 1371
Shipley, Annie, 740, 942
Austin V., 961
Bertha, 740
Blanche, 740
Carrie D., 981
Charles F., 981
Charles F., Jr., 981
Charlotte, 740
Denton R., 1292, 1293
Denton Robert, 1293
Dorsey, 740
Elias, 1292
Elinore, 1293
Eliza Ann, 981
Ernest, 981
Fannie E., 981, 1283
Florence Virginia, 961
Franklin, 981
Franklin F., 981
Frederick, 740
George, 740, 793
George E., 1286, 1357
George Upton, 961
George W., 981
Grace, 740
Harry F., 740, 1170
Harry F., Jr., 740
Helen, 740
J. Frederick, 981
Janet, 981
John, 826, 933, 1606
John J., 981
Joshua, 981
Maggie, 740
Margaret E., 981
Marie, 981
Marie G., 1293
Mary E., 981
Mildred, 981
Mollie May, 981
Mrs. Florence, 865
Nellie, 740
Nimrod O., 939
Oscar, 1293
Raymond, 981
Robert, 740

Roscoe Ralph, 961
Roy, 740
Ruth, 981
Sallie, 740
Sarah, 1306
Silas, 1293
Susan, 1293
Upton D. W., 1306
Vida, 981
Wallace D. W., 1292, 1293
William H., 980, 981
Shivers, Lucy, 1525
Shob, Margaret, 1024
Shoe, John A., 1194
Shoemaker, Elizabeth, 1291
Esther, 857
George W., 863
Henry, 759
Magdalena, 1019
Philip, 1611
Shook, Amelia, 1531
Daniel, 1237
Granison, 1134
Mary C., 1237
Shope, Catharine, 981
Charles B., 1575
Shores, Francis, 1488
Short, Abraham, 1612
Annie, 1565
John, 1565
Shouman, H. B., 1575
Shreeve, J., 1468
Shreeves, Nettie, 1279
Shriner, Annie, 1353
Blanche E., 1387
Cornelius, 796, 1068, 1352, 1353, 1414
Edward A., 1247, 1352, 1353
Edward D., 1352-1354
Edward Derr, 1353, 1456
Edward G., 1354
Elizabeth, 1596
Elizabeth R., 1069
G. W. B. , 702
G. W. B., 1168
George W. B., 1353, 1387
Jacob, 1069, 1222
James, 1588
Jasper, 732
Julia Catharine, 1267, 1507
Margaret, 1155, 1222
Mary C., 1353
Mrs. E. D., 1456

Mrs. E. L., 1352
Rosa E., 732
Shriver, Abraham, 711
  Catherine, 1178
  Christian, 828, 1618
  Eleanor, 710, 711
  Henry, 1178
  John, 1178
  Juliann, 1178
  Margaret, 1178
  Mary, 1219, 1609
  Rachel, 1139
  Rebecca, 761, 999, 1000,
    1060, 1447
Shroyer, Susannah, 1614
  Trenton C., 827
Shryock, Bertha, 741
  Christina, 740
  Florence T. R., 741
  George W., 740, 741
  Gracon E., 741
  Henry, 740, 741
  Henry V, 741
  John J., 741
  Mary E., 741
  Rebecca, 741
  Sarah A., 741
  Valentine, 740
  William H., 741
Shuff, Carrie, 1324
  Lucretia, 1348
  M. F., 1445
Shuford, M. L., 1453
Shulenberger, Adam, 1280
  Anthony, 1280
  Benjamin, 1279, 1280
  Benjamin, Jr., 1279
  Elizabeth, 1199, 1280
  Eva M., 1280
  John, 1199, 1279, 1280
  John Hackett, 1280
  Rachel E., 1280
  Robert, 1280
  Samuel, 1280
  William C. B., 1279, 1280
Shull, Annabel, 1434
  Anna Belle, 1268
  Elias, 1434
  L. V., 783
  Lewis, 923
  William, 1294
Shully, Frederick, 1024
  Harry, 1024
  Miriam, 1024
Shults, Susan, 1203
Shultz, Charles, 1383, 1534

Matilda, 1425
Theodore, 1425
Shuman, Joshua, 1613
  Mattie, 1310
  Sidney Ann B., 1613
Sicard, Wm. Floyd, 1330
Sickles, Daniel, 1535
Sidney, Philip, 939
Sidwell, F. H., 732
  Frank, 1057, 1070
  Thomas, 1053, 1057, 1151,
    1497
Siedling, George C., 1278
  George F. C., 1278
  Julia H. F., 1278
Siegel, Hanna, 1393
Sifford, John, 1361
Sigafoose, T. A., 926
Sigler, Amanda C., 1549
  Hannah, 1174, 1190
  John, 1549
  Joseph, 1097
  Mary L., 1316
  O. C., 873
  Oliver, 1316
  Samuel, 932, 1332
  Sarah, 986, 987, 1129
  William, 987
Silence, Baker, 763
  Henry, 763
  Stansburg, 763
Sim, Thornas, 785
Simm, Edward, 791, 1610
  Sarah, 1263
Simmons, Clara A., 1412
  Effie, 1275
  John A., 979
  John F., 1577
  Mary R., 728
  Richard, 1412
  Susan Fessler, 979
Simond, Mary Susan, 1124
Simpson, Christine Virginia,
    1076
  Clarence, 1264
  E. J., 1563
  Edward, 1263, 1264
  Effie, 1261
  Elizabeth, 795, 1025, 1026
  Elmer, 1264
  George, 1263
  Grafton, 1263
  Homer, 1262
  Ida, 1263, 1264
  Irene, 1264
  John, 1026

Joshua, 1263
Julia A., 1264
Lila, 1264
Loraine, 1076
Loraine, Jr., 1076
Lurenna, 1263
Paul, 1262
R. D., 1262
Rachel, 1263
Richard, 1181
Richard Wallace, 1263
Ridgely, 1052
Ruth, 1026
Sophia, 1263
T. W., 785
Thomas, 1263, 1323
Walter, 1262
Warfield, 1058, 1263,
    1264, 1498
Sims, Joseph, 1181
Sinclair, George, 920
Sines, Annie R., 1411
  Arthur, 1483
  William, 1411
Singer, Amy Belle, 1182
  Clarence Leroy, 1182
  Elmer, 1500
  Guy, 1182
  Helen M., 1500
  Jesse Markel, 1182
  Lester, 1500
  Oscar, 1500
  Paul Raymond, 1182
  Raymond, 1182
Singler, Westminster, 1462
Sinn, Edward, 702, 703, 815
  Fannie, 853
  Fannie E., 1492
  Kate, 815
  Laura V., 702
Sinnott, John T., 1548
Sipe, Harley, 984
Sipes, Henry, 886
Sites, Roanna Grace, 780
  Stewart, 780
  Stewart Frederick, 780
Six, Ariminta, 1052
  Carrie, 1243
  David, 1207
  David W., 1052
  Edward, 1243
  Harry, 830
  Henry, 773, 1252
  Samuel, 1052, 1220
  William, 1052
Skoggs, Joshua, 1306

Slagle, E. C., 950
  Peter, 860
  Ruth, 1570
Slake, Sarah, 1095, 1542
Slater, John, 1099, 1107, 1114
Slayman, Margaret C., 962
Slicer, Henry, 1069
  Thomas, 1069
  Waters-Burgee, 1069
Slick, Abendigo, 1143
  Amanda, 1143
  Maria, 1143
Slifer, Eliza, 1351
  Emanuel, 957
  Ezra, 1122, 1486
  Frank, 1362
  George, 989, 1486
  George W., 760
  Hannah, 806, 807, 1487
  Hezekiah, 1486
  Jacob, 1486
  John, 1486
  Laura, 1046, 1479
  Laura E., 1486
  Laura Etta, 1485
  Lydia, 1151
  Margaret, 1086
  Mary Catherine, 1486
  Morris, 1101
  Peter, 807, 1485, 1486
  Sarah Ellen, 1486
  William, 1174, 1189
Sloane, J. Q., 763
Slothour, Elizabeth, 1210
  Stephen, 1210
Smeltzer, Erean, 726
  Eve Ann, 781
  Sarah Catharine, 1459
Smith, A. M., 859
  A. W., 838
  Abalonia, 1219
  Ada Koogle, 1325
  Ada, 1518, 1619
  Ada M., 1307
  Adam, 738, 1235, 1538
  Agnes, 1273
  Albert, 1518, 1619
  Alice McPherson, 834
  Alvey J., 738
  Amanda, 869, 1221, 1602
  Andrew Derr, 798
  Andrew Johnson, 1271
  Ann Maria, 1091
  Ann Matilda, 1237, 1270,
    1284, 1518, 1619
  Anna Margaretta, 1178,

1179
  Anna Mary, 1251
  Anne, 1515
  Annie, 733, 1029, 1500,
    1508
  Annie M., 1307
  Barbara, 1340
  Baxter, 1436
  Benjamin F., 1012
  Bernard, 1060
  Bertha Belle, 1271, 1481
  Bertie, 1454
  Bertie Lenora, 737
  Bessie V., 1335
  Burley V., 1287
  C. E. 1419
  C. Edward, 1271
  C. P., 1302
  Calvin P., 1237, 1270, 1284,
    1518, 1619
  Caroline, 738
  Carroll, 1236, 1525
  Catharine, 1052, 1091, 1207,
    1215, 1604
  Catharine B., 1156
  Catherine, 959
  Charles, 759, 790, 1014,
    1029, 1106, 1215, 1216,
    1221, 1416, 1518, 1619
  Charles Arthur, 705
  Charles C., 704, 818, 832,
    1026
  Charles Edward, 1271
  Charles J., 1153
  Charles K., 1334
  Charles W., 1236, 1307
  Charles William, Jr., 1076
  Charlotte Patterson, 834
  Christian, 1052, 1211, 1230,
    1589
  Christiana, 1106
  Clara, 704, 1518, 1619
  Clara V., 832
  Claud I., 1307
  Conrad, 732, 1250, 1334
  Cora J., 1013
  Cover, 1285
  D. H., 740, 1170
  Daniel, 738, 857, 874, 883,
    955, 1221
  Donald L., 1236, 1561
  Dorothy, 1221
  Edith G., 1170
  Edward, 1215, 1221, 1307,
    1418
  Edward Chester, 835

  Edward Claud, 835
  Edward Joseph, 1216
  Edward L., 1108
  Effie, 1532
  Eliza Ann, 705
  Elizabeth, 709, 710, 838,
    1181, 1184, 1230,
    1237, 1270, 1271,
    1284, 1306, 1334,
    1363, 1478, 1518,
    1619
  Elizabeth B., 1055
  Elizabeth C., 798, 1294
  Elmer, 830
  Elmer E., 1271
  Elmer J., 1033, 1351,
    1352
  Emma, 704, 1271, 1518,
    1619
  Emma J., 832, 1511
  Emory L., 1339
  Estelle, 705
  Eudora S., 1236
  Eugene G., 1334
  Evaline, 832
  Evaline C., 704
  Evelyn, 1454
  Ezra, 932, 995, 1237,
    1270, 1284, 1289,
    1317, 1332, 1382,
    1518, 1619
  Ezra E., 738
  F. B., 765
  F. Lester, 1018
  Fairce E., 738
  Flora D., 918
  Florence, 1271
  Florence E., 1271
  Flossie, 1221
  Francis Fenwick, 1215,
    1216
  Francis R., 1525
  Frank, 797, 1160, 1336
  Frank B., 1314
  Franklin, 965
  Franklin Buchanan, 704,
    832, 833
  Franklin Buchanan, Jr.,
    834
  Frederick Lester, 1305
  Frederick Lester, Jr., 1306
  Frisby L., 738
  G. Baxter, 1285
  G. L., 1234
  George, 703, 704, 738,
    765, 832, 833, 1012,

1178, 1416, 1477
George A., 738
George E., 1012
George Edward, 705, 738
George Ignatius, 1306
George J., 1012
George M., 863
George W., 798
George William, 703, 704, 832, 964, 1060, 1143, 1563, 1572
George Wm., 714, 715
Grace, 924
Grayson Raymond, 1287
Guy, 1236
H. G., 1133
Hannah, 1193, 1194
Harmon R., 1444
Harriet, 1060, 1136, 1539
Harrison Osborn, 1221
Helen, 1060
Helen S., 1102
Hellen S., 1101
Hench E. M., 735
Henry, 959, 1170, 1287, 1516
Henry E., 1307
Herbert, 1307
Hiram J., 1307
Hiram T., 1012
Hoke, 1113
Horace E., 1307
Horace H., 1307, 1413
Horace M., 1307
Howard, 889
Howard L., 705, 1060
Howard T., 1060
I. N., 1115
I. Staton, 1351
Ida, 705
Ida E., 1236
Ida M., 738, 778
Ida Missouri, 1615
Isaac, 1221
Isabel, 1586
Isabella Lavinia, 1237, 1270, 1284, 1518, 1619
Iva, 1221
J. Newton, 738
Jacob, 959, 1216, 1340, 1347, 1379
Jacob C., 738
James, 804, 842, 1350, 1546
James A., 1251
James H., 763, 1029, 1443

James Lee, 1271
James M., 1270, 1284, 1508, 1518, 1619
James V., 1195
James W., 1235, 1236
Jennie, 1307, 1518, 1619
Jennie L., 1302
Jesse, 1223
Johanna Rebecca, 737
John, 737, 804, 996, 1052, 1106, 1154, 1215, 1237, 1270, 1271, 1284, 1289, 1341, 1351, 1388, 1498, 1501, 1508, 1518, 1519, 1589, 1600, 1618, 1619
John C, 1221
John C., 869
John Francis, 1215, 1216, 1609
John Gesey, 1525
John J., 1250, 1351
John L., 1496
John Luther, 1270, 1271
John Michael, 1518, 1519, 1619
John O., 982
John W., 698, 1220, 1221, 1519, 1615
John Walter, 937, 1216, 1225
John, Jr., 738
John, Sr., 737, 1518
Jonas D., 1012
Jonathan, 1221
Joseph, 735, 1077, 1215, 1307
Joshua, 754
Josiah, 899
Josiah F., 737, 738, 778, 868
Julia A., 1250
Kenneth, 1285
L. C., 996, 1154
Laura, 1221
Laura A., 1012
Layton Hamilton, 1221
Leander F., 1334
Lena, 1221
Leonard, 1215, 1216
Lester C., 884
Lewis, 1613
Lewis B., 869
Lewis E., 1307, 1416
Lewis V., 1013
Lillie, 1221,1615
Lillie M., 1615
Lizzie, 1218, 1221
Louisa Catharine, 1271

Lucinda, 1289
Luella I., 738
Lula, 1302
Magdalena, 1087
Mahlon, 1307
Malinda, 1221
Mamie, 1236
Margaret, 1237, 1270, 1284, 1307, 1350, 1518, 1619
Margaret A., 1250, 1334
Margaret Olynscia, 835
Marietta Susan, 857
Marshall, 1518, 1619
Martin, 1302
Mary, 736, 794, 857, 1070, 1086, 1215, 1237, 1270, 1284, 1451, 1518, 1595, 1619
Mary C., 1334
Mary E., 1352, 1387
Mary Elizabeth, 1388
Mary Evelyn, 737
Mary G., 1335
Mary I., 1012
Mary K., 705
Mary M., 1450
Mary Magdalena, 1181
Mary Matilda, 1083
Matilda, 1271
Maurice, 1445
May, 1236
Mildred O., 1335
Milford E., 1335
Molly, 1221
Morris O., 1271
Mrs. Franklin B., 809
Mrs. Mary C., 1152
Myra, 1271
Nancy, 1221
Nathan R., 937
Nettie M., 1335
Nicholas, 1307
Noah J., 1221
Nora, 1007
Oliver M., 1013
Perry G., 1226, 1307
Perry Green, 735
Peter, 1235, 1343
Philip Francis, 1271
Phoebe, 1478
R. A., 1389
R. H., 1302
Rachel, 1302
Ralph Hamilton, 1287

Raymond L., 738
Rebecca, 1317
Robert Guy, 835
Robert V., 1302
Roger B., 1236
Ross, 1236
Roy H., 1335
Rufus, 1324, 1332
Ruth, 1060
S., 790, 967
S. D. T., 1044
Salome, 859
Samuel, 959, 1094, 1194, 1251
Sarah, 765, 1029
Sarah A., 996, 1003, 1153, 1154
Sarah E., 995, 1012
Savilla, 1221
Silas, 1221
Solomon, 1219, 1221, 1298, 1495, 1511
Solomon U., 738
Sue I., 1317
Susan, 775, 1237, 1270, 1284, 1307, 1405, 1474, 1512, 1518, 1522, 1619
Susan C., 1516
Susan E., 1379
Susan Isabella, 1271
Susan M., 1287
Susan S., 1226
Susanna, 1121, 1163
Susanna S., 1226, 1227
Susannah Rebecca, 735
Teressa M., 738
Teressa M. , 868
Thomas, 1029, 1286, 1302
Thomas A., 999, 1029
Thomas Henry, 737
Thomas K., 738
Thomas L., 737, 1454
Valentine, 1012
Vernon R., 1236
Vernon T., 1235, 1236
Verona, 1454
Verona Irene, 737
Victor M., 778
Virgie M., 1307, 1413
Virginia, 705, 1060
Washington, 1585
Wheeler A., 1351, 1352
William, 733, 781, 863, 918, 996, 1153, 1307, 1336, 1350
William A., 1176, 1237,

1270, 1284, 1518, 1519, 1619
William C., 1409
William Charles, 1076
William E., 1038
William E. T., 1307
William Frances, 737
William H., 1518, 1519, 1527, 1619
William Howard, 735
William Lee, 705
William Meredith, 1216
William Peter, 1525
Zedekiah, 1122
Zelda J., 1271
Zelma Victoria, 1271
Smyth, Sarah Spencer, 1043
Snader, Edna, 1278
Elizabeth, 990
Ellwood, 1279
Jacob, 990
Mary, 902
Mary A., 932
Phillip, 1278
Snapp, George O., 853
Snider, Charlotte, 1411
Snively, Ann Louis, 1573, 1574
D. S., 927
E. D., 805
Isabelle, 805
Jacob, 1574
Mary, 805
Snook, ——, 1602
Adam, 1385
Alexander, 1427
Annie Irene, 1400
C. C., 820
Catharine, 820
Charles S., 746
Daniel, 745, 746, 1135, 1399
Daniel F., 746
Daniel J., 745, 746, 1399
Eliza, 1427
Elizabeth, 758, 1038, 1171, 1396, 1422, 1427
Ella, 1159
Frank F., 820
Grayson, 764
Henry, 758, 1038, 1171, 1422, 1427
Ida B., 820
J. C., 1102
Jacob, 745, 820, 1399
John A., 745, 1399
John H., 820
Julia, 745, 1302, 1399

Julia Ann, 1135
Lewis A., 745, 820, 1399
Lewis P., 1427
Lydia A., 902, 1317
Margaret M., 745, 1399
Mary, 820, 1423
Minerva, 1234, 1385
Minerva A., 1384
Morris, 1418
Nancy, 1385
Nelson A., 1427
Rebecca, 950
Simon, 745, 1402
Susan Elizabeth, 948
Susan M., 745, 1399
Thomas C., 1427
William, 948, 1159, 1508
William G., 746, 1317
Snoots, S. T., 1435
Snouffer, Benjamin, 1323
Benjamin J., 1322
Edward N., 1419
Elizabeth, 920
G. A. T., 970
George, 1102, 1322, 1413
George A. T., 818, 1322, 1323
Hattie H., 1412, 1413
Mary A., 1323
Susie E., 1323
Snovel, John, 1384
Snowden, Elizabeth, 836
J. M., 1130
Snyder, Adella, 1140
Amanda E., 1362 , 1430
Andrew, 1204, 1205
Beatrice Rosaline, 917
Catharine V., 893
Catherine, 1177
Catherine Margaret, 1309
Charles A., 917
Charles Augustus, 1309
Charlotte Blanche, 917
Christian Guttlieb, 1309
Clifford, 1560
Daniel, 812
Eliza, 917
Elmer E., 884
Elsie, 1204, 1205
Elsie Rosina, 1309
Eve, 917
Florence W., 982
Frederick, 917, 1309
George A., 917
George Randolph, 917
Harvey A., 917

Henry, 1178
Henry M., 1272
Hettie, 1297, 1546
Houston E., 917
Jacob F., 982
James Albert, 1308, 1309
James Alvey, 1309
John, 1159, 1214, 1309, 1586
John George, 917
John J., 982
Julia, 917
Laura, 1181, 1546
Leighton Albert, 1309
Leopold, 1308, 1309
Martin, 1019
Mary C., 917
Mary T., 982
Mary Theresa, 1309
Michael, 917
Ralph, 1309
Sarah, 1152, 1297
Sarah A., 781
Sarah R., 1586, 1587
Savilla C., 917
Solomon, 917
Susan C., 1185
Susan R., 1586
Susanna, 791
Virgie Anna, 1309
William, 922, 1534
William F., 982
William W., 917
Zelda May, 1309
Solena, Maria, 1072
Soley, J. R., 701
Sollers, Arianna, 785
Somers, Lavinia, 1570
Soper, Corilla, 878
Julius, 919
Massey, 1034
Souder, Margaret, 880
Peter, 880
Susan, 880
Souders, Carlton Remsberg, 1379
David A., 1379
David Paul, 1379
Soule, Edward, 814
Sowalter, Mary, 893
Spahr, Abraham, 1134
Harry, 1292
Rebecca Elizabeth, 1134
Spake, Carrie, 1525
Spalding, Basil, 835
Elias, 839

Elizabeth, 835, 836
Genevieve, 835
Gertrude, 844
John, 844
Josephine, 839
Julia, 835
Sarah F., 839
Spangler, Miriah, 779
Sparks, Joseph, 942
Sparrow, Edward L., 1522
Thomas, 1123
Spaulding, Elias, 1295, 1457
Josephine, 1295, 1296, 1457
Speacht, Jacob, 1602
Jane E., 1601, 1602
Speak, Charles, 771
Speaks, Richard J., 1172, 1299
Specht, Lewis, 947
Marion, 1606
Spence, Robert Trail, 720
Sperow, George R., 1400
Spicer, Mrs. Etta L., 865
Spilman, W. R., 1202
Spitler, David, 827
Eliza J., 744
Eliza Jane, 827
Spitzer, Alonzo R., 933
Alonzo Rader, 934
Eli, 934
Eli G., 933
Elizabeth, 934
Frank L., 934
Jacob, 934
John, 934
John Bowman, 934
Joseph F., 933, 934
Mary, 934
Nancy Catharine, 934
Sadie, 934
Spohn, Caroline, 716
Spong, Ellen, 901
Sponseller, Annie, 1610
Arthur, 1170, 1610
Author, 1578
Eugene, 1108, 1109, 1127, 1128
Catharine, 1610
Charles, 1611
Elizabeth, 1533
George, 1610
Harland, 1611
Jacob, 981, 1610
John, 1610
Lewis, 1611
Margaret N., 981
Mary, 1610

Nettie J., 1170
Thomas C. P., 1610
William, 1611
William Eugene, 1610
William H., 1610
Spotts, Elizabeth, 1472
Spouteller, Silas, 1463
Sprague, Harriet M., 774
Wm., 1127
Spring, Betsey, 1435
Christina, 1172
Springer, Catharine Mariah, 944
Christopher, 1160, 1360
Jane Louisa, 1160, 1360
Susan, 891
William, 1160, 1360
Sprinkle, Kernan, 1293
Sproukle, Isaac C., 830
Linnie, 830
Sproul, George, 1151
Spurrier, C. H., 1394
Constatine, 1547
Eliza, 693, 694
Emma, 1034
Thomas, 1034
Spurner, Delila, 1558
Spuyer, Clarence, 878
Everett, 878
Franklin, 878
Margaret, 878
Stella, 878
Stable, Harry H., 844
Stabler, Susan, 1243
Staffer, Mary S., 1023
Stagle, George W., 1086
Stahle, Henry J., 928
Stahley, Catharine, 889, 890
Charles A., 746
Charles B., 1386
Grayson, 952
Grayson H., 776
Lewis, 882
Stair, Georgia, 1613
Staley, Aaron, 1455
Aaron L., 1454, 1577
Amanda M., 908, 1410
Ann S., 902, 1317
Ann Salinda, 943, 1158
Antionett Frances, 1056
Antionette Jane, 1159
Carrie C., 908
Charles A., 943
Clara A., 1079
Cornelius, 1056, 1158, 1410

Cornelius A., 908
Daniel, 898, 943, 1158
Daniel O., 943, 1138
Daniel Octavius, 1158
Daniel Ruch, 1138
Daniel Thadeus, 1159
David, 1063
David L., 1021
Edward G., 1282
Edward M., 1334
Effie M., 908
Ella Maud, 1282
Ella Virginia, 1159
Estella, 955
Estella B., 943
Eva, 1402
Fleet, 724, 943, 1158
Frances C., 1080
Frederick, 908
George Lewis, 1282
Grayson H., 943, 1079
Harry M., 1603
Harvey D., 943
Ira McDuell, 1138, 1159
Irving E., 943
Jane E., 870
John, 1158
Joseph, 1158
Joseph E., 943, 1079
Joseph Edward, 1158
Julia, 1454
Julia A., 1335
Julia Cusack, 1159
Levi, 1333
Lewis, 943
Lewis Van Lear, 1158
Luther R., 1333
Mahlon, 943
Mahlon Franklin, 1158
Margaret, 1230
Margaret C., 775, 1021,
    1022
Marion J., 908
Marshall D., 943
Mary, 1454
Mary A. E., 1410
Mary Edna, 1159
Mary Louise, 1282
Millie Hedges, 943
Orsena P. A., 908
Peter S., 902, 1317
Reverdy, 1518, 1619
Reverdy T., 908
Rhuanna, 898
Robert Algeo, 1138
Sarah, 1333

Stephen, 1282
William, 1454
William Thaddeus, 1138
Worthington C., 908
Stambaugh, Edward, 1586
    Emily E., 1491
    Jacob, 1219
    John, 1491
    John Edward, 1518, 1619,
        1237, 1270, 1284
    Mollie E., 1586
Stamp, Eugene D., 933
    Nannie, 933
Stanford, Leland T., 1258
Stang, Luther A., 1573
Stansbury, Abraham, 741, 743
    Bertha B., 742
    Charity, 1452
    Cronon, 773
    Elizabeth, 707
    Etta A., 742
    Jemima, 773
    John, 741
    Martha R., 743
    N. C., 733
    Nicholas, 741-743, 773
    Noah Phillips, 742
Stanton, Mary, 948
Stark, Amanda, 881
Starr, Ann Beaumont, 1463
    Edna W., 1345
    Edwin, 1463
    John F., 1345
    Mary Margaret, 1463
Staub, Agnes, 1168
    Andrew Jackson, 1168
    Blanche V., 1168
    Catherine, 1168
    Charles Melvin, 1168
    Corrine Leslie, 1168
    Daniel, 874
    Edith, 1168
    Edward, 1168
    Emma, 1168
    Francis V, 1168
    Frank, 1168
    Jacob, 1168
    James Marshall, 1169
    Jerome, 1168
    Lucy, 1168
    Mary Pauline, 1169
    Mary Stone, 1168
    Meredith Henry Van-
        Ranseller, 1169
    Roger Lee, 1168
    Sarah C., 829, 1618

Stauffer, Allie, 1205
    Amy, 1259
    Ann Virginia, 1460
    Barbara, 1205, 1259
    Carl Maynard, 1199
    Carrie, 1205
    Catharine, 1393, 1394
    Clara B., 1206
    Clara Beaty, 1199
    Clara C., 1205
    Courtnay Elizabeth, 1260
    D. Edward, 703
    D. V., 710
    Daniel, 1205, 1259, 1524
    David, 1434, 1537
    David R., 1537
    David V., 1205
    Dorsey, 1532
    Elinor, 1205
    Elizabeth, 1205, 1259
    Frank N., 1206
    George Harris, 1206
    George W., 1098, 1205,
        1389, 1532
    Glenn Offutt, 1259
    Henry, 1205, 1259, 1260
    Henry Clay, 1259
    Henry G., 1259
    Henry Webster, 1205
    Irene, 1259
    J. D., 1270
    J. H., 1110, 1140, 1259,
        1319
    James Henry, 1260
    John, 1205, 1259
    John Dorsey, 1205
    John H., 1205
    Joseph, 1205, 1259
    Kitty, 1205, 1259
    Mary A., 1260
    Mary S., 1598
    Nan, 1259
    Oda Neidig, 1098
    Oda S., 1205
    Ralph, 1199
    Ralph W., 1205
    S. W., 703
    Simon Theodore, 1259
    Simon Theodore, Jr., 1260
    Simon Wesley, 1205,
        1259
    Susan, 1205, 1259
    Theodore, 1111, 1526
    William, 1460
Staumbaugh, ——, 1292
    Adelaide, 1292

Staup, Clarence, 1059
  Eugene D., 1277
  Eva M., 1277
  Genevieve, 1059
  Helen, 1059
  Jennie C., 1277
  John, 1277
  John J., 1277
  John W., 1277
  Mary S., 1277
  Milton E., 1277
  William H., 1277
Stayard, Nicola, 948
Stear, John, 828, 1618
Steck, Charles F., 1583, 1584
  Daniel, 1583
  Frederick, 1583
  Jeannette A., 1584
  Julia J., 1584
  Margaret, 1484
Steel, Charles Edward, 1495
Steele, James H., 1128
Stein, Alice C., 823
  Almetta E., 822, 823
  Elias, 822
  Florence M., 823
  Franklin, 823
  John, 822
  John F., 822
  Nannie M., 823
Steiner, Catharine, 1246
  Christian, 709
  Henry, 833
  Jacob, 1047, 1246
  Jesse R., 1388
  John, 1246
  Lewis Henry, 1043
  Phebe, 1133
  Walter Ralph, 1043
Stem, Anna, 1446
  Henry, 717
  Jennie, 1223
  William, 718, 769
Stemple, Catharine, 1356
  Catharine, 1296
Stephens, Amelia Catharine,
    1340
  John C., 891
  Mary M., 1158
  William, 1077, 1158, 1340,
    1349
Stephey, Elizabeth, 1180
Sterle, Charles Edward, 1298
Stern, Clara, 1369
Sterr, Charles, 1336
Steven, Walter, 1266, 1301

Stevens, Charles, 933
  Florence, 1327
  Frank M., 933
  Isaac L., 933
  James G., 933, 1277
  Laura, 1327
  Lucy, 933
  Reuben, 1327
  Thaddeus, 693
Stevenson, Henrietta, 783
  James, 938
  Samuel, 941
  Susanna, 783
Stewart, Archie, 1355
  B. T., 1098
  James, 1081
  Lillie S., 1081
  M., 1185
  Rosa J., 864
Stickle, Maria, 916, 917
Stickman (Stockman), Henry,
    1266
Stieg, Augustus, 1024
Stier, Mary Ann, 1008
Stilley, Ann Rebecca, 752
  Peter, 752
Stimmel, Catharine, 1270
  Edward, 1270
  Eleanor Carmack, 926, 927
  Elizabeth, 1205
  Elizabeth C., 1112, 1268,
    1269, 1270
  Ellen, 1270
  Jacob, 1270
  John, 1200, 1270, 1287
  John B., 1270
  Josephine, 1270
Stine, Alice, 1030
  John F., 874, 1030
Stitely, Ann Rosella, 1450
  Anna Laura, 1521
  Annie, 1500
  B. W., 1273
  Basil, 1007, 1110, 1140,
    1336, 1450
  Bradley P., 1007
  Caroline, 1007, 1499
  Catharine, 1007, 1499
  Catharine Bernella, 1070
  Catharine D. E., 1499
  Clara G., 1007
  Clarence, 1500
  Clarence Joseph, 1136
  D. W., 1136
  David, 1007, 1500
  David Oscar, 1136

  David R., 1070, 1249,
    1377, 1499
  David W., 1500
  Dessie I., 1007
  Donald, 1500
  Donald Grossnickle, 1136
  Edith Grace, 1500
  Elizabeth, 947, 1071,
    1520
  Elsie R., 1007
  Emory F., 1007
  Florence, 1071, 1521
  Florence Irene, 1007
  George, 1273
  George M., 1007
  George S., 1207
  George Washington, 1006,
    1007, 1499
  Harriet Elsie, 1500
  Harry W., 1007
  Ida M., 1007
  Isaac, 1070, 1219
  Isaac Earl, 1136, 1500
  Isaac P., 1499-1501
  Jacob, 1006, 1499, 1515
  Jacob Ephraim, 1007,
    1499
  Joel, 1007, 1499
  John Henry, 1007, 1499
  Laura, 1499
  Lydia Ann, 1083
  Margaret Rachel, 1500
  Mary, 1006, 1499
  Mary Adelaide, 1007
  Mary Catharine, 1500
  Nellie E., 1500
  Rosa E., 1007
  Samuel, 1499
  Samuel A., 1007 , 1499
  Samuel M. , 1006
  Susan, 1235, 1515
  Theresa, 1516
  Thomas Lee, 1007
  Zoir E., 1008
Stitley, Catharine L., 1168
  George W., 886
  Jacob, 1235
Stitzel, Louise, 1292
Stockman, Amanda, 957,
    1345, 1346
  Ella M., 1488
  Harry, 1502
  Henry, 1091
  John, 1488
  Mary, 1444
  Susan, 1426

Stocks, Laura, 1411
Stocksdale, Arthur Talbert, 798
  Bertha Gardner, 798
  Caroline, 798
  Charles R., 799
  Edward, 798
  Ellen M., 798
  Frederick, 798
  George, 798
  George W., 798
  George Washington, 798
  Helen T., 798
  J. W., 926
  John, 798
  John Thomas, 798
  Letitia, 798
  Mary, 798
  Mazie Stokes, 798
  Murray F., 798
  Naomi, 1338
  Nellie, 798
  Noah, 798
  Noah, Jr., 798
  Ruhana, 936, 938, 939
  Solomon, 798
  Talbert Claton, 798
  Tobias C., 798
  Viola, 799
  William Henry Harrison, 798
  Zula L., 799
Stockton, Mrs. Isabelle, 1296, 1457
Stoddard, John, 1026
Stokes, Harry, 791
  Henrietta Marian, 711
  Robert Y., 711
Stollemyer, David W., 748
Stone, Allen M., 953
  Carrie, 1548
  Celeste Grace, 952
  Charles G., 1547
  D. E., 937, 1452
  Daniel, 1547
  Daniel Edward, 1547
  Daniel Edwin, 1547
  Daniel Edwin, Jr., 1548
  David, 1421
  Elizabeth C., 1106
  Eugenia, 1547
  Halbert, 1548
  Henry, 1106
  John, 1174, 1190, 1238, 1382
  John T., 1106

Joseph, 952
  Lenora Owings, 1452
  Lenore, 1548
  Llewellyn, 1547
  Mary Eugenia, 811
  Sarah, 1336
  Sarah Jane, 1468
  Thomas, 1547
  William, 969, 1547
  William Huff, 1547
Stonebraker, Alforetta R., 1249
  John W., 853
  Samuel, 1249
  Sebastian, 930
Stoneburner, Christianna, 969
  Christina, 890
Stoner, Abraham, 742, 946, 1209
  Anne, 1377
  Augustus, 946, 1235, 1377, 1515
  Blanch, 743
  Clarence, 922, 1219
  Clarence E., 1350
  Dallas, 946
  Daniel, 742
  David, 742, 886, 1151, 1210, 1262
  Denton H., 946
  Elizabeth, 1069, 1209, 1607
  Emanuel, 742
  Emma, 1053, 1350, 1497
  Emory, 716
  Ephraim, 1350
  Frank, 1273, 1597
  Frank L., 854, 924, 1139, 1349, 1350, 1465
  George, 946
  H. Lee, 1209, 1210
  H. Y., 1408
  Hannah, 946
  Harry A., 1209
  Henry, 923
  Isaac, 1209
  J. C., 1472
  Jacob, 742, 1209
  Jane, 1209
  Jesse, 1350
  John, 1209
  John R., 742 , 1620
  John T., 743
  Lydia, 742
  Marshall C., 1209
  Mary Ann, 742, 923
  Mary E., 1408
  Oliver L., 1350

R., 741
  Rachel A., 1209
  Raymond, 1209
  Samuel, 742, 1209, 1493
  Sarah, 1209, 1262, 1513
  Solomon, 731, 1209, 1309
  Thomas M. A., 946
  Upton, 1273
  Virginia, 1209
  Walter, 1350
  William, 742
  William J., 743
Stoner (Steiner) , Christian, 1378
  Elizabeth, 1378
  Stephen, 1378
Stonesifer, Harry, 734
  Mahlon, 831
  Reuben, 705
Storm, Christena, 894
Storms, John, 1261
Storr, Andrew G., 1022
  Bertha M., 1022, 1023
  Charles, 764
  Charles H., 1022
  Elgie M., 1022
  Grant, 1396
  Henry, 812, 1023
  Henry C., 1022, 1603
  John, 1022
  John D., 1022, 1603
  Mary E., 1022, 1320
  Mary Elizabeth, 1603
  Pauline R., 1022
  Ruth E., 1022
Stotlemyer, George F., 995
  J. Newton, 986
Stottlemyer, Alice V., 748
  C., 738
  Caroline, 1347
  Christopher C., 868
  Clarence B., 748
  Claud U., 749
  Daniel, 748, 749, 951, 952, 984
  David, 748, 749, 952
  David, Jr., 749
  Elias R., 749, 952
  Franklin, 775
  Frederick, 749, 952
  George R., 868
  Henry, 749
  Henry F. C., 748, 749, 952
  Ida L., 748
  Inna M., 749
  Jacob, 952

Jacon, 749
John, 749, 1084, 1374, 1609
John M., 952
Jonathan, 749, 952
Joseph, 749, 810, 952, 1126, 1371
Kesiah, 1448
Leah, 749, 983, 984
Leah A., 952
Lester A., 748
Levi E., 748
Lydia, 749, 887
Lydia A., 748, 952
Margaret, 749, 952
Margaret A. R., 749
Martin, 768
Mary, 952
Mary E., 749
Nancy, 1148, 1373, 1374
Olga D., 749
Rosanna, 749, 951, 952
Rosie, 775
Susan, 862
Walter, 810
Welty, 1606
Welty M., 748
William Hamilton, 748
Worth B., 749
Stottlenger, Jonathan, 862
Stouffer, Benjamin F., 1099, 1107, 1114
D. V., 994
David T., 813
H. C., 1539
Helen T., 798
J. H., 1128
Stout, Julia, 1274
Charles M., 1519
Stover, Catharine, 870
Mollie, 1167
Strailman, Henry M., 1219
Jessie, 1320
Stranp, Ora, 756
Strasburg, Edward, 1221
John Wesley, 1083
Keziah, 1498
Olive, 1221
Solomon, 1498
Straton, Emma J., 1564
Stratton, Rhoda, 1594
Strausburg, Daniel F., 936
Mollie, 936
Strauss, Albert C., 1454
William, 1454
William C., 1454

Strawsberger, Frank S., 1277
Strawsburg, Anna Mary, 1501
Bessie V., 1501
Blanche Pearl, 1501
Cassie, 1501
Edward, 1501
Jacob, 1501
John Wesley, 1501
John, Jr., 1501
Josiah, 1501
Julia, 1501
Lettie O., 1501
Mary Alice Virginia, 1501
Naomi, 1501
Oscar, 1501
Rebecca, 1501
Roland, 1501
Samuel, 1501
Sarah, 1501
Sidney, 1501
William, 1501
William H., 1501
Winfried, 1501
Streams, Israel, 1442
Streit, Jane, 836, 837
Stribling, Carrie, 1473
Strider, Isaac, 1109
Strine, Amos, 1532
Annie, 1532
Benjamin, 1532
Bettie F., 1533
Calvin B., 1533
Catharine, 1500, 1532
Charles Milton, 1533
Floyd, 1533
Frank, 1532
George H., 1532
Isaac, 1532
James William, 1533
Jesse, 1530
John, 1532
John W., 1360
John William, 1532, 1533
Margaret, 1082, 1083
Minnie, 1533
Nannie Florence, 1532
Pierce, 1532
Polly, 1533
Rebecca, 1532
Rhoda E., 1532
Roy, 1530
Russell, 1533
Samuel M., 1532, 1533
Sarah Etta, 1533
Susan, 1532, 1286
Virgie, 1532

Walter Raymond, 1533
William, 1110, 1532
Stringer, Mrs. Lydia
Warfield, 1072
Strobel, Mary G., 786, 963
William D., 787
Strother, Florence J., 1390
Struble, Rebecca K. M., 1489
Stryker, Hattie, 916
Stuart, Charles, 1548
J. E. B., 825
Sheeler, 806
Wm. R., 1212
Stull, Addie B., 1481
Adam, 882, 998, 1410
Amelia M., 1132
Annie T., 950, 1403
Barbara, 998, 1410
Beulah, 1387
Bradley, 1399
C. Spencer, 1145
Caroline S., 1132
Carroll, 1387
Charles A., 950, 1403
Daniel, 950
Daniel E., 1132
Daniel Z., 1010, 1021, 1592
Dennis, 1575
Donald, 1387
Edward, 950, 989, 1049, 1525
Edward Joshua, 998
Effie G., 950, 1403
Eliza, 950
Elsie, 1266, 1301
Ethel, 758
Ethel M., 951
F. Stanley, 950, 1594
F——, 950
Fannie E., 1403
Fleet, 724
Florand I., 950
Florence I., 1403
Frank S., 950, 1403
Frederick A., 950, 1402
Frederick J., 1594
Frederick Stanley, 1402, 1403
Garland Lee, 1215
George, 1023, 1598
Georgianna, 707
Germetta, 950
Glenn, 758
Glenn C., 951
Hannah, 1132

Harold, 1403
Harry C., 950, 1403
Harry C. , 758
Howard D., 1227
Jacob, 950, 1402
Jennette V., 1403
John, 882, 998, 1215, 1410
John A., 1132
Joshua M., 1132
Julian B., 1132
Keefer, 1403
Leander, 761, 989, 999, 1446
Leander D., 1427
Lerah I., 1403
Lewis, 948, 1481
Mary, 1010, 1021, 1592
Michael, 1132
Minnie E., 989, 1525
Nettie T., 1575
Nevin W., 1403
Orange C., 758
Oscar C., 758
Paul, 758
Paul Worthington, 951
Phoebe, 1592
R. C., 950
R. G., 1200, 1286
Reta M., 1403
Reverdy C., 1403
Rhuanna M., 1132
Robert W., 950, 1403
Sophia, 948
Sterling, 1387
Susan, 950
Susanna, 1049
Theodore, 741
Wilhelmina, 1022
Wilhelmina S., 1023, 1598
William, 950
William H., 1132
William M., 1132
Stultz, Anna Mary, 1514
Stunkle, J. Frederick, 891
Stup, Ada L., 1063
   Carrie, 1064
   Charles, 1064
   Charles W., 1063
   Clara A. J., 902
   Curtis, 1063
   David, 1063
   David T., 1063
   Douglas, 1063
   Emanuel, 1063
   Fannie, 1063
   Franklin, 1134

George, 1064
Howard, 1064
Jesse D., 1063
Jessie, 1064
John J., 902
John L., 1063
Jonathan, 1063
Julia, 1064
Mary, 1063, 1064
Mary E., 1063
Maud H., 1064
Miranda, 1064
Randolph, 1063
Raymond, 1064
Rebecca, 1063
Sophia, 1063
Spencer, 908
William, 1063, 1250
Stupe, Catharine E., 796, 797, 1414, 1415
   Daniel, 797, 1415
   Emanuel, 1287
Stutler, Angeline, 1564
Sueor, Mary Catharine, 1309
Suit, S. T., 966
Sulcer, David C., 1173
Sullivan, John W., 956
Sulser, Catharine, 1378
Suman, Edgar D., 1108
   Elizabeth, 1250
   Ida, 1327
   Mary, 1018
   Rachel, 1039
Summers, ——, 1602
   Alta M., 1474
   Alva C. L., 986
   Amanda C. R., 1341
   Amy V., 740, 1579
   Andrew, 1406, 1523
   Andrew J., 775
   Annie E., 761, 986, 999, 1446
   Annie P. A., 1573
   Bertha, 837
   Bertha M., 740, 1579
   Calvin D. H., 986
   Carrie Z., 1341
   Catharine M., 1573
   Catharine Rebecca, 1542
   Catherine, 1468, 1469
   Catherine R., 740, 1579
   Charles, 989
   Charles W., 1474
   Charlotte S. R., 1573
   Chester F., 1474
   Clara, 965, 1382, 1572

Clayton, 955
Clayton Harp, 1077
Cora J., 1077
Cordelia F., 965, 1382, 1572, 1573
David W., 739, 964, 985, 986, 1341, 1572, 1579
Effie L., 1474
Eli, 1382
Eli H., 965
Elizabeth,965, 1382, 1572
Elizabeth A. C., 1382
Emma, 1385
Emma E., 1573
Estella, 740, 1579
Florence V., 1341
George S., 1341
George W., 739, 964, 985, 1340, 1341, 1571, 1578
George W. S., 1573
Gertrude E., 1380
Grayson B., 1474
Guy M., 1474
Harlen H., 1077
Harlom, 790, 967
Hattie B., 740
Hattie D., 1579
Heber, 1609
Henry, 1157
Henry W., 739, 964, 986, 1341, 1382 , 1571-1573, 1579
Ida F., 1341
Isaac J., 1473, 1474
J. Elmer, 985
J. J. Thomas, 1573
J. V., 1335
Jacob, 739, 771, 959, 960, 964, 985, 1340, 1341, 1571, 1578
Jacob V., 739, 964, 986, 1341, 1572, 1579
John, 986, 1469, 1579
John B., 739
John C. L., 740, 1579
John E. M., 986
John F., 759, 760
John H. L., 1341
John T., 964, 1341, 1572
John W., 965
Jonas, 837
Jonas V., 1077
Joshua, 739, 964, 986, 1341, 1542, 1572, 1578, 1579

Joshua H., 1573
Laura C., 1474
Lawson H., 1077
Leatha E., 1580
Lewis E., 1382
Lidy B. I., 1341
Lottie L., 740, 1579
Louis E., 965, 1572
Mallissa A., 740, 1579
Margaret A. M., 1573
Margaret C., 1573
Mary A. C., 1382
Mary A. S., 965, 1572
Mary B., 1580
Mary C., 1474
Mary E., 740, 1313, 1579
Mary Lizzie, 1077
Mary M., 1474
Mildred B., 965
Milton A., 1374
Milton V., 739, 740,
    1578-1580
Minnie C. V., 986
Mollie M., 1341
Morry, 775
Myra, 1406, 1523
Nelson D., 1341
Philip W., 965, 1382,
    1571-1573
Samuel, 739, 986, 1473,
    1474, 1579
Samuel M., 964 , 1340,
    1341, 1572
Samuel P., 1341
Samuel P. D., 1573
Sarah Frances, 1077
Sarah J., 1341
Seymore, 897
Simon P., 965, 1382, 1572
Susan E., 1474
Sylvester J., 1580
Vada M., 1579
Veda M., 740
Vernon A., 1580
Walter S., 740, 1579
Wesley T. J., 1341
William, 1313
William C., 965
William E., 1255, 1341
William H., 964, 965, 1382,
    1473, 1474, 1572
Sumwalt, John, 773
Sunday, Columbus, 1418
Sundaygill, Nina May, 1355
    Stanley, 1355
Sundergill, Edna, 1153

Suter, Henry, 977
Suters, Charles W. , 942
Sutherland,W. T., 944
Sutro, E., 1488
Sutton, R. M., 1128
Swadner, Jane R., 1118
Swamley, Elisha, 1122
    S. J., 799
Swan, Thomas, 1064
Swartz, John, 1025
    Joseph, 1564
Sweadner, Lydia, 1508, 1509
Swearingen, Rebecca, 824
    Van, 787
Sweeney, Anna Maria, 1527
Swigard, Annie, 993, 1147
Swinard, Phoebe, 771
Swoduer, Fanny, 1059
Swomley, Annie, 1152
    Anthony C., 1152
    Asa, 1152
    Daniel, 806, 1152
    Eldred, 1152
    Elisha, 1152
    Emma, 1152
    Fanny, 1152
    Henry, 1152
    Kate D., 1152
    Lydia Ann, 1152
    Mahlon, 1152, 1468
    Mahlon J., 1152
    Mattie Virginia, 1152
    Miriam A., 1152
    Nettie Rebecca, 1152
    Sally, 1152
Swope, Daniel, 1451
    Henry, 1452
    John, 1451
    Samuel, 1451
Sykes, John W., 1323
Symmons, Lydia Ann, 842
Tabb, Edith, 1116
    John, 1116
Tabler, Abraham, 1136, 1539
    Andrew J., 1217
    Andrew Jackson,1136,1539
    Anna, 1136
    Catherine Ann, 1136
    Charles, 1136
    Christian, 1136, 1539
    Ella Belle, 1540
    Ezra, 1136, 1539
    George, 933
    George S., 1136
    Harriet Irene, 1137
    Harriet Smith, 1136

Irene Alberta, 1136
Jacob, 1136, 1539
John, 1136, 1539
John Francis, 1137
John H., 1469
John W., 1136
Levi A., 1136
Lewis, 1136, 1539
Lloyd, 1540
Mary Elizabeth, 1136
Mary Margaret., 1137
Molly Catherine, 1540
Rachel E., 1137
Robert Lee, 1137
Washington, 1136, 1539
William, 1136, 1539
William H., 1136
Taft, William H., 841, 927,
    962
Taggart, Alfred, 850
Talbot, Charles, 916
    Howard, 1607
    Nancy, 915, 916
    Polly, 990
Taney, Edward, 802
    Joseph, 1235, 1515
    Roger B., 1613
    Roger Brooke, 744
Tarboe, John, 836
Tasker, Benjamin, 1026
Taughinbaugh, Alice M.,
    1012
Taylor, Eleanor E., 1370
    Frank I., 1202
    Hamilton, 1426
    John W., 1370
    Olivia, 916
    Richard, 1216
    William S., 1072
    Zachary, 1324
Temple, Samuel, 1289
Thomas, A. D., 912
    Abba L., 1432, 1433
    Abbie L., 1015
    Ada E., 1365
    Adaline, 958
    Adelaide S., 1365
    Agnes A., 958
    Alma, 1219
    Alpheus D., 1346
    Alpheus Douglas, 957
    Amos, 1413
    Amos S., 1412
    Ann M., 1165, 1166
    Ann Margaret, 1364
    Ann Mary, 1431, 1528

Ann Rebecca, 1349 1431, 1528
Anna B., 958
Annie, 1119, 1440
Annie E., 1207
Annie M., 1066, 1441
Archie A., 958
Austin K., 1367
Barbara, 1364, 1431, 1528
Benjamin, 1412
Bernard S., 1016
Bernard W., 1365
Bettie, 1018, 1365
C. F., 711
C. M., 1571
C. N., 927
C. William, 958
Caroline, 780
Carrie H., 1441
Catharine, 1378
Catherine, 957, 1431, 1528
Catherine F., 1441
Catherine G., 1365
Catherine Susan, 1431
Cephas M., 1015, 1016, 1366 1431, 1493, 1494, 1528
Charles, 1016, 1064
Charles A., 1366 , 1431, 1494, 1528
Charles E., 1088, 1346
Charles F., 1015, 1066 , 1440
Charles G., 1412
Charles Silas, 957, 1345, 1346
Charlott, 1567
Charlotte, 980, 1003, 1012, 1043, 1165, 1364, 1402, 1406, 1440
Charlotte E., 1412
Christian, 1364
Christian H., 1365
Clarence C., 1432
Clarence S., 1015
Claud E., 1016
Clayborn A., 1433
Clayonia, 786
Clifford, 863
Clinton C., 1015
Clyde E., 1432
Cornelius, 1366
Curtis W., 1015, 1366, 1538
Curtis W., 1431-1433, 1494, 1528

Cyrus S., 1433
Daisy E., 1346
Daniel B., 1441
Daniel D., 1412
Daniel P., 1015, 1416, 1432
Darius, 804, 805
David, 1018, 1364
David D., 1060
David O., 1205
Dolly, 1620
Dorothy Edith, 731
Edgar L., 1433
Edna M., 1433
Ella V., 1432
Eleanor S., 1015
Eli, 1364
Eliza M., 1015
Elizabeth, 1079, 1349
Ellen, 1080
Elmer E., 1433
Emily H., 1365
Emma A., 1018, 1346, 1365
Ethel Hargett, 1366
Etta J., 1433
Eva, 1015
Evelyn S., 1413
Ezra, 957
Ezra Michael, 957, 1345, 1346
Flora May, 1604
Francis, 787
Francis Granville, 1018, 1365
Franklin, 1402
Franklin C., 1441
Franklin G., 1440
G. F., 1434
G. Leicester, 1433, 1434
G. Leicester, Jr., 1434
Gabriel, 1015, 1364, 1378, 1431, 1440, 1528
Geneva E., 1432
George, 775, 1165, 1166, 1364, 1365, 1406, 1413, 1431, 1432, 1440, 1523, 1528
George C., 1015, 1433
George Franklin, 1432
George H., 958, 1494
George Leicester, 1432
George M., 1018, 1365
George P., 1364
Gertrude, 1266, 1301, 1507
Gertrude I., 1365
Grace H., 1441
Harry L., 1307, 1412, 1413

Helen Gertrude, 1346
Helen I., 1367
Henry, 1365, 1366, 1378, 1431, 1494, 1528
Hester C., 1064
Hiram, 1362
Hiram G., 1297, 1366
Irvin C., 1433
Irving H., 1367
J. B., 1412
J. F., 1056
J. F. , 1402
J. Fenton, 1018, 1364, 1365
J. Fenton, Jr., 1365
J. Franklin, 1043, 1366, 1407, 1432, 1434
J. G., 731
Jacob, 1037
Jacob D., 1349, 1604
Jacob L., 1349
Jennie, 1366
John, 980, 1003, 1015, 1364, 1365, 1378, 1431, 1432
John B., 993, 1412
John E., 1349
John Franklin, 1431, 1433, 1494, 1528
John H., 1359
John J., 1365
John Travers, 854
John W., 1416, 1432-1434
Jonathan A., 1015
Joseph, 1238, 1349, 1366, 1431, 1528
Joseph F., 1494
Joseph G., 1349
Josiah S., 1015, 1432
Julia E., 1432
Kathern, 1349
Kathern E., 1349
Katy C., 958
Lee C., 1432
Levi, 1412
Lewis E., 1015
Lewis M., 786
Lillian, 1367
Lottie, 1413
Lucille M., 1428
Lucy, 1366
M. Edith, 1016
Mabel L., 1346
Margaret, 1364
Margaret E., 1412
Margaret M., 1365

Maria E., 1015, 1198
Maria Susan, 1400, 1401
Mary, 1090, 1095, 1349, 1364, 1431, 1528, 1543
Mary A. , 1043
Mary Ann, 1496
Mary B., 1365
Mary C., 1026, 1027
Mary E., 958, 987, 1015, 1433
Mary Ellen, 1561
Mary F., 1349
Michael, 1015, 1431, 1528
Mildred, 1413
Mrs. C. F., 1321
Nannie A., 1349
Nellie Amanda, 1346
Nellie B., 1016
Nellie E., 1412
Nellie Leona, 1060
Nellie S., 1413
Nina V., 1346
Nina Virginia, 1346
Nora E., 1346
Otho, 931, 1027
Otho B., 931
Paul Crum, 1346
Paul S., 1433
Peter, 1015, 1198, 1207, 1431, 1494, 1528
Philip, 1601
Ralph G., 1433
Ralph J., 1016
Rebecca, 1366
Robert, 1077
Robert L., 1349
Roy Zachariah, 1366
Russell C., 1433
Ruth T., 1016
S. D., 829
S. Elizabeth, 1016
S. F., 1412
Samuel, 1027, 1152, 1364, 1528, 1597
Samuel C., 1431, 1494
Samuel Cornelius, 1528, 1529
Samuel D., 1018, 1019, 1135, 1365
Sarah A., 1027
Sarah Ella, 1440
Sophia, 931, 1364
Stephen, 1365, 1431, 1528
Stephen A., 1366 , 1431, 1432, 1434, 1494, 1528
Susan, 1366, 1431, 1494, 1528
Susan N., 958
Susan R., 1015
Susan Rebecca, 1015, 1432
Thelma E., 1413
Thomas, 1494
Thomas L., 1349
Thomas M., 1366, 1431
Valentine, 1364, 1378, 1440
Viola, 1366
Viola I., 1010, 1380
Virginia, 731
Wade Purcell, 1346
William, 1004
William H., 1092, 1364, 1365, 1440, 1441, 1494
Zachariah, , 1428, 1431, 1528
Zachariah G., 1365, 1366
Zacharias G., 1010, 1494
Thompson, Cassandra, 827
Charlotte D., 767, 768
Edward, 1426
J. A., 1491
John, 1539
Lloyd, 903
Marion, 1310
Richard, 768
Robert, 768
W. S., 1045, 1303
William, 1539
William J., 1475
Zan, 1054
Thorne, Walter H., 806
Thrasher, Albert, 879
Anna Margaret, 880
Annie, 851
Benjamin, 879, 880
Benjamin Albert, 880
John, 879
John Robert, 880
Margaret A., 880
Martha Theresa, 880
Robert K., 880
Robert Knight, 880
Thomas, 879
Thomas Lakin, 880
Thomas Souder, 879, 880
William, 879, 1044, 1483
William Johnstone, 880
Tibballs, Clara Birdell, 1142
Tice, Annie, 1567
Tidings, Elizabeth, 920
Tiernan, Ann, 824, 825
Charles B., 824
Luke, 824, 825
Patrick, 824
Paul, 824
Tiffany, L. McLane, 1213
Tilghman, Cecil, 1183
Floyd, 1183
Matthew, 1026
Tobrey, Mary, 763
Toby, Catherine, 886
Tome, Jacob, 721
Tomes, Lydia, 844
Samuel, 988
Toms, Abraham, 903
Addie E., 1028
Albert F., 1524
Alta J., 958, 1524
Annie M. E., 1028
Anzonettie, 958, 1524
Carrie S., 1524
Catharine, 904
Catherine, 1196
Claud E., 1373, 1521, 1522
Daniel, 867, 1470
Dorothy Gaver, 1028
Edgar R., 1524
Edna M., 959
Edward A., 747, 911, 1028, 1375
Elizabeth, 747, 955, 1086
Ella, 955
Ella C., 958, 1524
Ella E., 747
Elmer J., 1370, 1522
Emma, 959
Ezra, 746, 955, 958, 1176, 1374, 1522-1524
Fannie, 955
Fannie C., 958, 1524
Fannie M., 747, 1176
Flora M., 1522
Franklin G., 1028
Gail, 1524
George, 1391
George D., 747, 877, 955, 958, 1175, 1524
Gertrude, 1290
Gertrude E., 1028
Grayson E., 1524
Hannah, 861, 1359, 1381, 1541
Harry L., 960
Hubert W., 960
Isaiah E., 1522, 1524
Isaiah J., 1028 , 1580
Isiah E., 958
Jacob, 955, 1028

Jacob, Jr., 958, 1521-1524
Jacob, Sr.,958, 1521, 1523
Jay W., 898
Jennie, 1522
John, 903-905
John H., 958, 1521, 1522,
    1524
Joseph Harold, 1028
Joshua, 958, 1522, 1524
Josiah, 1522
Keefer S., 898
Laura, 911
Laura V., 746, 955, 958,
    1375, 1524
Lemuel, 960
Lemuel F., 955
Lemuel V., 747, 958, 1524
Lester A., 898
Lydia, 767, 960, 961
Mabel A., 1522
Mary E., 958, 1374, 1522,
    1524, 1580
Mary Estelle, 1028
Maynard G., 1524
Mehrl A., 1524
Millard F., 747, 955, 958,
    1523, 1524, 1617
Minnie, 1110
Nettie, 746, 955
Nora E., 1522
Norman R., 1524
O. J., 898
Orhum B., 959
Oscar R., 960
Otho J., 746, 955
Paul D., 1524
Raymond E., 898
Ruth G., 959
S. Ellen, 1522
Samuel, 767, 911, 1023,
    1375, 1598
Susan, 1271
Taylor, 1532
Vada C., 959
William, 904, 1196
William A., 959
William E., 1522
Willie E., 1028
Topper, James T., 1039
Townley, Mary, 940
Townsend, O. R., 1615
    Oscar R., 1614
Towson, Nathan, 1072
Tracey, Mary, 1377
Trail, Anna M., 722
    Annie E., 963

Ariana Teresa, 722
Arie T., 919
Arthur, 722
Beatrice, 1337
Bertha, 722
C. E. , 1592
Charles, 1314
Charles B., 709
Charles Bayard, 722,
    1336-1338
Charles Bayard, Jr., 1337
Charles E., 853, 900, 1018,
    1336, 1364, 1368
Charles Edward, 720, 722,
    1337
Charlotte, 770
Edward, 720
Florence, 722, 1337
Grace Winebrener, 1337
Henry, 722, 1338
Mary, 720
Theresa McElfresh, 1337
Trayer, Eliza Catherine, 1152
    Jacob, 1152
    Mart, 1531
Trego, Mary E. , 1553
    William, 1553
Tressler, Jerome, 715
Tribby, Lillia, 879
Tritapoe, Ada V., 1173
    Alvira E., 1173
    Charles W., 1172, 1299
    Earl E., 1173
    Edward H., 1173
    Eliza, 1299
    Ella, 1299
    Erma M., 1173
    Florence, 1299
    George A., 1299
    George H., 1172, 1298, 1299
    Gertrude A. , 1173
    Harry E., 1131, 1173
    Harry G., 1131, 1172, 1173
    Irma M., 1131
    John, 1172, 1299
    John L., 1299
    Margaret, 1299
    Margaret A., 1172
    Margaret Elizabeth, 1299
    Mary, 1299
    Mary E., 1172
    Michael, 1172, 1298
    Samuel E., 1172, 1173, 1299
    Susan E., 1131, 1173
    Velma G., 1173
Trite, Peter, 1613

Trout, Abigail Elizabeth,
    1200
    Annie, 878
    Belle, 1200, 1507
    Charles H., 1199, 1200
    Claude, 1200
    David, 1200
    Genoa, 1200
    George, 1200
    Glenn, 1200
    Grover Cleveland, 1200
    Jacob, 800
    John, 800, 1199
    Joseph, 796, 1415
    Margaret, 1200
    Melvin, 1200
    Norman, 1200
    Sally, 1200
    Samuel, 1200
    Wilbur, 1200
    William, 1200
    Wilmer Harry, 1200
Troxell, Anna Elizabeth, 734
    Catherine, 734
    Charles, 1506
    Elizabeth, 734
    Emma, 1231
    Florence, 1588
    Florida, 734
    Francis Katherine, 734
    Frederick, 734, 1336
    George, 816
    Henry, 830
    Irene, 734
    James W., 734, 773
    James Wilson, 734
    Jemima, 815, 816
    John, 1239
    Joseph, 734
    Marian, 734
    Martin D., 1516
    Mary, 734
    Naomi, 734
    Peter, 816
    Samuel, 1588
    Susan, 781
    Susan M., 1336
    Susan Rebecca, 734
    Thomas, 734
    Thomas Wilson, 734
    William, 749, 952
    William Barbour Russell,
        734
Trueman, Julia, 747, 1254
Truit, Charles E., 1249
Trundle, Ann Virginia, 1045,

1302
C. M., 1027
Charlotte, 920
H. Clayton, 1450
Hattie, 1060
Kate, 958
Lewis, 1045, 1303
Newton, 1207
William, 1045, 1303
Tucker, Charles, 1444
Daniel, 771
Henry St. George, 936, 938, 939
Laura V., 771
Milton, 1454
Rosa Virginia, 1444
Ruth, 1454
Turnbull, Charles, 1466
Turner, J. H., 994
Jane, 1028, 1029
Louis, 1136
Margaret, 1072
William, 956
Turney, Josephine, 975
Turrill, Howard F., 1264
Twain, Mark, 1331
Tyler, Annie L., 1399
D. Grafton, 1399
E. B., 1242
Edward Murray, 1398
Henrietta D., 711
Jessie M., 1399
John, 1398
Lucy A., 1399
Mary, 1398
Mary C., 1399
Mary Jane, 1399
Nellie C., 1399
Robert F., 1399
Robert Lee, 1398, 1399
Ruth R., 1399
Samuel, 1398, 1399
Samuel L., 1399
Susannah, 1184
Thomas, 1044
Thomas B., 1399
William, 720, 1376, 1398
William H., 1399
Tyson, B., 802
C.Dorsey, 1599
Catharine, 1599
Charles B., 1599
Elizabeth, 1599
G. Warring, 1173
George Waring, 1598, 1599
Henry, 1599

Jacob, 1599
Jacob B., 1598
Jonathan, 1598, 1599
John S., 1212
Mary, 1599
Ulery, Mrs. Rachel, 1298, 1495
Ulrich, George, 1134
John, 1324
Umberger, Amanda, 1306
Edith, 1306
Elizabeth, 1306
Ida, 1306
Isadora, 1306
Jennie, 1306
Jesse, 1306
John, 1306
John S., 1306
Johnnie, 1306
Lewis, 1533
Mary, 1306
Michael, 1306
Mollie, 1306
Nellie, 1306
Phoebe, 1306
Susan, 1306
Vinnie Elissa, 1306
William T., 1306
Umstead, Susan, 1119
Unger, E. C., 1144
Unkefer, Abdiel, 1449
Unverzagt, Charles H., 732
Daniel W., 732
Henry, 732
James T., 732
John, 732
John L., 732
Urey, Margaret, 1557
Urner, Catherine, 732
Eugenia, 992
Francis Hammond, 992
George Floyd, 992
Hammond, 991, 992
Helen Agnes, 992
J. Paul, 992
Jonas, 732, 733, 990, 1076, 1239
Joseph Walker, 992
Laura, 733, 992, 1239
Martin Jonas, 992
Milton G., 732, 818, 824, 905, 992, 1076, 1337
Milton G., Jr., 992
Milton George, 990, 991
Mollie T., 732
Olivia G., 732
Samuel, 732, 990, 1076

Samuel Amos, 732, 733
Susan E., 732
Walter G., 991
William J. , 1076
Utterback, Annie, 1418
Columbus, 1418
Cora, 1418
Edith M., 1418
Edward J., 1417, 1418
Ella, 1418
Ernest E., 1418
Garne L., 1418
Hazel B., 1418
James F., 1418
John L., 1418
John N., 1417, 1418
Lester I., 1418
Lewis, 1417
Lillian R., 1418
Mamie, 1418
Martha, 1418
Nellie V., 1418
Susie, 1418
Temple A., 1418
Thomas W., 1418
William W., 1418
Uttz, Ann Catherine, 747, 1254
Utz, Ada, 863
Addie Lucinda, 731
Annie, 731, 1309
Catherine, 731
Celia, 1263
Charles M., 731
Charles Monroe, 730-732
Charles Monroe, Jr., 732
Cora Alice, 731
Daniel, 730, 731
Dora Edith, 731
Elizabeth, 731, 1318
Ella, 1515
Eve, 731
Francis M., 731
Harvey, 731
Henry, 731
Isaac, 731
John, 731, 1377
John H., 886
John Samuel, 731
Joseph H., 731
Laura, 1263
Margie, 731
Mary, 731
Mary Ellen, 731
Norman, 731
Ruth, 731

Samuel H., 730, 731
Samuel Shriner, 732
Sarah, 731
Silas Kelley, 731
Susie Lucinda, 732
Valentine, A. J., 930
A. Ellsworth, 1588
Albert, 1587, 1588
Bertha, 1588
Clarence L., 1587, 1588
Dora, 1588
Elias T., 1587
Ethel L. V., 1588
Frances, 1588
Frederick E., 1588
G. H., 1587
Grayson H., 1231
H. A., 1491
Harry E., 1588
Ira, 856
Jacob, 1587
James, 1587, 1214
John J., 741
Josiah, 1164
Lewis, 1587
Maggie Cordelia, 1231
Mary E., 762, 829
Martha Ellen, 1164
Martin E., 1588
Mary, 1600
Mary E., 1617, 1618
Minerva D., 1587
Nathen L., 1588
Rose, 1588
Samuel, 1618, 733, 829
Sarah, 1587
Susan A., 1588
Sylvester, 1587
William, 1587, 1588
Van-Hulsteyn, J. C., 1428
Vanfossen, Arnold, 1559
Edith, 1476, 1477
Van Fossen, Levi, 1343
Van Sant, Ella, 1556
Ellen V., 1343
Emily, 1344
Moses, 1344
Van Wright, John, 1355
Vananda, James, 890
Mary, 889, 890
Vance, Charles, 895
Vanmeter, Smith, 1400
Vaughan, Elizabeth, 1141
Richards, 1141
Vaughn, Elizabeth, 1140
Veant, Aaron, 1564

Daniel J. L., 1564
John, 1564
Samuel, 828, 1618
Veitch, John W., 1563
Vennegn, Margaret, 1559
Vicers, William, 1306
Vickers, George, 721
Vilas, William F., 1365
Vincel, Catherine, 1483
George, 1173
John, 1483
Sarah E., 1172, 1173
Vincent, King, 943
Vinsell, Polly, 1435
Virts, Cornelius, 875
Cornelius William, 1094
Cornelius, Sr, 1094
Edgar C., 1094
Harvey Grimm, 1094
John, 1313
Nellie May, 1094
William, 1313
Zona C., 1094
von Schaeffer, Peter, 1254
von Schaffer, Peter, 747
Von Steinwyck, Bertha, 1245
Vosburg, Hattie H., 1431
Wachtel, Alice M., 961
Annie L. C., 960
Daniel, 959
Daniel J., 959
Elizabeth, 959, 1299
George W., 767, 959, 961
Hattie V., 961
Jacob, 959
Jacob S., 959
Lowlie Arbelon, 961
Margie Estella, 960
Martin Luther, 961
Mary, 959
Mary Ellen, 959
Rebecca, 959
Solomon, 959
Susan, 959
William Solomon, 961
Wachter, Ada C., 1132
Ada S., 1399
Adda E., 1594
Alice, 1283
Allen, 1399
Alma Rebecca, 1226
Amanda, 724, 1226
Amanda R., 1283
Andrew J., 1132, 1226,
1489, 1593
Ann Susan, 725

Augustus, 746
Bernice K., 725
Bessie R., 1489
Caleb, 1307
Caleb L., 1132, 1226,
1489, 1593
Carl, 1227
Caroline S., 1132
Carrie S., 1419
Carroll D., 725
Catharine E., 988, 1132,
1226, 1283, 1489,
1593
Charles L., 724, 725
Charles Vaughan, 725
Clara E., 1283
Daisy S. V., 1594
Daniel, 1399
Daniel H., 1132, 1226,
1283, 1399, 1489,
1593
Dennis J., 1132, 1226,
1283, 1489, 1593
Doctor R., 1132, 1226,
1283, 1489, 1593
Dona E., 1403, 1594
Dona G., 725
E. C., 1538
E. E., 1463
Edgar B., 725
Edgar L., 746
Edith M., 725
Effie E., 725
Elijah R., 1368
Ella M., 1227
Ellen M., 1227
Elliott L., 1227
Elmer R., 1489
Emma S., 1132
Esta M., 1368
Ezra C., 1132, 1226,
1419, 1489, 1593
Ezra O., 1283
Fannie P., 725
Fanny, 1294
Florence, 1616
George M., 725
George Marshall, 1132
George Reginald, 1132
Grayson P., 746
Gusta S., 1594
Guy Roscoe, 725
Harriet S., 1010, 1021,
1592
Harvey E., 1132
Hazel Marie, 1132

Henry M., 725
Howard C., 724, 1226
Ida M., 1283, 1399
Illie E., 1403
Jacob, 724, 1141, 1225
Jacob H., 1132, 1226, 1283,
    1489, 1593
John H., 724, 1226, 1283
John P., 1132, 1226, 1283,
    1403, 1489, 1593
Joshua, 1132
Julia A., 1419
Leander, 724, 725, 1141
Leslie D., 1227
Lewis, 927, 1284
Lewis F, 1283, 1489, 1593
Lewis F., 1131, 1226
Lillie E., 1594
Lloyd, 1022
Lloyd W., 1132
Luther, 1319, 1526
Luther H., 724, 1226
Luther H. , 1225
Lycurgus M., 724, 1226
M. L., 1402
Mamie L., 1489
Mamie S. E., 1227
Margaret S., 1603
Maria, 724, 725, 1225
Maria C., 1108
Marian E. C., 1283
Marietta, 1403
Marseles, 1250
Martin, 1108
Martin L., 1227
Mary Ann, 997, 998, 1410
Mary C., 1283
Mary E., 725, 1226
Mattie H., 1227
Maynard S., 746
Michael, 706, 724, 725,
    1225, 1226
Millard R., 1227
Milton, 998, 1410
Modena, 1484
Mrs. Eliza A. C., 1399
Philip, 988, 998, 1131,
    1226, 1283, 1410, 1489,
    1593
Philip, Jr., 1131, 1283,
    1489, 1593
Raymond H., 1594

Rena B., 1227
Reverdy A., 1132
Rosie C., 1489
Samuel, 1010, 1021, 1592
Stella M., 1489
Stiner R., 724, 1226
Susanna R., 1131, 1226,
    1283, 1489, 1593
Thomas J., 724, 1226
Thomas M. , 1132
Thomas Marshall, 1132
Uriah, 1010, 1021,1592
Victorine E., 725
Viola C., 1227
Virginia, 1368
Wesley A., 1132, 1226,
    1227, 1283, 1489, 1593
Wesley V., 1227
Wad, Emanuel, 1428
Wade, James P., 1045, 1303
Waesche, Catharine, 728
    Charles, 728
    Charles A., 1437
    Clinton, 728
    Daisy F., 728
    Donald, 728
    Edna, 728
    George, 728, 1437
    George E., 728
    Henry, 727, 728, 1437
    James T., 1437
    James Theodore, 728
    John, 728, 1437
    Joseph, 728, 1437
    Leonard R., 1437
    Leonard Randolph, 727, 728
    Margaret B., 1438
    Mary A., 728
    Mary C., 1438
    Mary Catharine, 1437
    Phoebe Grace, 728
    Rapold, 728
    Repold, 1437
    Russell R., 728
    William, 728, 1437
Wagaman, Amelia, 717
    Anna, 1541
    David, 717
    David A., 717
    Edith A., 717, 1063
    Elizabeth, 1541
    Fanny, 717

Flora E., 717
Frank, 1541
Howard R., 717
James, 1541
John, 717, 1541
Laura E., 717, 770
Lycurgus T., 717
Mary, 717, 1541
Mary A., 717
Morris R., 717
Rachael, 717
Richard, 717, 770, 1063
Samuel, 1541
Thomas E., 717
William, 717
William G., 717
Wagner, Alice, 1534
    Amelia J., 1141
    George, 1155
    John, 1534
    Joseph E., 1450
    Joseph F., 990
    Kate, 990
    Margaret E., 1449-1451
    Rachel, 1051, 1216, 1217
    William H., 1237
Waille, John, 1298
    Louisa, 1298
Walburn, James, 922
Walcott, Annie S., 792
    Harrison, 792
Walcutt, Annie S., 1251
Waldeck, Margaretta A., 1418
Waldermott, Sarah, 1563
Walk, F., 1098
Walker, Alice C., 1281
    Alice Catherine, 1272
    Basil, 1443
    Charles D., 710
    Charlotte, 862, 863, 1272
    Daisy W., 1497
    Edward, 863, 1272
    Eleanor Jennett, 1272
    Elisha, 1271, 1272
    Fannie J., 1497
    Francis, 1271, 1272
    George, 1271
    Hallie, 710, 881
    Hester, 1273
    J. C., 1008, 1281, 1466,
        1477
    Jacob, 1271

James, 710, 1272
James E., 881, 1357, 1562
James Edward, 709, 710
Jane R., 1118
Jane Rebecca, 1272
Jemima Florence, 1272
Jennie C., 1497
Jesse, 1271, 1272
Jesse Clinton, 1272
John C., 1008
John Calvin, 1271-1273
Lizzie E., 1497
Louise, 1273
Lydia A. N., 1272
Mary, 1272
Mary E., 1272
Nancy, 1443
Nettie May, 1497
Rebecca, 1272
Reuben, 1272
Rhoda, 1272, 1466
Sarah, 1272
William, 724, 828, 1272, 1618
William Norris, 1272
William R., 1497
William W., 709, 710 , 1461
Willie, 1497
Willie Anna, 710
Wallace, Albert, 981
Arther, 1511
Charles, 1511
E. A., 1548
Elizabeth, 981
Grafton, 981
Lew, 1264, 1354, 1590
R., 1033
Wallis, Albert, 982, 1282
Albert A., 1282
Albert E., 1282, 1283
Albert Grafton, 1283
Albert R., 1283
Elizabeth R., 1283
Margaret, 1282
Samuel, 1282
Severn Teackle, 1213
Walsh, William, 1559
Walter, Agnes, 965
Alice V., 982
Aloysius, 965
Ambrose, 965

Anselm, 965
Bernard, 965
Bertie E., 982
Catherine, 1324
Charles D., 966
Charles G., 965, 966, 982
Edward H., 982
Ella, 965
Fanny, 966
Florence M., 982
Francis J., 1100
George M., 965
Jacob W., 982
Jennie, 965
Jerome, 965
John, 965, 981
John S., 965
Joseph, 965
Lewis C., 982
Mary, 965
Robert, 965
Sarah, 1324
Sarah C., 982
Simon, 965
Stanislaus, 965
Vincent, 965
William B., 965
William F, 966
Walters, John, 1274
Waltman, P. T., 799
Peter, 883
Walton, Annie, 1286
Waltz, Alice Susan, 1273
Dessie Caroline, 1274
Elizabeth, 1273
Ellen, 1273
Emily J., 1511
Enoch, 1007, 1499, 1511
Enoch Joseph, 1273
Isaac, 1239, 1273
Jane, 1273
Jemima, 1273
Jesse, 1273
John, 966, 1273
Leonard E., 1274
Lewis, 1273
Margaret C., 1273
Marshall E., 1273
Mollie, 1513
Norman C., 1274
Ranson W., 1274
Rinehart, 1273

Samuel, 874
Sarah, 1229
Sarah A., 1273
Solomon, 1273
Sophia, 1239
Upton, 947, 1136, 1219
Upton R., 1182, 1273
Wampler, Francis, 860
Ward, Elizabeth, 1287
Julia, 835
Mary Helen, 1113
Singleton, 1486
William H., 798
Wardlaw, Helen, 919
Warehime, Dorothy Whipp, 1396
Mary Emma, 1395
O. C., 1473
Oliver Cornelius, 1395, 1396
Oliver W., 1395
Warfield, Abraham, 1318
Ann, 1071, 1520
Carrie E., 1540
Edward A., 1384
Edwin, 708, 714, 940
Elinore, 940
Eliza, 1086
Fanny L., 762
George, 1152
John, 940
Laura, 839
Luther, 1540
Mary, 1462
Perrigrene, 1449
S. D., 1049, 1497
Thomas, 1263
Warner, Addison M., 1081
Annie, 922
Anthony, 719
C. Anderson, 718-720
Carrie, 1081
Celina, 1370
Charles, 1009
Charles A., 718, 719
Clara R., 1011
Daniel M., 1082
David, 1081, 1514
David M., 1081
Elias, 1011
Eliza, 719
Elmer, 1492

Elmer C., 1081
Emanuel, 1081
Emily S., 719
Gardner, 719
George B., 1081
George C., 1081
Griswold E., 1582
Griswold Elliott, 1583
Guilford T., 720
Hamell, 719
Henrietta, 1583
Henrietta W., 1582
Isaac, 719
Jacob, 719
John, 761, 844, 999, 1060,
    1447, 1501
Joseph, 820, 1370
Laurean H., 720
Leslie T., 1081
Levi, 719
M. G., 1081
M. T., 1231
Margaret, 1081
Margaret H, 720
Martha, 1181
Penrose, 719
Rebecca J., 719
Robley A., 719
Salina, 1373
Selina, 1377
Susan, 819, 820
Upton E., 1081
William, 719
Warren, George, 742
Warrenfeltz, Annie E., 1467
C. F. S., 868
Caroline, 727, 1467
Catharine, 727
Charles E., 1467
Charles F. S., 726
Christina, 727, 1616
Christine, 882, 1588
Daniel, 726, 1348, 1541
Daniel P., 1467
Daniel T., 726
Elizabeth, 727
Eva Ann, 726, 1348 , 1617
Ezra, 748
Ezra A., 1467
Frank, 1467
George M., 726
Hannah, 727, 738

Henry M., 726, 868
Jacob, 727
Jacob W., 726 , 1467
John, 726, 727
John G., 726
Joshua, 1477
Josiah J., 726
Joshua P., 1467
Julia, 727
Lydia A., 748
Magdalena, 727
Margaret S., 727
Mary, 727, 1467
Mary A. E., 726
Mary Elizabeth, 1541
Mary J., 1545
Mary Jane, 727
Peter, 727
Philip, 727, 1467
Philip F., 726
Sarah, 726, 727, 1467
Solomon, 1467
Susan, 727, 1541
Uriah, 727, 1545
Washabaugh, Upton, 962
Washburn, Etta, 1130
Washington, George, 904, 1068,
    1205, 1232, 1477
John H., 1228
Wasky, Eli C., 1015
Wasler, Jonas, 1336
Waters, Ann F., 838
Ann Francis, 913
Ann P., 1448
Anna, 1574
Caroline, 1562
Carrie E., 913
Catherine A., 913
Charles, 1128, 1562
Charles C., 896, 1129
Charles E., 913
Eleanor, 1004
G. W., 913
Greenberry, 1469
Guy P., 913
Hannah H., 1128
Ignatius, 1448
Irene C., 1562
James, 838, 877, 913
James K., 896, 913, 994,
    1128, 1616
James Somerset, 896

Joel, 1069, 1461
John C., 913
John S., 1129
John T., 1128
Joseph G., 1574
Margaret, 758, 1128
Martha, 975
Mary A., 913
Mary E, 875
Mary E., 877, 913
Mary Elizabeth, 1554,
    1596
Nathaniel, 1073
Peter S., 913
Rachel, 1128
Richard, 896, 1004, 1128
S. R., 1128
Sallie, 1072
Sarah, 1128
Sarah Ann, 1448
Somerset R., 896, 1128
Susan, 848
Thomas, 1072
Ulysess, 1306
William L., 913
Watkins, Alice Olivia, 724
Bradley, 723
Denton, 878
Ernest, 724
Gassaway, 1216
George, 858
Joseph, 1216
Joseph L., 1054
Mazie Noreen, 724
Morris, 723
Noah, 1228
Ray Mount, 724
Sally Virginia, 724
Samuel, 723
Vernon T., 723, 724
William Thomas, 723, 724
Watson, Annie E., 718
Blanche C., 718
D. Steward, 718
Eliza, 718
Elizabeth M., 718
Emily, 737
Eugene A., 1565
Garland Brown Harwood,
    1565
George, 718
Grace, 1565

James, 718
James G., 718
Jennie Lee, 1305
John, 718
John M., 718
Laura V., 1565
Lyndon, 1565
Mollie, 1227
Oscar Lee, 1565
Robert, 718
Thomas S., 1565
Wade B., 1565
Watts, Janett Rogers, 1417
John Q., 1443
Ways, William H., 1010
Weagley, Vallietta S., 1161
Weams, William, 1225
Weant, Iva, 1517
Weast, Hiram, 1272
Weault, Alice, 1181
Weaver, Calvin, 955
Henry, 1569
Margaret, 1104, 1569
Mary, 798, 1124
Webb, Annie, 922
George W., 1152
Henry Randall, 1233
Joseph, 1231
Margaret, 1306
Mary Addison, 1233
Weber, Philip, 871
Webster, Ada S., 775, 1287,
1405, 1406, 1578
Ada S., 1522, 1523
Allen T., 1288
Charles, 775, 1287, 1406,
1523
Christina, 1287
Ella, 1287
George W., 1287, 1327
Harriet, 1287
Harriet S., 1063
Jacob, 1287
Leah A., 775
Luther, 1287
Mary A., 771
Thomas, 775, 1287, 1406,
1523
William, 1287
William T., 1287
Weddle, Leonard, 903
Tobias, 772

Weddrick, Annie M., 1410
Wedrick, Elizabeth, 797, 1415
Weeks, William, 966
Weidler, Frederick, 751
Weikert, Maria, 1053
Peter, 1053
Weimer, Barbara, 917
Deborah, 804, 805
Joseph, 804
Weinberg, Amelia, 1463
Clara, 1463
David, 1463
Henry, 1463
Isaac, 1463
Jeannette, 1463
Leah Frances, 1465
Leo, 1463, 1464, 1466
Mrs. Amelia, 1464
Samuel, 1463
Weiner, Mary, 1487
Weinterfield, Isaac B., 1118
Welch, Mary Grace, 1452
Welker, Charles, 1533
Laura, 1058
Margaret, 1621
Weller, Christian, 727
Frank, 843
Joel, 754
John, 886
Savannah, 1436
Welsh, Anna May, 1212
Luther, 818
Ruth Griffith, 818
Welty, Andrew, 723
Anna Valerie, 723
Annie C., 1358
Eva, 733
Frederick A., 723
Grayson, 733
Hammond, 1118
Harriet J., 1445, 1446
Henry, 1405
Howard, 733
Joseph Frederick, 723
Mary Frances., 723
Mary M., 733
Murray, 733
V. Rebecca, 733
William, 1083
Wenner, C. F., 1565
Charles F., 1032
Jacob, 1435

Margaret, 879, 1434, 1435
R. B., 1031, 1564, 1565
Wentz, Amanda, 1395
John, 1395
R. Robert M., 1040
Wenrick, Mary, 1532
Wertenbaker, Alanzella, 715
Alta V., 716
Elizabeth, 715
Ella, 715
Fleet V., 716
George W., 715, 716
John, 715
John H., 715
Katie G., 716
Laura, 715
Laura T., 716
Lewis, 715
Margie G., 716
Sarah, 743
Susan E., 1229
William O., 716
Wertheimer, Charles, 887,
888, 1117, 1368
Charles J., 889
David, 888
Emma C., 888
Francis Karley, 888
Frederick, 887, 888
Marcus, 888
Meyer, 888
Philip, 889, 1117
Rose, 888
Samuel, 888
Sarah, 888
West, Airy, 1448
Charles, 1447, 1448
Edward, 1448
Eliza, 1345
Elizabeth, 872
Erasmus, 872
George, 1605
George Washington, 872
John J., 1447, 1448
Joseph, 1345
Levin, 872, 1345
Margaret, 1448
Mary, 841, 872
Mary H., 872
Patrick McGill, 841, 872
Samuel, 1447, 1448
Sarah, 872

Susan, 872
Thomas, 1448
Thomas H., 872
William, 1448, 1605
Westcote, G., 1594
Henry, 1594
Wetmaght, Cordelia, 1351
Wetzel, Annie M., 962
David, 1588
Elizabeth, 1319
Josiah, 1456
Margaret, 1214
Maria, 1587, 1588
Mary, 1456
Susan, 1588
William, 1588
Weybright, Annie M., 932
D. Saylor, 933
Jacob, 932
Jesse P., 932
John, 932
John S., 932
Martha L., 932
Mary R., 932
Ruth Ella, 933
Samuel R., 932
Vernon J., 932
William, 1352
Whaley, Georgie F., 703
Wheeler, Ann, 835
Charlotte, 1138
Odell, 1115
Sarah Odell, 1115
Thomas Trueman, 1138
Whiltler, Albert, 1612
Amelia, 1612
Fredonia, 1612
Whip, Charlotte, 1313
L. O., 957
Newton, 1313
Susanna, 1015
Whipp, Carrie E., 1396
Cora, 1362
Cora May, 804
David M., 1396, 1473
David M., Jr., 1473
Ellen R. T., 1043
Emma M. , 1258
George T., 804, 1473
Lewis, 879
Lewis O., 1473
Mary, 1586

Mary Elizabeth, 1473
Peter, 1046
Samuel T., 1043, 1407
Charles Edgar, 1473
Whisner, Margaret, 1493
Margaret L., 1493
Michael, 1493
White, Catherine, 1013
E. V., 1137
Elijah, 712
Elizabeth, 1142
Emily Busby, 1594
Furr, 1115
John C., 1187
Joseph, 1013
Laurence A., 919
Lewis, 878
Lillian, 878
Mary, 1259
Murr, 878
Paul, 878
Stephen, 1045, 1303
Whitehill, James, 981, 1450,
1452
Whitmore, Abraham, 734
Agnes Viola, 1620
America, 1619
Ann, 1619
Ann Rebecca, 747
Anna, 1620
Anna Rebecca, 748
Anne Katharine Sabina, 1620
Arnold, 1168
Barbara, 734
Benjamin, 733, 734, 891
Berta I., 892
Bruce C., 995
Calvin E., 995
Charles N., 995
Charlotte B., 1620
Christian, 734
Daniel J., 995
David, 733, 734, 995
Elizabeth, 891
Ellen Rebecca, 1620
Ephraim, 734
Estella, 778
Francesanna, 891
Frederick, 734
George, 891, 1619
George H., 891
Giles, 891

Greenberry, 891
Hamilton, 1619
Harvey, 741
Harvey V., 995
Helen R., 995
Henry, 995
Jacob, 891, 1619
Jeremiah Washington,
1619, 1620
John, 1501, 1619
John H., 995
John J., 1620
John William, 1620
Joseph, 734
Levi, 734
Lucinda, 1619
Mahlon, 1436
Mary, 734
Mary C., 995
Mary Elizabeth, 1620
Mary Ellen, 733, 734
Mayme Margaret, 1620
Nicholas, 747, 801, 1592
Oscar H., 892
Pheba A., 995
Phoebe Ann Catherine,
1591, 1592
Polly, 891
Randolf N., 1010, 1021
Randolph, 1592
Samuel, 1619
Sarah, 891
Sarah G., 891
Simon, 734
Spencer J. H., 995
Stiner M., 995
Susan, 801
Susan Adelaide, 1620
Thomas P., 891
W. H., 892
William, 891, 1168, 1619
William J., 778
Whittaker, Elizabeth, 949
Whitter, Fanny, 894
Wib, Jacob E., 1371
Wickham, John B., 1525
Martha, 1524, 1525
Widegan, Christopher, 1431,
1528
Widerick, Anmareless, 1283
Widrick, Annie M., 998
Wiener, Andrew, 1121, 1122

Bertha Marie, 1122
Catherine, 1122
George, 1121
Henry M., 1121, 1122
Mary Ann, 1078, 1122,
  1189
Michael, 1121, 1122, 1189
Michael Jenkins, 1122
Wierman, Daniel, 805
Wiest, Maria, 725
Wikard, Maria, 1244
Wilcoxan, Fannie Alverta, 889
Wilcoxon, Andrew J., 997,
  1222
  Clara, 997, 1222
  D. Clinton, 1222
  Frances A. , 1117
  Frank M., 1222
  George E., 842, 997, 1222
  George Edward, 1222
  Jesse, 1036
  John, 1117
  Mrs. Hannah A., 1036
  William, 1222
Wild, Emma, 1390
Wilders, William, 1360
Wiles, A. G. P., 1387
  Americus, 800, 1387
  Americus G. P., 1286, 1589
  Barbara A., 723
  Belva Grace, 1387
  Bradley A., 1387
  Cassandra, 1387
  Charles, 1616
  Charles C., 1474
  Charles P., 1387
  Christian, 1341
  Cleggett B., 723
  Cornelia A., 1444
  Cota J., 723
  Earl, 1616
  Edith, 1387, 1616
  Eva M., 723
  George P., 723
  Hazel, 1616
  Helen, 1387, 1616
  Irving, 1331
  Iva, 1387
  Jacob, 1177
  Jacob B., 1444
  James, 1595
  Jane R., 723

Jennie, 1383
Jennie R., 849
Jesse C., 723
John, 1387
John E., 723
John W. T., 723
Lee McC., 723
Lela L., 723
Leslie, 1387
Lydia E., 1108
Mamie, 1387
Mamie M. R., 1589
Mary M., 1558
Merhl, 1387
Pauline, 1387
Peter, 722, 1387, 1558
Thomas, 722, 723, 849
Thomas E., 1587
Thomas J. L., 723
Thomas McCleary, 722, 723
Walter, 800
Walter S., 1387
William, 1108
William W., 722
Wilhide, Ada M., 1519
  Addie, 730, 1458
  Agnes, 1221
  Amanda, 1458
  Annie E., 1239
  Arnold R., 729, 730, 1457,
    1458
  Benjamin, 729, 1457, 1458
  Bessie M., 730
  Binnie E., 730
  Catherine, 729, 1458
  Charles E., 729, 730, 1458
  Clara, 730, 1458
  Clarence M., 730
  David B., 730, 1458
  Dorothy, 1053
  Elizabeth, 772
  Emma, 730, 1458
  Ernest C., 730
  Ethel, 1221
  Fannie K., 1458
  Florence, 730
  Florence E., 1458
  Frank, 1221
  Frederick, 729, 772, 1457,
    1458
  Frederick M., 729, 1458
  Gelena R., 730

Henry, 729, 730, 772,
  1221, 1458
Herbert, 729, 1458
Horras D., 730 , 1458
Isabella, 729, 730, 1458
J. Lloyd, 730
James, 729, 1458
Jennie, 730, 1458
John, 1458
John H., 730, 1458
John L., 1519
Josephine A., 729 , 1458
Julia, 1221
Leon, 730
Lewis M., 730, 1458
Lloyd, 1053
Louisa, 729, 1053, 1458
Maggie, 730, 1458
Maria, 1458
Martha A., 730
Mary Matilda, 1238
Merhl, 1053
Mettie M., 730
Mollie, 729
Morris J., 1053
Oscar, 730, 1458
Phoebe, 728
Randolph, 730
Randolph N., 1458
Raymond, 730, 1458
Rena, 1516
Rosa, 1508
Ross, 1508
Sally, 1508
Samuel, 707
Savilla, 729
Susan, 729, 1458
Vada M., 730
Vivian V., 730, 1458
Walter J., 730
Washington, 729, 1458
Washington E., 1458
Wilson, 729
Wilkinson, James, 1398
Will, Mary, 891
Willard, Abraham, 894,
  1407, 1453, 1573
  Ann M., 1178
  Annie, 1407, 1408
  Arthur D., 873, 1408
  Arthur D., Jr., 1408
  Callie Hersperger, 1453

Carlton, 1576
Catharine, 894, 1566, 1567
Catherine, 1408
Charles, 1030
Charles F. M., 1407
Charles Francis, 1093
Charles H., 1408
Clarke L., 1408
Clinton, 1481, 1576
Daniel, 1407
David, 1387
Dewalt, 894, 1030, 1407, 1408
Dewalt J., 1407, 1408
Edgar Harold, 1093
Edward, 894
Edward L., 1407, 1408
Eliza, 893
Elizabeth, 1407
Ezra, 1093
Frances, 1576
Frances E, 1213
Frances V., 1453
Fullerton, 1567
George, 1085
George A., 1014
George W., 1407
Hamilton, 1621
Harriet Janet, 1453, 1573
Henry, 957, 1345
Hugh, 1576
Ida M., 772
John, 894, 1567
John Henry, 1453
Joseph, 1576
Julia Ann, 894, 1453
Katherine, 1453
L. A., 1407
L. E., 1115
Laurence, 1576
Lena, 1321
Louis, 1408
Manzella, 1164, 1573
Marcissa, 1453
Mary, 1184, 1185, 1576, 1621
Mary Ann, 894, 1407
Mary E., 1407
Mary Elizabeth, 1453
Paul C., 1408
Paul Luther, 1408
Peter, 1149, 1164, 1407

Pierce, 1576
Sarah Ann, 1407
Thomas, 1324
Tilghman, 1183
Tilghman A., 1453
William, 894
William H., 1453
William K., 1127
Willcox, James M., 1211
Katherine, 1211
Willet, Elizabeth, 779
Willett, Benjamin, 845
Clifford, 763
Elton C. T., 763
Esther, 845
Willhide, Elizabeth, 1444
George E., 930
Harriet V., 755
Joseph, 755
Julia, 755
William, John, 1142
Williams, Annie, 839
Basil, 1295, 1456
Charles, 1447
Charles A. D., 1510
Cornelia, 1115
Courtnay May, 1510
Dorothy, 920
Dougless, 1510
E., 1264
Eunice, 865
Frank, 1220
Hannah, 970
Hannah Elizabeth, 1435
Henry, 710, 711, 805
Jacob, 1221
John, 1143, 1286
John C., 1435
John F., 1225
John H., 710, 1038, 1327
John T., 784
L. W., 1609
Lu, 1531
Margaret Jeannette, 711
Mary, 1143
Mrs. Jane, 1196
Otho Holland, 1353
Rebecca, 1181
Rob H., 842
Robert H., 1225
Roger, 1583
Samuel, 723, 1325

Sarah, 1062, 1189
Sarah E., 723, 724
W. S., 868
William, 1286
Williamson, Charles L., 1054
G. W., 1426
George, 1089
J. A., 1028
J. Alleine, 1550, 1551
Joseph Allein, 1551
Joseph Alleine, 1550
Julia P., 1551
Mary A., 1551
Roberta, 1551
T. R., 719
Thomas McGill, 1550, 1551
Williar, Adam, 1135
Augustus, 1601
Cecelia A., 1127
Effie D., 1436
Elizabeth, 1058
Emma Amanda, 1058
Florence L., 1058
Frank, 1058
Frank Ecker, 1601
George B., 1127
Herbert, 1058, 1601
Jacob, 1058, 1155
Jacob O., 1601
John A., 1058
Lillian, 1601
M. A., 1436
Margaret Hannah, 1601
Marguerite, 1058
Minnie, 1127
Paul, 1601
Prudence, 1058, 1601
Ralph, 1058, 1601
Rose Alberta, 1058
Williard, Alonza, 730, 1458
Annie Maria, 1179
Daisy, 1180
Julia, 1096
Willier, Augustus Henry, 1057, 1058
Celia, 1058
Charles, 1058
Commius, 1058
Emma Amanda, 1057
George, 1058
Herman, 1058

John, 1058
Margaret, 837, 1058
Willis, Ann Eliza, 1025
  Arietta, 1025
  Bennett, 1089
  David, 1089
  Eliza, 1025
  Eliza Ann, 1025
  Elizabeth Newkirk, 1025
  Frances Finley, 1025
  George A.,, 1089
  George Newkirk, 1025
  Hamilton, 1089
  Henry Newton, 1025
  Hugh, 1089
  Hugh Finley, 1025
  J. Houston, 1089
  James, 1089
  John, 1089
  Jonathan, 1089
  Keziah Ann, 1025
  L. O., 863
  Lavinia, 1089
  Levan C., 1024
  Levan Nicholas, 1025
  Levin C., 1025
  Levin Charles, 1025
  Louis O., 1025
  Louis Orndorf, 1024, 1025
  Margaret A., 1089
  Maria Louisa, 1025
  Martha, 1089
  Mary, 1089
  Mary Anderson, 1025
  Rebecca, 1089
  Russell, 1089
  Samuel, 1089
  Simon Peter, 1089
  Susan Ellen, 1025
  Thomas, 1089
  Thomas C., 1089
  William , 1089
  William Lewis, 1024, 1025
Willman, Mrs. E., 755
Wills, Harvey C., 868
  William O., 975
Willson, Martha, 860
  Martha Rebecca, 777
Willyard, Elizabeth, 1415,
  1416
Wilmer, R. H., 774
Wilson, Adam, 1556

Albert, 1556
Benjamin C., 1223
Charles, 726, 1008
Charles S., 959
Clara K., 1614
Cordelia, 1326, 1556
Daniel Duvall, 1557
Dora, 1557
Emma Louisa, 1354
Evan, 1556
Florence E., 1350
G. Albert, 1557
George Edward, 1557
George I., 726
Greenberry, 1556
H. B., 1243
Harry, 1054
Harry E., 1243, 1557
Harry Ellsworth, 1243, 1244
Herman M., 1244
J. W., 1243
Jesse R., 1556, 1557
Jesse R., Jr., 1557
John, 1132
John E., 1557
John T., 1243
John W., 987, 1129
Laura, 1129
Letitia, 1556
Mahalia, 987
Margaret Blackston, 1243
Mary, 1506
Mary E., 1557
Mary V., 825
Mattie, 1344
Myra, 1478
N. J., 725, 1140, 1354
Nathan, 1556
Nathan H., 1557
P. L., 1350
Rachel, 1557
Robert, 987
Samuel R., 1583
Sarah L., 1556
Senath Norris, 1243
Sharon, 1243
Susan, 734
Thomas, 804
Thomas J., 1614
Viola J., 987
William, 1243, 1306
William G., 1243

William H. H., 1243
William Murdock Beall,
  777
Wiltburger, Lee, 972
Wilter, R. G., 1427
Wimsatt, William Kurtz, 695
Winchel, William R., 1454
Windpigler, Amanda, 971
Windser, Flora, 762
  Thompson, 1063
Windsor, Antonia, 839
  Caroline, 763
Winebrener, Arie, 1342
  Charles, 1342
  Christian, 709, 1341, 1342
  D. C., 853, 1057, 1314,
    1337
  D. Charles, 708, 709
  David, 1342
  David C., 708, 709
  David C., 3rd, 709
  Emma, 1342
  George A., 1342
  Grace, 709, 1337
  Harriet, 1342
  Jacob, 1342
  Johann Christian, 708
  John, 1337, 1342
  Margaret, 1342
  Mary, 1342
  Philip, 708, 1341, 1342
  Philip Ritchie, 709
  Reverdy J., 1341, 1342
  Susan May, 709, 1057
Winebrenner, C. Mary, 1112,
  1268, 1269
  Christian, 1266, 1301,
    1507
  D. C., 765, 1254, 1268,
    1559
  George, 1305, 1536
  Harry, 1071, 1521
  John, 1112, 1212, 1268,
    1269, 1286
  Margaret, 1532
  Mary, 1212
  Philip, 1112, 1268, 1269
  William, 1532
Winegardner, Franklin, 1598
  Jacob F., 1598
Winemiller, Mary, 1136,
  1539

Winepigler, Amanda, 1021
Winfield, Cyrus, 1014
Winger, Elizabeth, 1092, 1093
Winsing, Annie, 1546
Winter, T. B., 920
Winters, Catherine, 1179
  Celiann, 1179
  Diana Agnes, 1179
  Elizabeth, 1179, 1180
  George Martin, 1179
  Henry, 1179
  John Henry Franklin, 1179
  Margaret, 1179
  Marthia Delia, 1179
  Mary, 1171
  Mary Isabella, 1179
  May, 1507
  Savilla, 1179
Wirtz, Mary, 1574
Wise, Ellen, 1005
  H. C., 1570
Wiseman, Amanda E., 897
  Enos, 897
  Lydia, 1218
Wisner, Albert, 1529
  Alesa, 1529
  Charles, 1529
  Charles Samuel, 1529
  Christian, 1529
  George, 1529
  Grace, 1529
  Harry Lewis, 1529
  John, 1529
  Leslie LeRoy, 1529
  Mary, 1529
  Maud M., 1529
  Nannie, 1529
  Neva, 1529
  Ray, 1529
  Ruth, 1529
  Wilfred, 1529
Wisong, Elizabeth, 1080
Witherow, Anna Isabelle, 805
  David, 805
  Jane Eleanor Elizabeth, 805
  Jeannette, 710
  John, 805, 1238
  Margaret B., 805, 806
  Ross Lafayette, 805
  Samuel, 805
  Sarah A., 805, 806
  Thomas Scott, 805

Withers, Catharine, 1223
  Charles B., 1270
Witmer, George, 743
  John, 1271
  Willamina, 743
Witmore, Barbara, 1408, 1409
  George, 1409
Witter, Alice, 1075
  Benjamin, 1075
  David, 1075
  Dolly, 1075
  Ellen, 1075
  Emanuel, 1075
  Grace, 1075
  Harry B., 1075
  Jacob, 812, 1075
  Jennie, 1075
  John F., 1075
  John H., 1075, 1493
  Martha, 1075
  Mary, 1075
  Mary C., 1075
  Nora T., 1075
  Robert G., 1075
  Ruby, 1075
  Susan, 1075
  Willis, 1075
Wittington, Robert, 1418
Wolf, Ann Mary, 1349
  Catherine, 911
  Daniel M., 826, 1606
  Daniel, Jr., 1369
  Dorothy, 886, 1180
  Frank, 1219
  Ida M., 1514
  Joel, 1228
  Rachael, 1119
  Sallie, 1351
  Sophia, 750
  Susan, 1529
  Tabitha, 1555
  Thomas, 886
  Webb, 1532
Wolfe, Abraham, 1195
  Abraham Lincoln, 1254
  Anna, 1221
  Annie Barbara, 924
  Annie Mary, 942
  Aquilla P., 1409
  Aquilla R., 1414
  Arrie Viola, 1414
  Catharine, 1414

Charles Edgar, 1070
Christiana, 1042, 1043,
  1406, 1407
Clara V., 1409
Daniel, 1070, 1151, 1194,
  1499
David, 1414
E. R., 1414
Eli R., 1409
Frank, 922
George, 1556
J. K. P., 784
Jacob, 1409
James K. P., 1409
Jinna A., 1409
John, 1043, 1085, 1407,
  1597
Joseph, 947
L. J., 1414
Lavinia, 1461
Leanna, 1085
Levi J., 1408, 1409
Lillie May, 1414
Margaret, 1155
Mary, 1194, 1195, 1409,
  1414, 1585
Mary C., 1409
Nancy, 1498
Rachel, 1556
Roger B., 1414
Samuel, 1408, 1409
Samuel J., 1414
Sarah, 1196, 1409, 1414
Sarah C., 1409
Susan, 1130, 1279, 1596,
  1597
William H., 886
William Nicholas, 1085
William R., 1409
William V., 1414
Wolff, Anna Mary, 1604
Wolford, William, 1374
Woltz, James, 1012
Wood, Alice E., 1008, 1224
  Anna Louise, 1008
  Basil, 716, 1166
  Caleb, 716
  Charles, 716, 717, 1272,
    1462, 1588
  Henry, 716, 1008
  Ira Newton, 1008
  J. E. R., 1540

James, 1500
John, 716, 1008
John W., 1008
Joseph, 1008, 1327
Joseph M., 1008
M. P., 840, 1561
Margaret H., 1008
Mary, 1292
Melvin P., 1008, 1272
R. Vinton, 1008
Charles
Woodruff, Robert, 1595
Woods, Maria, 1414
Woodward, Abraham, 1028
Dodge, 1028
Woog, Nannetta, 1265
Woolery, Hammond, 1548
Wootton, Eliza, 777
Martha, 777
Richard, 777
W. T., 822
Workens, Ella, 1486
Working, Elsie, 1446
James C., 1492
John, 1446
Margaret Ellen, 1526
Workings, Annie, 1275
Works, Charles, 1116
Worley, Elizabeth, 1452
Worman, Andrew, 929
Anna Elizabeth, 1352
Annie M., 1019
Elizabeth, 1247
Emma, 1450-1453
Emma O., 1420, 1422
Harry, 1054, 1272
Henry, 1222, 1422
Mary E., 1019
Mary O., 928, 929
Moses, 842
William D., 978, 1019
Worthan, Annie, 1306
David, 1306
Worthington, Ann, 1137
Clark, 728
Dorothy, 729
Glenn H., 717, 728, 925, 1537
John, 717, 728
John Clark., 729
John H., 728
John Henry, 728

John T., 728
Julia, 729
Kate, 717
Matilda, 1072
Matilda Merriwether, 1212
Nicholas, 1029
Nicholas D., 1072
Richard Alvey, 729
Ruth, 729
Sarah, 1241
T. C., 787
Thomas, 717
William, 1137
Wothington, Deye W., 1072
Wrenn, Emma Jane, 1218
Wright, Ann Rebecca, 990
Carl N., 1162
Caroline, 1195
Charles W., 1161, 1162
Charles W. , 969
Clotilda, 990
Edward E., 1087
Ellen, 1195
Elmo, 990
Emma A., 1161
Frank J., 1194
George, 1195
Henry, 990
Hester, 944
Hugh E., 1162
Isaac, 1194, 1195
Isadore, 990
James T., 1161
Jedediah, 944
Jennie V., 1161
Jesse, 937-941
Joel D., 990
John, 939, 990
John A., 990
John B., 836, 1162
John H., 990
John P., 1161
Julia A., 990
Lakin I., 1162
Lewis, 990
Lewis Clay, 990
Lewis M., 1161
Lulu A., 1162
Margaret, 941, 990
Margaret A., 1194, 1195
Margaret Jane, 936-939, 941
Mary, 1195

Nancy I., 1310
Nona H., 1162
Ocale T., 1162
Raymond, 990
Robert T., 1161
Samuel, 939, 1161
Sarah, 990, 1195, 1227
Sarah Jane, 942
Sophia, 990
Susanna, 939
Thomas, 990
William, 1161, 1194, 1195
William Henry, 990
Wylie, Edward A. Gill, 1331
W. Gill, 1331
Wysong, Amanda, 927
Yakey, Jane, 1316
Yantzey, Mary, 843
Yaste, Edward G., 763
Mary M., 843, 1220
Samuel, 843
Yeagaline, Louisa, 705
Yeakle, A. R., 959
Aquilla Reese, 1016
C. Kate, 1346
Edward, 1016
Henry, 1016
John, 1016
Katie, 1016
Marie Hane, 1017
Thomas, 1016
William, 1016, 1087, 1346
Yenglin, Joseph, 706
Yerbury, Sarah, 1241
Yerkes, Amanda Owen, 1093
Ellwood, 1093
Yerty, Elizabeth, 734
Yingling, A., 1007
Daniel, 1071, 1520
David G., 1153
Emanuel, 1500
Louisa, 1181, 1230, 1231
Mrs. Louisa Schwarber, 1252
Thomas, 990
Yonson, John, 1506
Yost, Daniel D., 1389
George, 1315
Harry S., 1390
May, 1389

Young, A. O., 1229
  Adaline, 1149, 1150
  Albert O., 1331, 1332
  Alexander, 744
  Alma G., 1103
  Amanda Catherine, 1083
  Amanda E., 1479
  Amanda J., 1480
  Amy Grace., 1332
  Anne L., 1543, 1544
  Barnett, 708
  Betsy, 1332
  Calvin W., 1332
  Catharine, 978, 1190, 1332
  Catherine, 1189
  Charles B., 708, 955, 958, 1524
  Charles T. K., 1079, 1120, 1121, 1521
  Charlotte Elizabeth, 1083
  Conrad, 931, 1120
  Daniel, 791, 931, 932, 1190, 1332, 1479, 1480, 1590, 1591
  Daniel H., 1120, 1121
  David, 932
  Devault, 707, 708
  Effie I., 1121
  Elias, Jr., 1352
  Elias, 1591
  Eliza, 744
  Elizabeth, 708, 744, 791, 932, 1289, 1591
  Ellen, 1325
  Elmer A., 708, 905
  Elmyra Virginia, 1095
  Eloise Newman, 745
  Emma, 932, 1174
  Emma E., 1479
  Emma M. , 1190
  Ezra, 1332
  Fannie, 1590
  Fanny, 1591
  Frank, 1103
  Frank R., 859
  Henry, 932, 1120, 1150, 1174, 1189, 1332, 1506
  Herman, 1590
  Hezekiah, 1120, 1340
  Hugh, 744
  Ira J., 931, 932, 1190, 1479, 1621

Isaac, 1480
Israel, 1590
Jacob, 707, 708, 830, 931, 932, 1083, 1190, 1332, 1479, 1591, 1621
Jacob D., 988, 1265, 1339
Jacob S., 1590
James, 744, 1590
John, 931, 988, 1265, 1339, 1380, 1480, 1514
John S. F., 1482
John W., 1116
Josephine, 744
Julia, 932, 1190, 1621
Julia Ann, 932, 1332
Julia C., 1479
Katherine, 932
Laura A., 1332
Lena, 932, 1332
Lewis, 932, 1332, 1549
Lewis Jacob, 1332
Lizzie, 1532
Luther F., 1332
Lydia, 1480
Lyra L., 1479
M. L., 951
Mahala, 1332
Maria, 1591
Marietta, 932
Martha, 780, 781, 830, 932, 1179, 1336
Martha E., 1190, 1479
Mary, 932, 1590
Mary A., 1332, 1549
Mary Virginia, 878
McClintock, 744, 870
Millard F., 1362
Mrs. Sarah F., 878
Myra L., 1190
Myra Loretta, 932
Myrah L., 1479
Nora, 1590
Olivar, 1134
Olive L., 1482
Peter, 756, 791
Rachel, 932
Robert, 1590
Samuel, 757
Sarah A. E., 708
Sobina, 1506
Sophia, 932, 1332
Stanley F., 1482

Susie, 1590
Velma Blanche, 1332
Virginia, 932
William Randolph, 707, 708
William S., 967
Windell S., 1121
Younkins, Esta May, 1482
Yourtee, Aaron B., 1244
  Abraham, 1244
  Amanda, 1244
  Barbara, 1244
  Bessie, 1244
  Catherine, 1244
  Daniel, 1244
  Edith, 1244
  Eli, 1244
  Elizabeth, 1244
  Ella M., 1244
  George W., 954, 1244
  George Wilmer, 1244
  Howard, 1244
  Jacob, 1244
  John, 1244
  L. R., 1164
  Mary, 1244
  Mary Ann, 1244
  Nancy, 1244
  Peter, 1244
  Sallie, 1244
  Samuel, 1244
  Sophia, 1244
Yunkins, R. C., 1013
Zacharias, D., 910
  Daniel, 870, 1169
  H. C., 1439
  Mary E., 734
Zecher, Alta, 1324
  Alta May, 1332
  Daniel D., 1332
  Estella, 1332
  George A., 1332
  John, 1086
  John S., 1332
  Martin, 1332
Zeigler, George A., 1128
  Margaret E., 1128
Zeiler, Harriet, 928
Zeller, Edward, 1335
Zellers, Charles E., 963
Zentmyer, Jacob, 1104
Zentz, Abraham, 705, 706

Abraham S., 707, 918, 1457
Adam R., 706, 707, 1239, 1457
Alice, 706
Anna, 705
Annie, 706
Annie R., 706
Benjamin, 706
Bessie D., 706, 906
Carrie Beatrice, 707
Charles E., 918
Chester, 1457
Daniel, 705, 706
Daniel W., 706, 1457
David, 705, 706
David G., 706, 707, 1457
David H., 707
Doctor W., 706
Dorothy, 707
Elma L., 707
Estee Blaine, 707
Evelyn J., 707
Ezra Monroe, 706
Fannie O., 707
Franklin, 705, 1457
George C., 706, 707, 1457
Harry A., 707
Hazel, 1239
Herbert L. H., 706
Howard G., 707
Jane, 705
Jennie Michael, 906
Jesse, 705
Jessie, 706
Laura V., 706
Leo Paul, 707
Levi, 706, 1108
Lillian, 707
Lottie, 1239
Lula May, 707
Mabel L., 707
Martin S., 707
Mary, 1457
Maurice A., 1457
Mildred, 1457
Myrtle May, 706
Newton M., 705, 788, 906
Pauline, 706
Raymond, 1457
Robert F., 706
Rolland R., 918
Sophronia, 706

Susan, 706
Whendell L. H., 918
William, 706
William R., 707
  Abraham S.
  Adam R
Zepp, George, 1462
Ziegler, Eliza, 1394
  Lucretia, 1360
Zimmerman, Ada, 892, 1168, 1538
  Albert, 1164, 1233
  Albert F., 1402
  Albert J., 998
  Albert M., 1411
  Alice, 1092, 1168
  Alice B., 1191
  Alice V., 1294, 1496
  Allen, 1164
  Alpha, 724
  Alvey O., 1168
  Amanda D., 934
  Andrew, 881, 998, 1410
  Ann March, 1307
  Ann Mariah, 1307
  Ann Rebecca, 1127
  Anna, 1294
  Anna Mary, 819
  Anne E., 1537
  Annie, 724, 882, 934, 998, 1410
  Annie E., 703
  Annie M., 1154
  Annie Rebecca, 1167
  Austin E., 998
  Benjamin, 881, 998, 1410, 1587
  Benjamin F., 1587
  Bernard F., 1402
  Bertha, 1060
  Bertha L., 935
  Bertha M., 998, 1090
  Bertie May, 882
  Bettie V., 703
  C. F., 821
  C. Herbert, 1402
  C. M., 1538
  Calvin C., 1190, 1191
  Carl S., 1164
  Caroline, 1090, 1313
  Carrie C., 882
  Catharine, 1490, 1587

Cephas H., 980, 996, 1003, 1153, 1154
Charles, 1537
Charles E., 1090, 1401, 1402, 1411
Charles H., 703
Charles W., 1294, 1496
Charlotte, 1482
Clara E., 934, 998, 1410
Clara H., 1164
Clara M., 1411
Claude W., 1497
Clayborne Milton, 1199
Clayton, 1200
Clayton Heberlig, 1199
Clayton M., 1198, 1199, 1537
Cora, 724
Cornelius, 998, 1410
Cornelius F., 980, 1003
Cornelius T., 1586, 1587
Curtis T., 980, 1003
Daisy M., 1043
Daniel, 1567
Daniel J., 954, 980, 1003, 1411
Daniel P., 1007, 1050 , 1499
Daniel Peter, 1167
David, 882, 998, 1410
David E., 934
David H., 1118, 1214
David M., 1586, 1587
David William, 1164
Earl Nicodemus, 1294
Edgar Allen, 1199
Edith Ellen, 1164
Edward, 908, 980, 998, 1003, 1164, 1567
Edward D., 1401, 1402
Edward J., 998, 1602
Edward Joshua, 997, 1410
Edward Joshua, Jr., 1409, 1410
Edwin S., 1497
Effie, 1168
Elias, 1090
Elinor R., 1164
Elizabeth, 882, 998, 1401, 1410, 1567
Elizabeth Cecelia, 1199
Elizabeth S., 980, 1003,

1402
Ellen, 1092
Elmer Crawford, 1294
Elsie, 1053
Elsie L., 1168
Emily V., 1433
Emma, 724, 1411
Emma F., 724
Emma J., 1497
Emma L., 1168
Emma V., 1402
Emory, 1164
Ephraim, 980, 1568
Ephraim B., 1199
Ephraim I., 1198
Ephraim J., 1015
Ethel M., 998
Ethel May, 1199
Ezra, 773, 816
Fannie, 1411
Fanny, 1164
Fannie D., 1602
Florence, 703, 1140, 1322
Francis M., 1411
Frank, 1289
Franklin, 1090
Franklin N., 998, 1410
G. Bernard, 1410
G. F. S., 702, 1599
George, 881, 882, 998,
  1090, 1110, 1169, 1307,
  1313, 1410, 1592
George C., 935
George Edgar, 1294
George H., 934, 1368, 1488
George W., 1090
George Willis, 1294, 1496
Gideon, 1433
Gideon M., 980, 1003,
  1042, 1043, 1406, 1567
Ginnevra Lucttia, 882
Grace B., 1168
Grace E., 935
Grace L., 1410
H. E., 838
H. Oscar, 1164
Hallie Roderick, 1294
Hallie V., 703
Harry E., 1163, 1164, 1214
Harry M., 1043
Harry W., 1497
Harvey L., 1407

Helen F., 703
Henry, 881, 980, 998, 1043,
  1190, 1198, 1402, 1406,
  1410, 1567
Henry O., 703, 1167, 1537
Hester C., 1198
Hester Z., 1335
Hiram Z., 735
Ira Leslie, 980
Isaac, 1043
Isaac C., 979, 980, 1003
Isaac Wesley, 1496
Isabella E., 703
Isabelle R., 980, 1003
Jackson, 1000
Jacob E., 998, 1410
Jane, 1022
Jennette L., 723
Jessie, 724
John, 881, 998, 1401, 1402,
  1410
John A. J., 724
John D., 1163, 1164
John David, 1167
John H., 1042, 1043, 1191,
  1406, 1407
John M., 1586
John Nicholas, 881, 882, 998,
  1410
Jonathan, 723
Joseph, 1169, 1191, 1443,
  1503
Josephus, 1090
Joshua, 1090
Joshua B., 980
Joshua J., 1572
Josiah, 1568
Josiah B., 1003, 1567
Katie May, 1043
Lavinia M., 1406
Lena, 724
Lester C., 1407
Levina, 1090
Lew Reno, 882
Lillian, 1497
Lottie K., 1411
Lula E., 1407
Lura, 724
Luther, 724, 728, 1164, 1284
Luther C., 980, 1003
Luther M., 1167
Mamie C., 980

Margaret A. M., 1572
Maria, 882, 998, 1205,
  1259, 1410
Marshall, 902, 1317
Marshall L., 997, 998,
  1410
Martha N., 1000
Mary, 931, 1090, 1167,
  1191
Mary A., 1497
Mary C., 1169
Mary E., 1043, 1169,
  1407, 1432, 1433
Mary Genevieve, 1199
Mary Jane, 724
Mehrl Henry, 703
Michael, 881, 882, 980,
  998, 1002, 1003, 1227,
  1401, 1402, 1410,
  1586, 1606
Millard C., 1411
Milton, 1529, 1530
Milton S., 1567, 1568
Minerva, 1109, 1110
Mrs. Cephas H., 996
Myra Susan, 1199
Nicholas Z., 1198
O. T., 927, 1322
Oda Helen, 1199
Peter, 1567
Peter T., 980, 1002, 1003
Polly, 882, 998, 1410
R. Clinton, 1402
Ralph B., 1199
Ralph L., 998
Ray Baxter, 1294
Raymond, 1164
Rebecca, 882, 998, 1410
Rhulda, 1587
Richard D., 1145
Robert C., 1402
Robert E., 703
Roger E., 1164
Ross J., 998
Roy Calvin, 1294
Roy F., 1497
Roy W., 1407
Rufus R., 1089
Ruth Marie, 1199
Ruth V., 1497
Sallie A., 1411
Sally, 1091, 1266

Samuel, 979, 1004, 1090, 1154
Samuel A., 1586
Sarah, 1260
Sarah A., 934
Sarah Ada, 703
Savanna, 882
Solomon, 703, 1167, 1260, 1313
Susan, 882, 980, 998, 1004, 1410
Susan Alice, 703
T. E., 1503
Theo., 1526
Theodore, 1234, 1319
Thomas L., 935
Wesley, 1294
William Henry, 1199
William, 851, 1164, 1297, 1568
William C., 1497
William D., 935, 1587
William G., 703, 1537
William H., 819, 934, 980, 1003, 1169, 1190
William M., 998, 1410
William N., 1043, 1406, 1407
Zachariah T., 1090
Zachary Elias, 1043
Zachery, 963
Zoie, 1168
Zittle, Mary A., 1404, 1405
Norina, 1324
Zober, Philip, 898
Zumbrum, Willis E., 903
Zumbrun, Annie Elizabeth, 1305
Charles, 956
Emma, 955, 956
Jacob, 956, 1305